I0818472
DIC WARE
MADE IN THE USA

AMERICA'S
TEST KITCHEN

Also by America's Test Kitchen

Dinner Tonight
Umma
When Southern Women Cook
Cocktails Illustrated
Food Gifts
America's Test Kitchen 25th Anniversary Cookbook
A Very Chinese Cookbook
Boards
Gatherings

The Sheet Pan
The Skillet
Cook It in Your Dutch Oven
Cook It in Cast Iron
Ultimate Air Fryer Perfection
Kitchen Gear

Baking for Two
Everyday Bread
The Cook's Illustrated Baking Book
The Perfect Cookie
The Perfect Pie
The Perfect Cake

The Science of Good Cooking
Cook's Science
The New Cooking School Cookbook: Fundamentals
The New Cooking School Cookbook: Advanced Fundamentals

Mostly Meatless
Vegan for Everybody
Vegan Cooking for Two
Vegetables Illustrated
How Can It Be Gluten Free Cookbook Collection

The Complete Anti-Inflammatory Cookbook
The Complete Plant-Based Cookbook
The Complete Beans and Grains Cookbook
The Complete Mediterranean Cookbook
The Complete Cooking for Two Cookbook, 10th Anniversary Edition
The Complete Diabetes Cookbook
The Complete Vegetarian Cookbook
The Complete One Pot
The Complete Autumn and Winter Cookbook
The Complete Summer Cookbook
The Complete Modern Pantry
The Complete Salad Cookbook

The Complete America's Test Kitchen TV Show Cookbook
The Complete Cook's Country TV Show Cookbook

For a full listing of all our books:

COOKSILLUSTRATED.COM
AMERICASTESTKITCHEN.COM

Praise for America's Test Kitchen Titles

"The book is a treasure for its endless kitchen wisdom, heart-filled recipes, and deep-rooted respect for all generations that came before. It showcases home cooking at its best, ranging from sauces, banchan (side dishes), and a slew of kimchi, to gurgling stews, tantalizing meats, and not-too-sweet fare."

Epicurious on *Umma: A Korean Mom's Kitchen Wisdom & 100 Family Recipes*

A Best Cookbook of 2024

Los Angeles Times* on *When Southern Women Cook

"This 'very' Chinese cookbook from a father-son duo is a keeper. The book—ATK's first devoted to Chinese cooking—proves that you can teach and entertain in the same volume . . . All in all, it's one of the most charming works I've seen in years, and I already want to get a second copy."

Washington Post* on *A Very Chinese Cookbook

"An exhaustive but approachable primer for those looking for a 'flexible' diet. Chock-full of tips, you can dive into the science of plant-based cooking or just sit back and enjoy the 500 recipes."

Minneapolis Star Tribune* on *The Complete Plant-Based Cookbook

"This comprehensive guide is packed with delicious recipes and fun menu ideas but its unique draw is the personal narrative and knowledge-sharing of each ATK chef, which will make this a hit."

Booklist* on *Gatherings

"True to its name, this smart and endlessly enlightening cookbook is about as definitive as it's possible to get in the modern vegetarian realm."

Men's Journal* on *The Complete Vegetarian Cookbook

"A mood board for one's food board is served up in this excellent guide . . . This has instant classic written all over it."

Publishers Weekly* (starred review) on *Boards: Stylish Spreads for Casual Gatherings

"Reassuringly hefty and comprehensive, *The Complete Autumn and Winter Cookbook* by America's Test Kitchen has you covered with a seemingly endless array of seasonal fare . . . This overstuffed compendium is guaranteed to warm you from the inside out."

NPR on *The Complete Autumn and Winter Cookbook*

"If you're one of the 30 million Americans with diabetes, *The Complete Diabetes Cookbook* by America's Test Kitchen belongs on your kitchen shelf."

Parade.com on *The Complete Diabetes Cookbook*

"Another flawless entry in the America's Test Kitchen canon, *Bowls* guides readers of all culinary skill levels in composing one-bowl meals from a variety of cuisines."

BuzzFeed Books on *Bowls*

"*The Perfect Cookie* . . . is, in a word, perfect. This is an important and substantial cookbook . . . If you love cookies, but have been a tad shy to bake on your own, all your fears will be dissipated. This is one book you can use for years with magnificently happy results."

HuffPost on *The Perfect Cookie*

"The book offers an impressive education for curious cake makers, new and experienced alike. A summation of 25 years of cake making at ATK, there are cakes for every taste."

Wall Street Journal* on *The Perfect Cake

"The go-to gift book for newlyweds, small families, or empty nesters."

Orlando Sentinel* on *The Complete Cooking for Two Cookbook

the complete
GRILLING
&
BARBECUE
cookbook
AMERICA'S TEST KITCHEN

Library of Congress Cataloging-in-Publication Data has been applied for.

ISBN 978-1-966027-04-1

America's Test Kitchen

21 Drydock Avenue, Boston, MA 02210

Printed in China

10 9 8 7 6 5 4 3 2 1

Distributed by Penguin Random House Publisher Services

Tel: 800-733-3000

Editorial Director, Books: Adam Kowit

Executive Food Editor: Dan Zuccarello

Deputy Food Editor: Stephanie Pixley

Executive Managing Editor: Debra Hudak

Project Editor: Cheryl Redmond

Senior Editor: Joe Gitter

Associate Editor: Claudia Catalano

Senior Photo Test Cook: José Maldonado

Test Cook: Malcolm Jackson, Hannah Smokelin, and Stephanie Winter

Kitchen Intern: Canela Almonte

Assistant Editor: Julia Arwine

Creative Director, Editorial: Lindsey Timko Chandler

Art Director and Designer: Nicole O'Toole

VP of Imagery: Casey Stenger

Senior Photography Producer: Meredith Mulcahy

Senior Staff Photographers: Steve Klise and Daniel J. van Ackere

Staff Photographer: Kritsada Panichgul

Additional Photography: Joseph Keller, Carl Tremblay, and Kevin White

Senior Food Stylist: Christine Tobin

Food Styling: Joy Howard, Sheila Jarnes, Catrine Kelty, Chantal Lambeth, Ashley Moore, Marie Piraino, Elle Simone Scott, Kendra Smith, and Sally Staub

Illustrations: Jay Layman

Project Manager, Books: Kelly Gauthier

Senior Print Production Specialist: Lauren Robbins

Production and Imaging Coordinator: Amanda Yong

Production and Imaging Specialist: Tricia Neumyer

Production and Imaging Assistant: Chloe Petraske

Copy Editor: Elizabeth Wray Emery

Proofreader: Vicki Rowland

Indexer: Elizabeth Parson

Chief Executive Officer: Dan Suratt

Chief Content Officer: Dan Souza

Senior Content Adviser: Jack Bishop

Executive Editorial Directors: Julia Collin Davison and Bridget Lancaster

Senior Director, Book Sales: Emily Logan

Contents

B
A

C

WELCOME TO

America's Test Kitchen

This book has been tested, written, and edited by the folks at America's Test Kitchen, where curious home cooks become confident cooks. Located in Boston's Seaport District in the historic Innovation and Design Building, it features 15,000 square feet of kitchen space including multiple photography and video studios. It is the home of *Cook's Illustrated* magazine and is the workday destination for more than 60 test cooks, editors, and cookware specialists. Our mission is to empower and inspire confidence, community, and creativity in the kitchen.

We start the process of testing a recipe with a complete lack of preconceptions, which means that we accept no claim, no technique, and no recipe at face value. We simply assemble as many variations as possible, test a half dozen of the most promising, and taste the results blind. We then construct our own recipe and continue to test it, varying ingredients, techniques, and cooking times until we reach a consensus. As we like to say in the test kitchen, "We make the mistakes so you don't have to." The result is our best version of every recipe. We use the same rigorous approach when we test equipment and taste ingredients.

All of this would not be possible without a belief that good cooking, much like good music, is based on a foundation of objective technique. Some people like spicy foods and others don't, but there is a right way to sauté, there is a best way to cook a pot roast, and there are measurable scientific principles involved in producing perfectly beaten, stable egg whites. Our ultimate goal is to investigate the fundamental principles of cooking to give you the techniques, tools, and ingredients you need to become a better cook. It is as simple as that.

Founded in 1992, ATK is the leading multimedia cooking resource serving millions of cooks like you with our trusted expertise. Come inside our kitchens on public television's most-watched cooking shows, *America's Test Kitchen* and *Cook's Country*. Watch every season and our original streaming series on your favorite streaming platforms.

We invite you to explore our app and website for access to thousands of rigorously tested recipes, unbiased product reviews, classes, videos, and more in one easy-to-use, ad-free digital experience.

Download the five-star-rated ATK app today.

cooks.io/subscribe

Follow us on Social

@TestKitchen

@TestKitchen

@AmericasTestKitchen

@AmericasTestKitchen

Getting Started

THE GRILL

THE FIRE

THE GEAR

THE FOOD

Fire Up the Grill

The practice of cooking outdoors with live fire is so ancient, it's practically in our DNA. Unlike many culinary tools we use today, grills don't promise to do the work for you. What they do promise—and deliver—is unmatched flavor and aroma, as well as an overall eating experience that's unique and special. When you serve a great meal off the grill to hungry, happy, impressed friends and family, you feel the pride and satisfaction that comes from mastering a skill and sharing the delicious results.

At America's Test Kitchen, we want you to feel that way every time you grill. We've gathered our best recipes, insights, and techniques from the past 30 years that will build your skill no matter what your level of experience is. Our comprehensive range of recipes includes full meals you can grill in under an hour, vibrant grilled sides and salads, company-worthy roasts, and delectable "grill-baked" goods. We also include a whole chapter of pitmaster-level barbecue so authentic that you'll be amazed you can produce it on your grill.

Our introduction is an essential guide to the way fire, fuel, equipment, and ingredients all interact to make memorable meals. We explain the science behind the techniques so you can customize your grill's heat output to the food you want to eat, add just the right amount of smokiness to your meal, season your food for the best texture and color, and make your cooking grate slick enough to turn out even delicate fish with ease.

If you know the secrets to great grilled steaks, burgers, and vegetables, you can cook them confidently even without a recipe, so we've included quick and thorough guides to those foods in special chapter sections, along with handy information on keeping lean pork juicy on the grill, achieving perfectly browned pizza crust with a clever charcoal "ring" arrangement, and more.

Useful tools and smart organization go a long way to make grilling both enjoyable and successful. We've sorted through and tested a staggering array of grilling equipment and narrowed it down to what works the best and helps you the most. And we show you how to set up a simple grillside prep station that will make cooking outside just as efficient as cooking inside.

Sometimes you want to make grilling a fun challenge or a celebration—and sometimes you just want to cook dinner without heating up the kitchen. You can do it all, using nothing more than your grill, your love of good food, and this book. Whatever your grilling goals or mood, we've got you covered. The groundwork for great grilling is in your hands.

THE GRILL

It Starts with Heat

People put a lot of thought into choosing the best grill—and rightly so—but for excellent grilled food, your most important tool is the heat you create in the grill, whether it comes from lit charcoal or gas flames. Understanding the way heat works will help you keep a cool head when it comes to grilling so that you can adjust the fire for the best outcome.

HOW HEAT WORKS IN THE GRILL

Heat travels in three main ways: conduction, convection, and radiation.

CONDUCTION

takes place when heat moves through direct contact between a hot object (such as a grill grate) and a cooler object (such as a steak). Conduction is responsible for the handsome grill marks foods develop from the grate, but apart from that it doesn't play a major role in grilling.

CONVECTION

is the movement of heat through currents in a fluid, such as air (scientifically, air is a fluid). The heat source heats the air, the air travels toward the food (hot air rises), and the heat is transferred from the air to the food. Convection is the primary way that a **gas grill** cooks: The gas burners generate a lot of hot airflow, which envelops and heats the food.

RADIANT HEAT

is the primary way that **charcoal grills** cook. The glowing coals pump out infrared rays that travel on straight, linear paths—like the beams of light they are—to heat the food. The metal "drip-catcher" bars on gas grills also emit some radiant heat.

Why do charcoal grills brown better than gas grills?

Quick browning on grilled foods comes mainly from radiant heat. Charcoal, once it has burned down to glowing coals and ash, emits almost all radiant heat. Gas, on the other hand, gives off very little radiant heat (though it burns about 75 percent hotter than charcoal). To compensate, manufacturers insert ceramic rods, metal bars, or lava rocks above the flames of gas grills to capture the energy from the burning fuel and convert it into radiant heat. But as the hot gases travel from the flames to these radiant surfaces, some are simply carried away by air currents. This makes it difficult to raise the temperature of the radiant emitters as high as that of glowing coals, putting most gas grills at a disadvantage when it comes to browning.

PUTTING GRILL HEAT TO WORK FOR YOU

You can achieve different cooking effects when grilling by dividing the grill into zones of direct and indirect heat.

DIRECT HEAT

Direct heat flows straight from the heat source to the food, in the form of radiant infrared rays as well as rising convective currents of hot air.

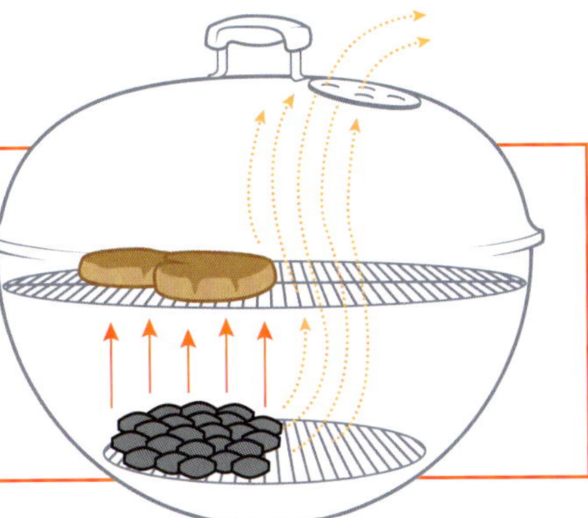

INDIRECT HEAT

Indirect heat is largely convection heat, as circulating hot air gently surrounds the food to cook it at a moderate temperature.

THE GRILL

Anatomy of a Grill

First things first: You can grill—and barbecue—amazing food with either a charcoal grill or a gas grill. (There are a handful of recipes in this book that require a charcoal grill, but a few hundred recipes that will work great on either kind.) Charcoal and gas grills both have plenty to recommend them, and many serious grillers own one of each. But if you need to make a choice, here are some things to consider.

CHARCOAL GRILLS

BENEFITS:

- Can achieve higher temperatures than most gas grills, leading to deeper searing and charring.
- Better control of heat and airflow thanks to adjustable vents in base and lid.
- Can produce stronger smoky flavors in longer-cooking foods such as brisket and ribs.

CHALLENGES:

- Managing a live charcoal fire is a bit of an art and requires more focused attention.
- Heat fades over time unless charcoal is replenished.
- Ash catcher must be emptied periodically.

OUR FAVORITE:
Weber Original Kettle Premium Charcoal Grill

UPGRADE PICK:
Weber Performer Deluxe Charcoal Grill with gas ignition system

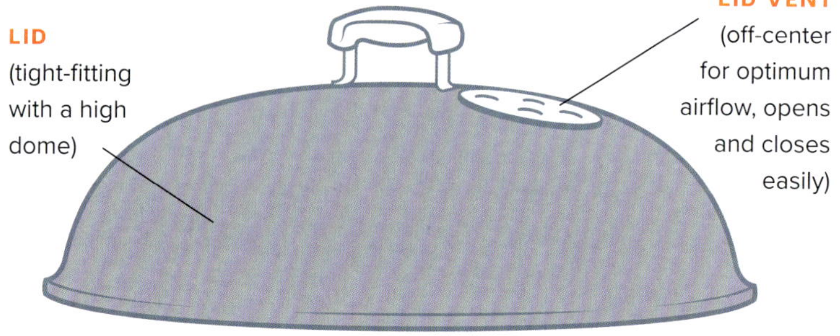

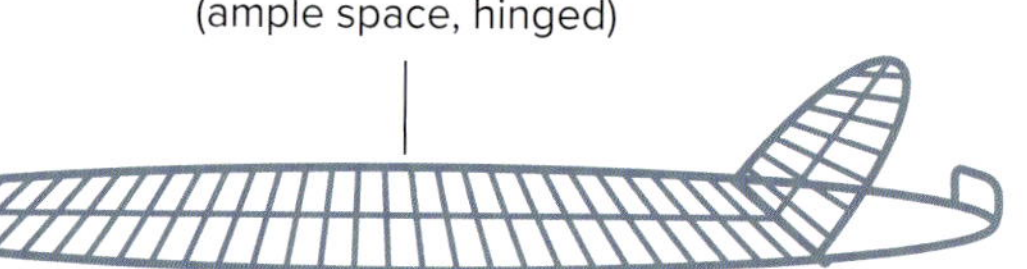

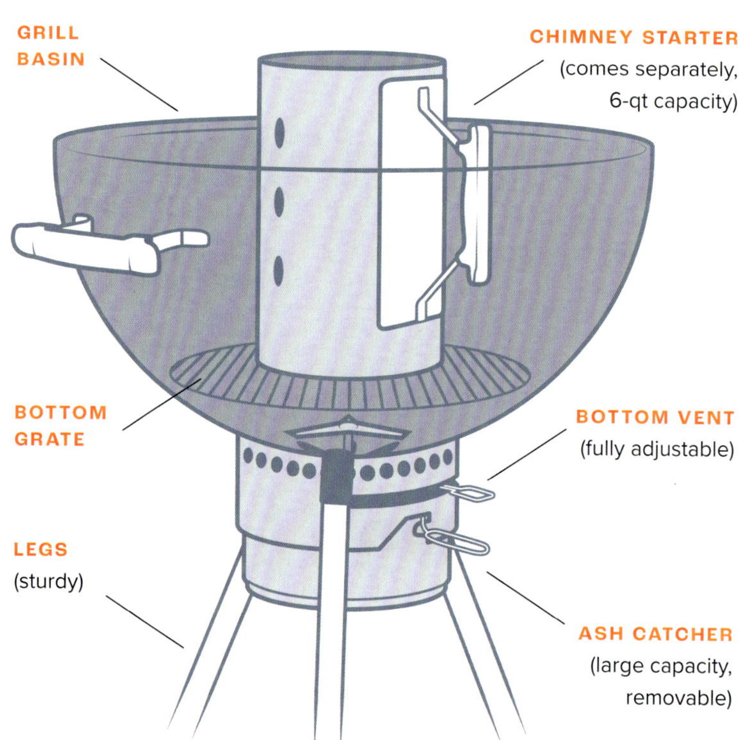

GAS GRILLS

BENEFITS:

- Convenience of lighting: Just turn on the gas, push a button, and go.
- Provides steady, consistent heat.
- Multiple burners can be adjusted or turned off to create different cooking configurations.

CHALLENGES:

- Requires checking that you have enough propane; tank must be returned to store for refills.
- Most models don't get ripping hot.
- Vents aren't usually adjustable, giving you little to no control over airflow and heat flow.
- Produces less-pronounced charred, smoky flavor especially in longer-cooked foods.
- Grease tray must be emptied periodically.

OUR FAVORITE:
Weber Spirit E-325 Gas Grill

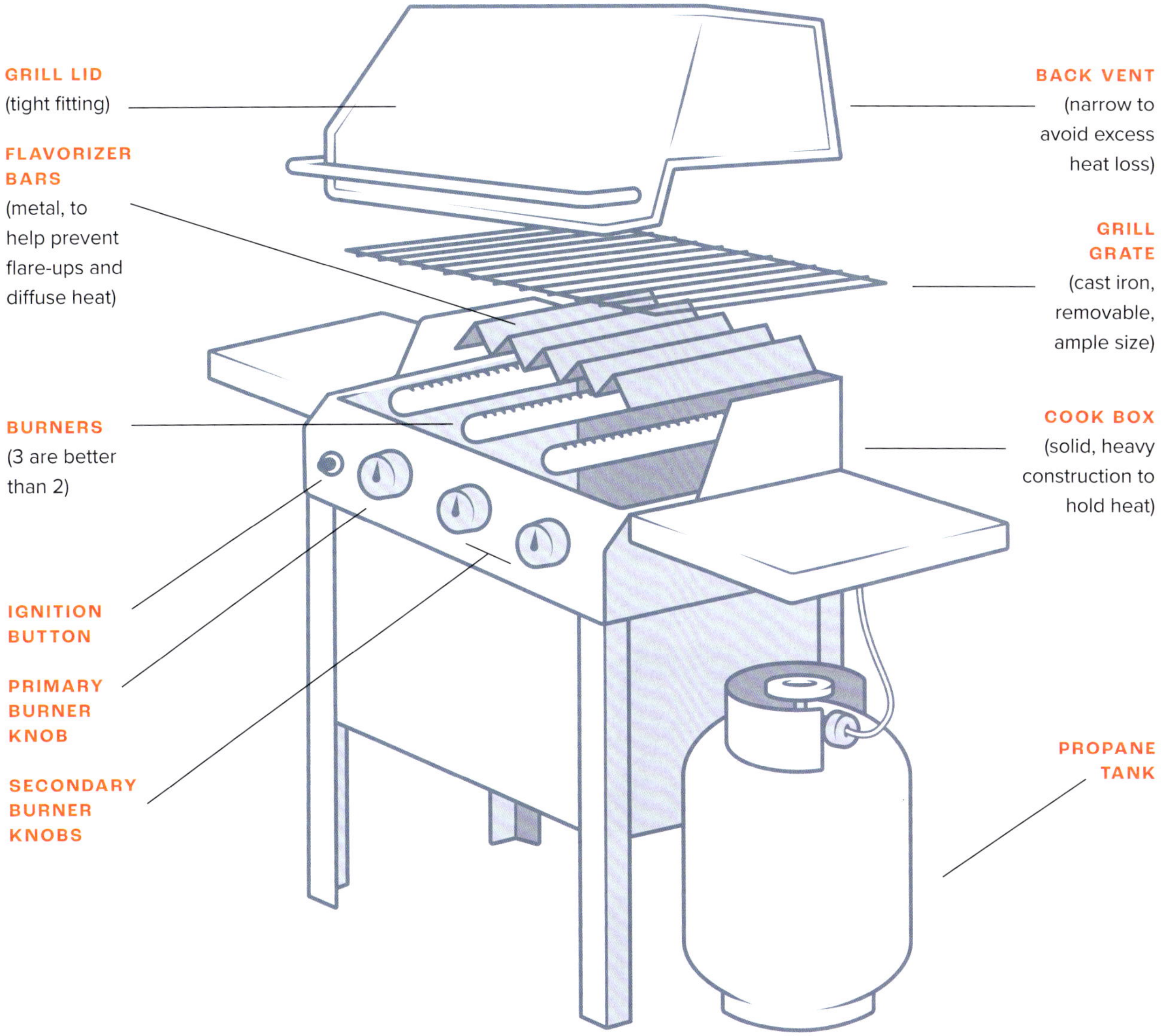

GRILL LID
(tight fitting)

FLAVORIZER BARS
(metal, to help prevent flare-ups and diffuse heat)

BURNERS
(3 are better than 2)

IGNITION BUTTON

PRIMARY BURNER KNOB

SECONDARY BURNER KNOBS

BACK VENT
(narrow to avoid excess heat loss)

GRILL GRATE
(cast iron, removable, ample size)

COOK BOX
(solid, heavy construction to hold heat)

PROPANE TANK

THE FIRE

All About Fuel

The choices of charcoal, the convenience of gas: No matter what you use, it's important to get to know your fuel, both for safety and so that you develop a sense of how it performs.

CHARCOAL

There are two types of charcoal: **lump** ▲ (also known as hardwood) and **briquettes**. ▼ While lump resembles the wood it comes from and briquettes are compact pucks made from sawdust and other materials, both are byproducts of the lumber industry.

Some lump charcoal enthusiasts claim that lump burns hotter than briquettes do, and that it makes food more flavorful. It's hard to make universal rules about whether lump or briquettes burn hotter overall: The heat of any fire depends on a large range of factors, including the mass, density, composition, and size of the charcoal; the way it's arranged (and the resulting air flow); and how the charcoal was made. As for flavor, charcoal in any form contributes aromatic smoke, but it lacks the more complex array of flavor molecules you get from burning raw wood. Lump charcoal is more expensive, and its irregular shapes and sizes means that each bag will have some unusable material; when you factor that in, the price difference can be significant. Because a full chimney of lump will burn faster than a full chimney of briquettes, you may need to use more of it or replenish it more frequently.

Our advice? For quick grilling, choose either kind of charcoal. If you're going to be grilling for more than 40 minutes, go for briquettes since they stay hot longer.

Can I reuse charcoal?

Sometimes the food is done, but the coals are not. You can save them and replace up to half the fresh coals called for in a recipe with used coals. Here's how.

SAVE

1 As soon as you're finished grilling, cover the grill and close the vents.

2 Once the coals are cool enough to handle, dump them into a small, lidded metal container, such as a garbage can.

REUSE

1 Before you light a new fire, place the used, cooled briquettes in a charcoal chimney starter and shake and rap it over the trash to dislodge loose ash. Temporarily remove the coals from the chimney starter.

2 To maximize airflow, place 1 part fresh coals in the chimney first and top them with 1 part used coals.

GAS

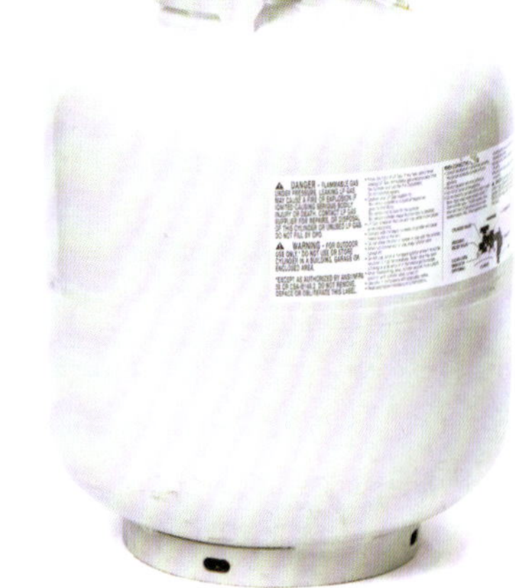

Convenience and reliability are big selling points in the choice of a gas grill over a charcoal grill. However, there are still things you need to pay attention to, particularly if you are using **propane**, ► which requires you to use refillable tanks (rather than natural gas, which requires you to connect your grill to a natural gas supply line).

While propane has an indefinite shelf life, propane tanks do not. In the United States, steel propane cylinders have to be inspected and recertified 12 years after manufacture and every five years after that. The date of manufacture is stamped on the collar at the top of the tank: 02 24 means the tank was manufactured in February 2024. Regardless of the tank's age, it should be free from dents and rust; if you see any damage, even on an unexpired tank, dispose of it properly by trading it in at your propane dealer or hardware store. And, especially at the beginning of grilling season, make sure to check the fuel hose for signs of wear (or chewing damage from critters).

BTUs—THE HIGHER THE BETTER?

The heat output of a gas grill is measured in British Thermal Units or BTUs, but this number doesn't tell the whole story. In addition to producing significant heat, a great grill retains that heat and spreads it across the grates. When we tested gas grills, one grill rated at 30,000 BTUs outperformed another rated at 55,000 BTUs, thanks to its superior ability to hold on to and disperse heat.

Check Your Fuel

In general, you should get between 10 and 20 hours of grilling from a 20-pound tank of propane—the larger the grill, the faster it uses up fuel. If your grill doesn't have a gas gauge, use this method:

1 Bring about 1 cup of water to boil. Pour water over side of tank.

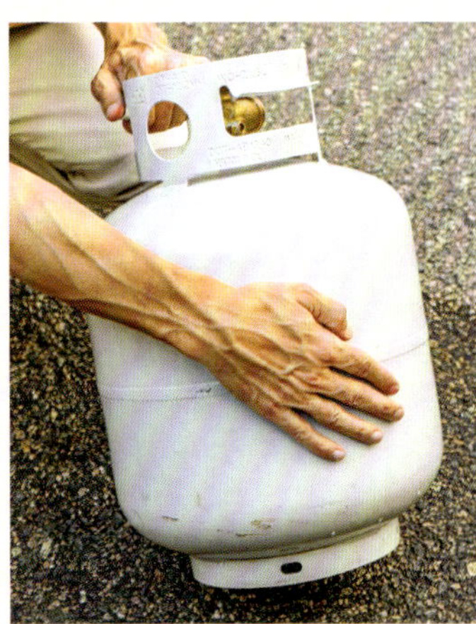

2 Where water has warmed metal, the tank is empty; where metal remains cool to touch, there is propane inside.

THE FIRE

Light It Up

There's more of an art to cooking with charcoal than with gas, and that starts with lighting the grill. Whichever kind of grill you're using, though, a clean, nonstick grate is your first key to success. Follow these steps and get ready to grill.

PREPPING A CHARCOAL GRILL

1 Remove the cooking grate. Fill a chimney starter with the amount of charcoal called for in the recipe and set it on the lower grate (make sure the bottom vent is open).

2 Light and wait until the charcoal is covered with fine gray ash (about 20 minutes), a sign that the coals are fully lit.

3 Pour the coals onto the lower grate as directed in the recipe. (Don't pour out the coals prematurely or you'll be left with unlit coals that may never ignite as well as a cooler fire.)

4 Set the cooking grate in place, cover the grill, and heat for 5 minutes.

How to Use a Chimney Starter

A chimney starter heats coals safely, evenly, and efficiently; we consider it a must-have for charcoal grilling. Our favorite model (see page 18) is roomy enough to hold sufficient charcoal for any grilling task.

To use a chimney starter, tuck a couple crumpled sheets of newspaper in the bottom chamber and pour the desired amount of charcoal into the top chamber. Set the chimney starter on the bottom grill grate and light the newspaper. In about 20 minutes (depending on the weather conditions and type of charcoal) the top layer of charcoal will be covered in a fine layer of white ash—the visual cue that it's ready to use.

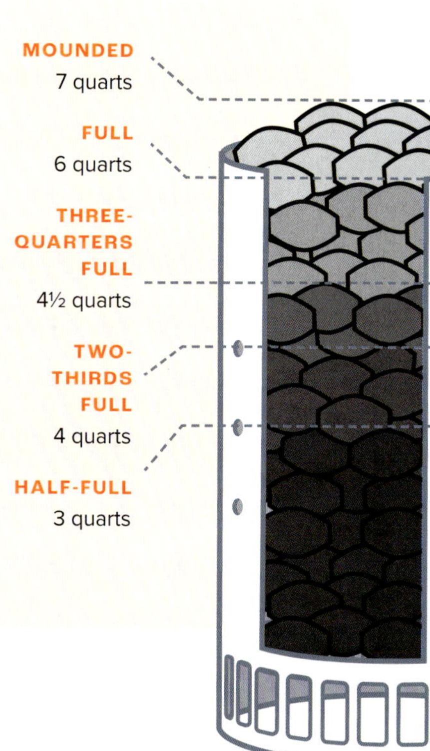

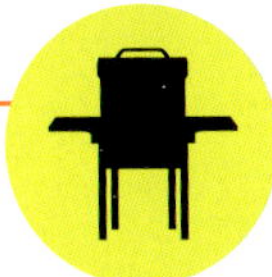

PREPPING A GAS GRILL

1 Open the lid.

2 Turn on the gas.

3 Light the burners as directed in the recipe.

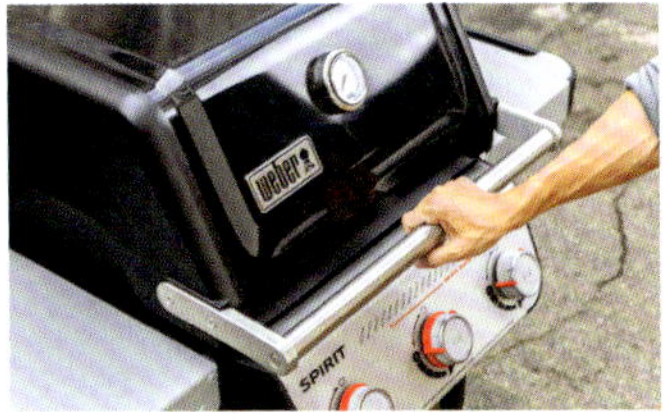

4 Cover the grill and heat for 15 minutes.

CLEANING AND OILING THE COOKING GRATE

If you don't want the burnt, sooty residue from last night's dinner flavoring tonight's meal, grill on a clean grate. You could clean the grate when you're done cooking, but why not enjoy your food while it's hot? Instead, spend a few minutes on the job before you start grilling. Scraping the grate clean gets rid of oil as well as burnt food residue, so it's important to also apply fresh oil every time you grill.

1 Once the grate is hot, scrape it thoroughly with a grill brush to remove all debris, which would cause food to stick. If you don't have a brush, a crumpled-up wad of aluminum foil held with a pair of long-handled tongs does a decent job.

2 Pour a few tablespoons of vegetable oil into a small bowl. Using long-handled tongs, dip a wad of paper towels in the oil and wipe the cooking grate several times. The oil offers a layer of protection against sticking.

3 The first coat or two of oil will burn off, so to build up a nonstick coating—especially important for delicate foods such as fish—continue dipping the wad of towels into the oil and slicking down the grate until it turns black and glossy.

HOW TO TURN YOUR GRILL INTO A NONSTICK COOKING SURFACE

When you place meat or seafood on the grill, its proteins form an almost instantaneous bond to the grate. This molecule-to-molecule fusion is stronger than the superficial bond caused by a sticky barbecue sauce or glaze. Your first line of defense against this bonding is to create a barrier between the food and the grill by cleaning and then oiling the grate.

When oil is applied to a hot cooking grate, it vaporizes almost instantly, leaving a black, weblike residue. As the oil heats up, its fatty-acid chains form polymers (that is, they stick together), creating a crisscross pattern over the surface of the metal. A single layer of these polymers won't prevent sticking, but applying and heating oil repeatedly builds up a thicker layer. The more delicate the food (think fish fillets), the more times you want to repeat oiling. Also, the hotter the grate the better, so for extra insurance you can briefly cover the grill during the oiling process to let the grate heat back up before continuing. After enough applications of oil, proteins will no longer come into direct contact with the metal and therefore won't be able to bond with it. That black, glossy appearance is your sign that the grate is ready for you to start grilling.

THE FIRE

Fine-Tune Your Fire

By piling lit coals into different arrangements on a charcoal grill, you can create hotter or cooler temperature zones to grill food of any size or shape. You can also make a hotter or cooler fire by using more or fewer coals. After preheating a gas grill, you can adjust the burners to mimic most charcoal configurations. Here are the setups we use most often for grilling and grill roasting. (For more about barbecue setups see page 218.)

SINGLE-LEVEL FIRE

Delivers uniform level of heat across entire cooking surface

GOOD FOR

Quick-cooking pieces of food such as shrimp, fish fillets, thin steaks, boneless chops or chicken breasts, and a wide range of vegetables

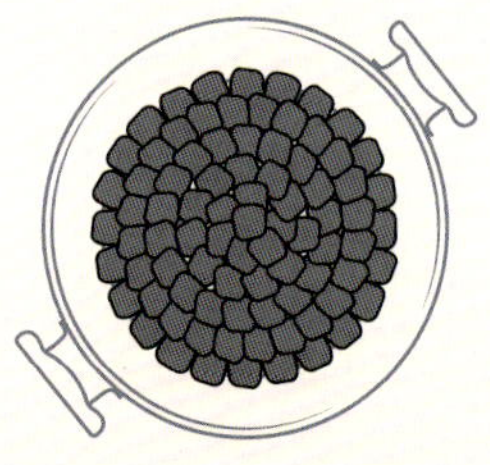

CHARCOAL METHOD

Distribute lit coals in even layer across bottom of grill.

GAS METHOD

Turn all burners to desired heat setting (low, medium, or high).

TWO-LEVEL FIRE

Creates two cooking zones: hotter zone for searing and slightly cooler zone for gentler cooking

GOOD FOR

Thick chops, bone-in poultry pieces, recipes with multiple foods that require different heat levels

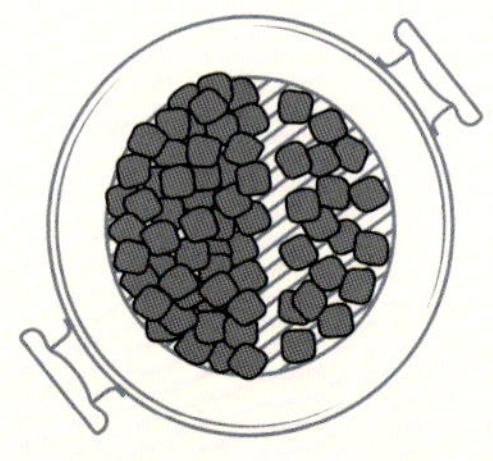

CHARCOAL METHOD

Evenly distribute two-thirds of lit coals over half of grill, then distribute remaining coals over other half.

GAS METHOD

Leave primary burner on high and turn other burner(s) to medium.

CONCENTRATED FIRE

Creates contained area of intense heat to sear quick-cooking foods

GOOD FOR

Burgers, scallops, pork cutlets

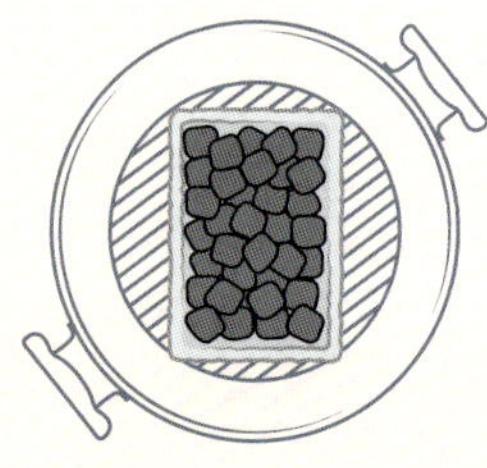

CHARCOAL METHOD

Poke holes in bottom of disposable aluminum roasting pan and set in center of grill; pour lit coals into pan.

GAS METHOD

Leave all burners on high.

HALF-GRILL FIRE

Creates two cooking zones with greater heat difference than two-level fire: one intensely hot side and one relatively cool side

GOOD FOR

Thick steaks, pork tenderloin, bone-in poultry pieces, foods that need both searing and gentle cooking

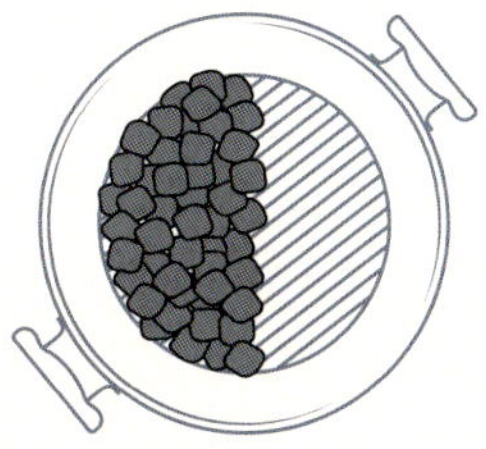

CHARCOAL METHOD

Distribute lit coals over half of grill, piling them in even layer; leave other half of grill free of coals.

GAS METHOD

Adjust primary burner to desired heat level and turn off other burner(s).

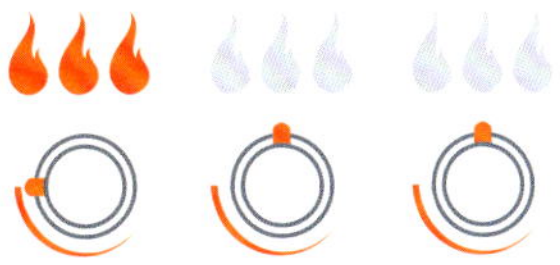

BANKED FIRE

Concentrates heat in smaller area than half-grill fire; can accommodate pan of water to prevent food from drying out

GOOD FOR

Large foods such as brisket, pork shoulder, or whole poultry; foods that need both browning and indirect cooking

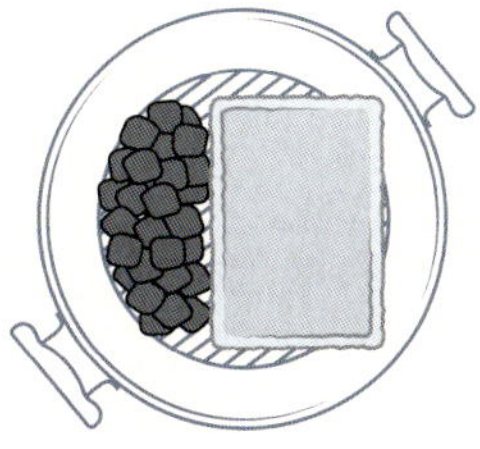

CHARCOAL METHOD

Place disposable aluminum roasting pan, if using, on 1 side of grill; bank lit coals steeply against other side.

GAS METHOD

Adjust primary burner to desired heat level and turn off other burner(s).

SPLIT FIRE

Creates cooler area between two heat sources so that food cooks evenly without needing to be rotated

GOOD FOR

Whole chickens, small roasts

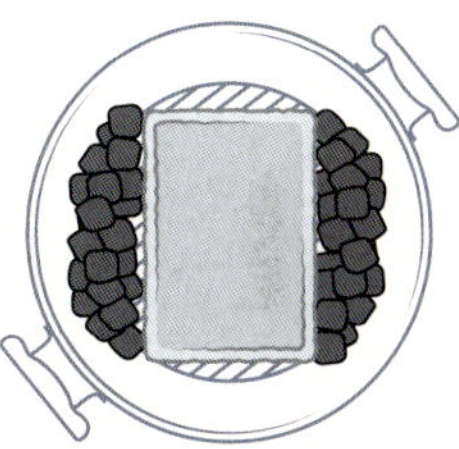

CHARCOAL METHOD

Place disposable aluminum roasting pan in center; pour lit coals in 2 steeply banked piles along long sides of pan.

GAS METHOD

Requires at least 3 burners: Leave primary burner and burner at opposite end of grill on medium-high or medium and turn off center burner(s).

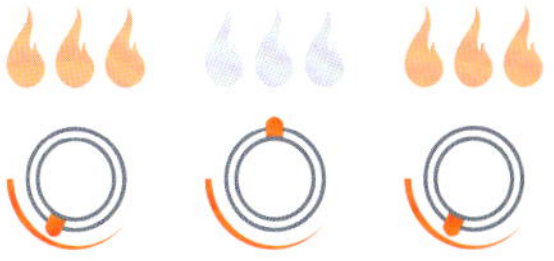

THE FIRE

Control Heat and Airflow

The coals are glowing and the grate is hot—but that's not all there is to grilling. Once the food hits the grill, you want to monitor and adjust the heat for the best results, whether that means a juicy burger with great char or a smoky, golden whole turkey. You might think that gas grills, with their temperature dials for each burner, have the edge in this department. But although charcoal grills seem rudimentary, they're very adaptable—perhaps more so than gas—if you know what to do with the vents and the lid.

THE VENTS

Grill vents are like the dials on your stovetop: They allow you to manipulate how hot the fire gets and how the food cooks.

Charcoal grills have a vent in the lid and a vent on the underside of the basin. In general, opening the vents completely allows more oxygen to reach the fire so that it burns hotter and faster, while opening the vents only partially lowers the temperature and prolongs the fire's duration. Because heat and smoke rise from the coals and are drawn out through the **top vent**, you can position the lid with the vent over the food maximize heat and smoke contact, or with the vent away from the food to minimize heat and smoke contact. The **bottom vent** is always at least partially open when cooking; air drawn through the bottom vent feeds the fire. Completely closing the top and bottom vents will kill charcoal fires quickly; you can save any unburned charcoal for the next time you grill.

Gas grills have vents, too, but they are not adjustable; when the lid is closed, hot air and smoke flow straight out the back of the grill. That's why it's important to choose a gas grill with a narrow vent and a thick, heat-retaining body.

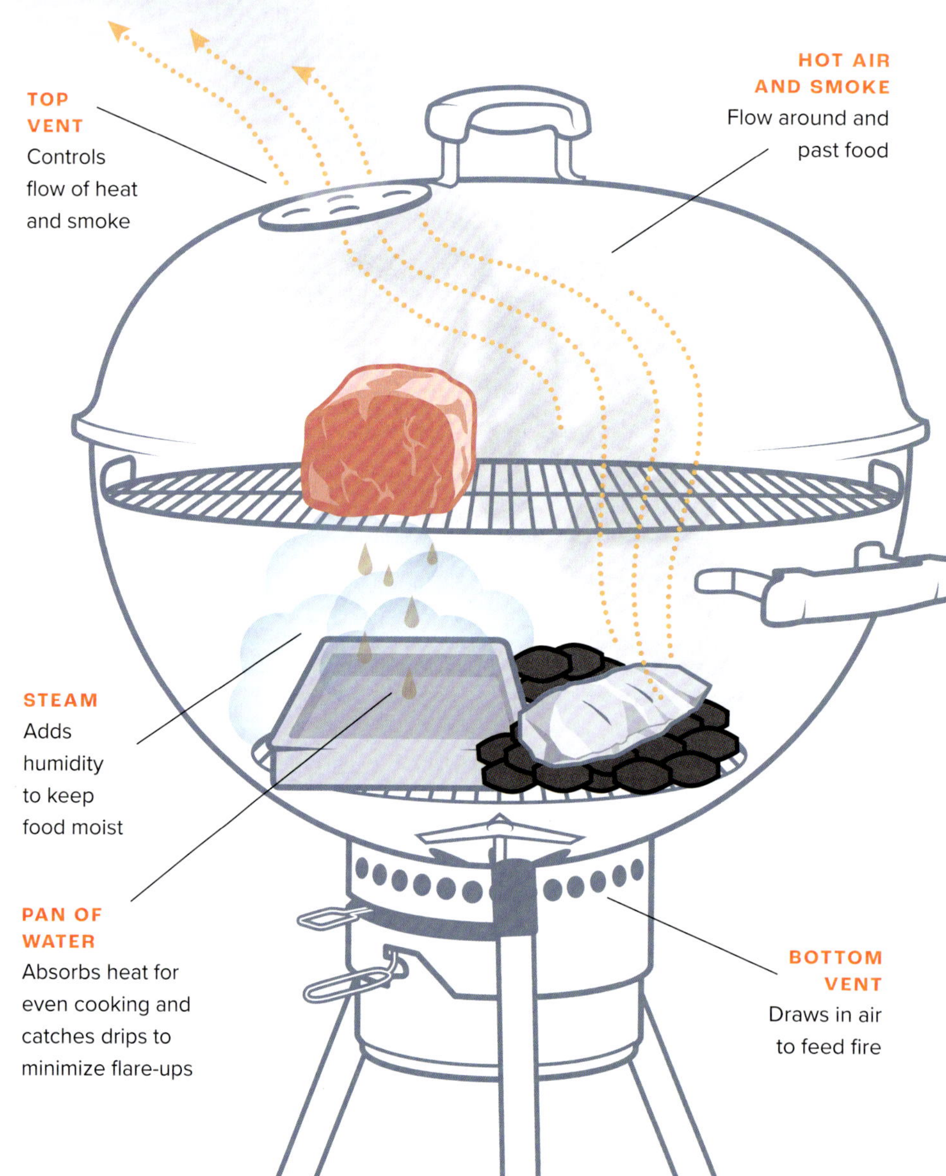

THE LID

An uncovered grill loses a lot of heat, and only the side of the food facing the flames gets hot. This is OK for thin, fast-cooking foods such as burgers, but for many dishes, trapping heat by keeping the lid down makes for more efficient cooking.

In general, heat loss is less of a problem with charcoal grills because they run hotter than gas grills. For that reason, the same recipe might call for covering a gas grill while leaving a charcoal grill uncovered. The lid on a charcoal grill is mostly used for low-and-slow cooking and smoking.

One major exception: If you're grilling in cold or windy weather, you should cook with the lid down regardless of what type of grill you're using, or you'll be wasting gas or burning through charcoal as the heat gets whisked away.

FIRE AND WATER

A pan of water placed under the cooking grate creates conditions inside the grill that you can use to your advantage in a few different ways.

First, the evaporating water increases humidity. This keeps the surface of the food moister. Because smoke adheres better to a moist surface, the pan of water boosts the effect of wood chips or chunks, helping transfer smoke flavor to the food. Higher humidity in the grill also slows down evaporation from the surface of the food. As meat loses moisture through evaporation, it creates a cooling effect that can cause the meat's temperature to stop rising, or "stall," particularly in low-and-slow grilling situations. Higher humidity counters this effect so that the meat can continue to cook.

Second, the pan of water absorbs a lot of heat energy, stabilizing the heat in the grill and keeping the whole setup a bit cooler, which promotes gentle, even cooking during longer grill times. Some people use a pan filled with rocks or an empty pan, but a dry pan absorbs heat only until its temperature matches that of the surrounding air. Water requires a constant flow of heat in order to evaporate, so it will moderate the heat during the entire grilling session (as long as the pan is topped up occasionally). Finally, a pan positioned directly under the food will catch drips and minimize flare-ups.

You can find all these principles at work in our recipes. The moist environment from the pan of water keeps Chicago Baby Back Ribs (page 230) moist and tender. Placing the water pan directly under our Simple Grill-Roasted Turkey (page 184) eliminates flare-ups, so the meat tastes roasted, not smoky or sooty. Humidity keeps the chicken skin in our Smoked Chicken Parts (page 139) moist so that the smoke from wood chips can adhere better. And it helps reduce evaporative cooling from our Barbecued Flat-Cut Brisket (page 242), so the cooking process doesn't stall.

Can I Trust My Grill's Thermometer?

Your grill thermometer may measure temperature accurately, but what temperature, exactly, is it measuring? If the thermometer (and therefore its sensor) is in the lid, that number on its dial tells you how hot the air near the lid is, not how hot the cooking surface is. The difference between the two can be as much as 50 to 100 degrees Fahrenheit, and it can vary even more when you open and close the lid. As long as you remember this, you can use a built-in thermometer to gauge whether your burners are working as they usually do. But for the best outcome, use a remote probe or instant-read thermometer (see page 18) and monitor the temperature of the food itself.

Summon the Smoke

The complex aroma and taste of smoked foods is irresistible. When you understand how smoke flavors food you can produce subtly or dramatically smoked foods on your grill. Here's what you need to know to add smoke to your grilling skill set.

Smoking is one of the oldest known methods of food preservation: Archeologists think this technique has been used for more than 3,000 years. But although smoke does have antimicrobial properties that help protect food from spoilage, in the age of refrigeration we primarily value smoke because it imparts unique and complex flavors to food. That's the effect achieved in the many barbecued and grilled recipes in this book that include wood chips or chunks. Here's how it works.

Smoke is a fragrant, visible suspension of particles in air that rises from burning materials such as wood. When wood burns, one of its primary components, lignin, breaks down to form hundreds of smoky aroma compounds that we associate with barbecue, such as guaiacol and syringol. The sugars in cellulose and hemicellulose, wood's other major components, break apart into additional flavor compounds, including some of the same molecules found in caramel, such as cyclotene, which is reminiscent of maple syrup. These aromas drift up in the form of smoke, which clings to the surface of food, imbuing it with flavor. Moisture on the surface of the food helps the flavorful compounds, which are mostly water-soluble, adhere and dissolve. Because of this, smoke flavor is absorbed most rapidly at the beginning of cooking, when the food contains more moisture.

HOW TO MAKE A FOIL PACKET FOR WOOD CHIPS

1 Spread wood chips in center of 15 by 12-inch piece of heavy-duty aluminum foil. Fold into 8 by 4-inch packet, fold to seal edges, and cut 2 evenly spaced 2-inch slits in top of packet.

2A Place foil packet on lit coals if using charcoal grill.

2B Place foil packet over primary burner if using gas grill.

We don't usually soak wood chips when smoking food; soaking delays the onset of smoke, since the wood can't smolder until the water is driven off.

A **foil packet** measuring 8 by 4 inches is just the right size to fit under the grates of most gas grills and won't block too much heat from the burner. Use heavy-duty foil, and not too big a piece: Multiple foil layers, with air trapped between them, end up insulating the chips from the heat, so they don't get hot enough to smoke.

Cutting slits in the packet is the key to wood chips that smolder but don't ignite. Two 2-inch-long slits should let in just enough oxygen for a steady smolder but not enough for the chips to burn. If the chips aren't smoking, insert the tip of a paring knife to gently widen the openings just a little at a time. (On a gas grill, make sure that the slits aren't blocked by the grate's bars when the packet is on the burner.)

CHOOSING AND USING WOOD CHIPS AND CHUNKS

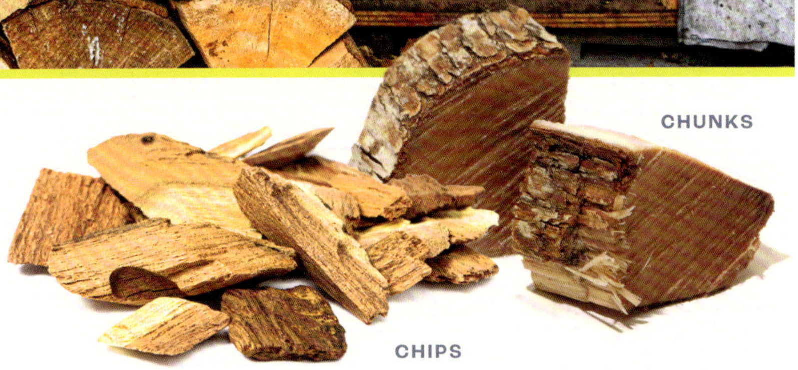

On a grill, we add smoke flavor with **wood chips** or (for a charcoal grill) **wood chunks**. A 3-inch wood chunk is the equivalent of 1 cup of chips. Each variety of wood provides a unique smoke flavor to your food. Here are some of the most common types.

CHUNKS

CHIPS

FRUIT
(Apple, Cherry, Peach)
Produces lightly sweet, mild smoke. Great for seafood and poultry.

HICKORY
A balanced though intense smoke that works with almost any food.

MAPLE
Relatively mild and tasty smoke good for pork and poultry; some tasters found it "resiny" on salmon.

MESQUITE
A potent smoke that works best with stronger-tasting cuts of beef, pork, lamb, and game.

OAK
A nutty and well-balanced smoke. The traditional choice for many pitmasters.

THE GEAR

The Essential Tools

You don't need a lot of gadgets for great grilled food, just a choice selection of efficient cookware, tools, and gear. Our essentials are workhorses that will give you better results. Our handy extras make grilling easier and more fun; depending on the kinds of foods you grill, you might consider them essential too.

CHIMNEY STARTER

Charcoal chimney starters light charcoal in a controlled manner and are our top choice for charcoal grilling. The **Weber Rapidfire Chimney Starter** features a roomy charcoal chamber, an insulated handle, and a helper handle to make it easier to precisely distribute the lit coals.

GRILL GLOVES

While heatproof gloves designed specifically for grilling may seem like overkill, we recommend them for novice and pro grillers alike. **WZQH Leather Forge Welding Gloves** are protective, sturdy and comfortable—and they come in four sizes.

GRILL BRUSH

With short metal bristles and a triangular head, the **Weber 12" Three-Sided Grill Brush** makes it easy to clean grill grates by sweeping the top of the grill or by holding the brush at an angle and wedging it between the bars.

INSTANT-READ THERMOMETER

The **ThermoWorks Thermapen ONE** has a large, grippy handle; a rotating screen with large, highly legible numbers; and a backlight that goes on when viewing conditions are dim. As its name indicates, it takes just 1 second to measure a temperature.

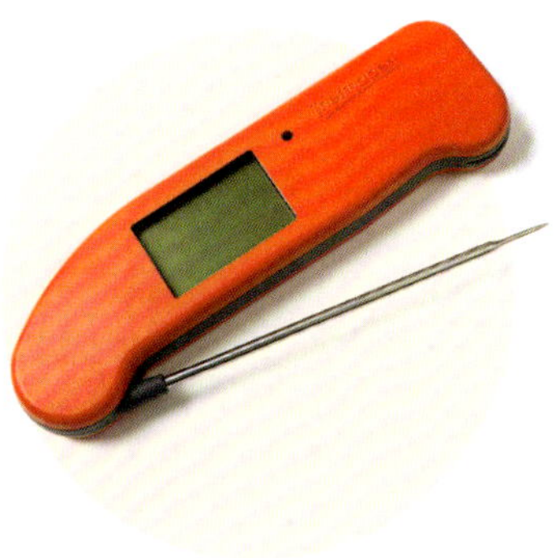

DISPOSABLE ALUMINUM PANS

Positioned beneath the grill grate on a charcoal grill, a **disposable aluminum pan** acts as a drip tray, cutting down on flare-ups. It can hold water to add humidity or it can corral a pile of lit briquettes for a concentrated fire. You can also use pans to braise food on the grill, such as Grilled Beer Brats and Onions (page 213). We like 13 by 9-inch moderately deep pans. For gas grills, you'll need **disposable aluminum pie plates**.

TONGS

You need long tongs to safely move food around the grill. We like **OXO Good Grips Grilling Tongs**, which are 16 inches long. They're lightweight but tough, with an easy locking tab and precise pincers that can grip spears of asparagus or racks of ribs.

SPATULA

When you're cooking on a hot grill, you need a spatula that's strong and agile, with a long handle. We love the **Char-Broil Comfort-Grip Grill Spatula** for its flared shape that fits into tight spaces and its comfortable, rounded handle. Particularly when the grill is really packed, this is your spatula.

FISH SPATULA

The unique long, flared head of a fish spatula enables you to nimbly navigate tight spaces on the grill and move delicate foods without breaking them. We use two for turning grilled whole fish and fish fillets. We especially like the proportions, flexibility, and curved shape of the **Wusthof Gourmet 7" Slotted Fish Spatula**.

BASTING BRUSH

Long-handled barbecue basting brushes allow you to safely apply oil or sauce to food on the grill without burning your fingers. The silicone bristles of the **OXO Good Grips Grilling Basting Brush** pick up an impressive volume of sauce.

SKEWERS

For most jobs, we prefer metal skewers, which are flameproof and reusable. Thin, flat **Norpro 12-Inch Stainless Steel Skewers** support thick kebabs, can be threaded through delicate foods without tearing them, and turn easily. For certain tasks, such as holding butterflied chicken flat on the grill, slender, disposable 12-inch **wooden or bamboo skewers** work better.

KITCHEN TWINE

Linen or cotton twine is indispensable for tying roasts and rolled, stuffed meats; it makes neat, even ties and stays in place without slipping or fraying. We found that linen twine pulls away from cooked meat most cleanly; however, cotton works almost as well and costs less. We like **Librett Cotton Butcher's Twine** because it releases string from the center of the ball, letting us pay it out with no danger of it rolling off the counter.

THE GEAR

The Handy Extras

SHEET PANS

Half-sheet and quarter-sheet rimmed baking pans have a host of uses for outdoor cooking prep. The 18 by 13-inch half-sheet size can hold cooked ribs or roasts or double as a pizza peel. The smaller 13 by 9-inch size makes a perfect caddy for jars of condiments or bowls of seasonings. Our winning sheets, **Nordic Ware Naturals Baker's Half Sheet** and **Nordic Ware Naturals Quarter Sheet**, are sturdy and warp resistant.

PLASTIC SQUEEZE BOTTLES

Beyond their uses for serving burger condiments, squeeze bottles make it easy to apply oil or barbecue sauce to foods on or off the grill. **TableCraft Widemouth Squeeze Bottles** are made of flexible plastic that's very easy to squeeze but won't deform.

PROBE THERMOMETER

A probe thermometer tells you when your food is ready without having to lift the grill lid and thus slow down the cooking process. It consists of a probe that's inserted into the food you're cooking and connects by a thin wire to a base that sits outside the grill. The base displays the readout so you can monitor the food's temperature. Clip-on probe thermometers are useful only as long as you're standing next to the grill, while remote-probe thermometers also transmit temperature data to portable receivers. We prefer this style, especially for longer-cooking foods such as barbecue or roasts, because you can walk away from the grill; the receiver lets you know when your food has reached its target temperature. The **ThermoWorks Smoke 2-Channel Alarm** is ready to use right out of the box. The base and receiver have clear displays that can be read in any light conditions, and the unit maintains a connection for up to 300 feet.

COOLER

A cooler comes in handy for more than camping trips or picnics: Having a cooler near your grill saves you travel time back and forth from the kitchen, keeps food at a safe temperature, and keeps beverages cold for the cook. Generally speaking, the more insulating power a cooler has, the heavier it is and the smaller the capacity for its size. The **Yeti Tundra 45** and **65** fall into this category. They're durable and easy to open and close, and ice lasts a whole week in them. The budget-friendly **Coleman 50 QT XTreme Wheeled Cooler** does a decent job of cooling, keeping ice for six days. Its wheels make it more portable, and it has a roomy interior.

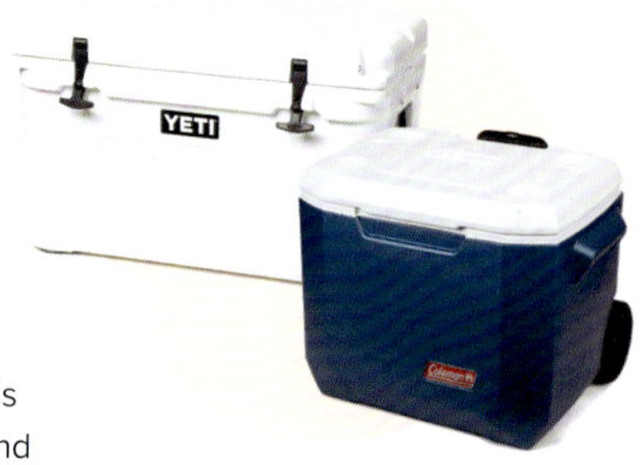

PLANCHA

A plancha is a flat griddle that fits on top of a charcoal or gas grill grate. Its flat surface allows you to use your grill like a flattop to put a good sear on smashed burgers or grill smaller foods such as shrimp or shishito peppers without losing them between the grate bars. We use the seasoned cast-iron **Lodge Pro-Grid Reversible Grill/ Griddle**, which is 20 by 10½ inches.

CAST-IRON SKILLET

A cast-iron skillet allows you to "bake" cakes, brownies, and biscuits on your grill. Our choice for outdoor cooking is the **Lodge Cast Iron Skillet**. You may already have this in your kitchen, but if not, you'll need to follow the seasoning instructions before using it on the grill. Some recipes in this book use a 12-inch skillet; others use a 10-inch skillet.

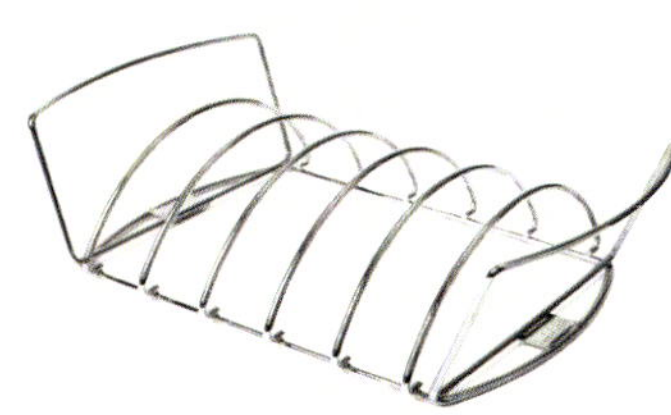

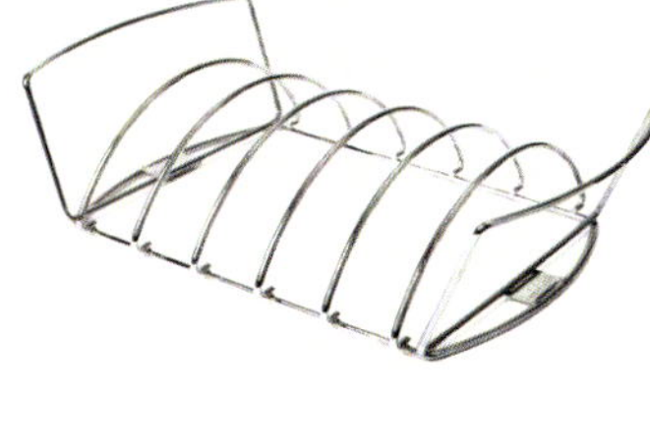

REVERSIBLE RIB RACK

If you want to make ribs for a crowd, you can double our rib recipes, but you need a way to fit more ribs on your grill. The large, sturdy stainless-steel **Weber Premium Grilling Rack** holds five full racks of barbecued ribs upright with plenty of space, so heat circulates freely.

MEAT SHREDDERS

Meat shredders pull apart large cuts of meat more quickly than a pair of forks, and they do a better job of keeping your hands protected from heat. **Bear Paws Meat Handlers** have thick, sharp tines and stay-cool plastic handles that help you lift hot meat easily and safely. Their widely spaced tines allow shredded meat to pass through them without getting stuck.

PIZZA PEEL

A pizza peel helps you transfer pizza or other flatbreads onto and off of a grill with ease. Peels can be wood or metal; for grilling we prefer the latter. Our favorite, the **American Metalcraft Pizza Peel 2814** does an excellent job of sliding under pizzas or breads to rotate or remove them.

SMOKER BOX

If you frequently use wood chips and want to avoid fussing with foil packets, a smoker box is a worthwhile purchase. Simply a small metal box with a vented lid, it can be filled with wood chips and placed directly on the coals in a charcoal grill or on the burner in a gas grill. The **GrillPro Cast Iron Smoker Box** is easy to use and clean; at just over an inch tall, it fits in almost any grill.

THE GEAR

Beyond Grilling

You can make an almost endless array of foods on your grill, but it's also fun to expand your outdoor cooking repertoire with specialized equipment. We particularly like rotisseries and pizza ovens.

GRILL ROTISSERIES

Purchasing a motorized rotisserie attachment for your grill is an investment that pays off in delectable spit-roasted meals. The combination of elevating food above the grill grate and continuous rotation promotes uniform cooking and consistent basting, which results in even browning and superlative juiciness.

A grill rotisserie consists of a long metal spit with two sets of prongs for holding food; a small motor at one end (which you plug into an electrical outlet) turns the spit continuously. For charcoal grills, a metal ring (about 6 inches tall) that supports the spit sits on the rim of a kettle-style grill. You put the grill's lid on top of the ring, forming an oven-like chamber while your meat cooks. We like the powerful motor and simple design of the **Weber 2290 22-inch Charcoal Kettle Rotisserie**.

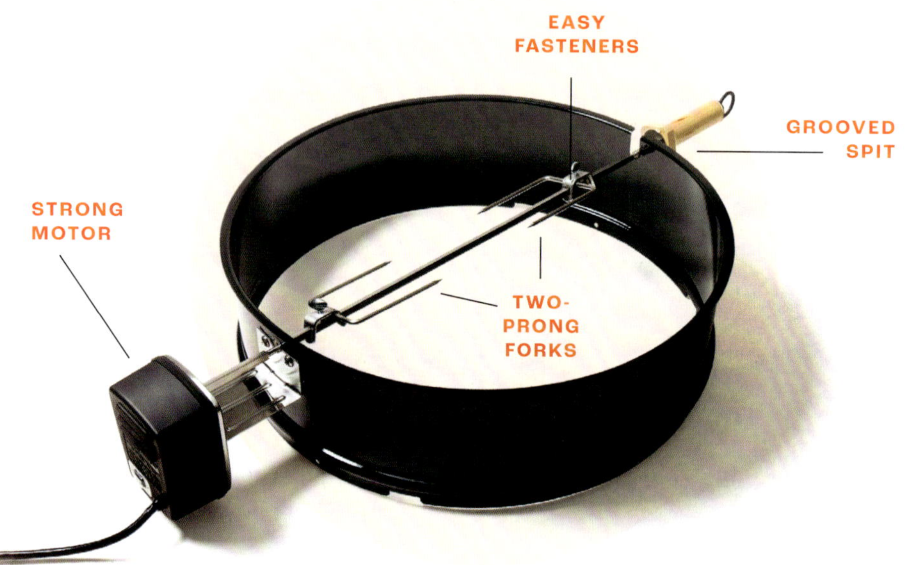

3 RECIPES FOR THE ROTISSERIE

Six Tips for Superb Rotisserie

1. On a charcoal grill, use a split fire setup (see page 13) with a 13 by 9-inch disposable aluminum pan in the center.
2. Confirm that there is enough vertical space for the food to rotate freely. (This is more of an issue for gas grill rotisserie setups.)
3. Use pliers to tighten the screws that clamp the forks snugly on the spit. These screws are small, slippery, and often greasy; pliers help you deal with them safely and effectively.
4. Oil and season the food before spearing it; an oil mister/sprayer is useful. For seasoning, salt, pepper, and herbs or a spritz of lemon work well.
5. Tie up any dangling bits on the food with kitchen twine to keep them from burning and to create a compact, uniform shape that will cook more evenly.
6. Lightly tighten the first fork on the spit (with the prongs facing in), slide the food onto the spit, and spear it firmly on the tines. Add the second fork and spear the food. Slide the food and forks to the center of the spit before screwing both forks in place. The food should turn with the spit on the grill, not spin around the spit.

Four Tips for Perfect Pizza

1 For ease of use and fire safety, set up your pizza oven on a sturdy, heatproof table.

2 An infrared thermometer is important to verify the correct pizza oven temperature. Check the temperature in the center of the oven, as there will be hot spots depending on the proximity of the cooking surface to the flame.

3 A thin metal pizza peel is a must for safely getting your pizza into and out of the oven.

4 To clean the pizza oven, let it cool completely and then flip the pizza stone. The residue left on the bottom will carbonize during your next pizza cooking session. Once the oven is cooled, you can flip the stone again and brush off the carbonized residue using a stiff-bristled brush. Continue this process after every use.

PIZZA OVENS

While you can make excellent pizza on your grill (see page 360), a portable pizza oven is a pizza lover's dream. These outdoor appliances reach temperatures similar to those of professional pizza ovens—meaning you can turn out pro-quality pizza right in your own backyard. Our recipe developed especially for an outdoor pizza oven is on page 363.

Pizza ovens are fueled by propane gas and/or wood or charcoal; we prefer gas-fueled ovens for their ease of use and their ability to maintain the necessary high temperatures for producing the professional results they promise. The best-performing ovens are well insulated, easily portable, and have burners placed at the back (rather than under the cooking surface), which allows them to produce great results in a variety of pizza styles. The **Ooni Koda 2** is our recommendation for most home cooks. It has a 14-inch stone and is a breeze to set up, and its powerful gas burner, located in the rear of the oven, makes attractively browned pizzas in just 2 minutes. A "flamekeeper visor shield" built into the opening of the oven helps brown toppings especially well. If you want the ability to make 16-inch pizzas, the Ooni Koda 16 does a great job, although it's heavier and bulkier.

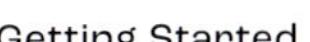

THE GEAR

Your Grill Station

You can think of your grill as an extension of your kitchen—or you can make your grill area a kitchen in its own right. The setup doesn't need to be fancy, or permanent. Just a few basic items and some smart organizing will save you from multiple trips inside as you prep and grill your meal.

YOUR PREP TABLE

A sturdy, **portable table** gives you a dedicated place to prep food that's separate from where you'll be eating. Make sure it's big enough to allow prep space as well as storage space and room to hold the tools you need.

- A small sheet pan holding plastic squeeze bottles of **oil**, **water**, and any **condiments** you need, along with prep bowls holding **salt**, **pepper**, and other **spices**.
- Another sheet pan holding **cutting boards** and **serving platters**. Having a stack of lightweight cutting boards or mats on hand makes it easy to avoid cross-contamination; use separate boards to hold raw meat and vegetables.
- A third sheet pan or a tray holding any **cooking utensils** that you need: spatulas, knives, scissors, metal skewers, and so on.

ALONGSIDE YOUR PREP TABLE

Here are some other handy items for your outdoor kitchen:

► A **dish tub** filled with warm soapy water is a great place to stash grilling utensils when you're done with them. Soaking the used tools gives you a head start on cleanup—no dried-on food to contend with.

► A **cooler** keeps raw meat and other foods safe until you use them and also holds cold drinks for the cooking crew.

► A **plastic storage tub** is handy for storing grill gear that can live outside for the season, such as grill gloves, grill brush, long tongs, grill lighter, stash of disposable aluminum roasting pans, and more.

► A **wide-mouthed trash barrel** makes an easy target for discards; a tight-fitting lid discourages flying pests and other critters.

► A **fire extinguisher** is a safety feature that every kitchen, outdoors or indoors, should have.

Safety First!

Part of the fun of outdoor cooking is the primal thrill of playing with fire. Here are four tips to keep that thrill accident-free.

1 LOCATION IS EVERYTHING

Always set up your grill at least 10 feet from your home on a flame-safe surface—a driveway or patio rather than grass or a wooden deck—and away from where children and pets might wander. Pay special attention when cooking with charcoal or wood in windy weather, as sparks can fly out of the grill or fire pit.

2 CLEANLINESS COUNTS

It's important that the interior basin of your gas or charcoal grill be cleaned a few times each season to wash away built-up food matter that can ignite (or lend off-flavors) to whatever you're cooking. Empty drip pans and ash-catchers frequently to reduce mess and minimize fire risk.

3 PREP FOOD CAREFULLY

Flare-ups are often caused by fat or by excess oily marinade dripping off the meat and catching fire. Trim meat carefully and pat dry any oil-marinated foods with paper towels before grilling. But in case a flare-up still happens, keep long tongs and grill gloves handy so that you can quickly and safely move the food to an area of the grill not directly over the fire. Briefly covering the grill can also help squelch flare-ups.

4 FOOD SAFETY MATTERS

It's easy to be tempted to skip basic food safety rules when cooking outside—but don't. Always use separate platters for raw and cooked foods to avoid cross-contamination, and always dispose of excess marinade for raw proteins. Also be mindful of basting brushes: If you brush something onto a protein early in cooking, use a clean brush and separate bowl of sauce for any finishing swipes of sauce.

THE GEAR

Deep-Clean Your Grill

Basic maintenance—scraping the grate clean after preheating, emptying the drip tray or the ash catcher when full—is a small price to pay after a delicious grilled meal. On the other hand, a thorough grill deep-cleaning is a messy, intimidating job that we'd rather avoid. But it's so important to do, both for safety reasons and to ensure that your grill works properly for the best results. Follow our steps for cleaning your charcoal or gas grill and you'll be glad you did it—honest. Depending on the length of your grilling season, aim to deep clean your grill every three months or at least twice a year.

DEEP-CLEANING A CHARCOAL GRILL

WHAT YOU'LL NEED

- Dish soap
- Rubber gloves
- Grill brush
- Plastic paint scraper or putty knife
- Grill cleaner or nonacidic oil (WD-40)
- Paper towels or rags

BEFORE YOU START

Empty any old charcoal and/or ashes. Hopefully you did this after your last cookout, but if not, do so now.

1 First, use a grill brush to scrape off any built-up carbon (black, flaky paint-like material) on the inside of the lid. Then remove the grates and use a plastic scraper to clean any gunk or buildup from the inside of the grill bowl, paying attention to the blades.

2 Inspect and wash the outside of the grill. If any surface rust has built up around the welded joints, use grill cleaner or nonacidic oil such as WD-40 to remove it. Then wash the exterior of the grill (warm, soapy water works just fine).

3 Check both grates and scrape off any superficial rust with the grill brush. If the rust is deep or it looks like the grates have totally corroded, you may need to replace the grates. No rust? Terrific. You can scrub and oil the cooking grate as usual the next time you heat up the grill.

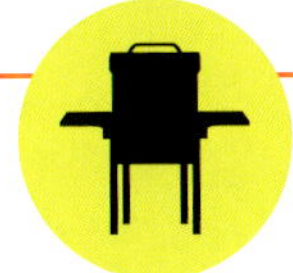

DEEP-CLEANING A GAS GRILL

WHAT YOU'LL NEED

Two plastic bins big enough to fit the cooking grates and grease tray

A tarp or cut-up trash bags to put under your work station

Dish soap

Rubber gloves

Grill brush or heavy-duty bristle brush

Grill floss (optional)

Grill grease spray (optional)

Plastic paint scraper or putty knife

Stainless-steel wool

Paper towels or rags

BEFORE YOU START

Make sure that your grill is fully cooled and the propane is turned off. Gloves are a must to protect your hands. Leave the grease tray and drip pan in place to start (you'll clean those at the end).

1 Lay a tarp or cut-up trash bags under your work station and/or grill. Fill one bin with warm soapy water and the other with clean water. The more you contain the mess from the start, the easier cleanup will be.

2 Using a wire grill brush, grill floss (if you have it), and a scraper, work over the grill, scraping everything directly into the grill's cookbox to control the mess. Pull out the grease tray and dump the accumulated scrapings as needed.

3 Set the grill grates (and flavorizer bars if your grill has them) in the soapy water to soak for a few minutes. Once the remaining debris is softened after soaking, scrub the grates and bars clean using stainless-steel wool and a bristle brush. Dip the grates and bars in the clean water bin and set them out to dry.

4 Clean the upper and lower cookbox from top to bottom, scraping everything into the grease tray. Leave the burner tubes in place, but give them a light scrape as well. (You can use a grill grease spray at this point.) Follow up with a bristle brush or steel wool. Once all the stuck-on gunk is removed, remove any remaining loose particles with a wet rag. Inspect and gently clean the igniters, making sure that they are clear of debris.

5 Replace the disposable pan inside your grease tray (if your grill has one) and scrape down the tray itself over a trash can. Soak the tray in the soapy water bin (if necessary), scrub it, and then rinse it in the clean water bin.

6 Scrub the inside cabinets, cooking knobs, and exterior with hot soapy water and a rag. Dump the water bins far away from your grilling and dining area. (There shouldn't be too much grease in either of them, but it's still a good idea to be conscious of where you're dumping them.)

THE FOOD

When Food Meets Grill

There's a scientific reason for the allure of grilled foods. The heat of the grill has real chemistry with food, creating browning and flavors that are unmatched by other cooking methods.

Browning Makes Food Nonstick

Along with developing savory flavor, fully browning a piece of meat has a second benefit: It makes the meat a little easier to release from the grill grate. When meat first starts to cook, its proteins unravel and bond to the iron in the grate; but as the Maillard reaction kicks in, the proteins increasingly react with each other and with sugars, which means they are no longer available to bond to the metal. If you find that meat sticks to the grate bars, give it a minute to brown a bit more, and try again.

BEAUTIFUL BROWNING

The rich color of a mahogany-crusted steak or bronze-skinned chicken on the grill is the visual cue that a process called the **Maillard reaction** is taking place. When that happens, meat's amino acids (the building blocks of protein) and sugars react with each other to form new flavor compounds, not just once, but continuously, so that as the temperature rises, the flavor continues to deepen along with the color. The compounds created depend on the specific amino acids or sugars present—one reason why a browned steak tastes different from a browned chicken breast.

Maillard browning appears in the form of distinctive dark grill marks from contact with the hot grate and—more significantly for flavor—as the overall browning produced by the radiant heat from the coals or gas flame. Grilling is excellent at producing browning because it generates the heat needed to quickly eliminate moisture on the meat's surface so it can reach the high temperatures necessary for browning to happen.

Vegetables and fruits develop great browning on the grill through **caramelization**, which occurs at even higher temperatures than Maillard browning and involves sugars alone. As the sugars degrade and darken, they form new flavor molecules that range from toasty to somewhat bitter.

TANTALIZING TASTE

If you had to describe grill flavor with one word, it might be "smoky." While you can certainly add smoke to delicious effect by using wood chips or chunks (see page 17), the simplest, most essential form of grill flavor comes from smoke produced by the food itself—at least if that food is meat. The appealing smokiness of grilled meats is a result of drippings that fall onto blazing-hot coals (or onto the heat diffusers of a gas grill). When they hit the heat source, these fat- and protein-laden juices combust in a puff of smoke, producing complex new flavor compounds, such as aldehydes and pyrazines formed by the breakdown of fats. These flavorful compounds immediately rise up and adhere to the food. In combination with the savory products of the chemical reactions associated with browning, these flare-ups are responsible for imparting the characteristic flavor of the grill. Because juices from vegetables and fruits are generally too watery to burst into flame, they won't produce the same effect, although applying oil (either by marinating or simply brushing on the surface) can cause flare-ups.

GRILLING FOR OPTIMAL TEXTURE

Great color and flavor can't disguise a dry, tough, or overly chewy texture. In the pursuit of tenderness and juiciness, the goal of grilling meat is to minimize the negative effects of heat while using it to promote positive effects.

As meat heats up, the proteins in the muscle fibers lose their bonds with each other, the connective tissue constricts, and the juices in meat (mostly water) are squeezed out, leading to dryness and toughness. The intramuscular (marbled) fat in meat melts, lubricating the muscle fibers and promoting the perception of tenderness. As the temperature of the meat continues to rise, **collagen**, the main protein in connective tissue, unwinds and eventually transforms into **gelatin**, which retains moisture and creates juiciness.

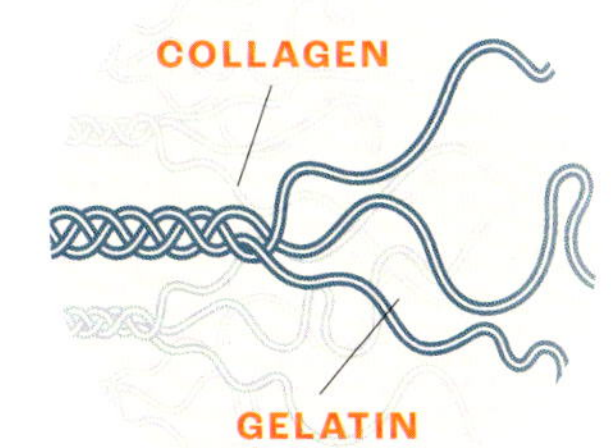

All of this means you don't grill a lean, tender filet mignon the same way you grill a well-marbled porterhouse or a collagen-rich brisket. Because the various types and cuts of meat have different ratios of lean meat to fat and different amounts of collagen—as well as different sizes and shapes—you get the best results when you tailor the level and type of heat, and the time spent on the grill, to the specific meat you're grilling. Lean steaks and chops are best grilled quickly over high, direct heat so that they brown before they can dry out. Larger cuts such as a whole turkey breast are grill-roasted over moderate indirect heat, which gives them time to evenly cook from center to edge. Tougher, collagen-rich cuts, such as brisket or pork shoulder, are grilled over gentle heat to keep the meat in the optimum temperature range as long as possible for collagen breakdown until they turn fall-apart tender.

THE FOOD

The Power of Salt and Seasonings

Lean meat needs help to stay juicy in the hot, dry environment of the grill. This is where the amazing properties of salt come in—literally.

SALT AND BRINES

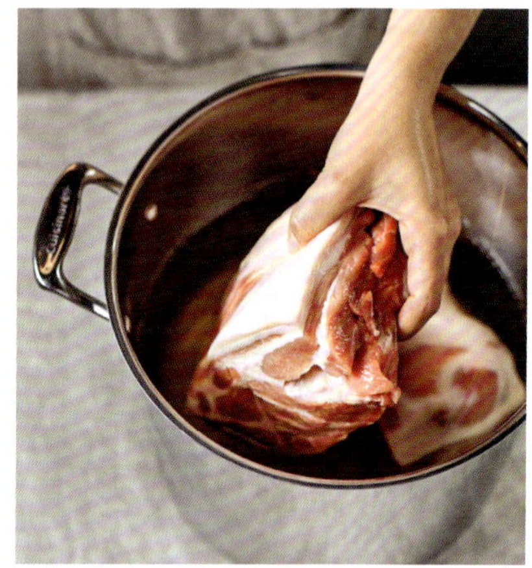

Salt is made up of two ions, sodium and chloride. Salt ions naturally move from an area of greater concentration to an area of lesser concentration by a process called diffusion. When meat is salted or brined, the concentration of salt outside the muscle is much higher than inside, so the salt diffuses into the muscle cells. The proteins readjust their shape, creating gaps that fill up with water. Some of the proteins are dissolved by the salt and form a gel capable of holding on to even more water. The rearrangement of the protein molecules also compromises the structural integrity of the meat so, in addition to being juicier, the meat is more tender.

Salting is also referred to as dry brining because it uses the meat's own moisture to create a brine. The salt sprinkled on meat initially draws some moisture from the meat to the surface and then dissolves into that moisture, forming a concentrated brine that slowly diffuses back into the meat.

Two key differences: Because salting uses moisture already in the meat, this method doesn't give meat any extra moisture, while with brining, there's a net gain. Brining also makes the surface of meat wetter than salting does. Since surface moisture can impede browning, in some situations salting is preferable.

MARINADES

You could think of marinade as a fancy brine—a highly seasoned liquid that's basically a vehicle for getting salt into the meat. The other ingredients commonly added to a marinade can't penetrate the meat to flavor it from the inside out. Most flavor molecules are either fat-soluble and thus repelled by the water in meat or simply too large to infiltrate the muscle fibers. No matter how long the meat marinates, these flavors stay on or near the surface.

So why do we use marinades? Because when the food has a high surface area to volume ratio (think cutlets, thin chops and steaks, and boneless chicken breasts), surface flavoring is significant. Our Grilled Flank Steak (page 48), for example, has plenty of real estate for the marinade ingredients to undergo flavorful transformations on the grill and enhance every bite.

Do Acids Tenderize Meat?

To tenderize meat, you have to break down muscle fiber and collagen, the connective tissue that makes meat tough, thus increasing the meat's ability to retain moisture. While acidic ingredients such as citrus juice, vinegar, yogurt, buttermilk, and wine do weaken collagen, their impact is confined to the meat's surface. We find that if left too long, acids turn the outermost layer of meat mushy, not tender. To minimize mushiness, we use acidic components sparingly, for short marinating times—or forgo them completely.

The enzyme in many plants—such as papain in papaya and bromelain in pineapple, to name two—can break down collagen in meat. But as with acids, their impact is limited to the meat's surface, where we find they likewise turn the meat mushy, not tender.

WHAT SEASONINGS DO—AND DON'T DO

The flavor molecules in **herbs** and **spices** are mainly fat soluble and not absorbed by meat. Adding oil to a marinade dissolves some of the fat-soluble flavors and helps them cling to the surface of meat where their flavors can bloom. **Onion** and **garlic** molecules are water-soluble but are too large to travel more than a few millimeters beyond the surface. Water-soluble **sugar** molecules are likewise too large to season deeply. However, sugar is useful in marinades (and some brines) for its sweet flavor and because it helps meat brown. The water-soluble glutamates found in **soy sauce** and **fish sauce** enter meat in a way and to a degree that's similar to **salt**; although they don't help meat retain moisture like salt does, glutamates boost savory flavor.

To prevent flare-ups and ensure properly browned meat, wipe off most of the excess marinade before grilling. Keep just a little marinade on the meat surface to maximize flavor.

THE FOOD

When Is Food Done?

The temperature of a steak or roast when you pull it off the grill isn't necessarily the temperature you want to serve it at. Here's why.

As meat cooks on the grill, its exterior gets hotter (and heats up more quickly) than the interior. Because heat always travels from a hotter to a cooler region, during cooking the heat steadily moves via conduction from the outside to the inside of the food. The process occurs as long as there's a difference in temperature between the two regions, so even after you remove the meat from the grill, it continues to cook using the heat energy stored in those outer layers, causing its internal temperature to rise. This is the phenomenon known as **carryover cooking**. The effect is greater in larger cuts of meat (and in foods cooked at higher temperatures) and makes it tricky to judge the ideal doneness temperature—remove a roast when the center is cooked just the way you like it and you may be eating overcooked meat. For the best results, we remove meat from the grill when it's shy of its final doneness temperature and let it rest while its internal temperature stabilizes.

HOW TO TEMP FOOD

When you're trying to figure out if the food is done, thermometer placement matters—here's how to get the most accurate results.

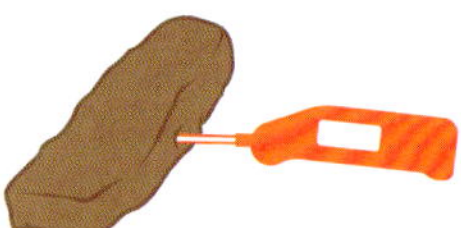

STEAKS AND CHOPS

Hold the steak or chop with tongs and insert the thermometer through the side of the meat. This method also works for chicken parts.

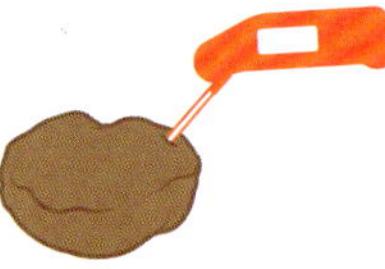

BURGERS

Leaving the burger on the grill, slide the tip of the thermometer into the top edge and angle it toward the center, making sure to avoid hitting the grate.

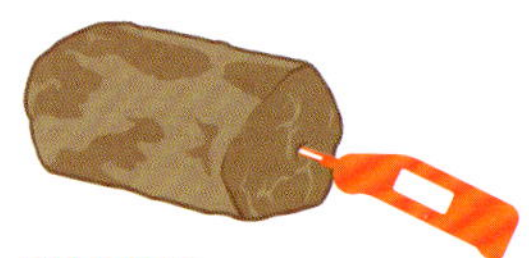

ROASTS

Insert the thermometer probe deep into the roast and then slowly draw it out. Look for the lowest temperature to find the center of the meat.

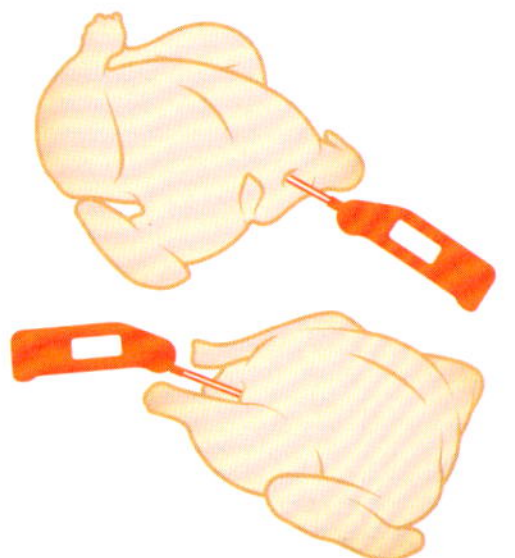

WHOLE POULTRY

Temp both the breast and the thigh. For the breast, insert the thermometer from the neck end, holding it parallel to the bird. (Avoid hitting the bone, which can give an inaccurate reading.) For the thigh, insert the thermometer at an angle away from the bone into the area between the drumstick and breast.

TEMPERATURE GUIDE FOR MEAT AND SEAFOOD

The significance of carryover cooking depends on many factors, including (but not limited to) the thickness and density of the meat and the grilling temperature and time. The doneness temperatures in our recipes take the effects of carryover cooking into account and suggest appropriate resting times. Here are our general guidelines.

BEEF/LAMB	COOK TO	SERVE AT
Rare	115°F–120°F	125°F
Medium-Rare	120°F–125°F	130°F
Medium	130°F–135°F	140°F
Medium-Well	140°F–145°F	150°F
Well-Done	150°F–155°F	160°F
BEEF/LAMB BURGERS		
Medium-Rare	125°F	125°F
Medium	130°F	130°F
Medium-Well	140°F	140°F
Well-Done	160°+F	160°+F
PORK		
Medium	140°F–145°F	150°F
Well-Done	150°F–155°F	160°F
Pork Burgers	150°F	150°F

POULTRY	COOK TO	SERVE AT
White Meat	160°F	160°F
Dark Meat	175°F	175°F
Turkey Burgers	160°F	160°F
SEAFOOD		
Lobster (tail)	140°F	140°F
Salmon, Salmon Burgers		
Farmed	125°F	125°F
Wild	120°F	120°F
Shrimp Burgers	140°F–145°F	140°F–145°F
Tuna		
Rare	110°F	110°F
Medium-Rare	125°F	125°F
Tuna Burgers	125°F	125°F
White-Fleshed Fish	130°F–135°F	130°F–135°F

Why You Should "Overcook" Some Foods

While most meats are best cooked just to an internal temperature at which they're safe to eat, items such as barbecued or grill-roasted dark-meat chicken, pork butt, and beef chuck often taste better when they're cooked longer. That's because these tough cuts are loaded with collagen; when the meat's internal temperature is between 140 and 195 degrees, the collagen breaks down into gelatin, which lubricates the muscle fibers, making them seem more moist and tender. It's also important to cook these cuts slowly; the longer they spend in that temperature range, the more tender the meat will be.

THE FOOD

Menus for Outdoor Meals

When you combine fresh air and grilled food, you get an eating experience that's casual, fun, and very satisfying. You can make the most of that vibe by cooking your entire meal outdoors. The keys are to choose compatible grill setups, do whatever prep you can before grilling, and coordinate the timing. Get started with these 12 menus.

Steak Tips with Grilled Sweet Potato Salad

SERVES 4 to 6 **SETUP** 6-qt single-level fire

51 Grilled Steakhouse Steak Tips
332 Grilled Sweet Potato Salad

Start the potatoes in the disposable pan on the grill; after moving them directly to the grate, add the steak tips to the grill. When the potatoes are done, prepare the salad while the steaks finish up on the grill.

Japanese Steakhouse Steak and Vegetables with Shishito Peppers

SERVES 6 **SETUP** 6-quart single-level fire with plancha

328 Blistered Shishito Peppers
68 Japanese Steakhouse Steak and Vegetables

Grill the shishitos and serve them to nibble on while you grill the steak and vegetables.

Grilled Thick-Cut Bone-In Pork Chops and Grilled Potatoes with Garlic and Rosemary

SERVES 4 **SETUP** 6-quart two-level fire

94 Grilled Thick-Cut Bone-In Pork Chops
325 Grilled Potatoes with Garlic and Rosemary

Prep the potato skewers while the pork chops are brining. A few minutes after sliding the pork chops to the cooler side of the grill, add the potatoes to the hotter side. After pulling the pork chops off the grill to rest, move the potatoes to the cooler side (or turn all burners to medium-low) to finish cooking.

Grilled Pork Tacos with Tomatillo-Avocado Salsa, Grilled Tortillas, and Grilled Plantains

SERVES 4 **SETUP** 6-quart single-level fire

119 Grilled Pork Tacos with Tomatillo-Avocado Salsa
369 Grilled Flour Tortillas
324 Grilled Plantains

Make the tortilla dough up to three days ahead of time. Grill the pork, tomatillos, and avocado, then grill the plantains (turning the burners to medium-high if using gas), and finally the tortillas (turning the burners to medium if using gas).

Grill-Roasted Butterflied Chicken and Grilled Carrots with Feta-Herb Sauce

SERVES 4 **SETUP** 7-quart half-grill fire

178 Grill-Roasted Butterflied Chicken
317 Grilled Carrots with Feta-Herb Sauce

Place the chicken on the cooler side of the grill; after rotating the chicken, add the carrots to the hotter side of the grill. When the carrots are done, remove them and arrange the carrots and sauce on the platter while the chicken finishes grilling and resting.

Grilled Chicken Caprese with Grilled Zucchini and Corn Salad

SERVES 4 **SETUP** 6-quart single-level fire

142 Grilled Chicken Caprese
335 Grilled Zucchini and Corn Salad

Grill the zucchini and corn; when they're done, grill the chicken and tomatoes. Chop the zucchini and corn, assemble the salad, and assemble the caprese.

Barbecued Chicken Thighs and Grilled Corn with Basil and Lemon Butter

SERVES 4 to 6 **SETUP** 7-quart banked fire with wood chips

253 Barbecued Chicken Thighs
319 Grilled Corn with Basil and Lemon Butter

Grill the thighs; while the thighs are resting, grill the corn on the hotter side of the grill. Set the disposable pan of butter on the cooler side and add the corn to it.

Turkey Burgers with Grilled Vegetables

SERVES 4 **SETUP** 6-quart single-level fire

340 Grilled Vegetable Platter
206 Classic Turkey Burgers

Grill the vegetables and then the turkey burgers.

Perfect Grilled Salmon and Grilled Vegetable Ratatouille

SERVES 4 **SETUP** 4½-quart single-level fire

285 Perfect Grilled Salmon
336 Grilled Vegetable Ratatouille

Grill vegetables for ratatouille, chop, and set aside. Grill salmon (turning burners to medium if using gas).

Grilled Whole Red Snapper with Panzanella

SERVES 4 to 6 **SETUP** 7-qt single-level fire

307 Grilled Whole Red Snapper
339 Grilled Panzanella

Make the dressing, grill the vegetables, then the bread. Grill the snapper; assemble the salad while the snapper grills and rests. Fillet the snapper.

Grilled Clams, Mussels, or Oysters with Soy-Citrus Sauce, Grilled Shrimp Boil Foil Packs, and Pull-Apart Dinner Rolls

SERVES 4 **SETUP** 7-quart banked fire

374 Pull-Apart Dinner Rolls
276 Grilled Clams, Mussels, or Oysters with Soy-Citrus Sauce
276 Grilled Shrimp Boil Foil Packs

Prepare and form the dinner roll dough. Prepare the shrimp foil packs while the dough rises. Grill-bake the dinner rolls, then spread the banked coals into an even layer (or turn all burners to high if using gas). Grill the clams, mussels or oysters, then grill the foil packs.

Grilled Vegetable and Halloumi Salad and Mana'eesh Za'atar

SERVES 4 to 6 **SETUP** 4½-quart single-level fire

337 Grilled Vegetable and Halloumi Salad
368 Mana'eesh Za'atar

Grill the vegetables; while they cool, grill the mana'eesh. Chop the vegetables for the salad.

Save Room for Dessert

To add a dessert (see chapter 8) to your menu, grill-bake it ahead of time and then, after grilling your meal, place the dessert over the dwindling heat of the coals to warm up while you enjoy dinner.

POLLO A LA BRASA

THE FOOD

Get Grilling

With hundreds of great grilling recipes in this book, the only question is: Where to start? We love them all, but here are some good choices if you're not sure what you're in the mood for.

12 Meals in Under 40 Minutes

10 Great Grilled Appetizers

6 Recipes for the Plancha

10 Recipes to Impress Your Guests

10 Recipes with Subtly Smoky Flavor

8 Recipes for Serious Barbecue

Five Smart Grilling Tips

1 Instead of using old newspapers to light a chimney starter, use your **empty bags of charcoal briquettes** to light the next fire. Cut or tear a charcoal bag (separating the paper layers) into pieces. Crumple up a few pieces, stuff them in the bottom of the chimney, and light. The charcoal residue on the bag will help the paper stay lit.

2 Before lighting your gas grill, **remove the warming rack** unless you know that you're going to need it. On most grills, the rack is very close to the cooking surface, and it can be hard to reach foods on the back of the grill without burning your hands on the hot metal.

3 You can keep your food safe and clean while still saving yourself from having to wash any extra dishes if you **reuse the same platter** to hold meat before and after cooking. Simply cover the dish with plastic wrap or foil before putting the meat on it. Remove the protective layer after all the meat is in the pan or on the grill and voilà—you have a clean platter ready for the cooked food.

4 Make sure you remember to turn off the gas tank after grilling with this simple trick: Jog your memory by slipping a **rubber band** around the knob of the gas tank. When you turn the tank on, place the rubber band around your wrist, and remove it only when you turn the tank off. As long as you're wearing the rubber band, you know that the tank is on.

5 Here's how to light your charcoal grill without a chimney starter: Open the bottom vent and place eight sheets of **balled-up newspaper** (or paper from a charcoal bag) beneath the bottom grate. Pile the charcoal in an even pile (use an empty half-gallon milk or juice carton, which holds about 2 quarts, to measure the coals) in the center of the grate and light the paper. After about 20 minutes, the coals will be covered with gray ash and ready to be rearranged for cooking.

1

Beef

SIMPLE STEAKS AND RIBS

MARINATED AND RUBBED

MAKE IT A MEAL

SKEWERS, TACOS, SANDWICHES, AND MORE

ROASTS

IN DEPTH

Grill an Amazing Steak

Marinades, sauces, and sides are all fantastic ways to dress up your steak—and this chapter has plenty of them—but sometimes you just want straight-up steak on the grill, something so simple that you don't even need a recipe. These tips have you covered.

CHOOSE A GREAT STEAK

We have grilling favorites all along the price spectrum; here's how they compare in terms of flavor and texture.

$

FLANK STEAK

(also called jiffy)

Thin, slightly chewy, and very flavorful.

$$

SKIRT STEAK

(also called fajita or Philadelphia)

Long and thin with a distinct grain and an especially beefy taste.

$$

SIRLOIN STEAK TIPS

(also called sirloin tips, flap meat, or steak tips)

Not particularly tender, but has a distinct grain and a robust beefiness.

$$$

TENDERLOIN STEAK

(also called filet mignon)

Quite lean and tender, with a very mild flavor.

$$$

STRIP STEAK

(also called top loin, shell, sirloin strip, Kansas City strip, or New York strip)

Lots of marbling with good texture and flavor.

$$$

RIB-EYE STEAK

(also called Spencer or Delmonico)

Smooth, fine texture; lots of marbling and very flavorful.

$$$

T-BONE STEAK

Two steaks in one: a fatty, flavorful strip and buttery tenderloin separated by the T-shaped bone.

$$$

PORTERHOUSE STEAK

Similar to a T-bone steak but larger overall and with a larger tenderloin.

TRIM SOME FAT

In addition to marbling, some steaks boast a fat cap and/or fat deposits within the muscle. When the fat renders and drips onto the fire, it causes flare-ups. To keep things from getting out of hand, trim large fat deposits away and trim the fat cap down to ⅛ to ¼ inch thick.

USE KOSHER SALT

We like to use kosher salt for sprinkling on meat (and other foods) because its larger crystals disperse evenly and are easy to handle.

SALT THE STEAKS

For flavorful steak with a nicely browned crust, timing is everything. A sprinkle of salt first draws moisture to the surface of the steaks and then travels into the meat, seasoning it deeply and altering its protein structure to make it more tender and juicy—but this takes a while. If you're in a hurry, salt the steaks right before grilling so that the salt doesn't have a chance to make the surface moist and impede browning. But if you have at least 45 minutes (or up to 24 hours), pat the steaks dry, season them with 1½ teaspoons of kosher salt per pound of meat, and let them rest uncovered in the cold, dry air of the fridge to evaporate moisture while the salt works its magic.

START THE FIRE

The recipes in this chapter use a variety of grill setups but a **two-level setup** is one that works well for steaks. The hotter zone quickly browns the meat; the cooler zone provides a lower-heat area to slide the steaks over while you temp them, while their interiors gently finish cooking, or while you wait out flare-ups on the hotter side.

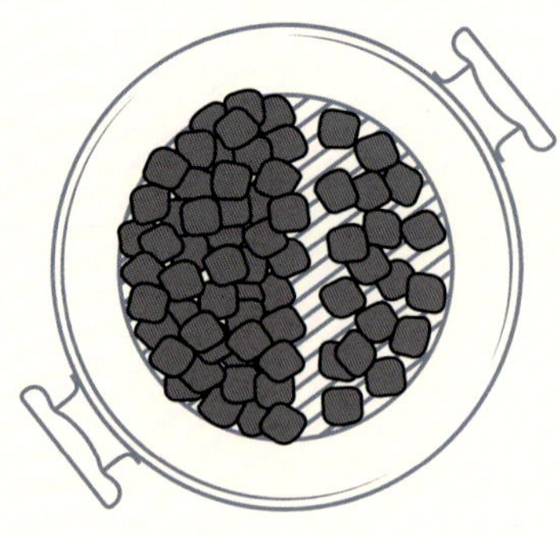

CONTROL THE FLARE AND MOVE IF NECESSARY

When fatty juices drip onto the fire, their fat ignites, their proteins and sugars transform into flavorful compounds, and their water turns to steam that carries the flames and flavors to the meat. Small, quick bursts create smoky, savory grill flavor but larger, prolonged flames will burn the food and deposit a layer of soot. Trimming the fat (see the tip on page 41) encourages the optimal amount of flare-up, but if big flare-ups occur, simply move the steaks away from the flames. Eventually, the fat will burn off and the fire will die down.

You might need to move the steaks around the grill to ensure that their browning and interior doneness are in sync. For example, move well-browned steaks that aren't up to temperature to the cooler side of the grill to finish cooking gently. Be aware that the hotter and cooler sides of a grill have hotter and cooler areas within them: Charcoal fires are hottest where the coals are glowing red as opposed to covered with gray ash; gas grills tend to be slightly cooler near their vents.

MONITOR DONENESS

Relatively thick steaks (1¼ to 1½ inches thick) typically cook through in 8 to 14 minutes; thinner ones are done in 4 to 8 minutes. Start temping them at the low end of that time range: Lift the steak off the grill and insert a thermometer through its side to check for desired doneness: 115 to 120 degrees for rare, 120 to 125 degrees for medium-rare, or 130 to 135 degrees for medium. The temperature will continue to rise a bit after you remove them from the grill.

COOK TIME

3/4–1"
THINNER STEAKS
4–8 minutes

1 1/4–1 1/2"
THICKER STEAKS
8–14 minutes

DONENESS

RARE
115–120°F

MEDIUM-RARE
120–125°F

MEDIUM
130–135°F

FOOD SCIENCE

Why Poking Meat During Cooking Does Not Cause Moisture Loss

A widespread belief holds that piercing meat with a fork during cooking allows precious juices to escape. To put this theory to the test, we cooked two sets of five steaks to medium-rare. We turned one set with a pair of tongs, the other by jabbing the steaks with a sharp fork. Both sets of steaks lost exactly the same amount of moisture during cooking—an average of 19.6 percent of their weight. The reason: Virtually all moisture that is lost when meat is cooked is a result of muscle fibers contracting in the heat and squeezing out their juices. Piercing does not damage the fibers enough to cause additional juices to leak out (any more than poking a wet sponge with a fork would expel its moisture). Bottom line? When it comes to the moisture level and tenderness of meat, cooking time and temperature are the most important factors.

LET IT REST

Muscle fibers in meat contract during cooking. To help them relax and hold on to more moisture when sliced, let steaks rest on a wire rack set in a rimmed baking sheet (to keep the crust dry), loosely covered with aluminum foil, for 5 to 10 minutes.

SLICE, SEASON, AND SERVE

Slice the steaks thin against the grain; this shortens muscle fibers and makes any cut seem more tender (especially important for flank and skirt steaks). And for a perfectly simple finishing touch, give the steak a light shower of flake sea salt (such as Maldon). The delicate saline crunch is especially welcome if you didn't have time to let the salted meat rest before grilling.

Char-Grilled Steaks

SERVES 4 to 6 · **TIME** 25 minutes plus 30 minutes freezing

Why This Recipe Works For grilled steak with a fabulous crust, you need the exterior of the meat to be dry. To help you achieve this goal, look no further than your pantry and your freezer. First, rub the steak with a mixture of salt, for seasoning, and cornstarch, which is a champ at absorbing moisture. Then pop the steak in the freezer, where the intensely dry environment will sufficiently dehydrate the steaks' exteriors in half an hour, a short enough stay to ensure that the interiors remain tender and juicy.

- 2 teaspoons kosher salt
- 1 teaspoon cornstarch
- 4 strip, rib-eye, or tenderloin steaks, 1½ inches thick, trimmed
- ½ teaspoon pepper

1 Combine salt and cornstarch in small bowl. Pat steaks dry with paper towels and rub with salt mixture. Place steaks on wire rack set in rimmed baking sheet and freeze until firm and dry to touch, at least 30 minutes or up to 1 hour. Sprinkle steaks with pepper.

2A FOR A CHARCOAL GRILL Open bottom vent completely. Light large chimney starter filled with charcoal briquettes (6 quarts). When top coals are partially covered with ash, pour evenly over grill. Set cooking grate in place, cover, and open lid vent completely. Heat grill until hot, about 5 minutes.

2B FOR A GAS GRILL Turn all burners to high; cover; and heat grill until hot, about 15 minutes. Leave burners on high.

3 Clean and oil cooking grate. Place steaks on grill and cook (covered if using gas) until meat registers 120 to 125 degrees (for medium-rare), 8 to 16 minutes, flipping halfway through cooking.

4 Transfer steaks to clean wire rack set in rimmed baking sheet, tent with aluminum foil, and let rest for 5 minutes. Serve.

Grilled Sugar Steak

SERVES 4 to 6 **TIME** 25 minutes plus 1 hour salting

Why This Recipe Works Is pouring sugar on steak a good idea? You bet. Picture a juicy, medium-rare steak with a delicate crust that delivers a fleeting moment of sweetness followed by a flood of meaty flavors. Using 2 parts sugar to 1 part salt creates the ideal clean sweetness without any bitterness. To ensure that the salt-sugar mixture stays on the steak rather than melts into a syrup that steams away on the grill, just season the meat, let it rest at room temperature for an hour, and season it again. The surface moisture from the first coating enables the second coating to stick. If your steaks are more than 1 inch thick, pound them to 1 inch. Be sure to let the steaks sit for at least 1 hour after seasoning. This recipe was developed using Diamond Crystal kosher salt. If you have Morton kosher salt, which is denser, use 1½ tablespoons salt; sprinkle 1¼ teaspoons sugar mixture per side of steaks in step 1 and ¾ teaspoon sugar mixture in step 2; you will have a little left over. Moving the steaks around the grill as they cook prevents the sugar from burning. Letting the steaks rest uncovered helps keep the crust in place.

- ¼ cup sugar
- 2 tablespoons kosher salt
- 4 (8-ounce) boneless strip steaks, 1 inch thick, trimmed
- ½ teaspoon pepper

1 Mix sugar and salt together in bowl. Pat steaks dry with paper towels and place in 13 by 9-inch baking dish. Sprinkle 1½ teaspoons sugar mixture evenly over top of each steak. Flip steaks and sprinkle second side of each steak with 1½ teaspoons sugar mixture. Cover with plastic wrap and let sit at room temperature for at least 1 hour or refrigerate for up to 24 hours.

2 Before grilling, transfer steaks to plate. (Steaks will be wet; do not pat dry.) Sprinkle steaks with ¾ teaspoon sugar mixture on each side, then sprinkle with pepper.

3A FOR A CHARCOAL GRILL Open bottom vent completely. Light large chimney starter mounded with charcoal briquettes (7 quarts). When top coals are partially covered with ash, pour evenly over half of grill. Set cooking grate in place, cover, and open lid vent completely. Heat grill until hot, about 5 minutes.

3B FOR A GAS GRILL Turn all burners to high; cover; and heat grill until hot, about 15 minutes. Leave all burners on high.

4 Clean and oil cooking grate. Place steaks on grill (hotter side if using charcoal) and cook (covered if using gas) until meat registers 120 to 125 degrees (for medium-rare), flipping halfway through cooking and moving as needed.

5 Transfer steaks to wire rack set in rimmed baking sheet and let rest for 5 minutes. Serve.

GRILLED SUGAR STEAK

Grilled Porterhouse or T-Bone Steaks

SERVES 4 **TIME** 45 minutes plus 30 minutes freezing

Why This Recipe Works Porterhouse and T-bone steaks are really two steaks in one—a tender New York strip steak on one side of the bone and a buttery, quicker-cooking tenderloin on the other—which makes grilling the meat evenly a challenge. As with boneless steaks, it's best to rub the steaks with cornstarch (which absorbs moisture) and salt (for flavor) and then put them in the freezer for a short spell to super-dry the surface (for a great crust). A two-level fire lets you sear the steaks over the hotter side and then slide them to the cooler side to cook through. The key is to position the steaks so that the tenderloin always faces the cooler side of the grill—this prevents it from overcooking. Be sure to buy steaks that are at least 1 inch thick.

- 2 teaspoons kosher salt
- 1 teaspoon cornstarch
- 2 (1¾-pound) porterhouse or T-bone steaks, 1 to 1½ inches thick, trimmed
- ½ teaspoon pepper

1 Combine salt and cornstarch in small bowl. Pat steaks dry with paper towels and rub with salt mixture. Place steaks on wire rack set in rimmed baking sheet and freeze until firm and dry to touch, at least 30 minutes or up to 1 hour. Sprinkle steaks with pepper.

2A **FOR A CHARCOAL GRILL** Open bottom vent completely. Light large chimney starter three-quarters filled with charcoal briquettes (4½ quarts). When top coals are partially covered with ash, pour evenly over half of grill. Set cooking grate in place, cover, and open lid vent completely. Heat grill until hot, about 5 minutes.

2B **FOR A GAS GRILL** Turn all burners to high; cover; and heat grill until hot, about 15 minutes. Leave primary burner on high and turn other burner(s) to low.

3 Clean and oil cooking grate. Place steaks on hotter side of grill with tenderloin sides facing cooler side of grill. Cook (covered if using gas) until dark crust forms, 6 to 8 minutes. Flip and turn steaks so that tenderloin sides are still facing cooler side of grill. Cook until dark brown crust forms on second side, 6 to 8 minutes.

4 Slide steaks to cooler side of grill and turn so that bone side is facing hotter side of grill. Cover and cook until meat registers 120 to 125 degrees (for medium-rare), 2 to 4 minutes, flipping halfway through cooking.

GRILLED PORTERHOUSE OR T-BONE STEAKS

5 Transfer to clean wire rack set in rimmed baking sheet, tent with aluminum foil, and let rest for 10 minutes. Transfer steaks to carving board, cut strip and tenderloin pieces off bones, then slice meat ¼ inch thick. Serve.

VARIATION

Grilled Porterhouse or T-Bone Steaks with Garlic

Rub halved garlic cloves over bone and meat on each side of steaks before sprinkling with pepper.

Grilling Porterhouse Steaks

1 Place steaks on hotter side with tenderloins facing cooler side; flip and turn to keep tenderloins facing cooler side.

2 Slide steaks to cooler side of grill, with bone sides facing fire. Cover grill to trap heat.

Grilled Cowboy-Cut Rib Eyes

SERVES 4 to 6 **TIME** 1 hour plus 1 hour salting

Why This Recipe Works Cowboy-cut rib eyes are 2-inch-thick, 1½-pound, bone-in behemoths that can cost a serious chunk of change. But these tender, beefy marbled steaks also offer serious advantages, including the fact that they stay on the grill longer than smaller steaks, soaking up more smoke and grill flavor. You want to make sure you know what you're doing when you throw them on the grill. Here's how to ace the challenge: Set up a half-grill fire, layering lit briquettes on top of unlit briquettes to help the fire stay hot long enough to finish the job. Start with room-temperature steaks and cook them gently over the cooler side of the grill before searing them over the hotter side. Your reward will be impressively seared steaks cooked to just the right temperature. Don't put the steaks on the grill until their internal temperature has reached 55 degrees; otherwise, the times and temperatures in this recipe will be inaccurate. This recipe was developed using Diamond Crystal kosher salt. If you have Morton kosher salt, which is denser, use 1 tablespoon.

- 2 (1½- to 2-pound) double-cut bone-in rib-eye steaks, 1¾ to 2 inches thick, trimmed
- 4 teaspoons kosher salt
- 2 teaspoons vegetable oil
- 2 teaspoons pepper

1 Pat steaks dry with paper towels and sprinkle all over with salt. Place steaks on wire rack set in rimmed baking sheet and let sit at room temperature until meat registers 55 degrees, about 1 hour. Before grilling, rub steaks with oil and sprinkle with pepper.

2A **FOR A CHARCOAL GRILL** Open bottom vent halfway. Arrange 4 quarts unlit charcoal briquettes in even layer over half of grill. Light large chimney starter one-third filled with charcoal briquettes (2 quarts). When top coals are partially covered with ash, pour evenly over unlit coals. Set cooking grate in place, cover, and open lid vent halfway. Heat grill until hot, about 5 minutes.

2B **FOR A GAS GRILL** Turn all burners to high; cover; and heat grill until hot, about 15 minutes. Turn primary burner to medium-high and turn off other burner(s). (Adjust primary burner as needed to maintain grill temperature around 300 degrees.)

3 Clean and oil cooking grate. Place steaks on cooler side of grill with bones facing fire. Cook, turning occasionally and keeping bones facing fire, until steaks register 95 degrees, 20 to 40 minutes.

4 If using charcoal, slide steaks to hotter side of grill. If using gas, remove steaks from grill; turn primary burner to high and heat until hot, about 5 minutes; and place steaks over primary burner. Cover and cook until well browned and meat registers 120 to 125 degrees (for medium-rare), about 8 minutes, flipping halfway through cooking.

5 Transfer steaks to clean wire rack set in rimmed baking sheet, tent with aluminum foil, and let rest for 15 minutes. Transfer steaks to carving board, cut meat from bone, and slice into ½-inch-thick slices. Serve.

Grilled Flank Steak

SERVES 4 **TIME** 35 minutes plus 1 hour salting

Why This Recipe Works Flank steak, a relatively thin cut, needs help to brown before it's cooked through. Using a 1:1 ratio of sugar to kosher salt encourages faster, deeper browning on the grill as well as seasoning the meat. We divide the steak into four pieces; this allows us to pull the tapered portions off the grill sooner, and it also shortens the steak's muscle fibers, which reduces the tendency to buckle. Flipping the steaks every 2 minutes during cooking further minimizes any buckling; prevents either side from developing a band of gray, overcooked meat just below the surface; and develops attractive grill marks. We cook the meat to 130 degrees because collagen-rich cuts such as flank are more tender when cooked to medium versus medium-rare, and we let it rest uncovered on a wire rack set in a rimmed baking sheet to avoid steaming the crust. Slicing the steak thin against the grain maximizes tenderness.

GRILLED FLANK STEAK

- 1 (1½- to 1¾-pound) flank steak, trimmed
- 2½ teaspoons kosher salt
- 2½ teaspoons sugar
- 1 teaspoon pepper

1 Pat steak dry with paper towels. Cut steak in half lengthwise, then cut each piece in half crosswise to create 4 steaks. Place steaks in 13 by 9-inch baking dish. Combine salt and sugar in small bowl. Sprinkle 2 teaspoons salt mixture over 1 side of steaks and press gently to adhere. Flip steaks and repeat with 2 teaspoons salt mixture. Cover and let sit at room temperature for 1 hour. Before grilling, sprinkle both sides of steaks with pepper and remaining salt mixture. (Steaks will be moist; do not pat dry.)

2A **FOR A CHARCOAL GRILL** Open bottom vent completely. Light large chimney starter mounded with charcoal briquettes (7 quarts). When top coals are partially covered with ash, pour evenly over grill. Set cooking grate in place, cover, and open lid vent completely. Heat grill until hot, about 5 minutes.

2B **FOR A GAS GRILL** Turn all burners to high; cover; and heat grill until hot, about 15 minutes. Leave all burners on high.

3 Clean and oil cooking grate. Place steak on grill and cook (covered if using gas), flipping every 2 minutes, until meat registers 130 degrees, 6 to 12 minutes. (Start checking temperature of thinner pieces after 6 minutes.) Transfer steaks to wire rack set in rimmed baking sheet and let rest for 10 minutes.

4 Transfer steaks to carving board, slice as thin as possible on bias against grain, and serve.

Better Browning with Sugar

Rubbing steaks with sugar and salt twice before grilling seasons the meat and helps thin cuts brown quickly. The first coat, applied an hour before cooking, denatures the steak's surface proteins so that they dry out and form a pellicle that develops Maillard browning and caramelizes deeply. The second, applied just before grilling, caramelizes and adds more seasoning and delicate crunch.

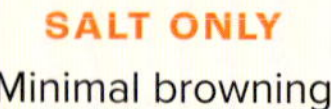
SALT ONLY
Minimal browning

SALT AND SUGAR
Deep browning

Bacon-Wrapped Filet Mignon

SERVES 4 **TIME** 40 minutes

Why This Recipe Works Is bacon the answer to all of life's culinary questions? Maybe not, but it does solve the conundrum of supremely tender yet lean and mild-to-a-fault filet mignon by adding both flavor and moisture. The combination of bacon and high heat (the typical heat for steaks) can spell disaster, but we have ways to make it work: We microwave the bacon between two plates, which keeps it from shrinking and makes it easier to wrap around the filets. To get the bacon crispy and caramelized, we sprinkle it with a little sugar. A second slice of raw bacon placed on top of each bacon-wrapped filet bastes the meat as it cooks, adding even more bacon flavor. To get a nice char from cooking beef over high heat and reduce flareups, we remove the extra bacon, move the steaks to the hottest part of the grill, and quickly sear them on one side until the meat is a perfect medium-rare.

- 8 slices bacon, divided
- ¼ cup sugar
- 1 teaspoon pepper, divided
- 4 (6- to 8-ounce) center-cut filets mignons, 1½ inches thick, trimmed
- 1 teaspoon kosher salt

1 Lay 4 slices bacon on large plate; weigh down with second plate; and microwave on high power until fat is rendered and bacon is slightly shriveled but still pliable, 1 to 3 minutes. Meanwhile, combine sugar and ½ teaspoon pepper in pie plate. Let bacon cool slightly, then dredge 1 side in sugar mixture.

2 Pat steaks dry with paper towels and sprinkle with salt and remaining ½ teaspoon pepper. Wrap 1 slice sugared bacon (sugared side out) around each filet, overlap ends, and secure with 2 toothpicks. Place 1 slice raw bacon on top of each steak, folding as needed to fit.

3A **FOR A CHARCOAL GRILL** Open bottom vent completely. Light large chimney starter filled with charcoal briquettes (6 quarts). When top coals are partially covered with ash, pour two-thirds evenly over half of grill, then pour remaining coals over other half of grill. Set cooking grate in place, cover, and open lid vent completely. Heat grill until hot, about 5 minutes.

3B **FOR A GAS GRILL** Turn all burners to high; cover; and heat grill until hot, about 15 minutes. Leave primary burner on high and turn other burner(s) to medium.

Wrapping the Steaks

1 Dredge 1 side of microwaved bacon slices in sugar mixture.

2 Wrap bacon (sugared side out) around each filet, overlapping ends, and secure with 2 toothpicks.

3 For extra bacon flavor, top bacon-wrapped filet with another slice of raw bacon. As bacon renders, it will baste and flavor steak.

4 Clean and oil cooking grate. Place steaks on cooler side of grill; cover; and cook until meat registers 100 degrees, 7 to 14 minutes. Remove bacon from top of steaks, place on cooler side, and cook until crispy; set aside for serving. Meanwhile, flip steaks; slide to hotter side of grill; and cook (covered if using gas) until meat registers 120 to 125 degrees (for medium-rare), 5 to 10 minutes.

5 Transfer steaks to plate, tent with aluminum foil, and let rest for 5 minutes. Remove toothpicks, crumble grilled bacon over top, and serve.

ULTIMATE CHARCOAL-GRILLED STEAKS

GRILLED BONELESS BEEF SHORT RIBS

Ultimate Charcoal-Grilled Steaks

SERVES 4 **TIME** 2 to 2½ hours

Why This Recipe Works Intensely seared steaks call for an intensely hot fire—so why not leave the coals in the chimney starter and brown the steaks right on top? We score, salt, and skewer the steaks and then bake them in a low oven for even cooking and to dry out their surfaces. Then we blast the steaks over the blazing-hot chimney for about a minute on each side. A bit of black pepper to finish is all the seasoning these beefy steaks need. Rib-eye steaks of a similar thickness can be substituted for the strip steaks, although they may produce more flare-ups. It is important to remove the fat caps on the steaks to limit flare-ups during grilling. You will need a charcoal chimney starter with a 7½-inch diameter and four 12-inch metal skewers for this recipe. If your chimney starter has a smaller diameter, skewer each steak individually and cook in four batches.

- 2 (1-pound) boneless strip steaks, 1¾ inches thick, fat caps removed
- 2 teaspoons kosher salt
- ½ teaspoon pepper, divided

1 Adjust oven rack to middle position and heat oven to 200 degrees. Cut each steak in half crosswise to create four 8-ounce steaks. Cut ⅟₁₆-inch-deep slits on both sides of steaks, spaced ¼ inch apart, in crosshatch pattern. Sprinkle evenly with salt.

2 Lay 2 steak halves flat on the counter, end to end, and skewer lengthwise with two 12-inch metal skewers; space skewers 1½ inches apart and space steaks ¼ inch apart. Repeat with remaining steak halves.

3 Place skewered steaks on wire rack set in rimmed baking sheet and cook in oven until centers of steaks register 120 degrees, flipping halfway through cooking and removing them as they come to temperature, 1½ hours to 1 hour 50 minutes. Tent skewered steaks (still on rack) with aluminum foil.

4 Light large chimney starter filled halfway with charcoal briquettes (3 quarts). When top coals are completely covered in ash, uncover steaks (reserving foil) and pat dry with paper towels. Using tongs, place 1 set of steaks directly over chimney so skewers rest on rim of chimney (meat will be suspended over coals). Cook until both sides are well browned and charred, about 1 minute per side. Using tongs, return first set of steaks to wire rack in sheet, sprinkle with ¼ teaspoon pepper, and tent with reserved foil. Repeat with second set of skewered steaks and remaining ¼ teaspoon pepper. Remove skewers from steaks and serve.

Grilled Boneless Beef Short Ribs

SERVES 4 to 6 **TIME** 30 minutes plus 1 hour salting

Why This Recipe Works With their rich marbling, intense beefiness, and satisfying chew, boneless beef short ribs rival a rib eye on the grill—at about half the cost. You've likely enjoyed this cut slowly braised until meltingly tender. But even quick, high-heat grilling can break down the well-distributed fat and abundant collagen in the ribs, bolstering their juiciness and imbuing them with rich, beefy flavor. We salt the ribs for an hour to ensure that they're seasoned throughout and then grill them over high heat to allow the drippings to flare up, creating great grill flavor. We turn the ribs frequently so that they cook evenly and gently, and we slice them against the grain for tenderness. We prefer these ribs cooked to medium. Serve with lemon wedges and flake sea salt.

- 2 pounds boneless beef short ribs, trimmed
- 2½ teaspoons kosher salt
- 1 teaspoon pepper

1 Cut ribs into 3- to 4-inch lengths. Sprinkle all sides with salt and pepper and let sit at room temperature for 1 hour.

2A FOR A CHARCOAL GRILL Open bottom vent completely. Light large chimney starter mounded with charcoal briquettes (7 quarts). When top coals are partially covered with ash, pour evenly over half of grill. Set cooking grate in place, cover, and open lid vent completely. Heat grill until hot, about 5 minutes.

2B FOR A GAS GRILL Turn all burners to high; cover; and heat grill until hot, about 15 minutes. Turn off 1 burner (if grill has more than 2 burners, turn off burner farthest from primary burner) and leave other burner(s) on high.

3 Clean and oil cooking grate. Place ribs on hotter side of grill. Cook (covered if using gas), turning every minute, until meat is well browned on all sides and registers 130 to 135 degrees (for medium) at thickest part, 8 to 14 minutes. (Ribs will be very pale after first turn but will continue to brown as they cook. This cut can quickly overcook; start checking temperature of smaller ribs after 8 minutes.)

4 Transfer ribs to carving board, tent with aluminum foil, and let rest for 10 minutes. Slice as thin as possible against grain and serve.

Grilled Steakhouse Steak Tips

SERVES 4 to 6 **TIME** 40 minutes plus 2 hours marinating

Why This Recipe Works For a steakhouse experience, all it takes is a well-balanced marinade and a trip to the backyard grill. Our marinade uses soy sauce for deep seasoning, dark brown sugar for complexity and a caramelized char, vegetable oil to distribute flavors, and tomato paste to help the marinade cling. Poking the meat with a fork before cutting it into chunks breaks the long, tough muscle fibers into shorter, more tender pieces and helps the meat to soak up the marinade. For peak flavor, marinate the tips for at least 2 hours; if it suits your schedule, there's no harm in soaking them for up to one day. Sirloin steak tips are sold as cubes, strips, or whole steaks that may be labeled "flap meat." For this recipe you'll need whole steaks weighing at least 8 ounces each. We prefer these steak tips cooked to medium for better browning and a less chewy texture.

- ⅓ cup soy sauce
- ⅓ cup vegetable oil
- 3 tablespoons packed dark brown sugar
- 5 garlic cloves, minced
- 1 tablespoon tomato paste
- 1 tablespoon paprika
- ½ teaspoon pepper
- ¼ teaspoon cayenne pepper
- 2½ pounds sirloin steak tips, trimmed

1 Whisk soy sauce, oil, sugar, garlic, tomato paste, paprika, pepper, and cayenne in bowl until sugar dissolves. Pat steak tips dry with paper towels, prick all over with fork, and cut into 2½-inch pieces. Combine marinade and beef in 1-gallon zipper-lock bag and toss to coat; press out as much air as possible and seal bag. Refrigerate for 2 to 24 hours, flipping bag occasionally.

2A FOR A CHARCOAL GRILL Open bottom grill vents completely. Light large chimney starter filled with charcoal briquettes (6 quarts). When top coals are partially covered with ash, pour evenly over grill. Set cooking grate in place, cover, and open lid vents completely. Heat grill until hot, about 5 minutes.

2B FOR A GAS GRILL Turn all burners to high; cover; and heat grill until hot, about 15 minutes. Leave all burners on high.

3 Clean and oil cooking grate. Place steak tips on grill. Cook (covered if using gas), turning often, until charred on all sides and meat registers 130 to 135 degrees (for medium), 8 to 10 minutes.

4 Transfer to platter, tent with aluminum foil, and let rest for 5 to 10 minutes. Serve.

Grilled Beef Teriyaki

SERVES 4 **TIME** 55 minutes plus 30 minutes marinating

Why This Recipe Works To optimize the meaty, caramelized flavor of teriyaki, we use a soy sauce–mirin marinade that keeps the beef juicy on the grill and promotes browning. Sugar adds balanced sweetness and scallions and ginger give it an aromatic boost. Grilling sirloin steak tips over high heat produces well-charred, slightly smoky meat, and slicing the meat against the grain before grilling it gives it a better texture and helps the glaze adhere firmly to each piece. Sirloin steak tips are sold as cubes, strips, or whole steaks that may be labeled "flap meat." For this recipe you'll need whole steaks weighing at least 8 ounces each. We prefer these steak tips cooked to medium for better browning and a less chewy texture. Serve with rice.

STEAK

- ⅓ cup soy sauce
- ¼ cup mirin
- 2 scallions, white parts minced, green parts sliced thin on bias
- 2 tablespoons vegetable oil
- 3 garlic cloves, minced
- 1 tablespoon grated fresh ginger
- 1 tablespoon sugar
- 1 teaspoon grated orange zest
- 2 pounds sirloin steak tips, trimmed

SAUCE

- ½ cup sugar
- ½ cup sake or vermouth
- ½ cup mirin
- ⅓ cup soy sauce
- 1 teaspoon grated fresh ginger
- 1 teaspoon cornstarch

1 FOR THE STEAK Combine soy sauce, mirin, scallion whites, oil, garlic, ginger, sugar, and orange zest in bowl. Cut steak tips with grain into 2 or 3 even pieces. (If total length of meat is 12 inches or less, cut into 2 pieces. If more than 12 inches, cut into 3 pieces.) Cut each piece on bias against grain into ½-inch-thick slices. Combine marinade and beef in 1-gallon zipper-lock bag and toss to coat; press out as much air as possible and seal bag. Refrigerate for 30 minutes to 1 hour, flipping bag every 15 minutes. Remove beef from marinade and pat dry with paper towels.

2 FOR THE SAUCE While steak tips marinate, whisk all ingredients together in small saucepan and bring to simmer over medium heat. Cook until syrupy and reduced to 1 cup, 12 to 15 minutes. Measure out and reserve ¾ cup sauce for serving.

3A FOR A CHARCOAL GRILL Open bottom vent completely. Light large chimney starter filled with charcoal briquettes (6 quarts). When top coals are partially covered with ash, pour evenly over half of grill. Set cooking grate in place, cover, and open lid vent completely. Heat grill until hot, about 5 minutes.

3B FOR A GAS GRILL Turn all burners to high; cover; and heat grill until hot, about 15 minutes. Leave all burners on high.

4 Clean and oil cooking grate. Place steak tips on grill (hotter side if using charcoal) and cook (covered if using gas) until dark brown on all sides, 6 to 8 minutes, turning as needed. Brush meat with 2 tablespoons sauce, flip, and cook for 30 seconds. Brush meat with remaining 2 tablespoons sauce, flip, and continue to cook 30 seconds longer.

5 Transfer to platter, tent with aluminum foil, and let rest for 5 to 10 minutes. Sprinkle with scallion greens and serve, passing reserved sauce separately.

Grilled Bourbon Steaks

SERVES 6 to 8 **TIME** 40 minutes plus 4 hours marinating

Why This Recipe Works Soaking meat in bourbon enhances its meatiness and helps create a char so flavorful that no sauce is necessary. To get the maximum amount of smoky bourbon flavor into boneless rib-eye steaks, we soak them for 4 hours in a mixture of bourbon, Worcestershire, shallot, garlic, salt, and pepper in two separate zipper-lock bags. Use a bourbon you'd be happy drinking.

MARINADE

- 1 cup bourbon
- 1 cup Worcestershire sauce
- 1 shallot, minced
- 2 garlic cloves, minced
- 2½ teaspoons kosher salt
- 2 teaspoons pepper

STEAKS

- 4 (1-pound) boneless rib-eye steaks, 1½ inches thick, trimmed
- 2 tablespoons vegetable oil
- ¾ teaspoon kosher salt
- ¾ teaspoon pepper

GRILLED BEEF TERIYAKI

1 FOR THE MARINADE Whisk all ingredients together in bowl.

2 FOR THE STEAKS Divide steaks between two 1-gallon zipper-lock bags, then divide marinade between bags and toss to coat. Press out as much air as possible, seal bags, and refrigerate for at least 4 hours or up to 24 hours, flipping bags occasionally.

3 Remove steaks from bags and pat dry with paper towels. Brush steaks all over with oil and sprinkle with salt and pepper.

4A FOR A CHARCOAL GRILL Open bottom vent completely. Light large chimney starter filled with charcoal briquettes (6 quarts). When top coals are partially covered with ash, pour evenly over grill. Set cooking grate in place, cover, and open lid vent completely. Heat grill until hot, about 5 minutes.

4B FOR A GAS GRILL Turn all burners to high; cover; and heat grill until hot, about 15 minutes. Leave all burners on high.

5 Clean and oil cooking grate. Place steaks on grill and cook (covered if using gas) until well charred and meat registers 120 to 125 degrees (for medium-rare), 12 to 16 minutes, flipping halfway through cooking.

6 Transfer steaks to wire rack set in rimmed baking sheet, tent with aluminum foil, and let rest for 10 minutes. Serve.

Grilled Flank Steak with Garlic-Shallot-Rosemary Marinade

SERVES 4 to 6 **TIME** 35 minutes plus 1 hour marinating

Why This Recipe Works Flank steak often gets the Italian dressing treatment; it's a quick and easy marinade. But the flavor comes at a cost—mushy gray meat caused by the acid in the vinegar. To really boost flavor without overtenderizing the meat, you want a fresh, aromatic marinade without acid. Because fat carries flavor so well, oil is the key ingredient. The challenge is to infuse garlic, shallot, and rosemary into the oil and then into the steak. Our solution has two parts: First, we mince the aromatics and combine them with the oil in a blender to create a marinade paste. Next, we use a novel "marinating" technique—prick the steak all over with a fork, rub it first with salt and then with the marinade paste, and let it sit for up to 24 hours. After marinating, the paste is wiped off to prevent burning, and the steak is ready for the grill. We use a two-level fire (which lets you move the thin part of the steak to the cooler side of the grill once it is done), and we cook the steak only to medium-rare to keep it nice and juicy. Other thin steaks with a loose grain, such as skirt steak or steak tips, can be substituted for the flank steak.

MARINADE

- 6 tablespoons extra-virgin olive oil
- 1 shallot, minced
- 6 garlic cloves, minced
- 2 tablespoons minced fresh rosemary

STEAK

- 1 (2- to 2½-pound) flank steak, trimmed
- 2 teaspoons kosher salt
- ½ teaspoon pepper

1 FOR THE MARINADE Process all ingredients in blender until smooth, about 30 seconds, scraping down sides of blender jar as needed.

2 FOR THE STEAK Pat steak dry with paper towels and place in 13 by 9-inch baking dish. Using dinner fork, prick steak about 20 times on each side. Rub both sides of steak evenly with salt, then with marinade. Cover with plastic wrap and refrigerate for at least 1 hour or up to 24 hours. Before cooking, wipe paste off steak with paper towels and sprinkle with pepper.

3A FOR A CHARCOAL GRILL Open bottom vent completely. Light large chimney starter filled with charcoal briquettes (6 quarts). When top coals are partially covered with ash, pour two-thirds evenly over half of grill, then pour remaining coals over other half of grill. Set cooking grate in place, cover, and open lid vent completely. Heat grill until hot, about 5 minutes.

3B FOR A GAS GRILL Turn all burners to high; cover; and heat grill until hot, about 15 minutes. Leave all burners on high.

4 Clean and oil cooking grate. Place steak on grill (hotter side if using charcoal) and cook (covered if using gas) until well browned on first side, 4 to 6 minutes. Flip steak and cook (covered if using gas) until meat registers 120 to 125 degrees (for medium-rare), 3 to 6 minutes.

5 Transfer steak to carving board, tent with aluminum foil, and let rest for 10 minutes. Slice steak on bias against grain into ¼-inch-thick pieces and serve.

GRILLED FLANK STEAK WITH GARLIC-GINGER-SESAME MARINADE

Grilled Marinated Skirt Steak

SERVES 4 **TIME** 35 minutes

Why This Recipe Works Intensely beefy skirt steak is a popular cut because its loose, open grain makes it an ideal candidate for soaking up a flavorful marinade. But while a marinade might add flavor, it can also lead to a steak that steams instead of browns. One way to avoid this dilemma and ensure a perfectly charred crust is to reverse the usual order of things: Grill first and marinate last. Sprinkled with just a bit of salt, pepper, and sugar, the steaks char nicely on the grill. Then you simply transfer the just-grilled steaks to a pan, poke them with a fork, pour a sweet and savory marinade over them, and let them soak up the flavorful liquid. Bonus: Since the marinade never touches raw meat, you can serve it on the side as a sauce. Keep the marinade at room temperature or it will cool down the steaks.

MARINADE

- ½ cup soy sauce
- ¼ cup Worcestershire sauce
- 2 scallions, sliced thin
- 2 tablespoons sugar
- 4 garlic cloves, minced
- 1 tablespoon Dijon mustard
- 2 teaspoons balsamic vinegar
- ½ teaspoon pepper
- ¼ cup vegetable oil

STEAK

- 1½ pounds skirt steak, trimmed and cut crosswise into 4-inch pieces
- 2 teaspoons sugar
- 1 teaspoon kosher salt
- ½ teaspoon pepper

1 FOR THE MARINADE Combine soy sauce, Worcestershire, scallions, sugar, garlic, mustard, vinegar, and pepper in bowl. Slowly whisk in oil until incorporated and sugar has dissolved; set aside.

2 FOR THE STEAK Pat steaks dry with paper towels and sprinkle evenly with sugar, salt, and pepper.

3A FOR A CHARCOAL GRILL Open bottom vent completely. Light large chimney starter mounded with charcoal briquettes (7 quarts). When top coals are partially covered with ash, pour evenly over half of grill. Set cooking grate in place, cover, and open lid vent completely. Heat grill until hot, about 5 minutes.

VARIATIONS

Grilled Flank Steak with Garlic-Ginger-Sesame Marinade

Substitute following mixture for marinade: Process ¼ cup toasted sesame oil, 3 tablespoons grated fresh ginger, 2 tablespoons vegetable oil, 2 minced scallions, and 3 minced garlic cloves in blender until smooth, about 30 seconds, scraping down sides as needed.

Grilled Flank Steak with Garlic-Chile Marinade

Substitute following mixture for marinade: Process 6 tablespoons vegetable oil, 6 minced garlic cloves, 2 minced scallions, 1 tablespoon minced canned chipotle chile in adobo sauce, and 1 seeded and minced jalapeño chile in blender until smooth, about 30 seconds, scraping down sides as needed.

3B FOR A GAS GRILL Turn all burners to high; cover; and heat grill until hot, about 15 minutes. Leave all burners on high.

4 Clean and oil cooking grate. Place steaks on grill (over hotter side if using charcoal). Cook (covered if using gas), flipping as needed, until well browned and meat registers 120 to 125 degrees (for medium-rare), 4 to 8 minutes.

5 Transfer steaks to 13 by 9-inch baking dish and poke all over with fork. Pour marinade over top, tent with aluminum foil, and let rest for 5 to 10 minutes.

6 Transfer steaks to carving board and pour marinade into serving bowl. Slice steak thin against grain and serve with marinade.

VARIATIONS

Grilled Thai Curry Marinated Skirt Steak

Substitute following mixture for marinade: Combine ⅓ cup soy sauce, ⅓ cup canned coconut milk, 2 tablespoons sugar, 2 tablespoons chopped fresh cilantro, 1 seeded and minced jalapeño chile, 1 teaspoon Thai red or green curry paste, and ½ teaspoon pepper in bowl. Slowly whisk in ¼ cup vegetable oil until incorporated and sugar has dissolved.

Grilled Hoisin-Scallion Marinated Skirt Steak

Substitute following mixture for marinade: Combine ½ cup soy sauce, ¼ cup hoisin sauce, 2 thinly sliced scallions, 2 tablespoons sugar, 1 to 2 teaspoons chili-garlic sauce, and 1 teaspoon grated fresh ginger in bowl. Slowly whisk in ¼ cup vegetable oil and 1 teaspoon toasted sesame oil until incorporated and sugar has dissolved.

Grilled Black Pepper–Honey Marinated Skirt Steak

Substitute following mixture for marinade: Combine ½ cup soy sauce, 3 tablespoons honey, 2 tablespoons Dijon mustard, 2 teaspoons pepper, and ½ teaspoon minced fresh thyme in bowl. Slowly whisk in ¼ cup vegetable oil until incorporated.

Grilled Shell Sirloin Steak with New Mexico Chile Rub

SERVES 6 to 8 **TIME** 1 hour plus 1 hour salting

Why This Recipe Works A good spice rub can work wonders on less-expensive steaks, counteracting flavor and texture deficiencies. Wet rubs and dry rubs both have their advantages, so why not use both? Tomato paste and fish sauce are two of the most potent carriers of glutamates, which amp up savory, meaty flavors; along with onion powder and garlic powder, they make a wet rub that deepens the flavor of the meat—without making it taste like fish or tomatoes. Toasted chiles and warm spices are the backbone of a dry rub that keeps its flavor over the intense heat of the grill. Spraying the rubbed steaks with oil helps the spices bloom, preventing a raw flavor. The end result is satisfying grilled steak with a crispy, crunchy crust. If New Mexico chiles aren't available, you can substitute California chiles.

STEAK

- 2 teaspoons tomato paste
- 2 teaspoons fish sauce
- 1½ teaspoons kosher salt
- ½ teaspoon onion powder
- ½ teaspoon garlic powder
- 2 (1½- to 1¾-pound) whole boneless shell sirloin steaks, 1 to 1¼ inches thick, trimmed

NEW MEXICO CHILE RUB

- 2 dried New Mexico chiles, stemmed, seeded, and torn into ½-inch pieces
- 4 teaspoons cumin seeds
- 4 teaspoons coriander seeds
- ½ teaspoon red pepper flakes
- ½ teaspoon black peppercorns
- 1 tablespoon sugar
- 1 tablespoon paprika
- ¼ teaspoon ground cloves
- Vegetable oil spray

1 FOR THE STEAK Combine tomato paste, fish sauce, salt, onion powder, and garlic powder in bowl. Pat steaks dry with paper towels. Cut ⅟₁₆-inch-deep slits on both sides of steaks, spaced ½ inch apart, in crosshatch pattern. Rub salt mixture evenly on both sides of steaks. Place steaks on wire rack set in rimmed baking sheet; let sit at room temperature for at least 1 hour.

2 **FOR THE NEW MEXICO CHILE RUB** Toast New Mexico chiles, cumin seeds, coriander seeds, pepper flakes, and peppercorns in 10-inch skillet over medium-low heat, stirring frequently, until just beginning to smoke, 3 to 4 minutes. Transfer to plate and let cool for 5 minutes. Grind spices in spice grinder or in mortar with pestle until coarsely ground. Transfer spices to bowl and stir in sugar, paprika, and cloves.

3 Sprinkle half of spice rub evenly over 1 side of steaks and press to adhere until spice rub is fully moistened. Lightly spray rubbed side of steak with oil spray, about 3 seconds. Flip steaks and repeat process of sprinkling with spice rub and coating with oil spray on second side.

4A **FOR A CHARCOAL GRILL** Open bottom vent completely. Light large chimney starter mounded with charcoal briquettes (7 quarts). When top coals are partially covered with ash, pour two-thirds evenly over half of grill, then pour remaining coals over other half of grill. Set cooking grate in place, cover, and open lid vent completely. Heat grill until hot, about 5 minutes.

4B **FOR A GAS GRILL** Turn all burners to high; cover; and heat grill until hot, about 15 minutes. Leave primary burner on high and turn other burner(s) to medium.

5 Clean and oil cooking grate. Place steaks on hotter side of grill and cook until nicely charred and meat registers 120 to 125 degrees (for medium-rare), 6 to 8 minutes, flipping steaks halfway through cooking. (If spices begin to burn, slide steaks to cooler side of grill to finish cooking.)

6 Transfer steaks to clean wire rack set in rimmed baking sheet, tent with aluminum foil, and let rest for 10 minutes. Transfer to carving board, slice thin against grain, and serve.

VARIATIONS

Grilled Shell Sirloin Steak with Ancho Chile–Coffee Rub

Substitute 1 dried ancho chile for New Mexico chiles, 2 teaspoons ground coffee for paprika, and 1 teaspoon cocoa powder for ground cloves.

Grilled Shell Sirloin Steak with Spicy Chipotle Chile Rub

Substitute 2 dried chipotle chiles for New Mexico chiles, 1 teaspoon dried oregano for paprika, and ½ teaspoon ground cinnamon for ground cloves.

GRILLED SHELL SIRLOIN STEAK WITH NEW MEXICO CHILE RUB

Grilled Spice-Rubbed Chuck Steaks

SERVES 4 to 6 **TIME** 45 minutes plus 6 hours seasoning

Why This Recipe Works The chuck eye comes from the border between the chuck and rib primal cuts (close to where rib eyes are cut from), which means this cut is more tender than other chuck cuts but has the same great beefy flavor. For consistent-size steaks, we buy a boneless chuck-eye roast and divide it into four equal portions. A dry rub creates a great crust on the grill, and a few key ingredients—chipotle powder, cocoa powder, and brown sugar—provide deep flavor. To ensure that the meat is perfectly cooked, we sear it over the hotter side of the grill and then let it finish slowly on the cooler side. Choose a roast without too much fat at the natural seam.

- 1 tablespoon kosher salt
- 1 tablespoon chipotle chile powder
- 1 teaspoon unsweetened cocoa powder
- 1 teaspoon packed brown sugar
- ½ teaspoon ground coriander
- ½ teaspoon granulated garlic
- 1 (2½- to 3-pound) boneless beef chuck-eye roast
- 2 tablespoons vegetable oil

1 Combine salt, chile powder, cocoa, sugar, coriander, and granulated garlic in bowl. Separate roast into 2 pieces along natural seam. Turn each piece on its side and cut in half lengthwise against grain. Remove silver skin and trim fat to ¼-inch thickness. Pat steaks dry with paper towels and rub all over with spice mixture. Transfer steaks to 1-gallon zipper-lock bag and refrigerate for at least 6 hours or up to 24 hours. Before cooking, brush steaks all over with oil.

2A FOR A CHARCOAL GRILL Open bottom vent halfway. Light large chimney starter filled with charcoal briquettes (6 quarts). When top coals are partially covered with ash, pour evenly over half of grill. Set cooking grate in place, cover, and open lid vent halfway. Heat grill until hot, about 5 minutes.

2B FOR A GAS GRILL Turn all burners to high; cover; and heat grill until hot, about 15 minutes. Turn primary burner to medium-high and secondary burner(s) to medium-low.

3 Clean and oil cooking grate. Place steaks over hotter side of grill and cook (covered if using gas) until well charred on both sides, about 10 minutes, flipping halfway through cooking. Slide steaks to cooler side of grill and cook (covered if using gas) until meat registers 120 to 125 degrees (for medium-rare), 5 to 8 minutes.

4 Transfer steaks to carving board, tent with aluminum foil, and let rest for 10 minutes. Slice thin against grain and serve.

GRILLED SPICE-RUBBED CHUCK STEAKS

Creating Chuck Steaks at Home

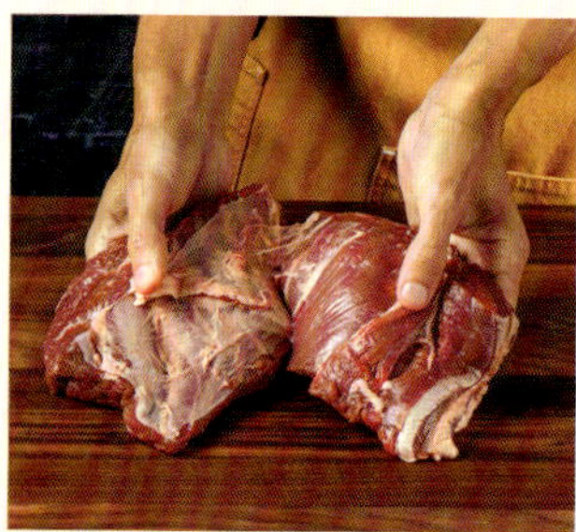
1 Use your hands to separate roast at natural seam.

2 Turn each piece on its side and cut it in half lengthwise, against grain.

3 Remove and discard chewy silver skin and any excess fat.

KALBI (KOREAN GRILLED FLANKEN-STYLE SHORT RIBS)

Kalbi (Korean Grilled Flanken-Style Short Ribs)

SERVES 4 **TIME** 40 minutes plus 24 hours marinating

Why This Recipe Works Sweet and savory Korean charred ribs are irresistible. This preparation is typically cooked over wood and made with beef short ribs cut thin, flanken-style, across the bones. (You can find this cut at Asian markets, especially ones that specialize in Korean ingredients.) Kalbi marinade usually gets its fruity sweetness from ripe Asian pear; canned pineapple is a reliable year-round stand-in. Green kiwi adds more sweetness plus enzymes that tenderize the meat. Aside from marinating the ribs for at least 24 hours, the biggest tip for success is to cook the kalbi for longer than you might think: You need to allow the fat to render and the connective tissue to break down. When the kalbi are done, the bones will pull away cleanly from the meat with little resistance. An 8-ounce can of pineapple chunks will yield enough for this recipe. We prefer the flavor of green kiwi to yellow kiwi for the marinade. We call for clear rice wine here; michiu, cheongju, or mirin can be used. Flanken-style short ribs are cut with a band saw and tend to have a fair amount of bone fragments stuck to them, which is why we rinse them in step 3. Kitchen shears make quick work of removing meat from the bones. Garnish the kalbi with sliced scallions, if desired. To enjoy the kalbi as ssam (a Korean style of eating in which morsels of meats, plus condiments and garnishes, are wrapped in leafy vegetables), we like to tuck bite-size pieces of beef into fresh lettuce leaves along with small amounts of short-grain white rice, kimchi, and ssamjang (seasoned soybean paste).

- ¾ cup packed dark brown sugar
- ⅔ cup soy sauce
- 1 cup coarsely chopped onion
- ½ cup canned pineapple chunks, plus 3 tablespoons juice
- ½ green kiwi, peeled
- 6 garlic cloves, smashed and peeled
- ¼ cup clear rice wine
- 2 tablespoons toasted sesame oil
- 3 pounds flanken-style beef short ribs, ¼ inch thick, trimmed

1 Combine sugar and soy sauce in small saucepan and cook over medium-high heat, stirring occasionally, until sugar is dissolved. Remove from heat and let cool completely.

2 Combine onion, pineapple and juice, kiwi, and garlic in blender and puree until smooth, about 30 seconds. Transfer onion mixture to 13 by 9-inch baking dish; stir in wine, oil, and soy sauce mixture.

STEAK AND POTATO SALAD WITH GRILLED LEMON DRESSING

3 Line rimmed baking sheet with triple layer of paper towels. Rinse ribs under cold running water to remove any bone fragments, then transfer to prepared sheet. Pat tops of ribs dry with additional paper towels.

4 Working with a few ribs at a time, transfer ribs to marinade, turn gently to coat, and submerge in marinade. Cover dish with plastic wrap and refrigerate for at least 24 hours or up to 2 days.

5A **FOR A CHARCOAL GRILL** Open bottom vent completely. Light large chimney starter three-quarters filled with charcoal briquettes (4½ quarts). When top coals are partially covered with ash, pour evenly over grill. Set cooking grate in place, cover, and open lid vent completely. Heat grill until hot, about 5 minutes.

5B **FOR A GAS GRILL** Turn all burners to high; cover; and heat grill until hot, about 15 minutes. Turn all burners to medium.

6 Clean and oil cooking grate. Place ribs on grill. Cook until evenly browned, about 12 minutes, flipping halfway through cooking and moving as needed to prevent flare-ups. Transfer ribs to platter, tent with aluminum foil, and let rest for 5 minutes. Serve.

Steak and Potato Salad With Grilled Lemon Dressing

SERVES 4 **TIME** 45 minutes

Why This Recipe Works This streamlined meal for the grill is inspired by tagliata, a popular Tuscan dish of sliced steak with arugula, lemon, and shaved Parmesan. Fingerling potatoes, parcooked in the microwave and grilled alongside boneless rib eyes, balance the peppery arugula with some earthy heft. We grill lemon halves to mellow their acidity to a caramelized sweetness and then use their juice to build a complex, nutty vinaigrette for our potato and arugula salad. Strip steaks can be substituted for the rib eyes, if desired.

- 2 (1-pound) boneless rib-eye steaks, 1½ inches thick, trimmed
- 5 teaspoons kosher salt, divided
- 1¼ teaspoons pepper, divided
- 1½ pounds fingerling potatoes, unpeeled
- ½ cup extra-virgin olive oil, divided
- 1 teaspoon grated lemon zest, plus 2 lemons, halved
- 1 shallot, chopped fine
- 1 teaspoon Dijon mustard

- 5 ounces (5 cups) baby arugula
- ½ teaspoon flake sea salt
- 1 ounce Parmesan cheese, shaved with vegetable peeler

1 Pat steaks dry with paper towels and sprinkle with 2 teaspoons kosher salt and ½ teaspoon pepper. Toss potatoes with 2 tablespoons oil, 2 teaspoons kosher salt, and ½ teaspoon pepper in large bowl. Microwave, covered, until potatoes are nearly tender, 9 to 12 minutes, stirring every 3 minutes.

2A **FOR A CHARCOAL GRILL** Open bottom vent completely. Light large chimney starter filled with charcoal briquettes (6 quarts). When top coals are partially covered with ash, pour evenly over grill. Set cooking grate in place, cover, and open lid vent completely. Heat grill until hot, about 5 minutes.

2B **FOR A GAS GRILL** Turn all burners to high; cover; and heat grill until hot, about 15 minutes. Leave all burners on high.

3 Clean and oil cooking grate. Place steak, potatoes, and lemon halves (cut sides down) on grill. Cook until potatoes and steak are well browned and meat registers 120 to 125 degrees (for medium-rare), 8 to 12 minutes, flipping as needed. Transfer steak, potatoes, and lemon to carving board.

4 Slice potatoes into ½-inch-thick rounds. Squeeze 3 tablespoons juice from 2 lemon halves. Whisk lemon juice and zest, shallot, mustard, remaining 1 teaspoon kosher salt and remaining ¼ teaspoon pepper together in large bowl. Whisking constantly, drizzle in remaining 6 tablespoons oil. Add arugula and potatoes and toss to combine. Transfer salad to serving platter.

5 Slice steak thin and arrange over salad. Sprinkle with flake sea salt and season with pepper to taste. Sprinkle with Parmesan and serve with remaining 2 lemon halves.

Grilled Strip Steaks and Zucchini with Olive Vinaigrette

SERVES 4 **TIME** 35 minutes

Why This Recipe Works A grill that's still hot after cooking steaks is just begging for a quick vegetable side, and easy-to-prep zucchini fits the bill. To keep the zucchini from falling through the grate, we cut it into generous, bias-cut slices. Store-bought olive tapenade makes the base for a quick, delicious vinaigrette that equally complements the grilled steaks and the zucchini. Look for tapenade (a mixture of chopped olives) in the Italian section of your local market.

- 2 (1-pound) strip steaks, 1½ inches thick, trimmed
- 3½ teaspoons kosher salt, divided
- 1¼ teaspoons pepper, divided
- ¼ cup extra-virgin olive oil
- 1 garlic clove, minced
- ¼ teaspoon red pepper flakes
- 4 zucchini (8 ounces each), sliced on bias ½ inch thick
- ¼ cup olive tapenade
- 1 tablespoon red wine vinegar
- 2 tablespoons pine nuts, toasted
- 1 tablespoon chopped fresh parsley

1 Pat steaks dry with paper towels and sprinkle with 2 teaspoons salt and ½ teaspoon pepper. Whisk oil, garlic, and pepper flakes together in small bowl. In large bowl, toss zucchini with 1 tablespoon oil mixture, 1 teaspoon salt, and ½ teaspoon pepper. Whisk tapenade, vinegar, remaining ½ teaspoon salt, and remaining ¼ teaspoon pepper into remaining oil mixture; set aside for serving.

2A **FOR A CHARCOAL GRILL** Open bottom vent completely. Light large chimney starter filled with charcoal briquettes (6 quarts). When top coals are partially covered with ash, pour evenly over grill. Set cooking grate in place, cover, and open lid vent completely. Heat grill until hot, about 5 minutes.

2B **FOR A GAS GRILL** Turn all burners to high; cover; and heat grill until hot, about 15 minutes. Leave all burners on high.

3 Clean and oil cooking grate. Place steaks on grill and cook (covered if using gas) until meat registers 120 to 125 degrees (for medium-rare), 8 to 16 minutes, flipping as needed. Transfer steaks to carving board, tent with aluminum foil, and let rest for 5 minutes. Meanwhile, place zucchini on grill and cook until charred and tender, 6 to 10 minutes, flipping as needed; transfer to platter.

4 Slice steaks and transfer to platter with zucchini. Drizzle with reserved tapenade mixture, and sprinkle with pine nuts and parsley. Serve.

Grilled Strip Steak and Potatoes with Blue Cheese Butter

SERVES 4 **TIME** 35 minutes

Why This Recipe Works When the family is craving meat and potatoes but you're craving being outdoors, this superfast recipe steps up to the plate. Strip steaks need just a little salt

GRILLED STRIP STEAK AND POTATOES
WITH BLUE CHEESE BUTTER

and pepper and about 10 minutes over a hot fire to taste their best. Skewered parcooked potatoes turn tender and browned in the amount of time it takes for the steaks to cook. A quick blue cheese–garlic butter evokes classic steakhouse flavors; dollop some of it on the just-grilled steak and toss the rest with the potatoes for wall-to-wall flavor. You will need four to five 12-inch metal skewers for this recipe.

- 1½ pounds small (1- to 2-inch-wide) red or yellow potatoes, unpeeled, halved
- 2 tablespoons extra-virgin olive oil, divided
- 2 teaspoons kosher salt, divided
- ½ teaspoon pepper, divided
- 4 tablespoons unsalted butter, softened
- 3 tablespoons crumbled blue cheese
- 2 tablespoons minced fresh chives
- 1 garlic clove, minced
- 2 (1-pound) strip steaks, 1 inch thick, trimmed

1 Toss potatoes with 1 tablespoon oil, ½ teaspoon salt, and ⅛ teaspoon pepper in bowl. Microwave, covered, until potatoes offer slight resistance when poked with tip of paring knife, about 6 minutes, stirring halfway through. Drain if necessary, then toss with remaining 1 tablespoon oil. Thread potatoes onto four or five 12-inch metal skewers.

2 Mash butter with blue cheese, chives, garlic, ½ teaspoon salt, and ⅛ teaspoon pepper with fork in large bowl until combined; set aside for serving. Pat steaks dry with paper towels and sprinkle with remaining 1 teaspoon salt and remaining ¼ teaspoon pepper.

3A **FOR A CHARCOAL GRILL** Open bottom vent completely. Light large chimney starter filled with charcoal briquettes (6 quarts). When top coals are partially covered with ash, pour evenly over grill. Set cooking grate in place, cover, and open lid vent completely. Heat grill until hot, about 5 minutes.

3B **FOR A GAS GRILL** Turn all burners to high; cover; and heat grill until hot, about 15 minutes. Leave all burners on high.

4 Clean and oil cooking grate. Place steaks and potatoes on grill. Cook (covered if using gas) until meat registers 120 to 125 degrees (for medium-rare) and potatoes are lightly charred and tender, 8 to 16 minutes, flipping as needed.

5 Transfer steaks to carving board, dollop with half of reserved blue cheese butter, tent with aluminum foil, and let rest for 5 minutes. Slide potatoes off skewers into bowl with remaining garlic butter and toss to coat. Slice steaks ½ inch thick. Serve with potatoes.

Beef Tenderloin with Pear, Grilled Onion, and Blue Cheese Salad

SERVES 4 **TIME** 30 minutes

Why This Recipe Works We give mild beef tenderloin steaks a flavor boost by serving them atop a crunchy, creamy, sweet-and-salty salad of endive, watercress, blue cheese, pear, and grilled red onion. To prevent the lean beef tenderloin from drying out, we use a two-level fire to create different levels of heat on opposite sides of the grill. The hotter side is perfect for searing the meat to develop flavor and color, while the cooler side allows the meat to gently finish cooking to the desired level of doneness, which keeps it moist. Grilling raw onion slices can lead to blackened, crunchy onions. To limit their time on the grill, we parcook them in the microwave first. Once they're softened, we grill them until they're very tender, with the perfect amount of char. Do your best to leave the onion slices intact when cooking so that they will be easier to maneuver around the grill.

- 1 red onion, sliced into ¾-inch-thick rounds (do not separate rings)
- 3 tablespoons extra-virgin olive oil, divided
- 1½ teaspoons kosher salt, divided
- ¾ teaspoon pepper, divided
- 4 (6- to 8-ounce) center-cut filets mignons, 1½ to 2 inches thick, trimmed
- 2 tablespoons balsamic vinegar
- 8 ounces (8 cups) watercress, trimmed
- 1 head Belgian endive (4 ounces), leaves separated and halved lengthwise
- 3 ounces blue cheese, crumbled (¾ cup)
- 1 Bosc pear, halved, cored, and sliced thin

1 Brush onion rounds with 1 tablespoon oil and sprinkle with ½ teaspoon salt and ¼ teaspoon pepper. Lay onion in single layer on plate and microwave until beginning to soften, about 3 minutes. (Handle onion gently to avoid separating rings.) Pat steaks dry with paper towels and sprinkle with remaining 1 teaspoon salt and remaining ½ teaspoon pepper.

2A **FOR A CHARCOAL GRILL** Open bottom vent completely. Light large chimney starter filled with charcoal briquettes (6 quarts). When top coals are partially covered with ash, pour two-thirds evenly over grill, then pour remaining coals over half of grill. Set cooking grate in place, cover, and open lid vent completely. Heat grill until hot, about 5 minutes.

2B FOR A GAS GRILL Turn all burners to high; cover; and heat grill until hot, about 15 minutes. Leave primary burner on high and turn other burner(s) to medium.

3 Clean and oil cooking grate. Place steaks on hotter side of grill and cook (covered if using gas) until well browned on both sides, 4 to 6 minutes, flipping as needed. Slide steaks to cooler side of grill and continue to cook until meat registers 120 to 125 degrees (for medium-rare), 5 to 9 minutes, flipping halfway through cooking. Transfer steaks to platter, tent loosely with aluminum foil, and let rest while finishing salad.

4 As steaks finish cooking, place onion rounds on hotter side of grill and cook until tender and spottily charred, about 4 minutes, flipping halfway through cooking; transfer to bowl.

5 Separate onion rounds into rings. Whisk vinegar and remaining 2 tablespoons oil together in large bowl. Add onion, watercress, endive, blue cheese, and pear and toss to coat. Serve with steaks.

Grilled Steak and Kale Salad

SERVES 4 **TIME** 45 minutes

Why This Recipe Works What happens when you throw lacinato kale on the grill? You get a surprising base for a hearty steak salad. The flavorful charring adds complexity to the hearty greens, which tenderize and wilt slightly over the intense heat but keep enough structure to stand up to the substantial toppings. Coating flank steak with a honey-Dijon rub enhances browning, and mustard and honey also flavor the vinaigrette. Grilled croutons and crumbled blue cheese and bacon add big, bold flavors to balance out the bitterness of the grilled kale. Lacinato kale is also sold as cavolo nero, black, dinosaur, or Tuscan kale; other types of kale are too tough for this recipe.

DRESSING

- 2 tablespoons red wine vinegar
- 2 teaspoons Dijon mustard
- 1 teaspoon honey
- 1 teaspoon kosher salt
- ½ teaspoon pepper
- ¼ cup extra-virgin olive oil

STEAK AND SALAD

- ¼ cup extra-virgin olive oil, divided
- 1 teaspoon Dijon mustard
- 1 teaspoon honey
- 2 teaspoons kosher salt, divided
- ½ teaspoon pepper
- 1 (1½-pound) flank steak, trimmed
- 1 (5-inch) piece baguette, cut on bias into ½-inch-thick slices
- 1 pound lacinato kale, tough stems trimmed
- 6 slices cooked bacon, crumbled (½ cup)
- 2 ounces blue cheese, crumbled (½ cup)

1 FOR THE DRESSING Whisk vinegar mustard, honey, salt, and pepper together in large bowl. Slowly whisk in oil; set aside for serving.

2 FOR THE STEAK AND SALAD Combine 1 tablespoon oil, mustard, honey, 1½ teaspoons salt, and pepper in bowl. Pat steak dry with paper towels, then rub all over with honey mixture. Brush bread all over with 1 tablespoon oil. Toss kale with remaining 2 tablespoons oil and remaining ½ teaspoon salt in large bowl.

3A FOR A CHARCOAL GRILL Open bottom vent completely. Light large chimney starter filled with charcoal briquettes (6 quarts). When top coals are partially covered with ash, pour evenly over grill. Set cooking grate in place, cover, and open lid vent completely. Heat grill until hot, about 5 minutes.

3B FOR A GAS GRILL Turn all burners to high; cover; and heat grill until hot, about 15 minutes. Leave all burners on high.

4 Clean and oil cooking grate. Place steak on grill and cook until browned and meat registers 120 to 125 degrees (for medium-rare), 6 to 10 minutes, flipping halfway through cooking. Transfer steak to carving board, tent with aluminum foil, and let rest. Place bread on grill and cook until browned, about 2 minutes, flipping halfway through cooking; transfer to plate. Place kale on grill and cook until charred and tender, 2 to 4 minutes, flipping halfway through cooking; transfer to cutting board.

5 Chop kale coarse. Whisk dressing to recombine, add kale, and toss to coat; transfer to serving platter. Cut steak in half lengthwise, then slice each half thin against grain. Tear bread into bite-size pieces. Top kale with steak, bread, bacon, and blue cheese and serve.

Grilled Cumin-Rubbed Flank Steak with Mexican Street Corn

SERVES 4 **TIME** 40 minutes

Why This Recipe Works Sweet summer corn picks up a smoky char on the grill and some cheesy richness from a Mexican street corn–inspired sauce. Mayonnaise does double duty as a flavorful fat for grilling the corn and then as the base of the sauce. A simple cumin and chili powder spice rub flavors the quick-cooking flank steak, which rests while the corn is grilling, so both are ready to eat at the same time.

- 1 tablespoon ground cumin
- 1½ teaspoons kosher salt, divided
- ¾ teaspoon chili powder, divided
- ½ teaspoon pepper
- ¼ cup mayonnaise
- ¼ cup grated Pecorino Romano cheese
- 2 tablespoons minced fresh cilantro
- 1 tablespoon lime juice, plus lime wedges for serving
- 1 garlic clove, minced
- 1 (1½- to 2-pound) flank steak, trimmed
- 4 ears corn, husks and silk removed

1 Combine cumin, 1 teaspoon salt, ½ teaspoon chili powder, and pepper in bowl. In separate bowl, combine mayonnaise, Pecorino, cilantro, lime juice, garlic, remaining ½ teaspoon salt, and remaining ¼ teaspoon chili powder.

2 Pat steak dry with paper towels and sprinkle with spice mixture. Brush corn with half of mayonnaise mixture.

3A FOR A CHARCOAL GRILL Open bottom vent completely. Light large chimney starter filled with charcoal briquettes (6 quarts). When top coals are partially covered with ash, pour evenly over grill. Set cooking grate in place, cover, and open lid vent completely. Heat grill until hot, about 5 minutes.

3B FOR A GAS GRILL Turn all burners to high; cover; and heat grill until hot, about 15 minutes. Leave all burners on high.

4 Clean and oil cooking grate. Place steak on grill and cook until meat registers 120 to 125 degrees (for medium-rare), 8 to 12 minutes, flipping as needed. Transfer steak to carving board, tent with aluminum foil, and let rest while cooking corn.

5 Place corn on grill and cook, turning often, until well browned on all sides, about 12 minutes. Transfer to platter and brush with remaining mayonnaise mixture. Cut corn in half and slice steak thin on bias against grain. Serve with lime wedges.

GRILLED STEAK AND KALE SALAD

GRILLED CUMIN-RUBBED FLANK STEAK WITH MEXICAN STREET CORN

FLANK STEAK WITH GRILLED GUACAMOLE SALAD

Flank Steak with Grilled Guacamole Salad

SERVES 4 **TIME** 35 minutes

Why This Recipe Works If you've never grilled avocados, now's the time. Along with red onion, limes, tomatoes, and jalapeño, buttery avocados gain intensity after a few minutes on the grill, making for a smoky-spicy salad that perfectly complements cumin-rubbed flank steak. You will need three 12-inch metal skewers for this recipe.

- 1 (1½-pound) flank steak, trimmed
- 6 tablespoons extra-virgin olive oil, divided
- 5 teaspoons kosher salt, divided
- 1 tablespoon ground cumin
- 1½ teaspoons pepper, divided
- 1 teaspoon grated lime zest, plus 2 limes, halved
- 1 red onion, sliced into ½-inch-thick rounds
- 10 ounces cherry tomatoes
- 2 avocados, halved and pitted
- 1 jalapeño chile
- 2 tablespoons minced fresh cilantro

1 Pat steak dry with paper towels and rub with 1 tablespoon oil. Combine 1 tablespoon salt, cumin, 1 teaspoon pepper, and lime zest in small bowl and rub on oiled steak. Push toothpick horizontally through each onion round. Thread tomatoes onto three 12-inch metal skewers. Brush onion, tomatoes, cut sides of avocados, and jalapeño with 1 tablespoon oil and sprinkle with 1 teaspoon salt and remaining ½ teaspoon pepper.

2A FOR A CHARCOAL GRILL Open bottom vent completely. Light large chimney starter filled with charcoal briquettes (6 quarts). When top coals are partially covered with ash, pour evenly over grill. Set cooking grate in place, cover, and open lid vent completely. Heat grill until hot, about 5 minutes.

2B FOR A GAS GRILL Turn all burners to high; cover; and heat grill until hot, about 15 minutes. Leave all burners on high.

3 Clean and oil cooking grate. Place steak, onion, tomatoes, avocados, jalapeño, and lime halves (avocados and limes cut sides down) on grill. Cook until meat registers 120 to 125 degrees (for medium-rare) and vegetables are charred, 5 to 10 minutes, flipping as needed. Transfer vegetables to platter. Transfer steak to carving board and let rest while making salad.

4 Stem and seed jalapeño, then chop fine. Squeeze 2 tablespoons juice from 2 lime halves. Whisk jalapeño, lime juice, remaining ¼ cup oil, and remaining 1 teaspoon salt together in bowl. Remove toothpicks from onion and cut rounds in half. Using spoon, scoop avocado flesh from skin and cut into ¾-inch wedges. Slide tomatoes off skewers and arrange with onion and avocados on platter. Drizzle dressing over vegetables and sprinkle with cilantro.

5 Slice steak thin on bias against grain. Serve with salad and remaining 2 lime halves.

Nam Tok (Grilled Thai Beef Salad)

SERVES 4 **TIME** 1 hour

Why This Recipe Works In the best versions of Thai grilled beef salad, known as nam tok, the cuisine's five signature flavor elements—hot, sour, salty, sweet, and bitter—come into balance, making for a light but satisfying dish perfectly suited for a weeknight or special-occasion summer dinner. A perfect medium-rare flank steak, seared over high heat to give it a nicely charred crust, provides the bitter element. The dressing of fish sauce, lime juice, sugar, and a mix of hot spices provides the remaining elements, and the final addition—toasted rice powder made in a food processor—adds extra body. If fresh Thai chiles are unavailable, substitute half of a serrano chile. Don't skip the toasted rice; it's integral to the texture and flavor of the dish. Any variety of white rice can be used. Toasted rice powder (kao kua) can also be found in many Asian markets; substitute 1 tablespoon rice powder for the white rice. Serve with rice.

- 1 teaspoon paprika
- 1 teaspoon cayenne pepper
- 1 tablespoon white rice
- 3 tablespoons lime juice (2 limes)
- 2 tablespoons fish sauce
- 2 tablespoons water
- ½ teaspoon sugar
- 1 (1½-pound) flank steak, trimmed
- 1 teaspoon kosher salt
- ¼ teaspoon white pepper
- 1 English cucumber, sliced ¼ inch thick on bias
- 1½ cups fresh mint leaves, torn
- 1½ cups fresh cilantro leaves
- 4 shallots, sliced thin
- 1 Thai chile, stemmed, seeded, and sliced thin into rounds

JAPANESE STEAKHOUSE STEAK AND VEGETABLES

1 Toast paprika and cayenne in 8-inch skillet over medium heat, shaking pan, until fragrant, about 1 minute; transfer to small bowl. Add rice to now-empty skillet and toast over medium-high heat, stirring constantly, until deep golden brown, about 5 minutes. Transfer to a separate small bowl and let cool for 5 minutes. When cool, grind rice with spice grinder, mini food processor, or mortar and pestle until it resembles fine meal, 10 to 30 seconds (you should have about 1 tablespoon rice powder).

2 Whisk lime juice, fish sauce, water, sugar, and ¼ teaspoon paprika mixture in large bowl and set aside for serving. Pat steak dry with paper towels and sprinkle with salt and white pepper.

3A **FOR A CHARCOAL GRILL** Open bottom vent completely. Light large chimney starter filled with charcoal briquettes (6 quarts). When top coals are partially covered with ash, pour in even layer over half of grill. Set cooking grate in place, cover, and open lid vent completely. Heat grill until hot, about 5 minutes.

3B **FOR A GAS GRILL** Turn all burners to high; cover; and heat grill until hot, about 15 minutes. Leave all burners on high.

4 Clean and oil cooking grate. Place steak on hotter side of grill and cook until beginning to char and beads of moisture appear on outer edges of meat, 5 to 6 minutes. Flip steak and continue to cook on second side until meat registers 120 to 125 degrees (for medium-rare), about 5 minutes. Transfer to carving board, tent with aluminum foil, and let rest for at least 10 minutes or up to 1 hour.

5 Line large platter with cucumber slices. Slice steak on bias against grain into ¼-inch-thick pieces and add to bowl with fish sauce mixture. Add mint, cilantro, shallots, Thai chile, and half of rice powder and toss to combine. Arrange steak over cucumber-lined platter. Serve, passing remaining rice powder and remaining paprika mixture separately.

Japanese Steakhouse Steak and Vegetables

SERVES 4 **TIME** 50 minutes

Why This Recipe Works The cast-iron plancha, with its seasoned nonstick surface and superior heat retention, is the perfect piece of equipment to create a hibachi-like experience on the grill. And rib-eye steak is a great cut of beef for this cooking method. It's very flavorful, with lots of marbling and a smooth, fine texture, and its generous thickness allows for a beautiful crust. To avoid overcrowding the food and thus steaming it, batch cooking is the way to go: The steak is cooked first and then the vegetables are cooked in two batches, where they absorb the flavorful drippings left on the plancha. A flavorful finishing sauce made with umami-heavy soy sauce and sweet mirin is added in the last few minutes of cooking the vegetables. You will need a cast-iron plancha measuring at least 20 by 10 inches.

- 3 tablespoons unsalted butter, melted
- 2 tablespoons soy sauce
- 2 garlic cloves, minced
- 2 (1-pound) boneless rib-eye steaks, 1½ inches thick, trimmed
- 2 tablespoons plus 2 teaspoons vegetable oil, divided
- 2 teaspoons kosher salt, divided
- 1¼ teaspoons white pepper, divided
- 2 zucchini (8 ounces each), halved lengthwise and sliced ¾ inch thick
- 2 onions, cut into ¾-inch pieces
- 6 ounces shiitake mushrooms, stemmed and halved if small or quartered if large
- 2 tablespoons mirin, divided

1 Combine melted butter, soy sauce, and garlic in small bowl; set aside. Pat steaks dry with paper towels. Rub steaks with 2 teaspoons oil and sprinkle with 1½ teaspoons salt and 1 teaspoon white pepper. In large bowl, toss zucchini, onions, mushrooms with remaining 2 tablespoons oil, remaining ½ teaspoon salt, and remaining ¼ teaspoon white pepper.

2A **FOR A CHARCOAL GRILL** Open bottom vent completely. Light large chimney starter filled with charcoal briquettes (6 quarts). When top coals are partially covered with ash, pour evenly over grill. Set cooking grate in place, center plancha on grill, cover, and open lid vent completely. Heat grill with plancha until hot, about 5 minutes.

2B **FOR A GAS GRILL** Turn all burners to high and heat grill until hot, about 15 minutes. Center plancha on grill, cover, and heat for an additional 5 minutes. Leave all burners on high.

3 Place steaks on plancha and cook, flipping every 2 minutes, until well browned and meat registers 120 to 125 degrees (for medium-rare), 10 to 13 minutes. Transfer steaks to carving board, tent with aluminum foil, and let rest.

4 Place half of mixed vegetables on hot plancha. Pat vegetables into even layer and cook, without stirring, until beginning to brown, about 3 minutes. Stir and continue to cook 2 minutes longer. Pour 1 tablespoon mirin and 1 tablespoon soy-garlic butter over vegetables and stir to combine. Cook until liquid has evaporated and vegetables are well browned, about 2 minutes longer. Transfer cooked vegetables to serving platter. Repeat cooking process with remaining vegetables, remaining 1 tablespoon mirin and 1 tablespoon soy-garlic butter.

5 Slice steaks ¼ inch thick and transfer to serving platter with vegetables. Drizzle steaks with remaining soy-garlic butter and serve.

Beef Satay with Spicy Peanut Dipping Sauce

SERVES 12 to 18 as an appetizer or 4 to 6 as a main dish
TIME 55 minutes plus 1½ hours freezing and marinating

Why This Recipe Works A savory, spicy peanut sauce complements strips of rich flank steak in this popular South Asian street food; it's a grilled appetizer that you could happily turn into a meal. Hot water loosens up the texture of the peanut butter, making it easier to mix in the lime juice, sriracha, fish sauce, and brown sugar. We partially freeze the meat to make it easier to slice into thin strips. You'll need about forty 6-inch wooden skewers for this recipe or, if serving as a main dish, twenty 12-inch metal skewers.

PEANUT SAUCE

- ½ cup creamy peanut butter
- ¼ cup hot water
- 2 tablespoons lime juice
- 2 tablespoons sriracha
- 1 tablespoon fish sauce
- 1 tablespoon packed dark brown sugar
- 2 scallions, sliced thin
- 1 tablespoon minced fresh cilantro
- 1 garlic clove, minced

SATAY

- 1 (2-pound) flank steak, trimmed
- ¼ cup fish sauce
- ¼ cup vegetable oil
- ¼ cup packed dark brown sugar
- ¼ cup minced fresh cilantro
- 4 scallions, sliced thin
- 2 tablespoons sriracha, plus extra to taste
- 2 garlic cloves, minced
- 40 (6-inch) wooden skewers, soaked in water for 30 minutes or 20 (12-inch) metal skewers

1 FOR THE PEANUT SAUCE Whisk peanut butter and hot water together in medium bowl. Whisk in lime juice, sriracha, fish sauce, sugar, scallions, cilantro, and garlic; transfer to serving bowl. (Sauce can be refrigerated for up to 24 hours; bring to room temperature before serving.)

2 FOR THE SATAY Cut flank steak in half lengthwise, place on large plate, and freeze until firm, about 30 minutes.

3 Slice each piece of steak across grain into ¼-inch-thick strips. Combine fish sauce, oil, sugar, cilantro, scallions, sriracha, and garlic in 1-gallon zipper-lock bag. Add steak strips and toss to coat; press out as much air as possible and seal bag. Refrigerate for 1 hour but no longer. Remove beef from bag and weave onto individual skewers: 1 piece per 6-inch skewer or 2 pieces per 12-inch skewer

4A FOR A CHARCOAL GRILL Open bottom vent completely. Light large chimney starter filled with charcoal briquettes (6 quarts). When top coals are partially covered with ash, pour evenly over grill. Set cooking grate in place, cover, and open lid vent completely. Heat grill until hot, about 5 minutes.

4B FOR A GAS GRILL Turn all burners to high; cover; and heat grill until hot, about 15 minutes. Leave all burners on high.

5 Clean and oil cooking grate. Place half of skewers on grill; cover; and cook until meat has cooked through and is lightly charred around edges, about 7 minutes, flipping halfway through cooking. Transfer to serving platter and cover with aluminum foil. Repeat with remaining skewers. Serve with peanut sauce.

Beef Kebabs with Lemon-Rosemary Marinade

SERVES 4 to 6 **TIME** 50 minutes plus 1 hour marinating

Why This Recipe Works Generous chunks of charred yet juicy beef, paired with browned, tender-firm vegetables—that's our kebab ideal. We use beefy, well-marbled steak tips and cut them into generous 2-inch cubes; just an hour in a flavor-packed marinade gives the meat plenty of seasoning. We grill the beef skewers over the center of a concentrated fire and the vegetable skewers around the cooler edges; both are perfectly done within minutes of each other. Sirloin steak tips are sometimes sold as whole steaks labeled "flap meat." For more information on how to cut onions for kebabs, see page 73. This recipe was developed using Diamond Crystal kosher salt. If you have Morton kosher salt, which is denser, use 1 tablespoon. You will need four 12-inch metal skewers for this recipe. We prefer these steak kebabs cooked to medium for better browning and a less chewy texture.

MARINADE

- 1 onion, chopped
- ⅓ cup beef broth
- ⅓ cup vegetable oil
- 3 tablespoons tomato paste
- 6 garlic cloves, chopped
- 2 tablespoons chopped fresh rosemary
- 2 teaspoons grated lemon zest
- 4 teaspoons kosher salt
- 1½ teaspoons sugar
- ¾ teaspoon pepper

BEEF AND VEGETABLES

- 2 pounds sirloin steak tips, trimmed and cut into 2-inch chunks
- 1 large zucchini, halved lengthwise and sliced 1 inch thick
- 1 large red bell pepper, stemmed, seeded, and cut into 1½-inch pieces
- 1 large red onion, cut into 1-inch pieces, 3 layers thick

1 FOR THE MARINADE Process all ingredients in blender until smooth, about 45 seconds. Measure out ¾ cup marinade and set aside for vegetables.

2 FOR THE BEEF AND VEGETABLES Combine remaining marinade and steak tips in 1-gallon zipper-lock bag and toss to coat; press out as much air as possible and seal bag. Refrigerate for 1 to 2 hours, flipping bag every 30 minutes. Gently combine zucchini, bell pepper, and onion with reserved marinade in bowl, cover, and let sit at room temperature for 30 minutes.

3 Remove steak tips from bag, pat dry with paper towels, and thread tightly onto two 12-inch metal skewers. Thread vegetables onto two 12-inch metal skewers in alternating pattern.

4A FOR A CHARCOAL GRILL Open bottom vent completely. Light large chimney starter mounded with charcoal briquettes (7 quarts). When top coals are partially covered with ash, pour evenly over center of grill, leaving 2-inch gap between grill wall and charcoal. Set cooking grate in place, cover, and open lid vent completely. Heat grill until hot, about 5 minutes.

4B FOR A GAS GRILL Turn all burners to high; cover; and heat grill until hot, about 15 minutes. Leave primary burner on high and turn other burner(s) to medium-low.

5 Clean and oil cooking grate. Place beef kebabs on hotter part of grill (in center if using charcoal) and place vegetable kebabs on cooler side of grill (at perimeter if using charcoal) . Cook (covered if using gas), turning kebabs every 3 to 4 minutes, until beef is well browned and meat registers 130 to 135 degrees (for medium), 12 to 16 minutes.

6 Transfer beef kebabs to platter and tent with aluminum foil. Continue cooking vegetable kebabs until tender and lightly charred, about 5 minutes longer. Serve.

VARIATIONS

Beef Kebabs with Red Curry Marinade
In marinade, omit lemon zest and rosemary. Add 3 tablespoons red curry paste, 2 teaspoons grated lime zest, ½ cup packed fresh basil leaves, and 2 teaspoons grated fresh ginger.

Beef Kebabs with North African Marinade
In marinade, omit lemon zest and rosemary. Add 20 cilantro sprigs, 2 teaspoons paprika, 1½ teaspoons ground cumin, and ½ teaspoon cayenne pepper.

BEEF KEBABS WITH LEMON-ROSEMARY MARINADE

Shashlik-Style Beef Kebabs

SERVES 4 to 6 **TIME** 1¼ hours plus 1 hour marinating

Why This Recipe Works Shashlik is a beloved street food in Russia, Kazakhstan, the Caucasus, and anywhere in the United States with immigrant communities from these areas. These flame-grilled kebabs have juicy, deeply seasoned, and well-charred meat that's been flavored with a punchy, oniony marinade. Ours combines chopped onion and garlic with tangy, assertive red wine vinegar; neutral vegetable oil; and a harmonious blend of warm spices. To get delicious charring in spite of the moisture from the marinade, we add a little sugar and grill the kebabs over a hot fire. A sweet, tangy sauce of caramelized onion and tart yogurt complements the rich, flame-kissed beef. Sirloin steak tips work great for kebabs because they have big beefy flavor and their loose grain enables them to soak up more marinade. Sirloin steak tips are sometimes sold as whole steaks labeled "flap meat." You will need four to six 12-inch metal skewers for this recipe. We prefer these steak kebabs cooked to medium for better browning and a less chewy texture.

A New Way to Grill High and Low

Meat and vegetables often need different heat levels to grill properly. Placing veggie skewers around the perimeter of the grill and meat skewers in the center over the coals allows each component to cook at its own pace.

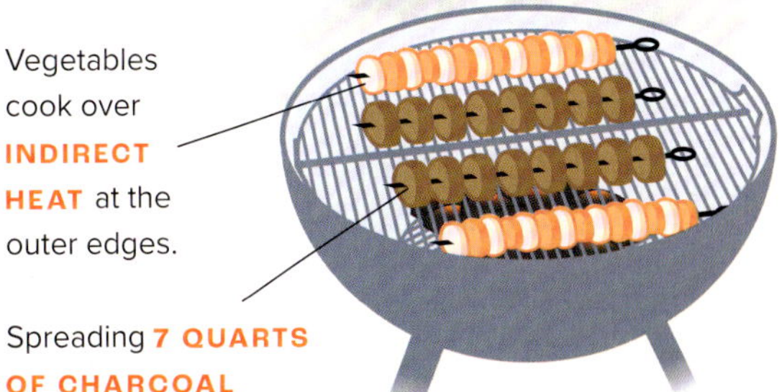

Vegetables cook over **INDIRECT HEAT** at the outer edges.

Spreading **7 QUARTS OF CHARCOAL** (instead of the usual 6) in the center of the grill creates a large area of direct, concentrated heat for the meat.

SHASHLIK-STYLE BEEF KEBABS

MARINADE

- ½ cup coarsely chopped onion
- ¼ cup vegetable oil
- 2 tablespoons red wine vinegar
- 4 garlic cloves
- 1 tablespoon soy sauce
- 1 tablespoon kosher salt
- 1 tablespoon sugar
- 1 teaspoon ground cumin
- ½ teaspoon pepper
- ½ teaspoon ground coriander
- ¼ teaspoon ground cinnamon
- ¼ teaspoon cayenne pepper
- 1 bay leaf, crumbled

BEEF AND SAUCE

- 2 pounds sirloin steak tips, trimmed and cut into 1-inch pieces
- 1 onion, chopped fine
- ⅓ cup water
- 1 tablespoon vegetable oil
- ½ cup plain whole-milk yogurt
- ⅓ cup chopped fresh cilantro
- 2 teaspoons lemon juice

1 **FOR THE MARINADE** Process all ingredients in blender until smooth, about 30 seconds. Measure out 2 tablespoons marinade and set aside for sauce.

2 **FOR THE BEEF AND SAUCE** Combine remaining marinade and steak tips in 1-gallon zipper-lock bag and toss to coat; press out as much air as possible and seal bag. Refrigerate for 1 to 2 hours, flipping bag every 30 minutes.

3 While steak tips marinate, combine onion, water, oil, and reserved marinade in 10-inch skillet. Cover and cook over medium-high heat, stirring occasionally, until liquid has evaporated and onion begins to brown, 5 to 7 minutes. Uncover; reduce heat to medium; and continue to cook until onion is well browned, 8 to 10 minutes. Transfer to serving bowl and stir in yogurt, cilantro, and lemon juice. Season with salt and pepper to taste; cover and refrigerate until serving.

4 Remove meat from bag and thread tightly onto four to six 12-inch metal skewers.

5A **FOR A CHARCOAL GRILL** Open bottom vent completely. Light large chimney starter mounded with charcoal briquettes (7 quarts). When top coals are partially covered with ash, pour evenly over half of grill. Set cooking grate in place, cover, and open lid vent completely. Heat grill until hot, about 5 minutes.

5B **FOR A GAS GRILL** Turn all burners to high; cover; and heat grill until hot, about 15 minutes. Leave all burners on high.

6 Clean and oil cooking grate. Place kebabs on grill (over hotter side if using charcoal). Cook (covered if using gas), turning as needed, until meat is well browned and registers 130 to 135 degrees (for medium), 8 to 12 minutes.

7 Transfer kebabs to platter, tent with aluminum foil, and let rest for 5 minutes. Serve with sauce.

Grilled Beef and Chorizo Skewers

SERVES 4 to 6 **TIME** 45 minutes

Why This Recipe Works Alambre Mexicano, a dish of skewered meat, chiles, and vegetables grilled over an open flame, is popular in northern Mexico. We use richly marbled steak tips for their beefy flavor and tender texture, as well as chorizo for its spice and assertive flavor profile. We toss the beef in a mixture of olive oil and spices—oregano for a peppery bite, garlic powder to add savoriness, and cumin for depth. We round out our kebabs with spicy jalapeños and sweet red onion. We briefly parcook the vegetables in the microwave so that they finish cooking at the same time as the meat. Stemming and seeding the jalapeños allows us to enjoy their flavor without making the dish overly spicy. Sirloin steak tips are sometimes sold as whole steaks labeled "flap meat." You will need four 12-inch metal skewers for this recipe. We prefer these steak kebabs cooked to medium for better browning and a less chewy texture. Serve with warm tortillas or rice.

- 1 large red onion, cut into 1-inch pieces, 3 layers thick
- 4 jalapeño chiles, stemmed, halved, seeded, and cut into 1-inch pieces
- 3 tablespoons extra-virgin olive oil, divided
- 1 tablespoon minced fresh oregano or 1 teaspoon dried
- ½ teaspoon garlic powder
- 1 teaspoon kosher salt
- ¼ teaspoon pepper
- ¼ teaspoon ground cumin
- 1 pound sirloin steak tips, trimmed and cut into 2-inch pieces
- 1 pound Mexican-style chorizo sausage links, cut into 2-inch lengths
- 2 tablespoons chopped fresh cilantro
- Lime wedges

1 Gently toss onion and jalapeños with 1 tablespoon oil in bowl; cover; and microwave until just tender, 3 to 5 minutes. In large bowl, combine oregano, garlic powder, salt, pepper, cumin, and remaining 2 tablespoons oil. Add steak tips and toss to coat. Thread steak tips, chorizo, onion, and jalapeños tightly onto four 12-inch metal skewers in alternating pattern.

2A **FOR A CHARCOAL GRILL** Open bottom vent completely. Light large chimney starter filled with charcoal briquettes (6 quarts). When top coals are partially covered with ash, pour evenly over grill. Set cooking grate in place, cover, and open lid vent completely. Heat grill until hot, about 5 minutes.

2B **FOR A GAS GRILL** Turn all burners to high; cover; and heat grill until hot, about 15 minutes. Leave all burners on high.

3 Clean and oil cooking grate. Place kebabs on grill and cook (covered if using gas), turning as needed, until well browned and meat registers 130 to 135 (for medium), 10 to 15 minutes.

4 Transfer kebabs to serving platter, tent with aluminum foil, and let rest for 5 minutes. Sprinkle with cilantro and serve with lime wedges.

GRILLED BEEF AND CHORIZO SKEWERS

Preparing Onions for Skewers

1 Peel onion, trim off stem and root ends, then quarter onion.

2 Pull onion apart into sections that are 3 layers thick; discard core.

3 Cut each section into 1-inch pieces.

Grilled Flank Steak Pinwheels with Prosciutto and Provolone

SERVES 4 to 6 **TIME** 55 minutes

Why This Recipe Works Stuffing and rolling a relatively thin, flat cut of beef into pinwheels turns it into something more exciting and colorful—but cheese that oozes onto the grill and stuffing that falls out in clumps are not our kind of excitement. To get tender beef and a juicy, flavorful filling that stays in place, the best cut to use is flank steak, thanks to its uniform shape and good, beefy taste. We butterfly the steak and pound it flat to make a nice base for the filling. The classic Italian-American combo of prosciutto and provolone is a winner for its salty savor and the way the dry cheese melts inside the pinwheel yet turns crisp where it's exposed to the grill. We also came up with variations that feature other salty, savory ingredients. To prevent the meat from shrinking on the grill, we roll up our flank steak, tie it with twine, and skewer it at 1-inch intervals before slicing and grilling. The twine keeps the steak from unraveling, while the skewers prevent the meat from shrinking. Depending on the size of the flank steak, you may have between eight and 12 pinwheels of stuffed meat at the end of step 3. Freezing the steak for 30 minutes will make butterflying it easier. Serve with lemon wedges.

- 2 tablespoons extra-virgin olive oil
- 2 tablespoons minced fresh parsley
- 1 small shallot, minced
- 2 garlic cloves, minced
- 1 teaspoon minced fresh sage
- 1 (2- to 2½-pound) flank steak, trimmed
- 4 ounces thinly sliced prosciutto
- 4 ounces thinly sliced provolone cheese
- 12 wooden skewers, soaked in water for 30 minutes
- ¾ teaspoon kosher salt
- ¾ teaspoon pepper

1 Combine oil, parsley, shallot, garlic, and sage in small bowl.

2 Lay steak on cutting board with grain running parallel to counter edge. Cut horizontally through meat, leaving ½-inch "hinge" along top edge. Open up steak; cover with plastic wrap; and pound into rough rectangle, trimming any ragged edges. Rub herb mixture evenly over surface of steak. Lay prosciutto evenly over steak, leaving 2-inch border along top edge. Cover prosciutto with even layer of provolone, leaving 2-inch border along top edge. Starting from bottom edge and rolling away from you, roll beef into tight log and place on cutting board seam side down.

3 Starting ½ inch from end of rolled steak, evenly space eight to twelve 14-inch pieces of kitchen twine at 1-inch intervals underneath steak. Tie middle string, then, working from outermost strings toward center, tightly tie all strings. Skewer beef directly through outer flap of steak near seam through each piece of string, allowing skewers to extend ½ inch on opposite side. Cut rolled steak between pieces of twine into 1-inch-thick pinwheels. Sprinkle with salt and pepper.

4A **FOR A CHARCOAL GRILL** Open bottom vent completely. Light large chimney starter three-quarters filled with charcoal briquettes (4½ quarts). When top coals are partially covered with ash, pour evenly over half of grill. Set cooking grate in place, cover, and open lid vent completely. Heat grill until hot, about 5 minutes.

4B **FOR A GAS GRILL** Turn all burners to high; cover; and heat grill until hot, about 15 minutes. Leave primary burner on high and turn off other burner(s).

5 Clean and oil cooking grate. Place pinwheels on hotter side of grill and cook until well browned on both sides, 6 to 11 minutes, flipping halfway through cooking. Slide pinwheels to cooler side of grill; cover; and cook until centers register 120 to 125 degrees (for medium-rare), 1 to 4 minutes (slightly thinner pinwheels may not need time on cooler side of grill).

6 Transfer pinwheels to large plate, tent with aluminum foil, and let rest for 5 minutes. Remove and discard skewers and twine and serve immediately.

VARIATIONS

Grilled Flank Steak Pinwheels with Spinach and Pine Nuts

Microwave 4 ounces chopped spinach, 1 tablespoon water, ½ teaspoon salt, and ½ teaspoon pepper in bowl until spinach is wilted and decreased in volume by half, 3 to 4 minutes. Let cool completely, then squeeze dry. Combine spinach and ¼ cup toasted pine nuts. Replace prosciutto with cooled spinach mixture.

Grilled Flank Steak Pinwheels with Sun-Dried Tomatoes and Capers

Combine ½ cup drained and chopped sun-dried tomatoes, ½ cup shredded Asiago cheese, and ¼ cup rinsed and chopped capers in bowl. Replace prosciutto with sun-dried tomato mixture.

GRILLED FLANK STEAK PINWHEELS WITH PROSCIUTTO AND PROVOLONE

How to Butterfly and Stuff Flank Steak

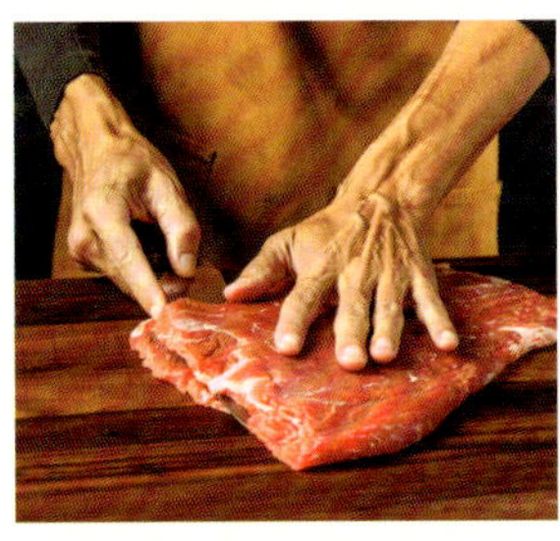

1 Lay steak on cutting board with grain running parallel to counter edge. Butterfly meat, leaving ½-inch "hinge" along top edge. Open up steak and pound flat.

2 Rub with herb mixture; layer with prosciutto and cheese, leaving 2-inch border at top. Roll away from you into tight log.

3 Place steak seam side down and tie with string at 1-inch intervals, starting at center.

4 Skewer steak directly through each string, allowing skewer to extend ½ inch on opposite side. Slice between skewers.

Tacos al Carbón

SERVES 4 **TIME** 40 minutes

Why This Recipe Works Tacos al carbón feature meat (usually steak) seasoned with a marinade or spices, cooked over a live fire, tucked into soft corn tortillas, and topped with garnishes such as charred scallions and lime juice. Thin, beefy flank steak cooks quickly and has lots of surface area for holding a spicy, smoky chipotle paste. Cutting the steak lengthwise to separate the thinner sides from the thicker center strip lets you cook all the meat just the way you want it. Frequent flipping helps the steaks stay flat and brown evenly. The scallions and jalapeños for the salsa pick up flavor from the meat as they grill. This steak's grill flavor is created when some of the fat and juices land on the fire, so choose a steak that has some visible fat deposits. Sour cream can be substituted for the crema, if desired.

- 3 tablespoons extra-virgin olive oil, divided
- 2 teaspoons minced canned chipotle chile in adobo sauce, plus 1 teaspoon adobo sauce, divided
- 2 teaspoons kosher salt, divided
- ¾ teaspoon ground cumin
- 1 (1½- to 1¾-pound) flank steak
- 2 jalapeño chiles
- 20 scallions
- 12 (6-inch) corn tortillas
- 1½ tablespoons lime juice, plus extra to taste, plus lime wedges for serving
- Fresh cilantro leaves
- Mexican crema

1 Combine 1 tablespoon oil, minced chipotle, 1½ teaspoons salt, and cumin in bowl. Trim fat on steak to ⅛-inch thickness. Cut steak lengthwise (with grain) into three 2- to 3-inch-wide strips. Rub steaks all over with chipotle mixture and transfer to rimmed baking sheet.

2A FOR A CHARCOAL GRILL Open bottom vent completely. Light large chimney starter mounded with charcoal briquettes (7 quarts). When top coals are partially covered with ash, pour evenly over half of grill. Set cooking grate in place, cover, and open lid vent completely. Heat grill until hot, about 5 minutes.

2B FOR A GAS GRILL Turn all burners to high; cover; and heat grill until hot, about 15 minutes. Turn off 1 burner (if grill has more than 2 burners, turn off burner farthest from primary burner) and leave other burner(s) on high.

3 Clean and oil cooking grate. Place steak and jalapeños on hotter side of grill. Cook (covered if using gas), flipping every 2 minutes, until meat is well browned and registers 120 to 125 degrees (for medium-rare) and jalapeños' skins are blistered and charred in spots, 7 to 12 minutes. Transfer steak to carving board and tent with aluminum foil. Transfer jalapeños to medium bowl and cover tightly.

4 Place scallions on hotter side of grill and cook until greens are well charred on 1 side, 1 to 2 minutes. Flip scallions, arranging so that greens are on cooler side while white and pale green parts are on hotter side. Continue to cook until whites are well charred, 1 to 2 minutes. Transfer to bowl with jalapeños and cover tightly.

5 Working in batches, grill tortillas on hotter side of grill, flipping as needed, until warm and lightly charred, about 1 minute; wrap tightly in foil to keep soft.

6 Without peeling, stem and seed jalapeños and reserve seeds. Chop jalapeños fine, chop scallions coarse, and transfer to bowl. Stir in remaining 2 tablespoons oil, lime juice, adobo sauce, and remaining ½ teaspoon salt. Season with lime juice, salt, and jalapeño seeds to taste. Slice steak thin against grain and transfer to serving platter. Serve, passing scallion salsa, tortillas, lime wedges, cilantro, and crema separately.

Grilled Skirt Steak Tacos with Roasted Poblanos

SERVES 6 **TIME** 55 minutes

Why This Recipe Works In this popular north Mexican taco filling, rich, smoky beef is perfectly complemented by sweet-hot poblano chiles and piquant onions. The combination is deliciously on point and very simple to put together. We grill the poblanos over a very hot fire, which leaves the skins charred and blistered while gently softening the flesh. Putting the peppers in a covered bowl when they come off the grill makes the bitter skins easier to peel off. A few minutes over the fire is enough to put good grill marks on the onions. Instead of marinating the skirt steak, we cover the cooked steak with a flavorful puree of onion, lime juice, garlic, cumin, and salt while it rests. Slicing the skirt steak thin ensures a tender texture. If you can't find skirt steak, you can substitute flank steak, although the meat will be a bit chewier. Serve the tacos with lime wedges and Mexican crema or sour cream.

TACOS AL CARBÓN

GRILLED SKIRT STEAK TACOS WITH ROASTED POBLANOS

4 onions (3 sliced crosswise into ½-inch-thick rounds, 1 chopped coarse)
6 tablespoons lime juice (3 limes)
3 garlic cloves, minced
4 teaspoons kosher salt, divided
½ teaspoon ground cumin
1½ pounds poblano chiles
1 tablespoon vegetable oil
1 teaspoon pepper, divided
2 pounds skirt steak, trimmed
18 (6-inch) corn tortillas

1 Process chopped onion, lime juice, garlic, 2 teaspoons salt, and cumin in food processor until smooth, about 20 seconds; set aside. Brush onion rounds and poblanos with oil and sprinkle with 1 teaspoon salt and ½ teaspoon pepper. Pat steak dry with paper towels and sprinkle with remaining 1 teaspoon salt and remaining ½ teaspoon pepper.

2A **FOR A CHARCOAL GRILL** Open bottom vent completely. Light large chimney starter filled with charcoal briquettes (6 quarts). When top coals are partially covered with ash, pour evenly over half of grill. Set cooking grate in place, cover, and open lid vent completely. Heat grill until hot, about 5 minutes.

2B **FOR A GAS GRILL** Turn all burners to high; cover; and heat grill until hot, about 15 minutes. Leave primary burner on high and turn off other burner(s).

3 Clean and oil cooking grate. Place poblanos on hotter side of grill and onion rounds on cooler side of grill. Cook (covered if using gas), turning as needed, until poblanos are blistered and blackened and onions are softened and golden, 6 to 12 minutes. Transfer onions to platter and cover to keep warm. Transfer poblanos to bowl and cover tightly.

4 Place steak on hotter side of grill. Cook (covered if using gas), flipping as needed, until well browned and meat registers 120 to 125 degrees (for medium-rare), 4 to 8 minutes. Transfer steak to 13 by 9-inch baking dish and poke all over with fork. Pour pureed onion mixture over top, cover, and let rest for 5 to 10 minutes.

5 Working in batches, grill tortillas on hotter side of grill, flipping as needed, until warm and lightly charred, about 1 minute; wrap tightly in foil to keep soft.

6 Peel poblanos, then slice thin. Separate onions into rings and chop coarse, then toss with poblanos. Remove steak from marinade, slice with grain into 4- to 6-inch-wide pieces, then slice thin against grain. Serve with warm tortillas and poblano-onion mixture.

Mesquite-Grilled Tacos Rasurados

SERVES 6 **TIME** 1¼ hours

Why This Recipe Works These hearty beef tacos—loaded with the heady mesquite smoke flavor that gives Tucson-style barbecue its distinctive character—are inspired by the tacos rasurados served at Tacos Apson in South Tucson, Arizona. We sear a rack of rich, fatty beef ribs to cook the meat; then, we separate it into individual ribs and return them to the grill to create a deeply savory crust and maximize the mesquite-grilled flavor. We serve the beef with bright, creamy aguamole and salsa tatemada, along with grilled spring onions and flour tortillas. Spring onions, or cebollitas, look like large scallions with round bulbs. If you can't find them, use scallions; they will cook more quickly. Small flareups can be extinguished with a water bottle; if they get difficult to manage, pull the ribs off the grill and let the fire die down before proceeding. You will need a charcoal grill and mesquite hardwood charcoal to make this recipe.

AGUAMOLE

- ⅔ cup water, divided
- ½ avocado
- 1 tablespoon lime juice
- 1 small garlic clove, minced
- 1½ teaspoons kosher salt

SALSA TATEMADA AND GARNISH

- 12 spring onions
- 7 jalapeño chiles
- 3 plum tomatoes
- ½ small onion, halved through root end into 2 wedges
- ¼ cup fresh cilantro leaves and stems
- 1½ teaspoons lime juice, plus extra for seasoning, plus lime wedges for serving
- 1 teaspoon kosher salt
- 1 cup finely chopped green cabbage

RIBS

- 1 (3½- to 4-pound) rack beef back ribs (about 7 bones)
- 3 tablespoons coarse sea salt, divided
- 12 (6-inch) flour tortillas, warmed

1 **FOR THE AGUAMOLE** Process ⅓ cup water, avocado, lime juice, garlic, and kosher salt in blender until smooth, about 10 seconds, adding remaining ⅓ cup water as needed to achieve pancake batter–like consistency. Season with salt to taste; set aside for serving.

2 Open bottom vent of charcoal grill completely. Light large chimney starter filled with mesquite hardwood charcoal (6 quarts). When top coals are partially covered with ash, pour evenly over half of grill. Set cooking grate in place, cover, and open lid vent completely. Heat grill until hot, about 5 minutes.

3 **FOR THE SALSA TATEMADA AND GARNISH** Clean and oil cooking grate. Place spring onions, jalapeños, tomatoes, and onion wedges on hotter side of grill. Cook, turning occasionally, until charred all over, 10 to 15 minutes, transferring items to platter as they finish cooking. (Spring onions will likely be done first, followed by jalapeños, then onion and tomatoes.)

4 **FOR THE RIBS** Adjust oven rack to middle position and heat oven to 200 degrees. Place ribs on hotter side of grill, bone side down. Sprinkle meaty side of ribs with 2¼ teaspoons coarse salt. Cook until well browned on first side, about 6 minutes, extinguishing any flare-ups with small squirts of water from squeeze bottle. Flip ribs and sprinkle bone side with 2¼ teaspoons coarse salt. Continue to cook until well browned on second side, about 6 minutes longer. (If flare-ups become too difficult, remove ribs from grill and let fire die down before proceeding.)

5 Transfer ribs to carving board. Cut rack between bones to separate ribs. Nestling 2 or 3 ribs together (bones oriented same way), return ribs to hotter side of grill, cut sides down. Sprinkle ribs with 2¼ teaspoons coarse salt and cook until well browned on cut sides, about 5 minutes.

6 Flip ribs so second cut sides are down; sprinkle with remaining 2¼ teaspoons coarse salt; and cook until well browned on second side, about 5 minutes. Transfer ribs to rimmed baking sheet and keep warm in oven while finishing salsa.

7 To finish salsa, core tomatoes, remove root ends from onion wedges, and stem 1 jalapeño. Process tomatoes, onion, stemmed jalapeño, cilantro, lime juice, and kosher salt in blender on low speed until coarsely chopped, about 7 seconds. Transfer to serving bowl; season with kosher salt and lime juice to taste.

8 Hold individual ribs vertically on carving board and, using chef's knife or boning knife, shave meat from ribs. Using chef's knife, chop meat into small, bite-size pieces. (For crispier meat, cook chopped meat in 12-inch nonstick skillet over medium-high heat until fat is rendered and meat is crisp all over, 3 to 5 minutes.)

9 Fill tortillas with meat, cabbage, salsa, and aguamole. Serve with spring onions, remaining 6 jalapeños, and lime wedges.

MESQUITE-GRILLED TACOS RASURADOS

Smoking the Ribs

1 Sear both sides of ribs on grill, sprinkling each side with coarse salt.

2 Remove rack from grill and cut into individual ribs.

3 Nestle 2 or 3 ribs together (with bones oriented same way). Grab rib bundles with tongs, return to grill, and brown on both cut sides.

Grilled Steak Fajitas

SERVES 4 to 6 **TIME** 1 hour plus 2 hours marinating

Why This Recipe Works Grilling accentuates the bold flavors of fajitas and suits their casual presentation: tender steak nestled into soft flour tortillas along with onions and colorful bell peppers. Skirt steak, the classic choice, has big, beefy flavor, and a marinade of soy sauce, garlic, and sweet-tangy pineapple juice amps up the meatiness even more. Cooking the steak to medium or medium-well means that it's firmer and thus easier to eat when combined with the vegetables. You'll char the bell peppers and onion over a hot fire and then move them to a pan on the cooler side of the grill to steam before tossing them with some marinade. Wrapping the tortillas in foil makes it easy to warm them gently on the grill. You will need a 13 by 9-inch disposable aluminum roasting pan. Serve with Pico De Gallo (page 398), Charred Guacamole (page 403), sour cream, and lime wedges.

- ¾ cup pineapple juice
- ½ cup plus 1 tablespoon vegetable oil, divided
- ¼ cup soy sauce
- 3 garlic cloves, minced
- 2 pounds skirt steak, trimmed and cut crosswise into 6 equal pieces
- 3 yellow, red, orange, or green bell peppers
- 1 large red onion, sliced into ½-inch-thick rounds
- 2 teaspoons kosher salt, divided
- ½ teaspoon pepper, divided
- 12 (6-inch) flour tortillas
- 1 (13 by 9-inch) disposable aluminum pan
- 1 tablespoon chopped fresh cilantro

1 Whisk pineapple juice, ½ cup oil, soy sauce, and garlic together in bowl. Measure out ¼ cup marinade and set aside for serving. Combine remaining marinade and steak in 1-gallon zipper-lock bag and toss to coat; press out as much air as possible and seal bag. Refrigerate for at least 2 hours or up to 24 hours, flipping bag occasionally.

2 Using paring knife, cut around stems of bell peppers and remove cores and seeds. Push toothpick horizontally through each onion round to keep rings intact while grilling. Brush bell peppers and onion with remaining 1 tablespoon oil and sprinkle with ½ teaspoon salt and ¼ teaspoon pepper. Remove steak from bag, pat dry with paper towels, and sprinkle with remaining 1½ teaspoons salt and remaining ¼ teaspoon pepper. Wrap tortillas in aluminum foil.

3A FOR A CHARCOAL GRILL Open bottom vent completely. Light large chimney starter filled with charcoal briquettes (6 quarts). When top coals are partially covered with ash, pour evenly over half of grill. Set cooking grate in place, cover, and open lid vent completely. Heat grill until hot, about 5 minutes.

3B FOR A GAS GRILL Turn all burners to high; cover; and heat grill until hot, about 15 minutes. Leave primary burner on high and turn other burner(s) to low.

4 Clean and oil cooking grate. Place bell peppers and onion on hotter side of grill and place tortilla packet on cooler side of grill. Cook vegetables (covered if using gas) until charred and tender, 8 to 13 minutes, turning as needed. Cook tortillas until warmed through, about 10 minutes, flipping halfway through cooking.

5 Remove tortillas from grill; keep wrapped and set aside. Transfer vegetables to disposable pan, cover pan tightly with foil, and place on cooler side of grill. (If using gas, cover and let grill reheat for 5 minutes.) Place steak on hotter side of grill and cook (covered if using gas) until charred and meat registers 135 to 140 degrees (for medium to medium-well), 4 to 8 minutes, flipping halfway through cooking. Transfer steak to carving board and tent with foil. Remove disposable pan from grill.

6 Carefully remove foil from disposable pan (steam may escape). Slice bell peppers into thin strips. Remove toothpicks from onion rounds and separate rings. Return vegetables to disposable pan and toss with cilantro and reserved marinade. Season with salt and pepper to taste. Slice steak thin against grain. Transfer steak and vegetables to serving platter. Serve with warmed tortillas.

Grilled Steak Sandwiches

SERVES 4 **TIME** 30 minutes

Why This Recipe Works With its beefy flavor and speedy grilling time, skirt steak rivals burgers as a go-to casual weeknight meal, especially when you put it in a sandwich. A bold blue cheese spread, which you can whip up in a food processor, tastes amazing slathered on the steak; peppery arugula and crisp red onion slices complete the gutsy flavor profile. We prefer these sandwiches on ciabatta rolls, but any sub rolls can be substituted.

GRILLED STEAK SANDWICHES

- ¾ cup mayonnaise
- 3 ounces blue cheese, crumbled (¾ cup)
- 1 tablespoon balsamic vinegar
- 1 tablespoon Dijon mustard
- ½ teaspoon pepper, divided
- 1 pound skirt steak, trimmed and cut crosswise into 4 equal pieces
- ½ teaspoon kosher salt
- 4 ciabatta sandwich rolls, halved lengthwise
- ¼ cup extra-virgin olive oil
- 2 ounces (2 cups) baby arugula
- 1 small red onion, halved and sliced thin

1 Process mayonnaise, blue cheese, vinegar, mustard, and ¼ teaspoon pepper in food processor until smooth, about 30 seconds; set aside for serving. Pat steak dry with paper towels and sprinkle with salt and remaining ¼ teaspoon pepper. Brush cut sides of rolls with oil.

2A FOR A CHARCOAL GRILL Open bottom vent completely. Light large chimney starter filled with charcoal briquettes (6 quarts). When top coals are partially covered with ash, pour evenly over grill. Set cooking grate in place, cover, and open lid vent completely. Heat grill until hot, about 5 minutes.

2B FOR A GAS GRILL Turn all burners to high; cover; and heat grill until hot, about 15 minutes. Leave burners on high.

3 Clean and oil cooking grate. Place steak on grill. Cook (covered if using gas) until meat registers 120 to 125 degrees (for medium-rare), 4 to 6 minutes, flipping halfway through cooking. Transfer to carving board, tent with aluminum foil, and let rest. Grill rolls, cut side down, until lightly toasted, 1 to 2 minutes.

4 Slice steak thin against grain. Spread blue cheese sauce on rolls. Divide steak, arugula, and onion evenly among rolls. Serve.

Grilled Free-Form Beef Wellington with Balsamic Reduction

SERVES 4 **TIME** 40 minutes

Why This Recipe Works This meal takes inspiration from beef Wellington, a classic combination of tender meat, sautéed mushrooms, and rich pâté wrapped in flaky puff pastry. We pared back the ingredient list and took the cooking outside to make this normally labor-intensive meal quick, easy, and accessible. Filets mignons and portobello mushrooms go on the grill first, followed by thick pieces of country bread—our answer to puff pastry. The grilled bread gets a schmear of duck liver pâté and is then topped with slices of the mushrooms and steaks. Reduced balsamic vinegar, drizzled over each stack, makes the perfect finishing touch.

- ½ cup balsamic vinegar
- 3 (8-ounce) filets mignons, 2 inches thick, trimmed
- 4 large portobello mushroom caps, 4 inches in diameter
- 2 tablespoons extra-virgin olive oil
- 1 teaspoon kosher salt
- ½ teaspoon pepper
- 4 thick slices rustic or country bread
- 4 ounces smooth duck liver pâté

1 Simmer vinegar in small saucepan over medium heat until reduced to 3 tablespoons, about 5 minutes; transfer to bowl. Pat steaks and mushrooms dry with paper towels, brush with oil, and sprinkle with salt and pepper.

2A FOR A CHARCOAL GRILL Open bottom vent completely. Light large chimney starter filled with charcoal briquettes (6 quarts). When top coals are partially covered with ash, pour two-thirds evenly over half of grill, then pour remaining coals over other half of grill. Set cooking grate in place, cover, and open lid vent completely. Heat grill until hot, about 5 minutes.

2B FOR A GAS GRILL Turn all burners to high; cover; and heat grill until hot, about 15 minutes. Leave primary burner on high and turn other burner(s) to medium.

3 Clean and oil cooking grate. Place steaks on hotter side of grill and cook (covered if using gas) until well browned on first side, 2 to 3 minutes. Slide steaks to cooler side of grill and cook, flipping as needed, until meat registers 120 to 125 degrees (for medium-rare), 5 to 9 minutes. Transfer steaks to carving board, tent with aluminum foil, and let rest.

4 Place mushrooms on hotter side of grill. Cook until tender and lightly browned, 8 to 10 minutes, flipping halfway through cooking; transfer to platter. Meanwhile, place bread on cooler side of grill and cook until golden brown, 1 to 1½ minutes, flipping halfway through cooking; transfer to platter.

5 Spread pâté over grilled bread. Slice mushrooms and lay on top of pâté. Slice steaks ¼ inch thick and lay on top of mushrooms. Drizzle with reduced balsamic vinegar and serve.

GRILLED FREE-FORM BEEF WELLINGTON WITH BALSAMIC REDUCTION

BALTIMORE PIT BEEF WITH TIGER SAUCE

Baltimore Pit Beef with Tiger Sauce

SERVES 10 **TIME** 1¾ to 2 hours plus 6 hours seasoning

Why This Recipe Works Baltimore's "barbecue" tradition involves superthin slices of grill-roasted beef piled on a soft bun with tiger sauce, a simple blend of mayonnaise and horseradish. Flavorful, tender, and affordable top sirloin roast makes a perfect stand-in for the huge whole top or bottom rounds used by Baltimore's pit beef joints. To get the salty, spicy, nearly blackened crust of pit beef, we cut the roast in half before adding our paprika-based spice rub to maximize surface area and speed up the flavoring process. To protect our roasts from developing an overcooked, gray ring around the edges, we wrap them in aluminum foil and start them over an indirect flame. Removing the foil and cranking up the grill creates that signature dark crust with a perfectly rosy interior. Top sirloin roast is also known as top butt or center-cut roast. Buy refrigerated prepared horseradish, not the shelf-stable kind, which contains preservatives and additives. This recipe was developed using Diamond Crystal kosher salt. If you have Morton kosher salt, which is denser, use 1 tablespoon.

TIGER SAUCE

- ½ cup mayonnaise
- ½ cup hot prepared horseradish
- 1 teaspoon lemon juice
- 1 garlic clove, minced

PIT BEEF

- 4 teaspoons kosher salt
- 1 tablespoon paprika
- 1 tablespoon pepper
- 1 teaspoon garlic powder
- 1 teaspoon dried oregano
- ¼ teaspoon cayenne pepper
- 1 (4- to 5-pound) top sirloin roast, trimmed and halved crosswise
- 10 kaiser rolls, split
- 1 onion, sliced thin

1 FOR THE TIGER SAUCE Whisk all ingredients together in bowl. Season with salt and pepper to taste, cover, and refrigerate until serving. (Sauce can be refrigerated for up to 2 days.)

2 FOR THE PIT BEEF Combine salt, paprika, pepper, garlic powder, oregano, and cayenne in small bowl. Pat roasts dry with paper towels and rub with 2 tablespoons seasoning mixture. Wrap meat tightly with plastic wrap and refrigerate for 6 to 24 hours.

3 Unwrap roasts and place end to end on long side of 18 by 12-inch sheet of aluminum foil. Loosely fold opposite long side of foil around top of roasts.

4A FOR A CHARCOAL GRILL Open bottom vent halfway. Light large chimney starter filled with charcoal briquettes (6 quarts). When top coals are partially covered with ash, pour evenly over half of grill. Set cooking grate in place, cover, and open lid vent halfway. Heat grill until hot, about 5 minutes.

4B FOR A GAS GRILL Turn all burners to high; cover; and heat grill until hot, about 15 minutes. Leave primary burner on high and turn off other burner(s).

5 Clean and oil cooking grate. Place wrapped roasts on cooler side of grill with foil-covered side closest to heat source. Cover (positioning lid vent over meat if using charcoal) and cook until meat registers 100 degrees, 45 minutes to 1 hour.

6 Transfer roasts to plate and discard foil. Turn all burners to high if using gas. If using charcoal, carefully remove cooking grate and light large chimney starter three-quarters filled with charcoal briquettes (4½ quarts). When top coals are partially covered with ash, pour evenly over spent coals. Set cooking grate in place and cover. Heat grill until hot, about 5 minutes.

7 Pat roasts dry with paper towels and rub with remaining spice mixture. Place meat on hotter side of grill. Cook (covered if using gas), turning occasionally, until charred on all sides and meat registers 120 to 125 degrees (for medium-rare), 10 to 20 minutes.

8 Transfer meat to carving board, tent with foil, and let rest for 15 minutes. Slice meat thin against grain. Divide steak and onion evenly among rolls, drizzle with sauce, and serve.

Grill-Roasted Top Sirloin with Garlic and Rosemary

SERVES 6 to 8 **TIME** 1½ to 2 hours plus 18 hours seasoning

Why This Recipe Works Smart grill work creates a show-stopping roast from humble top sirloin. The first step is applying a fragrant garlic-rosemary rub and letting the roast rest in the fridge for a day while the seasonings do their work. The second step is keeping the enzymes that tenderize meat active as long as possible; that means not raising the internal temperature of the roast too high too fast. We use a moderate half-grill fire so that we can sear the roast and give it a caramelized crust; then, we set it in a perforated roasting pan and let it cook slowly to a tender medium-rare. Cutting the roast into wafer-thin slices against the grain helps the beef taste even more tender. We prefer a top sirloin roast, but you can substitute a top round or bottom round roast. This recipe requires salting the beef for 18 to 24 hours, so you'll need to start the day before you plan to grill. This recipe was developed using Diamond Crystal kosher salt. If you have Morton kosher salt, which is denser, use 1 tablespoon. A pair of kitchen shears works well for punching the holes in the aluminum pan. Serve with Horseradish Cream Sauce with Chives (page 396).

- 6 garlic cloves, minced
- 2 tablespoons minced fresh rosemary
- 4 teaspoons kosher salt
- 1 tablespoon pepper
- 1 (3- to 4-pound) top sirloin roast, trimmed
- 1 (13 by 9-inch) disposable aluminum roasting pan

1 Combine garlic, rosemary, salt, and pepper in bowl. Sprinkle all sides of roast evenly with garlic mixture, wrap tightly in plastic wrap, and refrigerate for at least 18 hours or up to 24 hours. Before cooking, unwrap roast and pat dry with paper towels. Punch fifteen ¼-inch holes in center of disposable pan in area roughly same size as roast.

2A **FOR A CHARCOAL GRILL** Open bottom vent halfway. Light large chimney starter half filled with charcoal briquettes (3 quarts). When top coals are partially covered with ash, pour evenly over one-third of grill. Set cooking grate in place, cover, and open lid vent halfway. Heat grill until hot, about 5 minutes.

2B **FOR A GAS GRILL** Turn all burners to high; cover; and heat grill until hot, about 15 minutes. Leave all burners on high.

3 Clean and oil cooking grate. Place roast on grill (hotter side if using charcoal). Cook (covered if using gas) until well browned on all sides, 10 to 12 minutes, turning as needed.

4 Place roast in pan over holes. (If using gas, turn primary burner to medium and other burner(s) off; adjust burner as needed to maintain grill temperature between 250 and 300 degrees.) Set pan over cooler side of grill; cover; and cook until meat registers 120 to 125 degrees (for medium-rare), 40 minutes to 1 hour, rotating pan halfway through cooking.

5 Transfer roast to wire rack set in rimmed baking sheet and let rest for 20 minutes. Transfer to carving board, slice thin against grain, and serve.

VARIATION

Grill-Roasted Top Sirloin with Shallot and Tarragon

Substitute 1 minced shallot for garlic and 2 tablespoons minced fresh tarragon for rosemary.

California Barbecued Tri-Tip

SERVES 4 to 6 **TIME** 1¼ hours plus 1 hour seasoning

Why This Recipe Works Unlike other barbecue recipes, California barbecued tri-tip recipes call for cooking the meat over high heat and seasoning it with only salt, pepper, garlic, and a kiss of wood smoke. This produces a charred exterior and very rare center—but we wanted the outside cooked less and the inside cooked more. To achieve this, we push all the coals to one side of the grill, which creates a hot zone for searing and a cooler one for finishing the meat slowly. For nuanced smoke flavor, we add wood chips only after searing the meat. If using a charcoal grill, you can substitute two wood chunks for the wood chip packet. Tri-tip is cut from the bottom sirloin primal and is also known as bottom sirloin roast, bottom sirloin butt, or triangle roast. Santa Maria Salsa (page 398), named for the valley where this barbecue tradition originated, is a classic accompaniment.

- 2 tablespoons vegetable oil
- 6 garlic cloves, minced
- 1½ teaspoons kosher salt
- 1 (2-pound) beef tri-tip roast, trimmed
- 2 cups wood chips
- 1 teaspoon pepper
- ¾ teaspoon garlic salt

1 Combine oil, garlic, and salt in bowl. Pat roast dry with paper towels, poke each side about 20 times with fork, then rub all over with oil-garlic mixture. Wrap meat in plastic wrap and let sit at room temperature for 1 hour or refrigerate for up to 24 hours.

2 Using large piece of heavy-duty aluminum foil, wrap chips in 8 by 4½-inch foil packet. (Make sure chips do not poke holes in sides or bottom of packet.) Cut 2 evenly spaced 2-inch slits in top of packet. Unwrap meat, wipe off garlic paste using paper towels, and sprinkle with pepper and garlic salt.

3A **FOR A CHARCOAL GRILL** Open bottom vent halfway. Light large chimney starter filled with charcoal briquettes (6 quarts). When top coals are partially covered with ash, pour evenly over half of grill. Set cooking grate in place, cover, and open lid vent halfway. Heat grill until hot, about 5 minutes.

3B **FOR A GAS GRILL** Turn all burners to high; cover; and heat grill until hot, about 15 minutes. Leave all burners on high.

4 Clean and oil cooking grate. Place roast on grill (hotter side if using charcoal). Cook (covered if using gas), turning as needed, until well browned on all sides, 8 to 10 minutes. Transfer meat to plate.

5 Remove cooking grate and place wood chip packet directly on coals or primary burner. Set grate in place; cover grill; and let chips begin to smoke, about 5 minutes. If using gas, leave primary burner on high and turn off other burner(s).

6 Place roast on cooler side of grill. Cover (position lid vent over meat if using charcoal) and cook until meat registers 120 to 125 degrees (for medium-rare), about 20 minutes.

7 Transfer meat to carving board, tent with foil, and let rest for 15 to 20 minutes. Slice meat thin against grain (see One Cut, Two Grains) and serve.

CALIFORNIA BARBECUED TRI-TIP

One Cut, Two Grains

Tri-tip has two distinct sections with muscle fibers running in two different directions. Cutting the beef in half at the point where the muscle fibers change direction and then slicing the rested steak thin against the grain ensures that it is unfailingly tender.

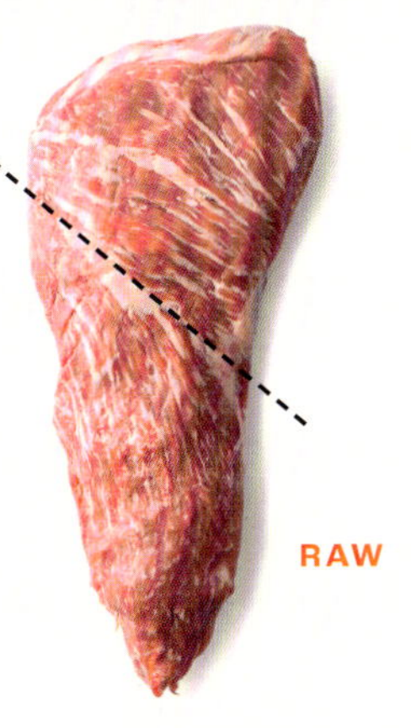

RAW

COOKED, BISECTED

COOKED, SLICED

Grill-Roasted Beef Tenderloin

SERVES 4 to 6 **TIME** 1¾ to 2¼ hours

Why This Recipe Works Grilling is a great way to add flavor to tenderloin in a way that enhances but doesn't overwhelm its delicate beefiness. To brown the outside without overcooking the interior, we rub the surface of the roast with baking soda. This raises the meat's pH, kicking the Maillard reaction into gear. Grill flavor also depends on drippings from the food, which hit the coals or heat diffusers, vaporize, and then waft up and stick to the meat. Because lean tenderloin produces very little in the way of drippings, we get some help from bacon. Three strips of bacon render their fat as they cook over direct heat, creating a steady stream of smoke that flavors the beef as it cooks over indirect heat. Center-cut beef tenderloin roasts are sometimes sold as Châteaubriand. You will need one 12-inch metal skewer for this recipe. This roast tastes great with Chermoula Sauce (page 394) or Argentinian Chimichurri Sauce (page 393).

- 2¼ teaspoons kosher salt
- 1 teaspoon pepper
- 2 teaspoons vegetable oil
- 1 teaspoon baking soda
- 1 (3-pound) center-cut beef tenderloin roast, trimmed and tied at 1½-inch intervals
- 3 slices bacon

1 Combine salt, pepper, oil, and baking soda in small bowl. Rub mixture all over roast and let sit while preparing grill.

2 Stack bacon slices. Keeping slices stacked, thread metal skewer through bacon 6 or 7 times to create accordion shape. Push stack together to compact into about 2-inch length.

3A **FOR A CHARCOAL GRILL** Open bottom vent halfway. Light large chimney starter three-quarters filled with charcoal briquettes (4½ quarts). When top coals are partially covered with ash, pour evenly over half of grill. Set cooking grate in place, cover, and open lid vent halfway. Heat grill until hot, about 5 minutes.

3B **FOR A GAS GRILL** Turn all burners to high; cover; and heat grill until hot, about 15 minutes. Turn primary burner to medium-high and turn off other burner(s). (Adjust primary burner as necessary to maintain grill temperature of 300 degrees.)

4 Clean and oil cooking grate. Place roast on hotter side of grill and cook until lightly browned on all sides, about 12 minutes, turning as needed. Slide roast to cooler side of grill, about 7 inches from heat source. Place skewered bacon on hotter side of grill. (For charcoal, place near center of grill, above edge of coals.

For gas, place above heat diffuser of primary burner. Bacon should be 4 to 6 inches from roast and drippings should fall on coals or heat diffuser and produce steady stream of smoke and minimal flare-ups. If flare-ups are large or frequent, slide bacon skewer 1 inch toward roast.) Cover and cook until meat registers 120 to 125 degrees (for medium-rare), 50 minutes to 1¼ hours.

5 Transfer roast to carving board, tent with aluminum foil, and let rest for 20 minutes. Remove twine, slice meat into ½-inch-thick pieces, and serve.

GRILL-ROASTED BEEF TENDERLOIN

Smoked Beef Tenderloin

SERVES 12 to 16 **TIME** 2½ hours plus 2 hours salting

Why This Recipe Works Smoking beef tenderloin on the grill gives this buttery, mild cut wall-to-wall flavor. We sprinkle the beef with a thyme-rosemary-salt mixture; then, we infuse olive oil with those same herbs plus garlic, pepper flakes, parsley, and balsamic vinegar and baste the meat with some of this potent sauce. We sear the tenderloin over the hotter side of a two-level fire and then move it to the cooler side where it gently cooks to medium-rare. A packet of wood chips adds subtle smoke. Chopped grilled scallions turn the remaining sauce into a vibrant accompaniment to this fantastic grilled tenderloin. For the most economical choice, buy a whole, untrimmed tenderloin from a big-box store and trim it yourself. This recipe was developed using Diamond Crystal kosher salt. If you have Morton kosher salt, which is denser, use 1½ tablespoons. If using a charcoal grill, you can substitute two wood chunks for the wood chip packet.

HERB SALT

- 2 tablespoons kosher salt
- 1 tablespoon minced fresh rosemary
- 2 teaspoons minced fresh thyme

BEEF

- 1 (6- to 7-pound) whole beef tenderloin, trimmed
- 2 bunches scallions, trimmed
- 1 tablespoon pepper
- 1½ cups wood chips

SAUCE

- ¾ cup extra-virgin olive oil
- 6 garlic cloves, chopped
- 1 sprig fresh rosemary
- 1 sprig fresh thyme
- ¼ teaspoon red pepper flakes
- ¼ cup minced fresh parsley
- 1 tablespoon balsamic vinegar
- 1 teaspoon pepper

1 **FOR THE HERB SALT** Rub all ingredients together in bowl using your fingers. Measure out and reserve 2 tablespoons separately for meat and 1 teaspoon for sauce.

2 **FOR THE BEEF** Tuck tail of tenderloin under by 2 to 4 inches to create more even shape, then tie with kitchen twine to secure. Tie remainder of tenderloin at 1-inch intervals. Sprinkle tenderloin all over with reserved 2 tablespoons herb salt, wrap in plastic wrap, and refrigerate for at least 2 hours or up to 2 days. Tie scallions into 2 separate bunches with kitchen twine.

Preparing an Untrimmed Tenderloin

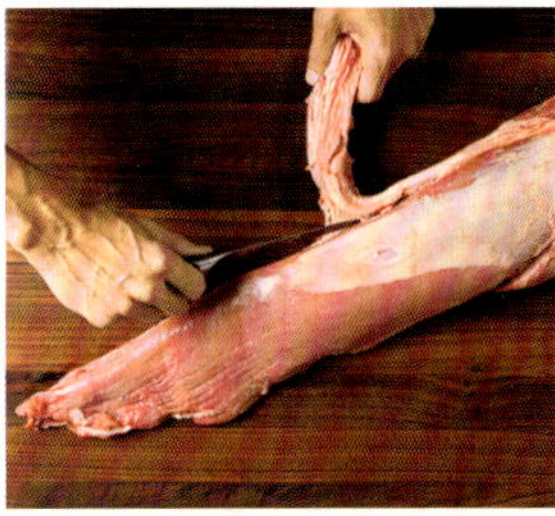

1 Use boning or chef's knife to remove fatty strip (or chain) that runs along side of tenderloin.

2 Insert tip of your knife under sinewy silver skin, then grab it and cut upward against silver skin to remove it. Use paper towel to grasp silver skin if slippery.

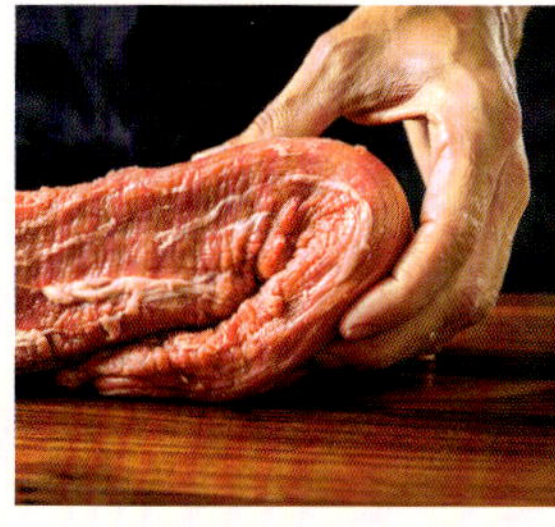

3 Fold narrow end under to make even shape that will cook more consistently.

4 Tie roast at 1-inch intervals with kitchen twine. Now you're ready to season, let rest, and grill.

3 **FOR THE SAUCE** Combine oil, garlic, rosemary, thyme, and pepper flakes in small saucepan. Bring to gentle simmer over low heat, stirring occasionally, and cook until garlic just begins to brown and herbs are fragrant, 8 to 10 minutes. Transfer sauce to bowl and let cool to room temperature. Discard herb sprigs. Stir in parsley, vinegar, pepper, and reserved 1 teaspoon herb salt. Measure out ¼ cup sauce for brushing on meat and scallions; set remaining sauce aside for serving.

4 Brush tenderloin all over with 3 tablespoons sauce, then sprinkle with pepper. Brush scallion bunches with remaining 1 tablespoon sauce.

5 Using large piece of heavy-duty aluminum foil, wrap wood chips in 8 by 4-inch foil packet. (Make sure chips do not poke holes in sides or bottom of packet.) Cut 2 evenly spaced 2-inch slits in top of packet.

6A **FOR A CHARCOAL GRILL** Open bottom vent halfway. Light large chimney starter filled with charcoal briquettes (6 quarts). When top coals are partially covered with ash, pour evenly over half of grill. Place wood chip packet on coals. Set cooking grate in place, cover, and open lid vent halfway. Heat grill until hot and wood chips are smoking, about 5 minutes.

6B **FOR A GAS GRILL** Remove cooking grate and place wood chip packet directly on primary burner. Set cooking grate in place; turn all burners to high; cover; and heat grill until hot and wood chips are smoking, about 15 minutes. Leave primary burner on high and turn off other burners. (Adjust primary burner as needed to maintain grill temperature between 350 and 375 degrees).

7 Clean and oil cooking grate. Place tenderloin and scallions on hotter side of grill. Cook (covered if using gas) until scallions are lightly charred and tenderloin is browned on first side, 3 to 5 minutes. Flip scallions and tenderloin and continue to cook on second sides until scallions are lightly charred and meat is browned, 3 to 5 minutes. Transfer scallions to plate. Move tenderloin to cooler side of grill, cover, and cook for 30 minutes.

8 Move thicker part of tenderloin to hotter side of grill and continue to cook, covered, until meat registers 120 to 125 degrees (for medium-rare), 10 to 20 minutes longer. Transfer tenderloin to carving board, tent with foil, and let rest for 30 minutes.

9 Chop scallions, stir into reserved sauce, and season with salt and pepper to taste. Remove twine from meat and slice into ½-inch-thick pieces. Season lightly with pepper and remaining herb salt, drizzle with sauce, and serve.

2

Pork + Lamb

SIMPLE CUTLETS, CHOPS, AND RIBS

MARINATED, RUBBED, AND GLAZED

MAKE IT A MEAL

SKEWERS, TACOS, AND SANDWICHES

ROASTS

IN DEPTH

Grilled Pork How-Tos

While meaty spareribs and hefty marbled roasts are justifiably famous as barbecue fare, quicker-cooking pork cuts can make for satisfying grilling. Get the most out of them with these tips.

HOW TO GRILL JUICY, FLAVORFUL LEAN PORK

Boneless pork chops, cutlets, loins, and tenderloins have a lot going for them: These lean, mild-mannered cuts are versatile and adapt to a wide range of flavor profiles; they cook quickly; and the lack of bones makes them easy to slice, serve, and eat. The downside? Because they're low in fat, they can easily become dried out over the dry heat of a grill. But you don't have to sacrifice flavor for convenience. The recipes in this chapter use smart strategies for adding moisture and flavor before, during, and/or after grilling.

BRINES AND MARINADES

At its simplest, a brine is a solution of salt and water that seasons meat, adds moisture, and helps the meat retain moisture, all of which are a boon for lean, mild pork. We often add sugar to enhance the natural sweetness of the pork, balance the saltiness of the brine, and promote browning. Marinades include salt, soy sauce, or other sodium-rich ingredients, and often some form of sugar. The difference is that the molecules in other marinade ingredients (such as garlic and herbs) are too large to penetrate deeply into meat. So marinades do most of their flavor-boosting work on the surface of mild pork cuts, both before and during grilling. (Learn more about salt, brines, and marinades on pages 30–31.)

GLAZES

Thin enough to be brushed on evenly yet sticky enough to cling, a glaze flavors the pork as it cooks on the grill. Glazes can be any flavor you dream up, but the common element is sugar, which caramelizes to create a browned, burnished surface. Applying the glaze in stages ensures that it sticks fast to create layers of lacquered flavor. The initial coat of glaze sets and dries slightly, becoming firm and tacky, before the second coat is added (either during or after grilling) so that the second coat has something to cling to.

SAUCES AND RELISHES

Once the pork is off the grill and on the plate, you can bolster its moisture, flavor, and visual appeal with a rich sauce or a juicy relish or salsa (see chapter 9 for plenty of options). It doesn't need to be complicated; sauces can be as simple as browned butter or a flavored compound butter that melts into a sauce. Relish and salsa ingredients can be raw or grilled alongside the pork. The bright acidity of citrus fruits, mango, pineapple, and tomatoes complements any cut of pork especially well.

HOW TO CHOOSE THE RIGHT CHOP

The prime pork chops for grilling are bone-in **rib chops** and bone-in **center-cut pork chops**, both cut from the loin. The bone provides a bit of insurance against overcooking and the meat closest to the bone has more marbling, which makes it more flavorful. You can easily identify rib chops by the curved bone that runs along one side and the one large eye of loin muscle. Because they come from the rib section of the loin, they have a relatively high fat content and rich flavor. Center-cut pork chops (also called top loin chops or loin chops) have a bone that divides the loin from the tenderloin muscle, which makes them look like a small T-bone steak. While tender and flavorful, center-cut chops are leaner than rib chops, so they're not quite as moist. Most boneless chops are cut from rib chops, although they can also come from center-cut chops.

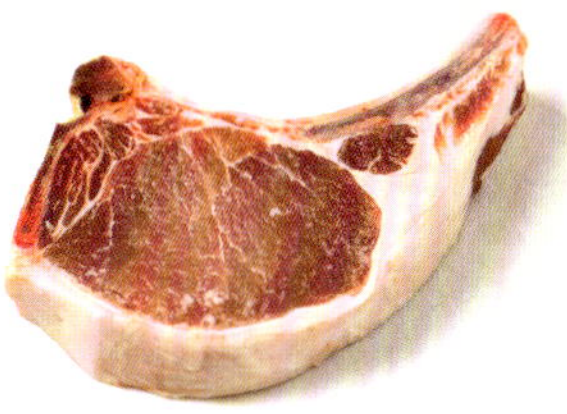

RIB CHOP

CENTER-CUT CHOP

HOW TO MAKE YOUR OWN CUTLETS

Prepackaged pork cutlets are often cut from the blade end of the ribs and can be ragged and unevenly cut, which results in uneven cooking. We prefer to make our own cutlets from **pork tenderloins**, boneless **country-style ribs**, or thin-cut boneless **pork chops**.

PREP

FOR TENDERLOIN

Remove silver skin and any extraneous fat. Cut crosswise into 4 equal pieces.

FOR COUNTRY-STYLE RIBS

Cut each rib lengthwise into 2 or 3 pieces about ⅜ inch thick.

FOR CHOPS

Trim any extraneous fat.

FLATTEN

Place on cutting board (cut side up for tenderloin and country-style ribs), cover with plastic wrap, and pound into ¼-inch-thick cutlets.

Easy Grilled Boneless Pork Chops

SERVES 4 to 6 **TIME** 45 minutes plus 30 minutes brining

Why This Recipe Works For juicy, well-charred grilled boneless pork chops, we start by brining to help the chops hold on to moisture during cooking and season them throughout. Then we coat them with the unlikely power duo of anchovy paste and honey for faster browning and big, meaty flavor. If your pork is enhanced, do not brine it in step 1. Anchovy fillets, rinsed, dried, and mashed fine, can be used instead of anchovy paste. Cutting slits through the fat of the pork chops prevents them from buckling during cooking. This recipe was developed using Diamond Crystal kosher salt. If you have Morton kosher salt, which is denser, use 4½ tablespoons. We like to serve these chops with Mango Mint Salsa (page 402).

- 6 (6- to 8-ounce) boneless pork chops, ¾ to 1 inch thick
- 6 tablespoons kosher salt for brining
- 1 tablespoon vegetable oil
- 1½ teaspoons honey
- 1 teaspoon anchovy paste
- ½ teaspoon pepper

1 Cut 2 slits, about 2 inches apart, through outer layer of fat and silver skin on each chop. Dissolve salt in 1½ quarts cold water in large container. Submerge chops in brine, cover, and let sit at room temperature for 30 minutes.

2 Whisk oil, honey, anchovy paste, and pepper together to form smooth paste. Remove pork from brine and pat dry with paper towels. Using spoon, spread half of oil mixture evenly over 1 side of each chop (about ¼ teaspoon per side).

3A FOR A CHARCOAL GRILL Open bottom vent completely. Light chimney starter filled with charcoal briquettes (6 quarts). When top coals are partially covered with ash, pour evenly over half of grill. Set cooking grate in place, cover, and open lid vent completely. Heat grill until hot, about 5 minutes.

3B FOR A GAS GRILL Turn all burners to high; cover; and heat grill until hot, about 15 minutes. Leave primary burner on high and turn off other burner(s).

4 Clean and oil cooking grate. Place chops, oiled side down, over hotter side of grill and cook until well browned on first side, 4 to 6 minutes. Spread remaining oil mixture evenly over top of chops; flip chops; and continue to cook until chops register 140 degrees, 4 to 6 minutes longer (if chops are well browned but register less than 140 degrees, slide to cooler side of grill to finish cooking). Transfer chops to plate and let rest for 5 minutes. Serve.

Grilled Thin-Cut Pork Chops

SERVES 4 to 6 **TIME** 45 minutes plus 30 minutes freezing

Why This Recipe Works Thin-cut pork chops easily dry out before they pick up char on the grill. Our fix: Salt the chops to keep the insides moist and partially freeze them to dry their surface so they brown quickly. Spreading softened butter and brown sugar over the chops results in a flavorful golden-brown crust when they come off the grill. For even more flavor, we serve them with a chive-mustard butter. Cutting slits through the fat of the pork chops prevents them from buckling during cooking.

- 6 (3- to 4-ounce) bone-in rib or center-cut pork chops, about ½ inch thick, trimmed
- 1½ teaspoons kosher salt
- 4 tablespoons unsalted butter, softened, divided
- 1 teaspoon packed brown sugar
- ½ teaspoon pepper
- 1 teaspoon minced fresh chives
- ½ teaspoon Dijon mustard
- ½ teaspoon grated lemon zest

1 Cut 2 slits, about 2 inches apart, through outer layer of fat and silver skin on each chop. Pat chops dry with paper towels and sprinkle with salt. Place chops on wire rack set in rimmed baking sheet and freeze until firm, at least 30 minutes or up to 1 hour.

2 Combine 2 tablespoons butter, sugar, and pepper in small bowl; set aside for grilling. Mix remaining 2 tablespoons butter, chives, mustard, and lemon zest in second small bowl and refrigerate until firm, about 15 minutes. (Chive butter can be refrigerated, covered, for up to 24 hours.)

3 Pat chops dry with paper towels. Spread butter-sugar mixture evenly over both sides of each chop.

4A FOR A CHARCOAL GRILL Open bottom vent completely. Light large chimney starter filled with charcoal briquettes (6 quarts). When top coals are partially covered with ash, pour evenly over grill. Set cooking grate in place, cover, and open lid vent completely. Heat grill until hot, about 5 minutes.

4B FOR A GAS GRILL Turn all burners to high; cover; and heat grill until hot, about 15 minutes. Leave all burners on high.

5 Clean and oil cooking grate. Place chops on grill; cover; and cook until well browned and meat registers 145 degrees, 6 to 8 minutes, flipping halfway through cooking. Transfer chops to platter and top with chilled chive butter. Tent with aluminum foil and let rest for 5 minutes. Serve.

EASY GRILLED BONELESS PORK CHOPS

VARIATIONS

Grilled Thin-Cut Pork Chops with Thyme and Ginger

Substitute 1 teaspoon grated fresh ginger, ½ teaspoon minced fresh thyme, and ½ teaspoon grated orange zest for chives, mustard, and lemon zest.

Spicy Grilled Thin-Cut Pork Chops with Cilantro and Lime

Substitute 1½ teaspoons chili-garlic sauce, 1 teaspoon minced fresh cilantro, and ½ teaspoon grated lime zest for chives, mustard, and lemon zest.

Mediterranean Grilled Thin-Cut Pork Chops

Substitute ½ teaspoon minced fresh oregano for chives and 1½ teaspoons black olive tapenade for mustard.

Grilled Thick-Cut Bone-In Pork Chops

SERVES 4 **TIME** 35 minutes plus 1 hour brining

Why This Recipe Works Generously cut chops are the way to go when you want big grilled pork flavor, but they aren't immune to drying out. An hour-long brine keeps the meat juicy; these chops spend enough time on the grill that, in spite of the added moisture, they still develop beautiful browning. We sear the chops over high heat and finish them over moderate heat so they slowly come up to the ideal 145 degrees. For a simple way to flavor the meat in the few minutes between grilling and serving, we top the grilled chops with a zesty chive, mustard, and lemon butter (you can serve them plain if you prefer). If your pork is enhanced, do not brine it in step 1. This recipe was developed using Diamond Crystal kosher salt. If you have Morton kosher salt, which is denser, use 4½ tablespoons in the brine.

- 6 tablespoons kosher salt for brining
- 4 (12-ounce) bone-in pork rib or center-cut chops, 1½ inches thick, trimmed
- 2 tablespoons unsalted butter, softened
- 1 teaspoon minced fresh chives
- ½ teaspoon Dijon mustard
- ½ teaspoon grated lemon zest
- ½ teaspoon pepper

1 Dissolve salt in 1½ quarts cold water in large container. Submerge chops in brine, cover, and refrigerate for 1 hour.

2 Meanwhile, combine butter, chives, mustard, and lemon zest in bowl and refrigerate until firm, about 15 minutes. (Chive butter can be refrigerated, covered, for up to 24 hours.)

3 Remove pork from brine and pat dry with paper towels. Cut 2 slits, about 2 inches apart, through outer layer of fat and silver skin on each chop. Sprinkle with pepper.

4A **FOR A CHARCOAL GRILL** Open bottom vent completely. Light large chimney starter filled with charcoal briquettes (6 quarts). When top coals are partially covered with ash, pour two-thirds evenly over grill, then pour remaining coals over half of grill. Set cooking grate in place, cover, and open lid vent completely. Heat grill until hot, about 5 minutes.

4B **FOR A GAS GRILL** Turn all burners to high; cover; and heat grill until hot, about 15 minutes. Leave primary burner on high and turn other burner(s) to medium-low.

5 Clean and oil cooking grate. Place chops on hotter side of grill. Cook (covered if using gas), until browned, about 6 minutes, flipping halfway through cooking. Slide chops to cooler side of grill and cook until meat registers 145 degrees, 7 to 9 minutes, flipping halfway through cooking. Transfer chops to platter and top with chilled chive butter. Tent with aluminum foil and let rest for 5 to 10 minutes. Serve.

Grilled Lamb Shoulder Chops

SERVES 4 **TIME** 35 minutes

Why This Recipe Works When done right, grilled lamb shoulder chops are juicy and tender, with just a touch of gamy richness and satisfying chew. We use a two-level fire so that the chops can develop a rich crust on the hotter side of the grill and then gently cook through on the cooler side. This method also reduces the potential for flare-ups, which can occur when lamb's abundant fat drips onto the hot coals. Look for lamb shoulder chops that are at least ¾ inch thick, since they're less prone to overcook. If you can find only chops that are ½ inch thick, reduce the cooking time on the cooler side of the grill by about 30 seconds on each side. These chops taste great drizzled with Sauce Verte (page 392).

- 4 (8- to 12-ounce) lamb shoulder chops (blade or round bone), ¾ to 1 inch thick, trimmed
- 2 tablespoons extra-virgin olive oil
- 1 teaspoon kosher salt
- ½ teaspoon pepper

1A **FOR A CHARCOAL GRILL** Open bottom vent completely. Light large chimney starter filled with charcoal briquettes (6 quarts). When top coals are partially covered with ash, pour two-thirds evenly over half of grill, then pour remaining coals over other half of grill. Set cooking grate in place, cover, and open lid vent completely. Heat grill until hot, about 5 minutes.

1B **FOR A GAS GRILL** Turn all burners to high; cover; and heat grill until hot, about 15 minutes. Leave primary burner on high and turn other burner(s) to medium.

2 Clean and oil cooking grate. Rub chops with oil and sprinkle with salt and pepper. Place chops on hotter side of grill and cook (covered if using gas) until well browned, about 4 minutes, flipping halfway through cooking. Slide chops to cooler side of grill and cook until meat registers 120 to 125 degrees (for medium-rare), 4 to 8 minutes. Transfer chops to large platter, tent with aluminum foil, and let rest for 5 minutes before serving.

GRILLED LAMB SHOULDER CHOPS

Grilled Lamb Loin or Rib Chops

SERVES 4 **TIME** 35 minutes

Why This Recipe Works Lamb loin and rib chops can be up to 1½ inches thick, so the challenge in grilling them is to cook the delicate meat through gently without overbrowning its exterior. While loin and rib chops are especially tender cuts of lamb, they tend to dry out if cooked past medium since they have less intramuscular fat than shoulder chops. Keep an eye on the grill to make sure the meat does not overcook. These chops are smaller than shoulder chops, so you will need two for each serving. A minimalist rub of olive oil, salt, and pepper is all the embellishment these beautifully charred and perfectly medium-rare chops need, but for a change of pace you can rub them with Herb Spice Rub or Herbes de Provence (page 411).

- 8 (4-ounce) lamb loin or rib chops, 1¼ to 1½ inches thick, trimmed
- 2 tablespoons extra-virgin olive oil
- ¾ teaspoon kosher salt
- ½ teaspoon pepper

1 Rub chops with oil and sprinkle evenly with salt and pepper.

2A **FOR A CHARCOAL GRILL** Open bottom vent completely. Light large chimney starter filled with charcoal briquettes (6 quarts). When top coals are partially covered with ash, pour two-thirds evenly over half of grill, then pour remaining coals over other half of grill. Set cooking grate in place, cover, and open lid vent completely. Heat grill until hot, about 5 minutes.

2B **FOR A GAS GRILL** Turn all burners to high; cover; and heat grill until hot, about 15 minutes. Leave primary burner on high and turn other burner(s) to medium.

3 Clean and oil cooking grate. Place chops on hotter side of grill and cook (covered if using gas), turning as needed, until nicely charred on both sides, 2 to 4 minutes. Slide chops to cooler part of grill and cook, turning as needed, until meat registers 120 to 125 degrees (for medium-rare), 6 to 9 minutes.

4 Transfer chops to platter, tent with aluminum foil, and let rest for 5 to 10 minutes. Serve.

ROSTICCIANA

Rosticciana (Tuscan Grilled Pork Ribs)

SERVES 4 to 6 **TIME** 55 minutes plus 1 hour salting

Why This Recipe Works Tuscan ribs, or rosticciana, offer a purer—and quicker—rib experience than smoky, saucy American barbecued ribs. Minimal seasonings allow the pork flavor to shine. Instead of low-and-slow cooking, these ribs are grilled over a medium-hot fire to create a crispy exterior and satisfying tender-yet-chewy interior. St. Louis–style spareribs offer bold, meaty flavor, and it's easy to peel the tough, papery membranes from the racks. We cut the racks into two-rib sections, which creates more surface area for flavorful browning. A rosemary, garlic, and lemon vinaigrette makes a bright contrast to the ribs' richness. Our variation adds wedges of radicchio, which you can grill over the still-hot fire until pleasantly charred and mellow while the finished ribs are resting. For more information on removing the membrane from the ribs, see page 219. When portioning the meat into two-rib sections, start at the thicker end of the rack. If you're left with a three-rib piece at the tapered end, grill it as such. Take the temperature of the meat between the bones.

RIBS

- 2 (2½- to 3-pound) racks St. Louis–style spareribs, trimmed, membrane removed, and each rack cut into 2-rib sections
- 2 teaspoons kosher salt
- 1 tablespoon vegetable oil
- 1 teaspoon pepper

VINAIGRETTE

- ¼ cup extra-virgin olive oil
- 2 garlic cloves, minced
- 1 teaspoon minced fresh rosemary
- 2 tablespoons lemon juice

1 FOR THE RIBS Pat ribs dry with paper towels, rub evenly with salt, and place on wire rack set in rimmed baking sheet. Let sit at room temperature for 1 hour. Before grilling, brush meat side of ribs with oil and sprinkle with pepper.

2 FOR THE VINAIGRETTE Combine oil, garlic, and rosemary in small bowl and microwave until fragrant and just starting to bubble, about 30 seconds. Stir in lemon juice; set aside for serving.

3A FOR A CHARCOAL GRILL Open bottom vent completely. Light large chimney starter filled with charcoal briquettes (6 quarts). When top coals are partially covered with ash, pour evenly over grill. Set cooking grate in place, cover, and open lid vent completely. Heat grill until hot, about 5 minutes.

3B **FOR A GAS GRILL** Turn all burners to high; cover; and heat grill until hot, about 15 minutes. Leave all burners on high.

4 Clean and oil cooking grate. Place ribs meat side down on grill. Cover and cook until meat side begins to develop spotty browning and light but defined grill marks, 4 to 6 minutes. Flip ribs and cook, covered, until second side is lightly browned, 4 to 6 minutes, moving ribs as needed to ensure even browning. Flip again and cook, covered, until meat side is deeply browned with slight charring and thick ends of ribs register 175 to 185 degrees, 4 to 6 minutes.

5 Transfer ribs to carving board and let rest for 10 minutes. Cut ribs between bones and serve, passing vinaigrette separately.

VARIATION

Rosticciana with Grilled Radicchio

Brush 3 heads radicchio, quartered, with 3 tablespoons extra-virgin olive oil and sprinkle with 1 teaspoon kosher salt and ¼ teaspoon pepper. While ribs rest in step 5, grill radicchio (covered if using gas), turning often, until edges are browned and wilted but centers are still slightly firm, about 5 minutes. Serve with ribs and vinaigrette.

Grilled Pork Cutlets

SERVES 4 to 6 **TIME** 40 minutes plus 30 minutes marinating

Why This Recipe Works Convenient pork cutlets make a great choice for a quick grilled meal—if you know how to get good grilled flavor on this lean, thin cut without it becoming leathery. To season the cutlets to the core, we give them a quick marinade. We use high heat to grill the cutlets, leaving them on one side for most of the cooking time so that they develop a nice char, and then finishing them for just 30 seconds on the other side. For even cooking, we make our own tender cutlets by pounding pork chops to a uniform thickness; that way we avoid the shredded edges and irregular sizes you often find in prepackaged cutlets. Since marinating is a key step in this recipe, we don't recommend using enhanced pork.

- ⅓ cup balsamic vinegar
- ⅓ cup extra-virgin olive oil
- 2 garlic cloves, minced
- 1 teaspoon minced fresh thyme
- ¾ teaspoon sugar
- 1½ teaspoons kosher salt
- ¼ teaspoon pepper
- 12 (3- to 4-ounce) thin-cut boneless pork chops, trimmed and pounded to ¼ inch thick

1 Combine vinegar, oil, garlic, thyme, sugar, salt, and pepper in 1-gallon zipper-lock bag. Add chops and toss to coat; press out as much air as possible and seal bag. Refrigerate for at least 30 minutes or up to 2 hours.

2A **FOR A CHARCOAL GRILL** Open bottom vent completely. Light large chimney starter filled with charcoal briquettes (6 quarts). When top coals are partially covered with ash, pour evenly over half of grill. Set cooking grate in place, cover, and open lid vent completely. Heat grill until hot, about 5 minutes.

2B **FOR A GAS GRILL** Turn all burners to high; cover; and heat grill until hot, about 15 minutes. Leave all burners on high.

3 Clean and oil cooking grate. Place cutlets on grill (hotter side if using charcoal) and cook until bottoms begin to turn opaque at edges, about 2 minutes. Flip cutlets and grill until just cooked through, about 30 seconds. Transfer to platter, tent with aluminum foil, and let rest for 5 minutes. Serve.

VARIATIONS

Grilled Pork Cutlets with Rosemary and Red Wine Vinegar

Substitute ⅓ cup red wine vinegar for balsamic vinegar, 1 teaspoon minced fresh rosemary for thyme, and ¾ teaspoon honey for sugar.

Grilled Pork Cutlets with Cilantro and Lime

Add ½ teaspoon ground cumin to marinade and substitute ⅓ cup lime juice (3 limes) for balsamic vinegar, 3 tablespoons minced fresh cilantro for thyme, and ¾ teaspoon brown sugar for granulated sugar.

Grilled Citrus-Marinated Pork Cutlets

SERVES 4 to 6 **TIME** 45 minutes plus 30 minutes marinating

Why This Recipe Works The signature Yucatán dish poc chuc begins with pork cutlets marinated in sour orange juice, annatto powder, and spices and aromatics. The pork is quickly grilled over a hot fire and then served with tortillas and garnishes. We use boneless country-style pork ribs, which stay moist during cooking even when pounded into thin cutlets. To echo the sour orange flavor, we marinate our cutlets in a simple lime juice mixture. Placing the cutlets over a concentrated fire browns the meat quickly without overcooking it. Before serving the cutlets, we top them with avocado, tomato, radishes, and cilantro for color and freshness. Since marinating is a key step in this recipe, we don't recommend using enhanced pork. Serve with warm tortillas or rice.

- 1½ pounds boneless country-style pork ribs, trimmed
- ⅓ cup lime juice (3 limes)
- ⅓ cup extra-virgin olive oil
- 3 garlic cloves, minced
- 1 tablespoon annatto powder
- ¾ teaspoon brown sugar
- 1½ teaspoons kosher salt
- ½ teaspoon pepper
- ½ teaspoon ground coriander
- 1 (13 by 9-inch) disposable aluminum roasting pan (if using charcoal)
- 1 avocado, halved, pitted, and cut into ½-inch pieces
- 1 tomato, cored and cut into ½-inch pieces
- 2 radishes, trimmed and sliced thin
- 2 tablespoons chopped fresh cilantro

1 Cut each rib lengthwise to create 2 or 3 cutlets about ⅜-inch wide. Pound cutlets to ¼-inch thickness between 2 sheets of plastic.

2 Combine lime juice, oil, garlic, annatto powder, sugar, salt, pepper, and coriander in 1-gallon zipper-lock bag. Add pork and toss to coat; press out as much air as possible and seal bag. Refrigerate for at least 30 minutes or up to 2 hours, flipping bag occasionally.

3 Before grilling, remove cutlets from bag and pat dry with paper towels. If using charcoal, use kitchen shears to remove and discard bottom of roasting pan; reserve pan collar.

4A FOR A CHARCOAL GRILL Open bottom vent completely. Light large chimney starter filled with charcoal briquettes (6 quarts). When top coals are partially covered with ash, place roasting pan collar in center of grill, oriented over bottom vent, and pour coals into even layer in collar. Set cooking grate in place, cover, and open lid vent completely. Heat grill until hot, about 5 minutes.

4B FOR A GAS GRILL Turn all burners to high; cover; and heat grill until hot, about 15 minutes. Leave all burners on high.

5 Clean and oil cooking grate. Place pork on grill (over coals if using charcoal) and cook until lightly browned on first side, about 2 minutes. Flip cutlets and continue to grill until just cooked through, about 30 seconds. Transfer cutlets to serving platter and sprinkle with avocado, tomato, radishes, and cilantro. Serve.

Garlic-Lime Grilled Pork Tenderloin Steaks

SERVES 4 to 6 **TIME** 1 hour plus 45 minutes marinating

Why This Recipe Works Here's a little grilled meat math: Increase the surface-to-volume ratio and you maximize the amount of flavorful browned crust. For pork tenderloins, this means cutting the roasts in half and pounding them into steaks, which increases their surface area by 30 percent. The more pork that touches the grill, the more flavor in every bite. Crosshatching the steaks opens up the surface even more and creates crispy edges. For a bold marinade, combine oil, lime juice and zest, garlic, fish sauce, and honey (to encourage browning). A two-level grill fire allows you to sear the steaks on the hotter side and then let them gently finish cooking on the cooler side. The steaks are served with a sauce made from a bit of reserved marinade whisked with mayo and cilantro. Since marinating is a key step in this recipe, we don't recommend using enhanced pork.

- 2 (1-pound) pork tenderloins, trimmed
- 1 tablespoon grated lime zest plus ¼ cup juice (2 limes)
- 4 garlic cloves, minced
- 4 teaspoons honey
- 2 teaspoons fish sauce
- 1½ teaspoons kosher salt
- ½ teaspoon pepper
- ½ cup vegetable oil
- 4 teaspoons mayonnaise
- 1 tablespoon chopped fresh cilantro

1 Slice each tenderloin in half crosswise to create 4 steaks total. Pound steaks to ¾-inch thickness between 2 sheets of plastic wrap. Cut ⅛-inch-deep slits on both sides of steaks, spaced ½ inch apart, in crosshatch pattern.

2 Whisk lime zest and juice, garlic, honey, fish sauce, salt, and pepper together in large bowl. Whisking constantly, drizzle in oil until combined. Measure out ½ cup marinade into separate bowl and whisk in mayonnaise; set sauce aside for serving. Combine remaining marinade and pork in 1-gallon zipper-lock bag and toss to coat; press out as much air as possible and seal bag. Let sit at room temperature for 45 minutes.

3A **FOR A CHARCOAL GRILL** Open bottom vent completely. Light large chimney starter filled with charcoal briquettes (6 quarts). When top coals are partially covered with ash, pour evenly over half of grill. Set cooking grate in place, cover, and open lid vent completely. Heat grill until hot, about 5 minutes.

3B **FOR A GAS GRILL** Turn all burners to high; cover; and heat grill until hot, about 15 minutes. Leave primary burner on high and turn off other burner(s).

4 Clean and oil cooking grate. Place pork on hotter side of grill and cook until well browned on both sides, 6 to 8 minutes, flipping halfway through cooking. Slide pork to cooler side of grill, with wider end of each steak facing hotter side of grill. Cover and cook until meat registers 140 degrees, 3 to 8 minutes longer. Transfer steaks to carving board and let rest for 5 minutes.

5 While steaks rest, microwave reserved sauce until warm, 15 to 30 seconds; stir in cilantro. Slice steaks ½ inch thick against grain. Drizzle with half of sauce and season with flake sea salt, if desired. Serve, passing remaining sauce separately.

VARIATIONS

Lemon-Thyme Grilled Pork Tenderloin Steaks

Substitute grated lemon zest and juice (2 lemons) for lime zest and juice. Add 1 tablespoon minced fresh thyme to lemon mixture with garlic. Omit cilantro.

Spicy Orange-Ginger Grilled Pork Tenderloin Steaks

Reduce lime zest to 1½ teaspoons and juice to 2 tablespoons. Add 1½ teaspoons grated orange zest plus 2 tablespoons juice, 2 teaspoons grated fresh ginger, and ¼ teaspoon cayenne to lime mixture with garlic.

GRILLED CITRUS-MARINATED PORK CUTLETS

GARLIC-LIME GRILLED PORK TENDERLOIN STEAKS

Grilled Hoisin-Glazed Pork Chops with Pineapple Salsa

SERVES 4 to 6 **TIME** 40 minutes

Why This Recipe Works Hoisin sauce not only provides a shortcut to giving fast-cooking bone-in pork chops a sweet-and-sour flavor profile; thanks to its sugar it also encourages delicious caramelization. Rings of fresh pineapple quickly develop a mellow sweetness on the grill; we add scallions, cilantro, jalapeño, fresh ginger, and smoky toasted sesame oil for a bright, complex salsa to serve with the chops.

- ½ cup hoisin sauce
- 3 tablespoons unseasoned rice vinegar
- 8 (3- to 4-ounce) bone-in center-cut pork chops, ½ inch thick, trimmed
- 1 teaspoon kosher salt
- ½ teaspoon pepper
- ½ pineapple, peeled, cored, and cut into ½-inch-thick rings
- 2 tablespoons toasted sesame oil, divided
- 3 scallions, sliced thin
- ¼ cup chopped fresh cilantro
- 1 jalapeño chile, stemmed, seeded, and minced
- 2 teaspoons grated fresh ginger

1 Whisk hoisin and vinegar together in bowl. Measure out 3 tablespoons and set aside for grilling. Pat pork chops dry with paper towels, sprinkle with salt and pepper, and brush chops all over with remaining hoisin mixture. Brush pineapple all over with 1 tablespoon oil.

2A **FOR A CHARCOAL GRILL** Open bottom vent completely. Light large chimney starter filled with charcoal briquettes (6 quarts). When top coals are partially covered with ash, pour evenly over grill. Set cooking grate in place, cover, and open lid vent completely. Heat grill until hot, about 5 minutes.

2B **FOR A GAS GRILL** Turn all burners to high; cover; and heat grill until hot, about 15 minutes. Leave all burners on high.

3 Clean and oil cooking grate. Place pineapple on grill and cook (covered if using gas) until charred, about 6 minutes, turning as needed. Transfer to cutting board.

4 Place chops on grill and cook (covered if using gas) until well browned and meat registers 140 degrees, about 6 minutes, flipping halfway through cooking. Transfer chops to platter and brush with reserved hoisin mixture. Tent with aluminum foil and let rest for 5 minutes.

5 Chop pineapple into ½-inch pieces and combine with scallions, cilantro, jalapeño, ginger, and remaining 1 tablespoon oil in bowl. Season with salt and pepper to taste. Serve pork with pineapple salsa.

Grill-Smoked Thick-Cut Pork Chops

SERVES 4 **TIME** 1¼ hours

Why This Recipe Works These chops have it all: a charred crust, ultramoist meat, and true smoke flavor. Thick-cut chops are a good choice for grill-smoking: More meat on the bone allows for more grilling time to infuse the meat with smoke without it drying out. We use a disposable aluminum pan to create a split fire. We put a packet of wood chips on the coals and start the chops over the cooler center of the grill, allowing the smoke plenty of time to do its job. Spearing the chops together with skewers provides further insurance against overcooking while they pick up smoky flavor; we make sure to leave a good inch between chops to allow air to circulate, and stand them upright on the grill. Then we remove the skewers, brush on some of the sauce, and finish the chops over the hot coals for a crusty char. Use the large holes of a box grater to grate the onion for the sauce. If you'd like to use wood chunks instead of wood chips when using a charcoal grill, substitute two medium wood chunks for the wood chip packet. You will need two 10-inch metal skewers for this recipe. Cutting slits through the fat of the pork chops prevents them from buckling during cooking. This recipe was developed using Diamond Crystal kosher salt. If you have Morton kosher salt, which is denser, use 1 tablespoon.

SAUCE

- ½ cup ketchup
- ¼ cup molasses
- 2 tablespoons grated onion
- 2 tablespoons Worcestershire sauce
- 2 tablespoons Dijon mustard
- 2 tablespoons cider vinegar
- 1 tablespoon packed light brown sugar

CHOPS

- 2 cups wood chips
- 4 (12-ounce) bone-in pork rib or center-cut chops, 1½ inches thick, trimmed
- 4 teaspoons kosher salt
- 2 teaspoons pepper
- 1 (13 by 9-inch) disposable aluminum roasting pan (if using charcoal)

Grill-Smoking Thick-Cut Pork Chops

1 Pass 2 skewers through loin muscle of each chop to provide stability when standing on grill.

2 Stand skewered chops, bone-side down, in center of cooking grate over pan so smoke can reach all sides.

3 Brush chops with sauce and transfer to hotter sides of grill to sear on both sides (brushing top of each chop again before flipping).

GRILL-SMOKED THICK-CUT PORK CHOPS

1 **FOR THE SAUCE** Bring all ingredients to simmer in small saucepan over medium heat. Cook, stirring occasionally, until reduced to about 1 cup, 5 to 7 minutes. Measure out ½ cup sauce for cooking and reserve remaining sauce for serving.

2 **FOR THE CHOPS** Using large piece of heavy-duty aluminum foil, wrap wood chips in 8 by 4-inch foil packet. (Make sure chips do not poke holes in sides or bottom of packet.) Cut 2 evenly spaced 2-inch slits in top of packet.

3 Pat pork chops dry with paper towels. Cut 2 slits, about 2 inches apart, through outer layer of fat and silver skin on each chop. Sprinkle salt and pepper evenly over chops. Place chops side by side, facing in same direction, on cutting board with curved rib bone facing down. Pass 2 metal skewers through loin muscle of each chop, close to bone, about 1 inch from each end, then pull chops apart to create 1-inch space between each.

4A **FOR A CHARCOAL GRILL** Open bottom vent halfway and place disposable pan in center of grill. Light large chimney starter filled with charcoal briquettes (6 quarts). When top coals are partially covered with ash, pour into 2 even piles on either side of disposable pan. Place wood chip packet on 1 pile of coals. Set cooking grate in place, cover, and open lid vent halfway. Heat grill until hot and wood chips are smoking, about 5 minutes.

4B **FOR A GAS GRILL** Remove cooking grate and place wood chip packet directly on primary burner. Set grate in place; turn all burners to high; cover; and heat grill until hot and wood chips are smoking, about 15 minutes. Turn all burners to medium-high. (Adjust burners as needed during cooking to maintain grill temperature between 300 and 325 degrees.)

5 Clean and oil cooking grate. Place skewered pork chops bone side down on grill (over pan if using charcoal). Cover and cook until meat registers 120 degrees, 28 to 32 minutes.

6 Remove skewers from chops. Lay chops flat on grate and brush top of each chop with 1 tablespoon sauce. Flip chops, slide to hotter sides of grill (if using charcoal) or turn all burners to high (if using gas) and cook until browned on first side, 2 to 6 minutes. Brush top of each chop with 1 tablespoon sauce, flip, and continue to cook until browned on second side and meat registers 145 degrees, 2 to 6 minutes longer.

7 Transfer chops to serving platter, tent with foil, and let rest for 5 to 10 minutes. Serve, passing reserved sauce separately.

Spice-Rubbed Pork Tenderloin with Grilled Tomato–Ginger Salsa

SERVES 4 to 6 **TIME** 45 minutes

Why This Recipe Works A bright, juicy grilled salsa makes a terrific side for lean pork—and puts the extra grill space to good use. We season the tenderloin with salt, cumin, and chipotle chile powder for smoky, savory flavor, as well as a touch of sugar to encourage browning. We sear the roast on the hotter side of a two-level fire to develop flavorful browning; then, we move it to the cooler side of the grill to gently finish cooking and add tomatoes and scallions to pick up some char on the hotter side. While the cooked pork rests, we combine the grilled vegetables with mint, lime juice, ginger, and garam masala for a quick salsa.

TENDERLOIN

- 1½ teaspoons kosher salt
- 1½ teaspoons sugar
- ½ teaspoon ground cumin
- ½ teaspoon chipotle chile powder
- 2 (12- to 16-ounce) pork tenderloins, trimmed

TOMATO-GINGER SALSA

- 1½ pounds plum tomatoes, cored, halved, and seeded
- 9 scallions
- 3 tablespoons plus 1 teaspoon extra-virgin olive oil, divided
- 3 tablespoons minced fresh mint
- 2 tablespoons lime juice, plus extra for seasoning
- 5 teaspoons grated fresh ginger
- ¼ teaspoon garam masala

1 **FOR THE TENDERLOIN** Combine salt, sugar, cumin, and chile powder in small bowl. Measure out ½ teaspoon spice rub and set aside for salsa. Pat pork dry with paper towels, rub with spice rub, and refrigerate until needed.

2 **FOR THE SALSA** Brush tomatoes and scallions with 1 teaspoon oil.

3A **FOR A CHARCOAL GRILL** Open bottom vent completely. Light large chimney starter filled with charcoal briquettes (6 quarts). When top coals are partially covered with ash, pour evenly over half of grill. Set cooking grate in place, cover, and open lid vent completely. Heat grill until hot, about 5 minutes.

3B **FOR A GAS GRILL** Turn all burners to high; cover; and heat grill until hot, about 15 minutes. Leave primary burner on high and turn off other burner(s).

4 Clean and oil cooking grate. Place tenderloins on hotter side of grill. Cover and cook, turning tenderloins every 2 minutes, until well browned on all sides, about 8 minutes.

5 Slide tenderloins to cooler side of grill; cover; and cook until pork registers 140 degrees, 12 to 17 minutes, turning tenderloins every 5 minutes. Meanwhile, place tomatoes and scallions on hotter side of grill and cook until softened and charred on both sides, 8 to 10 minutes, flipping halfway through cooking.

6 Transfer pork to carving board and tomatoes and scallions to plate; tent both with aluminum foil.

7 While tenderloins rest, roughly chop scallions. Combine scallions, tomatoes, remaining 3 tablespoons oil, mint, lime juice, ginger, garam masala, and reserved ½ teaspoon spice rub in food processor and pulse until coarsely chopped, 4 to 6 pulses. Transfer to bowl and season with salt and extra lime juice to taste. Slice tenderloins ½ inch thick. Serve with salsa.

SPICE-RUBBED PORK TENDERLOIN WITH GRILLED TOMATO-GINGER SALSA

Orange-Glazed Pork Tenderloin Roast

SERVES 4 **TIME** 1½ hours plus 1 hour brining

Why This Recipe Works Joining two pork tenderloins together takes them from casual supper to company-worthy roast. After brining and tying, we cook the roast over indirect heat and then move it over the flames to brown it. At this stage, we add a zesty orange glaze, which coats the roast on all sides for some beautiful charring. Since brining is a key step in having the two tenderloins stick together, we don't recommend using enhanced pork in this recipe. This recipe was developed using Diamond Crystal kosher salt. If you have Morton kosher salt, which is denser, use 4½ tablespoons. See page 104 for our glaze variations and more information on prepping the tenderloins.

TENDERLOIN

- 2 (1-pound) pork tenderloins, trimmed
- 6 tablespoons kosher salt for brining
- Vegetable oil
- ¼ teaspoon pepper

ORANGE GLAZE

- ½ cup orange marmalade
- 3 tablespoons orange juice concentrate
- 1 teaspoon grated lemon zest plus 1½ tablespoons juice
- 1 teaspoon minced fresh thyme
- 1 garlic clove, minced

1 **FOR THE TENDERLOIN** Lay tenderloins on cutting board, flat side (side opposite where silver skin was) up. Holding thick end of 1 tenderloin with paper towels and using dinner fork, scrape flat side lengthwise from end to end 5 times, until surface is completely covered with shallow grooves. Repeat with second tenderloin. Dissolve salt in 1½ quarts cold water in large container. Submerge tenderloins in brine, cover, and let sit at room temperature for 1 hour.

2 Remove tenderloins from brine and pat dry with paper towels. Lay 1 tenderloin, scraped side up, on cutting board and lay second tenderloin, scraped side down, on top so that thick end of 1 tenderloin matches up with thin end of other. Spray five 14-inch lengths of kitchen twine thoroughly with vegetable oil spray; evenly space twine underneath tenderloins and tie. Brush roast with oil and sprinkle with pepper.

3 **FOR THE GLAZE** Process marmalade, orange juice concentrate, lemon zest and juice, thyme, and garlic in food processor until smooth. Transfer mixture to small saucepan and cook over medium heat until slightly thickened, about 3 minutes. Measure out ¼ cup glaze and set aside for grilling; reserve remaining glaze for serving.

4A **FOR A CHARCOAL GRILL** Open bottom vent completely. Light large chimney starter filled with charcoal briquettes (6 quarts). When top coals are partially covered with ash, pour into steeply banked pile against side of grill. Set cooking grate in place, cover, and open lid vent completely. Heat grill until hot, about 5 minutes.

4B **FOR A GAS GRILL** Turn all burners to high; cover; and heat grill until hot, about 15 minutes. Leave primary burner on high and turn off other burner(s).

5 Clean and oil cooking grate. Place roast on cooler side of grill; cover; and cook until meat registers 115 degrees, 22 to 28 minutes, flipping and rotating halfway through cooking.

6 Slide roast to hotter side of grill and cook until lightly browned on all sides, 4 to 6 minutes. Brush top of roast with 1 tablespoon glaze, turn glaze side down, and cook until glaze begins to char, 2 to 3 minutes. Repeat glazing with remaining 3 sides of roast, until meat registers 140 degrees.

7 Transfer roast to carving board, tent with aluminum foil, and let rest for 10 minutes. Carefully remove twine and slice roast into ½-inch-thick slices. Serve with remaining glaze.

Turning Two Tenderloins into One Roast

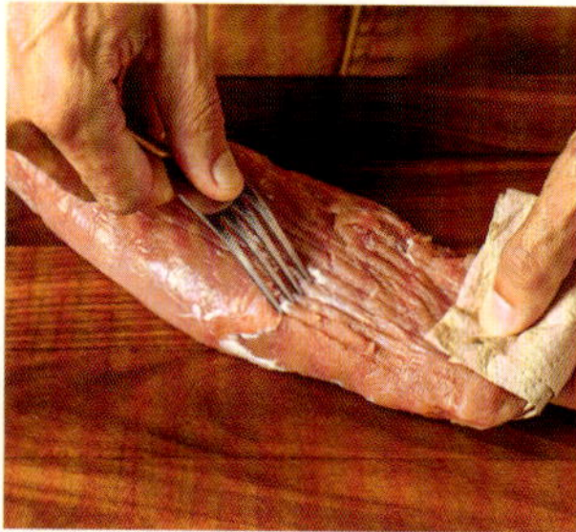

1 Scrape up flat sides of each tenderloin with fork until surface is covered with shallow grooves. This releases sticky proteins that act as "glue."

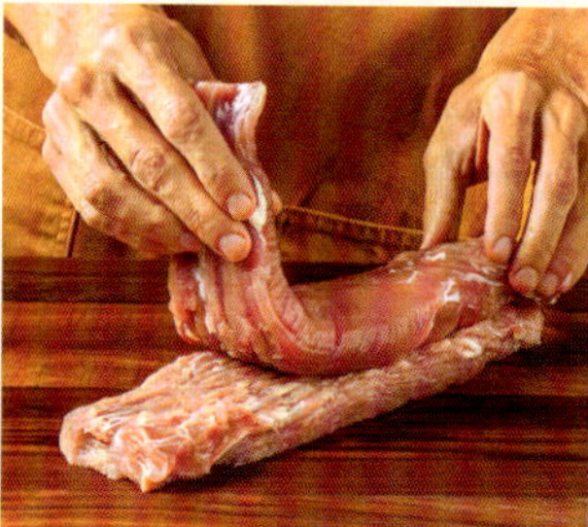

2 Arrange tenderloins with scraped sides touching and thick end of one nestled against thin end of other. Tie tenderloins together.

VARIATIONS

Miso-Glazed Pork Tenderloin Roast

Substitute following for orange glaze: Bring 3 tablespoons sake and 3 tablespoons mirin to boil in small saucepan over medium heat. Whisk in ⅓ cup white miso and ¼ cup sugar until smooth, about 30 seconds. Remove from heat and continue to whisk until sugar is dissolved, about 1 minute. Whisk in 2 teaspoons Dijon mustard, 1 teaspoon rice vinegar, ¼ teaspoon grated fresh ginger, and ¼ teaspoon toasted sesame oil until smooth.

Sweet and Spicy Hoisin-Glazed Pork Tenderloin Roast

Substitute following for orange glaze: Heat 1 teaspoon vegetable oil in small saucepan over medium heat until shimmering. Add 3 minced garlic cloves, 1 teaspoon grated fresh ginger, and ½ teaspoon red pepper flakes; cook until fragrant, about 30 seconds. Whisk in ½ cup hoisin sauce and 2 tablespoons soy sauce until smooth. Remove pan from heat and stir in 1 tablespoon rice vinegar.

SMOKED BOURBON PORK TENDERLOIN

Smoked Bourbon Pork Tenderloin

SERVES 4 **TIME** 1¼ hours plus 3 hours marinating

Why This Recipe Works With a little planning, you can grill up a smoky pork tenderloin dinner that'll satisfy barbecue cravings any night of the week. Don't let the 3-hour marinating time put you off; an all-day or even overnight stint adds even more flavor and lets you fit this meal into your schedule. We use bourbon as the marinade base and add soy sauce (as a brining agent), brown sugar, garlic, black pepper, and red pepper flakes. We set aside some of the marinade for glazing; the rest goes into a bag with a couple of mild, quick-cooking pork tenderloins. Smoky wood chips help bolster the flavor of the pork in addition to the marinade and glaze. With only about 30 minutes of grilling time required, this recipe lets you save the low-and-slow pork cuts for weekend cooking. Since marinating is a key step in this recipe, we don't recommend using enhanced pork. The longer the pork is brined, the more flavorful it will become. If you'd like to use wood chunks instead of wood chips when using a charcoal grill, substitute 2 wood chunks for the wood chip packet.

- ½ cup bourbon
- ½ cup soy sauce
- 3 tablespoons packed brown sugar
- 3 garlic cloves, smashed and peeled
- 1 teaspoon pepper
- ½ teaspoon red pepper flakes
- 2 (1-pound) pork tenderloins, trimmed
- 1 cup wood chips

1 Combine bourbon, soy sauce, sugar, garlic, pepper, and pepper flakes in medium saucepan. Bring to boil over medium-high heat and boil for 1 minute. Remove from heat and let cool completely. Measure out ¼ cup bourbon marinade and set aside for serving. (Marinade can be refrigerated for up to 3 days.)

2 Combine remaining marinade and pork in 1-gallon zipper-lock bag and toss to coat; press out as much air as possible and seal bag. Refrigerate for at least 3 hours or up to 24 hours, flipping occasionally.

3 Using large piece of heavy-duty aluminum foil, wrap wood chips in 8 by 4-inch foil packet. (Make sure chips do not poke holes in sides or bottom of packet.) Cut 2 evenly spaced 2-inch slits in top of packet.

4A **FOR A CHARCOAL GRILL** Open bottom vent completely. Light large chimney starter mounded with charcoal briquettes (7 quarts). When top coals are partially covered with ash, pour evenly over half of grill. Place wood chip packet on coals. Set cooking grate in place, cover, and open lid vent completely. Heat grill until hot and wood chips are smoking, about 5 minutes.

4B **FOR A GAS GRILL** Remove cooking grate and place wood chip packet directly on primary burner. Set cooking grate in place; turn all burners to high; cover; and heat grill until hot and wood chips are smoking, about 15 minutes. Leave primary burner on high and turn off other burner(s).

5 Clean and oil cooking grate. Place pork on cooler side of grill as far as possible from heat source, positioning tenderloins parallel to fire (if using charcoal) or burners (if using gas). Cover and cook until pork registers 135 degrees, 15 to 20 minutes, flipping and rotating halfway through cooking.

6 Brush top and sides of pork with half of reserved bourbon mixture. Flip pork, slide to hotter side of grill, and brush top with remaining reserved bourbon mixture. Cook, uncovered, until pork is lightly charred and registers 140 degrees, 3 to 5 minutes, flipping halfway through cooking.

7 Transfer pork to carving board, tent with foil, and let rest for 10 minutes. Slice ½ inch thick. Serve.

BARBECUED COUNTRY-STYLE RIBS

Barbecued Country-Style Ribs

SERVES 4 to 6 **TIME** 40 minutes plus 30 minutes brining

Why This Recipe Works Combining convenience and flavor, boneless country-style ribs make a great choice for easy grilling if you can deal with their dual nature: These well-marbled, tender slabs of pork contain both white meat and dark meat, which makes cooking them evenly a challenge. Our simple fix: Pound the ribs to an even ¾-inch thickness to "break down" the fattier dark meat and then brine them to keep the lean white meat juicy. A double layer of barbecue spice and sauce and a quick smoke on the grill turn these ribs into something to sing about. For easier pounding, cut any ribs that are longer than 5 inches in half crosswise. If you'd like to use wood chunks instead of wood chips when using a charcoal grill, substitute one medium wood chunk for the wood chip packet.

- 2 pounds boneless country-style pork ribs, trimmed
- 2 tablespoons kosher salt for brining
- ¾ cup packed dark brown sugar
- 2 tablespoons chili powder
- 2 tablespoons paprika
- 1 tablespoon dry mustard
- 1 tablespoon onion powder
- ¾ teaspoon pepper
- ¼ teaspoon cayenne pepper
- 6 tablespoons ketchup
- 1 tablespoon cider vinegar
- ¼ cup wood chips

1 Pound ribs to ¾-inch thickness between 2 sheets of plastic wrap. Dissolve salt in 2 cups cold water in large container. Submerge pork in brine, cover, and refrigerate for at least 30 minutes or up to 1 hour.

2 Meanwhile, combine sugar, chili powder, paprika, dry mustard, onion powder, pepper, and cayenne in shallow dish. Transfer half of mixture to bowl, stir in ketchup and vinegar, and set aside for cooking.

3 Remove pork from brine and pat dry with paper towels. Dredge pork in remaining spice mixture and transfer to plate. Using large piece of heavy-duty aluminum foil, wrap wood chips in 8 by 4-inch foil packet. (Make sure chips do not poke holes in sides or bottom of packet.) Cut 2 evenly spaced 2-inch slits in top of packet.

4A **FOR A CHARCOAL GRILL** Open bottom vent halfway. Light large chimney starter filled with charcoal briquettes (6 quarts). When top coals are partially covered with ash, pour evenly over half of grill. Place wood chip packet on coals. Set cooking grate in place, cover, and open lid vent halfway. Heat grill until hot and wood chips are smoking, about 5 minutes.

4B **FOR A GAS GRILL** Place wood chip packet directly on primary burner. Turn all burners to high; cover; and heat grill until hot and wood chips are smoking, about 15 minutes. Leave primary burner on high and turn off other burner(s).

5 Clean and oil cooking grate. Place pork on cooler side of grill; cover (positioning lid vent over meat if using charcoal); and cook until meat registers 125 degrees, 3 to 5 minutes. Brush pork with ketchup mixture, slide to hotter side of grill, and flip. Cover and cook until lightly charred, 2 to 3 minutes. Brush top of pork with ketchup mixture, flip, and cook, covered, until lightly charred and meat registers 145 degrees, 2 to 3 minutes. Transfer pork to platter, tent with foil, and let rest for 5 to 10 minutes. Serve.

St. Louis Barbecued Pork Steaks

SERVES 6 to 8 **TIME** 2 hours plus 2 hours seasoning

Why This Recipe Works In St. Louis, barbecued pork steaks are so popular that pork steaks are on permanent sale in family packs at the supermarket. The cut is a must-have for making this regional favorite, but if you don't live near St. Louis, you can create your own pork steaks: Cut a boneless pork butt roast in half crosswise, turn each piece on end, and slice 1-inch-thick steaks. A fragrant spice rub front-loads the steaks with flavor, and an untraditional grilling process—searing the steaks, simmering them in barbecue sauce in a pan right on the grill, and then searing them again—gives the steaks a nice char, candy-like edges, and succulent, slightly chewy interiors. Pork butt roast is also labeled Boston butt in the supermarket. If you can find pork steaks, increase the cooking time in the sauce to 1 to 1½ hours.

PORK STEAKS

- 1 tablespoon packed brown sugar
- 1 tablespoon paprika
- 2 teaspoons kosher salt
- 2 teaspoons dry mustard
- 2 teaspoons pepper
- 1 teaspoon onion powder
- 1 teaspoon garlic powder
- 1 teaspoon ground cumin
- ¼ teaspoon cayenne pepper
- 1 (5- to 6-pound) boneless pork butt roast, sliced crosswise into 2 pieces, trimmed, and each half cut into three or four 1-inch-thick steaks

BARBECUE SAUCE

- 2 cups mild lager, such as Budweiser
- 1½ cups ketchup
- ¼ cup A.1. Steak Sauce
- ¼ cup packed dark brown sugar
- 2 tablespoons cider vinegar
- 2 tablespoons Worcestershire sauce
- 1 teaspoon garlic powder
- 1 teaspoon hot sauce
- 1 teaspoon liquid smoke
- 1 (13 by 9-inch) disposable aluminum roasting pan

1 **FOR THE PORK STEAKS** Combine sugar, paprika, salt, dry mustard, pepper, onion powder, garlic powder, cumin, and cayenne in bowl. Pat steaks dry with paper towels and rub evenly with spice mixture. Wrap pork tightly in plastic wrap and refrigerate for at least 1 hour or up to 24 hours.

2 **FOR THE BARBECUE SAUCE** Whisk all ingredients together in bowl and transfer to disposable pan.

3A **FOR A CHARCOAL GRILL** Open bottom vent halfway. Light large chimney starter filled with charcoal briquettes (6 quarts). When top coals are partially covered with ash, pour evenly over grill. Set cooking grate in place, cover, and open lid vent halfway. Heat grill until hot, about 5 minutes.

3B **FOR A GAS GRILL** Turn all burners to high; cover; and heat grill until hot, about 15 minutes. Leave primary burner on high and turn off other burner(s). (Adjust primary burner as needed to maintain grill temperature of 350 degrees.)

4 Clean and oil cooking grate. Place pork steaks on grill and cook (covered if using gas) until well browned on both sides, about 10 minutes, flipping halfway through cooking.

5 Transfer pork steaks to sauce in pan and turn to coat thoroughly. Cover pan with aluminum foil and place on grill. Cover (positioning lid vent over pan if using charcoal) and cook steaks until fork-tender and register 190 degrees, 45 minutes to 1 hour.

6 Remove steaks from pan and cook until lightly charred around edges, about 10 minutes, flipping halfway through cooking. Skim excess fat from sauce and serve sauce with steaks.

Cutting Your Own St. Louis Pork Steaks

1 Halve pork butt crosswise and remove any large pieces of fat.

2 Rotate and stand each half on its cut end.

3 Cut each half into three or four 1-inch-thick steaks.

Grilled Pork Cutlets and Zucchini with Feta and Mint

SERVES 4 to 6 **TIME** 30 minutes

Why This Recipe Works These pork cutlets are the sum of a never-fail equation for an easy, flavor-packed meal on the grill: protein plus vegetable plus compound butter. We cut pork tenderloins into even cutlets, which we season simply and grill with tender zucchini halves. A blend of softened butter, salty feta, fresh mint, and orange zest turns into a luxurious sauce as it melts over the beautifully browned pork and zucchini.

- 2 (12- to 16-ounce) pork tenderloins, trimmed and cut crosswise into 4 equal pieces
- 2 teaspoons kosher salt, divided
- ½ teaspoon plus ⅛ teaspoon pepper, divided
- 4 tablespoons unsalted butter, softened
- 1 ounce feta cheese, crumbled (¼ cup)
- 1 tablespoon chopped fresh mint
- ½ teaspoon grated orange zest
- 4 small zucchini (6 ounces each), halved lengthwise
- 1 tablespoon vegetable oil

1 Lay pork pieces cut side down on cutting board, cover with plastic wrap, and pound to even ¼-inch thickness. Pat cutlets dry with paper towels and sprinkle with 1 teaspoon salt and ¼ teaspoon pepper.

2 Mash butter with feta, mint, orange zest, ½ teaspoon salt, and ¼ teaspoon pepper in bowl until combined; set aside for serving. Rub zucchini all over with oil and sprinkle with remaining ½ teaspoon salt and ⅛ teaspoon pepper.

3A **FOR A CHARCOAL GRILL** Open bottom vent completely. Light large chimney starter filled with charcoal briquettes (6 quarts). When top coals are partially covered with ash, pour evenly over grill. Set cooking grate in place, cover, and open lid vent completely. Heat grill until hot, about 5 minutes.

3B **FOR A GAS GRILL** Turn all burners to high; cover; and heat grill until hot, about 15 minutes. Leave all burners on high.

4 Clean and oil cooking grate. Place pork on grill and cook until lightly charred and registers 140 degrees, 4 to 6 minutes, flipping as needed. Transfer to serving platter, tent with aluminum foil, and let rest while grilling zucchini.

5 Place zucchini on grill and cook until tender, 5 to 7 minutes, flipping halfway through. Transfer zucchini to platter. Dollop pork and zucchini with reserved feta butter. Serve.

GRILLED PORK CUTLETS AND ZUCCHINI WITH FETA AND MINT

MOLASSES-GLAZED PORK CHOPS AND SWEET POTATOES WITH RED CABBAGE SLAW

GRILLED LAMB SHOULDER CHOPS WITH ZUCCHINI AND CORN SALAD

Molasses-Glazed Pork Chops and Sweet Potatoes with Red Cabbage Slaw

SERVES 4 **TIME** 45 minutes

Why This Recipe Works A molasses and cider vinegar mixture does double duty as a glaze for grilled pork chops and sweet potatoes and a dressing for a red cabbage slaw. Quickly simmering the glaze reduces it to a thicker, stickier consistency that clings to the pork chops and potatoes. With just a few minutes' head start in the microwave, sweet potatoes become plush and caramelized on the grill. Peanuts and cilantro add crunch and freshness to the slaw. Look for larger sweet potatoes, which make for more manageable slices.

- 1½ pounds sweet potatoes, unpeeled, sliced ½ inch thick
- 3 tablespoons extra-virgin olive oil, divided
- 1½ tablespoons kosher salt, divided
- 1¾ teaspoons pepper, divided
- ⅓ cup molasses
- 5 tablespoons cider vinegar, divided
- ½ teaspoon red pepper flakes
- ½ head red cabbage, halved, cored, and sliced thin (6 cups)
- ½ cup dry-roasted peanuts, chopped
- 3 tablespoons chopped fresh cilantro
- 4 (6- to 8-ounce) boneless pork chops, ¾ to 1 inch thick, trimmed

1 Toss potatoes with 1 tablespoon oil, 1 teaspoon salt, and ½ teaspoon pepper in bowl. Cover and microwave until softened, 6 to 8 minutes, stirring halfway through; drain well.

2 Combine molasses, ¼ cup vinegar, pepper flakes, and ½ teaspoon salt in small saucepan and bring to simmer over medium heat. Cook until thickened, 3 to 5 minutes; remove from heat. Measure 2 tablespoons mixture into large bowl and whisk in 1 teaspoon salt, ¼ teaspoon pepper, remaining 2 tablespoons oil, and remaining 1 tablespoon vinegar. Add cabbage, peanuts, and cilantro and toss to combine. Season with salt and pepper to taste.

3 Pat pork dry with paper towels and sprinkle with remaining 2 teaspoons salt and remaining 1 teaspoon pepper.

4A **FOR A CHARCOAL GRILL** Open bottom vent completely. Light large chimney starter filled with charcoal briquettes (6 quarts). When top coals are partially covered with ash, pour evenly over grill. Set cooking grate in place, cover, and open lid vent completely. Heat grill until hot, about 5 minutes.

4B **FOR A GAS GRILL** Turn all burners to high; cover; and heat grill until hot, about 15 minutes. Leave all burners on high.

5 Clean and oil cooking grate. Place pork on grill and cook until browned and meat registers 135 degrees, 8 to 12 minutes, flipping halfway through. After 4 minutes, place potatoes on grill and cook until browned and tender, 4 to 6 minutes, flipping halfway through. Brush pork and potatoes all over with remaining molasses mixture (you may not need all of it) and cook for 1 minute, flipping halfway through cooking. Transfer pork and potatoes to platter and let rest for 5 minutes. Serve with slaw.

Mojo Grilled Pork Chops with Black Bean and Orange Salad

SERVES 4 **TIME** 45 minutes

Why This Recipe Works To re-create the quintessential tart taste of Cuban mojo sauce, we mix olive oil with equal amounts of orange juice and lime juice and amp it up with a healthy dose of garlic and some ground cumin. Mojo often functions as both a marinade and a finishing sauce, and this recipe is no exception; in fact, we use it to dress a black bean and orange salad as well. A little brown sugar in the sauce promotes browning of the chops on the grill and adds balance to the dressing on the salad. Cutting slits through the fat of the pork chops prevents them from buckling during cooking.

- ⅓ cup extra-virgin olive oil
- 4 garlic cloves, minced
- 1 teaspoon ground cumin
- ¼ cup orange juice
- ¼ cup lime juice (2 limes)
- 1 tablespoon packed brown sugar
- 1 orange
- 2 (15-ounce) cans black beans, rinsed
- 1 avocado, halved, pitted, and cut into ½-inch pieces
- 1 small red onion, chopped fine
- 2 tablespoons minced fresh cilantro
- 1 teaspoon kosher salt
- ½ teaspoon pepper
- 4 (8- to 10-ounce) bone-in pork rib chops, ¾ to 1 inch thick

1 Microwave oil, garlic, and cumin in medium bowl until hot, about 30 seconds. Whisk in orange juice, lime juice, and sugar. Transfer ¼ cup dressing to large bowl for salad; set aside remaining dressing for serving.

2 Cut away peel and pith from orange, then quarter orange and slice crosswise into ¼-inch-thick pieces. Toss orange, beans, avocado, onion, and cilantro with ¼ cup reserved dressing and season with salt and pepper to taste.

3 Cut 2 slits, about 2 inches apart, through outer layer of fat and silver skin on each chop. Pat chops dry with paper towels, brush with remaining dressing, and sprinkle with salt and pepper.

4A **FOR A CHARCOAL GRILL** Open bottom vent completely. Light large chimney starter filled with charcoal briquettes (6 quarts). When top coals are partially covered with ash, pour two-thirds evenly over grill, then pour remaining coals over half of grill. Set cooking grate in place, cover, and open lid vent completely. Heat grill until hot, about 5 minutes.

4B **FOR A GAS GRILL** Turn all burners to high; cover; and heat grill until hot, about 15 minutes. Leave primary burner on high and turn other burner(s) to medium-low.

5 Clean and oil cooking grate. Place chops on hotter side of grill and cook (covered if using gas) until browned on both sides, 4 to 8 minutes, flipping halfway through cooking. Slide chops to cooler side of grill and cook until pork registers 145 degrees, 8 to 16 minutes, flipping halfway through cooking.

6 Transfer chops to platter, tent with aluminum foil, and let rest for 5 minutes. Drizzle chops with remaining dressing. Serve with salad.

Grilled Lamb Shoulder Chops with Zucchini and Corn Salad

SERVES 4 **TIME** 45 minutes

Why This Recipe Works If you ever feel like you're in a bit of a rut when it comes to choosing which meat to grill, inexpensive lamb shoulder chops are a fun way to mix things up. They're a great match for the grill because their distinctive gutsy flavor holds up beautifully to the smoke. A simple marinade of olive oil, garlic, salt, and pepper infuses the chops with flavor. Ears of corn and planks of zucchini get brushed with a similar marinade (plus red pepper flakes for some kick); once grill-charred, they become the stars of a summery salad that gets a punch from fresh basil, lemon juice, and feta. We like our lamb shoulder chops cooked to medium, as this cut can be tough if cooked any less than that.

- ½ cup extra-virgin olive oil, divided
- 3 garlic cloves, minced, divided
- 2 teaspoons kosher salt, divided
- ¾ teaspoon pepper, divided
- 4 (8- to 12-ounce) lamb shoulder chops (blade or round bone), ¾ to 1 inch thick, trimmed
- ⅛ teaspoon red pepper flakes
- 2 ears corn, husks and silk removed
- 3 zucchini, sliced lengthwise into ½-inch-thick planks
- 2 tablespoons chopped fresh basil
- 4 teaspoons lemon juice
- 2 ounces feta cheese, crumbled (½ cup)

1 Whisk 3 tablespoons oil, one-third of garlic, 1 teaspoon salt, and ½ teaspoon pepper together in 13 by 9-inch baking dish. Add lamb chops to marinade and turn to coat.

2 In large bowl, whisk pepper flakes with remaining 5 tablespoons oil, remaining two-thirds garlic, remaining 1 teaspoon salt, and remaining ¼ teaspoon pepper. Brush corn with 1 tablespoon oil mixture. Add zucchini to remaining oil mixture in bowl and toss to coat.

3A **FOR A CHARCOAL GRILL** Open bottom vent completely. Light large chimney starter three-quarters filled with charcoal briquettes (4½ quarts). When top coals are partially covered with ash, pour evenly over grill. Set cooking grate in place, cover, and open lid vent completely. Heat grill until hot, about 5 minutes.

3B **FOR A GAS GRILL** Turn all burners to high; cover; and heat grill until hot, about 15 minutes. Turn all burners to medium-high.

4 Clean and oil cooking grate. Place corn and zucchini on grill, reserving remaining oil mixture in bowl. Cook (covered if using gas), turning as needed, until corn is lightly charred all over and zucchini is well browned and tender, 10 to 15 minutes. Transfer corn and zucchini to cutting board. Turn all burners to high if using gas.

5 Place chops on grill; cover; and cook until browned and meat registers 130 to 135 degrees (for medium), 8 to 12 minutes, flipping halfway through cooking. Transfer chops to serving platter, tent with aluminum foil, and let rest.

6 Cut kernels from cobs. Slice zucchini on bias ½ inch thick. Add vegetables, basil, and lemon juice to bowl with reserved oil mixture and toss to combine. Season with salt and pepper to taste. Transfer salad to serving platter and sprinkle with feta. Serve with lamb chops.

Grilled Pork Tenderloin with Broccolini and Hazelnut Browned Butter

SERVES 4 **TIME** 40 minutes

Why This Recipe Works Broccolini offers a bold counterpoint to mellow pork tenderloin in this quick meal from the grill, and the bridge that connects them is a rich browned butter sauce with toasty hazelnuts. The hint of char from grilling transforms broccolini's straightforward bitterness into something more intriguing. Browning the butter takes just a few minutes; we stir ribbons of fresh basil into the warm butter before pouring it over the grilled pork and broccolini. If any broccolini stems are thicker than ½ inch, cut them in half lengthwise to ensure that they cook at the same rate as the smaller stems.

- 2 (1-pound) pork tenderloins, trimmed
- 1 teaspoon kosher salt, divided
- ½ teaspoon black pepper, divided
- 1 pound broccolini, trimmed
- 2 tablespoons extra-virgin olive oil
- 8 tablespoons unsalted butter
- ½ cup blanched hazelnuts, chopped
- 3 tablespoons shredded fresh basil
- 1 tablespoon lemon juice

1 Sprinkle pork with ½ teaspoon salt and ¼ teaspoon pepper. Toss broccolini with oil, ¼ teaspoon salt, and remaining ¼ teaspoon pepper.

2A **FOR A CHARCOAL GRILL** Open bottom vent completely. Light large chimney starter filled with charcoal briquettes (6 quarts). When top coals are partially covered with ash, pour evenly over grill. Set cooking grate in place, cover, and open lid vent completely. Heat grill until hot, about 5 minutes.

2B **FOR A GAS GRILL** Turn all burners to high; cover; and heat grill until hot, about 15 minutes. Leave all burners on high.

3 Clean and oil cooking grate. Place pork on grill and cook until well browned and meat registers 140 degrees, about 15 minutes, turning as needed. After 5 minutes, place broccolini on grill and cook until charred and tender, 8 to 10 minutes, turning as needed. Transfer pork to carving board and broccolini to platter; tent both with aluminum foil.

4 Cook butter, hazelnuts, and remaining ¼ teaspoon salt in 10-inch skillet over medium heat until nuts are toasted and butter is lightly browned, about 4 minutes. Off heat, stir in basil and lemon juice. Slice pork and transfer to platter with broccolini. Drizzle sauce over pork and broccolini. Serve.

Grilled Honey-Ginger Pork Tenderloin and Plums

SERVES 4 **TIME** 40 minutes

Why This Recipe Works This dish is a stellar example of the affinity between pork and fruit, summer-style. We baste pork tenderloins with a luscious honey-ginger butter sauce as they grill, which gives them a bronzed exterior. The plums are simply halved and pitted and grilled cut sides down until juicy and caramelized. Fresh lemon juice, stirred into some reserved sauce, adds brightness and ties everything together.

- 6 tablespoons unsalted butter
- 1 tablespoon grated fresh ginger
- 2 teaspoons minced fresh thyme
- 2 tablespoons honey
- 2 (1-pound) pork tenderloins, trimmed
- 2 teaspoons kosher salt
- ½ teaspoon pepper
- ¼ teaspoon ground cinnamon
- 4 plums, halved and pitted
- 1 tablespoon lemon juice

1 Melt butter in small saucepan over medium heat. Stir in ginger and thyme and cook until fragrant, about 30 seconds. Off heat, whisk in honey. Measure 2 tablespoons sauce into small bowl; set aside for serving. Cover remaining sauce in saucepan to keep warm.

2 Pat pork dry with paper towels and sprinkle with salt, pepper, and cinnamon.

3A **FOR A CHARCOAL GRILL** Open bottom vent completely. Light large chimney starter filled with charcoal briquettes (6 quarts). When top coals are partially covered with ash, pour evenly over grill. Set cooking grate in place, cover, and open lid vent completely. Heat grill until hot, about 5 minutes.

3B **FOR A GAS GRILL** Turn all burners to high; cover; and heat grill until hot, about 15 minutes. Leave all burners on high.

GRILLED HONEY-GINGER PORK TENDERLOIN AND PLUMS

4 Clean and oil cooking grate. Place tenderloins on grill and cook (covered if using gas) until browned on all sides and pork registers 140 degrees, 12 to 14 minutes, turning as needed. Brush with warm sauce and cook for 1 minute. Transfer pork to carving board, tent with aluminum foil, and let rest while cooking plums.

5 Lay plums cut side down on grill and cook until lightly caramelized, 2 to 4 minutes. Transfer to serving platter. Slice pork and transfer to serving platter. Pour any accumulated juices into reserved butter mixture and stir in lemon juice. Drizzle pork and plums with sauce. Serve.

Grilled Spice-Rubbed Pork Tenderloin with Charred Fingerling Potato Salad

SERVES 4 **TIME** 45 minutes

Why This Recipe Works Easy to cook and easy to love, pork tenderloins anchor this upgraded meat-and-potatoes meal from the grill. A quick rub of smoked paprika and warm spices burnishes the pork tenderloins. The accompanying potato salad is a simple but sophisticated composition of skewered and grilled fingerling potatoes, roasted red peppers, pecans, and scallions. Pulling the pork off the grill at 145 degrees and letting it rest ensures a juicy roast with a rosy center. Fingerling potatoes with a 1-inch diameter work best in this recipe; if they are thinner, you may not be able to skewer them with the cut sides facing down. You can substitute small, halved red potatoes, if necessary. You can substitute white wine vinegar for the white balsamic vinegar. You will need four 12-inch metal skewers for this recipe.

- 1½ pounds fingerling potatoes, unpeeled, halved lengthwise
- ¼ cup vegetable oil, divided
- 2½ teaspoons kosher salt, divided
- 1¼ teaspoons pepper, divided
- 1 tablespoon packed brown sugar
- 2½ teaspoons smoked paprika
- ⅛ teaspoon ground cinnamon
- ⅛ teaspoon ground allspice
- 2 (1-pound) pork tenderloins, trimmed
- 2 tablespoons white balsamic vinegar
- ¾ cup jarred roasted red peppers, sliced thin
- ½ cup pecans, toasted and chopped
- 2 scallions, sliced thin

1 Toss potatoes with 1 tablespoon oil, ½ teaspoon salt, and ¼ teaspoon pepper. Cover and microwave until softened, 6 to 8 minutes, stirring halfway through cooking. Drain potatoes well, then thread, cut side down, onto four 12-inch metal skewers.

2 Meanwhile, mix sugar, paprika, cinnamon, allspice, remaining 2 teaspoons salt, and remaining 1 teaspoon pepper together in bowl. Measure out 2 teaspoons spice mixture and set aside for salad. Pat pork dry with paper towels and rub evenly with remaining spice mixture.

3A FOR A CHARCOAL GRILL Open bottom vent completely. Light large chimney starter three-quarters filled with charcoal briquettes (4½ quarts). When top coals are partially covered with ash, pour evenly over grill. Set cooking grate in place, cover, and open lid vent completely. Heat grill until hot, about 5 minutes.

3B FOR A GAS GRILL Turn all burners to high; cover; and heat grill until hot, about 15 minutes. Turn all burners to medium-high.

4 Clean and oil cooking grate. Place pork and potatoes on grill. Cook (covered if using gas) until pork and potatoes are well browned on all sides and pork registers 145 degrees, 8 to 15 minutes, turning as needed. Transfer pork to carving board and potatoes to platter; tent both with aluminum foil.

5 Whisk vinegar, remaining 3 tablespoons oil, and reserved spice mixture together in large bowl. Carefully slide potatoes off skewers into bowl and add red peppers, pecans, and scallions. Toss potatoes gently to combine and season with salt and pepper to taste. Cut pork into ½-inch-thick slices. Serve with salad.

Pork Tenderloin and Peach Kebabs with Brown Rice Salad

SERVES 4 **TIME** 1 hour

Why This Recipe Works Pork and peaches were made for each other—and for the grill. Cutting mild pork tenderloin and juicy summer peaches into bite-size pieces and grilling them on skewers makes this delicious duo easy to serve and eat alongside a light but hearty brown rice and arugula salad. We cook the rice for the salad pasta-style, so it's ready in just 25 minutes. A sweet and mustardy balsamic mixture makes a quick marinade for the pork and a savory dressing for the salad. You will need seven 12-inch metal skewers for this recipe. Top the salad with chopped toasted pecans for added crunch.

- 1 cup long-grain brown rice
- 3½ teaspoons kosher salt, divided, plus salt for cooking rice
- 6 tablespoons balsamic vinegar
- 2 tablespoons packed brown sugar
- 2 tablespoons Dijon mustard
- ½ teaspoon pepper
- ¼ cup extra-virgin olive oil, divided
- 2 (12-ounce) pork tenderloins, trimmed and cut into 1-inch chunks
- 2 teaspoons minced fresh rosemary
- 2 peaches, halved, pitted, and cut into 1-inch chunks
- 5 ounces (5 cups) baby arugula

1 Bring 2 quarts water to boil in large saucepan over medium-high heat. Add rice and 2 teaspoons salt and cook, stirring occasionally, until rice is tender, about 25 minutes. Drain rice through fine-mesh strainer and rinse under cold water until chilled. Drain well and set aside.

GRILLED SPICE-RUBBED PORK TENDERLOIN WITH CHARRED FINGERLING POTATO SALAD

2 Meanwhile, whisk vinegar, sugar, mustard, pepper, and 2½ teaspoons salt together in large bowl. Measure ¼ cup mixture into separate large bowl, whisk in 3 tablespoons oil, and set aside for salad. Add pork, rosemary, and remaining 1 teaspoon salt to remaining mixture and toss to coat; let sit for 10 minutes.

3 Thread pork onto four 12-inch metal skewers. Thread peaches onto three 12-inch metal skewers and brush with remaining 1 tablespoon oil.

4A **FOR A CHARCOAL GRILL** Open bottom vent completely. Light large chimney starter filled with charcoal briquettes (6 quarts). When top coals are partially covered with ash, pour evenly over grill. Set cooking grate in place, cover, and open lid vent completely. Heat grill until hot, about 5 minutes.

4B **FOR A GAS GRILL** Turn all burners to high; cover; and heat grill until hot, about 15 minutes. Leave all burners on high.

5 Clean and oil cooking grate. Place pork and peach skewers on grill and cook until well charred on all sides and meat registers 140 degrees, 6 to 10 minutes, turning as needed. Transfer to platter. Add arugula and cooked rice to reserved vinaigrette and toss to combine. Season with salt and pepper to taste. Serve with pork and peaches.

Pinchos Morunos (Spanish Grilled Pork Kebabs)

SERVES 4 as a main dish or 8 as an appetizer
TIME 45 minutes plus 30 minutes brining

Why This Recipe Works Pinchos morunos is typically served in Spain as part of a tapas spread, but it works equally well as an entrée. We use convenient, tender country-style ribs in our version. To increase juiciness, we brine the pork briefly before cutting it into cubes and coating it with a robust spice paste. Because country-style ribs contain a mix of lighter loin meat and darker shoulder meat, we grill the light meat and dark meat on separate skewers so that each can cook to its ideal temperature. You will need four or five 12-inch metal skewers for this recipe. Look for country-style ribs with an even distribution of light and dark meat. If your pork is enhanced, do not brine it in step 1. This recipe was developed using Diamond Crystal kosher salt. If you have Morton kosher salt, which is denser, use 4½ tablespoons in the brine.

- 6 tablespoons kosher salt for brining
- 2 pounds boneless country-style pork ribs, trimmed
- ¼ cup vegetable oil
- 2 tablespoons lemon juice, plus lemon wedges for serving
- 6 garlic cloves, minced
- 1 tablespoon grated fresh ginger
- 2 teaspoons minced fresh oregano, divided
- 2 teaspoons smoked paprika
- 1 teaspoon ground coriander
- 1 teaspoon kosher salt
- ½ teaspoon ground cumin
- ½ teaspoon pepper
- ¼ teaspoon cayenne pepper

1 Dissolve 6 tablespoons salt in 1½ quarts cold water in large container. Submerge ribs in brine, cover, and let sit at room temperature for 30 minutes. Meanwhile, whisk oil, lemon juice, garlic, ginger, 1 teaspoon oregano, paprika, coriander, salt, cumin, pepper, and cayenne together in small bowl.

2 Remove pork from brine and pat dry with paper towels. Cut ribs into 1-inch chunks; place dark meat and light meat in separate bowls. Divide spice paste proportionately between bowls and toss to coat. Thread light and dark meat separately onto four or five 12-inch metal skewers (do not crowd pieces).

3A **FOR A CHARCOAL GRILL** Open bottom vent completely. Light large chimney starter filled with charcoal briquettes (6 quarts). When top coals are partially covered with ash, pour evenly over half of grill. Set cooking grate in place, cover, and open lid vent completely. Heat grill until hot, about 5 minutes.

3B **FOR A GAS GRILL** Turn all burners to high; cover; and heat grill until hot, about 15 minutes. Leave primary burner on high and turn off other burner(s).

4 Clean and oil cooking grate. Place dark meat on hotter side of grill and cook for 6 minutes. Turn dark meat, add light meat to hotter side of grill, and cook for 4 minutes. Turn all kebabs and continue to cook until well charred and dark meat registers 155 degrees and light meat registers 140 degrees, 4 to 8 minutes, turning as needed.

5 Transfer pork to serving platter, tent with aluminum foil, and let rest for 5 minutes. Remove pork from skewers, toss to combine, and sprinkle with remaining 1 teaspoon oregano. Serve, passing lemon wedges separately.

PINCHOS MORUNOS

The Dark (and Light) Side of Country-Style Ribs

These meaty, tender, boneless ribs are cut from the backbone where the shoulder meets the loin, and contain meat from both regions. Because the shoulder muscle uses energy for extended periods, it's rich in fat, which acts as fuel, and the red protein myoglobin, which accounts for its darker color. The lesser-worked loin area is leaner and lighter. The dark meat can be cooked to a higher temperature and still stay juicy, but the leaner light meat needs to be cooked to a lower temperature or it will be dry. Butchers usually cut them into individual ribs and package several ribs together.

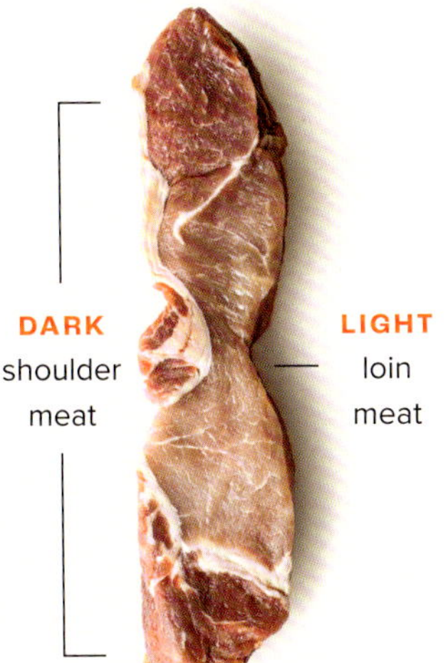

Grilled Pork Kebabs with Hoisin and Five-Spice

SERVES 4 **TIME** 50 minutes

Why This Recipe Works Kebabs amplify the appeal of glazed grilled pork tenderloin by increasing the pork's surface area, which allows lots of space for flavorful char. We salt the meat before cooking, which helps it hold on to moisture, and make a mixture of thick, sweet hoisin sauce and five-spice powder to flavor the skewers. We add cornstarch to the hoisin mixture to help it cling to the pork, and we reserve a small amount of the glaze to brush on halfway through grilling. Thanks to the cornstarch and the second glaze addition, each piece of moist, juicy pork boasts crusty char and a sticky coating. Because this is the kind of meal that you can put into heavy rotation, we've made a spicy-sweet variation and an American barbecue version. You will need four 12-inch metal skewers for this recipe. Spraying the meat with oil not only minimizes sticking but also helps the five-spice powder bloom, preventing a raw spice flavor.

- 2 (12-ounce) pork tenderloins, trimmed, and cut into 1-inch chunks
- 1 teaspoon kosher salt
- 1½ teaspoons five-spice powder
- ¾ teaspoon garlic powder
- ½ teaspoon cornstarch
- 4½ tablespoons hoisin sauce
- Vegetable oil spray
- 2 scallions, sliced thin

1 Toss pork with salt in large bowl and let sit at room temperature for 20 minutes. Meanwhile, combine five-spice powder, garlic powder, and cornstarch in bowl, then stir in hoisin. Measure out 1½ tablespoons hoisin mixture and set aside for grilling.

2 Toss pork with remaining hoisin mixture. Thread pork onto four 12-inch metal skewers, leaving ¼ inch between pieces. Spray meat generously with oil spray.

3A **FOR A CHARCOAL GRILL** Open bottom vent completely. Light large chimney starter filled with charcoal briquettes (6 quarts). When top coals are partially covered with ash, pour evenly over half of grill. Set cooking grate in place, cover, and open lid vent completely. Heat grill until hot, about 5 minutes.

3B **FOR A GAS GRILL** Turn all burners to high; cover; and heat grill until hot, about 15 minutes. Leave primary burner on high and turn off other burner(s).

GRILLED PORK KEBABS WITH HOISIN AND FIVE-SPICE

SHISH KEBAB WITH MINT, ROSEMARY, AND GARLIC MARINADE

4 Clean and oil cooking grate. Place skewers on hotter side of grill and cook until well charred, 3 to 4 minutes. Turn skewers; brush with reserved hoisin mixture; and continue to cook until well charred and meat registers 145 degrees, 3 to 4 minutes. Transfer to serving platter, tent with aluminum foil, and let rest for 5 minutes. Sprinkle with scallions and serve.

VARIATIONS

Grilled Pork Kebabs with Sweet Sriracha Glaze

Substitute 3 tablespoons packed brown sugar and 1½ tablespoons sriracha for five-spice powder, garlic powder, and hoisin sauce. Increase cornstarch to 1 teaspoon. Substitute ¼ cup minced fresh cilantro for scallions.

Grilled Pork Kebabs with Barbecue Glaze

Substitute 3 tablespoons ketchup, 1½ tablespoons packed brown sugar, 1 teaspoon chili powder, ¼ teaspoon liquid smoke, and pinch cayenne pepper for five-spice powder, garlic powder, and hoisin sauce. Increase cornstarch to ¾ teaspoon. Omit scallions.

Shish Kebab with Mint, Rosemary, and Garlic Marinade

SERVES 4 to 6 **TIME** 45 minutes plus 2 hours marinating

Why This Recipe Works When shish kebab is grilled just right, the chunks of lamb are well browned and the vegetables are crisp and tender. Choosing the components carefully will get you the best results. The shank end of a boneless leg of lamb is a great choice for shish kebab: It's inexpensive, requires little trimming, and yields a generous amount of meat. Red onions and bell peppers both work well with the timing and heat required to cook the lamb; plus, they add color and flavor to the kebabs without needing any special attention. The marinade is where you can have fun with this dish; we've got four delicious variations to choose from. A 2-hour soak gives the kebabs good flavor, but you can marinate them for 12 hours, or overnight. You will need twelve 12-inch metal skewers for this recipe.

MARINADE

- 10 fresh mint leaves
- 1½ teaspoons chopped fresh rosemary
- ½ tablespoon grated lemon zest plus 2 tablespoons juice
- 3 garlic cloves, peeled
- ½ cup extra-virgin olive oil
- 2 teaspoons kosher salt
- ⅛ teaspoon pepper

SHISH KEBAB

- 2¼ pounds boneless leg of lamb, trimmed, pulled apart at seams, and cut into 1-inch pieces
- 1 large red onion, cut into 1-inch pieces, 3 layers thick (see page 73)
- 3 bell peppers (1 red, 1 yellow, and 1 orange), stemmed, seeded, and cut into 1-inch pieces
- Lemon or lime wedges (optional)

1 FOR THE MARINADE Process all ingredients in food processor until smooth, about 1 minute, stopping to scrape down bowl as needed.

2 FOR THE SHISH KEBAB Combine marinade and lamb in 1-gallon zipper-lock bag and toss to coat; press out as much air as possible and seal bag. Refrigerate for at least 2 hours or up to 24 hours, flipping bag occasionally.

3 Remove lamb from marinade and pat dry with paper towels. Thread lamb, onion, and bell pepper tightly onto twelve 12-inch metal skewers in alternating pattern.

4A FOR A CHARCOAL GRILL Open bottom vent completely. Light large chimney starter filled with charcoal briquettes (6 quarts). When top coals are partially covered with ash, pour evenly over grill, then spread additional 6 quarts unlit briquettes over lit coals. Set cooking grate in place, cover, and open lid vent completely. Heat grill until hot, about 5 minutes.

4B FOR A GAS GRILL Turn all burners to high; cover; and heat grill until hot, about 15 minutes. Leave all burners on high.

5 Clean and oil cooking grate. Place kebabs on grill. Cook (covered if using gas), turning as needed, until meat is well browned and registers 120 to 125 degrees (for medium-rare) or 130 to 135 degrees (for medium), 7 to 9 minutes. Transfer kebabs to serving platter and serve with lemon wedges, if using.

VARIATIONS

Shish Kebab with Sweet Curry-Buttermilk Marinade

Substitute following mixture for marinade: Whisk ¾ cup buttermilk, 1 tablespoon lemon juice, 3 minced garlic cloves, 1 tablespoon packed brown sugar, 1 tablespoon curry powder, 1 teaspoon red pepper flakes, 1 teaspoon ground coriander, 1 teaspoon chili powder, 1 teaspoon kosher salt, and ⅛ teaspoon pepper together in bowl.

Shish Kebab with Cilantro, Raisin, and Garam Masala Marinade

Substitute following mixture for marinade: Process ½ cup extra-virgin olive oil, ½ cup fresh cilantro leaves, ¼ cup raisins, 1½ tablespoons lemon juice, 3 peeled garlic cloves, 1 teaspoon kosher salt, ½ teaspoon garam masala, and ⅛ teaspoon pepper in food processor until smooth, about 1 minute.

Shish Kebab with Parsley, Ginger, and Warm Spices Marinade

Substitute following mixture for marinade: Process ½ cup extra-virgin olive oil, ½ cup fresh parsley leaves, 1 seeded and coarsely chopped jalapeño chile, 2 tablespoons grated fresh ginger, 3 peeled garlic cloves, 1 teaspoon ground cumin, 1 teaspoon ground cardamom, 1 teaspoon ground cinnamon, 1 teaspoon kosher salt, and ⅛ teaspoon pepper in food processor until smooth, about 1 minute.

Grilled Pork Tacos with Tomatillo-Avocado Salsa

SERVES 4 **TIME** 45 minutes

Why This Recipe Works Pork tenderloin makes a quick-cooking taco filling on the grill. For flavorful charring in every bite, we split tenderloins in half lengthwise to maximize their grilling surface area, and we rub them with a tasty mixture of honey, lime zest, and coriander to perk up their mild flavor and increase browning. There's plenty of room on the grill to throw on some tomatillos, onions, and avocado at the same time; processed along with lime juice and cilantro, the grilled vegetables make a smoky-tangy salsa to top the pork. Serve with sliced jalapeños and crumbled cotija cheese.

GRILLED PORK TACOS WITH TOMATILLO-AVOCADO SALSA

2 tablespoons vegetable oil, divided
4 teaspoons kosher salt, divided
1 teaspoon grated lime zest plus 1 tablespoon juice
1 teaspoon honey
1 teaspoon ground coriander
2 (1-pound) pork tenderloins, trimmed and sliced in half lengthwise
8 ounces tomatillos, husks and stems removed, rinsed well and dried
1 avocado, halved and pitted
1 small onion (½ cut into 1-inch-thick wedges through root end, ½ chopped fine)
8–10 (6-inch) flour tortillas
¾ cup chopped fresh cilantro, divided

1 Combine 1 tablespoon oil, 2 teaspoons salt, lime zest, honey, and coriander in small bowl. Pat pork dry with paper towels and rub with seasoning mixture. Brush tomatillos, cut sides of avocado, and onion wedges with remaining 1 tablespoon oil and sprinkle with 1 teaspoon salt.

2A **FOR A CHARCOAL GRILL** Open bottom vent completely. Light large chimney starter filled with charcoal briquettes (6 quarts). When top coals are partially covered with ash, pour evenly over grill. Set cooking grate in place, cover, and open lid vent completely. Heat grill until hot, about 5 minutes.

2B **FOR A GAS GRILL** Turn all burners to high; cover; and heat grill until hot, about 15 minutes. Leave all burners on high.

3 Place pork, tomatillos, avocado (cut sides down), and onion wedges on grill. Cook (covered if using gas) until vegetables are charred and tender and pork registers 140 degrees, 6 to 12 minutes, flipping as needed. Transfer to cutting board and tent with aluminum foil.

4 Working in batches, grill tortillas, flipping as needed, until warm and soft, about 1 minute; wrap tightly in foil to keep soft.

5 Using spoon, scoop avocado flesh into food processor. Add lime juice, ¼ cup cilantro, tomatillos, onion wedges, and remaining 1 teaspoon salt and pulse until coarsely chopped, 4 to 6 pulses. Slice pork thin, arrange on tortillas, and top with salsa, chopped onion, and remaining ½ cup cilantro. Serve.

Tacos al Pastor

SERVES 8 to 10 **TIME** 2 hours plus 1 hour marinating

Why This Recipe Works Tacos al pastor boast a long history and an irresistible combination of spicy-sweet flavors designed to satisfy a hungry crowd. Traditionally, thin slices of marinated pork are layered on a rotating spit and roasted in front of an open flame; this recipe uses boneless pork butt roast, cut into thick "steaks," to make cooking the tacos a backyard-friendly event. First, the pork marinates in a potent paste of toasted guajillo and ancho chiles, garlic, pineapple juice, vinegar, and oregano. Next, the pork cooks slowly over indirect heat, ensuring moist and tender meat, and then the steaks get a final sear over a hot fire to char the outer edges. Lightly grilled pineapple adds sweet juiciness, while raw onion, cilantro, and lime punch things up. Slice the meat extra-thin to mimic the original, serve it with corn tortillas, and watch it disappear. Note that 1½ ounces guajillos is about six chiles; 1 ounce anchos is about two chiles. Pork butt roast is also labeled Boston butt in the supermarket. This recipe was developed using Diamond Crystal kosher salt. If you have Morton kosher salt, which is denser, use 1½ tablespoons.

1½ ounces dried guajillo chiles, stemmed
1 ounce dried ancho chiles, stemmed
½ cup cider vinegar
½ cup pineapple juice
2 tablespoons kosher salt
4 garlic cloves, peeled
1 tablespoon dried oregano
2 teaspoons ground cumin
1½ teaspoons pepper
½ teaspoon ground cinnamon
1 (2½-pound) boneless pork butt roast, cut crosswise into 1½-inch-thick steaks
1 pineapple, peeled, quartered lengthwise, and cored, 3 quarters set aside for another use
24 (6-inch) corn tortillas
Finely chopped onion
Fresh cilantro leaves
Lime wedges

1 Using kitchen shears, cut guajillos and anchos in half lengthwise and discard seeds. Cut guajillos and anchos into 1-inch pieces. Toast chiles in 12-inch skillet over medium heat, stirring often, until fragrant and darkened slightly, about 6 minutes. Immediately transfer chiles to bowl and cover with hot water. Let sit until soft, about 5 minutes.

2 Using slotted spoon, lift guajillos and anchos from water and transfer to blender; discard soaking water. Add vinegar, pineapple juice, salt, garlic, oregano, cumin, pepper, and cinnamon and process until smooth, about 1 minute, scraping down sides of blender jar as needed. Measure out ¼ cup marinade and set aside for grilling.

3 Combine remaining marinade and pork in 1-gallon zipper-lock bag and toss to coat; press out as much air as possible and seal bag. Refrigerate for at least 1 hour or up to 24 hours. Before grilling, remove pork from marinade (do not pat dry).

4A **FOR A CHARCOAL GRILL** Open bottom vent completely. Light large chimney starter filled with charcoal briquettes (6 quarts). When top coals are partially covered with ash, pour evenly over half of grill. Set cooking grate in place, cover, and open lid vent completely. Heat grill until hot, about 5 minutes.

4B **FOR A GAS GRILL** Turn all burners to high; cover; and heat grill until hot, about 15 minutes. Leave primary burner on high and turn off other burners. (Adjust primary burner as needed to maintain grill temperature of 350 degrees.)

5 Clean and oil cooking grate. Place pork on cooler side of grill. Cover and cook until pork registers 150 degrees, 50 minutes to 1 hour 10 minutes.

6 Brush tops of steaks with 2 tablespoons reserved marinade, slide to hotter side of grill, and flip, marinade side down. Brush second side of steaks with remaining 2 tablespoons reserved marinade. Place pineapple on hotter side of grill next to steaks. Cook (covered if using gas), turning as needed, until pork is well charred and registers 175 degrees, 12 to 16 minutes for charcoal or 24 to 30 minutes for gas. Cook pineapple until warmed through, flipping as needed, about 10 minutes. Transfer pork and pineapple to wire rack set in rimmed baking sheet, tent with aluminum foil, and let rest for 15 minutes.

7 Working in batches, grill tortillas on hotter side of grill, flipping as needed, until warm and lightly charred, about 1 minute; wrap tightly in foil to keep soft. Transfer pork and pineapple to carving board and slice thin. Season with salt to taste. Divide pork and pineapple evenly among tortillas and top with onion and cilantro. Serve with lime wedges.

TACOS AL PASTOR

GRILLED PORK BÁNH MÌ

Grilled Pork Bánh Mì

SERVES 4 **TIME** 55 minutes

Why This Recipe Works The most traditional versions of the Vietnamese sandwich called bánh mì feature grilled pork and pâté layered in a baguette and topped with pickled vegetables, fresh herbs, and various condiments. To bring the essence of this classic street food to your backyard, we rub pork tenderloin with five-spice powder before grilling, and we stir up a spicy mayo for slathering on the bread. To make the quick pickles, toss carrot and daikon radish in a mixture of rice vinegar, sugar, sriracha, and fish sauce, which gives the vegetables a sweet-spicy-salty flavor. You can prep the remaining ingredients while the pickles marinate, and the sandwiches come together quickly after that. You can substitute six red radishes for the daikon, if desired.

- ½ cup unseasoned rice vinegar
- 3 tablespoons sugar
- 1 carrot, peeled and cut into 2-inch-long matchsticks
- 1 (6-inch) piece daikon radish, peeled and cut into 2-inch-long matchsticks
- ¼ cup fish sauce, divided
- 2 tablespoons sriracha, divided
- ¾ cup mayonnaise
- 1 (1-pound) pork tenderloin, trimmed
- 2 teaspoons five-spice powder
- 1 (24-inch) baguette, cut into four 6-inch pieces and split horizontally, toasted on grill if desired
- ½ English cucumber, halved lengthwise and sliced thin
- 1 cup fresh cilantro leaves

1 Combine vinegar and sugar in bowl and microwave until sugar dissolves, about 1½ minutes. Add carrot, daikon, 2 tablespoons fish sauce, and 1 tablespoon sriracha to bowl and toss to combine. Let sit for 15 minutes, then drain and set aside. Meanwhile, whisk mayonnaise, remaining 2 tablespoons fish sauce, and remaining 1 tablespoon sriracha together in second bowl; set aside. Rub pork with five-spice powder.

2A FOR A CHARCOAL GRILL Open bottom vent completely. Light large chimney starter filled with charcoal briquettes (6 quarts). When top coals are partially covered with ash, pour evenly over grill. Set cooking grate in place, cover, and open lid vent completely. Heat grill until hot, about 5 minutes.

2B FOR A GAS GRILL Turn all burners to high; cover; and heat grill until hot, about 15 minutes. Leave all burners on high.

3 Clean and oil cooking grate. Place pork on grill and cook (covered if using gas) until browned on all sides and registers 140 degrees, 12 to 14 minutes, turning as needed. Transfer to carving board, tent with aluminum foil, and let rest for 5 minutes.

4 Slice pork thin against grain. Spread mayonnaise mixture evenly on cut sides of baguette pieces. Divide pickled vegetables, pork, cucumber, and cilantro evenly among baguette bottoms, close sandwiches, and serve.

Grilled Rosemary Pork Loin

SERVES 6 to 8 **TIME** 1½ hours

Why This Recipe Works Boneless pork loin has a built-in self-baster: its fat cap. Scoring the fat encourages it to melt and moisten the meat as it grills. We flavor the roast from the inside by butterflying the loin; applying a savory paste of finely minced garlic, rosemary, parsley, and olive oil; and then rolling the meat up and tying it. In less than an hour on the grill, we have a browned, juicy roast fragrant with garlic and herbs. Look for a relatively short, wide roast (about 7 to 8 inches long and 4 to 5 inches wide). Freezing the pork for 30 minutes will make butterflying it much easier.

- ⅓ cup minced fresh parsley
- 1½ tablespoons minced fresh rosemary
- 2 garlic cloves, minced
- 3 tablespoons extra-virgin olive oil, divided
- 2½ teaspoons kosher salt, divided
- 1¼ teaspoons pepper, divided
- 1 (2½- to 3-pound) boneless pork loin roast, fat cap trimmed to ⅓ inch

1 Combine parsley, rosemary, garlic, 2 tablespoons oil, 1½ teaspoons salt, and ¾ teaspoon pepper in bowl. Cut shallow slits through fat cap, spaced ½ inch apart, in crosshatch pattern, being careful not to cut into meat. With roast fat side up, cut horizontally through meat, one-third above bottom, stopping ½ inch from edge. Open roast and press flat; 1 side will be twice as thick. Continue cutting thicker side of roast in half, stopping ½ inch from edge; open roast and press flat. If uneven, cover with plastic wrap and use meat pounder to even out.

GRILLED ROSEMARY PORK LOIN

2 Spread herb mixture over cut side of pork, leaving ½-inch border on sides. Roll pork tightly and tie at 1-inch intervals with kitchen twine. (Roast can be refrigerated for up to 24 hours.) Rub roast with remaining 1 tablespoon oil and sprinkle with remaining 1 teaspoon salt and remaining ½ teaspoon pepper.

3A **FOR A CHARCOAL GRILL** Open bottom vent completely. Light large chimney starter filled with charcoal briquettes (6 quarts). When top coals are partially covered with ash, pour evenly over half of grill. Set cooking grate in place, cover, and open lid vent completely. Heat grill until hot, about 5 minutes.

3B **FOR A GAS GRILL** Turn all burners to high; cover; and heat grill until hot, about 15 minutes. Leave primary burner on high and turn off other burner(s).

4 Clean and oil cooking grate. Place roast on hotter side of grill. Cook (covered if using gas) until well browned on all sides, about 12 minutes, turning as needed. Slide roast to cooler side of grill and flip fat side up. Cover and cook until meat registers 140 degrees, 35 to 45 minutes.

5 Transfer pork to carving board, tent with aluminum foil, and let rest for 15 to 20 minutes. Remove twine, cut into ½-inch-thick slices, and serve.

Butterflying a Pork Loin

1 Place roast fat side up on cutting board. Starting about 1 inch from cutting board, cut horizontally, stopping about ½ inch before edge.

2 Cut into thicker half of roast again, starting about 1 inch from cutting board and stopping about ½ inch before edge.

Grill-Roasted Bone-In Pork Rib Roast

SERVES 6 to 8 **TIME** 1½ hours plus 6½ hours salting and resting

Why This Recipe Works A pork rib roast makes an impressive, deeply flavorful, and—if you choose the right cut—simple centerpiece dish. A center-cut rib roast is ideal; because the meat is a single muscle attached along one side to the bones, there's no need to tie the roast for a tidy presentation. This roast cooks over indirect heat for the duration, yet still develops a mahogany crust—no high-temperature sear needed. It's important to position the roast away—but not too far away—from the coals or flames with the bones facing away from the fire. Letting the roast rest for a full 30 minutes after it finishes on the grill allows the meat to reabsorb some of the juices lost during cooking. For easier carving, have the butcher remove the tip of the chine bone and cut the remainder of the chine bone from between the ribs (a technique called scoring). If using a charcoal grill, you can substitute one wood chunk for the wood chip packet. This recipe was developed using Diamond Crystal kosher salt. If you have Morton kosher salt, which is denser, use 1 tablespoon.

1 (4- to 5-pound) center-cut bone-in pork rib roast, chine bone removed, fat trimmed to ¼ inch
4 teaspoons kosher salt
1½ teaspoons pepper
1 cup wood chips

1 Pat roast dry with paper towels. Cut ¼-inch-deep slits through fat cap, spaced 1-inch apart, in crosshatch pattern, being careful not to cut into meat. Rub salt all over roast and into slits. Wrap roast in plastic wrap and refrigerate for at least 6 hours or up to 24 hours.

2 Unwrap roast (do not pat dry) and sprinkle with pepper. Using large piece of heavy-duty aluminum foil, wrap wood chips in 8 by 4-inch foil packet. (Make sure chips do not poke holes in sides or bottom of packet.) Cut 2 evenly spaced 2-inch slits in top of packet.

3A **FOR A CHARCOAL GRILL** Open bottom vent halfway. Light large chimney starter filled with charcoal briquettes (6 quarts). When top coals are partially covered with ash, pour into steeply banked pile against side of grill. Place wood chip packet on coals. Set cooking grate in place, cover, and open lid vent halfway. Heat grill until hot and wood chips are smoking, about 5 minutes.

3B **FOR A GAS GRILL** Remove cooking grate and place wood chip packet directly on primary burner. Set cooking grate in place; turn all burners to high; cover; and heat grill until hot and wood chips are smoking, about 15 minutes. Leave primary burner on high and turn off other burner(s). (Adjust primary burner as needed to maintain grill temperature of 350 degrees.)

4 Clean and oil cooking grate. Place roast meat side up on cooler side of grill, with bones facing away from coals and flames. Cover (position lid vent over meat if using charcoal) and cook until meat registers 140 degrees, 1¼ to 1½ hours.

5 Transfer roast to carving board, tent with foil, and let rest for 30 minutes. Carve into thick slices by cutting between ribs. Serve.

Cuban-Style Grill-Roasted Pork

SERVES 8 to 10 **TIME** 6 to 7 hours plus 20 hours brining, seasoning, and resting

Why This Recipe Works Roast pork marinated in citrus juices, garlic, olive oil, and spices—a dish known as lechon asado—is a star of Cuban cuisine. Traditionally made by spit-roasting a whole pig, it boasts crackling-crisp skin and bold-flavored meat with a texture somewhere between a juicy, sliceable American pork roast and fall-apart-tender pulled pork. Our grilled version uses a picnic shoulder (aka pork shoulder), an inexpensive, fatty, bone-in cut with a generous amount of skin attached. For bold flavor, we start by brining the pork in a potent solution that includes two heads of garlic and orange juice; then, we rub a similarly flavored paste into slits cut all over the pork. To streamline cooking, we grill the pork until our supply of coals dies down and then finish it in the oven. This recipe was developed using Diamond Crystal kosher salt. If you have Morton kosher salt, which is denser, use 3 cups in the brine and 1½ tablespoons in the paste. Serve with rice, black beans, and fried plantains.

PORK

1 (7- to 8-pound) bone-in, skin-on pork picnic shoulder roast
4 cups orange juice (8 oranges)
3 cups sugar
4 cups kosher salt
2 garlic heads, unpeeled, cloves separated and crushed

PASTE

12 garlic cloves, chopped coarse
2 tablespoons ground cumin
2 tablespoons dried oregano
2 tablespoons kosher salt
1½ teaspoons pepper
6 tablespoons orange juice
2 tablespoons distilled white vinegar
2 tablespoons vegetable oil

MOJO SAUCE

½ cup extra-virgin olive oil
4 garlic cloves, minced to a paste
2 teaspoons kosher salt
½ teaspoon ground cumin
¼ cup distilled white vinegar
¼ cup orange juice
¼ teaspoon dried oregano
⅛ teaspoon pepper

1 **FOR THE PORK** Cut 1-inch-deep slits (1 inch long) all over roast, spaced about 2 inches apart. Combine 6 quarts cold water, orange juice, sugar, salt, and garlic in large container and whisk to dissolve salt and sugar. Submerge pork in brine, cover, and refrigerate for 18 to 24 hours. Remove pork from brine and pat dry with paper towels.

2 **FOR THE PASTE** Pulse garlic, cumin, oregano, salt, and pepper in food processor to coarse paste, about 10 pulses. With processor running, add orange juice, vinegar, and oil and process until smooth, about 20 seconds. Rub paste all over roast and into slits. Wrap roast in plastic wrap and let sit at room temperature for 1 hour.

3 **FOR THE SAUCE** Heat oil in medium saucepan over medium heat until shimmering. Stir in garlic, salt, and cumin and cook until fragrant, about 30 seconds. Off heat, whisk in vinegar, orange juice, oregano, and pepper. Transfer to bowl and let cool to room temperature. (Sauce can be refrigerated for up to 24 hours; bring to room temperature before serving.)

4A **FOR A CHARCOAL GRILL** Open bottom vent halfway. Light large chimney starter three-quarters filled with charcoal briquettes (4½ quarts). When top coals are partially covered with ash, pour into steeply banked pile against side of grill. Set cooking grate in place, cover, and open lid vent halfway. Heat grill until hot, about 5 minutes.

4B **FOR A GAS GRILL** Turn all burners to high; cover; and heat grill until hot, about 15 minutes. Turn primary burner to medium-high and turn off other burner(s). (Adjust primary burner as needed to maintain grill temperature of 325 degrees.)

5 Clean and oil cooking grate. Make two ½-inch folds on long side of 18-inch length of aluminum foil to form reinforced edge. Place foil in center of cooking grate, with reinforced edge over hotter side of grill. Place roast, skin side up, on cooler side of grill so that it covers about one-third of foil. Lift and bend edges to shield sides of pork, tucking in edges. Cover (position lid vent over meat if using charcoal) and cook for 2 hours. During final 20 minutes of grilling, adjust oven rack to lower-middle position and heat oven to 325 degrees.

6 Transfer pork to wire rack set in rimmed baking sheet. Roast pork in oven until skin is browned and crisp and meat registers 190 degrees, 3 to 4 hours.

7 Transfer roast to carving board and let rest for 1 hour. Remove skin in 1 large piece. Scrape off and discard fat from top of roast and from underside of skin. Cut meat away from bone in 3 or 4 large pieces, then slice ¼ inch thick. Cut skin into strips. Whisk sauce to recombine and serve with pork.

A Shield for the Roast

An aluminum foil shield keeps the pork roast from getting too dark on the side closest to the heat—no rotation required.

Grilled Rack of Lamb with Garlic and Herbs

SERVES 4 to 6 **TIME** 55 minutes

Why This Recipe Works Rack of lamb and the grill have great chemistry. The intense heat of the coals produces a fantastic crust and melts the meat's abundance of fat, distributing flavor throughout while imparting a smokiness that complements lamb's rich, gamy flavor. But the rendering fat can cause flare-ups that scorch the meat and impart sooty flavors, ruining this pricey cut. To solve this problem, we trim the excess fat from racks of lamb and stack the coals on the sides of the grill, creating a cooler center where the fat can safely render before we move the lamb over direct heat to brown the exterior. A simple wet rub of robust herbs and oil enhances the meat's flavor without overwhelming it and helps create a well-browned crust. While most racks of lamb are sold frenched (meaning part of each rib bone is exposed), chances are there will still be some extra fat between the bones. Remove the majority of this fat, leaving an inch at the top of the small eye of meat. Also, make sure that the chine bone running along the bottom of the rack has been removed so it will be easy to cut between the ribs after cooking. Ask the butcher to do this; it's very hard to cut off at home. We prefer domestic lamb here for its less gamy flavor and better fat marbling.

- 4 teaspoons vegetable oil, divided
- 4 teaspoons minced fresh rosemary
- 2 teaspoons minced fresh thyme
- 2 garlic cloves, minced
- 2 (1½- to 1¾-pound) racks of lamb, fat trimmed to ⅛ inch, bones frenched
- 1 teaspoon kosher salt
- ½ teaspoon pepper
- 1 (13 by 9-inch) disposable aluminum roasting pan (if using charcoal)

1 Combine 1 tablespoon oil, rosemary, thyme, and garlic in bowl; set aside for grilling. Pat lamb dry with paper towels, rub with remaining 1 teaspoon oil, and sprinkle with salt and pepper.

2A FOR A CHARCOAL GRILL Open bottom vent completely and place disposable pan in center of grill. Light large chimney starter filled with charcoal briquettes (6 quarts). When top coals are partially covered with ash, pour into 2 even piles on either side of disposable pan. Set cooking grate in place, cover, and open lid vent completely. Heat grill until hot, about 5 minutes.

2B FOR A GAS GRILL Turn all burners to high; cover; and heat grill until hot, about 15 minutes. Leave primary burner on high and turn off other burner(s).

3 Clean and oil cooking grate. Place racks, bone side up, on cooler part of grill with meaty side very close to, but not quite over, hotter part of grill. Cover and cook until meat is lightly browned, faint grill marks appear, and fat has begun to render, 8 to 10 minutes.

4 Flip racks bone side down, slide to hotter part of grill, and cook until well browned, 3 to 4 minutes. Brush racks with herb mixture, flip bone side up, and cook until well browned, 3 to 4 minutes.

5 Stand up racks, leaning them against each other for support, and cook until bottoms are well browned and meat registers 120 to 125 degrees (for medium-rare), 3 to 8 minutes.

6 Transfer racks to carving board, tent with aluminum foil, and let rest for 15 to 20 minutes. Cut between ribs to separate chops and serve.

GRILLED RACK OF LAMB WITH GARLIC AND HERBS

Grilling Rack of Lamb

1 Place lamb racks, bone side up, on cooler part of grill with meaty side close to, but not quite over, hot coals. Cover and cook until meat is lightly browned.

2 Flip racks bone side down and slide to hotter part of grill. Cook until well browned, then brush with herb mixture, flip racks, and brown well on second side.

3 Stand racks up, leaning them against each other for support, and cook until bottom is well browned.

GRILLED BUTTERFLIED LEG OF LAMB

Grilled Butterflied Leg of Lamb

SERVES 6 to 8 **TIME** 1 hour

Why This Recipe Works When you want the impressive presentation and unforgettable flavor of a grilled leg of lamb, but at a slightly lower difficulty setting, a butterflied cut is the way to go. Simply a boneless leg of lamb that has been pounded to an even thickness, this cut is easy to cook evenly and thick enough to carve into attractive slices when done. Turning the meat regularly during grilling produces a crust that's nicely caramelized, not blackened. For the best-looking slices, slice the meat thin on an angle, disregarding the grain. We prefer domestic lamb here for its less gamy flavor and better fat marbling. Boneless leg of lamb can be sold wrapped in netting and might be a single piece or a mix of smaller pieces. For this recipe you'll want a single piece; ask your butcher if you're unsure what's under the netting. Often, the butcher will pound and trim the lamb for you. Sweet Mint-Almond Relish (page 406) makes a nice accompaniment.

- 1 (3½- to 4-pound) boneless leg of lamb, trimmed
- 2 tablespoons vegetable oil
- 2 teaspoons kosher salt
- 1 teaspoon pepper

1 Cover lamb with plastic wrap and pound to even thickness. Pat lamb dry with paper towels, then rub with oil and sprinkle with salt and pepper.

2A FOR A CHARCOAL GRILL Open bottom vent completely. Light large chimney starter filled with charcoal briquettes (6 quarts). When top coals are partially covered with ash, pour evenly over half of grill. Set cooking grate in place, cover, and open lid vent completely. Heat grill until hot, about 5 minutes.

2B FOR A GAS GRILL Turn all burners to high; cover; and heat grill until hot, about 15 minutes. Leave primary burner on high and turn other burner(s) to medium.

3 Clean and oil cooking grate. Place lamb fat side down on cooler side of grill. Cover and cook until well browned, about 10 minutes, rotating meat halfway through cooking.

4 Flip lamb fat side up and continue to cook, covered, on cooler side of grill for 5 minutes. Slide lamb to hotter side of grill; cover; and cook until meat registers 120 to 125 degrees (for medium-rare) or 130 to 135 degrees (for medium), 5 to 15 minutes.

5 Transfer lamb to carving board, tent with aluminum foil, and let rest for 20 minutes. Slice lamb thin on bias and serve.

Grilled Bone-In Leg of Lamb with Charred-Scallion Sauce

SERVES 10 to 12 **TIME** 2½ to 3 hours plus 12½ hours marinating and resting

Why This Recipe Works This cut is grand enough for any celebration, but its tapered shape means that, when cooked over a fire, the meat takes on a wide range of doneness. We start the leg of lamb on the cooler side of a half-grill fire before searing it over the hotter side to give the roast a charred exterior and a lovely medium-rare interior. A garlicky, lemony herb paste seasons the meat inside and out. For a sauce befitting this roast, we combine grill-charred scallions with a mixture of extra-virgin olive oil, red wine vinegar, parsley, and garlic. This recipe was developed using Diamond Crystal kosher salt. If you have Morton kosher salt, which is denser, use 1½ tablespoons in the rub in step 1. We prefer domestic lamb here for its less gamy flavor and better fat marbling. For an accurate temperature reading in step 5, insert your thermometer into the thickest part of the leg until you hit bone, then pull it about ½ inch away from the bone.

LAMB

- 12 garlic cloves, minced
- 2 tablespoons vegetable oil
- 2 tablespoons kosher salt
- 1½ tablespoons pepper
- 1 tablespoon fresh thyme leaves
- 1 tablespoon dried oregano
- 2 teaspoons finely grated lemon zest
- 1 teaspoon ground coriander
- 1 (8-pound) bone-in leg of lamb, trimmed

SCALLION SAUCE

- ¾ cup extra-virgin olive oil
- ¼ cup chopped fresh parsley
- 1 tablespoon red wine vinegar
- 2 garlic cloves, minced
- 1 teaspoon pepper
- ¾ teaspoon kosher salt
- ¼ teaspoon red pepper flakes
- 12 scallions, trimmed

1 FOR THE LAMB Combine garlic, oil, salt, pepper, thyme, oregano, lemon zest, and coriander in bowl. Place lamb on rimmed baking sheet and rub all over with garlic paste. Cover with plastic wrap and refrigerate for at least 12 hours or up to 24 hours. Before grilling, unwrap lamb (do not pat dry).

2 FOR THE SCALLION SAUCE Combine oil, parsley, vinegar, garlic, pepper, salt, and pepper flakes in bowl; set aside for serving.

GRILLED BONE-IN LEG OF LAMB WITH CHARRED-SCALLION SAUCE

ROTISSERIE LEG OF LAMB WITH CAULIFLOWER AND GRAPE SALAD

3A FOR A CHARCOAL GRILL Open bottom vent halfway. Light large chimney starter filled with charcoal briquettes (6 quarts). When top coals are partially covered with ash, pour evenly over half of grill. Set cooking grate in place, cover, and open lid vent halfway. Heat grill until hot, about 5 minutes.

3B FOR A GAS GRILL Turn all burners to high; cover; and heat grill until hot, about 15 minutes. Leave primary burner on high and turn off other burner(s). (Adjust primary burner as needed to maintain grill temperature between 350 and 400 degrees.)

4 Clean and oil cooking grate. Place scallions on hotter side of grill. Cook (covered if using gas) until lightly charred on both sides, about 6 minutes, turning as needed. Transfer scallions to plate.

5 Place lamb fat side up on cooler side of grill, parallel to fire. (If using gas, it may be necessary to angle thicker end of lamb toward hotter side of grill to fit.) Cover grill (position lid vent over lamb if using charcoal) and cook until thickest part of meat (½ inch from bone) registers 120 degrees, 1¼ hours to 1¾ hours.

6 Transfer lamb, fat side down, to hotter side of grill. Cook (covered if using gas) until well browned, 7 to 9 minutes. Transfer lamb fat side up to carving board, tent with aluminum foil, and let rest for 30 minutes.

7 Cut scallions into ½-inch pieces and stir into reserved oil mixture. Season sauce with salt and pepper to taste. Slice lamb thin and serve with sauce.

Rotisserie Leg of Lamb with Cauliflower and Grape Salad

SERVES 8 to 10 **TIME** 2½ hours plus 12½ hours chilling and resting

Why This Recipe Works A leg of lamb on the rotisserie is a culinary work of art. The key to making this cut taste great and remain juicy is a good, long salting period in a potent rub of garlic, anchovies, mustard, and rosemary. As the lamb turns on its spit, its flavorful juices and rendered fat drip onto a pan of cauliflower, onion, and grapes, which form the base of an elegant salad. This recipe uses a semi-boneless leg of lamb, which is what you most commonly find at the market; if, by chance, the leg has the full bone, have the butcher remove the hipbone and aitchbone for you. This recipe was developed for a 22-inch or larger kettle-style charcoal grill. You will need a motorized rotisserie attachment and two 13 by 9-inch disposable aluminum roasting pans.

LAMB AND SALAD

- ½ cup plus 2 tablespoons extra-virgin olive oil, divided
- 12 garlic cloves (6 halved, 6 minced)
- 4 sprigs fresh rosemary, cut into thirds, plus 2 teaspoons minced fresh rosemary
- 8 anchovy fillets (4 cut into thirds, 4 minced)
- 4¾ teaspoons kosher salt, divided
- 1 tablespoon Dijon mustard, divided
- 2 teaspoons grated lemon zest
- 1 teaspoon pepper
- 1 (6- to 8-pound) semi-boneless leg of lamb, fat trimmed to ¼ inch
- 1 large head cauliflower (3 pounds), cored and cut into 1-inch florets
- 1 red onion, halved and sliced thin
- 2 (13 by 9-inch) disposable aluminum roasting pans
- 9 ounces seedless red grapes
- 3 tablespoons balsamic vinegar
- 10 ounces (10 cups) baby arugula
- 1 fennel bulb, ¼ cup fronds chopped coarse, stalks discarded, bulb halved, cored, and sliced thin

SOUR CREAM SAUCE

- 1 cup sour cream
- ½ cup minced fresh parsley
- ¼ cup Dijon mustard

1 **FOR THE LAMB AND SALAD** Combine 2 tablespoons oil, minced garlic, minced rosemary, minced anchovies, 4 teaspoons salt, 2 teaspoons mustard, lemon zest, and pepper in bowl. Place lamb leg on rimmed baking sheet. Using paring knife, make twelve 1-inch-deep incisions into fat side of lamb. Stuff each opening with 1 garlic clove half, 1 piece rosemary sprig, and 1 piece anchovy. Tie lamb with kitchen twine at 1½-inch intervals and rub with garlic paste. Cover and refrigerate for at least 12 hours or up to 24 hours.

2 Thread rotisserie skewer lengthwise through center of lamb leg; center leg on skewer. Attach rotisserie forks to skewer and insert tines into lamb; secure forks by tightening screws. Toss cauliflower and onion with 2 tablespoons oil and ¼ teaspoon salt in disposable pan. Scatter grapes over top.

3 Open bottom vent of charcoal grill halfway and place second disposable pan in center of grill. Light large chimney starter filled with charcoal briquettes (6 quarts). When top coals are partially covered with ash, pour into 2 even piles on either side of disposable pan. Position rotisserie motor attachment on grill so that skewer runs parallel to coals. Cover; open lid vent halfway; and heat grill until hot, about 5 minutes.

4 Set pan with vegetables into pan in grill. Attach rotisserie skewer to motor and start motor. Cover and cook until thickest part of leg, ½ inch from bone, registers 120 to 125 degrees (for medium-rare), 1¼ hours to 1¾ hours.

5 Transfer lamb, still on skewer, to carving board. Transfer pan with vegetables to wire rack. Tent lamb with aluminum foil and let rest for 30 minutes.

6 **FOR THE SOUR CREAM SAUCE** Combine all ingredients in bowl and set aside for serving. (Sauce can be refrigerated for up to 2 days.)

7 Whisk vinegar, remaining ½ teaspoon salt, and remaining 1 teaspoon mustard together in large bowl. Whisking constantly, drizzle in remaining 6 tablespoons oil. Add grill-roasted vegetables, arugula, and sliced fennel and toss to combine. Season with salt and pepper to taste and sprinkle with fennel fronds. Using large wad of paper towels in each hand, carefully remove rotisserie forks and skewer from lamb. Carve lamb from bone and slice thin. Serve with salad and sauce.

VARIATION

Rotisserie Leg of Lamb with Cauliflower and Grape Salad for a Gas Grill

Cut onion into ½-inch-thick rounds, cut cauliflower into 2-inch pieces, and halve grapes. Brush onion and cauliflower with 2 tablespoons oil and sprinkle with ¼ teaspoon salt; set aside vegetables and grapes while cooking lamb. Remove cooking grate. Position rotisserie motor attachment on grill. Turn all burners to high; cover; and heat grill until hot, about 15 minutes. Turn outside burners to medium and center burner off (if using 2-burner grill, turn both burners to medium) and cook lamb as directed in step 4. (Adjust burners as needed to maintain grill temperature between 350 and 375 degrees.) While lamb rests, set cooking grate in place; turn all burners to medium-high; and heat grill until hot, about 5 minutes. Grill onion and cauliflower, covered, until lightly browned and tender, 10 to 15 minutes, turning as needed. Chop vegetables before tossing with arugula and fennel in step 7. Sprinkle salad with grapes before serving.

3

Poultry

SIMPLE CHICKEN PARTS

MARINATED, GLAZED, AND SAUCED

MAKE IT A MEAL

SKEWERS, TACOS, SANDWICHES, AND MORE

WHOLE CHICKENS, CORNISH GAME HENS, AND TURKEY

IN DEPTH

Roast Poultry Outdoors

If you love the flavor of roasted chicken but don't want to heat up your kitchen, grill roasting is the way to go. This relatively gentle grilling method relies on indirect heat and a closed lid to let larger cuts of meat come up to temperature without burning, and it produces whole chickens, game hens, turkeys, and turkey breasts with juicy meat and crispy, lightly charred skin. (It works wonders with other roasts, such as bone-in pork rib roast and beef tenderloin, as well.) Here's how to grill-roast.

BUILD WITH BRIQUETTES

For charcoal grills, regular briquettes are better suited to grill-roasting because they last longer than natural hardwood charcoal. A chimney's worth of briquettes can keep going up to 2 hours after the same amount of hardwood charcoal has turned to ash.

GET IN THE ZONE

There are two charcoal setups used for grill-roasting; each creates a hotter zone and a cooler zone.

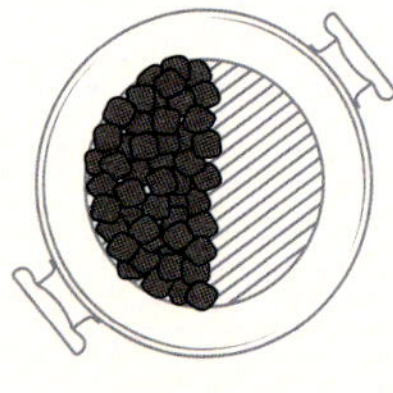

A **half-grill setup** (top) creates a dramatic heat level difference. Cuts that benefit from a deeply browned crust can be cooked over the cooler side and quickly seared over the hotter side.

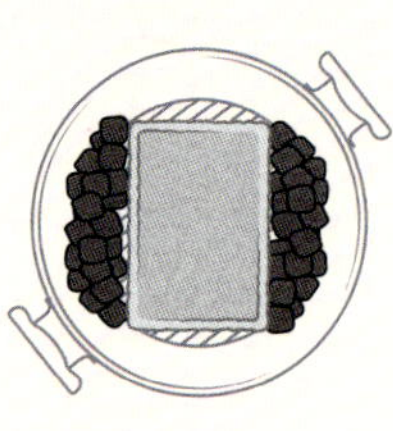

A **split-fire setup** (bottom) piles coals on either side of the grill, creating a cooler, evenly heated area in the middle. Since the two hotter areas have fewer coals that burn out faster than coals in a half-grill setup, the heat level is ideal for quicker-cooking roasts such as whole chickens, as well as foods that don't need to be seared.

On a gas grill, the burner setup can vary based on the recipe.

CATCH THE DRIPS

Some recipes for fattier cuts use a **disposable aluminum roasting pan** beneath the meat to catch drippings.

ADD WOOD FOR FLAVOR

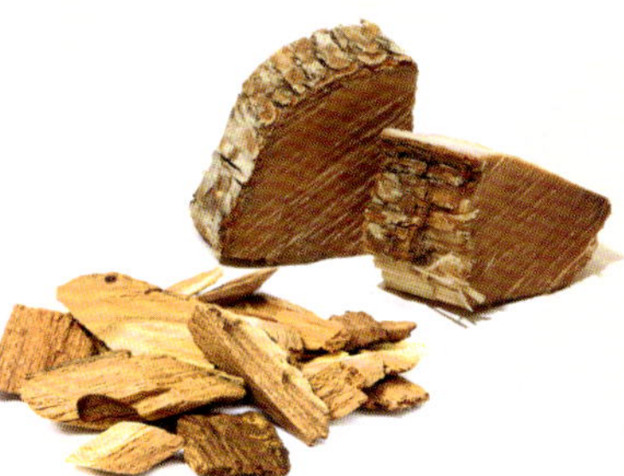

While added smoke isn't an essential component of grill-roasting, smokiness can enhance grill-roasted recipes. Place **wood chunks** directly on charcoal; **wood chips**, which can be used with charcoal or gas, should be wrapped in a foil packet. Because of the longer cooking times it's important not to over-smoke, especially with mild meats such as chicken. Follow individual recipe directions for the correct amount of chips or chunks.

CONTAIN THE HEAT

A closed lid creates the oven-like conditions necessary for grill-roasting. Open the vents on the lid and grill bottom only halfway; this prevents the coals from burning too fast and helps the grill retain heat. You'll need to take the temperature of the food to ensure that it's cooked properly: If you use an instant-read thermometer, try to minimize the number of times you open the lid.

If you have one, a **probe thermometer** is even better; it allows you to monitor the temperature of the roast while the grill is closed.

GRILLED BONELESS, SKINLESS CHICKEN BREASTS

Grilled Boneless, Skinless Chicken Breasts

SERVES 4 **TIME** 25 minutes plus 30 minutes brining

Why This Recipe Works Versatile grilled boneless, skinless chicken breasts can be served as is, but they can also be the jumping-off point for countless summer salads and sandwiches. To make sure they're as appealing as they are easy, we start by pounding them ½ inch thick so that they cook through evenly. Brining the chicken for 30 minutes seasons it and adds moisture that helps keep it juicy during cooking; we spike the salt water with just enough umami-rich fish sauce to add savory depth without any trace of fishiness, as well as honey that encourages browning and balances the salt. You can use that half-hour to light your grill and prep any other ingredients. Coating the chicken in a little oil before grilling keeps it from sticking to the grate, and cooking it over a hot fire ensures that it browns deeply.

- 4 (6- to 8-ounce) boneless, skinless chicken breasts, trimmed
- 3 tablespoons fish sauce
- 2 tablespoons honey
- 2 teaspoons kosher salt for brining
- ⅛ teaspoon pepper
- 1 tablespoon vegetable oil

1 Pound chicken breasts to ½-inch thickness between 2 sheets of plastic wrap. Whisk fish sauce, honey, salt, pepper, and ½ cup water together in bowl. Combine brine and chicken in 1-gallon zipper-lock bag and toss to coat; press out as much air as possible and seal bag. Refrigerate for 30 minutes.

2 Remove chicken from brine, letting excess drip off (do not pat dry) and place in bowl. Add oil and toss to coat.

3A **FOR A CHARCOAL GRILL** Open bottom vent completely. Light large chimney starter filled with charcoal briquettes (6 quarts). When top coals are partially covered with ash, pour evenly over grill. Set cooking grate in place, cover, and open lid vent completely. Heat grill until hot, about 5 minutes.

3B **FOR A GAS GRILL** Turn all burners to high; cover; and heat grill until hot, about 15 minutes. Leave all burners on high.

4 Clean and oil cooking grate. Place chicken skinned side down on grill and cook (covered if using gas) until chicken develops dark grill marks, 3 to 5 minutes. Gently release chicken from cooking grate; flip; and cook until chicken registers 160 degrees, 3 to 5 minutes. Transfer chicken to cutting board, tent with aluminum foil, and let rest for 5 minutes. Serve.

Grilled Bone-In Chicken Breasts

SERVES 6 **TIME** 50 minutes plus 30 minutes brining

Why This Recipe Works With crackling-crisp skin and moist, tender meat, grilled bone-in chicken breasts are simple grilled fare at its finest—salt, pepper, and a half-grill fire are all you need. We use a potent brine to quickly add moisture to the meat. After the pieces pick up some color on the hotter side of the grill, we move them to the cooler side to cook through, arranging the chicken so that the thicker sides face the fire. Covering the chicken with a piece of foil creates an oven within an oven, minimizing temperature fluctuations and promoting even cooking. Then it's back to direct heat to turn the skin crisp and brown. This recipe was developed using Diamond Crystal kosher salt. If you have Morton kosher salt, which is denser, use ½ cup. Don't brine the chicken for more than 1 hour, and don't skip the step of rinsing the chicken after brining, or it will taste too salty.

- ⅔ cup kosher salt for brining
- 6 (12-ounce) bone-in split chicken breasts, trimmed
- 1 teaspoon pepper

1 Dissolve salt in 2 quarts cold water in large container. Submerge chicken, cover, and refrigerate for at least 30 minutes or up to 1 hour. Remove chicken from brine, pat dry with paper towels, and sprinkle with pepper.

2A FOR A CHARCOAL GRILL Open bottom vent completely. Light large chimney starter filled with charcoal briquettes (6 quarts). When top coals are partially covered with ash, pour evenly over half of grill. Set cooking grate in place, cover, and open lid vent completely. Heat grill until hot, about 5 minutes.

2B FOR A GAS GRILL Turn all burners to high; cover; and heat grill until hot, about 15 minutes. Leave primary burner on high and turn off other burner(s).

3 Clean and oil cooking grate. Place chicken on hotter side of grill and cook until lightly browned on both sides, 10 to 14 minutes, flipping as needed. Slide chicken to cooler side of grill and arrange skin side down with thicker side of breast facing hotter side. Cover loosely with aluminum foil; cover grill; and cook until chicken registers 150 degrees, 15 to 25 minutes.

4 Flip chicken skin side up; slide to hotter side of grill; and cook until well browned, 4 to 6 minutes. Flip chicken skin side down and cook until well browned and registers 160 degrees, 2 to 3 minutes. Transfer chicken to platter, tent with foil, and let rest for 5 minutes. Serve.

GRILLED CHICKEN WINGS

Grilled Chicken Wings

SERVES 4 **TIME** 45 minutes plus 30 minutes brining

Why This Recipe Works Bronzed, juicy chicken wings are a real treat. But deep-frying them in the summertime? Not so much. Fortunately, grilling over moderate heat produces crisp, well-rendered, meltingly tender chicken wings that you won't be able to stop eating. A quick toss in cornstarch and spices both flavors the wings and prevents them from sticking to the grate. We begin grilling with the thicker skin side facing up to slowly render the fat and then we flip the wings at the end of cooking to crisp the skin. For the magic combination of moisture and tenderness, we brine the wings before grilling and leave them on the grill until they're 180 degrees, at which point their abundant collagen (responsible for chewiness) has turned to gelatin. This recipe was developed using Diamond Crystal kosher salt. If you have Morton kosher salt, which is denser, use ¾ cup. Don't brine the wings for more than 30 minutes, or they'll be too salty.

- 1 cup kosher salt for brining
- 2 pounds chicken wings, cut at joints, wingtips discarded
- 1½ teaspoons cornstarch
- 1 teaspoon pepper

1 Dissolve salt in 2 quarts cold water in large container. Prick chicken wings all over with fork. Submerge chicken in brine, cover, and refrigerate for 30 minutes.

2 Combine cornstarch and pepper in large bowl. Remove chicken from brine and pat dry with paper towels. Transfer wings to bowl with cornstarch and toss to coat evenly.

3A **FOR A CHARCOAL GRILL** Open bottom vent completely. Light large chimney starter half filled with charcoal briquettes (3 quarts). When top coals are partially covered with ash, pour evenly over grill. Set cooking grate in place, cover, and open lid vent completely. Heat grill until hot, about 5 minutes.

3B **FOR A GAS GRILL** Turn all burners to high; cover; and heat grill until hot, about 15 minutes. Turn all burners to medium-low.

4 Clean and oil cooking grate. Place wings fatty side up on grill and cook (covered if using gas) until browned, 12 to 15 minutes. Flip wings and grill until skin is crisp and lightly charred and chicken registers 180 degrees, about 10 minutes. Transfer chicken to platter, tent with aluminum foil, and let rest for 5 minutes. Serve.

VARIATIONS

BBQ Wings

Reduce pepper to ½ teaspoon. Add 1 teaspoon chili powder, 1 teaspoon paprika, ½ teaspoon garlic powder, ½ teaspoon dried oregano, and ½ teaspoon sugar to cornstarch with pepper.

Creole Grilled Chicken Wings

Add ¾ teaspoon dried oregano, ½ teaspoon garlic powder, ½ teaspoon onion powder, ½ teaspoon white pepper, and ¼ teaspoon cayenne pepper to cornstarch with pepper.

Tandoori Grilled Chicken Wings

Reduce pepper to ½ teaspoon. Add 1 teaspoon garam masala, ½ teaspoon ground cumin, ¼ teaspoon garlic powder, ¼ teaspoon ground ginger, and ⅛ teaspoon cayenne pepper to cornstarch with pepper.

The Power of Collagen

Chicken wings are white meat, but they cook more like dark meat, thanks to their high ratio of skin to meat. The robust amount of collagen in chicken-wing skin converts into moisture-holding gelatin at temperatures as low as 135 degrees—20 degrees lower than the temperature at which collagen found in chicken muscle converts. Since the meat in chicken wings is lean and delicate white meat, the extra gelatin from the skin is extremely helpful when cooking because it provides the perception of juiciness thanks to its moisture-holding capacity.

Prepping Chicken Wings

1 Cut off wingtip and discard.

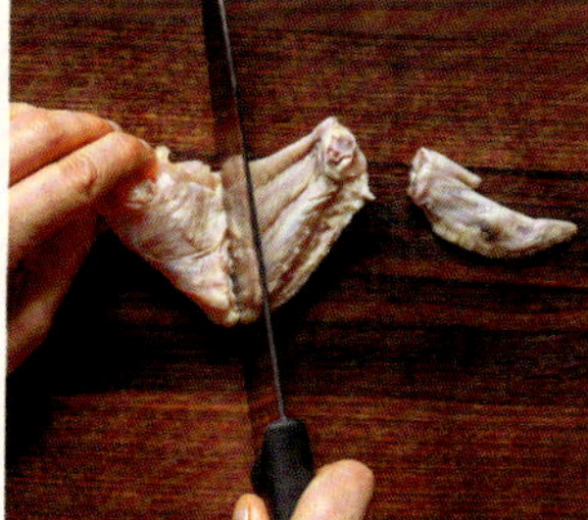

2 Using kitchen shears or sharp chef's knife, cut through joint between drumette and flat.

Smoked Chicken Parts

SERVES 6 to 8 **TIME** 1¾ hours plus 30 minutes brining

Why This Recipe Works Grill-roasting is often used for whole chickens, but this relatively low-temperature cooking method also works well for smoked chicken parts. We brine the chicken first to plump the meat with extra moisture. Mounding some lit coals on top of unlit briquettes on one side of the grill allows the heat to trickle down and light the cold coals, extending the life of the fire. A pan of water under the chicken on the cooler side of the grill stabilizes the temperature of the grill and provides humidity that helps prevent the breast pieces from drying out. Two packets of wood chips give the chicken all the smokiness it needs. If using a charcoal grill, you can substitute three wood chunks for the wood chip packets. This recipe was developed using Diamond Crystal kosher salt. If you have Morton kosher salt, which is denser, use 1½ cups. Don't brine the chicken for more than 1 hour, or it will be too salty.

- 2 cups kosher salt for brining
- 1 cup sugar for brining
- 6 pounds bone-in chicken pieces (split breasts, drumsticks, and/or thighs), trimmed
- 3 tablespoons vegetable oil
- 1 teaspoon pepper
- 3 cups wood chips
- 1 (13 by 9-inch) disposable aluminum roasting pan (if using charcoal) or 1 (9-inch) disposable aluminum pie plate (if using gas)

1 Dissolve salt and sugar in 4 quarts cold water in large container. Submerge chicken in brine, cover, and refrigerate for 30 minutes to 1 hour. Remove chicken from brine and pat dry with paper towels. Brush both sides of chicken with oil and sprinkle with pepper.

2 Using large pieces of heavy-duty aluminum foil, wrap wood chips into two 8 by 4-inch foil packets. (Make sure chips do not poke holes in sides or bottom of packets.) Cut 2 evenly spaced 2-inch slits in top of packets.

3A FOR A CHARCOAL GRILL Open bottom vent halfway, place disposable pan on 1 side of grill, and add 2 cups water to pan. Pile 2 quarts unlit charcoal briquettes against empty side of grill. Light large chimney starter filled halfway with charcoal briquettes (3 quarts). When top coals are partially covered with ash, pour on top of unlit briquettes, keeping coals steeply banked against side of grill. Place wood chip packets on coals. Set cooking grate in place, cover, and open lid vent halfway. Heat grill until hot and wood chips are smoking, about 5 minutes.

SMOKED CHICKEN PARTS

3B FOR A GAS GRILL Remove cooking grate and place wood chip packets directly on primary burner. Place disposable pie plate with 2 cups water on other burner(s). Set cooking grate in place; turn all burners to high; cover; and heat grill until hot and wood chips are smoking, about 15 minutes. Turn primary burner to medium-high and turn off other burner(s).

4 Clean and oil cooking grate. Place chicken skin side up as far away from fire as possible, with thighs closest to fire and breasts furthest away. Cover (positioning lid vent over chicken if using charcoal) and cook until breasts register 160 degrees and thighs/drumsticks register 175 degrees, 1¼ to 1½ hours.

5 Transfer chicken to cutting board, tent with foil, and let rest for 10 minutes. Serve.

Grilled Honey Mustard–Glazed Boneless, Skinless Chicken Breasts

SERVES 4 **TIME** 50 minutes plus 30 minutes brining

Why This Recipe Works Grilled glazed boneless chicken breasts make a quick and easy summer dinner. A two-level fire lets you control the grilling process to achieve perfect results. A quick brine ensures juiciness, but the real MVP here is a sprinkle of dry milk powder: Its lactose encourages quick browning and its powdery texture grabs on to the glaze. As for the glaze, it's painted on in layers as soon as the breasts get a quick sear on the hotter side of the grill and are flipped over. The timing here is important: Waiting until the chicken is seared keeps the glaze from burning, and applying the glaze immediately after the chicken is flipped means that more glaze stays on the chicken and less is stuck to the grill. This recipe was developed using Diamond Crystal kosher salt. If you have Morton kosher salt, which is denser, use 6 tablespoons. Don't brine the chicken for more than 1 hour, or it will be too salty.

GRILLED HONEY MUSTARD–GLAZED BONELESS, SKINLESS CHICKEN BREASTS

CHICKEN

- 4 (6- to 8-ounce) boneless, skinless chicken breasts, trimmed
- ½ cup sugar for brining
- ½ cup kosher salt for brining
- 2 teaspoons nonfat dry milk powder
- ¼ teaspoon pepper
- Vegetable oil spray

HONEY-MUSTARD GLAZE

- 2 tablespoons cider vinegar
- 1 teaspoon cornstarch
- 3 tablespoons Dijon mustard
- 3 tablespoons honey
- 2 tablespoons corn syrup
- 1 garlic clove, minced
- ¼ teaspoon ground fennel seeds

1 FOR THE CHICKEN Pound chicken to uniform thickness between 2 sheets of plastic wrap. Dissolve sugar and salt in 1½ quarts cold water in large container. Submerge chicken in brine, cover, and refrigerate for at least 30 minutes or up to 1 hour.

2 FOR THE GLAZE Whisk vinegar and cornstarch in small saucepan until cornstarch has dissolved. Whisk in mustard, honey, corn syrup, garlic, and fennel seeds. Bring mixture to boil over high heat. Cook, stirring constantly, until thickened, about 1 minute. Transfer to bowl.

3 Remove chicken from brine and pat dry with paper towels. Combine milk powder and pepper in bowl. Sprinkle half of milk powder mixture over 1 side of chicken breasts, then lightly spray with oil until powder is moistened. Flip chicken and repeat with remaining milk powder and more oil spray.

4A FOR A CHARCOAL GRILL Open bottom vent completely. Light large chimney starter mounded with charcoal briquettes (7 quarts). When top coals are partially covered with ash, pour two-thirds evenly over half of grill, then pour remaining coals over other half of grill. Set cooking grate in place, cover, and open lid vent completely. Heat grill until hot, about 5 minutes.

4B FOR A GAS GRILL Turn all burners to high; cover; and heat grill until hot, about 15 minutes. Leave primary burner on high and turn other burner(s) to medium-high.

5 Clean and oil cooking grate. Place chicken skinned side down on hotter side of grill and cook until browned on first side, 2 to 2½ minutes. Flip chicken; brush with 2 tablespoons glaze; and cook until browned on second side, 2 to 2½ minutes. Flip chicken, slide to cooler side of grill, brush with 2 tablespoons glaze, and cook for 2 minutes. Repeat flipping, brushing, and cooking for 2 minutes with remaining glaze until chicken registers 160 degrees, 5 to 8 minutes. Transfer chicken to plate, tent with aluminum foil, and let rest for 5 minutes. Serve.

VARIATIONS

Grilled Coconut Curry–Glazed Boneless, Skinless Chicken Breasts

Substitute following for honey-mustard glaze: Whisk 2 tablespoons lime juice and 1½ teaspoons cornstarch in small saucepan until cornstarch has dissolved. Whisk in ⅓ cup canned coconut milk, 3 tablespoons corn syrup, 1 tablespoon fish sauce, 1 tablespoon red curry paste, 1 teaspoon grated fresh ginger, and ¼ teaspoon ground coriander. Bring mixture to boil over high heat. Cook, stirring constantly, until thickened, about 1 minute. Transfer to bowl.

Grilled Spicy Hoisin-Glazed Boneless, Skinless Chicken Breasts

For a spicier glaze, use the larger amount of sriracha.

Substitute following for honey-mustard glaze: Whisk 2 tablespoons unseasoned rice vinegar and 1 teaspoon cornstarch in small saucepan until cornstarch has dissolved. Whisk in ⅓ cup hoisin sauce, 2 tablespoons corn syrup, 1–2 tablespoons sriracha, 1 teaspoon grated fresh ginger, and ¼ teaspoon five-spice powder. Bring mixture to boil over high heat. Cook, stirring constantly, until thickened, about 1 minute. Transfer to bowl.

Grilled Miso Sesame–Glazed Boneless, Skinless Chicken Breasts

Substitute following for honey-mustard glaze: Whisk 3 tablespoons unseasoned rice vinegar and 1 teaspoon cornstarch in small saucepan until cornstarch has dissolved. Whisk in 3 tablespoons white miso, 2 tablespoons corn syrup, 1 tablespoon toasted sesame oil, 2 teaspoons grated fresh ginger, and ¼ teaspoon ground coriander. Bring mixture to boil over high heat. Cook, stirring constantly, until thickened, about 1 minute. Transfer to bowl.

Grilled Molasses Coffee–Glazed Boneless, Skinless Chicken Breasts

Substitute following for honey-mustard glaze: Whisk 3 tablespoons balsamic vinegar and 1½ teaspoons cornstarch in small saucepan until cornstarch has dissolved. Whisk in ¼ cup molasses, 2 tablespoons corn syrup, 2 tablespoons brewed coffee, 1 minced garlic clove, and ¼ teaspoon ground allspice. Bring mixture to boil over high heat. Cook, stirring constantly, until thickened, about 1 minute. Transfer to bowl.

Grilled Citrus Chicken

SERVES 4 **TIME** 50 minutes plus 1 hour marinating

Why This Recipe Works To infuse perfectly grilled chicken breasts with bright citrus flavor, we immerse them in a salty brine/marinade of lemon, lime, and orange zest along with garlic, oil, water, sugar, salt, and pepper. As the chicken sits in the "brinerade," the salt penetrates the meat and helps lock in moisture as well as add flavor. We start the chicken breasts on the cooler side of the grill and cover them, which traps heat and keeps the breasts moist while cooking. After that, a quick stint over direct heat adds color and more grilled flavor. Since the oil-soluble zest in the marinade flavors only the exterior of the meat, we add more citrus flavor to the chicken with a bright, acidic sauce. Grilling the citrus halves before squeezing out their juice for the sauce caramelizes their sugars, which flavors the sauce, while chopped fresh mint adds brightness and zing. Don't marinate the chicken for more than 12 hours, or it will be too salty.

GRILLED CITRUS CHICKEN

CHICKEN AND CITRUS

- 3 tablespoons vegetable oil
- 3 tablespoons water
- 2 teaspoons lemon zest, plus 1 lemon cut in half
- 2 teaspoons lime zest, plus 1 lime cut in half
- 1 teaspoon orange zest, plus 1 orange cut in half
- 2 teaspoons sugar
- 2 garlic cloves, minced
- 1 tablespoon kosher salt
- ½ teaspoon pepper
- 4 (6- to 8-ounce) boneless, skinless chicken breasts, trimmed

SAUCE

- 1 teaspoon mayonnaise
- 1 teaspoon Dijon mustard
- 1 garlic clove, minced
- ½ teaspoon sugar
- ½ teaspoon kosher salt
- ⅛ teaspoon pepper
- ¼ cup vegetable oil
- 1 tablespoon minced fresh mint

1 **FOR THE CHICKEN AND CITRUS** Whisk oil, water, lemon zest, lime zest, orange zest, sugar, garlic, salt, and pepper together in bowl. Combine marinade and chicken in 1-gallon zipper-lock bag and toss to coat; press out as much air as possible and seal bag. Refrigerate for at least 1 hour or up to 12 hours.

2 Remove chicken from marinade, let excess marinade drip off (do not pat dry), and transfer to plate.

3 **FOR THE SAUCE** Whisk mayonnaise, mustard, garlic, sugar, salt, and pepper together in bowl; set aside for serving

4A **FOR A CHARCOAL GRILL** Open bottom vent completely. Light large chimney starter filled with charcoal briquettes (6 quarts). When top coals are partially covered with ash, pour evenly over half of grill. Set cooking grate in place, cover, and open lid vent completely. Heat grill until hot, about 5 minutes.

4B **FOR A GAS GRILL** Turn all burners to high; cover; and heat grill until hot, about 15 minutes. Leave primary burner on high and turn off other burner(s).

5 Clean and oil cooking grate. Place chicken skinned side down on cooler side of grill, with thicker ends facing coals. Cover and cook until light grill marks appear on first side, 6 to 9 minutes. Flip chicken and rotate so that thinner ends face coals. Cover and cook until chicken registers 140 degrees, 6 to 9 minutes.

6 Slide chicken to hotter side of grill and cook (uncovered if using charcoal; covered if using gas) until dark grill marks develop on both sides and chicken registers 160 degrees, 4 to 8 minutes, flipping halfway through cooking. Meanwhile, place citrus halves cut side down on hotter side of grill and cook until lightly charred, about 4 minutes; transfer to bowl. Transfer chicken to carving board, tent with aluminum foil and let rest while finishing sauce.

7 Squeeze 3 tablespoons orange juice, 1 tablespoon lemon juice, and 1 tablespoon lime juice from grilled citrus into sauce. Whisking constantly, slowly drizzle in oil until emulsified. Stir in mint and season with salt and pepper to taste. Slice chicken on bias ¼ inch thick, drizzle with sauce, and serve.

Grilled Chicken Caprese

SERVES 4 **TIME** 30 minutes

Why This Recipe Works The simple but inspired combination of tomato, mozzarella, and basil known as caprese salad is the essence of summer: vibrant, colorful, and fresh. Grilled chicken cutlets turn it into a meal. We cut the tomatoes into thick slices and set them on the grate with the chicken; the intense heat deepens their flavor and heightens their juiciness.

- 2 tablespoons chopped fresh basil
- 1 tablespoon red wine vinegar
- 2 garlic cloves, minced
- 2 teaspoons kosher salt, divided
- ¾ teaspoons pepper, divided
- 3 tablespoons extra-virgin olive oil
- 1 (6-ounce) fresh mozzarella ball, halved, sliced ¼ inch thick, and patted dry
- 1½ pounds chicken cutlets, ½ inch thick, trimmed
- 2 tomatoes, cored and cut into ½-inch slices

1 Combine basil, vinegar, garlic, 1 teaspoon salt, and ¼ teaspoon pepper in bowl. Slowly whisk in oil until thoroughly incorporated. Transfer 2 tablespoons vinaigrette to bowl and toss with mozzarella; reserve remaining vinaigrette for serving.

2 Pat chicken dry with paper towels and sprinkle with remaining 1 teaspoon salt and ½ teaspoon pepper.

3A **FOR A CHARCOAL GRILL** Open bottom vent completely. Light large chimney starter filled with charcoal briquettes (6 quarts). When top coals are partially covered with ash, pour evenly over grill. Set cooking grate in place, cover, and open lid vent completely. Heat grill until hot, about 5 minutes.

GRILLED CHICKEN CAPRESE

3B FOR A GAS GRILL Turn all burners to high; cover; and heat grill until hot, about 15 minutes. Leave all burners on high.

4 Clean and oil cooking grate. Place chicken and tomatoes on grill and cook until chicken is well browned and tomatoes are lightly charred, about 4 minutes, flipping as needed. Transfer chicken to platter, top with tomato slices, and drizzle with reserved vinaigrette. Cover with even layer of mozzarella, tent with aluminum foil and let rest for 5 to 10 minutes. Serve.

Monterey Chicken

SERVES 4 **TIME** 40 minutes plus 30 minutes marinating

Why This Recipe Works As invented by the Bonanza Steakhouse chain, Chicken Monterey consists of a marinated boneless chicken breast, flame-broiled and then topped with bacon strips and melted Monterey Jack cheese. To maximize that tasty char in our home-grilled version, we butterfly boneless, skinless chicken breasts to provide more surface contact with the grate. A simple mixture of honey, Dijon mustard, salt, and pepper makes a marinade that doubles as a basting sauce on the grill. While the chicken cooks on the hotter side of the grill, we let red onion slices—basted with the reserved fat from cooking the bacon—soften on the cooler side. To finish, we slide the chicken away from the fire and top it with the smoky onions and a mixture of cooked diced bacon and spicy shredded pepper Jack cheese.

- 4 (6- to 8-ounce) boneless, skinless chicken breasts, trimmed
- ½ cup Dijon mustard
- ¼ cup honey
- 2 teaspoons kosher salt
- ½ teaspoon pepper
- 4 slices bacon, cut into ½-inch pieces
- 6 ounces pepper Jack cheese, shredded (1½ cups)
- 4 (½-inch-thick) slices red onion
- Lime wedges

1 Working with 1 breast at a time and starting on thick side, cut chicken in half horizontally, stopping ½ inch from edge so that halves remain attached. Open up breast like book, creating single flat piece.

2 Whisk mustard, honey, salt, and pepper together in bowl to make marinade. Measure out ¼ cup marinade and set aside for cooking. Combine remaining marinade and chicken in 1-gallon zipper-lock bag and toss to coat; press out as much air as possible and seal bag. Refrigerate for 30 minutes to 1 hour.

MONTEREY CHICKEN

GRILLED PESTO CHICKEN

3 Meanwhile, cook bacon in 10-inch skillet over medium heat until crispy, 5 to 7 minutes. Using slotted spoon, transfer bacon to paper towel–lined plate, reserving bacon fat. When bacon is cool, toss with pepper Jack in bowl.

4 Push toothpick horizontally through each onion round to keep rings intact while grilling. Brush onion lightly with reserved bacon fat. Remove chicken from marinade, let excess marinade drip off (do not pat dry), and transfer to plate.

5A FOR A CHARCOAL GRILL Open bottom vent completely. Light large chimney starter filled with charcoal briquettes (6 quarts). When top coals are partially covered with ash, pour two-thirds evenly over half of grill, then pour remaining coals over other half of grill. Set cooking grate in place, cover, and open lid vent completely. Heat grill until hot, about 5 minutes.

5B FOR A GAS GRILL Turn all burners to high; cover; and heat grill until hot, about 15 minutes. Leave primary burner on high and turn other burner(s) to medium.

6 Clean and oil cooking grate. Place chicken on hotter side of grill and onion on cooler side of grill. Cover and cook until both are lightly charred, about 5 minutes. Flip onion and chicken and brush chicken with reserved honey-mustard mixture. Cover and cook until both are lightly charred on second side, about 5 minutes.

7 Remove onion from grill and slide chicken to cooler side of grill. Quickly remove toothpicks and separate onion rings. Divide onion rings evenly among chicken breasts. Divide bacon–pepper Jack mixture evenly over onion rings. Cover and cook until pepper Jack is melted and chicken registers 160 degrees, about 2 minutes. Transfer chicken to platter, tent with aluminum foil, and let rest for 5 minutes. Serve with lime wedges.

Grilled Pesto Chicken

SERVES 4 **TIME** 1¼ hours plus 1 hour marinating

Why This Recipe Works Basil pesto isn't just for pasta; we found a way to imbue chicken with basil and garlic flavor that holds up on the grill. We start with homemade pesto, which has a stronger flavor and is fresher than store-bought, and we use it three ways: First, we cut pockets into flavorful bone-in chicken breasts to fill with pesto and then we marinate the stuffed breasts in more pesto. The third dose of pesto comes in the form of a sauce to serve with the grilled chicken.

- 4 cups fresh basil leaves
- ¾ cup extra-virgin olive oil, divided
- 5 garlic cloves, peeled
- 1½ tablespoons lemon juice
- 2 teaspoons kosher salt, divided
- 2 ounces Parmesan cheese, grated (1 cup)
- ½ teaspoon pepper
- 4 (12-ounce) bone-in split chicken breasts, trimmed

1 Process basil, ½ cup oil, garlic, lemon juice, and 1½ teaspoons salt in food processor until smooth, about 1 minute, scraping down bowl as needed. Transfer ¼ cup to large bowl and set aside for marinade. Add Parmesan to mixture left in processor and pulse to incorporate, about 3 pulses. Transfer ¼ cup pesto to small bowl and set aside for stuffing. Add remaining ¼ cup oil to pesto left in processor and pulse to incorporate, about 3 pulses; set aside for serving.

2 Starting on thick side of breast, closest to breastbone, cut horizontal pocket in each breast. Sprinkle chicken, inside and out, with pepper and remaining ½ teaspoon salt. Place 1 tablespoon pesto reserved for stuffing in each pocket. Tie each chicken breast with 2 pieces kitchen twine to secure. In large bowl, rub chicken with pesto reserved for marinade, cover, and refrigerate for 1 hour.

3 Remove chicken from marinade, let excess marinade drip off (do not pat dry), and transfer to plate.

4A FOR A CHARCOAL GRILL Open bottom vent completely. Light large chimney starter filled with charcoal briquettes (6 quarts). When top coals are partially covered with ash, pour evenly over half of grill. Set cooking grate in place, cover, and open lid vent completely. Heat grill until hot, about 5 minutes.

4B FOR A GAS GRILL Turn all burners to high; cover; and heat grill until hot, about 15 minutes. Turn all burners to medium-low. (Adjust burners as needed to maintain grill temperature of 350 degrees.)

5 Clean and oil cooking grate. Place chicken skin side up on grill (cooler side if using charcoal). Cover and cook until chicken registers 155 degrees, 25 to 35 minutes.

6 Slide chicken to hotter side of grill (if using charcoal) or turn all burners to high (if using gas). Flip chicken skin side down; cover; and cook until well browned and chicken registers 160 degrees, 5 to 10 minutes.

7 Transfer chicken to platter, tent with aluminum foil, and let rest for 10 minutes. Remove twine, carve chicken, and serve with reserved pesto.

Sweet and Tangy Barbecued Chicken

SERVES 6 to 8 **TIME** 2 hours plus 6 hours seasoning

Why This Recipe Works Bone-in chicken pieces coated in a spicy-sweet barbecue sauce are a summer cookout classic. A rub of salt, onion and garlic powders, paprika, a touch of cayenne, and some brown sugar deeply seasons the meat and maintains a bold presence even after grilling. To ensure that all the chicken pieces cook at a slow, steady rate, we use a two-level heat setup. After browning the chicken pieces, we line up the fattier leg quarters closer to the coals and the leaner white meat farther from the heat; we also add a water pan underneath the cooler side to help the chicken cook slowly and evenly. Brushing on a homemade sauce in stages allows it to cling nicely to the skin and also develop layers of tangy-sweet flavor. This recipe was developed using Diamond Crystal kosher salt. If you have Morton kosher salt, which is denser, use 1 tablespoon in the spice rub. Use the large holes of a box grater to grate the onion for the sauce. When browning the chicken over the hotter side of the grill, move it away from any flare-ups.

CHICKEN

- 2 tablespoons packed dark brown sugar
- 1½ tablespoons kosher salt
- 1½ teaspoons onion powder
- 1½ teaspoons garlic powder
- 1½ teaspoons paprika
- ¼ teaspoon cayenne pepper
- 6 pounds bone-in chicken pieces (split breasts and/or leg quarters), trimmed
- 1 (13 by 9-inch) disposable aluminum roasting pan (if using charcoal) or 2 (9-inch) disposable aluminum pie plates (if using gas)

SAUCE

- 1 cup ketchup
- 5 tablespoons molasses
- 3 tablespoons cider vinegar
- 2 tablespoons Worcestershire sauce
- 2 tablespoons Dijon mustard
- ¼ teaspoon pepper
- 2 tablespoons vegetable oil
- ⅓ cup grated onion
- 1 garlic clove, minced
- 1 teaspoon chili powder
- ¼ teaspoon cayenne pepper

SWEET AND TANGY BARBECUED CHICKEN

1 FOR THE CHICKEN Combine sugar, salt, onion powder, garlic powder, paprika, and cayenne in bowl. Spread chicken out over rimmed baking sheet and sprinkle both sides evenly with spice rub. Cover with plastic wrap and refrigerate for at least 6 hours or up to 24 hours.

2 FOR THE SAUCE Whisk ketchup, molasses, vinegar, Worcestershire, mustard, and pepper together in bowl. Heat oil in medium saucepan over medium heat until shimmering. Add onion and garlic and cook until onion is softened, 2 to 4 minutes. Add chili powder and cayenne and cook until fragrant, about 30 seconds. Whisk in ketchup mixture and bring to boil. Reduce heat to medium-low and simmer gently for 5 minutes. Remove from heat. Measure out and reserve ⅔ cup sauce for cooking.

3A **FOR A CHARCOAL GRILL** Open bottom vent halfway, place disposable pan on 1 side of grill, and add 3 cups water to pan. Light large chimney starter filled with charcoal briquettes (6 quarts). When top coals are partially covered with ash, pour evenly over other half of grill (opposite disposable pan). Set cooking grate in place, cover, and open lid vent halfway. Heat grill until hot, about 5 minutes.

3B **FOR A GAS GRILL** Place 2 disposable pie plates, each filled with 1½ cups water, directly on 1 burner of gas grill (opposite primary burner). Turn all burners to high; cover; and heat grill until hot, about 15 minutes. Turn primary burner to medium-high and turn off other burner(s). (Adjust primary burner as needed to maintain grill temperature of 350 degrees.)

4 Clean and oil cooking grate. Place chicken skin side down on hotter side of grill and cook until browned and blistered in spots, 2 to 5 minutes. Flip chicken and cook until second side is browned, 4 to 6 minutes. Slide chicken to cooler side of grill and brush both sides with half of reserved sauce. Arrange chicken, skin side up, with leg quarters closest to fire and breasts farthest away. Cover (positioning lid vent over chicken if using charcoal) and cook for 25 minutes.

5 Brush both sides of chicken with remaining reserved sauce. Cover and cook until breasts register 160 degrees and leg quarters register 175 degrees, 25 to 35 minutes. Transfer chicken to serving platter, tent with aluminum foil, and let rest for 10 minutes. Serve, passing remaining sauce separately.

Barbecued Dry-Rubbed Chicken

SERVES 4 to 6 **TIME** 1 hour plus 30 minutes seasoning

Why This Recipe Works When you're making barbecued chicken, you could use barbecue sauce for an attractive, tasty glaze. Or you could employ a dry rub to flavor the meat thoroughly and allow for crispy skin. But why choose? This dry rub does double duty, both flavoring and glazing the chicken. Dark brown sugar duplicates the sweetness of barbecue sauce and melts reliably to help form a glaze. Chili powder and paprika, along with onion powder, dry mustard, and cayenne, help define that classic barbecue flavor. After applying the rub to bone-in mixed chicken parts, we give them a brief rest so that the rub can season the meat and draw moisture to the surface, which jump-starts the glazing process. Halfway through grilling, when the sugar has begun to melt, we dredge the chicken pieces in the dry rub again. The second coating adheres to the sticky base coat, and together they melt into a very nice lacquer. Grilling the chicken directly over medium-low heat lets the skin slowly render its fat. As the melting fat blends with the dry rub and enriches the glaze, the meat gently cooks through. A brief rest, covered, allows residual heat to melt any grains of sugar that survive the grill. The result is juicy grilled chicken with a full barbecue flavor and a light, even glaze. Apply the second coating of spice rub with a light hand, or it won't melt into a glaze.

- 3 tablespoons packed dark brown sugar
- 2 teaspoons chili powder
- 2 teaspoons paprika
- 1½ teaspoons pepper
- 1 teaspoon dry mustard
- 1 teaspoon onion powder
- 2 teaspoons kosher salt
- ¼ teaspoon cayenne pepper
- 3 pounds bone-in chicken pieces (split breasts cut in half, drumsticks, and/or thighs), trimmed

1 Combine sugar, chili powder, paprika, pepper, dry mustard, onion powder, salt, and cayenne in small bowl. Measure half of dry rub into shallow dish and set aside for cooking. Pat chicken dry with paper towels and rub remaining spice rub evenly over and under skin. Transfer chicken to plate, cover, and refrigerate for at least 30 minutes or up to 1 hour.

2A **FOR A CHARCOAL GRILL** Open bottom vent completely. Light large chimney starter half filled with charcoal briquettes (3 quarts). When top coals are partially covered with ash, pour evenly over grill. Set cooking grate in place, cover, and open lid vent completely. Heat grill until hot, about 5 minutes.

2B **FOR A GAS GRILL** Turn all burners to high; cover; and heat grill until hot, about 15 minutes. Turn all burners to medium-low.

3 Clean and oil cooking grate. Place chicken skin side down on grill and cook until skin is well browned and crisp, 15 to 20 minutes.

4 Lightly coat skin side of chicken with reserved rub, then return chicken to grill, skin side up. Cover and cook until rub has melted into glaze and breasts register 160 degrees and drumsticks/thighs register 175 degrees, 15 to 20 minutes. Transfer chicken to platter, tent with aluminum foil, and let rest for 10 minutes. Serve.

GRILLED JERK CHICKEN

Grilled Jerk Chicken

SERVES 4 **TIME** 1 hour plus 1 hour marinating

Why This Recipe Works Our bold, spicy-but-nuanced grilled jerk chicken starts with the jerk paste: Fiery habaneros (which are easier to find and less intense than the traditional Scotch bonnets), scallions, garlic, and 10 thyme sprigs give it a big, herby punch. Soy sauce adds depth, cider vinegar contributes brightness, and warm spices (allspice, cinnamon, and ginger) provide the characteristic jerk flavor, while brown sugar softens the spicy edge. After marinating bone-in chicken pieces in the paste, we cook them on the cooler side of the grill, covered, which helps the marinade to stick to the chicken and not slide off over direct heat and burn. Then we brush on a little reserved marinade for a fresh burst of jerk flavor and sear the chicken on the hotter side, where it picks up plenty of grill flavor. For a spicier dish, use the larger amount of habaneros. To make the dish less spicy, you can remove the seeds and ribs from the habaneros or substitute jalapeños. Use thyme sprigs with a generous amount of leaves; there's no need to separate the leaves from the stems. Keep a close eye on the chicken in step 6 since it can char quickly.

- 4 scallions
- ¼ cup vegetable oil
- ¼ cup soy sauce
- 2 tablespoons cider vinegar
- 2 tablespoons packed brown sugar
- 1–2 habanero chiles, stemmed
- 10 sprigs fresh thyme
- 5 garlic cloves, peeled
- 2½ teaspoons ground allspice
- 1 tablespoon kosher salt
- ½ teaspoon ground cinnamon
- ½ teaspoon ground ginger
- 3 pounds bone-in chicken pieces (split breasts cut in half, drumsticks, and/or thighs), trimmed
- Lime wedges

1 Process scallions, oil, soy sauce, vinegar, sugar, habanero(s), thyme sprigs, garlic, allspice, salt, cinnamon, and ginger in blender until smooth, about 30 seconds, scraping down sides of blender jar as needed. Measure out ¼ cup marinade and set aside for cooking.

2 Combine remaining marinade and chicken in 1-gallon zipper-lock bag and toss to coat; press out as much air as possible and seal bag. Refrigerate for 1 hour or up to 24 hours, flipping bag occasionally.

3 Remove chicken from marinade, let excess marinade drip off (do not pat dry), and transfer to plate.

4A FOR A CHARCOAL GRILL Open bottom vent completely. Light large chimney starter mounded with charcoal briquettes (7 quarts). When top coals are partially covered with ash, pour evenly over half of grill. Set cooking grate in place, cover, and open lid vent completely. Heat grill until hot, about 5 minutes.

4B FOR A GAS GRILL Turn all burners to high; cover; and heat grill until hot, about 15 minutes. Leave primary burner on high and turn off other burner(s).

5 Clean and oil cooking grate. Place chicken skin side up on cooler side of grill, with breast pieces farthest away from heat. Cover and cook until breasts register 160 degrees and drumsticks/thighs register 175 degrees, 22 to 30 minutes. Transfer chicken parts to platter as they finish cooking

6 Brush skin side of chicken with half of reserved marinade. Place chicken skin side down on hotter side of grill (if using charcoal) or turn all burners to high (if using gas). Brush with remaining reserved marinade and cook until lightly charred, 2 to 6 minutes, flipping halfway through cooking and moving pieces as needed to avoid flare-ups.

7 Transfer chicken to platter, tent with aluminum foil, and let rest for 10 minutes. Serve with lime wedges.

Peri Peri Grilled Chicken

SERVES 6 to 8 **TIME** 1½ hours plus 6 hours marinating

Why This Recipe Works The spicy grilled dish known as peri peri chicken has African roots; at its most basic, it is chicken marinated in a paste of garlic, herbs, spices, lemon juice, and fiery peri peri chiles and then grilled over a hot fire. Our version keeps the spicy yet complex profile while presenting a more accessible alternative to the hard-to-come-by peri peri peppers. We use a half-grill fire along with an aluminum pan filled with water to eliminate hot spots. For the spice paste, we start with a base of olive oil, garlic, shallot, lemon, bay leaves, paprika, and black pepper, plus five-spice powder for complexity. To mimic the fruity, complex heat of the peri peri peppers, we turn to dried arbol chiles and cayenne. Tomato paste and a final savory touch—chopped peanuts—give the dish a balanced richness and hint of sweetness. This recipe was developed using Diamond Crystal kosher salt. If you have Morton kosher salt, which is denser, use 6 tablespoons. When browning the chicken over the hotter side of the grill, move it away from the direct heat if any flare-ups occur. Serve with white rice.

PERI PERI GRILLED CHICKEN

Taste the Paste

In test after test, we have found that pastes that tasted exactly as spicy as we wanted before cooking had a more tempered flavor in the final dish. After some research, we learned that when exposed to high heat, capsaicin—the primary chemical compound responsible for the chile's heat—actually breaks down. After an hour on the grill, about 30 percent of the capsaicin will have broken down. To counteract this effect, your paste should taste just a bit spicier than you want prior to cooking. We call for using a relatively wide range of arbol peppers not only because tolerance for spiciness varies but also because the intensity of individual dried chiles can differ greatly. We suggest starting with four. Then, after mixing together the paste, give it a try and add up to six more chiles as necessary.

- ½ cup kosher salt
- 3 tablespoons extra-virgin olive oil
- 8 garlic cloves, peeled
- 2 tablespoons tomato paste
- 1 shallot, chopped
- 1 tablespoon sugar
- 1 tablespoon paprika
- 1 tablespoon five-spice powder
- 1 teaspoon pepper
- ½ teaspoon cayenne pepper
- 3 bay leaves, crushed
- 2 teaspoons grated lemon zest plus ¼ cup juice (2 lemons), plus lemon wedges for serving
- 4–10 arbol chiles, stems removed
- 6 pounds bone-in chicken pieces (split breasts cut in half, drumsticks, and/or thighs), trimmed
- ½ cup dry-roasted peanuts, chopped fine
- 1 (13 by 9-inch) disposable aluminum roasting pan (if using charcoal) or 2 (9-inch) disposable aluminum pie plates (if using gas)

1 Process salt, oil, garlic, tomato paste, shallot, sugar, paprika, five-spice powder, pepper, cayenne, bay leaves, lemon zest and juice, and 4 arbol chiles in blender until smooth paste forms, 10 to 20 seconds. Taste paste and add up to 6 additional arbol chiles, depending on desired level of heat (spice paste should be slightly hotter than desired heat level of cooked chicken); process until smooth.

2 Using metal skewer or tip of paring knife, poke skin side of chicken pieces 8 to 10 times. Combine chicken, peanuts, and spice paste in large container and toss until chicken is evenly coated. Cover and refrigerate for at least 6 hours or up to 24 hours.

3A **FOR A CHARCOAL GRILL** Open bottom vent halfway, place disposable pan on 1 side of grill, and add 3 cups water to pan. Light large chimney starter filled with charcoal briquettes (6 quarts). When top coals are partially covered with ash, pour evenly over other half of grill (opposite disposable pan). Set cooking grate in place, cover, and open lid vent halfway. Heat grill until hot, about 5 minutes.

3B **FOR A GAS GRILL** Place 2 disposable pie plates, each filled with 1½ cups water, directly on 1 burner of gas grill (opposite primary burner). Turn all burners to high; cover; and heat grill until hot, about 15 minutes. Turn primary burner to medium-high and turn off other burner(s). (Adjust primary burner as needed to maintain grill temperature of 350 degrees.)

4 Clean and oil cooking grate. Place chicken skin side down on hotter side of grill and cook until browned and blistered in spots, 2 to 5 minutes. Flip chicken and cook until second side is browned, 4 to 6 minutes.

5 Slide chicken, skin side up, to cooler side of grill with drumsticks/thighs closest to fire and breasts farthest away. Cover (positioning lid vent over chicken if using charcoal) and cook until breasts register 160 degrees and drumsticks/thighs register 175 degrees, 50 minutes to 1 hour.

6 Transfer chicken to serving platter, tent with aluminum foil, and let rest for 10 minutes. Serve with lemon wedges.

Thai-Style Grilled Chicken with Spicy Sweet-and-Sour Dipping Sauce

SERVES 4 **TIME** 55 minutes plus 1 hour brining and seasoning

Why This Recipe Works Coated in an herb and spice mixture and served with a sweet and spicy dipping sauce, Thai-style grilled chicken is wonderfully aromatic and complex. Our version seasons bone-in chicken breasts with a rub of cilantro, black pepper, lime juice, and garlic, accented with earthy coriander and fresh ginger. We place a thick layer of the rub under the skin as well as on top of it for flavoring throughout. The Thai flavors of this dish come through in the dipping sauce, a sweet and spicy blend of sugar, lime juice, distilled white vinegar, hot red pepper flakes, fish sauce, and garlic. We cook the chicken over a half-grill fire, searing it over the hotter side first to get good browning before moving it to the cooler side to cook through. This recipe was developed using Diamond Crystal kosher salt. If you have Morton kosher salt, which is denser, use ¾ cup. Some of the rub is inevitably lost to the grill, but the chicken will still be flavorful. Don't brine the chicken for more than 1 hour, or it will be too salty.

CHICKEN

- ½ cup sugar for brining
- 1 cup kosher salt for brining
- 4 (12-ounce) bone-in split chicken breasts, trimmed

DIPPING SAUCE

- ⅓ cup sugar
- ¼ cup distilled white vinegar
- ¼ cup lime juice (2 limes)
- 2 tablespoons fish sauce
- 3 small garlic cloves, minced
- 1 teaspoon red pepper flakes

RUB

- ⅔ cup chopped fresh cilantro
- 12 garlic cloves, minced
- ¼ cup lime juice (2 limes)
- 2 tablespoons grated fresh ginger
- 2 tablespoons pepper
- 2 tablespoons ground coriander
- 2 tablespoons vegetable oil

1 **FOR THE CHICKEN** Dissolve sugar and salt in 2 quarts cold water in large container. Submerge chicken in brine, cover, and refrigerate for 30 minutes to 1 hour. Remove chicken from brine and pat dry with paper towels.

2 **FOR THE DIPPING SAUCE** Whisk all ingredients together in bowl until sugar dissolves. Let stand for 1 hour at room temperature for flavors to meld.

3 **FOR THE RUB** Combine all ingredients in small bowl; work mixture with your fingers to thoroughly combine. Rub about 2 tablespoons rub under skin of each breast, then rub remaining rub evenly all over chicken. Place chicken in bowl, cover, and refrigerate for 30 minutes.

4A **FOR A CHARCOAL GRILL** Open bottom vent completely. Light large chimney starter filled with charcoal briquettes (6 quarts). When top coals are partially covered with ash, pour evenly over half of grill. Set cooking grate in place, cover, and open lid vent completely. Heat grill until hot, about 5 minutes.

4B **FOR A GAS GRILL** Turn all burners to high; cover; and heat grill until hot, about 15 minutes. Leave primary burner on high and turn other burner(s) to low.

5 Clean and oil cooking grate. Place chicken skin side down on hotter side of grill and cook until browned, 6 to 8 minutes, flipping halfway through cooking. Slide chicken to cooler side of grill, skin side up. Cover and cook until chicken registers 160 degrees, 10 to 15 minutes. Transfer chicken to platter and let rest, uncovered, for 10 minutes. Serve, passing dipping sauce separately.

GRILLED CHICKEN WITH ADOBO AND SAZÓN

Grilled Chicken with Adobo and Sazón

SERVES 4 to 6 **TIME** 1½ hours plus 3 hours marinating

Why This Recipe Works This juicy, intensely flavored grilled chicken gets its punch thanks to two dried seasonings from the Puerto Rican pantry: adobo, a blend of granulated garlic, salt, black pepper, and oregano; and sazón, a mixture that includes all the ingredients of adobo plus achiote, dried onion, cumin, and more herbs. We toss bone-in chicken parts in a mixture of vinegar and oil, and then rub the adobo-sazón seasoning over and under the skin and into pockets that we slash into the leg quarters. After the chicken marinates for at least 3 hours, we grill it mainly over indirect heat, browning the skin over high heat for the final few minutes of cooking. A punchy postmarinade made with lots of garlic and chopped cilantro as well as salt, white vinegar, black pepper, and olive oil contributes another layer of bright, savory flavor. Look for sazón with culantro and achiote (also called annatto) at the supermarket and avoid those without salt. You can substitute garlic powder for the granulated garlic. Breaking down a whole chicken lets you enjoy the delicacy that is the grilled backbone, but the recipe works fine with 4 to 4½ pounds of bone-in leg quarters and split breasts. A rasp grater makes quick work of turning the garlic into a paste.

ADOBO AND SAZÓN

- 4 teaspoons granulated garlic
- 2½ teaspoons commercial sazón
- 2 teaspoons kosher salt
- ½ teaspoon pepper
- ¼ teaspoon dried oregano

CHICKEN

- 1 (4- to 4½-pound) whole chicken, cut into 5 pieces (2 split breasts with wings, 2 leg quarters, and 1 backbone), giblets discarded
- 5 tablespoons distilled white vinegar, divided
- 5 tablespoons extra-virgin olive oil, divided
- 6 garlic cloves, minced to paste
- 1 teaspoon kosher salt
- ¼ cup chopped fresh cilantro
- ½ teaspoon pepper
- 1 (13 by 9-inch) disposable aluminum roasting pan

1 FOR THE ADOBO AND SAZÓN Combine all ingredients in bowl.

2 FOR THE CHICKEN Tuck wings behind chicken breasts. Place leg quarters skin side up on cutting board. Make 3 slashes through skin of each leg quarter: one across thigh, one across joint, and one across drumstick (each slash should reach bone). Flip leg quarters and make 1 more diagonal slash across back of drumsticks.

3 Toss chicken with 1 tablespoon vinegar and 1 tablespoon oil in large bowl, using your fingers to loosen skin from meat. Sprinkle adobo-sazón mixture over chicken pieces. Toss with your hands, rubbing mixture all over chicken, into slashes, and under skin. Cover and refrigerate chicken for at least 3 hours or up to 24 hours.

4 Combine garlic, salt, cilantro, pepper, remaining ¼ cup vinegar, and remaining ¼ cup oil to make paste, then add to disposable pan.

5A **FOR A CHARCOAL GRILL** Open bottom vent completely. Light large chimney starter mounded with charcoal briquettes (7 quarts). When top coals are partially covered with ash, pour evenly over half of grill. Set cooking grate in place, cover, and open lid vent completely. Heat grill until hot, about 5 minutes.

5B **FOR A GAS GRILL** Turn all burners to high; cover; and heat grill until hot, about 15 minutes. Turn primary burner to medium and turn other burner(s) to low. (Adjust primary burner as needed to maintain grill temperature between 400 and 425 degrees.)

6 Clean and oil cooking grate. Place chicken skin side up on cooler side of grill. Cover and cook until lightly browned on first side, 15 to 20 minutes. Flip chicken; cover; and cook until thickest part of breasts registers 150 degrees, 15 to 20 minutes. Meanwhile, place disposable pan with paste on hotter side of grill and cook until liquid begins to simmer and garlic begins to cook, 2 to 3 minutes. Remove disposable pan from grill.

7 Slide chicken to hotter side of grill and cook (covered if using gas) until skin is well browned, 2 to 3 minutes. Place disposable pan on cooler side of grill.

8 Flip chicken and cook until breasts register 160 degrees and legs register 175 degrees, 2 to 3 minutes. As chicken reaches temperature, transfer to disposable pan. Once all chicken is in disposable pan, cover with aluminum foil and slide to hotter side of grill. Cook until marinade is sizzling, 3 to 4 minutes. Remove pan from grill and let chicken rest for 10 minutes.

9 Cut each breast in half crosswise through the bone. Cut leg quarters through joint to separate thigh and drumstick. Place chicken on serving platter. Pour marinade from disposable pan into serving bowl. Serve, passing marinade separately.

Best Grilled Chicken Thighs with Mustard and Tarragon

SERVES 4 to 6 **TIME** 1¼ hours

Why This Recipe Works This easy grilling method lets time do the work of turning chicken thighs moist and tender, with crisp skin. We grill them skin side down over indirect heat until they register 185 to 190 degrees. The collagen in the meat and skin breaks down into gelatin, and the fat is thoroughly rendered, which allows the skin to become nicely crisp once we sear it over direct heat for the last few minutes of cooking. We coat the thighs with a bold-flavored paste, applying most of it to the flesh side so as not to introduce too much extra moisture to the skin, which would interfere with crisping. Briefly searing the flesh side before serving takes the raw edge off the paste on that side. Rosemary or thyme can be substituted for the tarragon.

MUSTARD AND TARRAGON PASTE

- 3 tablespoons Dijon mustard
- 5 garlic cloves, minced
- 1 tablespoon finely grated lemon zest, plus lemon wedges for serving
- 2 teaspoons minced fresh tarragon
- 1½ teaspoons kosher salt
- 1 teaspoon water
- ½ teaspoon pepper

CHICKEN

- ½ teaspoon kosher salt
- 8 (5- to 7-ounce) bone-in chicken thighs, trimmed

1 **FOR THE MUSTARD AND TARRAGON PASTE** Combine all ingredients in bowl.

2 **FOR THE CHICKEN** Place chicken skin side up on large plate. Sprinkle skin side with salt and spread one-third of paste evenly over top. Flip chicken and spread remaining paste evenly over flesh side. Refrigerate while preparing grill, or for up to 2 hours.

3A **FOR A CHARCOAL GRILL** Open bottom vent completely. Light large chimney starter mounded with charcoal briquettes (7 quarts). When top coals are partially covered with ash, pour evenly over half of grill. Set cooking grate in place, cover, and open lid vent completely. Heat grill until hot, about 5 minutes.

3B **FOR A GAS GRILL** Turn all burners to high; cover; and heat grill until hot, about 15 minutes. Leave primary burner on high and turn off other burner(s). (Adjust primary burner as needed to maintain grill temperature of 350 degrees.)

4 Clean and oil cooking grate. Place chicken skin side down on cooler side of grill, cover, and cook for 20 minutes. Rearrange chicken, keeping skin side down, so that pieces that were closest to edge are now closer to heat source and vice versa. Cover and cook until chicken registers 185 to 190 degrees, 15 to 20 minutes.

5 Slide chicken to hotter side of grill and cook until skin is nicely charred, about 5 minutes. Flip chicken and cook until lightly browned, 1 to 2 minutes. Transfer to platter, tent with aluminum foil, and let rest for 10 minutes. Serve with lemon wedges.

VARIATIONS

Best Grilled Chicken Thighs with Gochujang

Substitute following mixture for mustard and tarragon paste: Combine 3 tablespoons gochujang, 1 tablespoon soy sauce, 2 minced garlic cloves, 2 teaspoons sugar, and 1 teaspoon kosher salt in bowl. Omit lemon wedges.

Best Grilled Chicken Thighs with Garam Masala

For a spicier paste, use the larger amount of cayenne. Serve with lime wedges. Substitute following mixture for mustard and tarragon paste: Combine 3 tablespoons vegetable oil, 1½ tablespoons garam masala, 2 minced garlic cloves, 2 teaspoons grated fresh ginger, 2 teaspoons finely grated lime zest, 1¼ teaspoons kosher salt, and ⅛–¼ teaspoon cayenne pepper in bowl.

BEST GRILLED CHICKEN THIGHS WITH GOCHUJANG

Grilled Mojo Chicken

SERVES 4 to 6 **TIME** 1¾ hours plus 1 hour marinating

Why This Recipe Works Mojo chicken is all about that citrusy, garlicky marinade, traditionally built around the juice of sour oranges. To mimic their distinctive flavor, we use a combination of orange and lime juices as well as their zest. We take the raw edge off the garlic by toasting it in extra-virgin olive oil. Pineapple juice adds balancing sweetness to the marinade, while oregano, black pepper, and ground cumin give it a spicy backbone. Bone-in chicken leg quarters soak the up marinade well, especially when we slash them to allow the marinade direct access to the meat. For a fresh, extra-powerful dose of mojo flavor, we reserve part of the mojo mixture and make a sauce; we brush half on the chicken legs as they grill and spoon the rest over them before serving. Canned and bottled pineapple juices are both great in this recipe, but when it comes to the citrus, we highly recommend using freshly squeezed juice. This recipe was developed using Diamond Crystal kosher salt. If you have Morton kosher salt, which is denser, use 1½ tablespoons in the marinade.

- ⅓ cup extra-virgin olive oil
- 6 garlic cloves, minced
- ⅓ cup pineapple juice
- 1 tablespoon yellow mustard
- 2 teaspoons grated orange zest plus ⅓ cup juice
- 2 teaspoons grated lime zest plus ⅓ cup juice (3 limes)
- 1¼ teaspoons ground cumin
- ¾ teaspoon dried oregano
- 1 teaspoon pepper, divided
- 2 tablespoons kosher salt for marinade
- 6 (10-ounce) chicken leg quarters, trimmed
- 2 tablespoons coarsely chopped fresh cilantro
- 1 tablespoon minced jalapeño chile
- 2 teaspoons kosher salt

1 Heat oil and garlic in small saucepan over low heat, stirring often, until tiny bubbles appear and garlic is fragrant and straw-colored, 3 to 5 minutes. Let cool for at least 5 minutes. In medium bowl, whisk pineapple juice, mustard, orange zest and juice, lime zest and juice, cumin, oregano, and ¾ teaspoon pepper together. Slowly whisk in cooled garlic oil until emulsified.

2 Measure half of mojo mixture into small bowl and set aside for sauce. Whisk 2 tablespoons salt into remaining mojo mixture to make marinade.

GRILLED MOJO CHICKEN

GRILLED CHICKEN COBB SALAD

3 Pat chicken dry with paper towels and place skin side up on cutting board. Make 4 slashes through skin of each leg quarter: two across thigh, one across joint, and one across drumstick (each slash should reach bone). Flip leg quarters and make 1 more diagonal slash across back of drumsticks. Combine marinade and chicken in 1-gallon zipper-lock bag and toss to coat; press out as much air as possible and seal bag. Refrigerate for at least 1 hour or up to 24 hours.

4 Stir cilantro, jalapeño, salt, and remaining ¼ teaspoon pepper into mojo mixture reserved for sauce. Divide sauce in half; reserve half for cooking and remainder for serving. Remove chicken from marinade, let excess marinade drip off (do not pat dry), and transfer to plate.

5A **FOR A CHARCOAL GRILL** Open bottom vent completely. Light large chimney starter filled with charcoal briquettes (6 quarts). When top coals are partially covered with ash, pour two-thirds evenly over half of grill, then pour remaining coals over other half of grill. Set cooking grate in place, cover, and open lid vent completely. Heat grill until hot, about 5 minutes.

5B **FOR A GAS GRILL** Turn all burners to high; cover; and heat grill until hot, about 15 minutes. Turn primary burner to medium and turn other burner(s) to low.

6 Clean and oil cooking grate. Place chicken skin side up on cooler side of grill. Cover and cook until lightly browned on first side, about 15 minutes. Baste chicken on both sides with mojo reserved for cooking. Flip chicken skin side down; cover; and cook until leg-thigh joint registers 165 degrees, about 15 minutes.

7 Slide chicken to hotter side of grill and cook (covered if using gas) until skin is well browned, 3 to 5 minutes. Flip chicken and cook until leg-thigh joint registers 175 degrees, about 3 minutes. Transfer to platter and spoon mojo reserved for serving over top. Tent with aluminum foil and let rest for 10 minutes. Serve.

Grilled Chicken Cobb Salad

SERVES 4 **TIME** 40 minutes

Why This Recipe Works Time spent over live fire deepens the flavor of avocados and romaine lettuce to give this salad a smoky outdoor twist. You can prep the blue cheese dressing, hard-cooked eggs, and crispy bacon ahead, if you like, which makes mealtime cooking and assembly a snap. You'll grill boneless, skinless chicken breasts first; while they rest, the lettuce and avocados pick up some browning over the fire.

Slice the chicken and arrange it on a platter with the lettuce, avocados, eggs, bacon, and juicy cherry tomatoes; spoon the chunky, cheesy dressing over everything; and you've got an outdoor summertime meal that's as impressive as it is easy. Ripe but firm avocados are critical for successful grilling. If your avocados are overripe, skip seasoning and grilling them and simply peel and slice the avocados before assembling the salad.

- 2 ounces blue cheese, crumbled (½ cup)
- 6 tablespoons extra-virgin olive oil, divided
- 3 tablespoons red wine vinegar
- 4 teaspoons kosher salt, divided
- 1 teaspoon pepper, divided
- 3 romaine lettuce hearts (6 ounces each), halved lengthwise
- 2 ripe but firm avocados, halved and pitted
- 4 (6- to 8-ounce) boneless, skinless chicken breasts, trimmed and pounded to ¾-inch thickness
- 8 ounces cherry tomatoes, halved
- 4 hard-cooked large eggs, halved
- 6 slices bacon, cooked and crumbled (½ cup)
- 1 tablespoon chopped fresh chives

1 Combine blue cheese, ¼ cup oil, vinegar, 1 teaspoon salt, and ¼ teaspoon pepper in bowl; set aside for serving. Brush cut sides of lettuce and avocados with remaining 2 tablespoons oil and sprinkle with 1 teaspoon salt and ½ teaspoon pepper. Pat chicken dry with paper towels and sprinkle with remaining 2 teaspoons salt and ¼ teaspoon pepper.

2A **FOR A CHARCOAL GRILL** Open bottom vent completely. Light large chimney starter filled with charcoal briquettes (6 quarts). When top coals are partially covered with ash, pour evenly over grill. Set cooking grate in place, cover, and open lid vent completely. Heat grill until hot, about 5 minutes.

2B **FOR A GAS GRILL** Turn all burners to high; cover; and heat grill until hot, about 15 minutes. Leave all burners on high.

3 Clean and oil cooking grate. Place chicken on grill and cook until nicely browned and registers 160 degrees, 10 to 14 minutes, flipping as needed. Transfer chicken to carving board and tent with aluminum foil. Place lettuce and avocados on grill cut sides down and cook until charred in spots, about 2 minutes. Transfer to cutting board.

4 Using spoon, scoop avocado flesh from skin. Cut lettuce in half lengthwise. Slice chicken ¾ inch thick. Arrange lettuce, avocados, chicken, tomatoes, and eggs on serving platter. Sprinkle with bacon, drizzle with dressing, and sprinkle with chives. Serve.

GRILLED SPICED CHICKEN AND CARROTS WITH BULGUR

Grilled Spiced Chicken and Carrots with Bulgur

SERVES 4 **TIME** 45 minutes

Why This Recipe Works For a light but substantial companion to quick-cooking boneless, skinless chicken breasts, we pair grilled carrots with bulgur. Grilling the carrots brings out their sweetness, which we bolster with the warm, floral notes of the Indian spice blend garam masala. For ease of handling on the grill, we keep the carrots' long shape, splitting them lengthwise, and we precook them briefly in the microwave so that by the time the outsides are charred, the insides are tender. We slice the grilled carrots and toss them with the bulgur, feta cheese, and pine nuts and serve them with the chicken. A lemony tahini sauce drizzled over the top ties all the elements together. Trim off any very narrow tips from the carrots or they may burn on the grill.

- 1¼ cups medium-grind bulgur
- 3½ teaspoons plus pinch kosher salt, divided, plus salt for cooking bulgur
- 1 pound carrots, peeled and halved lengthwise
- ½ cup extra-virgin olive oil, divided
- 2 teaspoons garam masala, divided
- ½ teaspoon pepper, divided
- 3 tablespoons lemon juice, divided
- 2 tablespoons tahini
- 4 (6- to 8-ounce) boneless, skinless chicken breasts, trimmed
- 3 ounces feta cheese, crumbled (¾ cup)
- ¼ cup pine nuts, toasted

1 Bring 2 quarts water to boil in large saucepan. Add bulgur and 2 teaspoons salt. Reduce heat to medium-low and simmer until tender, 5 to 8 minutes. Drain bulgur and transfer to bowl.

2 Meanwhile, toss carrots with 1 teaspoon salt in large bowl. Cover and microwave until barely pliable, 3 to 4 minutes, shaking bowl halfway through cooking. Drain carrots and toss with 2 tablespoons oil, ½ teaspoon garam masala, and ¼ teaspoon pepper.

3 Whisk 1 tablespoon lemon juice, tahini, 2 tablespoons oil, and pinch salt together in bowl and set aside for serving. Pat chicken dry with paper towels and sprinkle with 2 teaspoons salt, remaining 1½ teaspoons garam masala, and remaining ¼ teaspoon pepper.

4A **FOR A CHARCOAL GRILL** Open bottom vent completely. Light large chimney starter filled with charcoal briquettes (6 quarts). When top coals are partially covered with ash, pour evenly over grill. Set cooking grate in place, cover, and open lid vent completely. Heat grill until hot, about 5 minutes

4B **FOR A GAS GRILL** Turn all burners to high; cover; and heat grill until hot, about 15 minutes. Leave all burners on high.

5 Clean and oil cooking grate. Place chicken and carrots on grill and cook until carrots are charred and chicken registers 160 degrees, 8 to 12 minutes, flipping as needed. Transfer chicken to carving board, tent with aluminum foil, and let rest while finishing salad. Transfer to carrots to cutting board.

6 Slice carrots on bias ½ inch thick and add to bowl with bulgur. Add feta, pine nuts, and remaining ¼ cup oil, remaining 2 tablespoons lemon juice, and remaining ½ teaspoon salt; toss to combine. Slice chicken thin on bias. Serve with bulgur and tahini sauce.

Grilled Chicken Panzanella

SERVES 6 to 8 **TIME** 40 minutes plus 30 minutes marinating

Why This Recipe Works Juicy grilled chicken turns this classic Italian bread salad into a meal. A loaf of ciabatta is split and charred alongside boneless, skinless chicken breasts on the grill before both are cut into equal-size pieces. The bread, charred on the edges, develops an appetizing "crunchewy" texture as it soaks up a vinaigrette that's sharp with Dijon mustard and minced shallot. Thinly sliced cucumber and chopped tomato offer juicy garden freshness. Add milky fresh mozzarella and lots of torn fresh basil and this main-dish salad is complete. If using breasts that are larger than 8 ounces and/or more than ¾ inch thick at the thicker end, halve the breasts horizontally before pounding. Ripe, in-season tomatoes are best here but if they are unavailable, supermarket vine-ripened tomatoes will work; plum tomatoes are too dry. Look for fresh mozzarella balls labeled "ciliegine"; if they're unavailable, cut one 8-ounce ball of fresh mozzarella into ½-inch pieces. The panzanella can be served warm or at room temperature.

- 1½–2 pounds boneless, skinless chicken breasts, trimmed
- ⅓ cup water
- 3 tablespoons fish sauce
- 2 tablespoons honey
- 2½ teaspoons kosher salt, divided
- ⅛ teaspoon plus ¼ teaspoon pepper, divided
- ½ cup extra-virgin olive oil
- 3 tablespoons wine vinegar
- 2 tablespoons minced shallot
- 1 teaspoon Dijon mustard
- 1 (1-pound) loaf ciabatta, halved horizontally
- 3 tablespoons vegetable oil, divided
- 1½ pounds tomatoes, cored and cut into ¾-inch pieces
- 1 English cucumber, quartered lengthwise and sliced ¼ inch thick
- 8 ounces cherry-size mozzarella balls, halved
- ¼ cup fresh basil leaves, torn

1 Pound chicken to ½-inch thickness between 2 sheets of plastic wrap. Whisk water, fish sauce, honey, 2 teaspoons salt, and ⅛ teaspoon pepper together in bowl. Combine marinade and chicken in 1-gallon zipper-lock bag and toss to coat; press out as much air as possible and seal bag. Refrigerate for 30 minutes.

2 Meanwhile, whisk olive oil, vinegar, shallot, mustard, remaining ½ teaspoon salt, and remaining ¼ teaspoon pepper in large bowl to make vinaigrette; set aside for serving.

3 Drizzle cut sides of bread evenly with 2 tablespoons vegetable oil. Open 1 corner of marinating bag, then pour out and discard marinade. Add remaining 1 tablespoon vegetable oil to bag and coat chicken evenly.

4A **FOR A CHARCOAL GRILL** Open bottom vent completely. Light large chimney starter filled with charcoal briquettes (6 quarts). When top coals are partially covered with ash, pour evenly over grill. Set cooking grate in place, cover, and open lid vent completely. Heat grill until hot, about 5 minutes.

4B **FOR A GAS GRILL** Turn all burners to high; cover; and heat grill until hot, about 15 minutes. Leave all burners on high

5 Clean and oil cooking grate. Place chicken on grill and cook (covered if using gas) until nicely marked on both sides and chicken registers 160 degrees, 6 to 10 minutes, flipping as needed. Meanwhile, place bread on grill and cook until well browned and charred at edges, 2 to 4 minutes, flipping as needed. Transfer bread and chicken to cutting board as they finish cooking; tent with aluminum foil.

6 Cut bread and chicken into ¾-inch pieces. Rewhisk vinaigrette to combine, then add bread, chicken, tomatoes, and cucumber and toss to combine. Season with salt and pepper to taste. Transfer salad to serving platter and top with mozzarella and basil. Serve.

GRILLED CHICKEN PANZANELLA

Grilled Chicken and Pita Salad

SERVES 4 **TIME** 40 minutes

Why This Recipe Works This grilled chicken salad is inspired by fattoush, a Levantine salad that combines fresh tomatoes and cucumbers with bright herbs and crisp pita. We make sure the pitas are just the right texture by brushing their craggy sides with plenty of olive oil before grilling them while the chicken rests. The oil soaks into the bread and prevents the pita chips from absorbing too much of the salad's moisture while still allowing them to take on some of its flavor. Ground sumac, lemon juice, and pomegranate molasses add bright, tangy sweetness to the dressing for this meal-worthy salad. Top with scallions, if desired.

- 7 tablespoons extra-virgin olive oil, divided
- 2 (8-inch) pitas, split open
- 2 tablespoons ground sumac, divided
- 4½ teaspoons kosher salt, divided
- 4 (6- to 8-ounce) boneless, skinless chicken breasts, trimmed
- 2 tablespoons lemon juice
- 1 tablespoon pomegranate molasses
- 3 romaine lettuce hearts (6 ounces each), halved and sliced thin
- 1 pound tomatoes, cored and cut into ¾-inch pieces
- 1 English cucumber, quartered lengthwise and sliced thin crosswise
- ½ cup chopped fresh mint

1 Brush 3 tablespoons oil over inner surface of pitas. Sprinkle with 1 teaspoon sumac and ½ teaspoon salt. Pat chicken dry with paper towels and sprinkle with 2 teaspoons sumac and 2 teaspoons salt.

2A **FOR A CHARCOAL GRILL** Open bottom vent completely. Light large chimney starter filled with charcoal briquettes (6 quarts). When top coals are partially covered with ash, pour evenly over grill. Set cooking grate in place, cover, and open lid vent completely. Heat grill until hot, about 5 minutes.

2B **FOR A GAS GRILL** Turn all burners to high; cover; and heat grill until hot, about 15 minutes. Leave all burners on high

3 Clean and oil cooking grate. Place chicken on grill and cook until it registers 160 degrees, about 10 minutes, flipping as needed. Transfer chicken to plate, tent with aluminum foil, and let rest for 5 minutes. Meanwhile, grill pitas until crisp and lightly charred, about 4 minutes, flipping as needed.

4 Whisk lemon juice, pomegranate molasses, remaining ¼ cup oil and remaining 2 teaspoons salt together in large bowl. Add lettuce, tomatoes, cucumber, mint, and remaining 1 tablespoon sumac. Break or cut pitas into bite-size pieces and add to bowl. Toss salad to combine and season with salt to taste. Slice chicken ½ inch thick and serve over salad.

GRILLED CHICKEN AND PITA SALAD

Grilled Chicken and Cabbage with Lemony Browned Butter Dressing

SERVES 4 **TIME** 35 minutes

Why This Recipe Works Coleslaw may be cabbage's usual summertime role, but this humble vegetable is also a natural choice for the grill. Cutting the dense head into wedges keeps it easy to manage on the cooking grate, where the flames transform its leaves from squeaky and sulfurous to sweet and tender. Browned butter, lemon, capers, and almonds elevate the lightly charred cabbage wedges to a sophisticated side for quick-grilled chicken breasts. Be sure to leave the core intact so that the cabbage wedges don't fall apart on the grill.

- 4 (6- to 8-ounce) boneless, skinless chicken breasts, trimmed
- 3½ teaspoons kosher salt, divided
- ¾ teaspoon pepper, divided
- ½ head green cabbage, cut into 8 wedges through core
- 2 tablespoons vegetable oil
- 2 teaspoons grated lemon zest, plus 2 lemons, halved
- 8 tablespoons unsalted butter
- ½ cup sliced almonds
- 2 tablespoons capers, rinsed and patted dry
- 2 tablespoons chopped fresh parsley

1 Pat chicken dry and sprinkle with 2 teaspoons salt and ½ teaspoon pepper. Brush cabbage all over with oil and sprinkle with 1 teaspoon salt and remaining ¼ teaspoon pepper.

2A FOR A CHARCOAL GRILL Open bottom vent completely. Light large chimney starter filled with charcoal briquettes (6 quarts). When top coals are partially covered with ash, pour evenly over grill. Set cooking grate in place, cover, and open lid vent completely. Heat grill until hot, about 5 minutes.

2B FOR A GAS GRILL Turn all burners to high; cover; and heat grill until hot, about 15 minutes. Leave all burners on high.

3 Clean and oil cooking grate. Place chicken, cabbage, and lemon halves cut side down on grill. Cook (covered if using gas) until lemons and cabbage are charred and chicken registers 160 degrees, 6 to 12 minutes, flipping as needed. Transfer lemons, cabbage, and chicken to carving board. Tent chicken with aluminum foil and let rest while making sauce.

4 Squeeze lemons to yield 3 tablespoons juice. Melt butter in 10-inch skillet over medium heat. Add almonds and capers and cook, stirring frequently, until butter is deep golden brown and has a nutty aroma and almonds are toasted, 4 to 6 minutes. Off heat, stir in lemon zest and juice and remaining ½ teaspoon salt, scraping up any browned bits.

5 Arrange cabbage on serving platter. Slice chicken ½ inch thick and arrange over cabbage. Drizzle with sauce and sprinkle with parsley. Serve.

Grilled Chicken, Shishitos, and Tomatoes with Miso-Garlic Butter

SERVES 4 **TIME** 45 minutes

Why This Recipe Works Earthy, mild shishito peppers are often skewered and grilled as a snack; encountering the occasional pepper with a kick is part of their appeal. Here we pair them with cherry tomatoes as a side to boneless chicken breasts and grill all three components quickly over a hot single-level fire. We drizzle everything with an umami-rich miso butter; a sprinkle of flake sea salt adds a delicate finishing crunch. To make flipping easier, we thread the shishito peppers onto doubled metal skewers. You will need seven 12-inch metal skewers for this recipe. Serve with rice or crusty bread.

- 4 tablespoons unsalted butter
- 2 tablespoons water
- 1 tablespoon white miso
- 2 teaspoons sugar
- 1 garlic clove, minced
- 1 teaspoon pepper, divided
- 4 (6- to 8-ounce) boneless, skinless chicken breasts, trimmed
- 3 teaspoons kosher salt, divided
- 10 ounces cherry tomatoes
- 8 ounces shishito peppers
- 1 tablespoon vegetable oil
- ½ teaspoon flake sea salt

1 Melt butter in small saucepan over medium heat. Whisk in water, miso, sugar, garlic, and ½ teaspoon pepper and cook until mixture is simmering and fragrant, 1 to 2 minutes. Remove from heat and cover to keep warm.

2 Pat chicken dry with paper towels and sprinkle with 2 teaspoons kosher salt and remaining ½ teaspoon pepper. Thread tomatoes onto three 12-inch metal skewers. Thread peppers onto 2 sets of two 12-inch metal skewers. Brush tomatoes and peppers with oil and sprinkle with remaining 1 teaspoon kosher salt.

3A **FOR A CHARCOAL GRILL** Open bottom vent completely. Light large chimney starter filled with charcoal briquettes (6 quarts). When top coals are partially covered with ash, pour evenly over grill. Set cooking grate in place, cover, and open lid vent completely. Heat grill until hot, about 5 minutes.

3B **FOR A GAS GRILL** Turn all burners to high; cover; and heat grill until hot, about 15 minutes. Leave all burners on high.

4 Clean and oil cooking grate. Place chicken, tomatoes, and peppers on grill and cook (covered if using gas) until vegetables are charred and blistered and chicken registers 160 degrees, 6 to 12 minutes, flipping as needed. Transfer chicken and vegetable to carving board, tent with aluminum foil, and let rest for 5 minutes.

5 Slide tomatoes and peppers off skewers onto platter. Slice chicken and transfer to platter. Drizzle chicken and vegetables with miso butter and sprinkle vegetables with flake sea salt. Serve.

Grilled Garam Masala Chicken with Radicchio and Naan

SERVES 4 **TIME** 45 minutes

Why This Recipe Works Take advantage of summer weather and use the grill to make this quick, no-fuss dish that calls to mind delectable tandoori chicken, with a vegetable side and a cooling yogurt sauce. Garam masala delivers a range of warm flavors in one convenient blend, and it makes for deeply flavorful chicken. We coat the chicken parts in a mixture of the garam masala and some salt before grilling. To round out the meal, we grill beautiful red radicchio; its crispy edges and bitter notes are an excellent complement to the richness of the chicken. To further balance out the flavors of the meal, we make a simple, bright sauce of plain yogurt, fresh lime juice, and chopped fresh cilantro for some color and kick. Quickly grilled store-bought naans complete this meal with Indian flavors.

- ¾ cup plain whole-milk yogurt
- 2 tablespoons fresh lime juice
- 2 tablespoons finely chopped fresh cilantro, divided
- 2½ teaspoons kosher salt, divided
- 1 tablespoon garam masala
- 3 pounds bone-in chicken pieces (split breasts cut in half crosswise, drumsticks, and/or thighs), trimmed
- 1 head radicchio (10 ounces), cut into 4 wedges through core
- 1 tablespoon extra-virgin olive oil
- ⅛ teaspoon pepper
- 2 naans, halved

1 Stir yogurt, lime juice, 1 tablespoon cilantro, and 1 teaspoon salt in small bowl; set aside for serving. Mix garam masala and 1 teaspoon salt together in bowl. Pat chicken dry with paper towels and sprinkle evenly with spice mixture. Brush radicchio with oil and sprinkle with remaining ½ teaspoon salt and pepper.

2A **FOR A CHARCOAL GRILL** Open bottom vent completely. Light large chimney starter filled with charcoal briquettes (6 quarts). When top coals are partially covered with ash, pour two-thirds evenly over half of grill, then pour remaining coals over other half of grill. Set cooking grate in place, cover, and open lid vent completely. Heat grill until hot, about 5 minutes.

2B **FOR A GAS GRILL** Turn all burners to high; cover; and heat grill until hot, about 15 minutes. Leave primary burner on high and turn other burner(s) to low.

3 Clean and oil cooking grate. Place chicken skin side down on cooler side of grill. Cover and cook until skin is well browned and breasts register 160 degrees and drumsticks/thighs register 175 degrees, 20 to 30 minutes, flipping as needed. Transfer chicken pieces to serving platter as they finish cooking. Tent with aluminum foil and let rest while grilling radicchio.

4 While chicken rests, place radicchio on hotter side of grill and cook until softened and lightly charred, 3 to 5 minutes, flipping as needed. Transfer radicchio to serving platter with chicken and tent with foil. Place naans on hotter side of grill and cook until warmed through, about 2 minutes, flipping as needed. Sprinkle chicken and radicchio with remaining 1 tablespoon cilantro. Serve with reserved sauce and naans.

GRILLED GARAM MASALA CHICKEN WITH RADICCHIO AND NAAN

GRILLED CHICKEN THIGHS WITH MANGO SLAW

Grilled Chicken Thighs with Mango Slaw

SERVES 4 **TIME** 35 minutes

Why This Recipe Works Meaty grilled chicken thighs find a perfect counterpoint in a fresh and fruity coleslaw. To keep this meal quick and breezy, we use boneless thighs and bagged coleslaw mix, which we augment with colorful mango, red bell pepper, red onion, and cilantro. Tajín Clásico Seasoning, made with chile peppers, lime, and sea salt, adds citrus tang and chile warmth to both the chicken and the slaw. Tajín Clásico Seasoning is available at most well-stocked grocery stores. If you can't find it, look for "chili-lime salt" in the spice aisle. Serve with sliced avocado.

- ¼ cup extra-virgin olive oil, divided
- 4 teaspoons Tajín Clásico Seasoning, divided
- 4 teaspoons honey, divided
- 3½ teaspoons kosher salt, divided
- 8 (3- to 5-ounce) boneless, skinless chicken thighs, trimmed
- ½ teaspoon grated lime zest plus 3 tablespoons juice (2 limes)
- 1 (14-ounce) bag coleslaw mix
- 1 mango, peeled, pitted, and cut into thin strips
- 1 red bell pepper, stemmed, seeded, and sliced thin
- 1 small red onion, sliced thin
- ¼ cup chopped fresh cilantro

1 Whisk 2 tablespoons oil, 1 tablespoon Tajín, 1 teaspoon honey, and 2 teaspoons salt together in large bowl. Add chicken and toss to coat, rubbing seasoning into chicken. In separate bowl, whisk lime zest and juice with remaining 2 tablespoons oil, remaining 1 teaspoon Tajín, remaining 1 tablespoon honey, and remaining 1½ teaspoons salt. Add coleslaw mix, mango, bell pepper, onion, and cilantro and toss to combine.

2A **FOR A CHARCOAL GRILL** Open bottom vent completely. Light large chimney starter filled with charcoal briquettes (6 quarts). When top coals are partially covered with ash, pour evenly over grill. Set cooking grate in place, cover, and open lid vent completely. Heat grill until hot, about 5 minutes.

2B **FOR A GAS GRILL** Turn all burners to high; cover; and heat grill until hot, about 15 minutes. Leave all burners on high.

3 Clean and oil cooking grate. Place chicken on grill and cook (covered if using gas) until well browned and registers 175 degrees, 10 to 14 minutes, flipping as needed. Transfer to platter, tent with aluminum foil, and let rest for 5 minutes. Serve chicken with slaw.

Go-To Grilled Chicken Kebabs

SERVES 6 **TIME** 35 minutes plus 1 hour marinating

Why This Recipe Works Boneless, skinless chicken thighs have a rich flavor and collagen that readily breaks down, making them an ideal choice for savory, juicy kebabs. Leaving the fat on the chicken contributes to charring and adds grill flavor. We toss the chicken pieces in a thick mixture of tomato paste, salt, sugar, fish sauce, garlic, and oil before threading them onto skewers and grilling them. A quarter-turn every couple minutes ensures even cooking and browning. If you have thin pieces of chicken, cut them larger than 1 inch and roll or fold them into 1-inch pieces. A rasp grater makes quick work of turning the garlic into a paste. You will need four 12-inch metal skewers for this recipe. We like to serve the kebabs with lettuce, tomato, Greek yogurt, hot sauce, and flatbread or tortillas, or with rice and grilled vegetables.

- ¼ cup tomato paste
- 3 tablespoons vegetable oil
- 2 tablespoons fish sauce
- 3 garlic cloves, minced to paste
- 1½ teaspoons sugar
- 1¼ teaspoons kosher salt
- ½ teaspoon pepper
- 2 pounds boneless, skinless chicken thighs, untrimmed, cut into 1-inch pieces

1 Whisk tomato paste, oil, fish sauce, garlic, sugar, salt, and pepper in medium bowl until smooth. Add chicken and toss to coat. Cover and refrigerate for at least 1 hour or up to 12 hours.

2 Thread chicken onto four 12-inch metal skewers, rolling or folding pieces as necessary to form 1-inch pieces and alternating leaner pieces with fattier pieces.

3A FOR A CHARCOAL GRILL Open bottom vent completely. Light large chimney starter three-quarters filled with charcoal briquettes (4½ quarts). When top coals are partially covered with ash, pour evenly over half of grill. Set cooking grate in place, cover, and open lid vent completely. Heat grill until hot, about 5 minutes.

3B FOR A GAS GRILL Turn all burners to high; cover; and heat grill until hot, about 15 minutes. Leave primary burner on medium-high and turn off other burner(s).

4 Clean and oil cooking grate. Place kebabs on hotter side of grill and cook until well browned and slightly charred on all sides and chicken registers 175 degrees, about 12 minutes, turning often. Remove kebabs from grill, tent with aluminum foil, and let rest for 5 minutes. Serve.

GO-TO GRILLED CHICKEN KEBABS

VARIATIONS

Go-To Grilled Chicken Kebabs with Harissa, Aleppo Pepper, and Mint

Reduce tomato paste to 2 tablespoons. Add 2 tablespoons harissa, 2 teaspoons ground dried Aleppo pepper, and 2 teaspoons dried mint to marinade in step 1.

Go-To Grilled Chicken Kebabs with Red Curry Paste and Lime

Reduce tomato paste to 2 tablespoons. Add 2 tablespoons Thai red curry paste and 2 teaspoons grated lime zest to marinade in step 1. Serve with lime wedges.

BARBECUED CHICKEN KEBABS

Barbecued Chicken Kebabs

SERVES 6 **TIME** 35 minutes

Why This Recipe Works These grilled chicken kebabs, lacquered with sweet and tangy barbecue sauce, work with both lean white meat and fattier dark meat. The secret is twofold: We use a salt rub on chunks of boneless, skinless breast and thigh meat to help them retain moisture. And, for incredible depth of flavor as well as juicy meat, we grind bacon to a paste and apply it to the salted meat. Combined with both sweet and smoked paprika and a little sugar, the bacony rub creates chicken that's juicy, tender, and full-flavored, with a smoky depth that complements the barbecue sauce. Use the large holes of a box grater to grate the onion for the sauce. We prefer flavorful dark thigh meat for these kebabs, but white meat can be used. Whichever you choose, don't mix white and dark meat on the same skewer, since they cook at different rates. If you have thin pieces of chicken, cut them larger than 1 inch and roll or fold them into 1-inch pieces. You will need four 12-inch metal skewers for this recipe.

SAUCE

- ½ cup ketchup
- ¼ cup molasses
- 2 tablespoons grated onion
- 2 tablespoons Worcestershire sauce
- 2 tablespoons Dijon mustard
- 2 tablespoons cider vinegar
- 1 tablespoon packed light brown sugar

CHICKEN

- 2 tablespoons paprika
- 4 teaspoons sugar
- 2 teaspoons kosher salt
- 2 teaspoons smoked paprika
- 2 slices bacon, cut into ½-inch pieces
- 2 pounds boneless, skinless chicken thighs or breasts, trimmed, cut into 1-inch pieces

1 FOR THE SAUCE Bring all ingredients to simmer in small saucepan over medium heat and cook, stirring occasionally, until reduced to about 1 cup, 5 to 7 minutes. Measure out ½ cup sauce and set aside for cooking.

2 FOR THE CHICKEN Combine paprika, sugar, salt, and smoked paprika in large bowl. Process bacon in food processor until smooth paste forms, 30 to 45 seconds, scraping down sides of bowl as needed. Stir bacon paste into spices until evenly combined. Add chicken and toss to coat. Thread chicken onto four 12-inch metal skewers, rolling or folding pieces as necessary to form 1-inch pieces.

3A FOR A CHARCOAL GRILL Open bottom vent completely. Light large chimney starter three-quarters filled with charcoal briquettes (4½ quarts). When top coals are partially covered with ash, pour evenly over half of grill. Set cooking grate in place, cover, and open lid vent completely. Heat grill until hot, about 5 minutes.

3B FOR A GAS GRILL Turn all burners to high; cover; and heat grill until hot, about 15 minutes. Turn all burners to medium-high.

4 Clean and oil cooking grate. Place kebabs on grill (hotter side if using charcoal). Cook (covered if using gas) until well browned on all sides and meat registers 160 degrees if using breasts, or 175 degrees if using thighs, 8 to 10 minutes, turning often. Brush top of kebabs with half of reserved sauce; turn; and cook until sauce is sizzling and browning in spots, about 1 minute. Brush kebabs with remaining reserved sauce, turn, and cook until sizzling and browning in spots, about 1 minute.

5 Transfer kebabs to serving platter, tent with aluminum foil, and let rest for 5 minutes. Serve, passing remaining sauce separately.

GRILLED CHICKEN SOUVLAKI WITH GREEN PEPPERS AND ONION

Grilled Chicken Souvlaki with Green Peppers and Onion

SERVES 4 **TIME** 1 hour

Why This Recipe Works At least as appealing as souvlaki's tangy, smoky flavor is how easily you can make it on the grill. Just give pieces of boneless chicken a quick brine while the grill heats, to prevent the meat from drying out, and then toss the chunks of chicken in olive oil, lemon juice, oregano, parsley, pepper, and honey right before grilling. Bell peppers and onion at the ends of each skewer make edible shields to protect the chicken while it cooks. Reserving some of the oil mixture to toss with the chicken once it comes off the grill ensures that the meat's exterior is brightly flavored and just as tender and moist as the interior. This tzatziki is fairly mild; if you like a more assertive flavor, double the garlic. A rasp grater makes quick work of turning the garlic into a paste. If you have thin pieces of chicken, cut them larger than 1 inch and roll or fold them into 1-inch pieces. This recipe was developed using Diamond Crystal kosher salt. If you have Morton kosher salt, which is denser, use 3 tablespoons. We like the chicken as a wrap, but you may skip the pitas and serve the chicken, vegetables, and tzatziki with rice. You will need four 12-inch metal skewers for this recipe.

TZATZIKI SAUCE

- 1 tablespoon lemon juice
- 1 small garlic clove, minced to paste
- ¾ cup plain Greek yogurt
- ½ cucumber, peeled, halved lengthwise, seeded, and diced fine (½ cup)
- 3 tablespoons minced fresh mint
- 1 tablespoon minced fresh parsley
- ¾ teaspoon kosher salt

CHICKEN

- ¼ cup kosher salt for brining
- 1½ pounds boneless, skinless chicken breasts, trimmed and cut into 1-inch pieces
- ⅓ cup extra-virgin olive oil
- 2 tablespoons minced fresh parsley
- 1 teaspoon finely grated lemon zest plus ¼ cup juice (2 lemons)
- 1 teaspoon honey
- 1 teaspoon dried oregano
- ½ teaspoon pepper
- 1 green bell pepper, quartered, stemmed, and seeded, each quarter cut into 4 chunks
- 1 small red onion, ends trimmed, peeled, and halved lengthwise, each half cut into 4 chunks
- 4 (8-inch) pitas

1 **FOR THE TZATZIKI SAUCE** Whisk lemon juice and garlic together in small bowl and let stand for 10 minutes. Stir in yogurt, cucumber, mint, parsley, and salt. Cover and set aside for serving.

2 **FOR THE CHICKEN** Dissolve salt in 1 quart cold water in large container. Submerge chicken in brine, cover, and refrigerate for 30 minutes. Meanwhile, combine oil, parsley, lemon zest and juice, honey, oregano, and pepper in medium bowl. Measure out ¼ cup oil mixture and set aside for serving.

3 Remove chicken from brine and pat dry with paper towels. Toss chicken with remaining oil mixture. Thread 4 pieces of bell pepper, concave side up, onto 1 skewer, followed by one-quarter of chicken and 2 chunks of onion; transfer to plate. Repeat with remaining 3 skewers. Lightly moisten 2 pitas with water. Sandwich 2 unmoistened pitas between moistened pitas and wrap stack tightly in lightly greased heavy-duty aluminum foil.

4A **FOR A CHARCOAL GRILL** Open bottom vent completely. Light large chimney starter mounded with charcoal briquettes (7 quarts). When top coals are partially covered with ash, pour evenly over half of grill. Set cooking grate in place, cover, and open lid vent completely. Heat grill until hot, about 5 minutes.

4B **FOR A GAS GRILL** Turn all burners to high; cover; and heat grill until hot, about 15 minutes. Leave primary burner on high and turn off other burner(s).

5 Clean and oil cooking grate. Place kebabs on hotter side of grill and cook until chicken and vegetables are well browned on all sides and chicken registers 160 degrees, 15 to 20 minutes, turning often. Using fork, push chicken and vegetables off skewers into bowl of reserved oil mixture and toss to combine; cover with foil and let rest while grilling pitas.

6 Meanwhile, place packet of pitas on cooler side of grill. Flip occasionally to heat, about 5 minutes.

7 Lay each warm pita on 12-inch square of foil. Spread each pita with 2 tablespoons tzatziki. Place one-quarter of chicken and vegetables in middle of each pita. Roll into cylindrical shape and serve.

Grilled Chicken Satay

SERVES 4 to 6 as a main dish or 10 to 12 as an appetizer
TIME 1¼ hours

Why This Recipe Works Gorgeously charred, robustly seasoned, crisp-edged grilled chicken: That's what you get with every bite of Malaysian chicken satay (satay ayam), one of Southeast Asia's quintessential street foods. It features skewers of grilled chicken coated in a deeply fragrant herbal paste. Our version uses fatty, collagen-rich chicken thighs cut into wide strips and stretched between two skewers; the more surface area, the more flavor. Loads of lemongrass, ginger, and galangal, plus garlic, shallots, pepper flakes, spices, and a touch of sugar make for a complex, aromatic paste that develops savory character when charred. We reserve part of the paste to use as a fragrant foundation for the peanut dipping sauce. If galangal is unavailable, increase the ginger to one 1½-inch piece. Use a Thai or Indonesian tamarind concentrate and not one from India, which is darker and has a more cooked flavor. Lime juice can be substituted for the tamarind concentrate. For a spicier dish, use the larger amount of red pepper flakes. You will need eight 12-inch metal skewers for this recipe.

AROMATIC PASTE

- 2 lemongrass stalks, trimmed to bottom 6 inches
- 3 shallots, chopped (⅔ cup)
- 3 tablespoons water
- 1 tablespoon vegetable oil
- 1 tablespoon packed brown sugar
- 3 garlic cloves, chopped
- 1 (1-inch) piece galangal, peeled and minced
- 1 (1-inch) piece ginger, peeled and sliced into ⅛-inch-thick coins
- 4 teaspoons kosher salt
- 1 teaspoon ground turmeric
- ½-¾ teaspoon red pepper flakes
- ½ teaspoon ground coriander
- ½ teaspoon ground cumin

PEANUT SAUCE

- ⅓ cup dry-roasted peanuts
- 2 tablespoons vegetable oil
- ¾ cup water, plus extra as needed
- 1 tablespoon tamarind juice concentrate
- 1 tablespoon packed brown sugar

CHICKEN

- 2 pounds boneless, skinless chicken thighs, trimmed and cut crosswise into 1- to 1½-inch-wide strips
- 2 tablespoons vegetable oil

GRILLED CHICKEN SATAY

1 **FOR THE AROMATIC PASTE** Halve lemongrass lengthwise and, using meat pounder, lightly crush on cutting board to soften. Mince lemongrass and transfer to food processor. Add shallots, water, oil, sugar, garlic, galangal, ginger, salt, turmeric, and pepper flakes and process until uniform paste forms, about 2 minutes, scraping down sides of bowl as necessary. Measure out ⅓ cup paste and set aside for peanut sauce.

2 Combine remaining paste, coriander, and cumin in bowl. Cover and microwave for 1½ minutes, stirring halfway through cooking. Transfer bowl to refrigerator and let cool while preparing sauce.

3 **FOR THE PEANUT SAUCE** Place peanuts in now-empty processor and process until coarsely ground, about 15 seconds. Heat oil and reserved ⅓ cup paste in medium saucepan over medium-low heat until paste starts to darken, about 5 minutes. Stir in water, tamarind, sugar, and peanuts and bring to boil, scraping up any browned bits. Reduce heat to maintain gentle simmer and cook, stirring occasionally, until sauce is reduced to about 1 cup, 8 to 10 minutes. Season with salt to taste, cover, and set aside for serving.

4 **FOR THE CHICKEN** Add chicken to cooled paste and toss to combine. Thread chicken onto 4 sets of two 12-inch metal skewers. (Hold 2 skewers 1 inch apart and thread chicken onto both skewers at once so that strips of chicken are perpendicular to skewers.) Do not crowd skewers; each set of skewers should hold 6 to 8 pieces of chicken. (Skewers can be refrigerated for up to 4 hours.) Brush both sides of skewers with oil.

5A **FOR A CHARCOAL GRILL** Open bottom vent completely. Light large chimney starter mounded with charcoal briquettes (7 quarts). When top coals are partially covered with ash, pour evenly over grill. Set cooking grate in place, cover, and open lid vent completely. Heat grill until hot, about 5 minutes.

5B **FOR A GAS GRILL** Turn all burners to high; cover; and heat grill until hot, about 15 minutes. Leave all burners on high.

6 Clean and oil cooking grate. Place skewers on grill and cook (covered if using gas) until browned and char marks appear on first side, about 5 minutes. Using large metal spatula, gently release chicken from grill. Flip skewers and cook until chicken registers 175 to 180 degrees, 3 to 5 minutes. Transfer skewers to large platter. Gently reheat peanut sauce, thinning with extra water, 1 tablespoon at a time, to desired consistency. Serve chicken, passing peanut sauce separately.

GRILLED CHICKEN TACOS WITH SALSA VERDE

Grilled Chicken Tacos with Salsa Verde

SERVES 4 **TIME** 40 minutes plus 30 minutes marinating

Why This Recipe Works Simple grilled chicken, which cooks up quickly with a nice, smoky char, makes a perfect taco filling, especially when accompanied by a piquant green tomatillo salsa. Because it's paired with other flavorful elements, the chicken needs only a brief stint in a garlic-lime marinade before being grilled over a hot fire. Grilling some of the salsa ingredients—sliced onion, a jalapeño chile, and half of the tomatillos—complements the smoky notes of the chicken. We pulse the grilled vegetables with additional raw tomatillos, cilantro, lime juice, and garlic for freshness and bite. The tortillas are also grilled briefly, until softened, so they wrap easily around the flavorful fillings. Serve with sliced avocado and sliced radishes.

- ¼ cup vegetable oil, divided
- 3 tablespoons lime juice (2 limes), divided
- 2 tablespoons water
- 5 cloves garlic, minced, divided
- 4½ teaspoons kosher salt, divided
- 1 teaspoon plus pinch sugar, divided
- ½ teaspoon pepper
- 1½ pounds boneless, skinless chicken breasts, trimmed
- 1 onion, peeled and cut into ½-inch-thick rounds
- 1 jalapeño chile, stemmed, halved, and seeded
- 1 pound tomatillos, husks and stems removed, rinsed well and dried, divided
- 12 (6-inch) corn tortillas
- ½ cup chopped fresh cilantro

1 Whisk 3 tablespoons oil, 1 tablespoon lime juice, water, half of garlic, 1 tablespoon salt, 1 teaspoon sugar, and pepper together in medium bowl. Add chicken and toss to coat. Cover and refrigerate for 30 minutes, stirring occasionally. Brush onion, jalapeño, and half of tomatillos with remaining 1 tablespoon oil and sprinkle with 1 teaspoon salt. Halve remaining tomatillos and set aside for making salsa just before serving.

2A **FOR A CHARCOAL GRILL** Open bottom vent completely. Light large chimney starter filled with charcoal briquettes (6 quarts). When top coals are partially covered with ash, pour evenly over grill. Set cooking grate in place, cover, and open lid vent completely. Heat grill until hot, about 5 minutes.

2B **FOR A GAS GRILL** Turn all burners to high; cover; and heat grill until hot, about 15 minutes. Leave all burners on high.

3 Clean and oil cooking grate. Place chicken and oiled vegetables on grill. Cook (covered if using gas), flipping as needed, until chicken registers 160 degrees and vegetables are lightly charred and soft, 10 to 15 minutes. Transfer chicken and vegetables to cutting board, tent with aluminum foil, and let rest while grilling tortillas.

4 Working in batches, grill tortillas, flipping as needed, until lightly charred, 30 to 60 seconds per side; wrap tightly in foil to keep soft.

5 Chop grilled vegetables coarse, then add to food processor. Add cilantro, remaining 2 tablespoons lime juice, remaining garlic, remaining ½ teaspoon salt, remaining pinch sugar and remaining tomatillos and pulse until salsa is slightly chunky, 16 to 18 pulses. Slice chicken thin on bias and serve with tortillas and tomatillo salsa.

Grilled Chicken Fajitas with Cilantro-Lime Sour Cream

SERVES 4 **TIME** 35 minutes

Why This Recipe Works Colorful, fresh, and supereasy, chicken fajitas are summer grilling in the fast lane. Chili powder, cumin, and lime juice flavor the quick and zesty marinade for boneless skinless breasts, which cook in a flash over a hot fire alongside onion and peppers. Cilantro, lime zest, and more lime juice elevate sour cream into a cooling topping. Tuck everything into grill-warmed tortillas and enjoy. These fajitas are great with only the cilantro-lime sour cream, but you can also serve them with your favorite fajita toppings, such as shredded Monterey Jack cheese, salsa, guacamole, lime wedges, or hot sauce.

- 3 tablespoons vegetable oil, divided
- 2½ teaspoons chili powder
- 3¼ teaspoons kosher salt, divided
- 1½ teaspoons ground cumin
- 1 teaspoon grated lime zest, plus 2 tablespoons lime juice (2 limes), divided
- 3 (6- to 8-ounce) boneless, skinless chicken breasts, trimmed
- 1 red onion, sliced into ½-inch-thick rounds
- 2 yellow, red, orange, or green bell peppers, quartered, stemmed, and seeded
- ¾ cup sour cream
- 3 tablespoons chopped fresh cilantro
- 8–12 (6-inch) flour tortillas

1 Combine 1½ tablespoons oil, chili powder, 1½ teaspoons salt, cumin, and 1½ tablespoons lime juice in large bowl. Add chicken and toss to coat. Push toothpick horizontally through each onion round to keep rings intact while grilling. Brush onion and bell peppers with remaining 1½ tablespoons oil and sprinkle with 1½ teaspoons salt.

2 Combine sour cream, cilantro, lime zest, and remaining 1½ teaspoons lime juice and remaining ¼ teaspoon salt in bowl; set aside for serving.

3A **FOR A CHARCOAL GRILL** Open bottom vent completely. Light large chimney starter filled with charcoal briquettes (6 quarts). When top coals are partially covered with ash, pour evenly over grill. Set cooking grate in place, cover, and open lid vent completely. Heat grill until hot, about 5 minutes.

3B **FOR A GAS GRILL** Turn all burners to high; cover; and heat grill until hot, about 15 minutes. Leave all burners on high.

4 Clean and oil cooking grate. Place chicken, onion, and bell peppers on grill and cook (covered if using gas) until chicken registers 160 degrees and vegetables are tender and lightly charred, 10 to 14 minutes, flipping as needed. Transfer chicken and vegetables to cutting board, tent with aluminum foil, and let rest while grilling tortillas.

5 Working in batches, grill tortillas, flipping as needed, until lightly charred, 30 to 60 seconds per side; wrap tightly in foil to keep soft.

6 Slice chicken crosswise into ¼-inch-thick pieces and peppers into thin strips. Remove toothpicks from onion and cut rounds in half. Serve with tortillas and sour cream sauce.

Grilled Chicken Nachos with Corn, Poblanos, and Black Beans

SERVES 6 to 8 **TIME** 50 minutes

Why This Recipe Works Nachos on the grill? Why not? Some of the components for nachos are even better when they're imbued with smoke and char. We soak boneless chicken breasts in a potent "brinerade" of water, fish sauce, honey, salt, and pepper and then brown them deeply over a hot fire. We also grill mildly spicy poblano chiles for an earthy, vegetal bite and fresh corn for pops of sweetness. We toss the grilled vegetables with drained canned black beans and a full pound of finely shredded sharp cheddar and then evenly distribute everything, along with bite-size pieces of the grilled chicken, among multiple layers of crisp tortilla chips in a disposable aluminum roasting pan. Briefly sliding the nachos back onto the grill melts the cheese and infuses the dish with tantalizing smoke flavor. If using breasts that are larger than 8 ounces and/or more than ¾ inch thick at the thicker end, halve the breasts horizontally before pounding. Use the smaller holes of a box grater to grate the cheese; a finer shred makes for more even distribution and melting. Serve with Mexican crema or sour cream, salsa and/or guacamole, fresh cilantro, and pickled jalapeños and/or onions.

- 1½–2 pounds boneless, skinless chicken breasts, trimmed
- ⅓ cup water
- 3 tablespoons fish sauce
- 2 tablespoons honey
- 2 teaspoons kosher salt
- ⅛ teaspoon pepper
- 5 teaspoons vegetable oil, divided
- 2 ears corn, husks and silk removed
- 2 poblano chiles, stemmed, halved, and seeded
- 1 pound sharp cheddar, Monterey Jack, or pepper Jack cheese, finely shredded (4 cups)
- 1 (15-ounce) can black beans, rinsed
- 12 ounces tortilla chips
- 1 (13 by 9-inch) disposable aluminum roasting pan
- 2 scallions, sliced thin
- Lime wedges

1 Pound chicken to ½-inch thickness between 2 sheets of plastic wrap. Whisk water, fish sauce, honey, salt, and pepper together in bowl. Combine marinade and chicken in 1-gallon zipper-lock bag and toss to coat; press out as much air as possible and seal bag. Refrigerate for 30 minutes.

2 Open 1 corner of marinating bag, then pour out and discard marinade. Add 1 tablespoon oil to bag and coat chicken evenly. Rub corn and poblanos with remaining 2 teaspoons oil.

3A **FOR A CHARCOAL GRILL** Open bottom vent completely. Light large chimney starter filled with charcoal briquettes (6 quarts). When top coals are partially covered with ash, pour evenly over grill. Set cooking grate in place, cover, and open lid vent completely. Heat grill until hot, about 5 minutes.

3B **FOR A GAS GRILL** Turn all burners to high; cover; and heat grill until hot, about 15 minutes. Leave all burners on high.

4 Clean and oil cooking grate. Place chicken on grill and cook (covered if using gas) until nicely marked on both sides and registers 160 degrees, 6 to 10 minutes, flipping as needed. Meanwhile, place corn and poblanos on grill and cook until corn is charred on all sides and poblanos are well blistered, 5 to 10 minutes, turning as needed. Transfer chicken and corn to cutting board as they finish cooking; tent with aluminum foil. Transfer poblanos to bowl and cover with foil. Turn all burners to medium (if using gas).

5 Peel and discard skin from poblanos and slice into ¼-inch-thick strips. Cut kernels from corn into bowl, then stir in cheddar, black beans, and poblanos. Cut chicken into ½-inch pieces.

6 Spread one-quarter of tortilla chips evenly in disposable pan. Sprinkle one-quarter of cheese mixture and one-quarter of chicken over top. Repeat layering of chips, cheese mixture, and chicken 3 more times. Place pan on grill; cover; and cook until cheese is melted, 5 to 7 minutes. Sprinkle with scallions and serve with lime wedges.

GRILLED CHICKEN NACHOS WITH CORN, POBLANOS, AND BLACK BEANS

GRILLED CHICKEN AND
VEGETABLE QUESADILLAS

Grilled Chicken and Vegetable Quesadillas

SERVES 4 as a main dish or 6 to 8 as an appetizer
TIME 40 minutes

Why This Recipe Works With the help of a plancha, you can turn out quesadillas on the grill as fast as your guests can devour them. Onion, bell pepper, zucchini, and chicken breasts all get a boost of grill flavor from being cooked right on the grate; then, the plancha is heated up and the assembled tortillas are pressed and griddled until they're evenly brown—and no melted cheese or bits of vegetable fall through the grate. For spicier quesadillas, use pepper Jack cheese in place of Monterey Jack. You will need a cast-iron plancha measuring at least 20 by 10 inches.

- 5 tablespoons extra-virgin olive oil, divided
- 3 garlic cloves, minced
- 1 onion, sliced into ½-inch-thick rounds
- 1 red bell pepper, quartered, stemmed, and seeded
- 1 small zucchini (6 ounces), sliced lengthwise into 4 planks
- 1½ pounds boneless, skinless chicken breasts, trimmed
- 1½ teaspoons kosher salt
- ½ teaspoon pepper
- 4 (12-inch) flour tortillas
- 8 ounces Monterey Jack cheese, shredded (2 cups)
- Lime wedges

1 Microwave ¼ cup oil and garlic together in bowl until bubbling, about 30 seconds. Push toothpick horizontally through each onion round to keep rings intact while grilling. Brush onion rounds, bell pepper, zucchini, and chicken with garlic-oil and sprinkle with salt and pepper.

2A FOR A CHARCOAL GRILL Open bottom vent completely. Light large chimney starter filled with charcoal briquettes (6 quarts). When top coals are partially covered with ash, pour evenly over grill. Set cooking grate in place, cover, and open lid vent completely. Heat grill until hot, about 5 minutes.

2B FOR A GAS GRILL Turn all burners to high; cover; and heat grill until hot, about 15 minutes. Leave all burners on high.

3 Clean and oil cooking grate. Place chicken and vegetables on grill and cook until lightly charred and chicken registers 160 degrees, 6 to 10 minutes, flipping as needed. Transfer vegetables and chicken to cutting board as they finish cooking.

4 Center plancha on now-empty grill. Turn all burners to medium-low (if using gas). Cover and heat plancha while assembling quesadillas.

5 Slice bell pepper, zucchini, and chicken thin. Remove toothpicks from onion rounds and separate into rings. Place tortillas on counter and brush with remaining 1 tablespoon oil. Flip tortillas oiled side down and sprinkle half of each with ¼ cup Monterey Jack, leaving ½-inch border. Layer vegetables and chicken over cheese and sprinkle with remaining Monterey Jack. Fold tortillas over filling and press gently to seal.

6 Place 2 quesadillas on plancha and press firmly to reseal. Cover and cook until quesadillas are crisp and golden brown on first side, 2 to 4 minutes. Using 2 spatulas, flip quesadillas and gently press down with spatula. Cook until second side is browned and crisp and cheese is melted, 2 to 4 minutes; transfer to cutting board. Repeat with remaining quesadillas. Cut each quesadilla into wedges and serve with lime wedges.

Grilled Chicken Sandwiches with Red Curry Slaw

SERVES 4 **TIME** 35 minutes

Why This Recipe Works Minimal prep and cooking makes these sandwiches a fantastic choice for your next cookout or campout. Red curry paste and fish sauce deliver big flavor to both the chicken marinade and the coleslaw dressing. The quick slaw adds cool, fresh crunch when tucked into toasty sub rolls along with the grilled chicken cutlets. If chicken cutlets are unavailable, make your own by halving four 6- to 8-ounce boneless, skinless chicken breasts horizontally and pounding them ½ inch thick. For a bit of extra heat, serve with sriracha or hot sauce.

- 2 tablespoons plus 2 teaspoons fish sauce, divided
- 2 tablespoons vegetable oil
- 2 tablespoons packed brown sugar
- 4 teaspoons red curry paste, divided
- ¼ teaspoon pepper
- 8 (3- to 4-ounce) chicken cutlets, ½ inch thick, trimmed
- ½ cup mayonnaise
- 1 tablespoon lime juice
- 1 (11-ounce) bag coleslaw mix
- 4 (6-inch) Italian sub rolls, split lengthwise

1 Whisk 2 tablespoons fish sauce, oil, sugar, 2 teaspoons curry paste, and pepper together in bowl. Add cutlets and toss to coat.

2 Whisk mayonnaise, lime juice, remaining 2 teaspoons fish sauce and remaining 2 teaspoons curry paste together in large bowl. Add coleslaw mix and toss to combine. Season with salt and pepper to taste.

GRILLED CHICKEN SANDWICHES WITH RED CURRY SLAW

CHICKEN SPIEDIES

3A **FOR A CHARCOAL GRILL** Open bottom vent completely. Light large chimney starter filled with charcoal briquettes (6 quarts). When top coals are partially covered with ash, pour evenly over grill. Set cooking grate in place, cover, and open lid vent completely. Heat grill until hot, about 5 minutes.

3B **FOR A GAS GRILL** Turn all burners to high; cover; and heat grill until hot, about 15 minutes. Leave all burners on high.

4 Clean and oil cooking grate. Place cutlets on grill and cook until lightly charred and cooked through, about 8 minutes, flipping as needed. Transfer cutlets to plate, tent with aluminum foil, and let rest for 5 minutes. Meanwhile, place rolls on grill and cook until toasted, about 1 minute. Divide cutlets and slaw evenly among rolls. Serve.

Chicken Spiedies

SERVES 6 **TIME** 45 minutes

Why This Recipe Works A grilled sandwich popular in upstate New York, the spiedie (pronounced "speedy") gets its named from "spiedo," Italian for "spit." Cubed meat marinates for up to a week before it's skewered and grilled. Our version gives you the trademark tangy brightness without the wait. Pricking the chicken with a fork allows the marinade to flavor the meat in only 30 minutes. The potent marinade keeps the chicken moist on the grill, and a final drizzle of reserved marinade mixed with lemon juice, vinegar, and mayonnaise reinforces the flavors. You will need six 12-inch metal skewers for this recipe.

- ½ cup extra-virgin olive oil
- 2 garlic cloves, minced
- 2 tablespoons finely chopped fresh basil
- 2 teaspoons grated lemon zest plus 1 tablespoon juice
- 2 teaspoons kosher salt
- ½ teaspoon pepper
- ½ teaspoon dried oregano
- ¼ teaspoon red pepper flakes
- 3 tablespoons mayonnaise
- 1 tablespoon red wine vinegar
- 4 (6- to 8-ounce) boneless, skinless chicken breasts, trimmed
- 6 (6-inch) sub rolls, slit partially open lengthwise and toasted if desired

1 Combine oil, garlic, basil, lemon zest, salt, pepper, oregano, and pepper flakes in large bowl. Transfer 2 tablespoons oil mixture to separate bowl and whisk in mayonnaise, vinegar, and lemon juice; cover sauce and refrigerate until serving.

2 Prick chicken breasts all over with fork and cut into 1¼-inch chunks. Add chicken to remaining oil mixture and toss to coat. Cover and refrigerate for at least 30 minutes or up to 3 hours.

3 Remove chicken from marinade (do not pat dry) and thread onto six 12-inch metal skewers.

4A **FOR A CHARCOAL GRILL** Open bottom vent completely. Light large chimney starter filled with charcoal briquettes (6 quarts). When top coals are partially covered with ash, pour evenly over grill. Set cooking grate in place, cover, and open lid vent completely. Heat grill until hot, about 5 minutes.

4B **FOR A GAS GRILL** Turn all burners to high; cover; and heat grill until hot, about 15 minutes. Leave all burners on high.

5 Clean and oil cooking grate. Place skewers on grill; cover; and cook until lightly charred and chicken is cooked through, 10 to 15 minutes, turning often. Transfer skewers to plate, tent with aluminum foil, and let rest for 5 minutes. Place skewers in sub rolls, remove skewers, and drizzle with reserved sauce. Serve.

Easy Grill-Roasted Whole Chicken

SERVES 4 **TIME** 1¾ hours

Why This Recipe Works This recipe brings the sublime simplicity of roast chicken to the grill. Grilling the chicken over indirect heat for the majority of the cooking time allows it to cook gently and evenly throughout, while finishing it directly over the fire ensures the skin crisps and browns. Using a wood chip packet subtly infuses the meat with smoky grill flavor. Draining the bird's cavity midway through cooking prevents the fatty juices from dripping onto the fire and causing flare-ups. We developed this recipe on a three-burner gas grill. If using a two-burner grill, place the wood chips on the primary burner and heat the grill with both burners on high. When the grill is hot, keep the primary burner on high and turn the secondary burner off; place the chicken on the cooler side, about 4 inches from the primary burner, and proceed with the recipe, adjusting both burners as needed to maintain 400 degrees and rotating the chicken halfway through cooking. If using a charcoal grill, you can substitute one small wood chunk for the wood chip packet.

- 1 tablespoon kosher salt
- ½ teaspoon pepper
- 1 (3½- to 4½-pound) whole chicken, giblets discarded
- 1 tablespoon vegetable oil
- ½ cup wood chips

1 Combine salt and pepper in bowl. Pat chicken dry with paper towels, then rub entire surface of chicken with oil. Sprinkle salt mixture all over chicken and rub in mixture with your hands to evenly coat. Tie legs together with kitchen twine and tuck wingtips behind back.

2 Using large piece of heavy-duty aluminum foil, wrap wood chips in 8 by 4-inch foil packet. (Make sure chips do not poke holes in sides or bottom of packet.) Cut 2 evenly spaced 2-inch slits in top of packet.

3A **FOR A CHARCOAL GRILL** Open bottom vent halfway. Light large chimney starter mounded with charcoal briquettes (7 quarts). When top coals are partially covered with ash, pour into 2 banked piles on either side of grill. Place wood chip packet on 1 pile of coals. Set cooking grate in place, cover, and open lid vent halfway. Heat grill until hot and wood chips are smoking, about 5 minutes. (Grill temperature will reach about 400 degrees and will fall to about 350 degrees by end of cooking.)

3B **FOR A GAS GRILL** Remove cooking grate and place wood chip packet directly on primary burner. Set grate in place; turn all burners to high; cover; and heat grill until hot and wood chips are smoking, about 15 minutes. Turn 2 outside burners to medium-high and turn off center burner. (Adjust outside burners as needed to maintain grill temperature of 400 degrees.)

4 Clean and oil cooking grate. Place chicken, breast side up with cavity facing toward you, in center of grill, making sure chicken is centered between hotter sides of grill. Cover (position lid vent over chicken if using charcoal) and cook until breast registers 130 degrees, 45 to 55 minutes.

5 Using long grill tongs, reach into cavity and carefully lift chicken by breast. Holding chicken over bowl or container, tilt chicken toward you to allow fat and juices to drain from cavity. Transfer chicken, breast side up, to hotter side of grill (without wood chip packet) and cook, covered, until back is deep golden brown, about 5 minutes. Using tongs, flip chicken breast side down; cover and cook until breast is deep golden brown, about 5 minutes.

6 Using tongs, flip chicken breast side up and return it to center of grill; take internal temperature of breast. If breast registers 155 degrees, transfer chicken to carving board. If breast registers less than 155 degrees, cover and cook in center of grill, checking temperature every 2 minutes, until it registers 155 degrees.

7 Transfer chicken to carving board and let rest, uncovered, for 15 minutes. Carve chicken and serve.

GRILL-ROASTED BUTTERFLIED CHICKEN

Grill-Roasted Butterflied Chicken

SERVES 4 **TIME** 1¾ hours plus 1 hour salting

Why This Recipe Works Butterflying a whole chicken puts more of the skin in contact with the grill, which makes it especially crisp. Threading skewers through the breast and drumsticks helps the chicken lie flat on the grill and keep it intact. To ensure juicy meat, we grill the chicken over the cooler side of a half-grill fire. A simple rub of brown sugar, salt, and pepper turns the skin a beautiful bronze; you can also heighten the flavor with a barbecue or ras el hanout rub variation.

- 1 (4-pound) whole chicken, giblets discarded
- 2 (12-inch) wooden skewers
- 1 tablespoon packed light brown sugar
- 2 teaspoons kosher salt
- 2 teaspoons pepper

1 With chicken breast side down, use kitchen shears to cut along both sides of backbone. Discard backbone and trim any excess fat or skin at neck. Flip chicken and use heel of your hand to flatten breastbone. Tuck wingtips behind back. Insert 1 skewer down length of chicken through thickest part of breast and drumstick. Repeat with second skewer on other half of chicken.

2 Combine sugar, salt, and pepper in bowl. Rub mixture evenly over skin side of chicken. Transfer chicken skin side up to plate and refrigerate, uncovered, for at least 1 hour or up to 24 hours.

3A **FOR A CHARCOAL GRILL** Open bottom vent completely. Light large chimney starter mounded with charcoal briquettes (7 quarts). When top coals are partially covered with ash, pour evenly over half of grill. Set cooking grate in place, cover, and open lid vent completely. Heat grill until hot, about 5 minutes.

3B **FOR A GAS GRILL** Turn all burners to high; cover; and heat grill until hot, about 15 minutes. Leave primary burner on high and turn off other burner(s). (Adjust primary burner as needed to maintain grill temperature between 350 and 400 degrees)

4 Clean and oil cooking grate. Place chicken skin side up on cooler side of grill (6 to 8 inches from heat source for gas grill) with skewers parallel to fire. Cover (position lid vent over chicken if using charcoal) and cook until breast registers 160 degrees and thighs register 175 degrees, about 1 hour, rotating chicken halfway through cooking.

5 Transfer chicken skin side up to carving board, tent with aluminum foil, and let rest for 15 minutes. Remove skewers, carve chicken, and serve.

VARIATIONS

Grill-Roasted Butterflied Chicken with Barbecue Spice Rub

Increase sugar to 3 tablespoons. Add 1 tablespoon paprika, 1 tablespoon chili powder, 2 teaspoons garlic powder, and ¼ teaspoon cayenne pepper to sugar rub. Rub one-third of spice mixture underneath skin, then rub remaining spice mixture all over chicken.

Grill-Roasted Butterflied Chicken with Ras el Hanout Spice Rub

Reduce salt to 1½ teaspoons and omit pepper. Add 2 tablespoons paprika, 4 teaspoons ground coriander, 4 teaspoons ground cumin, 1 teaspoon ground cardamom, 1 teaspoon ground cinnamon, ½ teaspoon ground cloves, ½ teaspoon ground nutmeg, and ½ teaspoon cayenne pepper to sugar rub. Rub one-third of spice mixture underneath skin, then rub remaining spice mixture all over chicken.

Butterflying a Chicken

1 Using kitchen shears, cut through bones on either side of backbone and trim any excess fat or skin at neck.

2 Flip chicken breast side up and use heel of your hand to flatten breastbone. Tuck wingtips behind back.

Grilled Wine-and-Herb-Marinated Chicken

SERVES 4 **TIME** 2 hours

Why This Recipe Works Dry white wine pairs beautifully with mild chicken and serves as the base for an herby marinade. Whizzing the marinade in a blender breaks down the herbs for optimal flavor and distribution, and poking holes in the chicken with a skewer helps the flavors of the marinade penetrate the bird. We butterfly the chicken so that it cooks more quickly and evenly. Skewering the breast and drumsticks helps the chicken lie flat on the grill and keeps it intact. We reserve a small amount of the marinade to brush on the chicken near the end of cooking; this adds complexity and freshness to the grilled meat. This recipe was developed using Diamond Crystal kosher salt. If you have Morton kosher salt, which is denser, use 3 tablespoons. Use a dry white wine, such as Sauvignon Blanc, for this recipe. An inexpensive wine will work just fine, but pick one that's good enough to drink on its own.

- 2 cups dry white wine
- 3 tablespoons lemon juice
- 3 tablespoons extra-virgin olive oil
- 2 tablespoons chopped fresh parsley
- 2 tablespoons chopped fresh thyme
- 2 tablespoons packed light brown sugar
- 4 garlic cloves, minced
- 1 teaspoon pepper
- ¼ cup kosher salt
- 1 (4-pound) whole chicken, giblets discarded
- 2 (12-inch) wooden skewers

1 Process wine, lemon juice, oil, parsley, thyme, sugar, garlic, and pepper in blender until emulsified, about 40 seconds. Measure out ¼ cup wine mixture and set aside for cooking. Add salt to remaining mixture in blender and process to make marinade, about 20 seconds.

2 With chicken breast side down, use kitchen shears to cut along both sides of backbone. Discard backbone and trim any excess fat or skin at neck. Flip chicken over and use heel of your hand to flatten breastbone. Tuck wingtips behind back. Poke holes all over chicken with skewer. Combine marinade and chicken in 1-gallon zipper-lock bag and toss to coat; press out as much air as possible and seal bag. Refrigerate for 2 to 3 hours.

3 Remove chicken from marinade and pat dry with paper towels. Insert 1 skewer down length of chicken through thickest part of breast and drumstick. Repeat with second skewer on other half of chicken.

4A FOR A CHARCOAL GRILL Open bottom vent completely. Light large chimney starter filled with charcoal briquettes (6 quarts). When top coals are partially covered with ash, pour evenly over half of grill. Set cooking grate in place, cover, and open lid vent completely. Heat grill until hot, about 5 minutes.

4B FOR A GAS GRILL Turn all burners to high; cover; and heat grill until hot, about 15 minutes. Turn primary burner to medium and other burner(s) to low. (Adjust primary burner as needed to maintain grill temperature between 350 and 375 degrees.)

5 Clean and oil cooking grate. Place chicken skin side down on cooler side of grill, with legs closest to hotter side of grill. Cover and cook until chicken is well browned and thighs register 160 degrees, 50 minutes to 1 hour 5 minutes.

6 Brush chicken with half of reserved wine mixture. Flip chicken skin-side up, slide to hotter side of grill, and brush with remaining reserved wine mixture. Cover and cook until breast registers 160 degrees and thighs register 175 degrees, 10 to 15 minutes.

7 Transfer chicken to carving board, tent with aluminum foil, and let rest for 15 minutes. Carve chicken and serve.

Thai Grilled Cornish Hens with Chili Dipping Sauce

SERVES 4 **TIME** 2 hours plus 6 hours marinating

Why This Recipe Works Our take on Thai grilled chicken starts with Cornish hens, which we butterfly and flatten so that they cook quickly and evenly on the grill. A thick marinade consisting of cilantro leaves and stems, garlic, white pepper, ground coriander, brown sugar, and fish sauce clings to the hens instead of sliding off. We start the hens skin side up over the cooler side of a half-grill fire, which gives the fatty skin time to render while the meat cooks; then, we finish them over the hotter side to crisp the skin. For a sweet-tangy-spicy dipping sauce, we simmer a mixture of equal parts white vinegar and sugar until slightly thickened and add plenty of minced garlic and Thai chiles for savory, fruity heat. If you can't find Thai chiles, substitute Fresno or red jalapeño chiles. This recipe was developed using Diamond Crystal kosher salt. If you have Morton kosher salt, which is denser, use 1 tablespoon in the marinade. Serve with rice.

HENS

- 4 (1¼- to 1½-pound) Cornish game hens, giblets discarded
- 1 cup fresh cilantro leaves and stems, chopped coarse
- 12 garlic cloves, peeled
- ¼ cup packed light brown sugar
- 2 teaspoons ground white pepper
- 2 teaspoons ground coriander
- 4 teaspoons kosher salt
- ¼ cup fish sauce

SAUCE

- ½ cup distilled white vinegar
- ½ cup granulated sugar
- 1 tablespoon minced Thai chiles
- 3 garlic cloves, minced
- ½ teaspoon kosher salt

1 FOR THE HENS Working with 1 hen at a time, place breast side down on cutting board and use kitchen shears to cut through bones on either side of backbone; discard backbone. Flip hen and press on breastbones to flatten. Trim any excess fat and skin.

2 Pulse cilantro leaves and stems, garlic, sugar, pepper, coriander, and salt in food processor until finely chopped, 10 to 15 pulses; transfer to small bowl. Stir in fish sauce to make marinade. Rub hens all over with marinade. Transfer hens and any excess marinade to four 1-gallon zipper-lock bags; press out as much air as possible and seal bags. Refrigerate for at least 6 hours or up to 24 hours, flipping bags halfway through marinating.

3 FOR THE SAUCE Bring vinegar to boil in small saucepan over high heat. Stir in sugar until dissolved. Reduce heat to medium-low and simmer until mixture is slightly thickened, about 5 minutes. Remove from heat and let cool completely. Stir in chiles, garlic, and salt and transfer to serving bowl. (Sauce can be refrigerated for up to 2 weeks. Bring to room temperature before serving.)

4 Remove hens from marinade (do not pat dry), tuck wingtips behind backs, and turn legs so drumsticks face inward toward breasts.

5A FOR A CHARCOAL GRILL Open bottom vent completely. Light large chimney starter filled with charcoal briquettes (6 quarts). When top coals are partially covered with ash, pour evenly over half of grill. Set cooking grate in place, cover, and open lid vent completely. Heat grill until hot, about 5 minutes.

THAI GRILLED
CORNISH HENS WITH
CHILI DIPPING SAUCE

5B FOR A GAS GRILL Turn all burners to high; cover; and heat grill until hot, about 15 minutes. Leave primary burner on high and turn off other burner(s). (Adjust primary burner as needed to maintain grill temperature between 350 and 400 degrees).

6 Clean and oil cooking grate. Place hens skin side up on cooler side of grill with legs and thighs facing coals. Cover and cook until skin is browned and breasts register 145 to 150 degrees, 30 to 35 minutes, rotating hens halfway through cooking.

7 Using tongs, carefully flip hens skin side down and slide to hotter side of grill. Cover and cook until skin is crisp, deeply browned, and charred in spots and breasts register 160 degrees and thighs register 175 degrees, 3 to 5 minutes, being careful to avoid burning.

8 Transfer hens, skin side up, to cutting board. Tent with aluminum foil and let rest for 10 minutes. Cut hens in half through breastbone and serve, passing dipping sauce separately.

Barbecue-Glazed Cornish Hens

SERVES 4 **TIME** 1½ hours plus 30 minutes brining

Why This Recipe Works Grilling has the potential to give Cornish hens great smoky flavor and really crisp skin, but there are potential pitfalls too. Rendered fat from the skin can cause flare-ups, and getting the skin crisp without overcooking the delicate breast meat is tricky. Our solutions: Use a banked-fire setup with a disposable roasting pan in the center to catch dripping fat. And butterfly the hens; this makes each bird a uniform thickness, which promotes even cooking, and also puts all of the skin on one side, which can face the coals and crisp more quickly. Our spice rub emphasizes the smoky flavor of the birds and also helps crisp the skin even further. To add smoke flavor to the hens, use the optional wood chips. If using a charcoal grill, you can substitute four wood chunks for the wood chip packet. This recipe was developed using Diamond Crystal kosher salt. If you have Morton kosher salt, which is denser, use ¾ cup.

HENS

- 4 (1¼- to 1½-pound) whole Cornish game hens, giblets discarded
- 1 cup kosher salt for brining

SPICE RUB

- 2 tablespoons packed brown sugar
- 1 tablespoon paprika
- 2 teaspoons garlic powder
- 2 teaspoons chili powder
- 1 teaspoon pepper
- 1 teaspoon ground coriander
- ⅛ teaspoon cayenne pepper
- 4 cups wood chips (optional)
- 1 (13 by 9-inch) disposable aluminum roasting pan (if using charcoal)

BARBECUE GLAZE

- ½ cup ketchup
- 2 tablespoons packed brown sugar
- 1 tablespoon soy sauce
- 1 tablespoon distilled white vinegar
- 1 tablespoon yellow mustard
- 1 garlic clove, minced

1 FOR THE HENS Working with 1 hen at a time, place breast side down on cutting board and use kitchen shears to cut through bones on either side of backbone; discard backbone. Flip hen and press on breastbones to flatten. Trim any excess fat and skin. Dissolve salt in 4 quarts cold water in large container. Submerge hens in brine, cover, and refrigerate for 30 minutes to 1 hour.

2 FOR THE SPICE RUB Combine all ingredients in bowl.

3 FOR THE GLAZE Combine all ingredients in small saucepan; bring to simmer; and cook, stirring occasionally, until thickened, about 5 minutes. Cover and set aside for grilling.

4 Remove hens from brine and pat dry with paper towels. Tuck wingtips behind backs and turn legs so that drumsticks face inward toward breasts. Rub hens evenly with spice mixture. If using wood chips, use large pieces of heavy-duty aluminum foil to wrap wood chips into two 8 by 4-inch foil packets. (Make sure chips do not poke holes in sides or bottom of packets.) Cut 2 evenly spaced 2-inch slits in top of packets.

5A FOR A CHARCOAL GRILL Open bottom vent completely and place disposable pan in center of grill. Light large chimney starter filled with charcoal briquettes (6 quarts). When top coals are partially covered with ash, pour into 2 even piles on either side of disposable pan. Place 1 wood chip packet, if using, on each pile of coals. Set cooking grate in place, cover, and open lid vent completely. Heat grill until hot and wood chips are smoking, about 5 minutes.

5B FOR A GAS GRILL If using wood chips, remove cooking grate and place wood chip packet directly on primary burner. Set grate in place; turn all burners to high; cover; and heat grill until hot and wood chips are smoking, about 15 minutes. Turn all burners to medium. (Adjust burners as needed during cooking to maintain grill temperature of 325 degrees.)

6 Clean and oil cooking grate. Place hens in center of grill (over disposable pan if using charcoal) skin side down. Cover (position lid vent over hens if using charcoal) and cook until thighs register 160 degrees, 20 to 30 minutes.

7 Using tongs, slide hens to hotter sides of grill (if using charcoal) or turn all burners to high (if using gas). Cover and cook until browned, about 5 minutes. Brush hens with half of glaze, flip, and cook for 2 minutes. Brush hens with remaining glaze; flip; and cook until breasts register 160 degrees and thighs register 175 degrees, 1 to 3 minutes.

8 Transfer hens to carving board, tent with foil, and let rest for 10 minutes. Cut hens in half through breastbone and serve.

VARIATION

Hoisin and Ginger–Glazed Cornish Hens

Substitute following mixture for barbecue glaze: Combine ¼ cup ketchup, ¼ cup hoisin sauce, 2 tablespoons unseasoned rice vinegar, 1 tablespoon soy sauce, 1 tablespoon toasted sesame oil, and 1 tablespoon grated fresh ginger in small saucepan. Bring to simmer and cook, stirring occasionally, until thickened, about 5 minutes.

SMOKED TURKEY BREAST

Smoked Turkey Breast

SERVES 6 to 8 **TIME** 2¼ hours plus 8 hours salting

Why This Recipe Works For smoked turkey with plump, juicy meat lightly perfumed with smoke, we chose a turkey breast, which cooks relatively quickly on the grill. Rubbing salt and brown sugar under and over the skin and refrigerating the turkey breast overnight allows the seasonings to penetrate the meat. Before grilling, we dry the skin and apply a second round of rub, replacing the salt with pepper for kick. Piercing the skin before grilling allows some of the fat to drain away, which helps crisp the skin. A small amount of wood chips—just ½ cup—adds enough smokiness without overwhelming the mild meat. After grilling for an hour and a half, the turkey has smoky, well-seasoned, juicy meat and golden, crisp skin. We prefer either a natural (unbrined) or kosher turkey breast for this recipe. If using a kosher turkey breast (rubbed with salt and rinsed during processing) or self-basting turkey breast (injected with salt and water), do not salt it in step 1, but do sugar. If the breast has a pop-up timer, remove it before cooking. If using a charcoal grill, you can substitute one small wood chunk for the wood chip packet.

3 tablespoons packed brown sugar, divided
1 tablespoon table salt
1 (5-pound) bone-in whole turkey breast, trimmed
2 teaspoons pepper
½ cup wood chips
1 (13 by 9-inch) disposable aluminum roasting pan (if using charcoal)

1 Combine 2 tablespoons sugar and salt in bowl. Pat turkey dry with paper towels. Using your fingers, gently loosen skin covering each side of breast. Rub sugar-salt mixture evenly over and under skin. Tightly wrap turkey with plastic wrap and refrigerate for 8 to 24 hours.

2 Combine remaining 1 tablespoon sugar and pepper in bowl. Unwrap turkey, pat dry with paper towels, and rub sugar-pepper mixture under and over skin. Poke skin all over with skewer.

3 Using large piece of heavy-duty aluminum foil, wrap wood chips in 8 by 4-inch foil packet. (Make sure chips do not poke holes in sides or bottom of packet.) Cut 2 evenly spaced 2-inch slits in top of packet.

4A **FOR A CHARCOAL GRILL** Open bottom vent halfway and place disposable pan in center of grill. Light large chimney starter filled with charcoal briquettes (6 quarts). When top coals are partially covered with ash, pour into 2 even piles on either side of disposable pan. Place wood chip packet on 1 pile of coals. Set cooking grate in place, cover, and open lid vent halfway. Heat grill until hot and wood chips are smoking, about 5 minutes.

4B **FOR A GAS GRILL** Remove cooking grate and place wood chip packet directly on primary burner. Set grate in place; turn all burners to high; cover; and heat grill until hot and wood chips are smoking, about 15 minutes. Turn all burners to medium-low. (Adjust burners as needed to maintain grill temperature of 350 degrees.)

5 Clean and oil cooking grate. Place turkey breast skin side up in center of grill (over disposable pan if using charcoal). Cover (position lid vent over turkey if using charcoal) and cook until skin is well browned and breast registers 160 degrees, about 1½ hours.

6 Transfer turkey to carving board, tent with foil, and let rest for 15 minutes. Carve turkey and serve.

SIMPLE GRILL-ROASTED TURKEY

Simple Grill-Roasted Turkey

SERVES 10 to 12 **TIME** 3 to 3½ hours plus 24¾ hours salting and resting

Why This Recipe Works Roasting your turkey on the grill frees up your oven for other dishes. We found a method that cooks the turkey gently and evenly and delivers traditional oven-roasted turkey flavor. We divide our coals into two piles on either side of the grill so that the turkey thighs receive the highest heat. A combination of lit coals and unlit briquettes yields a longer-burning fire, making replenishing coals unnecessary. The addition of a pan of water stabilizes the temperature inside the grill for even cooking and eliminates the flareups that would give the meat a smoky taste, and a quick salt rub before grilling yields seasoned meat and crispy skin. If using a self-basting turkey (such as a frozen Butterball) or a kosher turkey, don't salt in step 1, but do season with salt in step 2. This recipe was developed using Diamond Crystal kosher salt. If you have Morton kosher salt, which is denser, use 1 tablespoon inside the turkey cavity, 2 teaspoons on each side of the breast, 1 teaspoon on each leg, and 1 teaspoon in the rub in step 2. Check the wings halfway through roasting; if they are getting too dark, slide a small piece of foil between the wing and the cooking grate to shield the wings from the flame.

- 1 (12- to 14-pound) turkey, neck and giblets discarded
- ¼ cup plus 1 teaspoon kosher salt, divided
- 1 teaspoon pepper
- 1 teaspoon baking powder
- 1 tablespoon vegetable oil
- 1 (13 by 9-inch) disposable aluminum roasting pan (if using charcoal) or 2 (9-inch) disposable aluminum pie plates (if using gas)

1 Place turkey breast side down on cutting board. Make two 2-inch incisions below each thigh and breast along back of turkey (4 incisions total). Using your fingers or handle of wooden spoon, carefully separate skin from thighs and breast. Rub 4 teaspoons salt evenly inside cavity of turkey, 1 tablespoon salt under skin of each side of breast, and 1 teaspoon salt under skin of each leg.

2 Combine remaining 1 teaspoon salt, pepper, and baking powder in small bowl. Pat turkey dry with paper towels and rub evenly with baking powder mixture. Rub mixture thoroughly into skin, making sure to coat entire turkey evenly. Wrap turkey in plastic wrap and refrigerate for 24 to 48 hours.

3 Before grilling, unwrap turkey (do not pat dry). Tuck wings underneath turkey. Using your hands, rub turkey evenly with oil.

4A **FOR A CHARCOAL GRILL** Open bottom vent halfway, place disposable pan in center of grill, and add 3 cups water to pan. Arrange 1½ quarts unlit charcoal briquettes on either side of pan (3 quarts total). Light large chimney starter three-quarters filled with charcoal briquettes (4½ quarts). When top coals are partially covered with ash, pour evenly over unlit coals. Set cooking grate in place, cover, and open lid vent halfway. Heat grill until hot, about 5 minutes.

4B **FOR A GAS GRILL** Place disposable pie plates, each filled with 2 cups water, on burner over which turkey will be cooked (not primary burner). Turn all burners to high; cover; and heat grill until hot, about 15 minutes. Turn primary burner to medium-high and turn off other burner(s). (Adjust primary burner as needed to maintain grill temperature of 325 degrees.)

5 Clean and oil cooking grate. Place turkey breast side up over water-filled pan(s), with legs pointing toward fire for charcoal grill or side of turkey facing primary burner for gas. Cover (position lid vent over meat if using charcoal) and cook until breasts register 160 degrees and thighs/drumsticks register 175 degrees, 2½ to 3 hours, rotating turkey after 1¼ hours if using gas grill.

6 Transfer turkey to carving board and let rest, uncovered, for 45 minutes. Carve turkey and serve.

Is Pink Turkey Meat Safe to Eat?

We always use an instant-read thermometer to know when grilled poultry is done; the thickest part of the breast should be 160 degrees and the thickest part of the thigh should be 175 degrees. But even when the bird is fully cooked, the meat can occasionally be pink. Why is that? In general, the red or pink color in meat is due to the red protein pigment called myoglobin in the muscle cells that store oxygen. Legs and thighs, which get more exercise, require more oxygen; thus, they contain more myoglobin and are darker in color than the breast. As turkey (or chicken) roasts in the oven, the oxygen attached to the myoglobin is released, and the meat becomes lighter and browner in color. However, if there are trace amounts of other gases formed in a hot oven or grill, they may react to the myoglobin to produce a pink color, even if the turkey is fully cooked. So a pinkish tint doesn't necessarily mean turkey is underdone; temperature is a better indicator.

4

Burgers, Sausage + Ground Meat

IN DEPTH

Grill a Better Beef Burger

Outdoor cooking doesn't get much simpler than throwing burgers on a grill; but even for this seemingly basic recipe, paying attention to the details makes for a memorable meal.

1 Arrange ½-inch pieces of meat in single layer on rimmed baking sheet. Freeze until firm and starting to harden around edges but still pliable, 35 to 45 minutes.

2 Working in batches, pulse meat in food processor until finely ground into 1/16-inch pieces, stopping to redistribute meat as needed for an even grind.

3 Spread ground meat over sheet, discarding any long strands of gristle and large chunks of fat.

BE YOUR OWN BUTCHER

Grinding your own meat doesn't have to be intimidating or require special equipment. In fact, we've found that a food processor is as good a tool as an at-home meat grinder, producing a coarse grind that's perfect for burgers. A food processor doesn't grind the meat as finely as a commercial meat grinder, but stray pieces of gristle are obvious once the meat has been spread over a baking sheet and are easily removed.

HOW TO ACHIEVE PEAK BURGER

CHOOSE THE RIGHT MEAT

85%

The best preground beef for burgers is ground chuck. This will cook up into a juicier and more flavorful burger than ground sirloin or ground round. Unless a recipe specifically calls for fattier or leaner beef, 85 percent is our favorite choice for a burger with just the right amount of richness. If possible, have the butcher grind the meat for you. Avoid generically labeled "ground beef," which can come from any cut or combination of cuts and can have a fat content of up to 30 percent. Also avoid beef that looks brown, which indicates that it's not freshly ground, or that has juices at the bottom, which is a sign the meat may have been frozen.

HANDLE GENTLY

When shaping, don't overwork the ground beef; shape the patties with a gentle hand. If you pack the patties too tightly, the meat will bind too tightly, and you'll end up with tough, dry, chewy burgers. Our favorite technique is to start with a loosely packed ball of meat and then gently pat it down to a ¾-inch-thick disk. As soon as the patties hold together, stop. The meat will adhere as it cooks to create a cohesive burger.

SALT JUST THE OUTSIDE

Salt removes water from and dissolves some meat proteins, leaving the insoluble proteins bound together. Because of this, mixing salt into ground beef gives the patties a springy bite that's better suited to sausages than to burgers. Salt sprinkled on meat draws moisture from inside to the surface over time, so for moister, better-browned burgers, season them just before grilling.

MAKE A DIVOT

When we grill burgers, we always form a shallow indentation in the center of each patty before cooking it. That's because the collagen, or connective tissue, in ground meat shrinks when heated. This causes the bottom and sides of the meat to tighten like a belt, which forces the surface of the burger to expand. To prevent a bulging burger, press a slight divot into the center of each patty. When the collagen tightens, it will cause the divot to fill out so that it is level with the rest of the patty, ensuring that the patties emerge from the grill nice and flat.

FLIP ONLY ONCE

The burgers will stay together better and be less likely to break or tear if you leave them undisturbed until they're nicely browned on the first side and then flip them just once. This gives them time to develop a sturdy crust that will release easily from the grate. If you do have sticking issues, let the burgers sit on the grill for another 30 seconds before trying to remove them.

TAKE THE TEMP

If you want burgers cooked just the way you like them every time, an instant-read thermometer is your best tool. Insert the thermometer at an angle, not directly from the top. Pull each burger off the grill as soon as it hits the doneness level you want. See page 33 for doneness temperatures.

GIVE IT A REST

Let the cooked burgers sit on a wire rack set in a rimmed baking sheet or on a platter for 5 minutes before transferring them to buns. This allows the juices in the meat to redistribute within the burgers rather than soaking into the buns.

CLASSIC BEEF BURGERS

Classic Beef Burgers

SERVES 4 **TIME** 30 minutes

Why This Recipe Works Sometimes simple is best, and for quick weeknight burgers or a backyard barbecue for a crowd, that means store-bought ground beef. To produce tender, juicy burgers, you need the right cut with the ideal amount of fat; we find that 85 percent lean ground chuck makes burgers with rich flavor and a tender, moist texture. Slightly indenting, or dimpling, the center of each burger helps them cook to a perfectly even thickness.

- 1½ pounds 85 percent lean ground beef
- 1 teaspoon kosher salt
- ¼ teaspoon pepper
- 4 slices cheese (4 ounces) (optional)
- 4 hamburger buns, toasted if desired

1 Divide ground beef into 4 equal portions, then gently shape each portion into ¾-inch-thick patty. Using your fingertips, press center of each patty down until about ½ inch thick, creating slight divot. Just before cooking, sprinkle patties with salt and pepper.

2A FOR A CHARCOAL GRILL Open bottom vent completely. Light large chimney starter filled with charcoal briquettes (6 quarts). When top coals are partially covered with ash, pour evenly over grill. Set cooking grate in place, cover, and open lid vent completely. Heat grill until hot, about 5 minutes.

2B FOR A GAS GRILL Turn all burners to high; cover; and heat grill until hot, about 15 minutes. Leave all burners on high.

3 Clean and oil cooking grate. Place patties on grill, divot side up, and cook until well browned on first side, 2 to 4 minutes. Flip patties; top with cheese, if using; and cook until second side is browned and meat registers 120 to 125 degrees (for medium-rare) or 130 to 135 degrees (for medium), 3 to 5 minutes. Transfer burgers to platter and let rest for 5 minutes. Serve burgers on buns.

Grilled Well-Done Burgers

SERVES 4 **TIME** 30 minutes

Why This Recipe Works There are plenty of reasons to opt for a well-done burger: It makes the cooking more hands-off; it requires less precise timing; and, if you're trying to please multiple palates, it's far easier to cook all of the burgers to the same temperature. To keep them moist and tender, we add a panade—a paste of bread and milk. Minced garlic and tangy steak sauce punch up the flavor. Cooking the burgers over high heat creates a flavorful sear; the panade helps stem moisture loss over the hot fire for mouthwatering well-done burgers that will wow even the pickiest burger aficionado. Make sure to use 80 percent lean ground beef; a leaner ground beef will result in a drier burger.

- 1 slice hearty white sandwich bread, crust removed, torn into 1-inch pieces
- 2 tablespoons milk
- 2 teaspoons steak sauce
- 1 garlic clove, minced
- 1½ pounds 80 percent lean ground beef
- 1 teaspoon kosher salt
- ¼ teaspoon pepper
- 4 slices cheese (4 ounces) (optional)
- 4 hamburger buns, toasted if desired

1 Using fork, mash bread, milk, steak sauce, and garlic to paste in large bowl. Break ground beef into small pieces, add to bowl, and gently knead with your hands until well combined. Divide beef mixture into 4 equal portions, then gently shape each portion into ¾-inch-thick patty. Using your fingertips, press center of each patty down until about ½ inch thick, creating slight divot. Just before cooking, sprinkle patties with salt and pepper.

2A **FOR A CHARCOAL GRILL** Open bottom vent completely. Light large chimney starter filled with charcoal briquettes (6 quarts). When top coals are partially covered with ash, pour evenly over grill. Set cooking grate in place, cover, and open lid vent completely. Heat grill until hot, about 5 minutes.

2B **FOR A GAS GRILL** Turn all burners to high; cover; and heat grill until hot, about 15 minutes. Leave all burners on high.

3 Clean and oil cooking grate. Place patties on grill, divot side up, and cook (covered if using gas) until well browned on first side, 2 to 4 minutes. Flip patties; top with cheese, if using; and cook until second side is browned and meat registers 140 to 145 degrees (for medium-well) or 150 to 155 degrees (for well-done), 4 to 6 minutes. Transfer burgers to platter and let rest for 5 minutes. Serve burgers on buns.

Smashed Burgers

SERVES 2 **TIME** 30 minutes

Why This Recipe Works A plancha turns the grill into a diner flattop, so you can make thin, crispy-edged smashed burgers that outshine any fast-food version. Firmly pressing the meat with a small saucepan makes it spread and stick uniformly to the plancha, which helps guarantee deep browning. (Don't use a spatula; it won't flatten the burgers evenly.) The small patties cook through quickly; sandwiching a slice of American cheese between two patties helps them stick together while acting like a rich cheese sauce. A creamy, tangy burger sauce adds more richness. You can use 85 percent lean ground beef, but 90 percent lean will produce a dry burger. We strongly prefer Kraft Singles here for their meltability. To serve four, double the sauce and burger ingredients but use the same amount of oil. Transfer the first four cooked burgers to a wire rack set in a rimmed baking sheet, add the cheese, and keep warm (on the grill if there's room) while cooking the remaining four burgers. You will need a cast-iron plancha measuring at least 20 by 10 inches for this recipe.

SMASHED BURGERS

SAUCE

- 2 tablespoons mayonnaise
- 1 tablespoon minced shallot
- 1½ teaspoons finely chopped dill pickles plus ½ teaspoon brine
- 1½ teaspoons ketchup
- ⅛ teaspoon sugar
- ⅛ teaspoon pepper

BURGERS

- 2 hamburger buns
- 8 ounces 80 percent lean ground beef
- 2 tablespoons vegetable oil
- ¼ teaspoon kosher salt
- ⅛ teaspoon pepper
- 4 slices American cheese (4 ounces)

1 FOR THE SAUCE Stir all ingredients together in bowl.

2 FOR THE BURGERS Spread 1 tablespoon sauce on cut side of each bun top; set aside. Divide ground beef into 4 equal portions, then gently shape each portion into loose, rough ball (do not compress).

3A FOR A CHARCOAL GRILL Open bottom vent completely. Light large chimney starter three-quarters filled with charcoal briquettes (4½ quarts). When top coals are partially covered with ash, pour evenly over grill. Set cooking grate in place, center plancha on grill, cover, and open lid vent completely. Heat grill with plancha until hot, about 5 minutes.

3B FOR A GAS GRILL Turn all burners to high; cover; and heat grill until hot, about 15 minutes. Center plancha on grill, cover, and heat for an additional 5 minutes. Turn all burners to medium-high.

4 Heat oil on plancha until just smoking. Place beef balls about 3 inches apart on plancha. Use bottom of greased saucepan to firmly smash each ball until 4 to 4½ inches in diameter. Sprinkle patties with salt and pepper. Cook until at least three-quarters of each patty is no longer pink on top, about 2 minutes.

5 Use thin metal spatula to loosen patties from plancha. Flip patties and cook for 15 seconds. Transfer to platter. Transfer 1 burger to each bun bottom and top each with 1 slice American cheese; repeat with remaining burgers and cheese. Cap with prepared bun tops. Serve immediately.

Grind-Your-Own Sirloin Burgers

SERVES 4 **TIME** 35 minutes plus 1 hour 5 minutes freezing

Why This Recipe Works Although store-bought ground chuck makes a quick and satisfying burger, home-ground sirloin provides a loose, craggy texture and strong beefy flavor that make for a truly superior burger experience. We start with steak tips—which have good flavor, contain minimal gristly fat, and are available in small quantities—and use the food processor to grind them. Butter adds moisture and fat for juicy, tender burgers, and freezing the patties prior to grilling helps them hold together. To ensure quick, dramatic charring, we use a concentrated fire setup for intense, even heat. Sirloin steak tips are often sold as flap meat. When trimming the meat, remove any pieces of fat thicker than ⅛ inch along with any silver skin. After trimming, you should have about 1¾ pounds of meat. To double this recipe, spread the beef over two baking sheets in step 1 and process in eight batches.

- 2 pounds sirloin steak tips, trimmed and cut into ½-inch pieces
- 4 tablespoons unsalted butter, melted and cooled
- 1 teaspoon kosher salt
- ½ teaspoon pepper
- 1 (13 by 9-inch) disposable aluminum roasting pan (if using charcoal)
- 4 slices cheese (4 ounces) (optional)
- 4 hamburger buns, toasted if desired

1 Arrange steak tips in single layer on rimmed baking sheet and freeze until very firm and starting to harden around edges but still pliable, 35 to 45 minutes.

2 Working in 4 batches, pulse beef in food processor until finely ground into 1⁄16-inch pieces, about 20 pulses, stopping to redistribute meat as needed; return to sheet. Spread ground beef over sheet, discarding any long strands of gristle and large chunks of fat. Drizzle with melted butter and toss gently with fork to combine.

3 Divide ground beef into 4 equal portions, then gently shape each portion into ¾-inch-thick patty. Using your fingertips, press center of each patty down until about ½ inch thick, creating slight divot. (Patties can be refrigerated for up to 24 hours.)

4 Freeze patties for 30 minutes. Just before cooking, sprinkle patties with salt and pepper.

5A FOR A CHARCOAL GRILL Using skewer, poke 12 holes in bottom of disposable pan. Open bottom vent completely and place prepared pan in center of grill. Light large chimney starter two-thirds filled with charcoal briquettes (4 quarts). When top coals are partially covered with ash, pour into pan. Set cooking grate in place, cover, and open lid vent completely. Heat grill until hot, about 5 minutes.

5B FOR A GAS GRILL Turn all burners to high; cover; and heat grill until hot, about 15 minutes. Leave all burners on high.

6 Clean and oil cooking grate. Using spatula, place patties on grill, divot side up (over coals if using charcoal). Cook until well browned on first side and meat easily releases from grill, 4 to 7 minutes. Gently flip patties; top with cheese, if using; and cook until second side is well browned and meat registers 120 to 125 degrees (for medium-rare) or 130 to 135 degrees (for medium), 4 to 7 minutes. Transfer burgers to platter and let rest for 5 minutes. Serve burgers on buns.

VARIATION

Grind-Your-Own Sirloin Burgers for the Freezer

Uncooked patties can be frozen for up to 2 weeks. To freeze, stack patties, separated by parchment paper; wrap in plastic wrap; and place in zipper-lock freezer bag. Let frozen patties thaw at room temperature for 30 minutes before cooking.

Grind-Your-Own Ultimate Beef Burgers

SERVES 4 **TIME** 35 minutes plus 1 hour 5 minutes freezing

Why This Recipe Works This deluxe home-ground blend is a perfect combination of intense flavor and rich, tender texture. It starts with the bold beefiness that steak tips provide and then adds earthy depth of flavor from skirt steak and boneless short ribs for extra tenderness. Freezing the patties prior to grilling helps them hold together and keeps the insides pink, while a concentrated fire chars the outsides nicely. If you can't find skirt steak, you can substitute flank steak, though the flavor will be slightly milder. Sirloin steak tips are often sold as flap meat. When trimming the meat, remove any pieces of fat thicker than ⅛ inch along with any silver skin. After trimming, you should have about 1¾ pounds of meat. To double this recipe, spread the beef over two baking sheets in step 1 and pulse in the food processor in eight batches. We like to top these burgers with sautéed mushrooms and Pub-Style Burger Sauce (page 395).

GRIND-YOUR-OWN ULTIMATE BEEF BURGERS

- 1 pound skirt steak, trimmed and cut into ½-inch pieces
- 8 ounces boneless beef short ribs, trimmed and cut into ½-inch pieces
- 8 ounces sirloin steak tips, trimmed and cut into ½-inch pieces
- 1 teaspoon kosher salt
- ½ teaspoon pepper
- 1 (13 by 9-inch) disposable aluminum roasting pan (if using charcoal)
- 4 slices cheese (4 ounces) (optional)
- 4 hamburger buns, toasted if desired

1 Arrange skirt steak, short ribs, and steak tips in single layer on rimmed baking sheet and freeze until very firm and starting to harden around edges but still pliable, 35 to 45 minutes.

2 Working in 4 batches, pulse beef in food processor until finely ground into 1⁄16-inch pieces, about 20 pulses, stopping to redistribute meat as needed; return to sheet. Spread ground beef over sheet, discarding any long strands of gristle and large chunks of fat, and toss gently with fork to combine.

3 Divide ground beef into 4 equal portions, then gently shape each portion into ¾-inch-thick patty. Using your fingertips, press center of each patty down until about ½ inch thick, creating slight divot. (Patties can be refrigerated for up to 24 hours.)

4 Freeze patties for 30 minutes. Just before cooking, sprinkle patties with salt and pepper.

5A FOR A CHARCOAL GRILL Using skewer, poke 12 holes in bottom of disposable pan. Open bottom vent completely and place prepared pan in center of grill. Light large chimney starter two-thirds filled with charcoal briquettes (4 quarts). When top coals are partially covered with ash, pour into pan. Set cooking grate in place, cover, and open lid vent completely. Heat grill until hot, about 5 minutes.

5B FOR A GAS GRILL Turn all burners to high; cover; and heat grill until hot, about 15 minutes. Leave all burners on high.

6 Clean and oil cooking grate. Using spatula, place patties on grill, divot side up (over coals if using charcoal). Cook until well browned on first side and meat easily releases from grill, 4 to 7 minutes. Gently flip patties; top with cheese, if using; and cook until well browned on second side and meat registers 120 to 125 degrees (for medium-rare) or 130 to 135 degrees (for medium), 4 to 7 minutes. Transfer burgers to platter; let rest for 5 minutes. Serve burgers on buns.

VARIATION

Grind-Your-Own Ultimate Beef Burgers for the Freezer

Uncooked patties can be frozen for up to 2 weeks. To freeze, stack patties, separated by parchment paper; wrap in plastic wrap; and place in zipper-lock freezer bag. Let frozen patties thaw at room temperature for 30 minutes before cooking.

Grilled New Mexican Green Chile Cheeseburgers

SERVES 4 **TIME** 50 minutes

Why This Recipe Works This burger turns up the heat with two types of chiles for the ultimate fire-roasted flavor. Our Southwestern topping uses both mild Anaheim chiles and hot jalapeños for a complex combination that's slightly sweet and satisfyingly spicy. For intense smoky flavor, we roast the chiles along with an onion on the grill; once they develop a delicious char, we quickly chop them in the food processor with some garlic to create a chunky chile topping. Pureeing some of the topping and mixing it into the ground beef ensures bold chile flavor throughout. To keep our topping on the burgers—and off our plates—we layer American cheese on top; once melted, it holds the chile mixture in place. For more heat, include the jalapeño ribs and seeds. Traditional New Mexican chile burgers use Hatch chiles; if they are available in your area, feel free to substitute them for the jalapeños and Anaheims.

- 3 Anaheim chiles, stemmed, halved, and seeded
- 3 jalapeño chiles, stemmed, halved, and seeded
- 1 onion, sliced into ½-inch-thick rounds
- 1 garlic clove, minced
- 1½ pounds 85 percent lean ground beef
- 1 teaspoon kosher salt
- ¼ teaspoon pepper
- 4 slices American cheese (4 ounces)
- 4 hamburger buns, toasted if desired

1A FOR A CHARCOAL GRILL Open bottom vent completely. Light large chimney starter filled with charcoal briquettes (6 quarts). When top coals are partially covered with ash, pour evenly over grill. Set cooking grate in place, cover, and open lid vent completely. Heat grill until hot, about 5 minutes.

GRILLED NEW MEXICAN GREEN CHILE CHEESEBURGERS

1B FOR A GAS GRILL Turn all burners to high; cover; and heat grill until hot, about 15 minutes. Leave all burners on high.

2 Clean and oil cooking grate. Place Anaheims, jalapeños, and onion on grill and cook until lightly charred and tender, 4 to 8 minutes, turning as needed. Transfer vegetables to bowl, cover, and let sit for 5 minutes. Remove and discard skins from chiles. Separate onion rounds into rings.

3 Transfer chiles, onion, and garlic to food processor and pulse until coarsely chopped, about 10 pulses. Transfer all but ¼ cup mixture to bowl and season with salt and pepper to taste; set aside for serving. Continue to process remaining ¼ cup mixture until smooth, scraping down sides of bowl as needed, about 1 minute. (If mixture does not turn smooth, add up to 2 teaspoons water.)

4 Transfer pureed chile mixture to large bowl. Break ground beef into small pieces, add to bowl, and gently knead with your hands until well combined. Divide beef mixture into 4 equal portions, then gently shape each portion into ¾-inch-thick patty. Using your fingertips, press center of each patty down until about ½ inch thick, creating slight divot. Just before cooking, sprinkle patties with salt and pepper.

5 Place patties, divot side up, on grill. Cover and cook until well browned on first side, 2 to 4 minutes. Flip patties and top with chopped chile mixture and American cheese. Cover and cook until second side is well browned and meat registers 120 to 125 degrees (for medium-rare) or 130 to 135 degrees (for medium), 3 to 5 minutes. Transfer burgers to platter and let rest for 5 minutes. Serve burgers on buns.

Grilled Jucy Lucy Burgers

SERVES 4 **TIME** 40 minutes plus 30 minutes chilling

Why This Recipe Works This Minneapolis tavern offering is a unique twist on a classic cheeseburger: The cheese moves to the center of the burger to become a delicious, gooey surprise. To prevent the melted cheese from oozing out while the burgers are on the grill, we use a double-patty technique where we wrap a small patty around the cheese to create a barrier and then mold another patty around the first. These burgers need to be cooked to well-done to melt the cheesy center; adding a panade, as we do for our well-done burgers (see page 190) keeps them tender, not dry. Buy the American cheese from the deli counter and ask them to slice it into a ½-inch slab from which you can cut four big cubes to fill the center of the burgers. Allow the cooked cheeseburgers to rest for a full 5 minutes before eating them, or the hot, cheesy center will spurt out and could cause burns.

- 2 slices hearty white sandwich bread, torn into 1-inch pieces
- ¼ cup milk
- 1 teaspoon garlic powder
- 1½ pounds 85 percent lean ground beef
- 1 (½-inch-thick) slice American cheese (4 ounces), quartered
- 1 teaspoon kosher salt
- ¼ teaspoon pepper
- 4 hamburger buns, toasted if desired

1 Using fork, mash bread, milk, and garlic powder to paste in large bowl. Break ground beef into small pieces, add to bowl, and gently knead with your hands until well combined.

2 Divide beef mixture into 8 equal portions. Encase each American cheese piece within 1 portion of beef mixture to form mini burger patty. Mold second portion of meat around each mini patty and seal edges to form ball. Flatten ball to form ¾-inch-thick patty. Cover and refrigerate patties for at least 30 minutes or up to 24 hours. Just before cooking, sprinkle patties with salt and pepper.

3A FOR A CHARCOAL GRILL Open bottom vent completely. Light large chimney starter half filled with charcoal briquettes (3 quarts). When top coals are partially covered with ash, pour evenly over grill. Set cooking grate in place, cover, and open lid vent completely. Heat grill until hot, about 5 minutes.

3B FOR A GAS GRILL Turn all burners to high; cover; and heat grill until hot, about 15 minutes. Turn all burners to medium.

4 Clean and oil cooking grate. Place patties on grill and cook (covered if using gas), without pressing on them, until well browned and cooked through, 12 to 16 minutes, flipping halfway through cooking. Transfer burgers to platter and let rest for 5 minutes. Serve burgers on buns.

How to Form a Jucy Lucy

1 Encase 1 piece of cheese in 1 portion meat.

2 Mold second portion of meat around meat-encased cheese and seal to form ball.

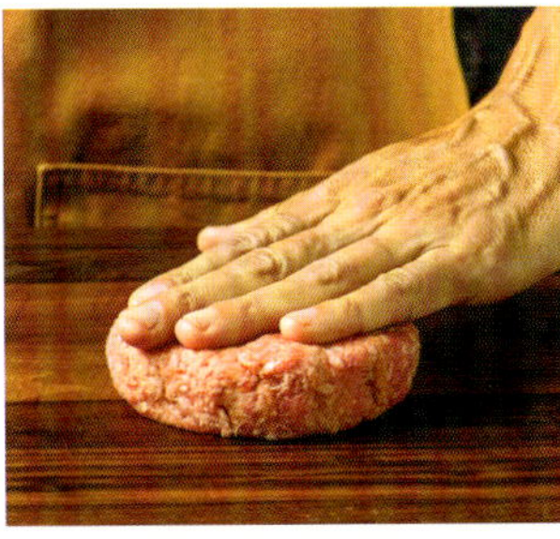

3 Flatten ball firmly with palm of your hand to form ¾-inch-thick patty.

Grilled Bayou Burgers with Spicy Mayonnaise

SERVES 4 **TIME** 45 minutes

Why This Recipe Works Andouille sausage, a staple of Cajun cooking, is the secret weapon in these rich and flavorful burgers, where it infuses mild ground pork with smoky, garlicky, peppery boldness. Whole-grain mustard and hot sauce boost the flavor even more. We top the burgers with cheddar cheese, grilled red onion, and a tangy mayonnaise-based sauce spiked with more mustard and hot sauce. We like to serve these burgers on onion rolls to complement the grilled onions, but standard hamburger buns can be substituted.

- 8 ounces andouille sausage, chopped fine
- ¼ cup whole-grain mustard, divided
- 1 tablespoon hot sauce, divided
- 1 pound ground pork
- 1 red onion, sliced into ½-inch-thick rounds
- 1 tablespoon vegetable oil
- 1 teaspoon kosher salt
- ¼ teaspoon pepper
- 4 slices cheddar cheese (4 ounces)
- ¼ cup mayonnaise
- 4 onion rolls, toasted if desired

1 Combine sausage, 2 tablespoons mustard, and 2 teaspoons hot sauce in large bowl. Break ground pork into small pieces, add to bowl, and gently knead with your hands until well combined. Divide meat mixture into 4 equal portions, then gently shape each portion into ¾-inch-thick patty. Using your fingertips, press center of each patty down until about ½ inch thick, creating slight divot.

2 Push toothpick horizontally through each onion round to keep rings intact while grilling. Brush onion with oil. Just before cooking, sprinkle patties with salt and pepper.

3A **FOR A CHARCOAL GRILL** Open bottom vent completely. Light large chimney starter filled with charcoal briquettes (6 quarts). When top coals are partially covered with ash, pour evenly over grill. Set cooking grate in place, cover, and open lid vent completely. Heat grill until hot, about 5 minutes.

3B **FOR A GAS GRILL** Turn all burners to high; cover; and heat grill until hot, about 15 minutes. Leave all burners on high.

4 Clean and oil cooking grate. Place onion rounds on grill and cook (covered if using gas) until softened and lightly charred, 6 to 12 minutes, flipping as needed. As they finish cooking, transfer onion rounds to bowl and cover to keep warm.

5 Place patties on grill, divot side up, and cook (covered if using gas) until well browned, 4 to 6 minutes. Flip patties; top with cheddar; and cook until second side is well browned and meat registers 150 degrees, 5 to 7 minutes. Transfer burgers to platter and let rest for 5 minutes.

6 Remove toothpicks from onion rounds and separate into rings. Whisk mayonnaise, remaining 2 tablespoons mustard, and remaining 1 teaspoon hot sauce together in bowl and season with salt and pepper to taste. Spread mayonnaise mixture on roll tops. Serve burgers on rolls, topped with onion.

Keep Onion Rounds Intact

For easy grilling, cut onions into ½-inch-thick rounds, then push toothpick completely through each round from side to side.

Grilled Teriyaki Pork Burgers

SERVES 4 **TIME** 50 minutes

Why This Recipe Works The Teri burger, as it's affectionately known in Hawaii, is all about big, bold flavors working in harmony. When it comes to adding those flavors, a glaze is simpler than a marinade and doesn't sog out the buns like a sauce would. For real clinging power, we add a little cornstarch to the glaze ingredients; briefly heating the mixture in the microwave activates the cornstarch's thickening properties and ensures just the right consistency. We grill the pineapple as well as the burgers—the grill accentuates the fruit's sweetness and deepens its flavor with some light caramelization. Tangy hot cherry peppers round out the burgers' Hawaiian flavor profile. You can substitute regular mayonnaise for the Japanese mayonnaise if desired. We prefer to use fresh pineapple rounds here, but canned pineapple rounds can be substituted.

- ⅓ cup soy sauce
- ¼ cup sugar
- 2 tablespoons mirin
- 1 tablespoon grated fresh ginger
- 2 teaspoons cornstarch
- 1 red onion, sliced into ½-inch-thick rounds
- 4 (½-inch-thick) pineapple rings
- 1 tablespoon vegetable oil
- 1 slice hearty white sandwich bread, torn into 1-inch pieces
- 2 scallions, sliced thin
- 2 tablespoons milk
- ¼ teaspoon pepper
- 1½ pounds ground pork
- ¼ cup Japanese-style mayonnaise, such as Kewpie, plus extra for serving
- 4 Hawaiian sweet rolls, toasted if desired
- 4 leaves iceberg lettuce
- ½ cup thinly sliced jarred hot cherry peppers

1 Microwave soy sauce, sugar, mirin, ginger, and cornstarch in bowl, whisking occasionally, until thickened, about 3 minutes. Divide glaze in half and reserve both, separately; cover both portions to keep warm. Push toothpick horizontally though each onion round to keep rings intact while grilling. Brush onion and pineapple with oil.

2 Using fork, mash bread, scallions, milk, and pepper to paste in large bowl. Break ground pork into small pieces, add to bowl, and gently knead with your hands until well combined. Divide pork mixture into 4 equal portions, then gently shape each portion into ¾-inch-thick patty. Using your fingertips, press center of each patty down until about ½ inch thick, creating slight divot.

3A FOR A CHARCOAL GRILL Open bottom vent completely. Light large chimney starter filled with charcoal briquettes (6 quarts). When top coals are partially covered with ash, pour evenly over grill. Set cooking grate in place, cover, and open lid vent completely. Heat grill until hot, about 5 minutes.

3B FOR A GAS GRILL Turn all burners to high; cover; and heat grill until hot, about 15 minutes. Leave all burners on high.

4 Clean and oil cooking grate. Place onion rounds and pineapple rings on grill and cook (covered if using gas) until softened and lightly charred, 6 to 12 minutes, flipping as needed. As they finish cooking, transfer onion and pineapple to platter and tent with aluminum foil.

5 Meanwhile, place patties on grill, divot side up, and cook until well browned, 4 to 6 minutes. Flip patties; brush with half of soy mixture; and cook until second side is well browned and meat registers 150 degrees, 5 to 7 minutes. Transfer burgers to platter, brush with remaining soy mixture, and let rest for 5 minutes.

6 Remove toothpicks from onion rounds and separate into rings. Spread mayonnaise on roll bottoms and top with lettuce. Serve burgers on rolls, topped with pineapple, onion, and cherry peppers, passing extra mayonnaise separately.

GRILLED TERIYAKI PORK BURGERS

Bún Chả

SERVES 4 to 6 **TIME** 50 minutes

Why This Recipe Works Vietnamese bún chả—a vibrant mix of grilled pork, crisp salad, and delicate yet resilient rice vermicelli, all united by a light yet vibrant sauce—is an ideal meal for a hot summer night. The noodles, salad, and nuoc cham sauce all come together quickly. A bit of baking soda raises the pH of ground pork, which helps the patties retain moisture and brown during their short grilling time. Briefly soaking the grilled patties in the sauce is a traditional step that further flavors the meat and imbues the sauce with grill flavor. We prefer the more delicate springiness of vermicelli made from 100 percent rice flour to those that include a secondary starch such as cornstarch. If you can find only the latter, just cook them longer—up to 12 minutes. For a less spicy sauce, use only half the Thai chile. For the cilantro, use the leaves and the thin, delicate stems, not the thicker ones close to the root. To serve, plate the components separately on the table so that everyone can combine them as they like.

BÚN CHẢ

NOODLES AND SALAD

- 8 ounces rice vermicelli
- 1 head Boston lettuce (8 ounces), torn into bite-size pieces
- 1 English cucumber, peeled, quartered lengthwise, seeded, and sliced thin on bias
- 1 cup fresh cilantro leaves and stems
- 1 cup fresh mint leaves, torn if large

SAUCE

- 1 small Thai chile, stemmed and minced
- 3 tablespoons sugar, divided
- 1 garlic clove, minced
- ⅔ cup hot water
- 5 tablespoons fish sauce
- ¼ cup lime juice (2 limes)

PORK PATTIES

- 1 large shallot, minced
- 1 tablespoon fish sauce
- 1½ teaspoons sugar
- ½ teaspoon baking soda
- ½ teaspoon pepper
- 1 pound ground pork

1 FOR THE NOODLES AND SALAD Bring 4 quarts water to boil in large pot. Stir in noodles and cook until tender but not mushy, 4 to 12 minutes. Drain noodles and rinse under cold running water until cool. Drain noodles very well, spread on large plate, and let stand at room temperature to dry. Arrange lettuce, cucumber, cilantro, and mint separately on large platter and refrigerate until ready to serve.

2 FOR THE SAUCE Using mortar and pestle (or on cutting board using flat side of chef's knife), mash Thai chile, 1 tablespoon sugar, and garlic to fine paste. Transfer to medium bowl and add hot water and remaining 2 tablespoons sugar. Stir until sugar is dissolved. Stir in fish sauce and lime juice, cover, and set aside for serving.

3 FOR THE PORK PATTIES Combine shallot, fish sauce, sugar, baking soda, and pepper in medium bowl. Break ground pork into small pieces, add to bowl, and gently knead with your hands until well combined. Shape pork mixture into 12 patties, each about 2½ inches wide and ½ inch thick.

4A FOR A CHARCOAL GRILL Open bottom vent completely. Light large chimney starter filled with charcoal briquettes (6 quarts). When top coals are partially covered with ash, pour evenly over half of grill. Set cooking grate in place, cover, and open lid vent completely. Heat grill until hot, about 5 minutes.

4B FOR A GAS GRILL Turn all burners to high; cover; and heat grill until hot, about 15 minutes. Leave all burners on high.

5 Clean and oil cooking grate. Place patties on grill (over coals if using charcoal; covered if using gas) and cook until well charred, 6 to 8 minutes, flipping as needed. Transfer grilled patties to bowl with sauce and toss gently to coat. Let stand for 5 minutes. Serve, passing noodles and salad separately. (Though it's not traditional, if preferred, remove grilled patties from sauce after 5 minutes and serve patties and sauce separately.)

Grilled Harissa Lamb Burgers

SERVES 4 **TIME** 40 minutes

Why This Recipe Works Harissa, a traditional North African condiment with an irresistibly complex chile flavor, pairs perfectly with lamb's earthy taste in this grilled burger. Cool, creamy mayonnaise provides a rich base for a spicy harissa-spiked sauce, and a blast of fresh mint and lemon zest balances out the harissa's heat.

- 3 tablespoons mayonnaise
- 2 tablespoons harissa, divided
- 1 tablespoon minced fresh mint
- 1½ teaspoons grated lemon zest, divided
- ½ teaspoon pepper, divided
- 1½ pounds ground lamb
- 1 red onion, sliced into ½-inch-thick rounds
- 1 tablespoon vegetable oil
- 1 teaspoon kosher salt
- 4 hamburger buns, toasted if desired
- 1 cup baby arugula

1 Combine mayonnaise, 1 tablespoon harissa, mint, and ½ teaspoon lemon zest in bowl and season with salt and pepper to taste; cover and refrigerate until ready to serve.

2 Combine remaining 1 tablespoon harissa, remaining 1 teaspoon lemon zest, and ¼ teaspoon pepper in large bowl. Break ground lamb into small pieces, add to bowl, and gently knead with your hands until well combined. Divide lamb mixture into 4 equal portions, then gently shape each portion into ¾-inch-thick patty. Using your fingertips, press center of each patty down until about ½ inch thick, creating slight divot.

3 Push toothpick horizontally through each onion round to keep rings intact while grilling. Brush onion with oil. Just before cooking, sprinkle with salt and remaining ¼ teaspoon pepper.

GRILLED HARISSA LAMB BURGERS

4A FOR A CHARCOAL GRILL Open bottom vent completely. Light large chimney starter filled with charcoal briquettes (6 quarts). When top coals are partially covered with ash, pour evenly over grill. Set cooking grate in place, cover, and open lid vent completely. Heat grill until hot, about 5 minutes.

4B FOR A GAS GRILL Turn all burners to high; cover; and heat grill until hot, about 15 minutes. Leave all burners on high.

5 Clean and oil cooking grate. Place onion rounds on grill and cook (covered if using gas) until softened and lightly charred, 6 to 12 minutes, turning as needed. As they finish cooking, transfer onion rounds to bowl and cover to keep warm.

6 Place patties on grill, divot side up, and cook until well browned on first side, 2 to 4 minutes. Flip patties and cook until second side is browned and meat registers 120 to 125 degrees (for medium-rare) or 130 to 135 (for medium), 3 to 5 minutes. Transfer burgers to platter and let rest for 5 minutes.

7 Remove toothpicks from onion rounds and separate into rings. Spread mayonnaise mixture on bun tops. Serve burgers on buns, topped with onion and arugula.

Grilled Lamb Kofte

SERVES 4 to 6 **TIME** 55 minutes plus 1 hour chilling

Why This Recipe Works A traditional favorite found all over the Middle East, kofte are boldly seasoned meat patties that are often formed around metal skewers and quickly cooked over live fire, which makes them tender and juicy on the inside and nicely charred on the outside. They can be stuffed into pitas, served with rice pilaf, or presented on a platter, as we do in this recipe. Corralling the coals into the center of the grill using a disposable pan concentrates the fire to create a smoky, crunchy coating of char on the meat. Kneading the ingredients together creates an almost sausage-like springiness, while gelatin helps the meat mixture retain juiciness without muting the flavors. Ground pine nuts add richness and keep the texture from being too bouncy. For the spices, we use a variation on the common Middle Eastern spice blend called baharat, which contains black pepper, cumin, coriander, and chile pepper. In the cooling yogurt sauce, we include a small amount of tahini, along with the traditional additions of garlic and lemon juice, to give the yogurt a depth to match that of the kofte itself. You will need eight 12-inch metal skewers for this recipe.

YOGURT-GARLIC SAUCE

- 1 cup plain whole-milk yogurt
- 2 tablespoons lemon juice
- 2 tablespoons tahini
- 1 garlic clove, minced

KOFTE

- ½ cup pine nuts
- 4 garlic cloves, peeled
- 1½ teaspoons smoked hot paprika
- 2 teaspoons kosher salt
- 1 teaspoon ground cumin
- ½ teaspoon pepper
- ¼ teaspoon ground coriander
- ¼ teaspoon ground cloves
- ⅛ teaspoon ground nutmeg
- ⅛ teaspoon ground cinnamon
- ½ cup grated onion, drained
- ⅓ cup minced fresh parsley
- ⅓ cup minced fresh mint
- 1½ teaspoons unflavored gelatin
- 1½ pounds ground lamb
- 1 (13 by 9-inch) disposable aluminum roasting pan, if using charcoal grill

GRILLED LAMB KOFTE

1 FOR THE YOGURT-GARLIC SAUCE Whisk all ingredients together in bowl. Cover and refrigerate until ready to serve.

2 FOR THE KOFTE Process pine nuts, garlic, paprika, salt, cumin, pepper, coriander, cloves, nutmeg, and cinnamon in food processor until coarse paste forms, 30 to 45 seconds. Transfer mixture to large bowl and add onion, parsley, mint, and gelatin. Break ground lamb into small pieces, add to bowl, and gently knead with your hands until well combined and mixture feels slightly sticky. Divide mixture into 24 equal portions, then gently shape each portion into 2-inch-long cylinder about 1 inch in diameter. Using eight 12-inch metal skewers, thread 3 cylinders onto each skewer, pressing gently to adhere. Transfer skewers to lightly greased baking sheet, cover with plastic wrap, and refrigerate for at least 1 hour or up to 24 hours.

3A FOR A CHARCOAL GRILL Using skewer, poke 12 holes in bottom of disposable pan. Open bottom vent completely and place pan in center of grill. Light large chimney starter two-thirds filled with charcoal briquettes (4 quarts). When top coals are partially covered with ash, pour into pan. Set cooking grate in place, cover, and open lid vent completely. Heat grill until hot, about 5 minutes.

3B FOR A GAS GRILL Turn all burners to high; cover; and heat grill until hot, about 15 minutes. Leave all burners on high.

4 Clean and oil cooking grate. Place skewers on grill (over coals if using charcoal) at 45-degree angle to grate bars. Cook (covered if using gas) until browned and meat easily releases from grill, 4 to 7 minutes. Flip skewers and cook until second side is browned and meat registers 160 degrees, about 6 minutes. Transfer skewers to serving platter and serve, passing yogurt sauce separately.

Grilled Adana-Style Kebabs

SERVES 4 to 6 **TIME** 1 hour plus 1 hour chilling

Why This Recipe Works In the Turkish city of Adana, the signature kebab is made from fatty lamb that's minced by hand and spiced with red pepper. The meat is pressed onto a long, flat skewer before being grilled over coals. Our backyard grill version begins with ground lamb and incorporates a heady blend of chopped onion, garlic, biber salçası (Turkish pepper paste), cumin, paprika, sumac, and cayenne pepper. To shape the kebabs correctly, we create makeshift shishes (skewers) by wrapping aluminum foil around a plank made from five wooden skewers. Thoroughly chilling the lamb skewers firms them up for grilling. We set the grilled kebabs on lavash and serve them with a vibrant, superfresh salad. Jarred biber salçası can be found in Middle Eastern grocery stores or online. Be sure to use the mild variety; if it's unavailable, you can substitute 3 tablespoons of tomato paste and increase the amount of paprika to 4 teaspoons. You can substitute 80 percent lean ground beef for the lamb, if desired. Pita can be substituted for the lavash. If you're using pita or smaller lavashes, you may want to use more than three. Serve with yogurt or Tzatziki sauce (page 395), if desired.

GRILLED ADANA-STYLE KEBABS

Making the Shishes

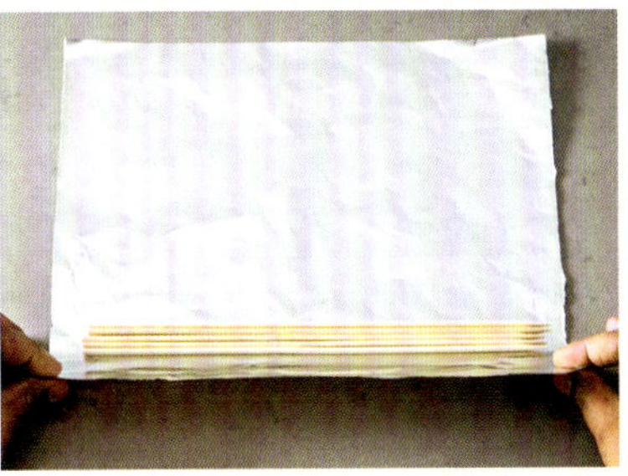

1 Place foil sheet on counter and place 5 bamboo skewers one-third of way up sheet. Fold bottom third of foil up and press down to secure over skewers.

2 Fold skewers over themselves, pressing foil down with each fold. Fold ends of foil down to form single wide, flat skewer.

Forming the Kebabs

1 Press ball of meat around middle of skewer.

2 Squeeze meat mixture to cover skewer in even layer. Use your thumb and forefinger to press ridges across meat mixture.

KEBABS

- 30 (12-inch) bamboo skewers
- 1 onion, chopped coarse
- 4 garlic cloves, chopped
- 3 tablespoons mild biber salçası
- 2 teaspoons kosher salt
- 2 teaspoons paprika
- 1 teaspoon ground cumin
- 1 teaspoon ground sumac
- 1 teaspoon pepper
- ½ teaspoon cayenne pepper
- 1½ pounds ground lamb
- 3 large rectangular lavashes, halved crosswise

SALAD

- 3 plum tomatoes, cored and chopped
- 2 small red onions, sliced thin
- 1 cup chopped fresh parsley
- ¼ cup extra-virgin olive oil
- ¼ cup lemon juice (2 lemons)
- 2 tablespoons ground sumac
- 1½ teaspoons kosher salt

1 **FOR THE KEBABS** Place 13 by 12-inch-long sheet of aluminum foil on counter with long side parallel to edge of counter. Place 5 skewers together (parallel to edge of counter) about one-third of way up sheet of foil. Fold bottom third of foil up over skewers and press foil down firmly to hold skewers in place. Fold skewers up and over themselves to wrap tightly in foil, pressing foil down firmly with each fold until you have a single 1-inch wide, flat skewer. Fold ends of foil over top and bottom of skewer and pinch firmly to seal. Repeat with remaining bamboo skewers and 5 additional pieces of foil to create 6 wide skewers; set aside.

2 Pulse onion and garlic in food processor until very finely chopped but not pureed, 15 to 20 pulses, scraping down sides of bowl as needed. Transfer to large bowl. Stir in biber salçası, salt, paprika, cumin, sumac, pepper, and cayenne. Break ground lamb into small pieces, add to bowl, and gently knead with your hands until well combined.

3 With your moistened hands, divide lamb mixture into 6 equal portions. Working with 1 portion and 1 skewer at a time, press lamb around middle of skewer. Squeeze lamb mixture to cover skewer and press into flat, 9-inch-long kebab, moistening your hands periodically if mixture begins to stick. Use your thumb and forefinger to press ridges evenly across entire length of kebab. (If lamb mixture becomes too warm to work with easily and shape onto skewers, transfer to freezer for 15 to 30 minutes to firm it up.) Transfer kebabs to lightly greased baking sheet. Cover kebabs with plastic wrap and refrigerate for at least 1 hour or up to 24 hours.

4 **FOR THE SALAD** Meanwhile, toss all ingredients together in large bowl. Cover and set aside for serving. (Salad can be held at room temperature for up to 2 hours.)

5A **FOR A CHARCOAL GRILL** Open bottom vent completely. Light large chimney starter mounded with charcoal briquettes (7 quarts). When top coals are partially covered with ash, pour evenly over grill. Set cooking grate in place, cover, and open lid vent completely. Heat grill until hot, about 5 minutes.

5B **FOR A GAS GRILL** Turn all burners to high; cover; and heat grill until hot, about 15 minutes. Leave all burners on high.

6 Clean cooking grate, then repeatedly brush grate with well-oiled paper towels until grate is black and glossy, 5 to 10 times. Cover grill and heat about 5 minutes longer. Uncover and wipe grate twice more with well-oiled paper towels.

7 Arrange lavash on large serving platter. Place kebabs on grill at 45-degree angle to grate bars. Cover and cook until well browned and meat easily releases from grill, 6 to 8 minutes, turning as needed. (If kebabs stick to cooking grate, use thin metal spatula to gently loosen before flipping with tongs). Top lavash with kebabs, tent with foil, and let rest for 5 minutes.

8 To remove kebabs from skewers, pinch piece of lavash around base of kebab and pull out skewer. Serve kebabs with salad and lavash.

Grilled Arayes with Parsley-Cucumber Salad

SERVES 4 to 6 **TIME** 1 hour

Why This Recipe Works Laced with herbs and warm spices, these Middle Eastern pressed and grilled lamb sandwiches are a street food favorite and all-around flavor bomb. The meat mixture is packed with seasoning: traditional cumin, coriander, and onion, as well as lemon zest, cayenne, and paprika. As the sandwiches cook, the lamb releases fat and juices into the bread, which helps it crisp up over the grill's heat. The bright yogurt-tahini sauce and an herb-based salad make this a meal. You can substitute 85 percent lean ground beef for the ground lamb, if desired. This recipe works best with ¼-inch-thick pitas that are fresh and pliable.

SAUCE

- 1 cup plain Greek yogurt
- ½ cup minced fresh mint
- 2 tablespoons tahini
- 1 tablespoon lemon juice
- 2 tablespoons extra-virgin olive oil
- ¼ teaspoon kosher salt

SALAD

- 2 tablespoons extra-virgin olive oil
- 1 tablespoon lemon juice
- ¼ teaspoon kosher salt
- 3 cups fresh parsley leaves
- 1 English cucumber, halved lengthwise and sliced thin
- 4 ounces feta cheese, sliced thin
- ½ cup walnuts, toasted and chopped coarse
- ¼ cup pomegranate seeds

LAMB

- 1 onion, cut into 1-inch pieces
- 1 cup fresh cilantro leaves
- ¼ cup extra-virgin olive oil
- 1 tablespoon grated lemon zest plus 2 tablespoons juice
- 1 tablespoon kosher salt
- 1 tablespoon ground coriander
- 1 tablespoon ground cumin
- 1 tablespoon paprika
- 1½ teaspoons pepper
- ½ teaspoon cayenne pepper
- ¼ teaspoon ground cinnamon
- 2 pounds ground lamb
- 4 (8-inch) pitas

1 **FOR THE SAUCE** Whisk all ingredients together in bowl. Cover and set aside until ready to serve.

2 **FOR THE SALAD** Whisk oil, lemon juice, and salt together in large bowl. Add parsley and cucumber and toss to coat. Transfer to serving platter and top with feta, walnuts, and pomegranate seeds. Cover and set aside until ready to serve.

3 **FOR THE LAMB** Pulse onion and cilantro in food processor until finely chopped, 10 to 12 pulses, scraping down sides of bowl as needed. Transfer mixture to large bowl and stir in oil, lemon zest, lemon juice, salt, coriander, cumin, paprika, pepper, cayenne, and cinnamon. Break ground lamb into small pieces, add to bowl, and gently knead with your hands until well combined.

GRILLED ARAYES WITH PARSLEY-CUCUMBER SALAD

4 Using kitchen shears, cut around circumference of each pita and separate into 2 halves. Place 4 thicker halves on counter, interior side up. Divide lamb mixture into 4 equal portions and place 1 portion in center of each pita half. Using spatula, gently spread lamb mixture into even layer, leaving ½-inch border. Top each lamb portion with 1 thinner pita half. Press each sandwich firmly until lamb mixture spreads to ¼ inch from edge of pita.

5A FOR A CHARCOAL GRILL Open bottom vent completely. Light large chimney starter two-thirds filled with charcoal briquettes (4 quarts). When top coals are partially covered with ash, pour evenly over grill. Set cooking grate in place, cover, and open lid vent completely. Heat grill until hot, about 5 minutes.

5B FOR A GAS GRILL Turn all burners to high; cover; and heat grill until hot, about 15 minutes. Turn all burners to medium-high.

6 Clean and oil cooking grate. Place sandwiches on grill; cover; and cook until first side is evenly browned and edges are starting to crisp, 7 to 10 minutes, moving sandwiches as needed to ensure even cooking. Flip sandwiches; cover; and cook until second side is evenly browned and edges are crispy, 7 to 10 minutes. Transfer sandwiches to cutting board and cut each into quarters, then transfer to platter and serve with sauce and salad.

Packing the Pita

Stuffing the lamb filling into a pita pocket can cause the bread to tear. Instead, separate each pita into two pieces. The bottom side, which has a pattern of marks on it (from the conveyor belt the breads sit on as they move through the oven), is more fragile. Use the sturdier top piece, which is usually slightly thicker, as the base to spread the filling on.

Classic Turkey Burgers

SERVES 4 **TIME** 35 minutes

Why This Recipe Works A lean, flavorful turkey burger is a delicious cookout alternative to the classic beef burger, and store-bought ground turkey makes a simple, satisfying patty. When we use preground turkey, we prefer the flavor of 93 percent lean ground turkey over lean white meat or all dark meat. Melted butter adds welcome richness and ensures moist, juicy burgers. A little bit of Worcestershire and Dijon mustard give the mild meat plenty of flavor and a pleasant tang. Be sure to use 93 percent lean ground turkey, not 99 percent fat-free ground turkey breast, or the burgers will be tough.

- 2 tablespoons unsalted butter, melted and cooled
- 2 teaspoons Worcestershire sauce
- 2 teaspoons Dijon mustard
- 1½ pounds ground turkey
- 1 teaspoon kosher salt
- ¼ teaspoon pepper
- 4 slices cheese (4 ounces) (optional)
- 4 hamburger buns, toasted if desired

1 Combine melted butter, Worcestershire, and mustard in large bowl. Break ground turkey into small pieces, add to bowl, and gently knead with your hands until well combined. Divide turkey mixture into 4 equal portions, then gently shape each portion into ¾-inch-thick patty. Using your fingertips, press center of each patty down until about ½ inch thick, creating slight divot. Just before cooking, sprinkle patties with salt and pepper.

2A FOR A CHARCOAL GRILL Open bottom vent completely. Light large chimney starter filled with charcoal briquettes (6 quarts). When top coals are partially covered with ash, pour evenly over grill. Set cooking grate in place, cover, and open lid vent completely. Heat grill until hot, about 5 minutes.

2B FOR A GAS GRILL Turn all burners to high; cover; and heat grill until hot, about 15 minutes. Leave all burners on high.

3 Clean and oil cooking grate. Place patties on grill, divot side up, and cook (covered if using gas) until well browned on first side and meat easily releases from grill, 4 to 6 minutes. Flip patties; top with cheese, if using; and cook until second side is browned side and meat registers 160 degrees, 5 to 7 minutes. Transfer burgers to platter and let rest for 5 minutes. Serve burgers on buns.

CLASSIC TURKEY BURGERS

GRILLED TURKEY BURGERS WITH SPINACH AND FETA

Grilled Turkey Burgers with Spinach and Feta

SERVES 4 **TIME** 35 minutes

Why This Recipe Works Ground turkey's neutral flavor makes it an ideal choice as the base for a burger with lots of mix-ins. Melted butter and feta cheese provide the ground meat with plenty of richness and flavor while also preventing the burgers from drying out. For textural interest, we add fresh baby spinach to the meat mixture. Chopped dill lends a hit of freshness, and minced garlic rounds out the flavors. Be sure to use 93 percent lean ground turkey, not 99 percent fat-free ground turkey breast, or the burgers will be tough.

- 2 ounces (2 cups) baby spinach, chopped
- 2 ounces feta cheese, crumbled (½ cup)
- 2 tablespoons unsalted butter, melted and cooled
- 2 teaspoons minced fresh dill
- 1 garlic clove, minced
- ¼ teaspoon pepper
- 1¼ pounds ground turkey
- 1 teaspoon kosher salt
- 4 hamburger buns, toasted if desired

1 Combine spinach, feta, melted butter, dill, garlic, and pepper in large bowl. Break ground turkey into small pieces, add to bowl, and gently knead with your hands until well combined. Divide turkey mixture into 4 equal portions, then gently shape each portion into ¾-inch-thick patty. Using your fingertips, press center of each patty down until about ½ inch thick, creating slight divot. Just before cooking, sprinkle patties with salt.

2A **FOR A CHARCOAL GRILL** Open bottom vent completely. Light large chimney starter filled with charcoal briquettes (6 quarts). When top coals are partially covered with ash, pour evenly over grill. Set cooking grate in place, cover, and open lid vent completely. Heat grill until hot, about 5 minutes.

2B **FOR A GAS GRILL** Turn all burners to high; cover; and heat grill until hot, about 15 minutes. Leave all burners on high.

3 Clean and oil cooking grate. Place patties on grill, divot side up, and cook (covered if using gas) until well browned on first side and meat easily releases from grill, 4 to 6 minutes. Flip patties and cook until second side is browned and meat registers 160 degrees, 5 to 7 minutes. Transfer burgers to platter and let rest for 5 minutes. Serve burgers on buns.

VARIATIONS

Grilled Turkey Burgers with Miso and Ginger

Omit spinach, feta, salt, and pepper. Whisk 2 tablespoons miso paste and 1 tablespoon water together in bowl until combined. Add miso mixture to turkey with melted butter. Substitute 1 teaspoon grated fresh ginger for dill and 2 minced scallions for garlic.

Grilled Turkey Burgers with Herbs and Goat Cheese

Omit spinach and garlic. Substitute ¾ cup crumbled goat cheese for feta. Add 1 large minced shallot and 2 tablespoons minced fresh parsley to turkey with melted butter.

Grind-Your-Own Turkey Burgers

SERVES 4 **TIME** 50 minutes plus 1 hour 5 minutes freezing

Why This Recipe Works For the meatiest-tasting turkey burgers, the obvious starting point is thigh meat, a cut that boasts a decent amount of fat and flavor. A food processor grinds the meat easily into fine pieces. We further process a small amount of the turkey with soy sauce, baking soda (to tenderize the meat by raising its pH), and gelatin; when mixed into the remaining turkey, this emulsion traps copious amounts of moisture and fat for juicy burgers. Finely chopped mushrooms keep the burger texture from being too dense and sausage-like. They also increase tenderness, provide extra moisture, and boost meatiness. Freezing the patties prior to grilling helps them hold together. If you are unable to find boneless, skinless turkey thighs, substitute one 2-pound bone-in thigh, skin and bones removed, trimmed. To double this recipe, spread turkey over two baking sheets in step 1 and pulse in food processor in six batches. When cooking turkey burgers, make sure they reach 160 degrees before removing them from the heat.

- 1½ pounds boneless, skinless turkey thighs, trimmed and cut into ½-inch pieces
- 1 tablespoon unflavored gelatin
- 3 tablespoons chicken broth
- 6 ounces white mushrooms, trimmed
- 1 tablespoon soy sauce
- Pinch baking soda
- 2 tablespoons plus 2 teaspoons vegetable oil, divided
- 1 teaspoon kosher salt
- ¼ teaspoon pepper
- 4 slices cheese (4 ounces) (optional)
- 4 hamburger buns, toasted if desired

1 Arrange turkey in single layer on rimmed baking sheet and freeze until very firm and starting to harden around edges but still pliable, 35 to 45 minutes.

2 Sprinkle gelatin over broth in small bowl and let sit until gelatin softens, about 5 minutes. Pulse mushrooms in food processor until coarsely chopped, about 7 pulses, stopping and redistributing mushrooms as needed; transfer to bowl and set aside. (Do not wash workbowl).

3 Working in 3 batches, pulse turkey in now-empty processor until ground into ⅛-inch pieces, about 20 pulses, stopping to redistribute meat as needed; transfer to separate large bowl. Return ½ cup (about 3 ounces) ground turkey to again-empty processor along with softened gelatin, soy sauce, and baking soda. Process until smooth, about 2 minutes, scraping down sides of bowl as needed. With processor running, slowly add 2 tablespoons oil until incorporated, about 10 seconds. Return mushrooms to processor with paste and pulse to combine, 3 to 5 pulses. Transfer mushroom mixture to bowl with turkey and knead with your hands until combined.

4 With your lightly greased hands, divide turkey mixture into 4 equal portions, then gently shape each portion into ¾-inch-thick patty. Using your fingertips, press center of each patty down until about ½ inch thick, creating slight divot. (Patties can be refrigerated for up to 1 hour.)

5 Freeze patties for 30 minutes. Just before cooking, brush 1 side of patties with 1 teaspoon oil and sprinkle with ½ teaspoon salt and ⅛ teaspoon pepper. Using spatula, gently flip patties, brush with remaining 1 teaspoon oil, and sprinkle with remaining ½ teaspoon salt and remaining ⅛ teaspoon pepper.

6A **FOR A CHARCOAL GRILL** Open bottom vent completely. Light large chimney starter filled with charcoal briquettes (6 quarts). When top coals are partially covered with ash, pour evenly over half of grill. Set cooking grate in place, cover, and open lid vent completely. Heat grill until hot, about 5 minutes.

6B **FOR A GAS GRILL** Turn all burners to high; cover; and heat grill until hot, about 15 minutes. Leave all burners on high.

7 Clean and oil cooking grate. Using spatula, place patties on grill, divot side up (over coals if using charcoal, covered if using gas), and cook until well browned on first side and meat easily releases from grill, 5 to 7 minutes. Flip; top with cheese, if using; and cook until second side is well browned and meat registers 160 degrees, 5 to 7 minutes. Transfer burgers to platter and let rest for 5 minutes. Serve on buns.

VARIATION

Grind-Your-Own Turkey Burgers for the Freezer

Uncooked patties can be frozen for up to 2 weeks. To freeze, stack patties, separated by parchment paper; wrap in plastic wrap; and place in zipper-lock freezer bag. Do not thaw frozen patties before cooking.

Grilled Southern Shrimp Burgers

SERVES 4 **TIME** 40 minutes plus 30 minutes chilling

Why This Recipe Works The ideal shrimp burger puts the sweet, briny flavor of shrimp front and center, with a texture that's chunky and moist but still cohesive. When it comes to binders and seasonings, less is more. A food processor quickly breaks down raw shrimp into a combination of fine and chunky shrimp pieces. We mix them with modest amounts of mayonnaise and fresh bread crumbs. Minced scallion and parsley, lemon zest, and a touch of cayenne pepper complement the shrimp flavor. Be sure to use raw, not cooked, shrimp here. Dry the shrimp thoroughly before processing to prevent a mushy texture. Handle the burgers gently when shaping and when grilling; if overhandled while being shaped, the burgers will be dense and rubbery, and if handled roughly during cooking, they will break apart. Serve with salad greens or on toasted hamburger buns with Classic Tartar Sauce (page 395).

- ¼ cup mayonnaise
- 2 scallions, minced
- 2 tablespoons minced fresh parsley
- 2 teaspoons grated lemon zest
- ½ teaspoon kosher salt
- ⅛ teaspoon pepper
- Pinch cayenne pepper
- 1 slice hearty white sandwich bread, torn into large pieces
- 1½ pounds extra-large shrimp (21 to 25 per pound), peeled, deveined, and patted dry
- Vegetable oil

1 Combine mayonnaise, scallions, parsley, lemon zest, salt, pepper, and cayenne in large bowl until uniform. Pulse bread in food processor to coarse crumbs, about 10 pulses. Transfer to small bowl; set aside. (Do not wash workbowl).

GRILLED SOUTHERN SHRIMP BURGERS

2 Pulse shrimp in now-empty food processor until some pieces are finely minced and others are coarsely chopped, about 7 pulses. Add shrimp to mayonnaise mixture and gently fold until just combined. Sprinkle bread crumbs over mixture and gently fold until incorporated.

3 Scrape shrimp mixture onto small baking sheet, divide into 4 equal portions, and loosely pack each into 1-inch-thick patty. Cover and refrigerate patties for at least 30 minutes or up to 3 hours.

4A **FOR A CHARCOAL GRILL** Open bottom vent completely. Light large chimney starter three-quarters filled with charcoal briquettes (4½ quarts). When top coals are partially covered with ash, pour evenly over grill. Set cooking grate in place, cover, and open lid vent completely. Heat grill until hot, about 5 minutes.

4B **FOR A GAS GRILL** Turn all burners to high; cover; and heat grill until hot, about 15 minutes. Turn all burners to medium-high.

5 Clean and oil cooking grate. Lightly brush tops of burgers with oil, lay them on grill oiled side down, and lightly brush other side with oil. Cook burgers, without pressing on them, until lightly browned and cooked through, 10 to 14 minutes, flipping them halfway through cooking. Transfer burgers to platter, tent with aluminum foil, and let rest for 5 minutes before serving.

Grilled Salmon Burgers

SERVES 4 **TIME** 40 minutes

Why This Recipe Works Although salmon is a fatty fish, salmon burgers tend to overcook quickly over the high heat of the grill. A couple tablespoons of mayonnaise adds enough fat and moisture to provide protection. We chop the fish by hand instead of using a food processor to make sure that we end up with a texture closer to ground meat than salmon mousse. For flavor, we keep things simple, with just fresh parsley, onion, lemon juice, and salt and pepper. After gently forming the burgers, we pop them in the refrigerator for a short time, which helps them hold their shape on the grill. Finally, we make sure to pull the burgers off the grill when they are just barely done. Be sure to refrigerate the burgers for at least 15 minutes before grilling. Coat a metal spatula with vegetable oil spray so that the burgers slide easily onto the grill. Serve these burgers on salad greens or toasted hamburger buns with Creamy Lemon-Herb Sauce (page 396).

- 1¼ pounds skinless salmon
- ¼ cup chopped fresh parsley
- 2 tablespoons mayonnaise
- 2 tablespoons finely grated onion
- 1 tablespoon lemon juice
- 1 teaspoon kosher salt
- Pinch pepper

1 Chop salmon into ¼-inch pieces. Using rocking motion, continue to chop salmon until it is coarsely chopped into pieces roughly ⅛ inch each. Transfer salmon to large bowl.

2 Add parsley, mayonnaise, onion, lemon juice, salt, and pepper to salmon and mix to combine. Divide mixture into 4 equal portions, then gently shape each portion into 1-inch-thick patty. Place patties on parchment paper–lined baking sheet and refrigerate for at least 15 minutes or up to 24 hours.

3A **FOR A CHARCOAL GRILL** Open bottom vent completely. Light large chimney starter filled with charcoal briquettes (6 quarts). When top coals are partially covered with ash, pour evenly over grill. Set cooking grate in place, cover, and open lid vent completely. Heat grill until hot, about 5 minutes.

3B **FOR A GAS GRILL** Turn all burners to high; cover; and heat grill until hot, about 15 minutes. Leave all burners on high.

4 Clean cooking grate, then repeatedly brush grate with well-oiled paper towels until grate is black and glossy, 5 to 10 times. Using greased spatula, place burgers on grill and cook (covered if using gas) until well browned on first side, 3 to 5 minutes. Flip burgers with greased metal spatula and cook (covered if using gas) until second side is well browned and burgers register 125 to 130 degrees, 3 to 4 minutes. Serve immediately.

Chili Cheese Dogs

SERVES 4 **TIME** 40 minutes

Why This Recipe Works Grilling the hot dogs for our chili cheese dogs adds a little extra something special to this already iconic food. We keep prep simple with a superfast ground beef chili and an easy microwave cheese sauce brightened with tart cherry pepper brine. Splitting the hot dogs means they pick up plenty of flavor from the grill and make a nice base for all the toppings. For the best texture, we recommend using American cheese from the deli counter (not individually wrapped slices).

GRILLED SALMON BURGERS

- 1 pound 85 percent lean ground beef
- 2 tablespoons chili powder
- 1 teaspoon kosher salt
- ½ teaspoon pepper
- ¼ cup tomato paste
- 1 cup water
- 8 ounces deli American cheese, chopped coarse
- ⅓ cup whole milk
- ¼ cup chopped jarred hot cherry peppers, plus 1 tablespoon brine
- 8 hot dogs
- 8 hot dog buns, toasted if desired
- ¼ cup finely chopped onion

1 Combine beef, chili powder, salt, and pepper in 12-inch nonstick skillet. Cook over medium-high heat, breaking up meat with wooden spoon, until beef is no longer pink, about 6 minutes. Stir in tomato paste and cook until paste begins to darken, about 1 minute. Add water and cook until sauce thickens and coats beef, about 4 minutes. Set aside and cover to keep warm.

2 Meanwhile, microwave American cheese, milk, and cherry pepper brine in bowl until cheese is fully melted, about 3 minutes, stirring occasionally. Cover to keep warm.

3 Split each hot dog lengthwise, stopping short of cutting completely in half, so that hot dogs are hinged on 1 side.

4A **FOR A CHARCOAL GRILL** Open bottom vent completely. Light large chimney starter filled with charcoal briquettes (6 quarts). When top coals are partially covered with ash, pour evenly over grill. Set cooking grate in place, cover, and open lid vent completely. Heat grill until hot, about 5 minutes.

4B **FOR A GAS GRILL** Turn all burners to high; cover; and heat grill until hot, about 15 minutes. Leave all burners on high.

5 Clean and oil cooking grate. Place hot dogs on grill and cook until well browned, about 8 minutes, flipping as needed. Meanwhile, grill buns cut side down until toasted, about 1 minute. As they finish cooking, transfer buns and dogs to platter.

6 Stir cheese sauce to recombine. Divide hot dogs, chili, and cheese sauce evenly among buns. Top with cherry peppers and onion. Serve.

CHILI CHEESE DOGS

GRILLED BEER BRATS AND ONIONS

Grilled Beer Brats and Onions

SERVES 8 to 12 **TIME** 55 minutes

Why This Recipe Works To do this Midwest favorite justice, we let the bratwurst marinate in the beer and seasonings in a disposable aluminum pan while we prepare the grill. We grill the onions before adding them to the pan with the sausages to braise on the grill; this gives the mixture serious flavor. Dijon mustard lends brightness and body to the sauce. After the braise, we throw the sausages directly onto the grill for a final crisping to give them good color and a great sear. For the beer, use a pale lager such as Budweiser.

- 2 pounds onions, sliced into ½-inch-thick rounds
- 3 tablespoons vegetable oil
- 1¼ teaspoons pepper, divided
- 3 cups beer
- ⅔ cup Dijon mustard
- 1 teaspoon sugar
- 1 teaspoon caraway seeds
- 1 (13 by 9-inch) disposable aluminum roasting pan
- 2 pounds bratwurst (8 to 12 sausages)
- 8–12 (6-inch) sub rolls, toasted if desired

1 Push toothpick horizontally though each onion round to keep rings intact while grilling. Brush onion with oil and sprinkle with ¼ teaspoon pepper. Combine beer, mustard, sugar, caraway seeds, and remaining 1 teaspoon pepper in disposable pan, then add bratwurst in single layer.

2A **FOR A CHARCOAL GRILL** Open bottom vent completely. Light large chimney starter filled with charcoal briquettes (6 quarts). When top coals are partially covered with ash, pour evenly over grill. Set cooking grate in place, cover, and open lid vent completely. Heat grill until hot, about 5 minutes.

2B **FOR A GAS GRILL** Turn all burners to high; cover; and heat grill until hot, about 15 minutes. Leave all burners on high.

3 Clean and oil cooking grate. Place onions on grill and cook until lightly charred, 6 to 10 minutes, flipping as needed. Transfer onions to disposable pan, remove toothpicks, and separate onions into rings. Place pan in center of grill, cover grill, and cook for 15 minutes.

4 Move pan to 1 side of grill. Transfer bratwurst directly to grill and cook until browned, about 5 minutes, turning as needed. Transfer bratwurst to platter and tent with aluminum foil. Continue to cook onion mixture in pan until sauce is slightly thickened, about 5 minutes. Serve bratwurst and onions with rolls.

Grilled Sausages with Bell Peppers and Onions

SERVES 6 **TIME** 1¼ hours

Why This Recipe Works Coordinated grilling is the key to getting all the components of this classic combination properly cooked. We cook the sausages gently on the cooler side of the grill until nearly done and then move them to the hotter side to develop nice grill marks and a slight char. For the vegetables, we jump-start their cooking in the microwave and then transfer them to a disposable aluminum pan set on the hotter side of the grill, which acts as a makeshift ballpark flat-top grill. Seasoned with vinegar, salt, and pepper, they reach the perfect tenderness as the sausages finish cooking. Just before serving, we transfer the sausages to the disposable pan, cover it with aluminum foil, and let everything rest for a few minutes. You can substitute hot Italian sausages for sweet, if desired. Small flare-ups are to be expected when grilling the sausages on the hotter side of the grill; they give the sausages color and flavor.

- 3 red bell peppers, stemmed, seeded, and cut into ¼-inch-wide strips
- 2 onions, halved and sliced ¼ inch thick
- 3 tablespoons distilled white vinegar
- 2 tablespoons sugar
- 1 tablespoon vegetable oil
- 1 teaspoon kosher salt
- ½ teaspoon pepper
- 1 (13 by 9-inch) disposable aluminum pan
- 2 pounds sweet Italian sausage (8 to 12 links)
- 12 (6-inch) sub rolls, toasted if desired

1 Toss bell peppers, onions, vinegar, sugar, oil, salt, and pepper together in bowl. Cover bowl and microwave until vegetables are just tender, about 6 minutes. Pour vegetables with any accumulated juices into disposable pan.

2A **FOR A CHARCOAL GRILL** Open bottom vent completely. Light large chimney starter filled with charcoal briquettes (6 quarts). When top coals are partially covered with ash, pour evenly over half of grill. Set cooking grate in place, cover, and open lid vent completely. Heat grill until hot, about 5 minutes.

2B **FOR A GAS GRILL** Turn all burners to high; cover; and heat grill until hot, about 15 minutes. Leave primary burner on high and turn off other burner(s). (Adjust primary burner as needed to maintain grill temperature between 350 and 400 degrees.)

GRILLED SAUSAGES WITH BELL PEPPERS AND ONIONS

3 Clean and oil cooking grate. Place disposable pan on hotter side of grill (over primary burner if using gas). Cover and cook for 20 minutes.

4 Place sausages on cooler side of grill and stir vegetable mixture; cover and cook for 8 minutes. Turn sausages and stir vegetable mixture again; cover and cook until sausages register 150 degrees and vegetables are softened and beginning to brown, about 8 minutes.

5 Transfer sausages to disposable pan with vegetables; slide disposable pan to cooler side of grill, then transfer sausages from disposable pan to hotter side of grill. Cook sausages, uncovered, turning often, until well browned and registering 160 degrees, 2 to 3 minutes (there may be flare-ups).

6 Return sausages to disposable pan with vegetables. Remove disposable pan from grill, tent with aluminum foil, and let rest for 5 minutes. Divide sausages and vegetables among rolls. Serve.

Grilled Sausages and Polenta with Arugula Salad

SERVES 4 to 6 **TIME** 30 minutes

Why This Recipe Works Grilled Italian sausages and sliced polenta deliver a speedy dinner with hearty, satisfying flavors. A rosemary and Parmesan vinaigrette flavors grilled slabs of convenient precooked polenta and also dresses a quick arugula and tomato salad. Handle the polenta minimally once it's on the grill; to avoid sticking, let the polenta char lightly before trying to turn it, and use a metal fish spatula. Avoid using pregrated Parmesan cheese here, as it will not dissolve properly in the dressing.

- 1 ounce Parmesan cheese, grated (½ cup)
- ⅓ cup extra-virgin olive oil
- 2 tablespoons red wine vinegar
- 1 teaspoon minced fresh rosemary
- 1 garlic clove, minced
- ½ teaspoon kosher salt
- ⅛ teaspoon pepper
- 1 (18-ounce) tube precooked polenta, sliced ½ inch thick
- 1½ pounds sweet or hot Italian sausage (6 to 8 links), pricked all over with fork
- 12 ounces cherry tomatoes, halved
- 5 ounces (5 cups) baby arugula

1 Whisk Parmesan, oil, vinegar, rosemary, garlic, salt, and pepper together in large bowl. Brush 3 tablespoons of dressing over polenta. Set remaining dressing aside for serving.

2A **FOR A CHARCOAL GRILL** Open bottom vent completely. Light large chimney starter filled with charcoal briquettes (6 quarts). When top coals are partially covered with ash, pour evenly over grill. Set cooking grate in place, cover, and open lid vent completely. Heat grill until hot, about 5 minutes.

2B **FOR A GAS GRILL** Turn all burners to high; cover; and heat grill until hot, about 15 minutes. Leave all burners on high.

3 Clean and oil cooking grate. Place sausages and polenta on grill and cook (covered if using gas) until both are lightly charred and sausages register 160 degrees, about 6 minutes, flipping as needed. (Handle polenta gently to avoid breaking.) Transfer sausages and polenta to serving platter.

4 Drizzle polenta with 2 tablespoons reserved dressing. Add tomatoes and arugula to remaining dressing and toss to coat; season with salt and pepper to taste. Serve sausages and polenta with salad.

GRILLED SAUSAGES AND POLENTA WITH ARUGULA SALAD

5

Barbecue

IN DEPTH

Barbecue with Long-Lasting Heat

Maintaining several hours of gentle heat is key to successfully barbecuing long-cooking foods. Here are two ways to achieve that on a charcoal grill.

LAYER UNLIT AND LIT COALS

Called the **Minion** method for its inventor, Joe Minion, this setup starts with placing a few quarts of unlit coals on the lower grate in a half-grill, banked, or split configuration (see page 13) and then adding lit coals on top. The burning charcoal eventually lights the coals beneath it, extending the overall burning time. This setup often, though not always, includes a pan of water and wood for smoke.

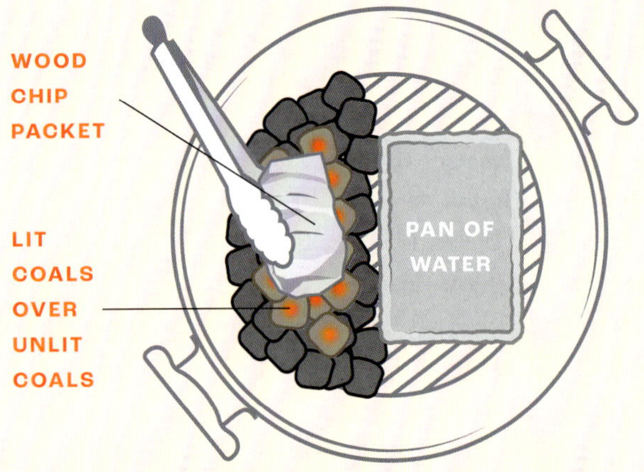

MAKE A CHARCOAL "C"

A charcoal formation in the shape of the letter C—often called a **charcoal snake**—creates a low, slow cooking environment by literally stretching out the fire. This setup starts with a semicircle of unlit briquettes; adding burning coals to one or both ends starts a chain reaction as the lit coals gradually light the coals next to them.

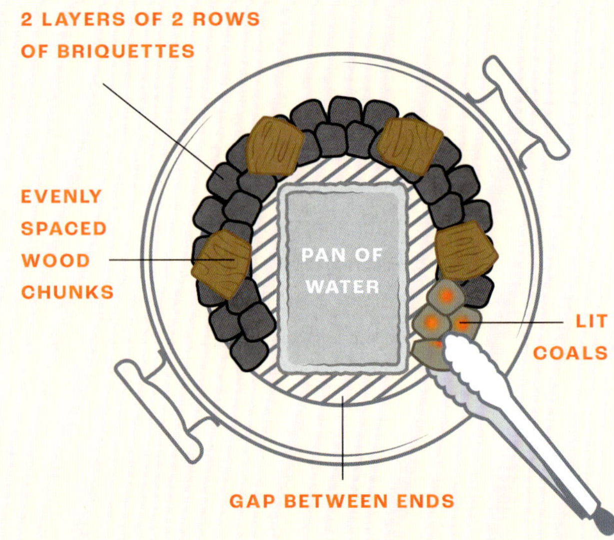

Ribs on the Grill

RIB ROUNDUP

The epitome of finger-lickin', pass-the-napkins barbecue for many, ribs are as satisfying to make as they are fun to eat. Both pork and beef ribs are cut from various sections along the animal's rib cage and can be processed in different ways. Here are the kinds you can buy.

PORK

BABY BACK RIBS
This cut comes from the section of the rib cage close to the backbone (the loin area). These small (about 2-pound) racks are tender and relatively lean.

SPARERIBS
These flavorful ribs come from near the pig's fatty belly. They're quite large, which makes them a challenge to fit on a grill, so we don't usually call for them.

ST. LOUIS–STYLE RIBS
These are spareribs that have been trimmed of skirt meat and excess cartilage to produce a narrower, rectangular rack that usually weighs around 3 pounds. They cook consistently and tend to stay more moist than baby backs.

BEEF

BEEF PLATE RIBS
These giant, meaty ribs are marbled with fat and collagen; over low, slow heat, they achieve a tender, juicy texture. They are rarely available prepackaged, so these ribs are a special-order item from your butcher.

ENGLISH-STYLE SHORT RIBS
Short ribs can be cut from anywhere along the cow's rib section, most often from the chuck or plate. Cut parallel to the bone, they feature a rectangular slab of meat along one side of the bone.

FLANKEN-STYLE SHORT RIBS
Found mainly in butcher shops, these ribs are about ¾ inch thick, cut across the ribs and grain, and they include two or three segments of rib bone. Flanken-style ribs are used for kalbi.

HOW TO REMOVE THE MEMBRANE

The thin, papery membrane on the underside of a rack of ribs helps keep the meat moist and flavorful. It's also somewhat chewy, which may or may not be desirable for the recipe, and its protective qualities aren't always necessary. Here's how to remove it.

1 LOOSEN EDGE
Using tip of paring knife, loosen edge of membrane on rack.

2 GRIP AND PULL
Using paper towel for grip, pull membrane off slowly. (It should come off in single piece.)

Lexington-Style Pulled Pork

SERVES 8 **TIME** 4¼ hours to 5¼ hours, plus 1½ hours seasoning and resting

Why This Recipe Works Lexington-style barbecue (named after Lexington, North Carolina, the self-proclaimed barbecue capital of the world) is unmistakably tender, sweet, and smoky. We coat the pork with a barbecue rub before starting it on the grill with wood chips. To reduce the cooking time, we finish it in the oven once the meat is flavored with smoke; the resulting meat is fall-apart tender. Pork butt roast is also labeled Boston butt in the supermarket; remove any elastic netting before rubbing with spices in step 1. If using a charcoal grill, you can substitute four wood chunks for the wood chip packets. This recipe was developed using Diamond Crystal kosher salt. If you have Morton kosher salt, which is denser, use 1½ tablespoons in the rub. Serve with hamburger buns or sandwich bread.

LEXINGTON-STYLE PULLED PORK

SPICE RUB AND PORK

- 2 tablespoons paprika
- 2 tablespoons pepper
- 2 tablespoons packed brown sugar
- 2 tablespoons kosher salt
- 1 (4- to 5-pound) boneless pork butt roast, with ¼-inch fat cap
- 4 cups wood chips

LEXINGTON BARBECUE SAUCE

- 1 cup water
- 1 cup cider vinegar
- ½ cup ketchup
- 1 tablespoon sugar
- 1½ teaspoons kosher salt
- ½ teaspoon pepper
- ½ teaspoon red pepper flakes

1 FOR THE SPICE RUB AND PORK Combine paprika, pepper, sugar, and salt in bowl. Pat meat dry with paper towels and rub evenly with spice mixture. Wrap meat in plastic wrap and let sit at room temperature for 1 hour or refrigerate for up to 24 hours.

2 FOR THE LEXINGTON BARBECUE SAUCE Whisk all ingredients in bowl until sugar and salt are dissolved.

3 Before grilling, unwrap pork (do not pat dry). Using large pieces of heavy-duty aluminum foil, wrap wood chips into two 8 by 4-inch foil packets. (Make sure chips do not poke holes in sides or bottom of packets.) Cut 2 evenly spaced 2-inch slits in top of packets.

4A FOR A CHARCOAL GRILL Open bottom vent halfway. Light large chimney starter three-quarters filled with charcoal briquettes (4½ quarts). When top coals are partially covered with ash, pour into steeply banked pile against side of grill. Place wood chip packets on coals. Set cooking grate in place, cover, and open lid vent halfway. Heat grill until hot and wood chips are smoking, about 5 minutes.

4B FOR A GAS GRILL Remove cooking grate and place wood chip packets directly on primary burner. Set cooking grate in place; turn all burners to high; cover; and heat grill until hot and wood chips are smoking, about 15 minutes. Turn primary burner to medium-high and turn off other burner(s). (Adjust primary burner as needed to maintain grill temperature of 300 degrees.)

5 Clean and oil cooking grate. Place meat on cooler side of grill. Cover (position lid vent over meat if using charcoal) and cook until pork has dark, rosy crust, about 2 hours. During final 20 minutes of grilling, adjust oven rack to lower-middle position and heat oven to 325 degrees.

6 Transfer pork to large roasting pan; cover pan tightly with foil; and roast pork in oven until fork slips easily into and out of meat, 2 to 3 hours. Remove pork from oven and let rest, covered, for 30 minutes.

7 When cool enough to handle, unwrap pork and pull meat into thin shreds, discarding excess fat and gristle. Toss pork with ½ cup barbecue sauce. Serve with remaining sauce.

South Carolina Pulled Pork

SERVES 8 **TIME** 4¼ hours to 5¼ hours, plus 1½ hours seasoning and resting

Why This Recipe Works Could be its winning flavor or the bright-yellow mustard sauce, but either way, this recipe's nickname—Carolina Gold—is more than justified. To achieve multidimensional mustard flavor, we coat boneless pork butt with a dry mustard spice rub. While the roast grills, we mix up a South Carolina barbecue sauce, which leans on yellow mustard, vinegar, brown sugar, and Worcestershire. We brush the pork with the sauce before transferring it to the oven. The tender cooked pork gets shredded and tossed with the remaining sauce. Pork butt roast is also labeled Boston butt in the supermarket; remove any elastic netting before rubbing with spices in step 1. If using a charcoal grill, you can substitute four wood chunks for the wood chip packets. This recipe was developed using Diamond Crystal kosher salt. If you have Morton kosher salt, which is denser, use 3 tablespoons in the rub. Serve with hamburger buns.

SPICE RUB AND PORK

- 3 tablespoons dry mustard
- ¼ cup kosher salt
- 1½ tablespoons packed light brown sugar
- 2 teaspoons pepper
- 2 teaspoons paprika
- ¼ teaspoon cayenne pepper
- 1 (4- to 5-pound) boneless pork butt roast, with ¼-inch fat cap
- 4 cups wood chips

MUSTARD BARBECUE SAUCE

- ½ cup yellow mustard
- ½ cup packed light brown sugar
- ¼ cup distilled white vinegar
- 2 tablespoons Worcestershire sauce
- 1 tablespoon hot sauce
- 2 teaspoons kosher salt
- 1 teaspoon pepper

SOUTH CAROLINA PULLED PORK

1 FOR THE SPICE RUB AND PORK Combine dry mustard, salt, sugar, pepper, paprika, and cayenne in bowl. Pat meat dry with paper towels and rub evenly with spice mixture. Wrap meat in plastic wrap and let sit at room temperature for 1 hour or refrigerate up to 24 hours.

2 FOR THE MUSTARD BARBECUE SAUCE Whisk all ingredients together in bowl until sugar and salt are dissolved. Measure out ½ cup sauce and set aside for cooking; reserve remaining sauce for serving.

3 Before grilling, unwrap pork (do not pat dry). Using large pieces of heavy-duty aluminum foil, wrap wood chips into two 8 by 4-inch foil packets. (Make sure chips do not poke holes in sides or bottom of packets.) Cut 2 evenly spaced 2-inch slits in top of packets.

4A FOR A CHARCOAL GRILL Open bottom vent halfway. Light large chimney starter three-quarters filled with charcoal briquettes (4½ quarts). When top coals are partially covered with ash, pour into steeply banked pile against side of grill. Place wood packets on coals. Set cooking grate in place, cover, and open lid vent halfway. Heat grill until hot and wood chips are smoking, about 5 minutes.

4B FOR A GAS GRILL Remove cooking grate and place wood chip packets directly on primary burner. Set cooking grate in place; turn all burners to high; cover; and heat grill until hot and wood chips are smoking, about 15 minutes. Turn primary burner to medium-high and turn off other burner(s). (Adjust primary burner as needed to maintain grill temperature of 300 degrees.)

5 Clean and oil cooking grate. Place meat on cooler side of grill. Cover (position lid vent over meat if using charcoal) and cook until pork has dark, rosy crust, about 2 hours. During final 20 minutes of grilling, adjust oven rack to lower-middle position and heat oven to 325 degrees.

6 Transfer pork to large roasting pan and brush evenly with ½ cup reserved sauce for cooking. Cover pan tightly with foil and roast pork in oven until fork slips easily into and out of meat, 2 to 3 hours.

7 Remove pork from oven and let rest, covered, for 30 minutes. When cool enough to handle, unwrap pork and pull meat into thin shreds, discarding excess fat and gristle. Toss pork with remaining sauce and serve.

Kalua Pork

SERVES 8 **TIME** 4¼ to 5¼ hours plus 6½ hours seasoning and resting

Why This Recipe Works If you've been to a luau in Hawaii, you've likely been lucky enough to experience kalua pork: a whole suckling pig, cooked over a fire of kiawe wood in a pit lined with rocks and banana leaves. To re-create this dish on a grill, we start with pork butt: Its balance of muscle and fat stays moist and flavorful during low, slow cooking. Kiawe is a species of mesquite; mesquite wood chips provide similar smoke. To replicate the earthy, grassy flavor given off by banana leaves, we rub the roast with a blend of green tea, brown sugar, salt, and pepper. Using both the grill and the oven gives us all the smoke and tenderness of pit cooking. We place the pork in an aluminum pan and cover the pan with foil to collect the juices and contain the steam. Pork butt roast is also labeled Boston butt in the supermarket; remove any elastic netting before rubbing with the tea mixture in step 1. If using a charcoal grill, you can substitute six mesquite wood chunks for the wood chip packets. This recipe was developed using Diamond Crystal kosher salt. If you have Morton kosher salt, which is denser, use 1 tablespoon. Serve with rice.

- 3 tablespoons green tea leaves (10 to 15 bags)
- 4 teaspoons kosher salt
- 1 tablespoon packed brown sugar
- 2 teaspoons pepper
- 1 (4- to 5-pound) boneless pork butt roast, with ¼-inch fat cap
- 1 (13 by 9-inch) disposable aluminum roasting pan
- 6 cups mesquite wood chips

1 Combine tea, salt, sugar, and pepper in bowl. Pat meat dry with paper towels and rub evenly with tea mixture. Wrap meat in plastic wrap and refrigerate for 6 to 24 hours.

2 Before grilling, unwrap pork (do not pat dry), place in disposable pan, and cover pan loosely with aluminum foil. Poke about twenty ¼-inch holes in foil. Using large pieces of heavy-duty foil, wrap wood chips into three 8 by 4-inch foil packets. (Make sure chips do not poke holes in sides or bottom of packets.) Cut 2 evenly spaced 2-inch slits in top of packets.

3A FOR A CHARCOAL GRILL Open bottom vent halfway. Light large chimney starter three-quarters filled with charcoal briquettes (4½ quarts). When top coals are partially covered with ash, pour into steeply banked pile against side of grill. Place wood chip packets on coals. Set cooking grate in place, cover, and open lid vent halfway. Heat grill until hot and wood chips are smoking, about 5 minutes.

3B **FOR A GAS GRILL** Remove cooking grate and place wood chip packets directly on primary burner. Set cooking grate in place; turn all burners to high; cover; and heat grill until hot and wood chips are smoking, about 15 minutes. Turn primary burner to medium-high and turn off other burner(s). (Adjust primary burner as needed to maintain grill temperature of 300 degrees.)

4 Place disposable pan on cooler side of grill. Cover (position lid vent over pan if using charcoal) and cook for 2 hours. During final 20 minutes of grilling, adjust oven rack to lower-middle position and heat oven to 325 degrees.

5 Transfer disposable pan from grill to rimmed baking sheet. Cover pan tightly with new sheet of foil and roast pork in oven until fork slips easily into and out of meat, 2 to 3 hours.

6 Remove pork from oven and let rest, covered, for 30 minutes. When cool enough to handle, unwrap pork and pull meat into thin shreds, discarding excess fat and gristle. Strain juices left in pan through fine-mesh strainer into fat separator. Let liquid settle, then return ¼ cup defatted pan juices to pork. Serve.

KALUA PORK

Tennessee Pulled Pork Sandwiches

SERVES 8 to 10 **TIME** 5¾ hours plus 18 hours marinating

Why This Recipe Works The signature sandwich at Papa KayJoe's in central Tennessee features pork that's shredded so fine it resembles pâté. This texture requires that the pork be cooked to a higher than usual temperature so that it's soft enough to break down. For our version, a combination of grill smoking and oven roasting does the job. Instead of hand-shredding, we use a stand mixer fitted with a paddle attachment to get a superfine shred. We like to serve our sandwich on hoecakes (thin cornmeal pancakes) as they do at Papa KayJoe's. If using a charcoal grill, you can substitute two wood chunks for the wood chip packet. This recipe was developed using Diamond Crystal kosher salt. If you have Morton kosher salt, which is denser, use 1½ tablespoons. Be sure to shred the pork while it's still hot in step 8. Serve with Hoecakes (page 224), pickles, and coleslaw.

PORK

- 1 (5- to 6-pound) bone-in pork butt roast, with ¼-inch fat cap
- 2 tablespoons kosher salt
- 1 (13 by 9-inch) disposable aluminum roasting pan
- 2 cups wood chips

TENNESSEE PULLED PORK SANDWICHES

BARBECUE SAUCE

- 1 cup ketchup
- ¼ cup cider vinegar
- ¼ cup water
- 2 tablespoons yellow mustard
- 1 tablespoon Worcestershire sauce
- 1 teaspoon granulated garlic
- 1 teaspoon pepper

1 **FOR THE PORK** Cut ¼-inch-deep slits through fat cap, spaced 1 inch apart, in crosshatch pattern, being careful not to cut into meat. Pat roast dry with paper towels and rub salt all over and into slits. Wrap meat in plastic wrap and refrigerate for 18 to 24 hours.

2 **FOR THE BARBECUE SAUCE** Combine all ingredients in medium saucepan and bring to boil over medium-high heat. Reduce heat to medium-low and simmer, whisking constantly, until slightly thickened, about 3 minutes. Transfer sauce to bowl and let cool completely.

3 Before grilling, unwrap pork (do not pat dry) and place fat side down in disposable pan. Using large piece of heavy-duty aluminum foil, wrap wood chips in 8 by 4-inch foil packet. (Make sure chips do not poke holes in sides or bottom of packet.) Cut 2 evenly spaced 2-inch slits in top of packet.

4A **FOR A CHARCOAL GRILL** Open bottom vent halfway. Light large chimney starter three-quarters filled with charcoal briquettes (4½ quarts). When top coals are partially covered with ash, pour evenly over half of grill. Place wood chip packet on coals. Set cooking grate in place, cover, and open lid vent halfway. Heat grill until hot and wood chips are smoking, about 5 minutes.

4B **FOR A GAS GRILL** Remove cooking grate and place wood chip packet directly on primary burner. Set cooking grate in place; turn all burners to high; cover; and heat grill until hot and wood chips are smoking, about 15 minutes. Turn primary burner to medium-high and turn off other burner(s). (Adjust primary burner as needed to maintain grill temperature of 300 degrees.)

5 Place disposable pan on cooler side of grill. Cover grill (with lid vent over pan if using charcoal) and cook for 2 hours. During final 20 minutes of grilling, adjust oven rack to lower-middle position and heat oven to 300 degrees.

6 Transfer disposable pan from grill to rimmed baking sheet. Cover pan tightly with foil and roast pork in oven until fork slips easily into and out of meat and meat registers 210 degrees, about 3 hours.

7 Remove pork from oven and carefully remove foil from pan (steam will escape). Remove blade bone from roast using tongs. Immediately transfer hot pork to bowl of stand mixer fitted with paddle attachment. Strain juices left in pan through fine-mesh strainer set over separate bowl; discard solids.

8 Mix pork on low speed until meat is finely shredded, about 1½ minutes. Add 1½ cups strained juices and mix until incorporated, about 15 seconds. Season with salt to taste, adding additional pork juices if desired. Serve.

Hoecakes

MAKES 16 hoecakes **TIME** 35 minutes

Papa KayJoe's makes their hoecakes with bacon fat.

- 3 cups (15 ounces) white cornmeal
- 2 tablespoons sugar
- 2 teaspoons baking powder
- 1½ teaspoons table salt
- 2 cups buttermilk
- 2 large eggs
- 2 tablespoons bacon fat or vegetable oil

1 Adjust oven rack to middle position and heat oven to 200 degrees. Set wire rack in rimmed baking sheet and place in oven. Whisk cornmeal, sugar, baking powder, and salt together in large bowl. Whisk buttermilk and eggs together in separate bowl. Whisk buttermilk mixture into cornmeal mixture until combined.

2 Heat 1 teaspoon fat in 12-inch nonstick skillet over medium heat until shimmering. Using level ¼-cup dry measuring cup, drop 3 evenly spaced scoops of batter into skillet, smoothing tops slightly.

3 Cook until small bubbles begin to appear on surface of cakes and edges are set, about 2 minutes. Flip and cook until second side is golden brown, about 2 minutes. Transfer hoecakes to prepared sheet in oven. Repeat with remaining fat and batter. Serve.

What Is Barbecue?

The most likely origins for the word "barbecue" can be traced back to the Taino, an indigenous population in and around the Caribbean, who built structures called barbacoas to smoke fish. Today, grilled foods are often referred to as barbecue as long as they're wearing that namesake sauce. Although we have several recipes that fit that description throughout this book, in this chapter, "barbecue" means 1) it's cooked low and slow, and 2) smoke is involved. Those two criteria leave a lot of room for variation, as is evident from regional barbecue traditions in the States.

In the eastern part of North Carolina, it's just not barbecue unless it's a whole hog cooked until the meat is succulent and the skin is crackling-crisp. The meat is literally picked from the bones and then lightly seasoned with a thin vinegar-and-pepper sauce. Western Carolinians go straight for the pork shoulder—the most marbled and meatiest chunk of the animal. Their Lexington-style sauce is enriched with just enough ketchup and sugar to take the edge off the acidity. And in South Carolina, thanks to the influence of German immigrants, the preferred sauce for their pulled pork gets its golden hue and its bite from mustard.

Texas barbecue is all about beef, specifically brisket and ribs. Seasonings are as simple as it gets—just salt and pepper—and, to keep the pure meat flavor front and center, sauce is optional. And in Memphis, Tennessee, "dry" pork spareribs are mopped (basted) with a vinegary liquid and rubbed with spices rather than sauced.

Unlike some other barbecue meccas, Kansas City, Missouri, is a melting pot of barbecue ingenuity. It's a city where beef and pork are represented in equal measure, and the uniqueness and bold character of a well-made barbecue sauce is valued above all else. Kansas City–style sauce is the archetype of American barbecue sauce: dark, thick, sweet, tangy, and tomatoey.

Of course, outside of these four American barbecue regions there is a whole world of sensational barbecue traditions, and we've included our takes on the signature recipes of some of them, from Alabama, South Dakota, and Hawaii to China and Peru. No matter which recipe you start with, you won't need a smoker: We've engineered all of them so that a charcoal grill (and in many cases, a gas grill) will give you real barbecue, by any definition.

North Carolina Barbecue Pork

SERVES 8 to 10 **TIME** 5¾ to 7¼ hours plus 19½ hours salting and resting

Why This Recipe Works When you're talking barbecue in North Carolina, you're talking pork, and a pork butt roast feeds a hungry crowd in style. A ring of charcoal, called a charcoal C, provides low, slow, indirect heat, so you'll need to refuel only once during the long cooking time. Wrapping the bone-in pork butt in foil when it reaches 170 degrees gives the meat plenty of time to absorb smoke flavor and develop a crusty bark without its exterior getting too bitter. There are two distinct styles of barbecue pork in North Carolina; we've got chopping and saucing options for both, so you can choose. This recipe was developed using Diamond Crystal kosher salt. If you have Morton kosher salt, which is denser, use 2 tablespoons. You will need a charcoal grill and a probe thermometer to make this recipe. You can use 4 cups wood chips, wrapped into two foil packets (see page 16) in place of the wood chunks. For more information on building a charcoal C setup, see page 218. Serve with hamburger buns.

- 3 tablespoons kosher salt
- 1½ tablespoons pepper
- 1 (6-pound) bone-in pork butt roast, with ¼-inch fat cap
- 1 (13 by 9-inch) disposable aluminum roasting pan
- 4 (3-inch) wood chunks
- 1 recipe Lexington-Style Barbecue Sauce or Eastern North Carolina–Style Barbecue Sauce (page 387)

1 Combine salt and pepper in bowl. Pat meat dry with paper towels and rub evenly with salt mixture. Wrap meat in plastic wrap and refrigerate for 18 to 24 hours. Before grilling, unwrap pork (do not pat dry).

2 Open bottom vent of charcoal grill halfway. Arrange 60 briquettes, 2 briquettes wide, around perimeter of grill to form C shape, overlapping slightly so briquettes touch. Place second layer of 60 briquettes, also 2 briquettes wide, on top of first. (Completed C will be 2 briquettes wide by 2 briquettes high.)

3 Space wood chunks evenly on top of C. Place disposable pan in center of grill, running lengthwise into gap of C, and fill with 4 cups water.

4 Light chimney starter filled with 15 briquettes (pile briquettes on 1 side of chimney so they catch). When coals are partially covered with ash, use tongs to place them at 1 end of C; do not let coals touch other end of C.

5 Set cooking grate in place, then clean and oil grate. Place pork fat side down on grill over water-filled pan. Insert temperature probe into thickest part of pork. Cover grill, positioning lid vent over gap in C, and open lid vent halfway. Cook, without opening grill, until pork registers 170 degrees, 4 to 5 hours. (Tail of C will not yet be lit.)

6 Place 1 large sheet of aluminum foil on rimmed baking sheet. Remove probe from pork. Using oven mitts, transfer pork fat side down to center of foil. Wrap pork tightly in foil, minimizing air pockets. Using additional sheets of foil, continue wrapping pork until completely covered and airtight. Make small mark on foil with marker to keep track of fat side.

7 Remove cooking grate. Pour 2 quarts unlit charcoal briquettes into gap in C, connecting unlit charcoal end with spent charcoal end. Replace cooking grate. Return wrapped pork to grill over water-filled pan, fat side down. Reinsert probe into thickest part of pork. Cover grill and continue to cook until pork registers 200 degrees, 1 to 1½ hours longer.

8 Remove probe. Transfer pork to carving board, fat side up, and let rest in foil for 1½ hours. Remove bone from pork. For Lexington style, chop pork with cleaver into 1-inch pieces. For eastern North Carolina style, chop pork into ¼-inch pieces. Toss with ⅔ cup sauce. Serve with remaining sauce.

NORTH CAROLINA BARBECUE PORK

South Carolina Smoked Fresh Ham

SERVES 8 to 10 **TIME** 6¼ hours plus 18 hours salting

Why This Recipe Works In certain corners of South Carolina, pitmasters swear by fresh ham, cut from the hindquarters of the hog and sold unsmoked and unseasoned. Fresh ham is leaner than traditional barbecue cuts such as shoulder, so cooking it takes a little know-how, but if it's done properly, the payoff is big: The meat is less soft and more chunky, and best of all, the crispy, bacon-like bits of skin can be chopped and mixed into it. Rubbing salt over the entire surface and letting it sit overnight helps season it throughout and keeps the meat moist. We smoke the meat on a grill for 2 hours before transferring it to a 300-degree oven to cook until it reaches an internal temperature of 200 degrees. We then crank the oven temperature up to 400 degrees and roast the skin on a baking sheet; this gives us plenty of crispy skin to mix in with the shredded ham. A vinegary mustard sauce, a hallmark of South Carolina barbecue, is just the contrast the sandwich needs. This recipe was developed using Diamond Crystal kosher salt. If you have Morton kosher salt, which is denser, use 1½ tablespoons. If using a charcoal grill, you can substitute two wood chunks for the wood chip packet. Serve with hamburger buns.

SOUTH CAROLINA SMOKED FRESH HAM

HAM

- 1 (6- to 8-pound) bone-in, skin-on shank-end fresh ham
- 2 tablespoons kosher salt
- 2 cups wood chips

MUSTARD SAUCE

- 1½ cups yellow mustard
- ½ cup cider vinegar
- 6 tablespoons packed brown sugar
- 2 tablespoons ketchup
- 2 teaspoons hot sauce
- 2 teaspoons Worcestershire sauce
- 1 teaspoon pepper

1 FOR THE HAM Pat ham dry with paper towels and rub all over with salt. Wrap ham in plastic wrap and refrigerate for 18 to 24 hours.

2 FOR THE MUSTARD SAUCE Whisk all ingredients together in bowl.

3 Before grilling, unwrap ham (do not pat dry). Using large piece of heavy-duty aluminum foil, wrap wood chips in 8 by 4-inch foil packet. (Make sure chips do not poke holes in sides or bottom of packet.) Cut 2 evenly spaced 2-inch slits in top of packet.

4A FOR A CHARCOAL GRILL Open bottom vent halfway. Light large chimney starter three-quarters filled with charcoal briquettes (4½ quarts). When top coals are partially covered with ash, pour evenly over half of grill. Place wood chip packet on coals. Set cooking grate in place, cover, and open lid vent halfway. Heat grill until hot and wood chips are smoking, about 5 minutes.

4B FOR A GAS GRILL Remove cooking grate and place wood chip packet directly on primary burner. Set cooking grate in place; turn all burners to high; cover; and heat grill until hot and wood chips are smoking, about 15 minutes. Turn primary burner to medium-high and turn off other burner(s). (Adjust primary burner as needed to maintain grill temperature of 300 degrees.)

5 Clean and oil cooking grate. Place ham flat side down on cooler side of grill. Cover grill (position lid vent over ham if using charcoal) and cook for 2 hours. During final 20 minutes of cooking, adjust oven rack to lower-middle position and heat oven to 300 degrees.

6 Transfer ham flat side down to 13 by 9-inch baking pan. Cover pan tightly with foil. Transfer to oven and roast until fork inserted in ham meets little resistance and meat registers 200 degrees, about 2½ hours.

7 Remove ham from oven and increase oven temperature to 400 degrees. Line rimmed baking sheet with foil. Using tongs, remove ham skin in 1 large piece. Place skin fatty side down on prepared sheet. Transfer to oven and roast until skin is dark and crispy and sounds hollow when tapped with fork, about 25 minutes, rotating sheet halfway through cooking. Tent ham with foil and let rest while skin roasts.

8 Transfer ham to carving board. Strain accumulated juices from pan through fine-mesh strainer set over bowl; discard solids. Trim and discard excess fat from ham. Remove bone and chop meat into bite-size pieces; transfer to large bowl.

9 When cool enough to handle, chop skin fine. Rewarm reserved ham juices in microwave for 1 minute. Add juices and chopped skin to ham and toss to combine. Season with salt to taste and serve with mustard sauce.

Crisping the Skin

The crackly skin is arguably the best part of a fresh ham, but it tends to steam and turn rubbery as the meat roasts. To crisp the skin, we pull it off in one piece once the ham is cooked through and roast it solo until it is dark brown. We then chop it and combine it with the chopped ham.

Barbecued Baby Back Ribs

SERVES 4 **TIME** 3½ to 4½ hours plus 2½ hours brining and resting

Why This Recipe Works The key to juicy, tender baby back ribs starts with the shopping: Buy the meatiest ribs you can find—as close to 2 pounds as possible. A brief stint in a standard salt-and-sugar brine ensures moist, well-seasoned ribs, while a simple spice rub of chili powder, cayenne, cumin, and brown sugar provides a good balance of sweet and spicy flavors. We barbecue the ribs for a couple of hours on the cooler side of the grill with wood chips and then move them to a baking sheet and cover them with foil to gently finish cooking in the oven. This recipe was developed using Diamond Crystal kosher salt. If you have Morton kosher salt, which is denser, use ¾ cup in the brine. If using a charcoal grill, you can substitute two wood chunks for the wood chip packet.

RIBS

- 1 cup kosher salt for brining
- ½ cup sugar for brining
- 2 (1½- to 2-pound) racks baby back ribs, trimmed
- 2 cups wood chips

SPICE RUB

- 4½ teaspoons paprika
- 1½ teaspoons chili powder
- 1½ teaspoons ground cumin
- 1½ teaspoons packed dark brown sugar
- 1½ teaspoons kosher salt
- 1 teaspoon white pepper
- ¾ teaspoon dried oregano
- ¾ teaspoon pepper
- ½ teaspoon cayenne pepper

1 **FOR THE RIBS** Dissolve salt and sugar in 4 quarts cold water in large container. Submerge racks in brine, cover, and refrigerate for 1 hour.

2 **FOR THE SPICE RUB** Meanwhile, combine all ingredients in small bowl.

3 Remove pork from brine, pat dry with paper towels, and rub evenly with spice rub. Let ribs sit at room temperature for 1 hour.

4 Using large piece of heavy-duty aluminum foil, wrap wood chips in 8 by 4-inch foil packet. (Make sure chips do not poke holes in sides or bottom of packet.) Cut 2 evenly spaced 2-inch slits in top of packet.

BARBECUED BABY BACK RIBS

5A FOR A CHARCOAL GRILL Open bottom vent halfway. Light large chimney starter three-quarters filled with charcoal briquettes (4½ quarts). When top coals are partially covered with ash, pour evenly over half of grill. Place wood chip packet on coals. Set cooking grate in place, cover, and open lid vent halfway. Heat grill until hot and wood chips are smoking, about 5 minutes.

5B FOR A GAS GRILL Remove cooking grate and place wood chip packet directly on primary burner. Set cooking grate in place; turn all burners to high; cover; and heat grill until hot and wood chips are smoking, about 15 minutes. Turn primary burner to medium-high and turn off other burner(s). (Adjust primary burner as needed to maintain grill temperature of 325 degrees.)

6 Clean and oil cooking grate. Place ribs meaty side down on cooler side of grill; ribs may overlap slightly. Cover (position lid vent over meat if using charcoal) and cook until ribs are deep red and smoky, about 2 hours, flipping and rotating racks halfway through cooking. During final 20 minutes of grilling, adjust oven rack to lower-middle position and heat oven to 325 degrees.

7 Transfer ribs to wire rack set in rimmed baking sheet. Cover tightly with foil and roast ribs in oven until fork slips easily into and out of meat, 1 to 2 hours.

8 Remove ribs from oven, loosen foil to release steam, and let rest for 30 minutes. Slice ribs between bones and serve.

Chicago-Style Barbecued Baby Back Ribs

SERVES 4 to 6 **TIME** 3½ to 4 hours plus 1½ hours seasoning and resting

Why This Recipe Works Achieving the moist, tender meat that defines Chicago ribs typically entails smoking the ribs at about 200 degrees for at least 8 hours. For our backyard low-and-slow version, the ribs pick up good color and smoke flavor over the grill and then finish up in the oven. Pans of water on the grill and in the oven allow the ribs to steam, making them extra moist and tender. Celery salt, allspice, and plenty of cayenne pepper flavor both the rub and the tangy, assertive Chicago-style barbecue sauce. For information on removing the membrane from ribs, see page 219. If using a charcoal grill, you can substitute one wood chunk for the wood chip packet.

SPICE RUB

- 1 tablespoon dry mustard
- 1 tablespoon paprika
- 1 tablespoon packed dark brown sugar
- 1½ teaspoons garlic powder
- 1½ teaspoons onion powder
- 1½ teaspoons celery salt
- 1 teaspoon cayenne pepper
- ½ teaspoon ground allspice

SAUCE

- 1¼ cups ketchup
- ¼ cup molasses
- ¼ cup cider vinegar
- ¼ cup water
- ⅛ teaspoon liquid smoke

RIBS

- 2 (2-pound) racks baby back ribs, trimmed and membrane removed
- 1 cup wood chips
- 1 (13 by 9-inch) disposable aluminum roasting pan (if using charcoal) or 1 (9-inch) disposable aluminum pie plate (if using gas)

1 **FOR THE SPICE RUB** Combine all ingredients in bowl. Measure out 2 tablespoons rub and set aside for sauce.

2 **FOR THE SAUCE** Whisk all ingredients and reserved 2 tablespoons spice rub together in bowl.

3 **FOR THE RIBS** Pat ribs dry with paper towels and rub evenly with remaining spice rub. Wrap ribs in plastic wrap and let sit at room temperature for 1 hour or refrigerate for up to 24 hours.

4 Before grilling, unwrap ribs (do not pat dry). Using large piece of heavy-duty aluminum foil, wrap wood chips in 8 by 4-inch foil packet. (Make sure chips do not poke holes in sides or bottom of packet.) Cut 2 evenly spaced 2-inch slits in top of packet.

5A **FOR A CHARCOAL GRILL** Open bottom vent halfway, place disposable pan on 1 side of grill, and add 2 cups water to pan. Light large chimney starter three-quarters filled with charcoal briquettes (4½ quarts). When top coals are partially covered with ash, pour into steeply banked pile against other side of grill. Place wood chip packet on coals. Set cooking grate in place, cover, and open lid vent completely. Heat grill until hot and wood chips are smoking, about 5 minutes.

5B **FOR A GAS GRILL** Remove cooking grate and place wood chip packet directly on primary burner. Place disposable pie plate with 2 cups water on other burner(s). Set cooking grate in place; turn all burners to high; cover; and heat grill until hot and wood chips are smoking, about 15 minutes. Turn primary burner to medium-high and turn off other burner(s). (Adjust primary burner as needed to maintain grill temperature of 325 degrees.)

6 Clean and oil cooking grate. Place ribs meaty side down on cooler side of grill; ribs may overlap slightly. Cover (position lid vent over meat if using charcoal) and cook until ribs are deep red and smoky, about 1½ hours, flipping and rotating racks halfway through cooking. During final 20 minutes of grilling, adjust oven rack to middle position and heat oven to 250 degrees.

7 Set wire rack in rimmed baking sheet and add just enough water to cover pan bottom. Transfer ribs to rack and cover tightly with foil. Roast ribs in oven until fork slips easily into and out of meat, 1½ to 2 hours.

8 Remove ribs from oven (being careful of hot water in pan). Transfer ribs to platter, tent with foil, and let rest for 30 minutes. Brush ribs evenly with half of sauce. Slice ribs between bones and serve with remaining sauce.

Honey-Mustard Barbecued Baby Back Ribs

SERVES 4 to 6 **TIME** 3½ to 4 hours plus 1½ hours seasoning and resting

Why This Recipe Works Honey-mustard barbecued ribs feature a sticky, sweet sauce with just a touch of heat. We start with lean, tender baby back ribs and cook them over indirect heat for a couple hours, so they pick up smoky flavor and develop a rich brown crust, before transferring them to a low oven to finish cooking. Our deeply flavored sauce includes garlic, honey, Worcestershire, and both Dijon and whole-grain mustard. For even more mustard flavor, we use a rub with dry mustard and whole mustard seeds for the ribs. We brush the ribs with the sauce twice: once before they go into the oven and again just before serving, for a nice sheen. This recipe was developed using Diamond Crystal kosher salt. If you have Morton kosher salt, which is denser, use 1½ tablespoons. For information on removing the membrane from a rack of ribs, see page 219. If using a charcoal grill, you can substitute two wood chunks for the wood chip packet.

- ¼ cup mustard seeds
- 2 tablespoons dry mustard
- 2 tablespoons packed brown sugar
- 2 tablespoons kosher salt
- 1 tablespoon garlic powder
- 1 tablespoon pepper
- 2 (2-pound) racks baby back ribs, trimmed and membrane removed
- 1 recipe Honey-Mustard Barbecue Sauce (page 389)
- 2 cups wood chips

1 Combine mustard seeds, dry mustard, sugar, salt, garlic powder, and pepper in bowl. Pat ribs dry with paper towels and rub evenly with spice mixture. Wrap ribs in plastic wrap and let sit at room temperature for 1 hour or refrigerate for up to 24 hours. Measure out ½ cup barbecue sauce and set aside for cooking; reserve remaining sauce for serving.

2 Before grilling, unwrap ribs (do not pat dry). Using large piece of heavy-duty aluminum foil, wrap wood chips in 8 by 4-inch foil packet. (Make sure chips do not poke holes in sides or bottom of packet.) Cut 2 evenly spaced 2-inch slits in top of packet.

3A **FOR A CHARCOAL GRILL** Open bottom vent halfway. Light large chimney starter three-quarters filled with charcoal briquettes (4½ quarts). When top coals are partially covered with ash, pour into steeply banked pile against side of grill. Place wood chip packet on coals. Set cooking grate in place, cover, and open lid vent halfway. Heat grill until hot and wood chips are smoking, about 5 minutes.

3B **FOR A GAS GRILL** Remove cooking grate and place wood chip packet directly on primary burner. Set cooking grate in place; turn all burners to high; cover; and heat grill until hot and wood chips are smoking, about 15 minutes. Turn primary burner to medium-high and turn off other burner(s). (Adjust primary burner as needed to maintain grill temperature of 325 degrees.)

4 Clean and oil cooking grate. Place ribs meaty side down on cooler side of grill; ribs may overlap slightly. Cover (position lid vent over meat if using charcoal) and cook until ribs are deep red and smoky, about 2 hours, flipping and rotating racks halfway through cooking. During final 20 minutes of grilling, adjust oven rack to middle position and heat oven to 325 degrees.

5 Remove ribs from grill, brush evenly with ½ cup reserved sauce, and wrap tightly with foil. Lay foil-wrapped ribs on rimmed baking sheet and roast in oven until fork slips easily into and out of meat, 1 to 2 hours.

6 Remove ribs from oven and let rest, still wrapped, for 30 minutes. Unwrap ribs and brush evenly with some of sauce reserved for serving. Slice ribs between bones and serve with remaining sauce.

South Dakota Corncob-Smoked Baby Back Ribs

SERVES 4 to 6 **TIME** 4¾ to 5¼ hours

Why This Recipe Works The South Dakota tradition of smoking ribs on a rig fueled by corncobs produces meat with a nutty smokiness that's much more subtle than what you get with hardwoods such as hickory or oak. For home-barbecued ribs with that same mild sweetness, layer charcoal in the grill with fresh corncobs (with the kernels removed) and a foil packet of cornmeal. The cornmeal gives the ribs an initial blast of smoky flavor, and the fresh cobs offer long-lasting smoke and a nutty aroma. Baste the ribs with a simple ketchup-based barbecue sauce with plenty of garlic and some celery seeds and you'll have sticky, sweet ribs that you won't be able to get enough of. For information on removing the membrane from a rack of ribs, see page 219. You will need a charcoal grill to make this recipe.

SAUCE

- 1 cup ketchup
- ¼ cup water
- 1 tablespoon pepper
- 1 tablespoon onion powder
- 1 tablespoon Worcestershire sauce
- 1 tablespoon light corn syrup
- 1 tablespoon granulated garlic
- 2 teaspoons celery seeds
- ½ teaspoon liquid smoke

RIBS

- 5 tablespoons packed light brown sugar
- 2 teaspoons kosher salt
- ½ teaspoon pepper
- 2 (2-pound) racks baby back ribs, trimmed and membrane removed
- 1 cup cornmeal
- 1 (13 by 9-inch) disposable aluminum roasting pan
- 6 corncobs, kernels removed and reserved for another use

1 **FOR THE SAUCE** Whisk all ingredients together in medium bowl; set aside.

2 **FOR THE RIBS** Combine sugar, salt, and pepper in bowl. Pat ribs dry with paper towels and rub evenly with sugar mixture. Using large piece of heavy-duty aluminum foil, wrap cornmeal in foil packet and cut several vent holes in top.

3 Open bottom vent of charcoal grill halfway, place disposable pan on 1 side of grill, and add 2 quarts water to pan. Arrange 3 quarts unlit charcoal briquettes on other side of grill. Place corncobs on top of unlit briquettes. Light large chimney starter half filled with charcoal briquettes (3 quarts). When top coals are partially covered with ash, pour over cobs and unlit briquettes. Place cornmeal packet on coals. Set cooking grate in place, cover, and open lid vent halfway. Heat grill until hot and cornmeal is smoking, about 5 minutes.

4 Clean and oil cooking grate. Place ribs side by side on grill, meaty side up, lengthwise over water-filled pan. Cover, positioning lid vent over meat, and cook until ribs are deep red and fork slips easily into and out of meat, 3½ to 4 hours, rotating and switching ribs every hour. (Do not flip ribs.) During last 30 minutes of cooking, baste ribs with sauce every 10 minutes, rotating and switching ribs each time.

5 Transfer ribs to carving board, tent with foil, and let rest for 15 to 20 minutes. Slice ribs between bones and serve with remaining sauce.

SOUTH DAKOTA CORNCOB-SMOKED BABY BACK RIBS

Layering the Fire

In South Dakota, they smoke their ribs on huge custom barbecue rigs using dried corncobs as the sole fuel. To adapt the method to a backyard kettle grill, we layer unlit and lit charcoal with fresh corncobs and a foil packet of cornmeal. This configuration produces 4 hours of steady, corn-tinged smoke.

Barbecued Pork Spareribs

SERVES 6 **TIME** 3¾ to 4¼ hours plus 1½ hours seasoning and resting

Why This Recipe Works Authentic barbecued ribs are melt-in-your-mouth, fall-off-the-bone tender, with a deeply smoky, meaty flavor. But these irresistibly satisfying ribs come at a cost: They can take a full day in the barbecue pit to develop that deep, smoky flavor. Is there a way to make the magic happen sooner? For bold flavor fast, we apply a spice rub to the ribs; the spices fully infuse the meat in just 1 hour. Indirect heat closely approximates the results of barbecue pit masters. After cooking the ribs on the cooler side of the grill to absorb smoky flavor, we transfer them to the oven to finish, coated with barbecue sauce and covered with foil to keep them moist. St. Louis–style ribs are also simply called spareribs. For information on removing the membrane from a rack of ribs, see page 219. Use our all-purpose barbecue sauce or one of its variations, or feel free to use your favorite store-bought sauce. For extra flavor, consider reserving any accumulated meat juices after the meat has rested and stirring them into the sauce. If using a charcoal grill, you can substitute two wood chunks for the wood chip packet.

- 2 (2½- to 3-pound) racks St. Louis–style spareribs, trimmed and membrane removed
- ¾ cup Barbecue Spice Rub (page 410)
- 2 cups wood chips
- ½ cup Easy All-Purpose Barbecue Sauce (page 386), plus extra for serving

1 Pat ribs dry with paper towels and rub evenly with spice rub. Let ribs sit at room temperature for 1 hour.

2 Using large piece of heavy-duty aluminum foil, wrap wood chips in 8 by 4-inch foil packet. (Make sure chips do not poke holes in sides or bottom of packet.) Cut 2 evenly spaced 2-inch slits in top of packet.

3A FOR A CHARCOAL GRILL Open bottom vent halfway. Light large chimney starter two-thirds filled with charcoal briquettes (4 quarts). When top coals are partially covered with ash, pour evenly over half of grill. Place wood chip packet on coals. Set cooking grate in place, cover, and open lid vent halfway. Heat grill until hot and wood chips are smoking, about 5 minutes.

3B FOR A GAS GRILL Remove cooking grate and place wood chip packet directly on primary burner. Set cooking grate in place; turn all burners to high; cover; and heat grill until hot and wood chips are smoking, about 15 minutes. Turn primary burner to medium-high and turn off other burner(s). (Adjust primary burner as needed to maintain grill temperature between 300 and 325 degrees.)

4 Clean and oil cooking grate. Place ribs meaty side down on cooler side of grill; ribs may overlap slightly. Cover (position lid vent over meat if using charcoal) and cook until ribs are deep red and smoky, about 2 hours, flipping and rotating racks halfway through cooking. During final 20 minutes of grilling, adjust oven rack to lower-middle position and heat oven to 325 degrees.

5 Transfer ribs to wire rack set in rimmed baking sheet and brush evenly with sauce. Cover tightly with foil and roast in oven until fork slips easily into and out of meat, 1 to 2 hours.

6 Remove ribs from oven and let rest, still covered, for 30 minutes. Unwrap ribs, slice between bones, and serve with remaining sauce.

Memphis-Style Barbecued Spareribs

SERVES 6 **TIME** 3¼ to 4¼ hours plus 1 hour seasoning

Why This Recipe Works Rather than smothering ribs in sauce, Memphis pitmasters rely on a potent spice rub to infuse the meat with unmistakable flavor. Our pantry-friendly combination of salt, brown sugar, paprika, chili powder, pepper, garlic powder, onion powder, and cayenne creates a perfectly balanced rub that helps create a spicy, bark-like crust. We use a half-grill fire and stow a pan of water underneath the cooking grate on the cooler side of the grill, where it absorbs heat and works to keep the temperature stable, as well as helps keep the meat moist. In true Memphis style, we baste the ribs with a mop of apple juice and cider vinegar to add flavor and moisture. After an hour and a half, we transfer the ribs to a wire rack set in a rimmed baking sheet and cook them in a moderate oven until tender and thick-crusted. St. Louis–style ribs are also simply called spareribs. This recipe was developed using Diamond Crystal kosher salt. If you have Morton kosher salt, which is denser, use 1½ tablespoons. If using a charcoal grill, you can substitute one small wood chunk for the wood chip packet.

MEMPHIS-STYLE BARBECUED SPARERIBS

SPICE RUB

- 2 tablespoons paprika
- 2 tablespoons packed light brown sugar
- 2 tablespoons kosher salt
- 2 teaspoons chili powder
- 1½ teaspoons pepper
- 1½ teaspoons garlic powder
- 1½ teaspoons onion powder
- 1½ teaspoons cayenne pepper
- ½ teaspoon dried thyme

RIBS

- 2 (2½- to 3-pound) racks St. Louis–style spareribs, trimmed
- ½ cup apple juice
- 3 tablespoons cider vinegar
- ¾ cup wood chips
- 1 (13 by 9-inch) disposable aluminum roasting pan (if using charcoal) or 1 (9-inch) disposable aluminum pie plate (if using gas)

1 **FOR THE SPICE RUB** Combine all ingredients in bowl.

2 **FOR THE RIBS** Pat ribs dry with paper towels and rub evenly with spice rub. Let ribs sit at room temperature for 1 hour.

3 Combine apple juice and vinegar in small bowl. Using large piece of heavy-duty aluminum foil, wrap wood chips in 8 by 4-inch foil packet. (Make sure chips do not poke holes in sides or bottom of packet.) Cut 2 evenly spaced 2-inch slits in top of packet.

4A **FOR A CHARCOAL GRILL** Open bottom vent halfway, place disposable pan on 1 side of grill, and add 2 cups water to pan. Light large chimney starter three-quarters filled with charcoal briquettes (4½ quarts). When top coals are partially covered with ash, pour into steeply banked pile against other side of grill. Place wood chip packet on coals. Set cooking grate in place, cover, and open lid vent completely. Heat grill until hot and wood chips are smoking, about 5 minutes.

4B **FOR A GAS GRILL** Remove cooking grate and place wood chip packet directly on primary burner. Place disposable pie plate with 2 cups water on other burner(s). Set cooking grate in place; turn all burners to high; cover; and heat grill until hot and wood chips are smoking, about 15 minutes. Turn primary burner to medium-high and turn off other burner(s). (Adjust primary burner as needed to maintain grill temperature of 325 degrees.)

5 Clean and oil cooking grate. Place ribs side by side on grill, meaty side up, lengthwise over water-filled pan. Cover (position lid vent over meat if using charcoal) and cook until ribs are deep red and smoky, about 1½ hours, brushing with apple juice mixture and flipping and rotating racks halfway through cooking. During final 20 minutes of grilling, adjust oven rack to lower-middle position and heat oven to 300 degrees.

6 Set wire rack in rimmed baking sheet and add just enough water to cover pan bottom. Transfer ribs to rack and brush top of each rack with 2 tablespoons apple juice mixture. Roast ribs (uncovered) for 1 hour. Brush ribs with remaining apple juice mixture and cook until fork slips easily into and out of meat, 1 to 2 hours.

7 Remove ribs from oven (being careful of hot water in pan). Transfer ribs to cutting board and let rest for 15 minutes. Slice ribs between bones and serve.

Kansas City–Style Barbecued Spareribs

SERVES 6 **TIME** 4¾ hours plus 1½ hours seasoning and resting

Why This Recipe Works The ribs served in Kansas City are straightforward, assertively spiced, well lacquered, and tender to the bone. Using a C-shaped arrangement of charcoal briquettes keeps the fire going slowly for 4 hours without interruption. The simple dry rub—just salt, pepper, and granulated garlic—provides ample bark while the ribs smoke; and a pantry-friendly sauce of ketchup, brown sugar, spices, and a touch of corn syrup gives the ribs a glazed appearance. We apply the sauce at the halfway point so that it tightens on the ribs as they cook and then again when the ribs come off the grill for an extra flavor boost. St. Louis–style ribs are also simply called spareribs. This recipe was developed using Diamond Crystal kosher salt. If you have Morton kosher salt, which is denser, use 1½ tablespoons in the rub. The corn syrup helps give the sauce a nice shine when applied to the ribs, but you can omit it, if desired. You will need a charcoal grill for this recipe. For more information on building a charcoal C setup, see page 218.

RIBS

- 2 tablespoons kosher salt
- 2 tablespoons pepper
- 1 tablespoon granulated garlic
- 2 (2½- to 3-pound) racks St. Louis–style spareribs, trimmed
- 5 (3-inch) wood chunks
- 1 (13 by 9-inch) disposable aluminum roasting pan

SAUCE

- ¼ cup ketchup
- ¼ cup packed brown sugar
- 2 tablespoons cider vinegar
- 2 tablespoons light corn syrup
- 1 teaspoon Worcestershire sauce
- 1 teaspoon pepper
- 1 teaspoon kosher salt
- ½ teaspoon granulated garlic
- ¼ teaspoon ground cumin

1 **FOR THE RIBS** Combine salt, pepper, and granulated garlic in bowl. Pat ribs dry with paper towels. Rub bone side of ribs with one-third of spice mixture, then rub meat side of ribs with remaining two-thirds of spice mixture. Let ribs sit at room temperature for 1 hour.

2 **FOR THE SAUCE** Meanwhile, whisk all ingredients together in small saucepan and cook over medium heat until sugar is dissolved; set aside.

3 Open bottom vent of charcoal grill halfway. Arrange 40 briquettes, 2 briquettes wide, around perimeter of grill to form C shape, overlapping slightly so briquettes touch. Place second layer of 40 briquettes, also 2 briquettes wide, on top of first. (Completed C will be 2 briquettes wide by 2 briquettes high.)

4 Space wood chunks evenly on top of C. Place disposable pan in center of grill, running lengthwise into gap of C, and fill with 6 cups water.

5 Light chimney starter filled with 10 briquettes (pile briquettes on 1 side of chimney so they catch). When coals are partially covered with ash, use tongs to place them at 1 end of C; do not let coals touch other end of C.

6 Set cooking grate in place, then clean and oil grate. Place ribs side by side on grill, meaty side up, lengthwise over water-filled pan. Cover, positioning lid vent over meat, and open lid vent halfway. Cook, without opening grill, for 2 hours.

7 Open grill and rotate ribs 180 degrees. Brush meaty side of ribs with half of barbecue sauce. Cover grill, positioning lid vent over ribs. Cook, without opening grill, for 2 hours.

8 Transfer ribs meaty side up to rimmed baking sheet. Brush meaty side of ribs with remaining sauce. Cover sheet tightly with aluminum foil and let ribs rest for 30 minutes. Slice ribs between bones and serve.

KANSAS CITY–STYLE BARBECUED SPARERIBS

Blood Bros.–Inspired Gochujang-Glazed Spareribs

SERVES 6 **TIME** 6¼ to 7¾ hours plus 20 minutes resting

Why This Recipe Works This recipe is inspired by the spicy-sweet gochujang-glazed ribs served at Blood Bros. BBQ in Houston, Texas. We rub the ribs with a simple mix of gochugaru (Korean chile flakes), sesame seeds, brown sugar, granulated garlic, salt, and pepper and then cook them on a long-lasting charcoal C setup until they're tender to the bone. We brush a potent gochujang glaze on the ribs when they come off the grill. St. Louis–style ribs are also simply called spareribs. This recipe was developed using Diamond Crystal kosher salt. If you have Morton kosher salt, which is denser, use 1 tablespoon. You will need a charcoal grill and a probe thermometer to make this recipe. You can substitute 5 cups wood chips wrapped into three foil packets (see page 16) for the wood chunks.

RIBS AND RUB

- 1½ tablespoons kosher salt
- 1 tablespoon gochugaru
- 5 teaspoons sesame seeds, toasted, divided
- 1 tablespoon packed brown sugar
- 2 teaspoons pepper
- 1½ teaspoons granulated garlic
- 2 (2½- to 3-pound) racks St. Louis–style spareribs, trimmed
- 5 (3-inch) wood chunks
- 1 (13 by 9-inch) disposable aluminum pan
- 2 scallions, sliced thin

GLAZE

- ¼ cup gochujang
- ¼ cup soy sauce
- ¼ cup packed brown sugar
- 2 tablespoons ginger ale
- 2 tablespoons toasted sesame oil

1 **FOR THE RIBS AND RUB** Combine salt, gochugaru, 1 tablespoon sesame seeds, sugar, pepper, and granulated garlic in bowl. Pat ribs dry with paper towels. Rub bone side of ribs evenly with about one-third of spice mixture. Flip ribs and rub meaty side evenly with remaining two-thirds of spice mixture.

2 Open bottom vent of charcoal grill halfway. Arrange 40 briquettes, 2 briquettes wide, around perimeter of grill to form C shape, overlapping slightly so briquettes touch. Place second layer of 40 briquettes, also 2 briquettes wide, on top of first. (Completed C will be 2 briquettes wide by 2 briquettes high.)

3 Space wood chunks evenly on top of C. Place disposable pan in center of grill, running lengthwise into gap of C, and fill with 6 cups water.

4 Light chimney starter filled with 10 briquettes (pile briquettes on 1 side of chimney so they catch). When coals are partially covered with ash, use tongs to place them at 1 end of C; do not let coals touch other end of C.

5 Set cooking grate in place, then clean and oil grate. Place ribs side by side on grill, meaty side up, lengthwise over water pan. Cover grill, positioning lid vent over ribs, and open lid vent halfway. Cook, without opening grill, for 2 hours.

6 Open grill and rotate ribs 180 degrees. Continue to cook, without opening grill, for 1½ to 2 hours longer.

7 **FOR THE GLAZE** Meanwhile, whisk all ingredients in bowl until sugar is dissolved.

8 Transfer ribs to rimmed baking sheet, meaty side up. Brush each rack with 3 tablespoons glaze. Tent with aluminum foil and let rest for 20 minutes. Sprinkle ribs with scallions and remaining 2 teaspoons sesame seeds. Slice ribs between bones and serve with remaining glaze.

Chinese-Style Barbecued Spareribs

SERVES 6 **TIME** 5 to 6 hours

Why This Recipe Works Chinese sticky ribs are marinated in boldly aromatic seasonings, slow-roasted until they retain a hint of satisfying chew, and then glazed and broiled to deeply caramelized perfection. Barbecued ribs, on the other hand, are rubbed with spice and smoked low and slow until they fall off the bone. Here we combine the best of both worlds for ribs that are tender; seasoned to the bone; kissed with smoke; and covered with a garlicky, gingery glaze. We start the ribs in the oven, braising them right in the marinade for deep seasoning, and finish them on the grill over indirect heat. Instead of wood chips, we briefly soak eight black tea bags in water, wrap them in foil (so they burn slower and smoke longer), and set them on the coals. The mellow tea smoke complements the seasonings perfectly. Adding a cup of red currant jelly to the braising liquid and meat juices makes a thick, sticky glaze. We glaze and flip the ribs every 30 minutes for the last 1 to 1½ hours of cooking, which ensures beautifully shellacked ribs. St. Louis–style ribs are also simply called spareribs. For information on removing the membrane from a rack of ribs, see page 219.

- 1½ cups ketchup, divided
- 1 cup soy sauce
- 1 cup hoisin sauce
- 1 cup sugar
- ½ cup dry sherry
- 6 garlic cloves, minced
- 2 tablespoons grated fresh ginger
- 2 teaspoons toasted sesame oil
- 1½ teaspoons cayenne pepper
- 8 bags black tea, preferably orange spice or Earl Grey
- 2 (2½- to 3-pound) racks St. Louis–style spareribs, trimmed and membrane removed
- 1 (13 by 9-inch) disposable aluminum roasting pan
- 1 cup red currant jelly

1 Adjust oven rack to middle position and heat oven to 300 degrees. Whisk 1 cup ketchup, soy sauce, hoisin, sugar, sherry, garlic, ginger, oil, and cayenne in large bowl; measure out ½ cup and set aside for glaze. Cover tea bags with water in small bowl and soak for 5 minutes. Squeeze water from tea bags. Using large piece of heavy-duty aluminum foil, wrap soaked tea bags in foil packet and cut several vent holes in top.

2 Cut rib racks in half and place meaty side down in disposable pan. Pour remaining ketchup mixture over ribs. Cover pan tightly with foil and cook in oven until fat has rendered and meat begins to pull away from bones, 2 to 2½ hours.

3 Transfer ribs to large plate. Pour pan juices into fat separator; let liquid settle and reserve 1 cup defatted pan juices. Simmer reserved pan juices in medium saucepan over medium-high heat until reduced to ½ cup, about 5 minutes. Stir in jelly, reserved ketchup mixture, and remaining ½ cup ketchup and simmer until reduced to 2 cups, 10 to 12 minutes. Measure out ⅔ cup glaze and set aside for serving.

4A **FOR A CHARCOAL GRILL** Open bottom vent halfway. Light large chimney starter filled with charcoal briquettes (6 quarts). When top coals are partially covered with ash, pour evenly over half of grill. Place tea packet on coals. Set cooking grate in place, cover, and open lid vent halfway. Heat grill until hot and tea is smoking, about 5 minutes.

4B **FOR A GAS GRILL** Remove cooking grate and place tea packet directly on primary burner. Set cooking grate in place; turn all burners to high; cover; and heat grill until hot and tea is smoking, about 15 minutes. Leave primary burner on high and turn off other burner(s).

TEXAS SMOKED SAUSAGES

SHREDDED BARBECUED BEEF

5 Clean and oil cooking grate. Place ribs meaty side down on cooler side of grill; ribs may overlap slightly. Cover and cook until ribs are smoky and edges begin to char, about 30 minutes. Brush ribs with glaze, flip, rotate, and brush again. Cover and continue to cook, brushing with glaze every 30 minutes, until ribs are fully tender and glaze is browned and sticky, 1 to 1½ hours. (Cover edges of ribs loosely with foil if they begin to burn.)

6 Transfer ribs to cutting board, tent with foil, and let rest for 10 minutes. Slice ribs between bones and serve with reserved glaze.

Texas Smoked Sausages

SERVES 4 **TIME** 1¼ hours

Why This Recipe Works Smoked sausages are a staple of Texas barbecue, a legacy of German butchers who settled in the area; they're aggressively seasoned with cayenne and garlic and smoke until the casing is wrinkled. You don't need homemade sausage or a smoker to re-create these for yourself; all it takes is hot Italian sausage (an easy stand-in for the original Texas hot links), wood chips, and time. We set up a half-grill fire with two wood chip packets and set the sausages on the cooler side. To get great smoke flavor, we leave them there for 45 minutes, until their skins deepen to a dark, slightly wrinkled red, like the sausages from a real Texas barbecue joint. Best of all, despite the long cooking time, they stay extremely moist and juicy. If using a charcoal grill, you can substitute three wood chunks for the wood chip packets. You can substitute raw kielbasa, bratwurst, or—if you can find them—Texas hot links for the Italian sausage.

- 3 cups wood chips
- 2 pounds hot Italian sausage (8 to 12 links)
- 8–12 (6-inch) sub rolls, toasted if desired

1 Using large pieces of heavy-duty aluminum foil, wrap wood chips in two 8 by 4-inch foil packets. (Make sure chips do not poke holes in sides or bottom of packets.) Cut 2 evenly spaced 2-inch slits in top of packets.

2A **FOR A CHARCOAL GRILL** Open bottom vent halfway. Light large chimney starter filled with charcoal briquettes (6 quarts). When top coals are partially covered with ash, pour evenly over half of grill. Place wood chip packet on coals. Set cooking grate in place, cover, and open lid vent halfway. Heat grill until hot and wood chips are smoking, about 5 minutes.

2B **FOR A GAS GRILL** Remove cooking grate and place wood chip packets directly on primary burner. Set cooking grate in place; turn all burners to high; cover; and heat grill until hot and wood chips are smoking, about 15 minutes. Leave primary burner on high and turn off other burner(s).

3 Clean and oil cooking grate. Place sausages on cooler side of grill and cover (position lid vent over sausages if using charcoal); cook until sausages are well browned and cooked through, about 45 minutes, turning every 15 minutes. Serve with rolls.

Shredded Barbecued Beef

SERVES 8 to 10 **TIME** 5 to 6 hours plus 1½ hours salting and resting

Why This Recipe Works For backyard beef with big flavor without the big time commitment, we cut a chuck-eye roast into quarters: The smaller pieces of beef absorb more smoke flavor and cook much faster. After cooking the meat in a disposable roasting pan on the cooler side of the grill for a couple hours, we flip the pieces, wrap the pan in foil, and place it in the oven to finish cooking. We take advantage of the flavorful beef fat, using it to sauté the onion for the barbecue sauce. Chili powder and pepper add bite, while ketchup, vinegar, coffee, Worcestershire sauce, brown sugar, and the beef juices round out the flavors. This recipe was developed using Diamond Crystal kosher salt. If you have Morton kosher salt, which is denser, use 1½ tablespoons. If you prefer a smooth barbecue sauce, strain the sauce before tossing it with the beef in step 6. If using a charcoal grill, you can substitute three wood chunks for the wood chip packets. We like to serve this beef on white bread with plenty of pickle chips.

- 2 tablespoons kosher salt
- 3½ teaspoons pepper, divided
- 1 teaspoon cayenne pepper
- 1 (5- to 6-pound) boneless beef chuck-eye roast, trimmed and quartered
- 1 (13 by 9-inch) disposable aluminum roasting pan
- 3 cups wood chips
- 1 onion, chopped fine
- 4 garlic cloves, minced
- ½ teaspoon chili powder
- 1¼ cups ketchup
- ¾ cup brewed coffee
- ½ cup cider vinegar
- ½ cup packed brown sugar
- 3 tablespoons Worcestershire sauce

1 Combine salt, 1 tablespoon pepper, and cayenne in small bowl. Pat meat dry with paper towels and rub evenly with spice mixture. Wrap meat in plastic wrap and let sit at room temperature for 1 hour or refrigerate for up to 24 hours.

2 Before cooking, unwrap meat (do not pat dry) and transfer to disposable pan. Using large pieces of heavy-duty aluminum foil, wrap wood chips into two 8 by 4-inch foil packets. (Make sure chips do not poke holes in sides or bottom of packets.) Cut 2 evenly spaced 2-inch slits in top of packets.

3A **FOR A CHARCOAL GRILL** Open bottom vent halfway. Light large chimney starter half filled with charcoal briquettes (3 quarts). When top coals are partially covered with ash, pour into steeply banked pile against side of grill. Place wood chip packets on coals. Set cooking grate in place, cover, and open lid vent halfway. Heat grill until hot and wood chips are smoking, about 5 minutes.

3B **FOR A GAS GRILL** Remove cooking grate and place wood chip packets directly on primary burner. Set cooking grate in place; turn all burners to high; cover; and heat grill until hot and wood chips are smoking, about 15 minutes. Turn primary burner to medium and turn other burner(s) off. (Adjust primary burner as needed to maintain grill temperature between 250 and 300 degrees.)

4 Place disposable pan on cooler side of grill. Cover (position lid vent over meat if using charcoal) and cook until meat is deep red, about 2 hours. During final 20 minutes of grilling, adjust oven rack to lower-middle position and heat oven to 300 degrees.

5 Flip meat in pan, cover pan tightly with foil, and roast in oven until fork slips easily into and out of beef, 2 to 3 hours.

6 Transfer meat to large bowl, tent with foil, and let rest for 30 minutes. While meat rests, skim fat from accumulated juices in pan; reserve 2 tablespoons fat. Strain defatted juices; reserve ½ cup juice. Combine onion and reserved fat in medium saucepan and cook over medium heat until onion has softened, about 10 minutes. Add garlic and chili powder and cook until fragrant, about 30 seconds. Stir in ketchup, coffee, vinegar, sugar, Worcestershire, remaining ½ teaspoon pepper, and reserved meat juices and simmer until thickened, about 15 minutes. Using 2 forks, pull meat into shreds, discarding any excess fat or gristle. Toss meat with ½ cup barbecue sauce. Serve with remaining sauce.

Texas-Style Smoked Beef Ribs

SERVES 6 to 8 **TIME** 6¼ to 7 hours plus 30 minutes resting

Why This Recipe Works Pork ribs may reign supreme across most of the United States, but in Texas, ribs mean beef ribs. They differ from barbecued pork ribs in nearly every way, from their Flintstonian size to their unapologetically meaty flavor. While pork ribs often cook until the meat slips off the bone, beef ribs retain some chew. And don't expect a sticky coat of sauce; beef ribs need no distractions. We start with racks of beef plate ribs, each with 1 to 1½ inches of meat on top of the bone to ensure that they won't shrink down too much during cooking. It takes steady smoke to infuse the ribs with big flavor to match their big size. On a backyard grill, that means using a C-shaped arrangement of coals with wood chunks arranged on top. Cooking the ribs to 210 degrees ensures that the collagen melts thoroughly, resulting in ultratender meat. You will need a charcoal grill to make this recipe. Beef plate ribs are substantially larger than short ribs; you may need to special-order these. You can substitute 5 cups wood chips wrapped into three foil packets (see page 16) for the wood chunks. This recipe was developed using Diamond Crystal kosher salt. If you have Morton kosher salt, which is denser, use 2 tablespoons. For more information on building a charcoal C setup, see page 218.

- 3 tablespoons kosher salt
- 3 tablespoons pepper
- 2 (4- to 5-pound) racks beef plate ribs, 1 to 1½ inches of meat on top of bone, trimmed
- 5 (3-inch) wood chunks
- 1 (13 by 9-inch) disposable aluminum roasting pan

1 Combine salt and pepper in bowl. Pat ribs dry with paper towels and rub evenly with salt mixture.

2 Open bottom vent of charcoal grill halfway. Arrange 60 briquettes, 2 briquettes wide, around perimeter of grill to form C shape, overlapping slightly so briquettes touch. Place second layer of 60 briquettes, also 2 briquettes wide, on top of first. (Completed C will be 2 briquettes wide by 2 briquettes high.)

3 Space wood chunks evenly on top of C. Place disposable pan in center of grill, running lengthwise into gap of C, and fill with 6 cups water.

4 Light chimney starter filled with 15 briquettes (pile briquettes on 1 side of chimney so they catch). When coals are partially covered with ash, use tongs to place them at 1 end of C; do not let coals touch other end of C.

5 Set cooking grate in place, then clean and oil grate. Place ribs side by side on grill, meaty side up, crosswise over water-filled pan. Cover, positioning lid vent over meat, and open lid vent halfway. Cook until ribs farthest from coals register 210 degrees, 5½ to 6¼ hours.

6 Transfer ribs to carving board, tent with aluminum foil, and let rest for 30 minutes. Cut ribs between bones and serve.

Barbecued Flat-Cut Brisket

SERVES 8 to 10 **TIME** 6 hours plus 2½ hours brining and resting

Why This Recipe Works Deeply smoky beef brisket gets its flavor and tenderness from hours of low and slow roasting over indirect heat. We deliver pit master–caliber beef with a hybrid grill-oven roasting method. To keep the brisket moist during extended cooking, we brine it in a sugar and salt solution. Layering unlit briquettes in a steeply banked pile on one side of the grill and then pouring hot coals on top keeps the fire going without the need to refuel. A pan of water placed next to the coals generates enough moisture to produce the trademark pink smoke ring below the crust's surface. A mixture of sugar, salt, and pepper rubbed into the scored fat cap, along with the smoke and keeping the lid closed, helps the brisket develop its signature thick, dark crust. To finish, we move the brisket to a moderate oven where the steady, even heat turns it perfectly tender. This recipe was developed using Diamond Crystal kosher salt. If you have Morton kosher salt, which is denser, use 1 cup in the brine in step 1 and 2 tablespoons in the rub in step 3. If using a charcoal grill, you can substitute two wood chunks for the wood chip packet. Serve with Texas-Style Barbecue Sauce (page 389), sliced white bread or saltines, pickle chips, and thinly sliced onion.

- 1 (5- to 6-pound) beef brisket, flat cut, fat trimmed to ¼ inch
- 1⅓ cups kosher salt for brining
- ½ cup sugar for brining
- 3 tablespoons kosher salt
- 2 tablespoons sugar
- 2 tablespoons pepper
- 2 cups wood chips
- 1 (13 by 9-inch) disposable aluminum roasting pan (if using charcoal) or 1 (9-inch) disposable aluminum pie plate (if using gas)

Smoking the Ribs

1 Evenly space wood chunks on top of charcoal C. Place disposable pan in center of grill so that short end of pan faces gap. Fill with 6 cups water.

2 Light chimney starter filled with 15 briquettes (pile on 1 side of chimney to make them easier to ignite). When coals are partially covered with ash, use tongs to place them at 1 end of C.

3 Position ribs side by side, meaty side up, crosswise over water-filled pan.

TEXAS-STYLE SMOKED BEEF RIBS

1 Cut ¹⁄₁₆-inch-deep slits on both sides of brisket, spaced 1 inch apart, in crosshatch pattern, being careful not to cut into meat. Dissolve 1⅓ cups salt and ½ cup sugar in 4 quarts cold water in large container. Submerge brisket in brine, cover, and refrigerate for 2 hours.

2 Using large piece of heavy-duty aluminum foil, wrap wood chips in 8 by 4-inch foil packet. (Make sure chips do not poke holes in sides or bottom of packet.) Cut 2 evenly spaced 2-inch slits in top of packet.

3 Combine salt, sugar, and pepper in bowl. Remove brisket from brine, pat dry with paper towels, and rub sugar mixture over and into slits.

4A **FOR A CHARCOAL GRILL** Open bottom vent halfway, place disposable pan on 1 side of grill, and add 2 cups water to pan. Arrange 3 quarts unlit charcoal briquettes into steeply banked pile against side of grill. Light large chimney starter two-thirds filled with charcoal briquettes (4 quarts). When top coals are partially covered with ash, pour evenly over unlit coals. Place wood chip packet on coals. Set cooking grate in place, cover, and open lid vent halfway. Heat grill until hot and wood chips are smoking, about 5 minutes.

4B **FOR A GAS GRILL** Remove cooking grate and place wood chip packet directly on primary burner. Place disposable pie plate with 2 cups water on other burner(s). Set cooking grate in place; turn all burners to high; cover; and heat grill until hot and wood chips are smoking, about 15 minutes. Turn primary burner to medium-high and turn off other burner(s). (Adjust primary burner as needed to maintain grill temperature of 300 degrees.)

5 Clean and oil cooking grate. Place brisket fat side down over water-filled pan with thickest side facing coals and flames. Cover (position lid vent over meat if using charcoal) and cook for 3 hours. During final 20 minutes of grilling, adjust oven rack to lower-middle position and heat oven to 325 degrees.

6 Transfer brisket to wire rack set in foil-lined rimmed baking sheet. Roast brisket (uncovered) in oven until tender and meat registers 195 degrees, about 2 hours. Transfer brisket to carving board, tent with foil, and let rest for 30 minutes. Slice brisket against grain into long, thin slices and serve.

Beef Brisket

A **FULL BRISKET**, which comes from the lower chest of the cow, ranges from 8 to 20 pounds. It's a tough cut made up of two overlapping muscles—the fatty, thicker point cut and the leaner, thinner flat cut—that are separated by a line of fat. Their grains run perpendicular to each other.

The knobby **POINT CUT** overlaps the rectangular **FLAT CUT**. The point cut has more marbling, while the flat cut is lean but topped with a thick fat cap. Because the flat cut (sometimes labeled "first cut") is easy to find, cheap, and fairly uniform in shape, it's the cut we generally call for in our recipes. Make sure to trim the fat cap according to the instructions in whatever recipe you are using.

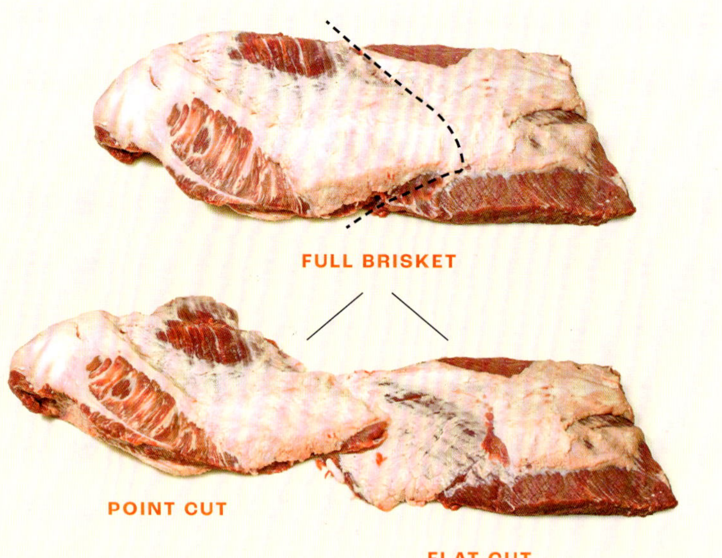

Texas-Style Barbecued Whole Brisket

SERVES 12 to 15 **TIME** 6¼ to 8¼ hours plus 14 hours salting and resting

Why This Recipe Works A properly smoked Texas brisket holds irresistible appeal: It's ultrabeefy, tender, and juicy inside, with a dark, peppery, smoky bark (crust). Legendary Texas barbecue joints don't even offer sauce; instead they season the meat sparingly and confidently with salt, pepper, and smoke. Tough, collagen-rich brisket needs slow, indirect cooking. For those who love a grilling challenge, brisket is the crowning achievement of backyard barbecue mastery: It feeds a crowd and looks and tastes incredible. To start, overnight seasoning enhances the brisket's flavor. For low, slow, indirect heat, you'll arrange a long line of briquettes in a C formation. Cooking the brisket fat side down provides a protective barrier against the direct heat of the fire, as does wrapping it in foil toward the end of cooking. A 2-hour rest before serving allows the juices time to redistribute evenly, and a cooler helps hold in the residual heat perfectly. This recipe was developed using Diamond Crystal kosher salt. If you have Morton kosher salt, which is denser, use 3 tablespoons. We call for a whole beef brisket here, with the flat and point cuts intact; you may need to special-order this cut. You can substitute 5 cups wood chips wrapped into three foil packets (see page 16) for the wood chunks. You will need a charcoal grill, a probe thermometer, and a cooler to make this recipe.

- 1 (10- to 12-pound) whole beef brisket, fat cap trimmed to ¼ to ½ inch
- ¼ cup kosher salt
- ¼ cup pepper
- 5 (3-inch) wood chunks
- 1 (13 by 9-inch) disposable roasting aluminum pan

1 With brisket positioned point side up, use sharp knife to remove excess fat from deep pocket where flat and point are attached. Trim and discard short edge of flat if less than 1 inch thick. Flip brisket and remove any large deposits of fat from underside.

2 Combine salt and pepper in bowl. Place brisket on rimmed baking sheet and sprinkle all over with salt mixture. Cover with plastic wrap and refrigerate for at least 12 hours or up to 24 hours.

3 Open bottom vent of charcoal grill halfway. Arrange 60 briquettes, 2 briquettes wide, around perimeter of grill to form C shape, overlapping slightly so briquettes touch. Place second layer of 60 briquettes, also 2 briquettes wide, on top of first. (Completed C will be 2 briquettes wide by 2 briquettes high.)

TEXAS-STYLE BARBECUED WHOLE BRISKET

Why Is Brisket Pink?

Championship barbecued brisket always contains a thick smoke ring—the pink layer just beneath the meat's surface. But smoke doesn't play much of a role—it's actually caused by reactions that occur when meat is cooked for a long time at a low temperature in a closed chamber. The fire emits gases that dissolve in the moisture on the surface of the meat to create new compounds similar to the nitrates that keep deli meats pink. We find that placing a pan of water in the grill adds enough moisture for a proper smoke ring.

4 Space wood chunks evenly on top of C. Place disposable pan in center of grill, running lengthwise into gap of C, and fill with 6 cups water.

5 Light chimney starter filled with 15 briquettes (pile briquettes on 1 side of chimney so they catch). When coals are partially covered with ash, use tongs to place them at 1 end of C; do not let coals touch other end of C.

6 Set cooking grate in place, then clean and oil grate. Place brisket, fat side down with point end facing gap in C, on grill over water-filled pan. Insert temperature probe into side of upper third of point. Cover grill, positioning lid vent over gap in C, and open lid vent halfway. Cook, without opening grill, until meat registers 170 degrees, 4 to 5 hours. (Tail of C will not yet be lit.)

KANSAS CITY BARBECUED BRISKET

BARBECUED BURNT ENDS

7 Place 2 large sheet of aluminum foil on rimmed baking sheet. Remove probe from brisket. Using oven mitts, transfer brisket fat side down to center of foil. Wrap brisket tightly in foil, minimizing air pockets. Using additional sheets of foil, continue wrapping brisket until completely covered and airtight. Make small mark on foil with marker to keep track of fat side.

8 Remove cooking grate. Pour 3 quarts unlit charcoal briquettes into gap in C, about halfway around perimeter of grill over gap in C and spent coals. Replace cooking grate. Return wrapped brisket fat side down to grill in same position over water-filled pan. Reinsert probe into point. Cover grill and continue to cook until meat registers 205 degrees, 1 to 2 hours longer.

9 Remove probe. Transfer foil-wrapped brisket point side up to cooler, close cooler, and let rest for 2 to 3 hours. Transfer brisket fat side up to carving board and unwrap. Slice flat against grain ¼ inch thick, stopping at point. Rotate point 90 degrees and slice against grain ¼ inch thick. Serve.

Kansas City Barbecued Brisket

SERVES 8 to 10 **TIME** 7 to 7½ hours plus 6 hours marinating

Why This Recipe Works Tender, mildly smoky Kansas City–style brisket is abundantly coated with a sweet, peppery spice rub and bathed in a tangy, ketchup-based sauce—the more, the better. Scoring the fat cap on the brisket helps it render and lets the potent spice rub penetrate the meat. We set the brisket in a disposable aluminum pan on the cooler side of the grill for gentle cooking. After a couple of hours of letting it smoke on the grill, we add our homemade barbecue sauce to the pan, cover it, and move it to the oven, where the steamy environment fully tenderizes the meat. Finally, we let the brisket rest in the turned-off oven so that it can reabsorb some of its lost juices, ensuring moist, tender meat. If using a charcoal grill, you can substitute two wood chunks for the wood chip packet. This recipe was developed using Diamond Crystal kosher salt. If you have Morton kosher salt, which is denser, use 1 tablespoon.

- 1½ tablespoons paprika
- 1½ tablespoons packed brown sugar
- 4 teaspoons kosher salt
- 1 tablespoon chili powder
- 1 tablespoon pepper
- 1 teaspoon granulated garlic
- 1 teaspoon onion powder

- 1 (5- to 6-pound) beef brisket, flat cut, fat trimmed to ¼ inch
- 1 (13 by 9-inch) disposable aluminum roasting pan
- 2 cups wood chips
- 1 cup ketchup
- 1 cup water
- 3 tablespoons molasses
- 1 tablespoon hot sauce

1 Combine paprika, sugar, salt, chili powder, pepper, garlic, and onion powder in bowl. Cut ¹⁄₁₆-inch-deep slits on both sides of brisket, spaced ½ inch apart, in crosshatch pattern, being careful not to cut into meat. Pat brisket dry with paper towels. Rub spice mixture all over brisket and into slits. Wrap brisket in plastic wrap and refrigerate for 6 to 24 hours.

2 Before grilling, unwrap brisket, pat dry with paper towels, and place in disposable pan. Using large piece of heavy-duty aluminum foil, wrap wood chips in 8 by 4-inch foil packet. (Make sure chips do not poke holes in sides or bottom of packet.) Cut 2 evenly spaced 2-inch slits in top of packet. Whisk ketchup, water, molasses, and hot sauce together in bowl; set aside for cooking.

3A **FOR A CHARCOAL GRILL** Open bottom vent halfway. Light large chimney starter filled with charcoal briquettes (6 quarts). When top coals are partially covered with ash, pour evenly over half of grill. Place wood chip packet on coals. Set cooking grate in place, cover, and open lid vent halfway. Heat grill until hot and wood chips are smoking, about 5 minutes.

3B **FOR A GAS GRILL** Remove cooking grate and place wood chip packet directly on primary burner. Set cooking grate in place; turn all burners to high; cover; and heat grill until hot and wood chips are smoking, about 15 minutes. Leave primary burner on high and turn off other burner(s). (Adjust primary burner as needed to maintain grill temperature of 350 degrees.)

4 Place pan on cooler side of grill. Cover (position lid vent over meat if using charcoal) and cook for 2 hours. During final 20 minutes of grilling, adjust oven rack to lower-middle position and heat oven to 300 degrees.

5 Remove pan from grill and pour reserved ketchup mixture over brisket. Cover pan tightly with foil and roast brisket in oven until tender and registers 195 degrees, 2½ to 3 hours.

6 Turn off oven and let brisket rest in oven for 1 hour. Transfer brisket to carving board. Skim fat from sauce. Slice brisket against grain into long, thin slices and serve with sauce.

Barbecued Burnt Ends

SERVES 8 to 10 **TIME** 6¼ hours plus 3 hours brining and resting

Why This Recipe Works For many, the best part of any barbecued meat is the dark, smoky, crusty, crispy bark. Burnt ends, the bark-iest kind of barbecue, usually come from generously marbled point-cut brisket, which is smoked for over 12 hours until the exterior is almost black and the meat is smoky and ultratender. We use the more readily available, leaner flat-cut brisket. To maximize surface area, we cut the meat into strips. Two hours in a brine solution keeps the meat moist through cooking. A combined grill-oven cooking method provides the burnished exterior and tender meat characteristic of true burnt ends. Look for a brisket with a significant fat cap. Although we don't usually soak wood chips, here we soak half of the chips to extend the total smoking time. If using a charcoal grill, you can substitute four wood chunks for the wood chip packets. This recipe was developed using Diamond Crystal kosher salt. If you have Morton kosher salt, which is denser, use 1½ cups in the brine in step 1. If you don't have ½ cup of juices from the rested brisket, add beef broth.

BRISKET AND RUB

- 2 cups kosher salt for brining
- ½ cup granulated sugar for brining
- 1 (5- to 6-pound) beef brisket, flat cut, fat trimmed to ¼ inch
- ¼ cup packed brown sugar
- 2 tablespoons pepper
- 1 tablespoon kosher salt
- 4 cups wood chips
- 1 (13 by 9-inch) disposable aluminum roasting pan (if using charcoal) or 2 (9-inch) disposable aluminum pie plates (if using gas)

BARBECUE SAUCE

- ¾ cup ketchup
- ¼ cup packed brown sugar
- 2 tablespoons cider vinegar
- 2 tablespoons Worcestershire sauce
- 2 teaspoons granulated garlic
- ¼ teaspoon cayenne pepper

1 **FOR THE BRISKET AND RUB** Dissolve 2 cups salt and granulated sugar in 4 quarts cold water in large container. Slice brisket with grain into 1½-inch-thick strips. Submerge brisket strips in brine, cover, and refrigerate for 2 hours.

2 Combine brown sugar, pepper, and salt in bowl. Remove brisket from brine, pat dry with paper towels, and rub evenly with sugar mixture.

3 Before grilling, soak 2 cups of wood chips in water for 15 minutes, then drain. Using large piece of heavy-duty aluminum foil, wrap soaked chips in 8 by 4-inch foil packet. (Make sure chips do not poke holes in sides or bottom of packets.) Cut 2 evenly spaced 2-inch slits in top of packets. Make second packet using remaining 2 cups unsoaked chips.

4A FOR A CHARCOAL GRILL Open bottom vent halfway, place disposable pan on 1 side of grill, and add 2 quarts water to pan. Arrange 3 quarts unlit charcoal briquettes evenly on other side of grill and place soaked wood chip packet on top. Light large chimney starter half filled with charcoal briquettes (3 quarts). When top coals are partially covered with ash, pour evenly over unlit coals and packet. Place unsoaked wood chip packet on top. Set cooking grate in place, cover, and open lid vent halfway. Heat grill until hot and wood chips are smoking, about 5 minutes.

4B FOR A GAS GRILL Remove cooking grate and place both wood chip packets directly on primary burner. Place disposable pie plates, each filled with 2 cups water, on other burner(s). Set cooking grate in place; turn all burners to high; cover; and heat grill until hot and wood chips are smoking, about 15 minutes. Leave primary burner on medium and turn off other burner(s). (Adjust primary burner as needed to maintain grill temperature of 275 degrees.)

5 Clean and oil cooking grate. Place strips of brisket over water-filled pan. Cover (position lid vent over meat if using charcoal) and cook for 3 hours (do not flip or rearrange strips during cooking). During final 20 minutes of grilling, adjust oven rack to lower-middle position and heat oven to 275 degrees.

6 Transfer brisket to rimmed baking sheet and cover tightly with foil. Roast brisket in oven until fork slips easily in and out of meat and meat registers about 210 degrees, about 2 hours. Remove brisket from oven and let rest (covered) for 1 hour. Remove foil, transfer brisket to carving board, and pour accumulated juices into fat separator.

7 FOR THE BARBECUE SAUCE Combine all ingredients with ½ cup defatted brisket juices in medium saucepan. Bring to simmer over medium heat and cook until slightly thickened, about 5 minutes.

8 Cut brisket strips crosswise into 1- to 2-inch chunks. Combine brisket chunks and barbecue sauce in large bowl and toss to combine. Serve.

Why Brine Beef?

We've found that soaking delicate lean white meat—such as pork, chicken, turkey, and even shrimp—in a salted water solution, or brine, before cooking results in moist, well-seasoned meat. So why not give beef the same treatment? In general, beef has a higher fat content than lean white meat, so it doesn't need the brine to remain juicy. Secondly, quick-cooking, tender beef cuts such as strip steaks or tenderloin roasts should ideally be cooked only to about 125 degrees (for medium-rare). In comparison, pork and chicken require a higher cooking temperature (around 145 for pork, 160 for white meat poultry, and 175 for dark meat poultry) and are, therefore, in greater danger of drying out. Tougher cuts of beef, however, such as chuck roast or brisket, are cooked to more than 200 degrees. Their extensive marbling of fat and collagen melts and acts as a natural moisturizer, but we found that in a long-cooking, high-temperature grilled brisket recipe, brining further ensures that the beef stays moist even after hours of grill-roasting.

Barbecued Pulled Chicken

SERVES 6 to 8 **TIME** 1¾ to 2¼ hours

Why This Recipe Works Barbecuing is an ideal method for cooking fatty cuts of pork or beef, but relatively lean chicken needs a little finessing. For excellent barbecued pulled chicken, we use whole chicken legs, which combine rich flavor, low cost, and resistance to overcooking. We grill the legs gently but thoroughly over indirect heat, using wood chips so they absorb plenty of smoke flavor along the way. Once the chicken is cooked, we hand-shred half and machine-process the other half to produce the perfect texture. Tossed with a quick barbecue sauce, this pulled chicken becomes truly bun-worthy. Chicken leg quarters consist of drumsticks attached to thighs; often, also attached are backbone sections that must be trimmed away. If using a charcoal grill, you can substitute two wood chunks for the wood chip packet. Serve with hamburger buns or sandwich bread.

BARBECUED PULLED CHICKEN

CHICKEN

- 8 (14-ounce) chicken leg quarters, trimmed
- 1½ teaspoons kosher salt
- 1 teaspoon pepper
- 2 cups wood chips
- 1 (16 by 12-inch) disposable aluminum roasting pan (if using charcoal)

SAUCE

- 1 large onion, peeled and quartered
- ¼ cup water
- 1½ cups ketchup
- 1½ cups apple cider
- ¼ cup molasses
- ¼ cup cider vinegar, divided
- 3 tablespoons Worcestershire sauce
- 3 tablespoons Dijon mustard
- ½ teaspoon pepper
- 1 tablespoon vegetable oil
- 1½ tablespoons chili powder
- 2 garlic cloves, minced
- ½ teaspoon cayenne pepper
- Hot sauce

1 FOR THE CHICKEN Pat chicken dry with paper towels and sprinkle with salt and pepper. Using large piece of heavy-duty aluminum foil, wrap wood chips in 8 by 4-inch foil packet. (Make sure chips do not poke holes in sides or bottom of packet.) Cut 2 evenly spaced 2-inch slits in top of packet.

2A FOR A CHARCOAL GRILL Open bottom vent halfway and place disposable pan in center of grill. Light large chimney starter three-quarters filled with charcoal briquettes (4½ quarts). When top coals are partially covered with ash, pour into 2 even piles on either side of disposable pan. Place wood chip packet on 1 pile of coals. Set cooking grate in place, cover, and open lid vent halfway. Heat grill until hot and wood chips are smoking, about 5 minutes.

2B FOR A GAS GRILL Remove cooking grate and place wood chip packet directly on primary burner. Set cooking grate in place; turn all burners to high; cover; and heat grill until hot and wood chips are smoking, about 15 minutes. Turn all burners to medium-high. (Adjust burners as needed during cooking to maintain grill temperature of 300 degrees.)

3 Clean and oil cooking grate. Place chicken skin side up on grill (over disposable pan if using charcoal). Cover (position lid vent over meat if using charcoal) and cook until chicken registers 185 degrees, 1 to 1½ hours, rotating chicken pieces halfway through cooking. Transfer chicken to carving board, tent with foil, and let rest until cool enough to handle.

4 FOR THE SAUCE Meanwhile, process onion and water in food processor until mixture resembles slush, about 30 seconds. Strain through fine-mesh strainer set over liquid measuring cup, pressing on solids with silicone spatula (you should have ¾ cup strained onion juice); discard solids.

5 Whisk onion juice, ketchup, cider, molasses, 3 tablespoons vinegar, Worcestershire, mustard, and pepper together in bowl. Heat oil in large saucepan over medium heat until shimmering. Stir in chili powder, garlic, and cayenne and cook until fragrant, about 30 seconds. Stir in ketchup mixture; bring to simmer; and cook over medium-low heat until slightly thickened, about 15 minutes (you should have about 4 cups of sauce). Transfer 2 cups sauce to serving bowl; leave remaining sauce in saucepan.

6 Remove and discard skin from chicken. Using your fingers, pull meat off bones, separating larger pieces (which fall off bones easily) from smaller, drier pieces into 2 piles.

7 Pulse smaller chicken pieces in food processor until just coarsely chopped, 3 or 4 pulses, stirring with silicone spatula between pulses. Add chopped chicken to sauce in saucepan. Pull larger chicken pieces into thin shreds and add to saucepan. Stir in remaining 1 tablespoon vinegar; cover; and heat chicken over medium-low heat, stirring occasionally, until heated through, about 10 minutes. Add hot sauce to taste. Serve with remaining sauce.

Grilling Chicken for a Crowd

Slide 2 chicken leg quarters into each slot of a 6-slot roasting rack. This way, all 12 legs will fit on the grill and finish cooking at once.

VARIATIONS

Barbecued Pulled Chicken with Peach Sauce

Substitute 1 cup water and ¾ cup peach preserves for apple cider and molasses in sauce.

Barbecued Pulled Chicken for a Crowd

SERVES 10 to 12

This technique works well on a charcoal grill but not so well on a gas grill. If your gas grill is large and can accommodate more than eight legs, follow the master recipe, adding as many legs as will comfortably fit in a single layer.

Increase amount of charcoal briquettes to 6 quarts. Use 12 chicken legs and slot them into V-shaped roasting rack set on top of cooking grate over disposable aluminum pan. Increase cooking time in step 3 to 1½ to 1¾ hours. In step 5, remove only 1 cup of sauce from saucepan. In step 7, pulse chicken in food processor in 2 batches.

SMOKED BARBECUED CHICKEN WINGS

Smoked Barbecued Chicken Wings

SERVES 4 to 6 **TIME** 1½ hours plus 1 hour brining

Why This Recipe Works Pronounced smokiness; tender, juicy meat; crisp, fully rendered skin; and a barbecue-inspired spice rub all add up to wings with a major "wow" factor. To allow the wings to cook through and smoke for just the right amount of time, we build a two-level fire in the grill, start them over indirect heat, and then move them directly over the coals to sear and crisp the skin. An irresistibly savory sauce of melted butter, cider vinegar, and ketchup gives these char-kissed wings a beautiful sheen. If using a charcoal grill, you can substitute two wood chunks for the wood chip packet. For more information on cutting chicken wings, see page 138. This recipe was developed using Diamond Crystal kosher salt. If you have Morton kosher salt, which is denser, use 6 tablespoons in the brine. Don't brine the chicken for more than 3 hours, or it will be too salty.

WINGS

- ½ cup kosher salt for brining
- ¼ cup sugar for brining
- 3 pounds chicken wings, cut at joints, wingtips discarded
- 2 teaspoons paprika
- 2 teaspoons chili powder
- 1¼ teaspoons dried oregano
- 1¼ teaspoons pepper
- 1¼ teaspoons garlic powder
- 1 teaspoon sugar
- ¼ teaspoon cayenne pepper
- 2 cups wood chips

SAUCE

- 4 tablespoons unsalted butter
- 2 tablespoons cider vinegar
- 2 tablespoons ketchup
- ½ teaspoon kosher salt

1 FOR THE WINGS Dissolve ½ cup salt and ¼ cup sugar in 2 quarts cold water in large container. Submerge wings in brine, cover, and refrigerate for at least 1 hour or up to 3 hours. Combine paprika, chili powder, oregano, pepper, garlic powder, sugar, and cayenne in large bowl. Measure out 1 tablespoon spice mixture and set aside for sauce.

2 FOR THE SAUCE Melt butter in small saucepan over medium-low heat. Add 1 tablespoon reserved spice mixture and cook until fragrant, about 30 seconds. Carefully add vinegar (mixture will bubble). Bring to simmer, then remove from heat. Whisk in ketchup and salt, cover, and set aside.

3 Remove wings from brine, pat dry with paper towels, then toss wings with remaining spice mixture until well coated.

4 Using large piece of heavy-duty aluminum foil, wrap wood chips in 8 by 4-inch foil packet. (Make sure chips do not poke holes in sides or bottom of packet.) Cut 2 evenly spaced 2-inch slits in top of packet.

5A **FOR A CHARCOAL GRILL** Open bottom vent completely. Light large chimney starter mounded with charcoal briquettes (7 quarts). When top coals are partially covered with ash, pour evenly over half of grill. Place wood chip packet on coals. Set cooking grate in place, cover, and open lid vent completely. Heat grill until hot and wood chips are smoking, about 5 minutes.

5B **FOR A GAS GRILL** Remove cooking grate and place wood chip packet directly on primary burner. Set grate in place; turn all burners to high; cover; and heat grill until hot and wood chips are smoking, about 15 minutes. Leave primary burner on high and turn off other burner(s). (Adjust primary burner as needed to maintain grill temperature of 400 degrees.)

6 Clean and oil cooking grate. Place wings fatty side up on cooler side of grill (6 to 8 inches from heat source for gas grill), arranging drumettes closest to fire. Cover (position lid vent over chicken if using charcoal) and cook until wings are darkened and register at least 180 degrees, 40 minutes to 1 hour, flipping halfway through cooking.

7A **FOR A CHARCOAL GRILL** Slide half of wings to hotter side of grill and cook, uncovered, until charred in spots, 2 to 6 minutes, flipping as needed. Transfer wings to platter and tent with foil. Repeat with remaining wings.

7B **FOR A GAS GRILL** Turn all burners to high and cook, uncovered, until wings are charred in spots, 10 to 14 minutes, flipping as needed. Transfer wings to platter and tent with foil.

8 Meanwhile, reheat sauce over medium heat, about 2 minutes. Toss wings with sauce in bowl. Serve.

BARBECUED CHICKEN THIGHS

Barbecued Chicken Thighs

SERVES 4 to 6 **TIME** 2 hours plus 1 hour seasoning

Why This Recipe Works Braising chicken thighs makes them meltingly tender, and you can do it right on the grill. First we set a pan of spice-rubbed chicken thighs in a mixture of barbecue sauce and chicken broth over the cooler side of a banked fire. After 30 minutes, we remove the thighs from the pan, apply a sticky glaze and more spice rub, and set them right on the grate. Smoke from a wood chip packet gently perfumes the meat. We prefer Frank's RedHot Original Cayenne Pepper Sauce for this recipe. If you use Tabasco, reduce the amount to 2 teaspoons in the broth mixture and 1 teaspoon in the glaze. You can substitute garlic powder for the granulated garlic. If using a charcoal grill, you can substitute two wood chunks for the wood chip packet.

- 2 tablespoons packed brown sugar, divided
- 1 tablespoon kosher salt
- 1 tablespoon paprika
- 1 teaspoon pepper
- 1 teaspoon white pepper
- ¾ teaspoon granulated garlic
- 8 (5- to 7-ounce) bone-in chicken thighs, trimmed
- 1 (13 by 9-inch) disposable aluminum roasting pan
- ½ cup plus 2 tablespoons bottled barbecue sauce, divided
- ½ cup chicken broth
- 7 garlic cloves (6 sliced thin, 1 minced)
- 3 tablespoons Worcestershire sauce
- 3 tablespoons hot sauce, divided
- 2 tablespoons apple jelly
- 1½ cups wood chips

1 Combine 1 tablespoon sugar, salt, paprika, pepper, white pepper, and granulated garlic in bowl. Measure out 4 teaspoons spice mixture and set aside for cooking. Place chicken in disposable pan and rub all over with remaining spice mixture. Flip chicken skin side down and let sit at room temperature for 1 hour.

2 Meanwhile, whisk ½ cup barbecue sauce, broth, sliced garlic, Worcestershire sauce, and 2 tablespoons hot sauce together in bowl; set aside for cooking. In separate bowl, microwave jelly until melted, about 30 seconds. Stir minced garlic, remaining 2 tablespoons barbecue sauce, remaining 1 tablespoon sugar, and remaining 1 tablespoon hot sauce into jelly to make glaze; set aside for cooking.

3 Using large piece of heavy-duty aluminum foil, wrap wood chips in 8 by 4-inch foil packet. (Make sure chips do not poke holes in sides or bottom of packet.) Cut 2 evenly spaced 2-inch slits in top of packet.

4A FOR A CHARCOAL GRILL Open bottom vent completely. Light large chimney starter mounded with charcoal briquettes (7 quarts). When top coals are partially covered with ash, pour into steeply banked pile against side of grill. Place wood chip packet on coals. Set cooking grate in place, cover, and open lid vent completely. Heat grill until hot and wood chips are smoking, about 5 minutes.

4B FOR A GAS GRILL Remove cooking grate and place wood chip packet directly on primary burner. Set grate in place; turn all burners to high; cover; and heat grill until hot and wood chips are smoking, about 15 minutes. Leave primary burner on high and turn off other burners. (Adjust primary burner as needed to maintain grill temperature between 350 and 400 degrees.)

5 Clean and oil cooking grate. Pour barbecue sauce mixture over chicken in pan. Place pan on cooler side of grill, cover (positioning lid vent over chicken if using charcoal) and cook for 30 minutes (chicken will be about 140 degrees).

6 Remove pan from grill. Using tongs, transfer chicken skin side up to cooler side of grill. (Discard cooking liquid.) Brush chicken with half of glaze, then sprinkle with reserved spice rub. Cover and cook for 15 minutes.

7 Brush chicken skin with remaining glaze. Cover and cook until glaze has set and chicken registers 175 degrees, 25 to 30 minutes. Transfer chicken to platter, tent with foil, and let rest for 10 minutes. Serve.

Alabama Barbecued Chicken

SERVES 6 to 8 **TIME** 2 hours plus 1 hour chilling

Why This Recipe Works Alabama chicken with white barbecue sauce can be traced to a single place: the Big Bob Gibson Bar-B-Q restaurant in Decatur. The sauce—creamy and tart, with hints of sweetness and heat—perfectly complements the hickory-smoked chicken. We cut two chickens in half for quicker, easier grilling, and center them between two piles of coals for fast, indirect cooking. When they come off the grill, we brush them with our version of Big Bob's sauce, a mayonnaise-based mixture spiked with cider vinegar, sugar, horseradish, and a touch of cayenne. Applying the sauce twice flavors the hot chicken through and through. Hickory wood chips are traditional here; however, any type of wood chips will work well. If using a charcoal grill, you can substitute 2 wood chunks for the wood chip packet.

SAUCE

- ¾ cup mayonnaise
- 2 tablespoons cider vinegar
- 2 teaspoons sugar
- ½ teaspoon prepared horseradish
- 1 teaspoon kosher salt
- ½ teaspoon pepper
- ¼ teaspoon cayenne pepper

CHICKEN

- 2 teaspoons kosher salt
- 1 teaspoon pepper
- ½ teaspoon cayenne pepper
- 2 (3½- to 4-pound) whole chickens, giblets discarded
- 2 cups wood chips
- 1 (13 by 9-inch) disposable aluminum roasting pan (if using charcoal)

ALABAMA BARBECUED CHICKEN

1 **FOR THE SAUCE** Process ingredients in blender until smooth, about 1 minute. Refrigerate for at least 1 hour or up to 2 days.

2 **FOR THE CHICKEN** Combine salt, pepper, and cayenne in small bowl. Working with 1 chicken at a time, place breast side down on cutting board. Use kitchen shears to cut along both sides of backbone. Discard backbone and trim any excess fat or skin at neck. Flip chicken and cut in half lengthwise through center of breastbone. Tuck wingtips behind backs. Pat chickens dry with paper towels and rub evenly with spice mixture.

3 Using large piece of heavy-duty aluminum foil, wrap wood chips in 8 by 4-inch foil packet. (Make sure chips do not poke holes in sides or bottom of packet.) Cut 2 evenly spaced 2-inch slits in top of packet.

4A **FOR A CHARCOAL GRILL** Open bottom vent halfway and place disposable pan in center of grill. Light large chimney starter filled with charcoal briquettes (6 quarts). When top coals are partially covered with ash, pour into 2 even piles on either side of disposable pan. Place wood chip packet on 1 pile of coals. Set cooking grate in place, cover, and open lid vent halfway. Heat grill until hot and wood chips are smoking, about 5 minutes.

4B **FOR A GAS GRILL** Remove cooking grate and place wood chip packet directly on primary burner. Set grate in place; turn all burners to high; cover; and heat grill until hot and wood chips are smoking, about 15 minutes. Turn all burners to medium. (Adjust burners as needed to maintain grill temperature of 350 degrees.)

5 Clean and oil cooking grate. Place chickens skin side down on grill (over disposable pan if using charcoal). Cover (positioning lid vent over chicken if using charcoal) and cook chicken until well browned on bottom and thighs register 120 degrees, 35 to 45 minutes.

6 Flip chickens skin side up. Cover and cook chicken until skin is golden brown and crisp and breasts register 160 degrees and thighs register 175 degrees, 15 to 20 minutes.

7 Transfer chickens to carving board and brush with 2 tablespoons sauce. Tent chickens with foil and let rest for 10 minutes. Brush chickens with remaining sauce, carve, and serve.

Smoked Bourbon Chicken

SERVES 6 to 8 **TIME** 2½ hours plus 1 hour marinating

Why This Recipe Works Bourbon and smoke are a flavor match made in heaven. A bourbon and soy marinade that doubles as a mopping sauce takes grilled chicken to its flavorful max. Because smoke is attracted to moisture, keeping the skin moist pulls the smoke to the chicken like a magnet. For plenty of surface area to achieve this effect, we split the birds in half and cut slashes into the meat. Giving the chicken halves a good soak in a portion of the savory-sweet marinade before cooking and basting them on the grill every 15 minutes ensures plenty of bourbon flavor. If using a charcoal grill, you can substitute one wood chunk for the wood chip packet. Use all of the basting liquid in step 7.

- 1¼ cups bourbon
- 1¼ cups soy sauce
- ½ cup packed brown sugar
- 1 shallot, minced
- 4 garlic cloves, minced
- 2 teaspoons pepper
- 2 (3½- to 4-pound) whole chickens, giblets discarded
- 1 cup wood chips
- 4 (12-inch) wooden skewers

SMOKED BOURBON CHICKEN

1 Bring bourbon, soy sauce, sugar, shallot, garlic, and pepper to boil in medium saucepan over medium-high heat and cook for 1 minute. Remove from heat and let cool completely. Measure out ¾ cup marinade and set aside for cooking.

2 Working with one chicken at a time, place breast side down on cutting board. Use kitchen shears to cut along both sides of backbone. Discard backbone and trim any excess fat or skin at neck. Flip chicken and cut in half lengthwise through center of breastbone. Cut ½-inch-deep slits across breasts, thighs, and legs, about ½ inch apart. Tuck wingtips behind backs.

3 Combine remaining marinade and chicken halves in two 1-gallon zipper-lock bags and toss to coat; press out as much air as possible and seal bag. Refrigerate for at least 1 hour or up to 24 hours, flipping occasionally.

4 Remove chickens from marinade and pat dry with paper towels. Insert 1 skewer lengthwise through thickest part of breast down through thigh of each chicken half.

5 Using large piece of heavy-duty aluminum foil, wrap wood chips in 8 by 4-inch foil packet. (Make sure chips do not poke holes in sides or bottom of packet.) Cut 2 evenly spaced 2-inch slits in top of packet.

6A FOR A CHARCOAL GRILL Open bottom vent halfway. Light large chimney starter filled with charcoal briquettes (6 quarts). When top coals are partially covered with ash, pour into steeply banked pile against side of grill. Place wood chip packet on coals. Set cooking grate in place, cover, and open lid vent halfway. Heat grill until hot and wood chips are smoking, about 5 minutes.

6B FOR A GAS GRILL Remove cooking grate and place wood chip packet directly on primary burner. Set grate in place; turn all burners to high; cover; and heat grill until hot and wood chips are smoking, about 15 minutes. Leave primary burner on high and turn off other burners. (Adjust primary burner as needed to maintain grill temperature between 350 and 400 degrees.)

7 Clean and oil cooking grate. Place chicken halves skin side up on cooler side of grill with legs pointing toward fire. Cover (position lid vent over chicken if using charcoal) and cook, basting every 15 minutes with reserved bourbon mixture, until breasts register 160 degrees and thighs register 175 degrees, 1¼ to 1½ hours, switching placement of chicken halves after 45 minutes. (All of bourbon mixture should be used.) Transfer chicken to carving board, tent with foil, and let rest for 15 minutes. Carve chicken and serve.

POLLO A LA BRASA

Pollo a la Brasa (Peruvian Rotisserie Chicken)

SERVES 8 **TIME** 2½ hours plus 24 hours marinating

Why This Recipe Works Making this wildly popular dish just might convince you that your rotisserie attachment is your smartest-ever grilling investment. We soak two chickens in a beer-based marinade that includes soy sauce, lime juice, mustard, garlic, and spices. A serving sauce made with ají amarillo (Peruvian yellow chile pepper) paste and huacatay (black mint) paste amps up the flavors even more. This recipe was developed using Diamond Crystal kosher salt. If you have Morton kosher salt, which is denser, use 2 tablespoons. You will need a motorized rotisserie attachment. If using a charcoal grill, you can substitute one wood chunk for the wood chip packet. Our gas grill instructions are for a three-burner grill. If using a two-burner grill, we recommend halving the recipe and cooking with both burners turned to medium-low (do not halve the wood chip amount). This dish is traditionally served with french fries and salad.

SAUCE

- ¾ cup mayonnaise
- 3 tablespoons ají amarillo paste
- 1½ tablespoons lime juice
- 1 garlic clove, minced to paste
- 1½ teaspoons jarred huacatay paste

CHICKEN

- 1 cup cerveza negra or amber ale
- ¼ cup finely grated garlic
- ¼ cup lime juice (2 limes)
- ¼ cup soy sauce
- 2 tablespoons minced fresh rosemary
- 8 teaspoons kosher salt
- 4 teaspoons yellow mustard
- 2 teaspoons pepper
- 2 teaspoons dried oregano
- 2 teaspoons ground cumin
- 2 (4- to 4½-pound) whole chickens, giblets discarded
- 1 cup wood chips
- 1 (13 by 9-inch) disposable aluminum roasting pan

1 FOR THE SAUCE Whisk all ingredients until smooth. (Sauce can be refrigerated for up to 1 week.)

2 FOR THE CHICKEN Whisk beer, garlic, lime juice, soy sauce, rosemary, salt, mustard, pepper, oregano, and cumin together in liquid measuring cup. Using your fingers or handle of wooden spoon, gently loosen skin covering chicken breasts and leg quarters. Using paring knife, poke 10 to 15 holes in fat deposits on skin of backs. Tuck wingtips underneath chickens.

3 Place 1 chicken in bowl with cavity end up. Slowly pour half of marinade between skin and meat and rub marinade inside cavity, outside skin, and under skin to distribute. Transfer chicken to 1-gallon zipper-lock bag and add marinade left in bowl to bag; seal bag. Repeat with remaining chicken and remaining marinade. Refrigerate for 24 hours, flipping bags halfway through marinating.

4 Transfer chickens to rimmed baking sheet. Tie knot around each chicken tail with 12-inch piece of kitchen twine, then tie legs together and secure to tail using ends of twine. Tuck wingtips behind back. Turn chickens breast side up and line them up so that breast ends touch. Thread rotisserie skewer lengthwise through chickens. Center chickens on skewer, leaving 1-inch gap between chickens. Attach rotisserie forks to skewer and insert tines into chicken thighs; secure forks by tightening screws.

5 Using large piece of heavy-duty aluminum foil, wrap wood chips in 8 by 4 ½-inch foil packet. (Make sure chips do not poke holes in sides or bottom of packet.) Cut 2 evenly spaced 2-inch slits in top of packet.

6A FOR A CHARCOAL GRILL Open bottom vent halfway and place disposable pan in center of grill. Light large chimney starter filled with charcoal briquettes (6 quarts). When top coals are partially covered with ash, pour into 2 even piles on either side of disposable pan. Place wood chip packet on 1 pile of coals. Position rotisserie motor attachment on grill so that skewer runs parallel to coals. Cover and open lid vent halfway. Heat grill until hot and wood chips are smoking, about 5 minutes.

6B FOR A GAS GRILL Remove cooking grate and place wood chip packet directly on primary burner. Position rotisserie motor attachment on grill and turn all burners to high. Cover and heat grill until hot and wood chips are smoking, 15 to 25 minutes. Turn 2 outside burners to medium and turn off center burner. (Adjust outside burners as needed to maintain grill temperature between 350 and 375 degrees.)

7 Attach rotisserie skewer to motor and start motor. Cover and cook until breasts register 160 degrees and thighs register 175 degrees, 1¼ hours to 1½ hours.

8 Transfer chickens, still on skewer, to carving board and let rest for 15 minutes. Using large wad of paper towels in each hand, carefully remove rotisserie forks and skewer from chickens. Carve chickens, transfer to platter, and serve with sauce.

BEER CAN CHICKEN

Beer Can Chicken

SERVES 6 to 8 **TIME** 2¼ hours

Why This Recipe Works While it may sound like a gimmick, beer can chicken is the real deal: A whole chicken is rubbed with spices and then propped upright on an open can of beer and placed on the grill, using the bird's drumsticks to form a tripod. The beer simmers and turns to steam as the chicken roasts, which makes the meat remarkably juicy and rich-textured, similar to braised chicken. And the dry heat crisps the skin and renders the fat. The results are too good not to share, so this recipe makes two chickens. Banking the coals on either side of the grill makes a cooler spot in the middle where the chickens can cook through evenly and gently. Wood chips contribute a pleasing smoky flavor that doesn't overwhelm the chicken. A simple but flavorful blend of brown sugar, paprika, salt, pepper, and cayenne provides a rub that's rich and a little bit spicy, the perfect complement to the smokiness imparted by the fire. This recipe was developed using Diamond Crystal kosher salt. If you have Morton kosher salt, which is denser, use 1½ tablespoons. If using a charcoal grill, you can substitute four wood chunks for the wood chip packets. Inexpensive beer is fine; avoid those with strong hoppy or bitter flavors. Do not use 16-ounce cans; their height will make the chickens less stable.

SPICE RUB

- 2 tablespoons packed light brown sugar
- 2 tablespoons paprika
- 2 tablespoons kosher salt
- 1 tablespoon pepper
- 1 teaspoon cayenne pepper

CHICKEN

- 2 (12-ounce) cans mild beer
- 4 crumbled bay leaves
- 2 (3- to 3½-pound) whole chickens, giblets discarded
- 4 cups wood chips
- 1 (13 by 9-inch) disposable aluminum roasting pan (if using charcoal)

GLAZE

- 2 tablespoons packed light brown sugar
- 2 tablespoons ketchup
- 2 tablespoons distilled white vinegar
- 1 teaspoon hot sauce

1 FOR THE SPICE RUB Mix all ingredients together in bowl. Measure out 1 tablespoon and set aside for glaze.

2 FOR THE CHICKEN Measure out 1 cup beer from each can; reserve 2 tablespoons beer for glaze, and discard (or drink) the rest. Enlarge drinking hole in can using church key can opener (this will help steam to escape during cooking). Crumble 2 bay leaves into each beer can and set aside for cooking.

3 Using your fingers, gently loosen skin covering breasts and legs. Rub remaining spice rub inside cavity, on skin, and under skin to distribute. Using paring knife, poke 10 to 15 holes in fat deposits on skin of back. Tuck wingtips underneath chickens. Pat chickens dry with paper towels.

4 FOR THE GLAZE Combine all ingredients with reserved 1 tablespoon spice rub and 2 tablespoons beer in medium bowl.

5 Place beer cans in separate large, shallow bowls and spray cans with vegetable oil spray. Slide chickens over cans so that chickens stands upright, with can inside chicken cavities.

6 Using large pieces of heavy-duty aluminum foil, wrap wood chips into two 8 by 4-inch foil packets. (Make sure chips do not poke holes in sides or bottom of packets.) Cut 2 evenly spaced 2-inch slits in top of packets.

7A **FOR A CHARCOAL GRILL** Open bottom vent halfway and place disposable pan in center of grill. Light large chimney starter two-thirds filled with charcoal briquettes (4 quarts). When top coals are partially covered with ash, pour into 2 even piles on either side of disposable pan. Place wood chip packet on 1 pile of coals. Set cooking grate in place, cover, and open lid vent halfway. Heat grill until hot and wood chips are smoking, about 5 minutes.

7B **FOR A GAS GRILL** Remove cooking grate and place wood chip packet directly on primary burner. Set grate in place; turn all burners to high; cover; and heat grill until hot and wood chips are smoking, about 15 minutes. Turn all burners to medium. (Adjust burners as needed to maintain grill temperature of 325 degrees.)

8 Clean and oil cooking grate. Place chickens (on cans) on grill (over disposable pan if using charcoal); use drumsticks to help stabilize them. Cover (position lid vent over chicken if using charcoal) and cook until skin is well browned and very crisp, 40 minutes to 1 hour. Brush with glaze and grill, covered, until breasts register 160 degrees and thighs register 175 degrees, about 20 minutes.

9 With large wad of paper towels in each hand, transfer chickens (still on cans) to carving board, keeping cans upright; let rest, uncovered, for 15 minutes. Using wads of paper towels, carefully lift chickens off cans and onto carving board. Carve chickens and serve.

Let Off Some Steam

Use church key can opener to enlarge hole in top of can to allow maximum amount of steam to escape.

Peruvian Garlic-Lime Chicken

SERVES 4 **TIME** 2¼ hours plus 24 hours marinating

Why This Recipe Works The even heat provided by a rotisserie gives traditional pollo a la brasa unmatched crispy skin and juicy meat. But if you don't own a grill rotisserie, you can get a similar effect using our grill setup for beer-can chicken: coals banked on two sides of the grill, with the bird propped on a beer can over the cooler center. While the chicken cooks, you'll rotate the can a quarter turn every 15 minutes, which produces a rotisserie-like effect for remarkably succulent, smoky meat packaged in well-rendered, uniformly mahogany skin. Before it hits the grill, the chicken picks up flavor in a beer-based marinade that includes soy sauce, lime juice, mustard, garlic, dried thyme, black pepper, and cumin. Inexpensive beer is fine; avoid those with strong hoppy or bitter flavors. Do not use a 16-ounce can because its height will make the chicken less stable. This recipe was developed using Diamond Crystal kosher salt. If you have Morton kosher salt, which is denser, use 1 tablespoon. We developed this recipe on a three-burner gas grill. If using a two-burner grill, turn both burners to high and place the wood chips on the primary burner while the grill heats. When the grill is hot, turn the primary burner to medium and turn the secondary burner off; stand the chicken on the cooler side of the grill, about 4 inches from the primary burner, and proceed with the recipe, adjusting the primary burner as needed to maintain 350 to 375 degrees. If using a charcoal grill, you can substitute one wood chunk for the wood chip packet. Serve with french fries, salad, and Ají Verde and/or Ají Amarillo (both on page 397).

- 1 (12-ounce) can mild beer, divided
- 2 tablespoons finely grated garlic
- 2 tablespoons lime juice
- 2 tablespoons soy sauce
- 4 teaspoons kosher salt
- 2 teaspoons yellow mustard
- 1 teaspoon pepper
- 1 teaspoon dried thyme
- 1 teaspoon ground cumin
- 1 (4- to 4½-pound) whole chicken, giblets discarded
- 1 cup wood chips
- 1 (13 by 9-inch) disposable aluminum roasting pan (if using charcoal)

1 Whisk ½ cup beer, garlic, lime juice, soy sauce, salt, mustard, pepper, thyme, and cumin together in liquid measuring cup. Refrigerate remaining beer, still in can, until ready to grill. Using your fingers, gently loosen skin covering breast and legs. Using paring knife, poke 10 to 15 holes in fat deposits on skin of back. Tuck wingtips underneath chicken.

2 Place chicken in bowl. Slowly pour marinade between skin and meat. Rub marinade inside cavity, on skin, and under skin to distribute. Cover and refrigerate for 24 hours, turning chicken occasionally.

3 Place beer can in large, shallow bowl and spray can with vegetable oil spray. Slide chicken over can so that chicken stands upright, with can inside chicken cavity.

4 Using large piece of heavy-duty aluminum foil, wrap wood chips in 8 by 4-inch foil packet. (Make sure chips do not poke holes in sides or bottom of packet.) Cut 2 evenly spaced 2-inch slits in top of packet.

5A **FOR A CHARCOAL GRILL** Open bottom vent halfway and place disposable pan in center of grill. Light large chimney starter two-thirds filled with charcoal briquettes (4 quarts). When top coals are partially covered with ash, pour into 2 even piles on either side of disposable pan. Place wood chip packet on 1 pile of coals. Set cooking grate in place, cover, and open lid vent halfway. Heat grill until hot and wood chips are smoking, about 5 minutes.

5B **FOR A GAS GRILL** Remove cooking grate and place wood chip packet directly on primary burner. Set grate in place; turn all burners to high; cover; and heat grill until hot and wood chips are smoking, about 15 minutes. Turn 2 outside burners to medium and turn off center burner. (Adjust outside burners as needed to maintain grill temperature between 350 and 375 degrees.)

6 Clean and oil cooking grate. Place chicken (on can) in center of grill (over disposable pan if using charcoal); use drumsticks to stabilize it. Orient chicken so that wings facing piles of coals (or outer burners on gas grill) are at 3 and 9 o'clock. Cover grill (with top vent open for charcoal grill) and cook for 15 minutes. Using tongs and wad of paper towels, rotate chicken 90 degrees so wings are at 6 and 12 o'clock. Continue cooking and turning chicken at 15-minute intervals until breast registers 160 degrees and thighs register 175 degrees, 1 hour to 1¼ hours.

7 With large wad of paper towels in each hand, transfer chicken (still on can) to clean bowl, keeping can upright; let rest, uncovered, for 15 minutes. Using wads of paper towels, carefully lift chicken off can and onto carving board. Carve chicken and serve.

Beer Cans on the Grill

Is grilling a chicken perched on an open beer can really a good idea? Beer can interiors are coated with an epoxy that contains Bisphenol A (BPA), which some studies have linked to cancer and other harmful health effects. To evaluate the effects of cooking chicken on a beer can, we roasted two whole birds, one set on an open beer can containing 6 ounces of beer and the other on a stainless-steel vertical roaster with the same amount of beer poured into the reservoir. After roasting the chickens, we collected their drippings and stripped each carcass, grinding the meat and skin to create homogeneous samples. We sent the samples to a lab to be evaluated for BPA content. In each chicken, the BPA measured less than 20 micrograms per kilogram, leading us to believe that the beer can cooking method is safe. (The Food and Drug Administration's current standard for exposure is 50 micrograms per kilogram of body weight for adults, or 3,400 micrograms per day for a 150-pound person.) But if you'd rather not use a beer can, you can use a vertical roaster.

Smoked Prime Rib with Horseradish Sauce

SERVES 8 to 10 **TIME** 3¼ to 4 hours plus 24¾ hours salting and resting

Why This Recipe Works Smoking a prime rib elevates this already grand cut of meat to an entirely new level of flavor. Since this prime rib is done in the Texas style (which is meant to highlight the beef flavor), the only seasonings are kosher salt and black pepper. Applying this simple rub at least 24 hours (or up to four days) in advance of cooking allows the salt to penetrate and fully season the meat; the salting process helps keep the meat juicy too. A charcoal C grill setup supplies sufficient heat to cook the roast through without recharging, so you can relax with your guests. We recommend ordering the prime rib ahead of time from your butcher; make sure you ask specifically for a first-cut (it is more uniform and tender) standing rib roast. The roast should have an even fat cap on top and three big bones. You will need a charcoal grill and a probe thermometer to make this recipe. You can substitute 3 cups wood chips wrapped into

SMOKED PRIME RIB WITH HORSERADISH SAUCE

two foil packets (see page 16) for the wood chunks. This recipe was developed using Diamond Crystal kosher salt. If you have Morton kosher salt, which is denser, use 1½ tablespoons to season the meat in step 1. For more information on building a charcoal C setup, see page 218.

PRIME RIB

- 1 (6- to 7-pound) first-cut beef standing rib roast (3 bones), fat cap trimmed to ¼ inch
- 2 tablespoons kosher salt
- 1 tablespoon pepper
- 3 (3-inch) wood chunks
- 1 (13 by 9-inch) disposable aluminum roasting pan

HORSERADISH SAUCE

- ½ cup mayonnaise
- ⅓ cup prepared horseradish
- 2 tablespoons lemon juice
- 1 garlic clove, minced
- 1 teaspoon Worcestershire sauce
- 1 teaspoon pepper
- ¾ teaspoon kosher salt
- Pinch cayenne pepper

1 FOR THE PRIME RIB Cut ¼-inch-deep slits through fat cap, spaced 1 inch apart, in crosshatch pattern, being careful not to cut into meat. Pat roast dry with paper towels and rub salt and pepper all over and into slits. Place roast on large plate and refrigerate, uncovered, for at least 24 hours or up to 4 days.

2 FOR THE HORSERADISH SAUCE Combine all ingredients in bowl. Cover and refrigerate for at least 30 minutes or up to 2 days.

3 Open bottom vent of charcoal grill halfway. Arrange 40 briquettes, 2 briquettes wide, around half of perimeter of grill to form C shape, overlapping slightly so briquettes touch. Place second layer of 40 briquettes, also 2 briquettes wide, on top of first. (Completed C should be 2 briquettes wide by 2 briquettes high.)

4 Space wood chunks evenly on top of C. Place disposable pan in center of grill, running lengthwise into gap of C, and fill with 6 cups water.

5 Light chimney starter filled with 15 briquettes (pile briquettes against 1 side of chimney so they catch). When coals are partially covered with ash, use tongs to place them at 1 end of C; do not let coals touch other end of C.

6 Set cooking grate in place, then clean and oil grate. Place roast fat side up over water-filled pan, with bones facing gap in C. Insert temperature probe into center of roast. Cover grill, positioning lid vent over roast, and open vent halfway. Cook, without opening grill, until meat registers 115 degrees (for medium-rare), 2½ to 3¼ hours.

7 Transfer roast to carving board, tent with aluminum foil, and let rest for 45 minutes. Carve meat from bones and slice into ½-inch-thick pieces. Serve with sauce.

No Bone? No Problem!

If all you can find is boneless prime rib, here's how to mimic the protective bones with aluminum foil.

1 Fold 12- to 14-foot sheet of aluminum foil in half lengthwise and then in half lengthwise again; gently roll and scrunch it into narrow tube.

2 Coil foil tube into tight disk about 6 inches across. Flatten to form rectangle.

3 Tie foil "bone" to roast (where real bones were removed) and proceed with recipe.

BARBECUED GLAZED PORK ROAST

Barbecued Glazed Pork Roast

SERVES 6 **TIME** 2¾ to 3¼ hours plus 6½ hours seasoning and resting

Why This Recipe Works No meat takes to smoke and fire quite like pork, which soaks up the smoke as it slowly renders to a succulent finish. Smoked pork often means a pork shoulder that's slow-cooked, hand-pulled, and piled high on a bun to form a gloriously sloppy sandwich. Delicious? You bet. Dinner party fare? Not really. But swap in a center-cut, bone-in rib roast and you have a sliceable, elegant roast that remains true to the smoky, porky nature of the beast. Deeply cross-hatching the fat cap helps the fat to render and also provides access for a simple rub to flavor the roast. We grill it low and slow, and once much of the fat has been rendered we baste the roast with a thick, sweet sauce (in a disposable pan on the grill) for the last half of cooking, which gives the pork a flavorful, shellacked crust. For easier carving, have the butcher remove the tip of the chine bone and cut the remainder of the chine bone from between the ribs (a technique called scoring). If using a charcoal grill, you can substitute two wood chunks for the wood chip packet.

- 1 (4- to 5-pound) center-cut bone-in pork rib roast, chine bone removed, fat trimmed to ¼ inch
- 5 tablespoons plus 1 teaspoon packed brown sugar, divided
- 1 tablespoon kosher salt
- 1½ teaspoons pepper
- 1 teaspoon paprika
- ½ teaspoon garlic powder
- 2 cups wood chips
- 1½ cups ketchup
- 1½ cups apple juice
- 3 tablespoons cider vinegar
- 1 tablespoon Worcestershire sauce
- 1 tablespoon yellow mustard seeds
- 1–2 teaspoons hot sauce
- 1 (13 by 9-inch) disposable aluminum roasting pan

1 Combine 1 teaspoon sugar, salt, pepper, paprika, and garlic powder in bowl. Cut ¼-inch-deep slits through fat cap, spaced ½ inch apart, in crosshatch pattern, being careful not to cut into meat. Pat roast dry with paper towels and rub spice mixture all over and into slits. Wrap roast in plastic wrap and refrigerate for at least 6 or up to 24 hours.

2 Before cooking, unwrap roast (do not pat dry). Using large piece of heavy-duty aluminum foil, wrap wood chips in 8 by 4-inch foil packet. (Make sure chips do not poke holes in sides or bottom of packet.) Cut 2 evenly spaced 2-inch slits in top of packet.

3A **FOR A CHARCOAL GRILL** Open bottom vent halfway. Arrange 3 quarts of unlit charcoal briquettes over half of grill. Light large chimney starter filled with charcoal briquettes (6 quarts). When top coals are partially covered with ash, pour evenly over unlit coals. Place wood chip packet on coals. Set cooking grate in place, cover, and open lid vent halfway. Heat grill until hot and wood chips are smoking, about 5 minutes.

3B **FOR A GAS GRILL** Remove cooking grate and place wood chip packets directly on primary burner. Set cooking grate in place; turn all burners to high; cover; and heat grill until hot and wood chips are smoking, about 15 minutes. Leave primary burner on high and turn off other burners. (Adjust primary burner as needed to maintain grill temperature of 350 degrees.)

4 Clean and oil cooking grate. Place roast meat side up on cooler side of grill, with bones facing coals and flames. Cover (position lid vent over meat if using charcoal) and cook until pork registers between 90 and 100 degrees, about 1 hour.

5 Whisk ketchup, apple juice, vinegar, Worcestershire, mustard seeds, hot sauce, and remaining 5 tablespoons sugar together in disposable pan until sugar dissolves. Place pan on grill and transfer roast to pan. Spoon sauce over roast. Slide pan to cooler side of grill and cover (position lid vent over meat if using charcoal). Cook, basting meat with sauce every 15 minutes, until pork registers 140 degrees, 45 minutes to 1¼ hours.

6 Remove pan from grill, tent roast with foil, and let pork rest in sauce for 30 minutes. Transfer pork to carving board and pour sauce into serving vessel, skimming off fat as necessary. Carve pork in between ribs into thick chops. Serve, passing sauce at table.

Holiday Smoked Turkey

SERVES 10 to 12 **TIME** 4¼ hours plus 30 minutes resting

Why This Recipe Works Smoking your holiday turkey is a fun and effective route to moist, tender, richly flavored meat. For this recipe, we consulted a true pro, James Beard Award–winning pit master Rodney Scott. Adapting a recipe from his book, *Rodney Scott's World of BBQ* (2021), we start with a spatchcocked turkey (meaning the backbone is removed and the bird is laid out flat) for even cooking, and we sprinkle it thoroughly with a just-spicy-enough rub. While Scott's recipe is designed for a ceramic smoker, ours is made for the more common kettle charcoal grill. We use a charcoal C setup and light both ends at the outset. This technique makes for a nice low, long burn from two directions, which helps the turkey cook evenly. Four wood chunks provide bursts of smoke throughout cooking. An acidic mop flavors and tenderizes the turkey, which acquires a beautiful bronzed exterior by the time the breast meat reaches 160 degrees. This recipe was developed using Diamond Crystal kosher salt. If you have Morton kosher salt, which is denser, use 1½ tablespoons. You will need a charcoal grill and a probe thermometer to make this recipe. For more information on building a charcoal C setup, see page 218.

MOP

- 2 cups distilled white vinegar
- 2 thin lemon slices
- ¼ cup granulated sugar
- 1 tablespoon pepper
- 2 teaspoons cayenne pepper
- ½ teaspoon red pepper flakes

RUB

- 2 tablespoons kosher salt
- 1 tablespoon monosodium glutamate
- 1 tablespoon pepper
- 1 tablespoon paprika
- 1 tablespoon chili powder
- 1 tablespoon packed light brown sugar
- 1½ teaspoons garlic powder
- 1½ teaspoons onion powder
- ¼ teaspoon cayenne pepper

TURKEY

- 1 (12- to 14-pound) turkey, neck and giblets discarded
- 4 (3-inch) wood chunks
- 1 (13 by 9-inch) disposable aluminum roasting pan

1 **FOR THE MOP** Combine all ingredients in medium saucepan and bring to simmer over medium-high heat. Cook until sugar is dissolved, about 2 minutes. Remove from heat and let cool completely. Discard lemon slices. (Mop can be refrigerated for up to 2 months.)

2 **FOR THE RUB** Combine all ingredients in bowl.

3 **FOR THE TURKEY** With turkey breast side down, use kitchen shears to cut along both sides of backbone, staying as close as possible to backbone. Discard backbone and trim any excess fat or skin at neck. Flip turkey and press down firmly on breast with heels of your hands to flatten breastbone. Tuck wingtips behind back. Sprinkle rub all over both sides of turkey.

4 Open bottom vent of charcoal grill halfway. Arrange 50 charcoal briquettes, 2 briquettes wide, around perimeter of grill to form C shape, overlapping slightly so briquettes touch. Place second layer of 50 briquettes, also 2 briquettes wide, on top of first. (Completed C will be 2 briquettes wide by 2 briquettes high.)

5 Space wood chunks evenly on top of C. Place disposable pan in center of grill, running lengthwise into gap of C, and fill with 6 cups water.

6 Light chimney starter filled with 20 briquettes. When coals are partially covered with ash, use tongs to pile 10 coals on each end of charcoal C, where briquettes meet water pan, so both ends of C ignite.

HOLIDAY SMOKED TURKEY

Grill Setup

This "two-headed snake" (you light both ends of the charcoal simultaneously) provides hours of heat and smoke to gently cook and flavor the turkey.

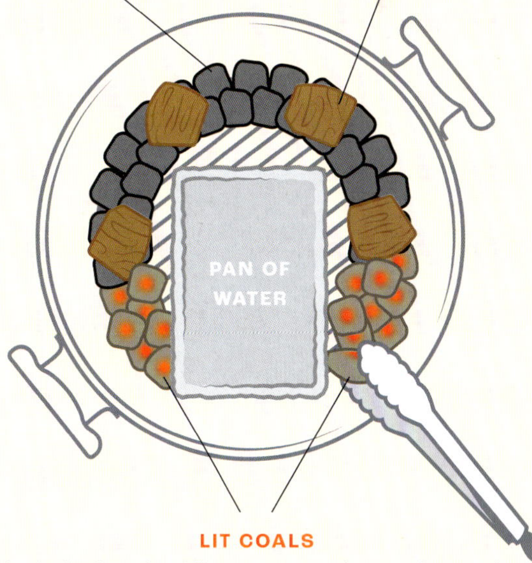

7 Set cooking grate in place, then clean and oil grate. Place turkey skin side down over water-filled pan, with drumsticks pointing toward arc in charcoal C. Cover grill, position lid vent over turkey, and open lid vent halfway. Cook, undisturbed, for 2 hours.

8 Baste turkey liberally with mop. Using oven mitts or grill mitts, flip turkey skin side up, positioning it over water pan with drumsticks facing same direction. Baste turkey liberally with more mop (you may not need all of it; discard any extra).

9 Insert temperature probe into thickest part of breast. Cover grill and cook until breast registers 160 degrees (check temperature of both sides of breast) and thighs register 175 degrees, about 1 hour.

10 Transfer turkey to rimmed baking sheet. Let rest for 30 to 40 minutes. Carve turkey and transfer to serving platter. Serve.

6

Seafood

SHELLFISH

SALMON

SWORDFISH AND TUNA

WHITE FISH FILLETS

WHOLE FISH

IN DEPTH

Fish on the Grill

Because fish is more delicate than meat, it has a reputation of being fussy to grill. But with a few simple tips and techniques, you can easily enjoy a wide variety of great meals that imbue fish with grill flavor.

WHOLE FISH ON THE GRILL

Whole fish makes an easy, quick, delicious, and impressive grilled meal. Grilling whole fish is a fairly streamlined process. You can serve it as fillets or let folks dig in with their own forks and knives.

We like grilling **black sea bass**, **branzino**, **mackerel**, **red snapper**, and **trout** whole, and all five of these are easy to find at a good fish counter. Black sea bass, branzino (European sea bass), and red snapper are similar in size and should be filleted after cooking to serve two. Mackerel and trout are nice because each fish serves one.

Usually, these fish will be scaled and gutted (ask your fishmonger to do this for you if they're not); you may just need to snip off the fins with kitchen scissors before cooking. Trout often have their backbones and pin bones removed for even less fuss. But for any of these fish, it's a good idea to look out for translucent pin bones when eating—they're part of the whole-fish experience.

BLACK SEA BASS

BRANZINO

MACKEREL

RED SNAPPER

TROUT

HOW TO FLIP FISH ON THE GRILL

To turn delicate fish on the grill without breaking it, use two thin metal spatulas; fish spatulas work best.

WHOLE FISH

1 Using spatula, lift bottom of thick backbone edge of fish from cooking grate just enough to slide second spatula under fish.

2 Remove first spatula, then use it to support raw side of fish as you use second spatula to flip fish.

FISH FILLETS

Place 1 spatula on each side of fillet and use spatulas to gently roll fillet onto opposite side.

DONENESS TEST

An instant-read thermometer is a useful tool for checking doneness in fish, but it's also handy to know how to use a more primitive test—nicking the fish with a paring knife and then peeking into the interior to judge color and flakiness. Whitefish, such as cod and trout, should be cooked to medium (about 135 degrees)—that is, the flesh should be opaque but still moist and just beginning to flake; salmon is best cooked to medium-rare (about 125 degrees), with the center still translucent; and tuna is best when rare (about 110 degrees), with only the outer layer opaque and the rest of the fish translucent.

HOW TO FILLET A GRILLED WHOLE FISH

1 Use sharp knife to make vertical cut just behind head from top of fish to belly.

2 Make horizontal cut along back of fish from head to tail.

3 Starting at head and working toward tail, use metal fish spatula to lift top fillet away from bones.

4 Lift and remove tail and skeleton and cut away head from remaining fillet. Discard head and skeleton.

FOOD SCIENCE

What Makes Fish Delicate

Compared to land animals, fish have much shorter muscle fibers and their muscle contains much less connective tissue. Fish collagen (the main protein in connective tissue) is more fragile than that of land animals and transforms into gelatin at lower temperatures. These factors make fish prone to flaking apart on the grill.

As with meat, there are differences between varieties of fish that call for different grilling strategies. Oiling the grate well (see page 11) is always a good start, and keeping the skin on fish also helps hold it together while grilling. Some fish, such as tuna and swordfish, have stronger intermuscular structure and can be grilled like steaks. For very delicate fish like cod, we sometimes avoid contact with the grate altogether by grilling it in a foil pouch.

GAMBAS A LA PLANCHA

Gambas a la Plancha

SERVES 4 to 6 as an appetizer **TIME** 40 minutes

Why This Recipe Works This iconic tapas dish is supremely satisfying and elemental—a simple food that you eat with your hands, straight off the grill if you're impatient. The shrimp are traditionally served with their heads on so that after gently twisting apart the head and body, you can suck the flavorful juices out of the head. Brining the shrimp before grilling keeps them especially plump and juicy. Employing a plancha gives the shrimp the flavor of the grill while allowing them to retain those juices that would otherwise be lost between the bars of the grate. A lemony garlic paste adheres perfectly and then coats your fingers as you peel and eat the shrimp. If head-on shrimp are unavailable, you can substitute extra-large, unpeeled, head-off shrimp. We prefer shrimp that have not been treated with salt or additives such as sodium tripolyphosphate (STPP). You will need a cast-iron plancha measuring at least 20 by 10 inches. A rasp grater makes quick work of turning the garlic into a paste. This recipe was developed using Diamond Crystal kosher salt. If you have Morton kosher salt, which is denser, use 6 tablespoons.

- ½ cup kosher salt for brining
- ¼ cup sugar for brining
- 2 pounds shell-on, head-on extra-large shrimp (10 to 15 per pound)
- 2 tablespoons extra-virgin olive oil
- 2 large garlic cloves, minced to paste
- 2 teaspoons lemon juice, plus 1 lemon, halved
- 1 teaspoon smoked paprika
- ¼ teaspoon cayenne pepper

1 Dissolve salt and sugar in 2 quarts cold water in large container. Submerge shrimp in brine, cover, and refrigerate for 15 minutes. Drain shrimp.

2 Combine oil, garlic, lemon juice, paprika, and cayenne in large bowl. Add shrimp and toss to coat. (Shrimp can be refrigerated for up to 1 hour.)

3A **FOR A CHARCOAL GRILL** Open bottom vent completely. Light large chimney starter filled with charcoal briquettes (6 quarts). When top coals are partially covered with ash, pour evenly over grill. Set cooking grate in place, center plancha on grill, cover, and open lid vent completely. Heat grill with plancha until hot, about 5 minutes.

3B **FOR A GAS GRILL** Turn all burners to high; cover; and heat grill until hot, about 15 minutes. Center plancha on grill, cover, and heat for 5 more minutes. Leave all burners on high.

4 Arrange half of shrimp on plancha in even layer and cook until shells are bright pink and just beginning to char and shrimp are opaque throughout, 2 to 6 minutes, flipping halfway through cooking. Transfer shrimp to platter and repeat with remaining shrimp. Meanwhile, cook lemon halves, cut side down, on open space of plancha until well charred, 2 to 4 minutes; set aside for serving. Serve shrimp warm or at room temperature, with lemon.

GRILLED CHIPOTLE SHRIMP

Grilled Chipotle Shrimp

SERVES 4 as a main dish or 6 to 8 as an appetizer
TIME 25 minutes

Why This Recipe Works Grilling shrimp comes with one big inherent challenge: getting nice char on the shrimp while keeping them tender and moist. To prevent overcooking, we use larger shrimp so that they can stay on the grill for a few seconds longer. We nestle them together on pairs of wooden skewers, which insulates individual shrimp and helps prevent them from drying out. We use mayonnaise here as a marinade; because it's oil-based, it enhances browning and prevents sticking, all while staying where we want it—on the shrimp. Canned chipotle chiles, fresh cilantro, lime juice, and spices add a big pop of flavor. The skewered shrimp are easy to transfer directly from grill to plate as a main course, or you can remove them from the skewers and load up a platter to serve as an appetizer. For this recipe, we like using jumbo shrimp (16 to 20 per pound), but extra-large shrimp (21 to 25 per pound) work as well, although you will need more skewers and the cooking time will be about 3 minutes . We prefer shrimp that have not been treated with salt or additives such as sodium tripolyphosphate (STPP).

- ¼ cup mayonnaise
- ¼ cup chopped fresh cilantro
- 3 tablespoons chopped canned chipotle chile in adobo sauce, plus 1 tablespoon adobo sauce
- 5 garlic cloves, minced
- 1 tablespoon lime juice, plus lime wedges for serving
- 1 teaspoon ground cumin
- 1 teaspoon paprika
- 1 teaspoon sugar
- 1 teaspoon kosher salt
- 2 pounds jumbo shrimp (16 to 20 per pound), peeled and deveined
- 8 (10-inch) wooden skewers

1 Whisk mayonnaise, cilantro, chipotle and adobo sauce, garlic, lime juice, cumin, paprika, sugar, and salt together in large bowl. Add shrimp and toss to coat.

2 Thread shrimp tightly, all facing same direction, onto sets of 2 skewers.

3A **FOR A CHARCOAL GRILL** Open bottom vent completely. Light large chimney starter mounded with charcoal briquettes (7 quarts). When top coals are partially covered with ash, pour evenly over grill. Set cooking grate in place, cover, and open lid vent completely. Heat grill until hot, about 5 minutes.

3B **FOR A GAS GRILL** Turn all burners to high; cover; and heat grill until hot, about 15 minutes. Leave all burners on high.

4 Clean cooking grate, then repeatedly brush grate with well-oiled paper towels until grate is black and glossy, 5 to 10 times. Place shrimp on grill and cook (covered if using gas), flipping as needed, until lightly charred and opaque throughout, about 4 minutes. Serve with lime wedges.

GRILLED JALAPEÑO-LIME SHRIMP SKEWERS

Grilled Jalapeño-Lime Shrimp Skewers

SERVES 4 **TIME** 30 minutes plus 30 minutes marinating

Why This Recipe Works Grill char and spicy heat can enhance the delicately sweet and briny flavor of shrimp. After skewering the shrimp, we sprinkle one side with sugar and grill this side over direct heat for a few minutes for quick browning. Then we flip the skewers and finish cooking them on the cooler side of the grill. We mix up a zesty—but not punishingly spicy—marinade with jalapeños, garlic, and lime juice and set a bit of it aside so we can give the grilled shrimp a quick dip before serving. We prefer shrimp that have not been treated with salt or additives such as sodium tripolyphosphate (STPP). Use the larger amount of jalapeños for a spicier marinade. You will need four 12-inch metal skewers for this recipe.

MARINADE

- 1–2 jalapeño chiles, stemmed, seeded, and chopped
- 3 tablespoons extra-virgin olive oil
- 6 garlic cloves, minced
- 1 teaspoon grated lime zest plus 5 tablespoons juice (3 limes)
- ½ teaspoon ground cumin
- 1 teaspoon kosher salt
- ¼ teaspoon cayenne pepper

SHRIMP

- 1½ pounds extra-large shrimp (21 to 25 per pound), peeled and deveined
- ½ teaspoon sugar
- 1 tablespoon minced fresh cilantro

1 FOR THE MARINADE Process all ingredients in food processor until smooth, about 15 seconds. Measure out 2 tablespoons marinade and set aside for serving. Transfer remaining marinade to bowl.

2 FOR THE SHRIMP Pat shrimp dry with paper towels, add to bowl with remaining marinade, and toss to coat. Cover and refrigerate for at least 30 minutes or up to 1 hour. Remove shrimp from marinade (do not pat dry) and thread tightly onto four 12-inch metal skewers, alternating direction of heads and tails. Sprinkle 1 side of skewered shrimp with sugar.

3A FOR A CHARCOAL GRILL Open bottom vent completely. Light large chimney starter filled with charcoal briquettes (6 quarts). When top coals are partially covered with ash, pour evenly over half of grill. Set cooking grate in place, cover, and open lid vent completely. Heat grill until hot, about 5 minutes.

3B FOR A GAS GRILL Turn all burners to high; cover; and heat grill until hot, about 15 minutes. Leave all burners on high.

4 Clean cooking grate, then repeatedly brush grate with well-oiled paper towels until grate is black and glossy, 5 to 10 times. Place shrimp sugared side down on grill (hotter side if using charcoal) and cook until lightly charred, 3 to 4 minutes. Flip skewers and slide to cooler side of grill (if using charcoal). Cover and cook until second side of shrimp is no longer translucent, 1 to 2 minutes. Using tongs, slide shrimp off skewers into clean bowl and toss with reserved marinade. Transfer shrimp to platter and sprinkle with cilantro. Serve.

VARIATIONS

Grilled Caribbean Shrimp Skewers

Serrano chiles can be used here in place of the habanero chiles.

For marinade, substitute following mixture for pureed marinade in step 1: Process 1–2 seeded and chopped habanero chiles; ¼ cup pineapple juice; 2 tablespoons extra-virgin olive oil; 3 minced garlic cloves; 1 teaspoon grated lime zest; 1 teaspoon grated fresh ginger; 1 teaspoon kosher salt; ¼ teaspoon ground allspice; 1 teaspoon packed brown sugar; and 1 teaspoon dried thyme until smooth, about 15 seconds. For shrimp, substitute fresh parsley for cilantro.

Grilled Red Chile–Ginger Shrimp Skewers

For marinade, substitute following mixture for pureed marinade in step 1: Process 1–3 seeded and chopped small red chiles; 3 tablespoons rice vinegar; 2 tablespoons soy sauce; 1 tablespoon toasted sesame oil; 1 tablespoon grated fresh ginger; 1 minced scallion; 2 teaspoons sugar; and 1 minced garlic clove until smooth, about 15 seconds. For shrimp, substitute 1 thinly sliced scallion for cilantro and serve with lime wedges.

Grilled Shrimp Skewers with Chili Crisp and Napa Cabbage Slaw

SERVES 4 **TIME** 30 minutes

Why This Recipe Works Chili crisp, aka lao gan ma, or "godmother sauce," is magical when applied to sweet, briny shrimp fresh off the grill. The skewered, grilled, and seasoned shrimp get an easy-prep side: a refreshing slaw of napa cabbage, scallions, and cilantro, with dry-roasted peanuts for a salty crunch. We prefer shrimp that have not been treated with salt or additives such as sodium tripolyphosphate (STPP). You will need four 12-inch metal skewers for this recipe.

- 2 pounds jumbo shrimp (16 to 20 per pound), peeled and deveined
- ¼ cup vegetable oil, divided
- ¼ teaspoon pepper
- 2 tablespoons white wine vinegar
- 1 teaspoon kosher salt
- 1 small head napa cabbage (1½ pounds), cored and sliced thin
- 4 scallions, sliced thin on bias
- 1 cup fresh cilantro leaves
- ¼ cup salted dry-roasted peanuts, chopped
- ¼ cup chili crisp, plus extra for serving

1 Thread shrimp tightly onto four 12-inch metal skewers, alternating direction of heads and tails. Pat shrimp dry with paper towels, then brush with 1 tablespoon oil and sprinkle with pepper.

2 Whisk remaining 3 tablespoons oil, vinegar, and salt together in large bowl. Add cabbage, scallions, and cilantro and toss to coat. Season with salt and pepper to taste. Sprinkle with peanuts; set aside for serving.

3A FOR A CHARCOAL GRILL Open bottom vent completely. Light large chimney starter mounded with charcoal briquettes (7 quarts). When top coals are partially covered with ash, pour evenly over grill. Set cooking grate in place, cover, and open lid vent completely. Heat grill until hot, about 5 minutes.

3B FOR A GAS GRILL Turn all burners to high; cover; and heat grill until hot, about 15 minutes. Leave all burners on high.

4 Clean cooking grate, then repeatedly brush grate with well-oiled paper towels until grate is black and glossy, 5 to 10 times. Place shrimp on grill and cook (covered if using gas), turning as needed, until lightly charred and opaque throughout, about 4 minutes. Using tongs, slide shrimp off skewers onto serving platter and brush with chili crisp. Serve shrimp with slaw, passing extra chili crisp separately.

GRILLED SHRIMP TACOS WITH JICAMA SLAW

Grilled Shrimp Tacos with Jicama Slaw

SERVES 6 **TIME** 35 minutes

Why This Recipe Works The shrimp in these fresh-tasting, easy-to-make grilled tacos are coated with an ultraflavorful spice rub. For a lively slaw to accompany the spicy shrimp, we thinly slice delicately flavored, crunchy jicama and toss it with orange juice, red onion, and fresh cilantro. We prefer shrimp that have not been treated with salt or additives such as sodium tripolyphosphate (STPP). To cut the jicama, use the shredding disk of a food processor, a V-slicer, or a sharp chef's knife. You will need four 12-inch metal skewers for this recipe. Serve with chopped onion, diced avocado, thinly sliced radishes, and Mexican crema (to make your own crema, see page 397).

- 1 pound jicama, peeled and cut into 3-inch-long matchsticks
- ¼ cup thinly sliced red onion
- 3 tablespoons chopped fresh cilantro
- 1 teaspoon grated orange zest plus ⅓ cup juice
- 2 teaspoons kosher salt, divided
- 3 tablespoons vegetable oil
- 1 tablespoon minced fresh oregano or 1 teaspoon dried
- 2 teaspoons chipotle chile powder
- 1 teaspoon garlic powder
- 2 pounds extra-large shrimp (21 to 25 per pound), peeled, deveined, and tails removed
- 18 (6-inch) corn tortillas
- Lime wedges

1 Combine jicama, onion, cilantro, orange zest and juice, and 1 teaspoon salt in bowl; cover and refrigerate until ready to serve.

2 Whisk oil, oregano, chile powder, garlic powder, and remaining 1 teaspoon salt together in large bowl. Pat shrimp dry with paper towels, add to spice mixture, and toss to coat. Thread shrimp tightly onto four 12-inch metal skewers, alternating direction of heads and tails.

3A **FOR A CHARCOAL GRILL** Open bottom vent completely. Light large chimney starter mounded with charcoal briquettes (7 quarts). When top coals are partially covered with ash, pour evenly over grill. Set cooking grate in place, cover, and open lid vent completely. Heat grill until hot, about 5 minutes.

3B **FOR A GAS GRILL** Turn all burners to high; cover; and heat grill until hot, about 15 minutes. Leave all burners on high.

4 Clean cooking grate, then repeatedly brush grate with well-oiled paper towels until grate is black and glossy, 5 to 10 times. Place shrimp on grill and cook (covered if using gas) until lightly charred on first side, about 4 minutes. Flip shrimp, pushing them together on skewer if they separate, and cook until opaque throughout, about 2 minutes. Transfer to platter and cover with aluminum foil.

5 Working in batches, grill tortillas, turning as needed, until warm and soft, about 1 minute; wrap tightly in aluminum foil to keep soft.

6 Slide shrimp off skewers onto cutting board and cut into ½-inch pieces. Serve with tortillas, jicama slaw, and lime wedges.

Grilled Shrimp, Corn, and Avocado Salad

SERVES 4 **TIME** 40 minutes

Why This Recipe Works Grill-charred fresh corn and sweet jumbo shrimp are a favorite light summertime meal, combined here with crisp romaine hearts in a dinner salad. Avocados keep their buttery, grassy flavor but become crisped and smoky when grilled. Lime on the grill is also a slam dunk: It develops a caramelized flavor element that adds nuance to its acidity and makes for a superstar salad dressing. Extra-large shrimp (21 to 25 per pound) can be substituted for jumbo shrimp; reduce the total cooking time in step 4 by about 1 minute. We prefer shrimp that have not been treated with salt or additives such as sodium tripolyphosphate (STPP). You will need four 12-inch metal skewers for this recipe.

- 2 ripe but firm avocados, halved and pitted
- 6 tablespoons extra-virgin olive oil, divided
- 3 ears corn, husks and silk removed
- 2 teaspoons kosher salt, divided
- 1 teaspoon pepper, divided
- 2 pounds jumbo shrimp (16 to 20 per pound), peeled and deveined
- 2 teaspoons grated lime zest plus 2 limes, halved
- 3 romaine lettuce hearts (6 ounces each), halved lengthwise and chopped

1 Rub cut sides of avocados with 1 teaspoon oil. Rub corn all over with 2 teaspoons oil and sprinkle with 1 teaspoon salt and ½ teaspoon pepper. Thread shrimp tightly onto four 12-inch metal skewers, alternating direction of heads and tails. Pat shrimp dry with paper towels, then brush with 1 tablespoon oil and sprinkle with ½ teaspoon salt and ¼ teaspoon pepper.

2A FOR A CHARCOAL GRILL Open bottom vent completely. Light large chimney starter filled with charcoal briquettes (6 quarts). When top coals are partially covered with ash, pour evenly over grill. Set cooking grate in place, cover, and open lid vent completely. Heat grill until hot, about 5 minutes.

2B FOR A GAS GRILL Turn all burners to high; cover; and heat grill until hot, about 15 minutes. Leave all burners on high.

3 Clean and oil cooking grate, then repeatedly brush grate with well-oiled paper towels until grate is black and glossy, 5 to 10 times. Place corn on grill and cook (covered if using gas), turning as needed, until charred on all sides, 10 to 13 minutes. Meanwhile, place avocados and lime halves cut sides down on grill and cook until lightly charred, about 2 minutes. Transfer corn, avocados and limes to cutting board as they finish cooking.

4 Place shrimp on grill and cook (covered if using gas) until lightly charred and opaque throughout, about 4 minutes, flipping halfway through cooking. Using tongs, slide shrimp off skewers into clean bowl and toss with 1 tablespoon oil and lime zest.

5 Scoop flesh from charred avocado halves and cut into 1-inch pieces. Cut kernels from cobs. Juice limes to yield ¼ cup. Whisk lime juice, remaining 3 tablespoons oil, remaining ½ teaspoon salt, and remaining ¼ teaspoon pepper together in large bowl. Add romaine, avocado, corn, and shrimp to dressing and toss gently to combine. Season with salt and pepper to taste. Serve.

Grilled Shrimp Boil Foil Packs

SERVES 4 **TIME** 45 minutes

Why This Recipe Works This quick and easy dinner brings all the elements of a shrimp boil—shrimp, potatoes, corn, and sausage—out to the grill, in single-serving foil packs. We give them that traditional shrimp boil flavor with Old Bay, lemon, and butter. To ensure that the potatoes cook through on the grill, we parcook them in the microwave first. We prefer shrimp that have not been treated with salt or additives such as sodium tripolyphosphate (STPP). Use small red potatoes measuring 1 to 2 inches in diameter. To keep the packs from tearing, use heavy-duty aluminum foil.

- 1 pound small red potatoes, unpeeled, halved
- 10 tablespoons unsalted butter, cut into 1-tablespoon pieces, divided
- ½ teaspoon kosher salt
- ¼ teaspoon pepper
- 1½ pounds extra-large shrimp (21 to 25 per pound), peeled and deveined
- 3 ears corn, husks and silk removed, each cut into 3 pieces
- 8 ounces andouille sausage, sliced ½ inch thick
- 2 tablespoons Old Bay seasoning
- 4 garlic cloves, minced
- 1 tablespoon lemon juice, plus lemon wedges for serving
- 2 tablespoons chopped fresh parsley

1 Toss potatoes with 2 tablespoons butter, salt, and pepper in large bowl. Microwave, covered, until potatoes begin to release moisture, about 5 minutes. Toss potatoes to coat with now-melted butter and let cool slightly, about 5 minutes. Toss potatoes with shrimp, corn, andouille, Old Bay, garlic, and lemon juice.

2 Cut four 16 by 12-inch sheets of aluminum foil. Spread one-quarter of shrimp mixture over half of each piece of foil. Evenly distribute remaining 8 tablespoons butter over shrimp mixture. Fold foil over mixture and crimp edges tightly to seal.

3A FOR A CHARCOAL GRILL Open bottom vent completely. Light large chimney starter filled with charcoal briquettes (6 quarts). When top coals are partially covered with ash, pour evenly over grill. Set cooking grate in place, cover, and open lid vent completely. Heat grill until hot, about 5 minutes.

3B FOR A GAS GRILL Turn all burners to high; cover; and heat grill until hot, about 15 minutes. Leave all burners on high.

4 Place packets on grill; cover; and cook until potatoes are fully tender and shrimp is cooked through, about 12 minutes. Remove packets from grill. When cool enough to handle, carefully cut packets open and sprinkle with parsley. Serve with lemon wedges.

Grilled Clams, Mussels, or Oysters with Soy-Citrus Sauce

SERVES 4 to 6 as an appetizer **TIME** 25 minutes

Why This Recipe Works Grill one, two, or all three types of briny-sweet mollusks to elicit plenty of oohs and aahs at your next outdoor gathering. They look fancy, but they're incredibly simple. There's no shucking necessary—when they're open, they're done. While the grill heats, you'll want to scrub the shells carefully to rid them of any grit, and you can also stir together the drizzling sauce. Once the shellfish are on the grill, the keys to success are to not move them around too much and to handle them carefully once they open: As you transfer the open bivalves with tongs to a platter, hold them steady so as not to spill any of their flavorful juices. Always look for tightly closed clams, mussels, and oysters (avoid any that are gaping; they may be dying or dead).

- ½ cup soy sauce
- 1 tablespoon lemon juice
- 1 tablespoon lime juice
- 1 scallion, sliced thin
- 1 teaspoon grated fresh ginger
- 30–35 mussels (about 2 pounds), scrubbed and debearded, or 24 clams or oysters
- Lemon wedges

1 Combine soy sauce, lemon juice, lime juice, scallion, and ginger in small bowl. Set sauce aside for serving.

2A FOR A CHARCOAL GRILL Open bottom vent completely. Light large chimney starter filled with charcoal briquettes (6 quarts). When top coals are partially covered with ash, pour evenly over grill. Set cooking grate in place, cover, and open lid vent completely. Heat grill until hot, about 5 minutes.

2B FOR A GAS GRILL Turn all burners to high; cover; and heat grill until hot, about 15 minutes. Leave all burners on high.

3 Clean and oil cooking grate. Place shellfish directly on cooking grate, cupped side down if grilling oysters. Cook (covered if using gas), without turning, until shellfish open, 3 to 6 minutes for mussels and oysters or 6 to 12 minutes for clams.

4 Using tongs, carefully transfer opened shellfish to flat serving platter, trying to preserve juices. Discard top shells and loosen meat in bottom shells before serving, if desired. Serve with soy-citrus sauce and lemon wedges.

GRILLED CLAMS, MUSSELS, OR OYSTERS WITH SOY-CITRUS SAUCE

Serving Clams, Mussels, and Oysters

The easiest way to serve grilled clams, mussels, or oysters is to divide them among small plates and give each person a small fork. However, if you want guests to eat them while milling about, try this: Holding each clam, mussel, or oyster in a dish towel as it comes off the grill, pull off and discard the top shell and then slide a paring knife under the meat to detach it from the bottom shell. By the time you have done this to each clam, mussel, or oyster, the shells should have cooled enough to permit everyone to pick them up and slurp the meat directly from the shells.

Grilled Scallops with Chile-Lime Vinaigrette

SERVES 4 **TIME** 40 minutes

Why This Recipe Works A quick blast of heat works wonders for scallops, deeply browning their exteriors while leaving their centers plump and moist. It's the perfect job for the grill. To get them lightly charred on the outside, tender inside, and tinged with smoke flavor, we build a concentrated fire, corralling the coals in a disposable aluminum pan set in the bottom of the grill. We lightly coat the scallops with a slurry of vegetable oil, flour, cornstarch, and sugar and then thread them onto pairs of metal skewers. The slurry keeps the scallops from sticking, the sugar promotes browning, and the double skewers prevent the scallops from spinning when turned. Choose from a trio of boldly flavored vinaigrettes to complement these juicy, smoky scallops. We recommend buying "dry" scallops, which don't have chemical additives and taste better than "wet." Dry scallops look ivory or pinkish; wet scallops are bright white. This recipe was developed with large sea scallops (sold 10 to 20 per pound). You will need eight to twelve 12-inch metal skewers for this recipe. If you prefer, serve the grilled scallops with lemon wedges instead of the vinaigrette.

SCALLOPS

- 1½ pounds large sea scallops, tendons removed
- 1 (13 by 9-inch) disposable aluminum roasting pan (if using charcoal)
- 2 tablespoons vegetable oil
- 1 tablespoon all-purpose flour
- 1 teaspoon cornstarch
- 1 teaspoon sugar
- ½ teaspoon kosher salt
- ½ teaspoon pepper

CHILE-LIME VINAIGRETTE

- 1 teaspoon finely grated lime zest plus 3 tablespoons juice (2 limes)
- 1 tablespoon sriracha
- 2 tablespoons honey
- 2 teaspoons fish sauce
- ½ cup vegetable oil

1 FOR THE SCALLOPS Place scallops on rimmed baking sheet lined with clean dish towel. Place second clean dish towel on top of scallops and press gently on towel to blot liquid. Let scallops sit at room temperature, covered with towel, for 10 minutes. Thread scallops onto sets of two 12-inch metal skewers all facing same direction. Return skewered scallops to towel-lined sheet; refrigerate, covered with second towel, while preparing grill.

2 FOR THE CHILE-LIME VINAIGRETTE Whisk lime zest and juice, sriracha, honey, and fish sauce until combined. Whisking constantly, slowly drizzle in oil until emulsified; set aside for serving.

3 Before cooking, whisk oil, flour, cornstarch, and sugar together in small bowl. Brush both sides of skewered scallops with oil mixture and sprinkle with salt and pepper.

4A FOR A CHARCOAL GRILL Light large chimney starter mounded with charcoal briquettes (7 quarts). Poke twelve ½-inch holes in bottom of disposable pan and place in center of grill. When top coals are partially covered with ash, pour into disposable pan.

4B FOR A GAS GRILL Turn all burners to high; cover; and heat grill until hot, about 15 minutes. Leave all burners on high.

5 Clean cooking grate, then repeatedly brush grate with well-oiled paper towels until grate is black and glossy, 5 to 10 times. Place scallops on grill (over coals if using charcoal). Cook (covered if using gas) without moving scallops until lightly browned, 2½ to 4 minutes. Carefully flip skewers and cook until second side is browned, sides of scallops are firm, and centers are opaque, 2 to 4 minutes. Serve immediately with vinaigrette.

VARIATIONS

Grilled Scallops with Basil Vinaigrette

Substitute following mixture for Chile-Lime Vinaigrette: Pulse 1 cup packed fresh basil leaves, 3 tablespoons minced fresh chives, 2 tablespoons champagne vinegar, 2 minced garlic cloves, 2 teaspoons sugar, 2 teaspoons kosher salt, and ½ teaspoon pepper in blender until coarsely chopped. With blender running, slowly drizzle in ⅔ cup vegetable oil until emulsified, scraping down sides of blender jar as necessary.

Grilled Scallops with Barbecue Sauce Vinaigrette

Substitute following mixture for Chile-Lime Vinaigrette: Whisk 3 tablespoons barbecue sauce, 2 tablespoons cider vinegar, 1 tablespoon ketchup, 2 teaspoons sugar, and 1 teaspoon kosher salt together in medium bowl. Whisking constantly, slowly drizzle in ½ cup vegetable oil until emulsified.

GRILLED SCALLOPS WITH CHILE-LIME VINAIGRETTE

GRILLED BACON-WRAPPED SCALLOPS

Grilled Bacon-Wrapped Scallops

SERVES 4 **TIME** 40 minutes

Why This Recipe Works Smoky, salty bacon beautifully accents sweet, succulent scallops, and taking this duo to the grill makes a great thing even better. We microwave the bacon to render its fat; then, a two-level fire cooks both scallops and bacon to perfection. A spritz of juice from grilled lemons and a sprinkling of chopped chives gives the dish a bright finish. We recommend buying "dry" scallops, which don't have chemical additives and taste better than "wet." Dry scallops look ivory or pinkish; wet scallops are bright white. Use regular bacon, as thick-cut bacon will take too long to crisp on the grill. When wrapping the scallops, the bacon slice should fit around both scallops, overlapping just enough to be skewered through both ends. This recipe was developed with large sea scallops (sold 10 to 20 per pound). You will need four 12-inch metal skewers for this recipe.

- 12 slices bacon
- 24 large sea scallops, tendons removed
- 3 tablespoons unsalted butter, melted
- 1 teaspoon kosher salt
- ⅛ teaspoon pepper
- 2 lemons, halved
- ¼ cup chopped fresh chives

1 Place 4 layers paper towels on large plate and arrange 6 slices bacon over towels in single layer. Top with 4 more paper towels and remaining 6 slices bacon. Cover with 2 layers of paper towels; place second large plate on top and press gently to flatten. Microwave until fat begins to render but bacon is still pliable, about 4 minutes.

2 Toss scallops, melted butter, salt, and pepper together in bowl until scallops are thoroughly coated with butter. Press 2 scallops together, side to side, and wrap with 1 slice bacon, trimming excess as necessary. Thread onto metal skewer through bacon. Repeat with remaining scallops and bacon, threading 3 bundles onto each of 4 skewers.

3A **FOR A CHARCOAL GRILL** Open bottom vent completely. Light large chimney starter filled with charcoal briquettes (6 quarts). When top coals are partially covered with ash, pour two-thirds evenly over half of grill, then pour remaining coals over other half of grill. Set cooking grate in place, cover, and open lid vent completely. Heat grill until hot, about 5 minutes.

3B **FOR A GAS GRILL** Turn all burners to high, cover, and heat grill until hot, about 15 minutes. Leave primary burner on high and turn other burner(s) to medium.

4 Clean and oil cooking grate. Place skewers, bacon side down, and lemon halves, cut side down, on cooler side of grill. Cook (covered if using gas) until bacon is crispy on first side, about 4 minutes. Turn skewers onto other bacon side and cook until crispy, about 4 minutes. Turn skewers scallop side down, slide to hotter side of grill, and cook (without turning) until sides of scallops are firm and centers are opaque, about 4 minutes. Transfer skewers to platter, squeeze lemons over top, and sprinkle with chives. Serve.

Grilled Lobsters

SERVES 2 as a main dish or 4 as an appetizer
TIME 30 minutes

Why This Recipe Works Grilling maximizes the sweetness of lobster, but it can be tricky to do right: Because lobster cooks quickly, there's only a small window of opportunity to develop grill flavor. And the claws take longer to cook than the tails, which tend to curl up tightly as they grill. A little butchering takes care of these issues. We split the lobsters lengthwise, which tames the tails and also helps the smoky grill flavor penetrate the meat. To help speed the cooking of the claws, we crack the shells by whacking them with the back of a chef's knife or pounding them lightly with a meat pounder so that the heat can better reach the meat. A buttery stuffing with panko, garlic, and parsley adds flavor partway through grilling. We also brush the lobsters with garlic butter before and during grilling for even richer flavor. Lobsters that are 1½ to 2 pounds fit comfortably on the cooking grate and can stay on the grill long enough to absorb plenty of flavor. Add the tomalley to the stuffing if you like. If you'd rather not butcher a live lobster, have the fishmonger do it for you at the store; just make sure to cook and eat it within a few hours.

- 2 (1½- to 2-pound) live lobsters
- ¼ cup panko bread crumbs
- 1 teaspoon vegetable oil
- 6 tablespoons unsalted butter, melted
- 2 cloves garlic, minced
- 2 tablespoons minced fresh parsley
- 1 teaspoon kosher salt, divided
- ¼ teaspoon pepper, divided
- Lemon wedges

1 Place lobsters in large bowl and freeze for 30 minutes. Toss panko with oil in bowl until evenly coated. Microwave, stirring frequently, until panko is light golden brown, about 2 minutes; set aside.

2A FOR A CHARCOAL GRILL Open bottom vent completely. Light large chimney starter filled with charcoal briquettes (6 quarts). When top coals are partially covered with ash, pour evenly over grill. Set cooking grate in place, cover, and open lid vent completely. Heat grill until hot, about 5 minutes.

2B FOR A GAS GRILL Turn all burners to high; cover; and heat grill until hot, about 15 minutes. Leave all burners on high.

3 Meanwhile, combine melted butter and garlic in bowl. In second bowl, combine toasted panko, parsley, ½ teaspoon salt, ⅛ teaspoon pepper, and 2 tablespoons garlic butter; set aside. Split lobsters in half lengthwise, then clean and devein lobsters. Using back of chef's knife or meat pounder, whack each claw to crack open slightly. Sprinkle tail meat with remaining ½ teaspoon salt and remaining ⅛ teaspoon pepper and brush lobster meat evenly with 2 tablespoons garlic butter.

4 Clean cooking grate, then repeatedly brush grate with well-oiled paper towels until grate is black and glossy, 5 to 10 times. Place lobsters, cut side down, on grill and cook (covered if using gas) until tail meat just begins to turn opaque, about 2 minutes.

5 Transfer lobsters, cut side up, to rimmed baking sheet. Divide panko mixture evenly among lobster halves and drizzle with remaining 2 tablespoons garlic butter. Return lobsters, shell side down, to grill and cook (covered if using gas) until panko mixture begins to bubble and tail meat is opaque and registers 140 degrees, 4 to 6 minutes. Serve lobsters with lemon wedges.

VARIATION

Grilled Lobsters with Tarragon-Chive Butter

In step 3, add 2 teaspoons minced fresh chives and 1 teaspoon minced fresh tarragon to garlic butter. Replace parsley in panko mixture with 2 tablespoons minced fresh chives and 2 teaspoons minced fresh tarragon.

GRILLED LOBSTERS

Preparing Lobsters for the Grill

1 Plunge chef's knife into body at point where shell forms "T" to kill lobster. Move blade straight down through head. (Freezing lobster for 5 to 10 minutes first will sedate it.)

2 Turn lobster around and, while holding upper body with your hand, cut through body toward tail.

3 Remove and discard stomach and intestinal tract. Remove green tomalley; reserve if desired. Remove rubber bands, then crack claw shells slightly by whacking them with back of chef's knife or meat pounder.

GRILLED LOBSTER TAILS

Grilled Lobster Tails

SERVES 4 **TIME** 30 minutes

Why This Recipe Works When you want to grill a meal to impress, you can't miss with lobster. Using frozen lobster tails makes this dinner easy to prep, serve, and eat. We cut the tails in half to speed up the cooking time and expose the meat for optimum flavor and browning from the grill. The exposed meat is also the perfect bed for a good dose of butter and some garlicky bread crumbs. For the best flavor, thaw the lobster tails slowly in the refrigerator for 24 hours before cooking. Handle the lobsters gently after the crumb topping is added in step 4.

- 6 tablespoons unsalted butter, melted
- 3 garlic cloves, minced
- ½ cup panko bread crumbs
- 3 tablespoons minced fresh parsley
- 1 teaspoon kosher salt, divided
- ¼ teaspoon pepper, divided
- 4 (4½- to 6-ounce) frozen lobster tails, thawed and patted dry
- Lemon wedges

1 Combine melted butter and garlic in bowl. Toast panko in 10-inch skillet over medium heat, stirring often, until golden, about 4 minutes. Transfer panko to small bowl, let cool slightly, then stir in parsley, ½ teaspoon salt, ⅛ teaspoon pepper, and 3 tablespoons garlic butter. Using sharp knife, cut lobster tails in half lengthwise and devein (if necessary). Sprinkle lobster meat with remaining ½ teaspoon salt and ⅛ teaspoon pepper.

2A **FOR A CHARCOAL GRILL** Open bottom vent completely. Light large chimney starter filled with charcoal briquettes (6 quarts). When top coals are partially covered with ash, pour evenly over grill. Set cooking grate in place, cover, and open lid vent completely. Heat grill until hot, about 5 minutes.

2B **FOR A GAS GRILL** Turn all burners to high; cover; and heat grill until hot, about 15 minutes. Leave all burners on high.

3 Clean cooking grate, then repeatedly brush grate with well-oiled paper towels until grate is black and glossy, 5 to 10 times. Place lobster tails, cut side down, on grill and cook (covered if using gas) until tail meat just begins to turn opaque, about 3 minutes. Transfer lobsters, cut side up, to rimmed baking sheet. Drizzle with remaining 3 tablespoons garlic butter and gently pack panko mixture into tail.

4 Return lobster tails, shell side down, to grill and cook (covered if using gas) until meat is opaque and registers 140 degrees, 4 to 8 minutes. Serve lobster tails with lemon wedges.

Paella on the Grill

SERVES 8 **TIME** 1½ hours

Why This Recipe Works Grilled paella has a subtle smokiness and is a great dish for outdoor entertaining. We use a large, sturdy roasting pan that maximizes the amount of socarrat, the prized caramelized rice crust that forms on the bottom of the pan. We build a long-lasting fire and streamline the cooking process to make this start-to-finish on the grill in a manageable amount of time. To ensure that the various components finish cooking at the same time, we stagger the addition of the proteins—chicken thighs followed by the shrimp, clams, and chorizo. We also place the chicken on the perimeter of the pan, where it finishes cooking gently after grilling, and the seafood and sausage in the center, where they're partially submerged in the liquid, so they cook through gently; once the liquid reduces, the steam keeps them warm. This recipe was developed using a light-colored 16 by 13.5-inch tri-ply roasting pan; however, it can be made in any heavy roasting pan that measures at least 14 by 11 inches. If your roasting pan is dark in color, the cooking times will be on the lower end of the ranges given. The recipe can also be made in a 15- to 17-inch paella pan. If littlenecks are unavailable, use 1½ pounds shrimp in step 1 and season them with 1½ teaspoons salt.

- 1½ pounds boneless, skinless chicken thighs, trimmed and halved crosswise
- 3½ teaspoons kosher salt, divided
- 1 teaspoon pepper
- 12 ounces jumbo shrimp (16 to 20 per pound), peeled and deveined
- 6 tablespoons extra-virgin olive oil, divided
- 6 garlic cloves, minced and divided
- 1¾ teaspoons hot smoked paprika, divided
- 3 tablespoons tomato paste
- 4 cups chicken broth
- 1 (8-ounce) bottle clam juice
- ⅔ cup dry sherry
- Pinch saffron threads (optional)
- 1 onion, chopped fine
- ½ cup jarred roasted red peppers, chopped fine
- 3 cups Arborio rice
- 1 pound littleneck clams, scrubbed
- 1 pound Spanish-style chorizo sausage, cut into ½-inch pieces
- 1 cup frozen peas, thawed
- Lemon wedges

1 Pat chicken dry with paper towels and sprinkle evenly with 2 teaspoons salt and pepper. Toss shrimp with 1 tablespoon oil, ½ teaspoon garlic, ¼ teaspoon paprika, and ½ teaspoon salt in bowl.

2 Heat 1 tablespoon oil in medium saucepan over medium heat until shimmering. Add remaining garlic and cook, stirring constantly, until garlic sticks to bottom of saucepan and begins to brown, about 1 minute. Stir in tomato paste and remaining 1½ teaspoons paprika and cook, stirring constantly, until dark brown bits form on bottom of saucepan, about 1 minute. Stir in broth, clam juice, sherry, and saffron, if using. Increase heat to high and bring to boil. Remove saucepan from heat and set aside.

3A **FOR A CHARCOAL GRILL** Open bottom vent completely. Light large chimney starter mounded with charcoal briquettes (7 quarts). When top coals are partially covered with ash, pour evenly over grill. Using tongs, arrange 20 unlit briquettes evenly over coals. Set cooking grate in place, cover, and open lid vent completely. Heat grill until hot, about 5 minutes.

3B **FOR A GAS GRILL** Turn all burners to high; cover; and heat grill until hot, about 15 minutes. Leave all burners on high.

4 Clean and oil cooking grate. Place chicken on grill and cook until both sides are lightly browned, 5 to 7 minutes total. Transfer chicken to plate. Clean cooking grate.

5 Place roasting pan on grill (turning burners to medium-high if using gas) and add remaining ¼ cup oil. When oil begins to shimmer, add onion, red peppers, and remaining 1 teaspoon salt. Cook, stirring frequently, until onion begins to brown, 4 to 7 minutes. Add rice (turning burners to medium if using gas) and stir until grains are well coated with oil.

6 Arrange chicken around perimeter of pan. Pour broth mixture and any accumulated juices from chicken over rice. Smooth rice into even layer, making sure nothing sticks to sides of pan and no rice rests atop chicken. When liquid reaches gentle simmer, place shrimp in center of pan in single layer. Arrange clams in center of pan, evenly distributing with shrimp and pushing hinge sides of clams into rice slightly so that they stand up. Distribute chorizo evenly over surface of rice. Cook (covered if using gas), moving and rotating pan to maintain gentle simmer across entire surface of pan, until rice is almost cooked through, 12 to 18 minutes. (If using gas, heat can also be adjusted to maintain simmer.)

PAELLA ON THE GRILL

7 Sprinkle peas evenly over paella; cover grill; and cook until liquid is fully absorbed and rice on bottom of pan sizzles, 5 to 8 minutes. Continue to cook, uncovered, checking bottom of pan frequently with metal spoon, until uniform golden-brown crust forms, 8 to 15 minutes longer. (Rotate and slide pan around grill as necessary to ensure even crust formation.) Remove pan from grill, cover with aluminum foil, and let stand for 10 minutes. Serve with lemon wedges.

PERFECT GRILLED SALMON

Perfect Grilled Salmon

SERVES 4 **TIME** 25 minutes

Why This Recipe Works For great grilled salmon fillets that really don't stick, we start with fillets that are 1 to 1½ inches thick, so they develop nice color on the grill by the time they're cooked through. We pat the fillets dry and then brush them with a mixture of mayonnaise, honey, and fish sauce. The mayo provides fat that prevents sticking and contributes protein and sugar that aid browning. The honey also encourages browning, and fish sauce adds savory depth that enhances the salmon's flavor. Starting the fish flesh side down diagonally over a hot grill ensures that the flesh sears when the grill is at its hottest, and the angle makes attractive grill marks. To ensure uniform cooking, buy a 1½- to 2-pound center-cut salmon fillet and cut it into four pieces. If using wild salmon, which tends to be thinner and leaner, check for doneness earlier and cook it just until it registers 120 degrees.

- ¼ cup mayonnaise
- 2 teaspoons fish sauce
- ½ teaspoon honey
- 4 (6- to 8-ounce) skin-on salmon fillets, 1 to 1½ inches thick
- 1½ teaspoons kosher salt
- ½ teaspoon pepper
- Lemon wedges

1 Combine mayonnaise, fish sauce, and honey in small bowl. Pat salmon fillets dry with paper towels. Refrigerate mayonnaise mixture and salmon while heating grill. Combine salt and pepper in second small bowl.

2 Brush skin side of fillets with thin, even coating of mayonnaise mixture. Sprinkle with half of salt mixture. Flip fillets and brush top of flesh side with thin, even coating of mayonnaise mixture (you may not need all of it). Sprinkle flesh side all over with remaining salt mixture.

Positioning Salmon on the Grill

Start fillets **FLESH SIDE DOWN** to firm up flesh, making it more resilient when flipped.

Place fish **DIAGONALLY** across grate bars to create attractive grill marks.

3A FOR A CHARCOAL GRILL Open bottom vent completely. Light large chimney starter two-thirds filled with charcoal briquettes (4 quarts). When top coals are partially covered with ash, pour evenly over grill. Set cooking grate in place, cover, and open lid vent completely. Heat grill until hot, about 5 minutes.

3B FOR A GAS GRILL Turn all burners to high; cover; and heat grill until hot, about 15 minutes. Turn all burners to medium.

4 Clean cooking grate, then repeatedly brush grate with well-oiled paper towels until grate is black and glossy, 5 to 10 times. Place salmon flesh side down on grill, diagonal to grate. Cook (covered if using gas), without moving fillets, until flesh side is well marked and releases easily from grill, 3 to 5 minutes.

5 Using 2 fish spatulas, flip fillets to skin side. Cook (covered if using gas) until centers are still translucent when checked with tip of paring knife and register 125 degrees (for medium-rare), 3 to 5 minutes. Transfer to platter and serve.

Grilled Honey Mustard–Glazed Salmon

SERVES 4 **TIME** 30 minutes

Why This Recipe Works A glaze not only creates a glossy, deeply caramelized crust on grilled salmon; its flavor also permeates the flesh, making the last bite of fish every bit as good as the first. We marinate the fish in soy sauce and maple syrup to season it throughout (the syrup also helps the marinade cling to the fish). After searing the marinated salmon over high heat, we brush it on both sides with honey-mustard glaze and then pull it to the cooler side of the grill to cook through. A final brush with glaze adds shine. To ensure uniform cooking, buy a 1½- to 2-pound center-cut salmon fillet and cut it into four pieces. If using wild salmon, which tends to be thinner and leaner, check for doneness earlier and cook it just until it registers 120 degrees.

HONEY-MUSTARD GLAZE

- ¼ cup honey
- 2 tablespoons soy sauce
- 3 tablespoons Dijon mustard

SALMON

- ⅓ cup soy sauce
- ⅓ cup maple syrup
- 4 (6- to 8-ounce) skin-on salmon fillets, 1 to 1½ inches thick
- ½ teaspoon pepper
- Lemon wedges

1 FOR THE GLAZE Bring honey and soy sauce to simmer in small saucepan over medium-high heat and cook until thickened slightly, 3 to 4 minutes. Off heat, whisk in mustard. Measure out 2 tablespoons glaze and set aside for serving.

2 FOR THE SALMON Whisk soy sauce and maple syrup together in 13 by 9-inch baking dish. Place salmon fillets skin side up in baking dish (do not coat salmon skin with marinade) and refrigerate fish while heating grill. Before cooking, remove salmon from marinade and sprinkle with pepper.

3A FOR A CHARCOAL GRILL Open bottom vent completely. Light large chimney starter filled with charcoal briquettes (6 quarts). When top coals are partially covered with ash, pour two-thirds evenly over grill, then pour remaining coals over half of grill. Set cooking grate in place, cover, and open lid vent completely. Heat grill until hot, about 5 minutes.

3B FOR A GAS GRILL Turn all burners to high; cover; and heat grill until hot, about 15 minutes. Leave primary burner on high and turn other burner(s) to medium.

4 Clean cooking grate, then repeatedly brush grate with well-oiled paper towels until black and glossy, 5 to 10 times. Place salmon flesh side down on grill, diagonal to grate. Cook (covered if using gas), without moving fillets, until grill marks form, 1 to 3 minutes. Using 2 fish spatulas, flip fillets; brush with glaze and cook until salmon is opaque about halfway up thickness of fillets, 3 to 5 minutes.

5 Brush fillets again with glaze, flip, and slide to cooler side of grill (if using charcoal) or turn all burners to medium-low (if using gas). Cook until centers are still translucent when checked with tip of paring knife and register 125 degrees (for medium-rare), 1 to 3 minutes longer.

6 Transfer fillets to serving platter, brush with reserved 2 tablespoons glaze, and serve with lemon wedges.

VARIATION

Grilled Maple Soy–Glazed Salmon

Omit Dijon and substitute ¼ cup maple syrup for honey in glaze.

GRILLED SALMON CAESAR SALAD

Grilled Salmon Caesar Salad

SERVES 4 **TIME** 35 minutes

Why This Recipe Works The grill excels at transforming ordinary salad components—in this case, romaine lettuce, bread, and salmon fillets—into something quite extraordinary by adding a slightly smoky, charred flavor. We make a quick Caesar dressing and brush some of it onto the romaine hearts, which helps them pick up flavorful char without wilting. Cut the bread on an extreme bias for larger pieces that are easy to handle on the grill. To ensure uniform cooking, buy a 1½- to 2-pound center-cut salmon fillet and cut it into four pieces. If using wild salmon, which tends to be thinner and leaner, check for doneness earlier and cook it just until it registers 120 degrees.

- 1 ounce Parmesan cheese, grated (½ cup), plus extra for serving
- ½ cup mayonnaise
- 6 tablespoons extra-virgin olive oil, divided
- 2 tablespoons lemon juice
- 1 tablespoon Worcestershire sauce
- 1 garlic clove, minced
- 2½ teaspoons kosher salt, divided
- 1 teaspoon pepper, divided
- 1 (12-inch) baguette, cut on bias into 4-inch-long, 1-inch-thick slices
- 3 romaine lettuce hearts (18 ounces), halved lengthwise through cores
- 4 (6- to 8-ounce) skin-on salmon fillets, 1 to 1½ inches thick

1 Whisk Parmesan, mayonnaise, ¼ cup oil, lemon juice, Worcestershire, garlic, 1 teaspoon salt, and ½ teaspoon pepper together in bowl. Measure out and reserve ½ cup for cooking.

2 Brush bread with remaining 2 tablespoons oil. Brush cut sides of romaine with 6 tablespoons reserved dressing. Sprinkle salmon fillets with remaining 1½ teaspoons salt and remaining ½ teaspoon pepper and brush all over with remaining 2 tablespoons reserved dressing.

3A **FOR A CHARCOAL GRILL** Open bottom vent completely. Light large chimney starter filled with charcoal briquettes (6 quarts). When top coals are partially covered with ash, pour evenly over grill. Set cooking grate in place, cover, and open lid vent completely. Heat grill until hot, about 5 minutes.

3B **FOR A GAS GRILL** Turn all burners to high; cover; and heat grill until hot, about 15 minutes. Leave all burners on high.

4 Clean cooking grate, then repeatedly brush grate with well-oiled paper towels until grate is black and glossy, 5 to 10 times. Place bread on grill and cook, flipping as needed, until well toasted, 2 to 4 minutes; transfer to platter. Place romaine cut side down on grill and cook until lightly charred, 1 to 2 minutes; transfer to platter with bread.

5 Place salmon flesh side down on grill, diagonal to grate (reducing heat to medium if using gas). Grill (covered if using gas) until well marked and centers are translucent when checked with tip of paring knife and register 125 degrees (for medium-rare), 8 to 12 minutes, using 2 fish spatulas to flip salmon halfway through cooking. Transfer salmon to platter with salad. Serve with remaining dressing and extra Parmesan.

Grilled Salmon with Charred Red Cabbage Slaw

SERVES 4 **TIME** 35 minutes

Why This Recipe Works Red cabbage caramelizes beautifully on the grill. Balanced with sweet shredded Asian pear and nutty toasted sesame oil, it's the star sidekick to buttery salmon. Use a small head of cabbage so that each wedge has enough core to hold together. If you can find only a large head, peel off the leaves until it weighs 1¼ pounds. To ensure uniform cooking, buy a 1½- to 2-pound center-cut salmon fillet and cut it into four pieces. If using wild salmon, which tends to be thinner and leaner, check for doneness earlier and cook just until it registers 120 degrees.

- 1 small head (1¼ pounds) red cabbage, cut through core into 1-inch-wide wedges
- 3 tablespoons plus 2 teaspoons extra-virgin olive oil, divided
- 2 teaspoons kosher salt, divided
- 2 teaspoons pepper, divided
- 4 (6- to 8-ounce) skin-on salmon fillets, 1 to 1½ inches thick
- 2 teaspoons grated lime zest (2 limes), limes halved
- 1 tablespoon toasted sesame oil
- 1 Asian pear, unpeeled, cored and shredded

1 Rub cabbage all over with 1 tablespoon olive oil and sprinkle with ½ teaspoon salt and ½ teaspoon pepper. Pat salmon fillets dry with paper towels, rub all over with 2 teaspoons olive oil, and sprinkle flesh side with 1 teaspoon salt and 1 teaspoon pepper.

2A **FOR A CHARCOAL GRILL** Open bottom vent completely. Light large chimney starter filled with charcoal briquettes (6 quarts). When top coals are partially covered with ash, pour evenly over grill. Set cooking grate in place, cover, and open lid vent completely. Heat grill until hot, about 5 minutes.

2B **FOR A GAS GRILL** Turn all burners to high; cover; and heat grill until hot, about 15 minutes. Leave all burners on high.

3 Clean and oil cooking grate. Grill cabbage and lime halves cut sides down (covered if using gas) until lightly charred and cabbage is beginning to wilt, 4 to 8 minutes, flipping cabbage halfway through cooking. Transfer to cutting board to cool.

4 Clean grate again, then repeatedly brush grate with well-oiled paper towels until grate is black and glossy, 5 to 10 times. Place salmon flesh side down on grill, diagonal to grate. Cover and cook (reducing heat to medium if using gas) until well marked and centers are translucent when checked with tip of paring knife and register 125 degrees (for medium-rare), 8 to 12 minutes, using 2 fish spatulas to flip salmon halfway through cooking. Transfer to serving platter.

5 Once lime halves and cabbage are cool enough to handle, juice limes to yield ¼ cup and slice cabbage thin, discarding core. Whisk lime zest and juice, sesame oil, remaining 2 tablespoons olive oil, remaining ½ teaspoon salt, and remaining ½ teaspoon pepper together in large bowl. Add sliced cabbage and shredded pear, toss to coat, and season with salt and pepper to taste. Serve with grilled salmon.

Smoked Salmon Tacos

SERVES 4 to 6 **TIME** 1¼ hours plus 4 hours seasoning

Why This Recipe Works Once you taste the sweet-smoky fish, creamy mustard sauce, and crunchy slaw in these creative California-style tacos, you'll forget how unexpected they sound as taco ingredients. An apricot glaze heightens the salmon's appealing sweetness. Green apple, celery, and carrot come together as a crisp, satisfying slaw, while spicy brown mustard punches up the sauce. If you can find them, applewood chips impart the best flavor to the fish; however, hickory chips are widely available and work fine here. If you'd like to use wood chunks when using a charcoal grill, substitute one medium wood chunk for the wood chip packet. To ensure uniform cooking, buy a 1½- to 2-pound center-cut salmon fillet and cut it into four pieces. Cooking to medium-well makes the fillets easier to flake over a tortilla. If using wild salmon, check for doneness earlier and cook it until it registers 130 degrees. This recipe was developed using Diamond Crystal kosher salt. If you have Morton kosher salt, which is denser, use 3 tablespoons.

SALMON

- 1 cup packed brown sugar for salting salmon
- ¼ cup kosher salt for salting salmon
- 1 tablespoon granulated garlic
- 4 (6- to 8-ounce) skin-on salmon fillets, 1 to 1½ inches thick
- 1 cup wood chips
- 2 tablespoons apricot preserves
- 1 tablespoon water

TACOS

- ½ cup mayonnaise
- ¼ cup spicy brown mustard
- 2 teaspoons lemon juice
- ¼ teaspoon ground cumin
- 1 small Granny Smith apple, peeled and chopped fine
- 1 small celery rib, chopped fine
- 1 small carrot, peeled and shredded
- 12 (6-inch) flour tortillas
- 3 ounces (3 cups) mesclun greens

1 FOR THE SALMON Combine sugar, salt, and granulated garlic in bowl. Combine sugar mixture and salmon in 1-gallon zipper-lock bag and toss to coat; press out as much air as possible and seal bag. Refrigerate for at least 4 hours or up to 24 hours.

2 Using large piece of heavy-duty aluminum foil, wrap wood chips in 8 by 4-inch foil packet. (Make sure chips do not poke holes in sides or bottom of packet.) Cut 2 evenly spaced 2-inch slits in top of packet.

SMOKED SALMON TACOS

3 FOR THE TACOS Whisk mayonnaise, mustard, lemon juice, and cumin together in bowl. Combine apple, celery, and carrot in second bowl; set aside for serving.

4 Before cooking, remove salmon from sugar mixture; discard sugar mixture. Rinse excess sugar mixture from salmon and pat salmon dry with paper towels. Whisk preserves and water together in small bowl; microwave until mixture is fluid, about 30 seconds. Brush tops and sides of salmon fillets evenly with apricot mixture.

5A FOR A CHARCOAL GRILL Open bottom vent completely. Light large chimney starter half filled with charcoal briquettes (3 quarts). When top coals are partially covered with ash, pour evenly over half of grill. Place wood chip packet on coals. Set cooking grate in place, cover, and open lid vent completely. Heat grill until hot and wood chips are smoking, about 5 minutes.

5B FOR A GAS GRILL Remove cooking grate and place wood chip packet directly on primary burner. Set cooking grate in place; turn all burners to high; cover; and heat grill until hot and wood chips are smoking, about 15 minutes. Turn primary burner to medium and turn off other burner(s).

6 Clean cooking grate, then repeatedly brush grate with well-oiled paper towels until grate is black and glossy, 5 to 10 times. Place salmon skin side down on cooler side of grill with thicker ends facing fire. Cover grill (position lid vent over salmon if using charcoal) and cook until centers of fillets register 135 degrees (for medium-well), 28 to 35 minutes. Transfer salmon to plate, tent with foil, and let rest for 5 minutes. (If skin sticks to cooking grate, insert fish spatula between skin and fillet to separate and lift fillet from skin.)

7 Working in batches, grill tortillas on hotter side of grill, turning as needed, until lightly charred, 30 to 60 seconds per side; wrap tightly in foil to keep soft.

8 Remove and discard salmon skin. Flake salmon into bite-size pieces and season with salt to taste. Divide salmon evenly among tortillas, about ⅓ cup per tortilla. Serve, topping each taco with desired amounts of mesclun, mayonnaise mixture, and apple mixture.

Wood-Grilled Salmon Fillets

SERVES 4 **TIME** 1¼ hours

Why This Recipe Works We love the way that grilling salmon on a cedar plank perfumes the fish with subtle wood flavor; our adaptation opens up the flavor possibilities by using wood chips. To corral the chips, we make individual foil trays, toss soaked chips into each tray, lay skin-on salmon fillets on top, and set the trays on a grill to cook. Poking slits in the bottom of the foil allows more heat to reach the wood chips, helping them release more of their woodsy flavor. When the fillets are done, we slip a thin metal spatula between the skin and salmon and transfer the now-skinless fillets to serving plates. To keep the trays from tearing, use heavy-duty aluminum foil. To ensure uniform cooking, buy a 1½- to 2-pound center-cut salmon fillet and cut it into four pieces. If using wild salmon, check for doneness earlier and cook it just until it registers 120 degrees. Use whatever kind of wood chips you like; apple and cherry work especially well with the salmon.

- 1½ teaspoons sugar
- 1 teaspoon kosher salt
- ¼ teaspoon pepper
- 4 (6- to 8-ounce) skin-on salmon fillets, 1¼ inches thick
- 1 tablespoon extra-virgin olive oil
- 2 cups wood chips, soaked in water for 15 minutes and drained

1 Combine sugar, salt, and pepper in small bowl. Pat salmon dry with paper towels. Brush flesh side of salmon with oil and sprinkle with sugar mixture. Using 4 large sheets of heavy-duty aluminum foil, crimp edges of each sheet to make 4 trays, each measuring 7 by 5 inches. Using tip of paring knife, make several small slits in bottom of each tray. Divide wood chips evenly among trays and lay 1 fillet skin side down on top of wood chips in each tray.

2A FOR A CHARCOAL GRILL Open bottom vent completely. Light large chimney starter filled with charcoal briquettes (6 quarts). When top coals are partially covered with ash, pour evenly over grill. Set cooking grate in place, cover, and open lid vent completely. Heat grill until hot, about 5 minutes.

2B FOR A GAS GRILL Turn all burners to high; cover; and heat grill until hot, about 15 minutes. Leave all burners on high.

3 Clean and oil cooking grate. Place trays with salmon on grill; cover; and cook until centers of fillets are still translucent when checked with tip of paring knife and register 125 degrees (for medium-rare), about 10 minutes. Remove trays from grill. Slide metal spatula between skin and flesh of fish and transfer to platter. Serve.

VARIATIONS

Barbecued Wood-Grilled Salmon Fillets

Add ¾ teaspoon chili powder and ¼ teaspoon cayenne pepper to sugar mixture. Omit oil and brush salmon with mixture of 1 tablespoon Dijon mustard and 1 tablespoon maple syrup before sprinkling with sugar mixture.

Lemon-Thyme Wood-Grilled Salmon Fillets

Add 2 teaspoons minced fresh thyme and 1½ teaspoons grated lemon zest to sugar mixture. Omit oil and brush salmon with 2 tablespoons Dijon mustard before sprinkling with sugar mixture.

WOOD-GRILLED SALMON FILLETS

Preparing Wood-Grilled Salmon

1 Crimp edges of 4 large sheets of heavy-duty aluminum foil to form four 7 by 5-inch trays. Cut small slits in bottoms of trays.

2 Place soaked wood chips in foil trays and arrange salmon, skin side down, directly on top of wood chips.

3 Once salmon is cooked, slide metal spatula between flesh and skin; fish should release easily.

Grill-Smoked Side of Salmon

SERVES 6 **TIME** 2 hours

Why This Recipe Works This backyard-friendly recipe captures both the intense, meaty flavor of hot-smoked salmon and the firm but silky texture of the cold-smoked type—without a huge investment of time. It's easy: We brine a skin-on salmon fillet and then slow-roast it on the cooler side of a half-grill fire for about an hour and a half. The resulting salmon is plush and moist—and just smoky enough. It makes a delicious meal either warm from the grill or at room temperature. If the skin sticks to the grill, slide a thin metal spatula between the fillet and the skin and leave the skin behind. This recipe was developed using Diamond Crystal kosher salt. If you have Morton kosher salt, which is denser, use 7½ tablespoons. Serve with Herb Yogurt Sauce (page 396) and lemon wedges.

- 5 tablespoons sugar for brining
- ½ cup plus 2 tablespoons kosher salt for brining
- 1 (2½-pound) skin-on salmon fillet
- 2 tablespoons vegetable oil
- 1½ teaspoons paprika
- 1 teaspoon ground white pepper
- 2 cups wood chips

1 Dissolve sugar and salt in 2 quarts cold water in large container. Submerge salmon in brine, cover, and refrigerate for 15 minutes. Remove salmon from brine, pat dry, and rub with oil. Place salmon on rimmed baking sheet and sprinkle with paprika and white pepper.

2 Meanwhile, using large piece of heavy-duty aluminum foil, wrap wood chips in 8 by 4-inch foil packet. (Make sure chips do not poke holes in sides or bottom of packet.) Cut 2 evenly spaced 2-inch slits in top of packet.

3A **FOR A CHARCOAL GRILL** Open bottom grill vent halfway. Light large chimney starter half filled with charcoal briquettes (3 quarts). When top coals are partially covered with ash, pour evenly over half of grill. Place wood chip packet on coals. Set cooking grate in place, cover, and open lid vent halfway. Heat grill until hot and wood chips are smoking, about 5 minutes.

3B **FOR A GAS GRILL** Remove cooking grate and place wood chip packet directly on primary burner. Set cooking grate in place; turn all burners to high; cover; and heat grill until hot and wood chips are smoking, about 15 minutes. Turn primary burner to medium and turn off other burner(s). (Adjust primary burner as needed to maintain grill temperature around 275 degrees.)

GRILL-SMOKED SIDE OF SALMON

4 Clean cooking grate, then repeatedly brush grate with well-oiled paper towels until grate is black and glossy, 5 to 10 times. Gently slide salmon from sheet onto cooler side of grill, skin-side down and perpendicular to grate bars. Cover (position lid vent over fish if using charcoal) and cook until center of salmon is translucent when checked with tip of paring knife and registers 125 degrees (for medium-rare), about 1½ hours. Using 2 thin metal spatulas, gently remove salmon from grill. Let rest for 5 minutes. Serve salmon hot or at room temperature.

Grilled Swordfish Steaks

SERVES 4 **TIME** 40 minutes

Why This Recipe Works Compared to other fish, swordfish has a low difficulty setting when it comes to grilling, as its dense, meaty flesh generally keeps the steaks from falling apart. Even better, thick swordfish steaks can stay on the grill for a relatively long time, picking up smoky flavor and dark grill marks that make the fish especially appealing. Building a two-level fire lets you move the seared fish to the cooler side to finish cooking through evenly. Serve with Italian Salsa Verde (page 393).

- 4 (6- to 8-ounce) skin-on swordfish steaks, 1 to 1½ inches thick
- 2 tablespoons extra-virgin olive oil
- 1 teaspoon kosher salt
- ¼ teaspoon pepper

1 Pat swordfish dry with paper towels, rub all over with oil, and sprinkle with salt and pepper.

2A FOR A CHARCOAL GRILL Open bottom vent completely. Light large chimney starter filled with charcoal briquettes (6 quarts). When top coals are partially covered with ash, pour two-thirds evenly over half of grill, then pour remaining coals over other half of grill. Set cooking grate in place, cover, and open lid vent completely. Heat grill until hot, about 5 minutes.

2B FOR A GAS GRILL Turn all burners to high; cover; and heat grill until hot, about 15 minutes. Leave primary burner on high and turn other burner(s) to medium-high.

3 Clean cooking grate, then repeatedly brush grate with well-oiled paper towels until grate is black and glossy, 5 to 10 times. Place swordfish on hotter side of grill, perpendicular to grate bars, and cook (covered if using gas) until streaked with dark grill marks, 6 to 9 minutes, flipping halfway through cooking. Slide swordfish to cooler side of grill and cook until centers of swordfish are no longer translucent when checked with tip of paring knife and register 130 to 135 degrees, 3 to 6 minutes, flipping halfway through cooking. Transfer to platter and let rest for 10 minutes. Serve.

Grilled Swordfish Salmoriglio

SERVES 4 **TIME** 35 minutes

Why This Recipe Works Lemony, garlicky, oregano-infused salmoriglio is a workaday Sicilian staple, stirred together from basic ingredients and always on hand to season grilled foods, notably swordfish. We use a nearly 1:1 ratio of lemon juice to olive oil for a bracing sauce and add lemon zest to boost its aroma. As the cooked fish rests in the salmoriglio, it sheds juices that slightly dilute the sauce's acidity and balance its flavor. Applying it to the swordfish before and after cooking, as well as alongside the fish for serving, means every bite is full of flavor. If your swordfish steaks are larger (about 1 pound each), cut them in half to make four smaller steaks.

- 1 tablespoon dried oregano
- 2 teaspoons grated lemon zest plus ¼ cup juice (2 lemons)
- 2 garlic cloves, minced
- 2 teaspoons kosher salt, divided
- 1 teaspoon pepper, divided
- ⅓ cup extra-virgin olive oil
- 4 (6- to 8-ounce) skinless swordfish steaks, 1 to 1½ inches thick
- 2 tablespoons chopped fresh parsley, divided

1 Whisk oregano, lemon zest and juice, garlic, 1¼ teaspoons salt, and ½ teaspoon pepper in bowl until salt is dissolved. Whisk in oil.

2 Arrange swordfish in single layer 13 by 9-inch baking dish. Pour half of marinade over fish, flipping steaks to ensure both sides are evenly covered. Refrigerate for at least 20 minutes or up to 45 minutes. Whisk 1½ tablespoons parsley into remaining marinade and set aside for serving.

3 Before cooking, remove fish from marinade (do not pat dry). Sprinkle both sides with remaining ¾ teaspoon salt and remaining ½ teaspoon pepper.

4A FOR A CHARCOAL GRILL Open bottom vent completely. Light large chimney starter filled with charcoal briquettes (6 quarts). When top coals are partially covered with ash, pour evenly over half of grill. Set cooking grate in place, cover, and open lid vent completely. Heat grill until hot, about 5 minutes.

4B FOR A GAS GRILL Turn all burners to high; cover; and heat grill until hot, about 15 minutes. Leave primary burner on high and turn other burner(s) to medium-high.

GRILLED SWORDFISH SALMORIGLIO

5 Clean cooking grate, then repeatedly brush grate with well-oiled paper towels until grate is black and glossy, 5 to 10 times. Place swordfish on hotter side of grill and cook (covered if using gas), flipping every 2 minutes, until steaks develop dark grill marks and register 130 to 135 degrees, 7 to 11 minutes.

6 Transfer fish to clean shallow pan or dish and pour reserved marinade over top. Tent with aluminum foil and let rest until centers register 140 degrees, 5 to 10 minutes. Transfer steaks to serving platter or individual plates and sprinkle with remaining 1½ teaspoons parsley. Transfer sauce in pan to small bowl. Serve, passing sauce separately.

Grilled Swordfish Tacos with Grilled Pineapple Salsa

SERVES 6 **TIME** 1 hour plus 30 minutes marinating

Why This Recipe Works Fish tacos from the Yucatán Peninsula—snapper or grouper bathed in a chile-citrus mixture, wrapped in banana leaves, and grilled—are a culinary work of art. We borrow the flavor profile but use a simpler approach with swordfish steaks cut into strips. A thick paste featuring ancho and chipotle chile powders, oregano, coriander, and just enough citrus juice to make it spreadable develops deep, flavorful charring on the grill without promoting sticking. A little tomato paste provides a layer of savory-sweet intensity, and a mix of orange and lime juices mimics Mexican sour oranges. We serve these tacos with a refreshing grilled pineapple salsa, sliced avocado, and crunchy iceberg lettuce.

- 3 tablespoons vegetable oil, divided
- 1 tablespoon ancho chile powder
- 2 teaspoons chipotle chile powder
- 2 garlic cloves, minced
- 1 teaspoon dried oregano
- 1 teaspoon ground coriander
- 2 teaspoons kosher salt
- 2 tablespoons tomato paste
- ½ cup orange juice
- 6 tablespoons lime juice (3 limes), divided, plus lime wedges for serving
- 2 pounds skinless swordfish steaks, 1 inch thick, cut into 1-inch-wide strips
- 1 pineapple, peeled, quartered, cored, and each quarter halved lengthwise
- 1 jalapeño chile
- 18 (6-inch) corn tortillas

- 1 red bell pepper, stemmed, seeded, and cut into ¼-inch pieces
- 2 tablespoons minced fresh cilantro, plus extra for serving
- ½ head iceberg lettuce (4½ ounces), cored and sliced thin
- 1 ripe avocado, halved, pitted, and sliced thin

1 Heat 2 tablespoons oil, ancho chile powder, and chipotle chile powder in 8-inch skillet over medium heat, stirring constantly, until fragrant, 2 to 3 minutes. Stir in garlic, oregano, coriander, and salt and cook until fragrant, about 30 seconds. Add tomato paste and, using spatula, mash into spice mixture until combined, about 20 seconds. Stir in orange juice and 2 tablespoons lime juice. Cook, stirring constantly, until thoroughly mixed and reduced slightly, about 2 minutes. Transfer chile mixture to large bowl and let cool for 15 minutes.

2 Add swordfish to bowl with chile mixture and stir gently to coat steaks. Cover and refrigerate for at least 30 minutes or up to 2 hours. Before cooking, remove swordfish from chile mixture (do not pat dry). Brush pineapple with remaining 1 tablespoon oil.

3A **FOR A CHARCOAL GRILL** Open bottom vent completely. Light large chimney starter mounded with charcoal briquettes (7 quarts). When top coals are partially covered with ash, pour evenly over grill. Set cooking grate in place, cover, and open lid vent completely. Heat grill until hot, about 5 minutes.

3B **FOR A GAS GRILL** Turn all burners to high; cover; and heat grill until hot, about 15 minutes. Leave all burners on high.

4 Clean cooking grate, then repeatedly brush grate with well-oiled paper towels until grate is black and glossy, 5 to 10 times. Place swordfish, pineapple, and jalapeño on grill. Cover and cook until swordfish, pineapple, and jalapeño have begun to brown, 3 to 5 minutes. Flip swordfish, pineapple, and jalapeño. Cover and cook until second sides of pineapple and jalapeño are browned and swordfish registers 130 to 135 degrees, 3 to 5 minutes. Transfer swordfish to large platter, flake into pieces, and tent with aluminum foil. Transfer pineapple and jalapeño to cutting board.

5 Working in batches, grill tortillas, turning as needed, until warm and soft, about 1 minute; wrap tightly in foil to keep soft.

6 When cool enough to handle, chop pineapple and jalapeño fine. Transfer to bowl and stir in bell pepper, cilantro, and remaining ¼ cup lime juice. Season with salt to taste. Top tortillas with flaked swordfish, salsa, lettuce, and avocado. Serve with lime wedges and extra cilantro.

GRILLED SWORDFISH TACOS WITH GRILLED PINEAPPLE SALSA

GRILLED SWORDFISH SKEWERS WITH CAPONATA

Grilled Swordfish Skewers with Caponata

SERVES 4 to 6 **TIME** 40 minutes

Why This Recipe Works A Sicilian-inspired grilled caponata packs enough flavor power to hold its own alongside robust grilled swordfish skewers. Grilled eggplant, cherry tomatoes, and scallions form the base of the caponata, along with kalamata olives. We grill lemons and use their sweet, mellow juice to tie the caponata together. Cumin, cinnamon, and coriander give the mixture depth, and we also rub coriander into the swordfish, which makes the flavor pop. If swordfish isn't available, you can substitute halibut. You will need six 12-inch metal skewers for this recipe.

- ¼ cup extra-virgin olive oil, divided
- 1½ tablespoons honey
- 1 tablespoon grated lemon zest, plus 2 lemons, halved
- 5 teaspoons ground coriander, divided
- 2 garlic cloves, minced
- 2½ teaspoons kosher salt, divided
- 1 teaspoon ground cumin
- ½ teaspoon pepper, divided
- ¼ teaspoon ground cinnamon
- ⅛ teaspoon ground nutmeg
- 1½ pounds skinless swordfish steaks, 1¼ inches thick, cut into 1¼-inch pieces
- 12 ounces cherry tomatoes
- 1 small eggplant (12 ounces), cut crosswise on bias into ½-inch-thick ovals
- 6 scallions, trimmed
- ¼ cup pitted kalamata olives, chopped
- 2 tablespoons chopped fresh basil

1 Whisk 2 tablespoons oil, honey, lemon zest, 2 teaspoons coriander, garlic, 1½ teaspoons salt, cumin, ¼ teaspoon pepper, cinnamon, and nutmeg together in large bowl. Microwave, stirring occasionally, until fragrant, about 1 minute; set aside for serving.

2 Pat swordfish dry with paper towels and sprinkle with remaining 1 tablespoon coriander, remaining 1 teaspoon salt, and remaining ¼ teaspoon pepper. Thread swordfish onto three 12-inch metal skewers. Thread tomatoes onto three separate 12-inch metal skewers. Brush swordfish, tomatoes, eggplant, and scallions with remaining 2 tablespoons oil.

3A **FOR A CHARCOAL GRILL** Open bottom vent completely. Light large chimney starter filled with charcoal briquettes (6 quarts). When top coals are partially covered with ash, pour evenly over grill. Set cooking grate in place, cover, and open lid vent completely. Heat grill until hot, about 5 minutes.

3B **FOR A GAS GRILL** Turn all burners to high; cover; and heat grill until hot, about 15 minutes. Leave all burners on high.

4 Clean cooking grate, then repeatedly brush grate with well-oiled paper towels until grate is black and glossy, 5 to 10 times. Place swordfish, tomatoes, eggplant, scallions, and lemon halves on grill. Cook (covered if using gas), turning as needed, until swordfish flakes apart when gently prodded with paring knife and registers 130 to 135 degrees and tomatoes, eggplant, scallions, and lemon halves are softened and lightly charred, 5 to 15 minutes. Transfer items to serving platter as they finish cooking and tent with aluminum foil to keep warm. Let swordfish rest while finishing caponata.

5 Once lemons are cool enough to handle, squeeze into fine-mesh strainer set over bowl, extracting as much juice as possible. Add juice to spiced oil–honey mixture, whisk to combine, and stir in olives.

6 Using tongs, slide tomatoes off skewers onto cutting board. Chop tomatoes, eggplant, and scallions coarse; transfer to bowl with olives and toss gently to combine. Season with salt and pepper to taste. Remove swordfish from skewers, sprinkle with basil, and serve with caponata.

Grilled Swordfish and Pineapple Skewers with Couscous

SERVES 4 **TIME** 45 minutes

Why This Recipe Works Pineapple provides a sweet and tangy contrast to meaty swordfish and punchy red onion for these quick-cooking kebabs; as they grill, the flavors of the components mellow and mingle. We serve them on a bed of quick-cooking couscous that we infuse with curry and stud with crunchy sliced almonds. You will need eight 12-inch metal skewers for this recipe. Serve with chopped fresh mint if you like.

- 1½ cups water
- 1 teaspoon curry powder
- ½ cup extra-virgin olive oil, divided
- 1½ tablespoons kosher salt, divided
- 1¼ cups couscous
- ½ cup sliced almonds, toasted
- 2 tablespoons honey
- 1 teaspoon grated lemon zest plus ¼ cup juice (2 lemons)
- ¼ teaspoon cayenne pepper
- 1½ pounds skinless swordfish steaks, 1 inch thick, cut into (1-inch) pieces
- 1 small pineapple, peeled, cored, and cut into 32 (1-inch) pieces
- 1 large red onion, cut into 1-inch pieces

1 Bring water, curry powder, 3 tablespoons oil and 1½ teaspoons salt to boil in medium saucepan over medium-high heat. Stir in couscous, cover, and let sit off heat for 5 minutes. Stir in almonds, transfer to platter, and cover until ready to serve.

2 Whisk remaining 5 tablespoons oil, honey, lemon zest and juice, cayenne, and remaining 1 tablespoon salt together in large bowl. Measure out ⅓ cup marinade and set aside for serving. Pat swordfish dry with paper towels. Add swordfish, pineapple, and onion to remaining marinade and toss to coat.

3 Thread 2 to 3 onion pieces, then 1 swordfish piece, then 1 pineapple piece onto each of eight 12-inch metal skewers. Repeat pattern 3 more times on each skewer and finish each skewer with 2 to 3 onion pieces.

4A **FOR A CHARCOAL GRILL** Open bottom vent completely. Light large chimney starter filled with charcoal briquettes (6 quarts). When top coals are partially covered with ash, pour evenly over grill. Set cooking grate in place, cover, and open lid vent completely. Heat grill until hot, about 5 minutes.

4B **FOR A GAS GRILL** Turn all burners to high; cover; and heat grill until hot, about 15 minutes. Leave all burners on high.

5 Clean cooking grate, then repeatedly brush grate with well-oiled paper towels until grate is black and glossy, 5 to 10 times. Place skewers on grill and cook (covered if using gas), turning as needed, until swordfish registers 130 to 135 degrees, 8 to 12 minutes. Transfer skewers to platter and lay on top of couscous. Drizzle with reserved marinade and serve.

Grilled Tuna Steaks with Red Wine Vinegar–Mustard Vinaigrette

SERVES 6 **TIME** 25 minutes

Why This Recipe Works The perfect grilled tuna is an exercise in contrasts: a hot, smoky, charred exterior wrapped around a cool, delicately flavored, tender, and moist center that pairs with nearly any flavoring you can dream up. A simple vinaigrette helps create this ideal: Oil provides moisture, honey promotes browning, and vinegar adds a bold punch of flavor. Our four vibrant vinaigrettes build on this foundation with potent ingredients such as fresh cilantro, garlic, soy sauce, and Dijon mustard. We prefer this tuna served rare or medium-rare. If you like your tuna cooked medium, observe the timing for medium-rare and then tent the steaks with aluminum foil for 5 minutes. To achieve a nicely grilled exterior and a rare center, use steaks that are at least 1 inch thick.

- 3 tablespoons plus 1 teaspoon red wine vinegar
- 2 tablespoons chopped fresh thyme or rosemary
- 2 tablespoons Dijon mustard
- 2 teaspoons honey
- 1½ teaspoons kosher salt, divided
- Pinch plus ½ teaspoon pepper, divided
- ¾ cup extra-virgin olive oil
- 6 (8-ounce) skinless tuna steaks, 1 inch thick

1 Whisk vinegar, thyme, mustard, honey, 1 teaspoon salt, and pinch pepper together in large bowl. Whisking constantly, slowly drizzle in oil until mixture is lightly thickened and emulsified. Measure out ¾ cup vinaigrette and set aside for grilling.

2 Before cooking, pat tuna dry with paper towels. Generously brush both sides of tuna with remaining vinaigrette and sprinkle with remaining ½ teaspoon salt and remaining ½ teaspoon pepper.

3A **FOR A CHARCOAL GRILL** Open bottom vent completely. Light large chimney starter filled with charcoal briquettes (6 quarts). When top coals are partially covered with ash, pour evenly over half of grill. Set cooking grate in place, cover, and open lid vent completely. Heat grill until hot, about 5 minutes.

3B **FOR A GAS GRILL** Turn all burners to high; cover; and heat grill until hot, about 15 minutes. Leave all burners on high.

4 Clean cooking grate, then repeatedly brush grate with well-oiled paper towels until grate is black and glossy, 5 to 10 times. Place tuna on grill (on hotter side if using charcoal) and cook (covered if using gas) until grill marks form and bottom is opaque, 1 to 3 minutes. Flip tuna and cook until steaks are opaque at perimeter and translucent red at center when checked with tip of paring knife and register 110 degrees (for rare), about 1½ minutes; or until steaks are opaque at perimeter and reddish pink at center and register 125 degrees (for medium-rare), about 3 minutes. Serve, passing reserved vinaigrette separately.

VARIATIONS

Grilled Tuna Steaks with Chermoula Vinaigrette

Substitute minced fresh parsley for thyme and add ¼ cup minced fresh cilantro, 4 minced garlic cloves, 1 teaspoon paprika, 1 teaspoon ground cumin, and ½ teaspoon ground coriander to vinaigrette.

Grilled Tuna Steaks with Provençal Vinaigrette

Substitute 2 tablespoons minced fresh parsley and 1 tablespoon minced fresh oregano for thyme and add 2 rinsed, patted dry, and minced anchovy fillets and 1 minced garlic clove to vinaigrette.

Grilled Tuna Steaks with Soy-Ginger Vinaigrette

For a spicier vinaigrette, increase the amount of red pepper flakes.

Substitute unseasoned rice vinegar for red wine vinegar and 2 thinly sliced scallions for thyme. Omit salt and add 3 tablespoons soy sauce, 1 tablespoon toasted sesame oil, 2 teaspoons grated fresh ginger, and ½ teaspoon red pepper flakes to vinaigrette.

GRILLED TUNA STEAKS WITH RED WINE VINEGAR–MUSTARD VINAIGRETTE

GRILLED TUNA STEAKS WITH CUCUMBER-MINT FARRO SALAD

Grilled Tuna Steaks with Cucumber-Mint Farro Salad

SERVES 4 **TIME** 1 hour

Why This Recipe Works Cooking your entire meal on the grill has major appeal, but there's also something to be said for a side dish that you can assemble ahead of time in the kitchen: At mealtime, a quick stint at the grill gets you to the finish line. Here, chewy farro is punctuated by crisp cucumber, juicy tomatoes, and peppery arugula. A creamy yogurt dressing makes the salad a cooling complement to the honey-brushed grill-seared tuna. We prefer the flavor and texture of whole farro; pearl farro can be used, but the texture may be softer. Do not use quick-cooking or presteamed farro. The cooking time for farro can vary greatly across brands, so begin to check for doneness after 10 minutes. We prefer this tuna served rare or medium-rare. If you like your tuna cooked medium, observe the timing for medium-rare and then tent the steaks with aluminum foil for 5 minutes.

- 1½ cups whole farro
- 2 teaspoons kosher salt, divided, plus salt for cooking farro
- 6 tablespoons extra-virgin olive oil, divided
- 2 tablespoons lemon juice
- 2 tablespoons plain Greek yogurt
- ¼ teaspoon pepper, divided
- 1 English cucumber, halved lengthwise, seeded, and sliced ¼ inch thick
- 6 ounces cherry tomatoes, halved
- 2 ounces (2 cups) baby arugula
- 3 tablespoons chopped fresh mint
- 2 teaspoons honey
- 1 teaspoon water
- 2 (8- to 12-ounce) skinless tuna steaks, 1 inch thick, halved crosswise

1 Bring 4 quarts water to boil in Dutch oven. Add farro and 1 tablespoon salt and cook until grains are tender with slight chew, 15 to 30 minutes. Drain farro, spread evenly on rimmed baking sheet, and let cool for about 10 minutes.

2 Whisk 3 tablespoons oil, lemon juice, yogurt, 1 teaspoon salt, and ⅛ teaspoon pepper together in large bowl. Add drained farro, cucumber, tomatoes, arugula, and mint and toss gently to combine. Season with salt and pepper to taste; set aside for serving.

3 Whisk remaining 3 tablespoons oil, honey, water, remaining 1 teaspoon salt, and remaining ⅛ teaspoon pepper together in bowl. Pat tuna dry with paper towels and generously brush with oil-honey mixture.

4A FOR A CHARCOAL GRILL Open bottom vent completely. Light large chimney starter filled with charcoal briquettes (6 quarts). When top coals are partially covered with ash, pour evenly over half of grill. Set cooking grate in place, cover, and open lid vent completely. Heat grill until hot, about 5 minutes.

4B FOR A GAS GRILL Turn all burners to high; cover; and heat grill until hot, about 15 minutes. Leave all burners on high.

5 Clean cooking grate, then repeatedly brush grate with well-oiled paper towels until grate is black and glossy, 5 to 10 times. Place tuna on grill (on hotter side if using charcoal) and cook (covered if using gas) until grill marks form and bottom is opaque, 1 to 3 minutes. Flip tuna and cook until steaks are opaque at perimeter and translucent red at center when checked with tip of paring knife and register 110 degrees (for rare), about 1½ minutes; or until steaks are opaque at perimeter and reddish pink at center and register 125 degrees (for medium-rare), about 3 minutes. Serve tuna with farro salad.

Grilled Blackened Red Snapper Fillets

SERVES 6 **TIME** 40 minutes

Why This Recipe Works Snapper blackened with pungent, smoky Cajun-style spices is a New Orleans classic that usually involves a superhot cast-iron skillet—and a kitchen full of tear-inducing smoke. But the dish is a winner, so we take the heat out of the kitchen and move it to the grill. To prevent the fillets from sticking, we make sure the grill is hot and the grate is well oiled. The fillets tend to curl up, but simply scoring the skin is an easy fix. Finally, to give the fish its flavorful blackened-but-not-burnt coating, we bloom the spice mixture in melted butter, let it cool, and then apply the coating to the snapper. While the fish cooks through, the spice crust becomes deeply flavorful.

- 2 tablespoons paprika
- 2 teaspoons onion powder
- 2 teaspoons garlic powder
- ¾ teaspoon ground coriander
- 1½ teaspoons kosher salt
- ¼ teaspoon pepper
- ¼ teaspoon cayenne pepper
- ¼ teaspoon white pepper
- 3 tablespoons unsalted butter
- 6 (6- to 8-ounce) skin-on red snapper fillets, 1 inch thick

GRILLED RED CURRY MAHI-MAHI WITH PINEAPPLE SALSA

GRILLED COD AND SUMMER SQUASH PACKETS

1 Combine paprika, onion powder, garlic powder, coriander, salt, pepper, cayenne, and white pepper in bowl. Melt butter in 10-inch skillet over medium heat. Add spice mixture and cook, stirring often, until fragrant and spices turn dark rust color, 2 to 3 minutes. Transfer mixture to shallow dish and let cool completely.

2 Pat snapper dry with paper towels. Using sharp knife, make shallow diagonal slashes 1 inch apart through skin, being careful not to cut into flesh. Rub spice mixture evenly all over each fillet (use all of spice mixture).

3A **FOR A CHARCOAL GRILL** Open bottom vent completely. Light large chimney starter filled with charcoal briquettes (6 quarts). When top coals are partially covered with ash, pour evenly over half of grill. Set cooking grate in place, cover, and open lid vent completely. Heat grill until hot, about 5 minutes.

3B **FOR A GAS GRILL** Turn all burners to high; cover; and heat grill until hot, about 15 minutes. Leave all burners on high.

4 Clean cooking grate, then repeatedly brush grate with well-oiled paper towels until grate is black and glossy, 5 to 10 times. Place snapper fillets skin side down on grill (on hotter side if using charcoal), perpendicular to grate bars. Cook until skin is very dark brown and crisp, 3 to 5 minutes. Using 2 fish spatulas, flip snapper and cook until second side is dark brown, fish flakes apart when gently prodded with paring knife, and snapper registers 130 to 135 degrees, about 5 minutes. Serve.

Grilled Red Curry Mahi-Mahi with Pineapple Salsa

SERVES 4 **TIME** 25 minutes

Why This Recipe Works Mahi-mahi's hearty, meaty texture makes it a prime candidate for the grill, and it takes well to robust flavors. Convenient store-bought red curry paste adds a kick; we brush it over the fillets before throwing them on the grill, where they cook through in just a few minutes. A zesty, bright pineapple salsa perfectly complements mahi-mahi's sweet, delicate taste.

- 2 cups ¼-inch pineapple pieces
- 1 scallion, sliced thin
- ¼ cup minced fresh cilantro
- 2 tablespoons vegetable oil, divided
- ½ teaspoon kosher salt
- ½ teaspoon pepper
- 1 tablespoon red curry paste
- 4 (6- to 8-ounce) skin-on mahi-mahi fillets, 1 inch thick

1 Combine pineapple, scallion, cilantro, 1 tablespoon oil, salt, and pepper in bowl; set aside for serving. Combine curry paste with remaining 1 tablespoon oil in separate bowl. Pat mahi-mahi dry with paper towels, then brush flesh side with curry paste mixture.

2A FOR A CHARCOAL GRILL Open bottom vent completely. Light large chimney starter filled with charcoal briquettes (6 quarts). When top coals are partially covered with ash, pour evenly over grill. Set cooking grate in place, cover, and open lid vent completely. Heat grill until hot, about 5 minutes.

2B FOR A GAS GRILL Turn all burners to high; cover; and heat grill until hot, about 15 minutes. Leave all burners on high.

3 Clean cooking grate, then repeatedly brush grate with well-oiled paper towels until grate is black and glossy, 5 to 10 times. Place mahi-mahi skin side up on grill, perpendicular to grate bars. Cook (covered if using gas) until well browned on first side, about 3 minutes. Using 2 fish spatulas, flip mahi-mahi and cook until fish flakes apart when gently prodded with paring knife and registers 130 to 135 degrees, 3 to 8 minutes. Transfer fillets to platter and serve with pineapple salsa.

Grilled Cod and Summer Squash Packets

SERVES 4 **TIME** 30 minutes

Why This Recipe Works This all-in-one meal of grilled fish and vegetables captures the flavors of summer in a tidy package. Tomatoes and summer squash cook at the same rate as cod fillets, and the foil packets ensure that you don't lose a drop of juices to the flames. Before cooking the vegetables, you'll boost their flavors by tossing them with some potent garlic oil, reserving the rest to drizzle on before serving. Briny capers and lemon slices perk up the packets. Black sea bass, haddock, hake, or pollock may be substituted for the cod.

- ½ cup extra-virgin olive oil
- 2 shallots, sliced thin
- 6 garlic cloves, sliced thin
- 1 tablespoon kosher salt, divided
- 1¼ teaspoons pepper, divided
- 1 pound summer squash, sliced ¼ inch thick
- 12 ounces plum tomatoes, sliced ½ inch thick
- ¼ cup capers, rinsed
- 4 (6- to 8-ounce) skinless cod fillets, 1 inch thick
- 1 lemon, sliced into ¼-inch-thick rounds
- 2 tablespoons minced fresh parsley

1 Spray centers of four 18 by 14-inch sheets of aluminum foil with vegetable oil spray. Microwave oil, shallots, garlic, 2 teaspoons salt, and 1 teaspoon pepper in large bowl until garlic begins to brown, about 2 minutes. Add squash, tomatoes, and capers to garlic oil and toss to coat.

2 Pat cod dry with paper towels and sprinkle with remaining 1 teaspoon salt and remaining ¼ teaspoon pepper. Divide vegetable mixture evenly among centers of each piece of foil; reserve garlic oil in bowl. Top each vegetable pile with cod fillet, then lay lemon slices evenly over top. Bring short sides of foil together and crimp to seal. Crimp remaining open ends of packets to seal.

3A FOR A CHARCOAL GRILL Open bottom vent completely. Light large chimney starter filled with charcoal briquettes (6 quarts). When top coals are partially covered with ash, pour evenly over grill. Set cooking grate in place, cover, and open lid vent completely. Heat grill until hot, about 5 minutes.

3B FOR A GAS GRILL Turn all burners to high; cover; and heat grill until hot, about 15 minutes. Leave all burners on high.

4 Clean and oil cooking grate. Place packets squash side down on grill and cook until cod registers 130 to 135 degrees, about 10 minutes. (To check temperature, poke thermometer through foil of 1 packet and into fish.) Carefully open packets, sprinkle with parsley, and drizzle with reserved garlic oil to taste. Serve.

Temping Foil-Wrapped Fish

Here's a way to test for doneness (135 degrees) without opening the packets: Before cooking, mark an "X" on the outside of the foil where the fish is the thickest with a permanent marker. Insert an instant-read thermometer through the "X" into the fish.

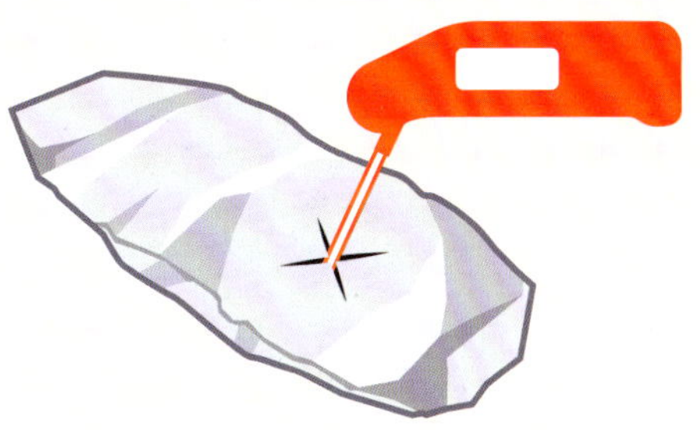

Grilled Halibut with Spicy Orange and Fennel Salad

SERVES 4 **TIME** 40 minutes

Why This Recipe Works Halibut fillets stay intact on the grill while picking up plenty of smoky flavor and appealing char marks. A spicy grilled orange and fennel salad provides a wonderful contrast to the rich fish. Swordfish or mahi-mahi can be substituted for the halibut. For a spicier dish, use the larger amount of chili paste. If your fennel doesn't have fronds, substitute basil or parsley leaves or use more mint.

- ½ cup extra-virgin olive oil, divided
- 3 tablespoons white wine vinegar
- 1–2 teaspoons Calabrian chili paste
- 2 teaspoons kosher salt, divided
- 2 oranges plus ½ teaspoon grated orange zest
- 1 large shallot, sliced thin
- 2 fennel bulbs, each cut through core into 8 wedges, base trimmed, stalks discarded, ¼ cup fronds torn
- 4 (6- to 8-ounce) skin-on halibut fillets, 1 to 1½ inches thick
- ¼ cup fresh mint leaves

1 Whisk ¼ cup oil, vinegar, chili paste, ½ teaspoon salt, and orange zest together in medium bowl. Stir in shallot; set aside for serving.

2 Cut away peel and pith from oranges, then slice crosswise into 1-inch-thick rounds. Brush fennel and oranges with 2 tablespoons oil and sprinkle with ½ teaspoon salt. Pat halibut dry with paper towels, brush with remaining 2 tablespoons oil, and sprinkle with remaining 1 teaspoon salt.

3A FOR A CHARCOAL GRILL Open bottom vent completely. Light large chimney starter mounded with charcoal briquettes (7 quarts). When top coals are partially covered with ash, pour evenly over grill. Set cooking grate in place, cover, and open lid vent completely. Heat grill until hot, about 5 minutes.

3B FOR A GAS GRILL Turn all burners to high; cover; and heat grill until hot, about 15 minutes. Leave all burners on high.

4 Clean and oil cooking grate. Place fennel and oranges on grill and cook, turning as needed, until lightly charred on all sides, 8 to 10 minutes; transfer to plate. Clean grate again, then repeatedly brush grate with well-oiled paper towels until grate is black and glossy, 5 to 10 times. Place halibut on grill and cook until fish flakes when gently prodded with paring knife and registers 130 to 135 degrees, 10 to 15 minutes, using 2 fish spatulas to flip halfway through cooking. Carefully transfer halibut to cutting board, tent with aluminum foil, and let rest while assembling salad.

5 Arrange fennel and oranges attractively on platter, top with fennel fronds and mint, and drizzle with shallot mixture. Remove skin from fillets by slipping knife or thin metal spatula between them. Serve halibut with salad.

Grilled Whole Trout with Marjoram and Lemon

SERVES 4 **TIME** 40 minutes

Why This Recipe Works When you're grilling a whole trout, getting a beautifully browned, moist, and tender fish off the grill in one piece can be challenging. The key is making sure the fish releases from the grill before the interior overcooks. Applying a mixture of honey and mayonnaise to its exterior helps the trout to brown more quickly; once its skin is charred and crisp, it naturally releases from the grill. We prefer marjoram in this recipe, but thyme or oregano can be substituted. For information on flipping a whole fish on the grill, see page 268.

- 2 teaspoons minced fresh marjoram
- 1 teaspoon grated lemon zest, plus lemon wedges for serving
- 2 teaspoons kosher salt
- 4 (10- to 12-ounce) boneless whole rainbow trout, gutted, fins snipped off with scissors
- 1 teaspoon pepper
- 2 tablespoons mayonnaise
- ½ teaspoon honey
- 1 (13 by 9-inch) disposable aluminum pan (if using charcoal)

1 Place marjoram, lemon zest, and salt on cutting board and chop until finely minced and well combined. Rinse trout under cold running water and pat dry with paper towels. Lay trout flesh side up and sprinkle evenly with marjoram mixture and pepper. Close up fish and let stand for 10 minutes. Stir mayonnaise and honey together. Brush mayonnaise mixture evenly over entire exterior of each fish.

2A FOR A CHARCOAL GRILL Poke twelve ½-inch holes in bottom of disposable pan. Open bottom vent completely and place disposable pan in center of grill. Light large chimney starter two-thirds filled with charcoal briquettes (4 quarts). When top coals are partially covered with ash, pour into even layer in disposable pan. Set cooking grate over coals with bars parallel to long side of disposable pan, cover, and open lid vent completely. Heat grill until hot, about 5 minutes.

GRILLED HALIBUT WITH
SPICY ORANGE AND FENNEL SALAD

2B FOR A GAS GRILL Turn all burners to high; cover; and heat grill until hot, about 15 minutes. Leave all burners on high.

3 Clean cooking grate, then repeatedly brush grate with well-oiled paper towels until grate is black and glossy, 5 to 10 times. Place trout on grill (over coals if using charcoal and covered if using gas) and cook until skin is browned and beginning to blister, 2 to 4 minutes. Using 2 fish spatulas, carefully flip fish. Cook until second side is browned, beginning to blister, and thickest part of trout registers 130 to 135 degrees, 2 to 4 minutes. Transfer fish to platter and let rest for 5 minutes. Serve with lemon wedges.

VARIATIONS

Grilled Whole Trout with Lime and Coriander

Substitute 1 teaspoon ground coriander for marjoram, and lime zest and wedges for lemon zest and wedges.

Grilled Whole Trout with Orange and Fennel

Substitute 1 teaspoon ground fennel for marjoram and orange zest for lemon zest.

GRILLED WHOLE TROUT WITH MARJORAM AND LEMON

Grilled Stuffed Trout

SERVES 4 **TIME** 1 hour

Why This Recipe Works One of our favorite ways to prepare trout is stuffed with a simple filling prior to grilling. Oiling the fish as well as the cooking grate helps avoid any sticking issues. Bacon is a classic pairing with trout, and spinach, red bell pepper, and onion make ideal additions. To control moisture, we precook the stuffing before it goes into the fish and brighten the flavors with a shot of cider vinegar. In less than 15 minutes on the grill, the trout become perfectly browned and smoky-sweet. For information on flipping a whole fish on the grill, see page 268.

- 4 slices bacon, cut into ¼-inch pieces
- 1 onion, halved and sliced thin
- 1 red bell pepper, stemmed, seeded, and chopped
- 2 teaspoons kosher salt, divided
- 8 ounces (8 cups) baby spinach
- 2 teaspoons cider vinegar
- 4 (7- to 10-ounce) whole trout, scaled, gutted, and fins snipped off with scissors
- 1 tablespoon vegetable oil
- ¼ teaspoon pepper
- Lemon wedges

1 Cook bacon in 12-inch skillet over medium heat until browned and crispy, about 8 minutes. Using slotted spoon, transfer bacon to paper towel–lined plate, leaving fat in skillet. Return skillet to medium-high heat; add onion, bell pepper, and 1 teaspoon salt; and cook until vegetables are softened and begin to brown, 5 to 7 minutes.

2 Stir in spinach and vinegar and cook until spinach is wilted and all extra moisture has evaporated, about 5 minutes. Transfer mixture to colander and let drain for 10 minutes. Stir in cooked bacon and season with salt and pepper to taste.

3 Rinse trout under cold water, then pat dry with paper towels. Rub exterior of trout with oil, then sprinkle exteriors and cavities with remaining 1 teaspoon salt and pepper. Divide spinach mixture evenly among cavities, about a generous ¼ cup per fish.

4A FOR A CHARCOAL GRILL Open bottom vent completely. Light large chimney starter filled with charcoal briquettes (6 quarts). When top coals are partially covered with ash, pour evenly over grill. Set cooking grate in place, cover, and open lid vent completely. Heat grill until hot, about 5 minutes.

4B FOR A GAS GRILL Turn all burners to high; cover; and heat grill until hot, about 15 minutes. Leave all burners on high.

5 Clean cooking grate, then repeatedly brush grate with well-oiled paper towels until grate is black and glossy, 5 to 10 times. Lay trout on grill, perpendicular to grate bars. Cook (covered if using gas) until flesh flakes when prodded with paring knife and filling is hot and thickest part of fish registers 130 to 135 degrees, 10 to 14 minutes, flipping trout gently halfway through cooking.

6 Transfer trout to wire rack, tent with aluminum foil, and let rest for 5 minutes. Serve with lemon wedges.

Grilled Whole Red Snapper

SERVES 4 **TIME** 45 minutes

Why This Recipe Works Roasting whole snapper on the grill is as simple as oven-roasting it and delivers an impressive fish dinner in mere minutes. The skin protects the fish and seals in flavor while the bones keep the fish moist. We make shallow diagonal slashes on the skin to ensure even cooking and seasoning (and to help gauge doneness more easily) and then give the fish a light coating of oil and a sprinkling of salt and pepper. We love the simplicity of this preparation because it allows the flavor imparted from the grill to really come through. After grilling, a few simple cuts yield four delicious fillets (see page 269 for more information). You can substitute black sea bass or branzino for the snapper. Avoid fish weighing more than 2 pounds; they will be hard to maneuver on the grill. To take the temperature, insert the thermometer into the fish through the opening by the gills.

- 2 (1½-pound) whole red snapper, scaled, gutted, and fins snipped off with scissors
- 3 tablespoons extra-virgin olive oil
- 2 teaspoons kosher salt
- ½ teaspoon pepper

1 Rinse snapper under cold water, then pat dry with paper towels. Using sharp knife, make 3 shallow diagonal slashes 2 inches apart through skin on both sides of fish, being careful not to cut into flesh. Rub exterior of snapper with oil, then sprinkle exterior and cavity with salt and pepper.

2A **FOR A CHARCOAL GRILL** Open bottom vent completely. Light large chimney starter filled with charcoal briquettes (6 quarts). When top coals are partially covered with ash, pour evenly over grill. Set cooking grate in place, cover, and open lid vent completely. Heat grill until hot, about 5 minutes.

2B **FOR A GAS GRILL** Turn all burners to high; cover; and heat grill until hot, about 15 minutes. Leave all burners on high.

GRILLED WHOLE RED SNAPPER

3 Clean cooking grate, then repeatedly brush grate with well-oiled paper towels until grate is black and glossy, 5 to 10 times. Place snapper on grill, perpendicular to grate bars. Cook (covered if using gas) until browned and crisp, 6 to 7 minutes. Using 2 fish spatulas, flip snapper; cook (covered if using gas) until flesh is no longer translucent at center, second side is blistered and crisp, and fish registers 130 to 135 degrees, 6 to 8 minutes. Transfer snapper to plate and let rest for 10 minutes.

4 Fillet each snapper by making vertical cut just behind head from top of fish to belly. Make another cut along top of snapper from head to tail. Starting at head and working toward tail, gently slide fish spatula between top fillet and bones to separate; transfer fillet to serving platter. Gently lift tail and peel skeleton and head from bottom fillet; discard head and skeleton. Transfer second fillet, skin side up, to platter. Serve.

7

Vegetable Dishes + Vegetarian Mains

VEGETABLE SIDES

SALADS AND PLATTERS

BURGERS, SANDWICHES, AND MORE

TOFU AND TEMPEH

IN DEPTH

Grilling Basics for Vegetables and Fruits

Throwing some vegetables and/or fruit onto the grate during a grilling session is a smart way to take advantage of still-hot coals or extra space on the grate. You can grill a side dish or dessert—or you can save what you grill for later, to be tucked into sandwiches or tossed into salads. Grilling softens vegetables and fruits, mellows their flavor, intensifies their sweetness through caramelization, and adds complexity through charring.

GETTING STARTED

You'll find plenty of recipes in this chapter for sides, salads, and platters. Here's a quick guide to prepping and grilling vegetables and fruits—some classic choices and others you may not have thought of.

1 Prepare a medium-hot fire: On a charcoal grill, use 4½ quarts of coals spread evenly over the grill. If you've already got food cooking on a hotter setup, grill the vegetables or fruits after the other items have come off the grill and the coals have cooled off a little.

2 Cut vegetables and fruits into large pieces to increase the surface area for charring and decrease chances of falling through the grate. You can cut them into smaller pieces before serving.

3 Place vegetables and fruits on a baking sheet and use a basting brush to coat them with oil (alternatively, toss them with oil in a bowl).

4 Grill cut sides down first to best control the charring that develops before flipping them to finish on the sturdier skin sides. (Or follow individual directions at right.) Move the pieces relatively frequently to avoid scorching, and cook until they're just tender and streaked with grill marks.

APPLES

Prep: Cut in half through core, then remove core and stem.

Grill: cut side down for 5 to 6 minutes; cut side up for 5 to 6 minutes

BABY BOK CHOY

Prep: Halve heads lengthwise through stem; rinse but don't dry.

Grill: 6 to 7 minutes, turning once

BANANAS

Prep: Leave skin on; cut in half lengthwise using sharp paring knife.

Grill: cut side down for 2 minutes; cut side up for 2 minutes

BELL PEPPERS

Prep: Halve lengthwise; remove core, seeds, and ribs. Cut each half in thirds lengthwise.

Grill: 7 to 9 minutes, turning once

CHERRY TOMATOES

Prep: Remove stems, thread onto skewers.

Grill: 3 to 6 minutes, turning often, until streaked with dark grill marks

ENDIVE

Prep: Halve lengthwise through core, keeping core intact to keep leaves together.

Grill: 5 to 7 minutes, turning once

FENNEL

Prep: Trim fronds and cut thin slice from base. Slice bulb vertically through base ¼ inch thick, leaving core intact.

Grill: 7 to 9 minutes, covered with an aluminum pan, turning once

MANGOS

Prep: Peel, pit, and cut into 4 pieces.

Grill: 5 minutes for larger pieces and 4 minutes for smaller pieces, turning all pieces once

ONIONS

Prep: Cut crosswise into ½-inch-thick slices; press toothpick into slice parallel to counter.

Grill: 10 to 12 minutes, turning once

PEACHES AND PLUMS

Prep: Cut in half and remove pit.

Grill: cut side down for 4 minutes, cut side up for 2 minutes

PEARS

Prep: Cut in half lengthwise. Remove core with melon baller or sturdy teaspoon measure. Use paring knife to cut out stem.

Grill: cut side down for 5 minutes, cut side up for 5 minutes

PINEAPPLES

Prep: Cut into half-circles.

Grill: 6 minutes, turning once

RADICCHIO

Prep: Quarter heads lengthwise.

Grill: 5 minutes, turning each wedge twice so that all sides spend time facing the fire, until edges are brown and wilted but centers are still firm

SCALLIONS

Prep: Choose scallions that measure at least ¼ inch in diameter. Trim root end; discard any loose or wilted outer layers.

Grill: 4 to 5 minutes, turning once

WHITE/CREMINI MUSHROOMS

Prep: Trim stems, thread onto skewers.

Grill: 6 to 7 minutes, turning often, until golden brown

ZUCCHINI/SUMMER SQUASH

Prep: Slice lengthwise into ½-inch-thick planks.

Grill: 8 to 10 minutes, turning once

How to Get Great Grilled Fruit

- Use ripe but firm fruit.
- Choose smaller plums, peaches, apples, and pears so they will heat through to the center before burning.
- Leave skin intact; the skin keeps the fruit from falling apart.
- Be sure to clean your cooking grate thoroughly before adding the fruit.

Grilled Artichokes with Lemon Butter

SERVES 4 to 6 **TIME** 1¼ hours

Why This Recipe Works Grilling artichokes brings out their nutty flavor. We parboil them first in a broth with lemon juice, red pepper flakes, and salt to ensure that they're completely tender and thoroughly seasoned. Tossing them in extra-virgin olive oil before grilling helps develop a flavorful char. A simple microwaved blend of lemon zest and juice, garlic, and butter is perfect for dipping or drizzling. Look for artichokes that are bright green, with tightly packed leaves; avoid soft artichokes or those with brown splotches. The leaves should not appear feathery or dried out. A rasp grater makes quick work of turning garlic into a paste. To eat the artichokes, use your teeth to scrape the flesh from the inner part of the exterior leaves. The tender inner leaves, heart, and stem are entirely edible.

GRILLED ARTICHOKES WITH LEMON BUTTER

- 4 (8- to 10-ounce) artichokes
- 1 teaspoon kosher salt, plus salt for boiling artichokes
- ½ teaspoon red pepper flakes
- 2 teaspoons grated lemon zest plus 1½ tablespoons juice, plus 1 lemon, halved
- 6 tablespoons unsalted butter
- 1 garlic clove, minced to paste
- ¼ teaspoon pepper
- 2 tablespoons extra-virgin olive oil

1 Cut off and discard bottom ¼ inch of each artichoke stem. Remove any leaves attached to stems. Using vegetable peeler, peel away outer layer of stems. Pull bottom row of tough outer leaves downward to break off at base. Cut off and discard top quarter of each artichoke. Using scissors, cut off sharp tips of remaining leaves all around artichokes.

2 Combine 3 quarts water, 6 tablespoons salt, and pepper flakes in Dutch oven. Squeeze juice from halved lemon into pot and add spent halves. Bring to boil over high heat. Add artichokes, cover, and reduce heat to medium-low. Simmer until tip of paring knife inserted into base of artichoke slips easily in and out, 25 to 28 minutes, stirring occasionally.

3 Meanwhile, combine butter, garlic, pepper, salt, and lemon zest in bowl. Microwave at 50 percent power, stirring occasionally, until melted and fragrant, about 2 minutes. Stir in lemon juice and season with salt and pepper to taste.

4 Set wire rack in rimmed baking sheet. Place artichokes stem side up on prepared rack and let drain for 10 minutes. Cut artichokes in half lengthwise. Using spoon, scoop out fuzzy choke, leaving small cavity in center of each half. Before grilling, brush artichokes with oil.

5A FOR A CHARCOAL GRILL Open bottom vent completely. Light large chimney starter filled with charcoal briquettes (6 quarts). When top coals are partially covered with ash, pour evenly over grill. Set cooking grate in place, cover, and open lid vent completely. Heat grill until hot, about 5 minutes.

5B FOR A GAS Turn all burners to high; cover; and heat grill until hot, about 15 minutes. Leave all burners on high.

6 Clean and oil cooking grate. Place artichokes on grill and cook (covered if using gas) until lightly charred, 4 to 8 minutes, flipping halfway through cooking. Transfer artichokes to platter and tent with aluminum foil. Briefly rewarm lemon butter in microwave, if necessary, and serve with artichokes.

Prepping Artichokes for the Grill

1 Cut off bottom ¼ inch of stem; remove leaves attached to stem. Using vegetable peeler, peel stem.

2 Pull bottom row of tough outer leaves downward toward stem and break off at base.

3 Cut off and discard top quarter. Use scissors to cut off sharp tips of remaining leaves.

Grilled Asparagus

SERVES 4 to 6 **TIME** 25 minutes

Why This Recipe Works For superb grilled asparagus, we use thicker spears, which can take the heat long enough to develop good char and retain a meaty, crisp-tender texture. With a simple medium-hot fire, the spears are on and off the grill in less than 10 minutes. Brushing them with butter rather than oil before grilling yields crispy, nutty asparagus and is the perfect opportunity to add some flavor. Use asparagus that is at least ½ inch thick near the base. Do not use pencil-thin asparagus; it cannot withstand the heat and will overcook.

- 1½ pounds thick asparagus spears, trimmed
- 3 tablespoons unsalted butter, melted
- ½ teaspoon kosher salt
- ¼ teaspoon pepper

1 Brush asparagus with melted butter and sprinkle with salt and pepper.

2A FOR A CHARCOAL GRILL Open bottom vent completely. Light large chimney starter three-quarters filled with charcoal briquettes (4½ quarts). When top coals are partially covered with ash, pour evenly over grill. Set cooking grate in place, cover, and open lid vent completely. Heat grill until hot, about 5 minutes.

2B FOR A GAS GRILL Turn all burners to high; cover; and heat grill until hot, about 15 minutes. Turn all burners to medium-high.

3 Clean and oil cooking grate. Place asparagus on grill and cook until just tender and browned, 4 to 10 minutes, turning halfway through cooking. Transfer asparagus to platter and serve.

VARIATIONS

Grilled Asparagus with Chili-Lime Butter

Add 1 teaspoon grated lime zest, ½ teaspoon chili powder, ¼ teaspoon cayenne pepper, and ⅛ teaspoon red pepper flakes to melted butter.

Grilled Asparagus with Cumin Butter

Add 2 minced small garlic cloves, 1 teaspoon grated lemon zest, ½ teaspoon ground cumin, and ½ teaspoon ground coriander to melted butter.

Grilled Asparagus with Garlic Butter

Add 3 minced small garlic cloves to melted butter.

Grilled Asparagus with Orange-Thyme Butter

Add 1 teaspoon grated orange zest and 1 teaspoon minced fresh thyme to melted butter.

Grill-Roasted Bell Peppers with Sherry Vinaigrette

SERVES 4 **TIME** 55 minutes

Why This Recipe Works Grill roasting is an easy way to add smoky flavor to sweet bell peppers. To get them softened but not mushy, we start by steaming the peppers in a disposable pan with a mixture of olive oil, garlic, salt, and pepper; then, we transfer them to the cooking grate to blacken. The leftover oil in the pan makes the base for a tangy vinaigrette, which we toss with the peeled peppers. Take care not to overroast the peppers—when the skin of a pepper puffs up and turns black, it has reached the optimal point for both flavor and texture.

- ¼ cup extra-virgin olive oil
- 3 garlic cloves, peeled and smashed
- 1 teaspoon kosher salt
- ¼ teaspoon pepper
- 1 (13 by 9-inch) disposable aluminum pan
- 6 red bell peppers
- 1 tablespoon sherry vinegar

1 Combine oil, garlic, salt, and pepper in disposable pan. Using paring knife, cut around stems of peppers and remove cores and seeds. Place peppers in pan and turn to coat with oil. Cover pan tightly with aluminum foil.

2A **FOR A CHARCOAL GRILL** Open bottom vent completely. Light large chimney starter filled with charcoal briquettes (6 quarts). When top coals are partially covered with ash, pour evenly over half of grill. Set cooking grate in place, cover, and open lid vent completely. Heat grill until hot, about 5 minutes.

2B **FOR A GAS GRILL** Turn all burners to high; cover; and heat grill until hot, about 15 minutes. Leave all burners on high.

3 Clean and oil cooking grate. Place pan on grill (hotter side if using charcoal). Cover and cook until peppers are just tender and skins begin to blister, 10 to 15 minutes, rotating and shaking pan halfway through cooking.

4 Remove pan from heat and carefully remove foil. Using tongs, remove peppers from pan, allowing juices to drip back into pan, and place on grill (hotter side if using charcoal). Cover and cook peppers, turning as needed, until skins are blackened, 10 to 15 minutes.

5 Transfer juices and garlic in pan to medium bowl and whisk in vinegar. Remove peppers from grill, return to now-empty pan, and cover tightly with foil. Let peppers steam for 5 minutes. Using spoon, scrape blackened skin off each pepper. Quarter peppers lengthwise, add to vinaigrette in bowl, and toss to combine. Season with salt and pepper to taste, and serve.

VARIATION

Grill-Roasted Peppers with Rosemary

Add 1 sprig rosemary to oil in step 1; discard rosemary sprig after grilling. Substitute 1 tablespoon red wine vinegar for sherry vinegar.

Grilled Broccoli with Lemon and Parmesan

SERVES 4 **TIME** 40 minutes

Why This Recipe Works Grilling broccoli adds flavorful char to the vivid green vegetable, making it a summertime barbecue treat. To avoid toughness and promote even cooking, we peel the stalks with a vegetable peeler and divide the broccoli crowns into spears with florets measuring 3 to 4 inches wide and stems that are ½ to ¾ inch thick. To ensure tender broccoli, we wrap it in an aluminum foil packet and let it steam first on the grill, flipping the packs halfway through grilling. We then remove the spears and place them directly on the grill to char. Grilled lemon halves add brightness and grill flavor, while shredded Parmesan provides a salty bite. To keep the packs from tearing, use heavy-duty aluminum foil. Use the large holes of a box grater to shred the Parmesan.

- ¼ cup extra-virgin olive oil, plus extra for drizzling
- 1 tablespoon water
- 1½ teaspoons kosher salt
- ½ teaspoon pepper
- 2 pounds broccoli
- 1 lemon, halved
- ¼ cup shredded Parmesan cheese

1 Cut two 26 by 12-inch sheets of heavy-duty aluminum foil. Whisk oil, water, salt, and pepper together in large bowl.

2 Trim stalk ends so each entire head of broccoli measures 6 to 7 inches long. Using vegetable peeler, peel away tough outer layer of broccoli stalks (about ⅛ inch). Cut stalks in half lengthwise (halved stalks should be ½ to ¾ inch thick and florets 3 to 4 inches wide). Add broccoli spears to oil mixture and toss well to coat.

3 Divide broccoli between sheets of foil, cut side down and alternating direction of florets and stems. Bring short sides of foil together and crimp tightly. Crimp long ends to seal packs tightly.

4A **FOR A CHARCOAL GRILL** Open bottom vent completely. Light large chimney starter filled with charcoal briquettes (6 quarts). When top coals are partially covered with ash, pour evenly over half of grill. Set cooking grate in place, cover, and open lid vent completely. Heat grill until hot, about 5 minutes.

4B **FOR A GAS GRILL** Turn all burners to high; cover; and heat grill until hot, about 15 minutes. Leave all burners on high.

5 Clean and oil cooking grate. Place packs on grill (over coals if using charcoal), cover, and cook for 8 minutes, flipping packs halfway through cooking. Transfer packs to rimmed baking sheet and, using scissors, carefully cut open, allowing steam to escape away from you. (Broccoli should be bright green and fork inserted into stalks should meet some resistance.)

6 Discard foil and place broccoli and lemon halves cut side down on grill (over coals if using charcoal). Grill (covered if using gas), turning broccoli as needed, until broccoli stalks are fork-tender and well charred, and lemons are well charred on cut side, 6 to 8 minutes. Return broccoli and lemons to sheet as they finish cooking.

7 Transfer broccoli to cutting board and cut into 2-inch pieces; transfer to platter. Season with salt and pepper to taste. Squeeze lemon over broccoli to taste, sprinkle with Parmesan, and drizzle with extra oil. Serve.

VARIATION

Grilled Broccoli with Sweet Chili Sauce

Omit lemon and Parmesan. Whisk 4 teaspoons toasted sesame oil, 2½ teaspoons sugar, 2 teaspoons chili-garlic sauce, 1 teaspoon distilled white vinegar, and ½ teaspoon kosher salt together in bowl; drizzle grilled broccoli with mixture before serving.

GRILLED BROCCOLI WITH LEMON AND PARMESAN

Maximize the Fire

One of the biggest perks of grilling boneless, skinless chicken breasts; steaks; chops; or fish fillets is that they cook quickly. So when you have extra time and ingredients—especially when you're grilling over charcoal and don't want to waste the still-hot coals—go ahead and grill something to serve on the side. This can be a quick-cooking vegetable (asparagus, summer squash, corn) or an ingredient that you turn into a garnish or sauce.

Grilled Butternut Squash

SERVES 4 to 6 **TIME** 40 minutes

Why This Recipe Works Like roasting, grilling brings out the best in butternut squash; in early fall, while grilling is still possible and squash fills markets, this dish is a no-brainer. We peel the squash to remove not only the tough outer skin but also the rugged fibrous layer of white flesh just beneath; this ensures that it's supremely tender. Parboiling the squash before grilling helps jump-start the cooking process so that the squash can finish cooking on the grill relatively quickly.

- 1 small butternut squash (about 2 pounds), peeled, seeded, and cut into ½-inch-thick slices
- 3 tablespoons extra-virgin olive oil
- 1 teaspoon kosher salt, plus extra for boiling squash
- ½ teaspoon pepper

1 Place squash slices in large pot and cover with 2 quarts cold water. Add 1 teaspoon salt and bring to boil over high heat. Reduce heat to medium and simmer until squash is barely tender, about 3 minutes. Drain squash in colander, being careful not to break squash slices. Transfer squash to large bowl, drizzle with oil, and sprinkle with salt and pepper; gently turn squash to coat.

2A FOR A CHARCOAL GRILL Open bottom vent completely. Light large chimney starter three-quarters filled with charcoal briquettes (4½ quarts). When top coals are partially covered with ash, pour evenly over grill. Set cooking grate in place, cover, and open lid vent completely. Heat grill until hot, about 5 minutes.

2B FOR A GAS GRILL Turn all burners to high; cover; and heat grill until hot, about 15 minutes. Turn all burners to medium-high.

3 Clean and oil cooking grate. Place squash on grill and cook until dark brown caramelization occurs and flesh becomes very tender, 8 to 10 minutes, flipping halfway through cooking. Serve hot, warm, or at room temperature.

VARIATION

Spicy Grilled Butternut Squash with Garlic and Rosemary

Omit pepper. Add 2 tablespoons brown sugar, 1 teaspoon chopped fresh rosemary, 1 minced garlic clove, and ½ teaspoon red pepper flakes to boiled squash with oil and salt in step 1.

GRILLED BUTTERNUT SQUASH

Cutting Up Squash for Grilling

1 Using sharp vegetable peeler or chef's knife, remove skin and fibrous threads just below skin from squash.

2 Trim off top and bottom and cut squash crosswise where narrow neck and wide curved bottom meet.

3 Cut squash base in half lengthwise, then scoop out and discard seeds and fibers. Slice both sections into ½-inch-thick pieces.

Grilled Cabbage

SERVES 4 **TIME** 35 minutes plus 45 minutes salting

Why This Recipe Works Cabbage is an underdog vegetable—except for coleslaw, few people give it much thought—but fire transforms it into a soft, sweet, deliciously smoky dish. We slice it into thick wedges, keeping the core intact. To get the inside to cook before the exterior overcooks, we salt the cabbage wedges, which draws out moisture: The moisture turns to steam on the grill, helping the interior of the wedges cook through. A simple lemon-herb vinaigrette, which we brush on the cabbage both before and after grilling, adds bright flavor. Leave the core intact so the cabbage wedges don't fall apart on the grill.

- 2 teaspoons kosher salt
- 1 head green cabbage (2 pounds), cut into 8 wedges through core
- 1 tablespoon minced fresh thyme
- 2 teaspoons minced shallot
- 2 teaspoons honey
- 1 teaspoon Dijon mustard
- ½ teaspoon grated lemon zest plus 2 tablespoons juice
- ¼ teaspoon pepper
- 6 tablespoons extra-virgin olive oil

1 Sprinkle salt evenly over cabbage wedges and let sit for 45 minutes. Combine thyme, shallot, honey, mustard, lemon zest and juice, and pepper in bowl. Slowly whisk in oil until incorporated. Measure out ¼ cup vinaigrette and set aside for serving. Before grilling, brush 1 cut side of cabbage wedges with half of vinaigrette.

2A **FOR A CHARCOAL GRILL** Open bottom vent completely. Light large chimney starter half-filled with charcoal briquettes (3 quarts). When top coals are partially covered with ash, pour evenly over grill. Set cooking grate in place, cover, and open lid vent completely. Heat grill until hot, about 5 minutes.

2B **FOR A GAS GRILL** Turn all burners to high; cover; and heat grill until hot, about 15 minutes. Turn all burners to medium.

3 Clean and oil cooking grate. Place cabbage vinaigrette side down on grill and cook (covered if using gas) until well browned, 7 to 10 minutes. Brush tops of wedges with remaining vinaigrette. Flip cabbage and cook (covered if using gas) until second side is well browned and fork-tender, 7 to 10 minutes. Transfer cabbage to platter and drizzle with reserved vinaigrette for serving. Season with salt and pepper to taste. Serve.

Grilled Carrots with Feta-Herb Sauce

SERVES 4 **TIME** 45 minutes

Why This Recipe Works Grilling carrots gives them an enchanting smokiness and crispy char. Leaving them whole makes them easy to maneuver on the grill. Because carrots are dense, we start them in the microwave; once we transfer them to the fire they cook through until tender and creamy. After grilling the carrots, we toss them with garam masala and fresh lemon juice. A quick and easy blender sauce of rich, briny feta; creamy yogurt; fresh herbs; olive oil; lemon; and a bit of fresh garlic makes a delicious bed for these chargrilled beauties, and pistachios and mint provide a colorful, crunchy crown. Look for carrots that are 1 to 1½ inches in diameter at the larger end. Smaller carrots may need to be cooked for a slightly shorter time. Larger carrots can be halved lengthwise to work with this recipe.

GRILLED CARROTS WITH FETA-HERB SAUCE

SAUCE

- 4 ounces feta cheese, crumbled (1 cup)
- ¼ cup plain whole-milk yogurt
- ¼ cup fresh parsley leaves
- ¼ cup fresh mint leaves
- 2 tablespoons lemon juice
- 2 tablespoons extra-virgin olive oil
- 1 large garlic clove, smashed and peeled
- 1 teaspoon honey
- ¼ teaspoon pepper
- 2 tablespoons water

CARROTS

- 2 pounds carrots, peeled
- 2 tablespoons extra-virgin olive oil, divided
- 2 teaspoons kosher salt
- 2 teaspoons garam masala
- 2 teaspoons lemon juice
- ¼ cup shelled pistachios, toasted and chopped coarse
- 2 tablespoons torn fresh mint

1 FOR THE SAUCE Process feta, yogurt, parsley, mint, lemon juice, oil, garlic, honey and pepper in blender until smooth, about 1 minute, scraping down sides of blender jar as needed. Add water, 1 tablespoon at a time, as needed for sauce to come together. Transfer to small bowl and set aside for serving.

2 FOR THE CARROTS Toss carrots, 1 tablespoon oil, and salt together in large bowl. Cover and microwave carrots until pliable but firm, about 9 minutes, shaking bowl to redistribute every 3 minutes. Transfer carrots to rimmed baking sheet (discard any juices in bowl) and toss with remaining 1 tablespoon oil.

3A FOR A CHARCOAL GRILL Open bottom vent completely. Light large chimney starter filled with charcoal briquettes (6 quarts). When top coals are partially covered with ash, pour evenly over grill. Set cooking grate in place, cover, and open lid vent completely. Heat grill until hot, about 5 minutes.

3B FOR A GAS GRILL Turn all burners to high; cover; and heat grill until hot, about 15 minutes. Leave all burners on high.

4 Clean and oil cooking grate. Place carrots on grill perpendicular to bars. Grill (covered if using gas), turning as needed, until charred on all sides, 8 to 12 minutes. Return carrots to sheet and toss gently with garam masala and lemon juice.

5 Spread ⅓ cup sauce over serving platter. Arrange carrots on top of sauce. Sprinkle with pistachios and mint. Serve warm or at room temperature, passing remaining sauce separately.

GRILL-ROASTED WHOLE CAULIFLOWER WITH TAHINI-YOGURT SAUCE

Grill-Roasted Whole Cauliflower with Tahini-Yogurt Sauce

SERVES 4 to 6 **TIME** 1¼ hours

Why This Recipe Works You don't need to cook a large cut of meat to present an entrée off the grill that will impress your guests: This whole head of cauliflower, brined for optimum seasoning and caramelization and gorgeously golden from turmeric, is both dramatic and delicious. Parcooking the cauliflower in the microwave ensures that it's tender throughout by the time the exterior is deeply charred. Creamy tahini-yogurt sauce underscores the smoky element, and pistachios add crunch. Choose a cauliflower head with plenty of leaves, if you like; cauliflower leaves are edible and become delightfully crispy on the grill. Look for a head of cauliflower with densely packed florets that feels heavy for its size.

TAHINI-YOGURT SAUCE

- ½ cup tahini
- ¼ cup plain Greek yogurt
- ¼ cup water, plus extra as needed
- 3 tablespoons lemon juice
- 1 garlic clove, minced

CAULIFLOWER

- 1 head cauliflower (2 pounds)
- ½ cup kosher salt for brining
- ½ cup sugar for brining
- ¼ cup extra-virgin olive oil
- 1½ teaspoons ground turmeric
- ¼ teaspoon pepper
- 2 tablespoons chopped toasted pistachios
- 2 tablespoons chopped fresh parsley

1 FOR THE TAHINI-YOGURT SAUCE Whisk all ingredients in bowl until combined. Adjust consistency with extra water as needed and season with salt and pepper to taste. (Sauce can be refrigerated for up to 2 days.)

2 FOR THE CAULIFLOWER Trim stem of cauliflower, keeping leaves intact, so that it sits flat. Dissolve salt and sugar in 2 quarts cold water in large bowl. Holding cauliflower upside down by stem, gently dunk in brine and let sit for 5 minutes. Flip and continue to submerge for 1 minute until evenly moistened (do not pat dry). Transfer cauliflower stem down to large plate and cover with inverted large bowl. Microwave until cauliflower is translucent and tender and paring knife inserted in thickest stem of florets (not into core) meets no resistance, 8 to 14 minutes.

3 Carefully transfer cauliflower to paper towel–lined plate and pat dry. Whisk oil, turmeric, and pepper together in small bowl, then brush cauliflower with oil mixture.

4A FOR A CHARCOAL GRILL Open bottom vent completely. Light large chimney starter filled with charcoal briquettes (6 quarts). When top coals are partially covered with ash, pour evenly over half of grill. Set cooking grate in place, cover, and open lid vent completely. Heat grill until hot, about 5 minutes.

4B FOR A GAS GRILL Turn all burners to high; cover; and heat grill until hot, about 15 minutes. Leave primary burner on high and turn off other burner(s). (Adjust primary burner as needed to maintain grill temperature of 350 to 400 degrees.)

5 Clean and oil cooking grate. Place cauliflower stem side down on cooler side of grill (6 to 8 inches from heat source for gas grill). Cover and cook until cauliflower is deeply browned and leaves are charred and crisp, 35 to 55 minutes, rotating cauliflower halfway through cooking. Using spatula and tongs, transfer cauliflower to plate.

6 Spread two-thirds of tahini-yogurt sauce over serving platter. Center cauliflower stem side down on sauce and sprinkle with pistachios and parsley. Cut into wedges and serve, passing remaining sauce separately.

Grilled Corn with Basil and Lemon Butter

SERVES 4 to 6 **TIME** 30 minutes

Why This Recipe Works Fresh corn and the hot lick of the grill flame are a perfect matchup. To take this pairing to the next level, we first char the husked corn ears over a hot fire and then sizzle them with basil-and-lemon-flavored butter in a disposable pan right on the grill. Trapped moisture from the melting butter turns to steam, encouraging the kernels to cook through, and along the way the corn gets coated in rich butter. Our flavored butter variations combine sweet and spicy elements to create options for every palate. Use a disposable aluminum roasting pan that is at least 2¾ inches deep.

BASIL AND LEMON BUTTER

- 6 tablespoons unsalted butter, softened
- 2 tablespoons chopped fresh basil
- 1 tablespoon minced fresh parsley
- 1 teaspoon finely grated lemon zest
- 1 teaspoon kosher salt
- ¼ teaspoon pepper

CORN

- 1 (13 by 9-inch) disposable aluminum roasting pan
- 8 ears corn, husks and silk removed
- 2 tablespoons vegetable oil
- 1 teaspoon kosher salt
- ½ teaspoon pepper

1 FOR THE BASIL AND LEMON BUTTER Combine all ingredients in small bowl.

2 FOR THE CORN Place flavored butter in disposable pan. Brush corn evenly with oil and sprinkle with salt and pepper.

3A FOR A CHARCOAL GRILL Open bottom vent completely. Light large chimney starter three-quarters filled with charcoal briquettes (4½ quarts). When top coals are partially covered with ash, pour evenly over grill. Set cooking grate in place, cover, and open lid vent completely. Heat grill until hot, about 5 minutes.

GRILLED CORN WITH CHIPOTLE-CILANTRO BUTTER

3B **FOR A GAS GRILL** Turn all burners to high; cover; and heat grill until hot, about 15 minutes. Turn all burners to medium-high.

4 Clean and oil cooking grate. Place corn on grill and cook, turning as needed, until lightly charred on all sides, 5 to 9 minutes. Transfer corn to disposable pan and cover tightly with aluminum foil.

5 Place disposable pan on grill and cook, shaking pan frequently, until butter is sizzling, about 3 minutes. Remove pan from grill and carefully remove foil, allowing steam to escape away from you. Serve corn, spooning any butter in pan over individual ears.

VARIATIONS

Grilled Corn with Honey Butter

Substitute following mixture for Basil and Lemon Butter: Combine 6 tablespoons softened unsalted butter, 2 tablespoons honey, 1 teaspoon kosher salt, and ¼ teaspoon red pepper flakes in small bowl.

Grilled Corn with Chipotle-Cilantro Butter

Substitute following mixture for Basil and Lemon Butter: Combine 6 tablespoons softened unsalted butter, 2 tablespoons minced fresh cilantro, 1 tablespoon minced fresh parsley, 1 teaspoon minced canned chipotle chile in adobo sauce, ½ teaspoon finely grated orange zest, and 1 teaspoon kosher salt in small bowl.

Grilled Corn with New Orleans "Barbecue" Butter

Substitute following mixture for Basil and Lemon Butter: Combine 6 tablespoons softened unsalted butter, 1 minced garlic clove, 1 tablespoon Worcestershire sauce, 1 teaspoon tomato paste, ½ teaspoon minced fresh rosemary, ½ teaspoon minced fresh thyme, and ½ teaspoon cayenne pepper in small bowl.

Grilled Corn with Spicy Old Bay Butter

Substitute following mixture for Basil and Lemon Butter: Combine 6 tablespoons softened unsalted butter, 1 tablespoon hot sauce, 1 tablespoon minced fresh parsley, 1½ teaspoons Old Bay seasoning, and 1 teaspoon finely grated lemon zest in small bowl.

Elote

SERVES 6 **TIME** 25 minutes

Why This Recipe Works In Mexico, street vendors add kick to grilled corn by slathering it with a creamy, spicy, cheesy sauce. The corn takes on an irresistibly sweet, smoky, charred flavor, which is heightened by the lime juice and chili powder in the sauce. For our own rendition, we ditch the husks, coat the ears with oil to prevent sticking, and grill them directly on the grate over a hot fire so that the corn can develop plenty of char. If Mexican crema is not available, you can make your own; see page 397. If you can find queso fresco or Cotija, use either in place of the Pecorino Romano. If you prefer the corn spicy, add the optional cayenne pepper.

- 1½ ounces Pecorino Romano cheese, grated (¾ cup)
- 7 tablespoons Mexican crema
- 3 tablespoons minced fresh cilantro
- 4 teaspoons lime juice
- 1 garlic clove, minced
- ¾ teaspoon chili powder, divided
- ¼ teaspoon pepper
- ¼ teaspoon cayenne pepper (optional)
- 4 teaspoons vegetable oil
- ½ teaspoon kosher salt
- 6 ears corn, husks and silk removed

1 Combine Pecorino; mayonnaise; sour cream; cilantro; lime juice; garlic; ¼ teaspoon chili powder; pepper; and cayenne, if using, in large bowl. In second large bowl, combine oil, salt, and remaining ½ teaspoon chili powder. Add corn to oil mixture and toss to coat evenly.

2A **FOR A CHARCOAL GRILL** Open bottom vent completely. Light large chimney starter filled with charcoal briquettes (6 quarts). When top coals are partially covered with ash, pour evenly over half of grill. Set cooking grate in place, cover, and open lid vent completely. Heat grill until hot, about 5 minutes.

2B **FOR A GAS GRILL** Turn all burners to high; cover; and heat grill until hot, about 15 minutes. Leave all burners on high.

3 Clean and oil cooking grate. Place corn on grill (hotter side if using charcoal) and cook (covered if using gas), turning as needed, until lightly charred on all sides, 7 to 12 minutes. Transfer corn to bowl with cheese mixture and toss to coat evenly. Serve.

Grilled Eggplant with Yogurt Sauce

SERVES 6 to 8 **TIME** 35 minutes

Why This Recipe Works The biggest challenge when preparing eggplant in any form is excess moisture; that's why grilling is such an ideal method for cooking eggplant. On the grill, the moisture evaporates or drips away, and the eggplant browns and crisps beautifully. Cutting ¼-inch-thick slices produces a charred exterior and tender flesh. For flavor, we quickly infuse olive oil with garlic and red pepper flakes in the microwave and brush it on the eggplant slices before grilling. A tablespoon of the infused oil mixed with yogurt, lemon, and fresh herbs makes a flavorful sauce to drizzle on at the end.

- 6 tablespoons extra-virgin olive oil
- 5 garlic cloves, minced
- ⅛ teaspoon red pepper flakes
- ½ cup plain whole-milk yogurt
- 3 tablespoons minced fresh mint
- 1 teaspoon grated lemon zest plus 2 teaspoons juice
- 1 teaspoon ground cumin
- 1 teaspoon kosher salt, divided
- ½ teaspoon pepper
- 2 pounds eggplant, sliced into ¼-inch-thick rounds

1 Microwave oil, garlic, and pepper flakes in bowl until garlic is golden and crisp, about 2 minutes. Strain oil through fine-mesh strainer into clean bowl; reserve oil and crispy garlic separately.

2 Combine 1 tablespoon strained garlic oil, yogurt, mint, lemon zest and juice, cumin, and ¼ teaspoon salt in bowl; set aside for serving. Brush eggplant thoroughly with remaining garlic oil and sprinkle with pepper and remaining ¾ teaspoon salt.

3A **FOR A CHARCOAL GRILL** Open bottom vent completely. Light large chimney starter three-quarters filled with charcoal briquettes (4½ quarts). When top coals are partially covered with ash, pour evenly over grill. Set cooking grate in place, cover, and open lid vent completely. Heat grill until hot, about 5 minutes.

3B **FOR A GAS GRILL** Turn all burners to high; cover; and heat grill until hot, about 15 minutes. Turn all burners to medium-high.

4 Clean and oil cooking grate. Place half of eggplant on grill. Cook (covered if using gas), turning as needed, until browned and tender, 8 to 10 minutes. Transfer to platter and repeat with remaining eggplant. Before serving, drizzle with yogurt sauce and sprinkle with crispy garlic mixture.

Baba Ghanoush

SERVES 4 **TIME** 55 minutes plus 50 minutes cooling and resting

Why This Recipe Works The bedrock technique for this deeply flavored dip is cooking the eggplant over an open flame until the skin is charred (it gets discarded) and the interior is meltingly tender. First, pierce the eggplant skins to encourage moisture to evaporate and to prevent them from bursting open. Then, place them on the grill for about 30 minutes, until they're fully tender and smoky. While the eggplants cool, combine the garlic, lemon juice, and salt; let the mixture sit to temper the garlic's pungency. Whisking a generous amount of tahini (along with olive oil) into the eggplant ensures that the dip is rich and creamy. A rasp grater makes quick work of turning garlic into a paste. If the only eggplants you can find weigh more than 12 ounces, you may need to go a little heavier on the salt and lemon juice when seasoning to taste in step 6. The finished product should be assertive but not overpowering.

- 2 (12-ounce) eggplants
- 1 tablespoon lemon juice, plus extra for seasoning
- 2 teaspoons kosher salt
- 1 garlic clove, minced to paste
- ¼ cup tahini
- ¼ cup extra-virgin olive oil, divided
- 1 tablespoon chopped fresh parsley

1 Poke each eggplant about 6 times with paring knife.

2A **FOR A CHARCOAL GRILL** Open bottom vent completely. Light large chimney starter filled with charcoal briquettes (6 quarts). When top coals are partially covered with ash, pour evenly over grill. Set cooking grate in place, cover, and open lid vent completely. Heat grill until hot, about 5 minutes.

2B **FOR A GAS GRILL** Turn all burners to high; cover; and heat grill until hot, about 15 minutes. Leave all burners on high.

3 Clean and oil cooking grate. Place eggplants on grill; cover; and cook, turning as needed, until skin is charred and eggplant is very tender, about 30 minutes.

4 Transfer eggplants to plate and let cool completely, about 30 minutes. Meanwhile, combine lemon juice, salt, and garlic in medium bowl and let sit while eggplants cool.

5 Working with 1 eggplant at a time, split lengthwise on 1 side through skin and peel back skin to expose flesh. Using spoon, scoop out eggplant flesh; discard eggplant skin. Chop eggplant flesh fine with chef's knife and transfer to bowl with lemon juice mixture.

6 Add tahini and 2 tablespoons oil to eggplant mixture and whisk to combine. Let baba ghanoush sit for 20 minutes to allow flavors to blend, stirring occasionally. Season with extra lemon juice and salt to taste. Spread baba ghanoush in shallow bowl and drizzle with remaining 2 tablespoons oil. Sprinkle with parsley and serve.

Grilled White Mushrooms

SERVES 4 to 6 **TIME** 35 minutes

Why This Recipe Works Few foods benefit as much from the high, dry heat of live-fire cooking as mushrooms do. After grilling the mushrooms directly on the grate, we gather them in a disposable pan and toss them with melted butter, parsley, soy sauce, lemon juice, thyme, and garlic. We then set the pan back on the grill and stir the mushrooms for a few minutes while they absorb the flavors. For even cooking, choose mushrooms of a uniform size. Medium mushrooms (1 to 2 inches in diameter) are best here; large mushrooms take much longer to cook. Season and oil the mushrooms just before grilling, or they will develop a wrinkled appearance and slimy texture. A rasp grater makes quick work of turning garlic into a paste.

- 2 tablespoons unsalted butter, softened
- 2 tablespoons minced fresh parsley
- 1½ tablespoons soy sauce
- 1 tablespoon lemon juice
- 2 teaspoons minced fresh thyme
- 1 garlic clove, minced to paste
- 1 (13 by 9-inch) disposable aluminum pan
- 2 pounds white mushrooms, stems trimmed flush with caps
- 2 tablespoons extra-virgin olive oil
- 1 teaspoon kosher salt
- ½ teaspoon pepper

1 Combine butter, parsley, soy sauce, lemon juice, thyme, and garlic in disposable pan. Before grilling, toss mushrooms with oil, salt, and pepper in large bowl.

2A **FOR A CHARCOAL GRILL** Open bottom vent completely. Light large chimney starter filled with charcoal briquettes (6 quarts). When top coals are partially covered with ash, pour evenly over grill. Set cooking grate in place, cover, and open lid vent completely. Heat grill until hot, about 5 minutes.

2B **FOR A GAS GRILL** Turn all burners to high; cover; and heat grill until hot, about 15 minutes. Leave all burners on high.

3 Clean and oil cooking grate. Place mushrooms gill side up on grill and cook (covered if using gas) until mushrooms have released some liquid and have some grill marks, about 6 minutes. Flip and cook (covered if using gas) until second side is well browned, 4 to 6 minutes.

4 Transfer mushrooms to disposable pan and place pan on grill. Cook (covered if using gas), stirring frequently, until butter has melted and mushrooms have absorbed liquid and appear glazed, about 3 minutes. Serve.

BABA GHANOUSH

GRILLED WHITE MUSHROOMS

Grilled Marinated Portobello Mushrooms

SERVES 6 to 8 **TIME** 25 minutes plus 1 hour marinating

Why This Recipe Works These portobello mushrooms are plump, juicy, and slightly charred, with all the smoky flavor of the grill, thanks to an old tool of the campfire trade: aluminum foil. Wrapped individually in packets of foil, the mushrooms cook through in about 10 minutes; we then unwrap them and pop them back on the heat for just a minute to sear in the grilled flavor. We cook them gill side up the whole time to trap the juices and flavor in the meaty mushrooms without sacrificing any of the grill's smoky attributes. We prefer large, 5- to 6-inch portobellos here; however, if you can't find large ones, use six 4- to 5-inch portobellos, which are usually sold three to a package; decrease their grilling time wrapped in foil to about 8 minutes. Removing the gills from the mushrooms prevents a muddy flavor. To keep the packs from tearing, use heavy-duty aluminum foil.

- ½ cup extra-virgin olive oil
- 3 tablespoons lemon juice
- 6 garlic cloves, minced
- ½ teaspoon kosher salt
- 4 portobello mushrooms (5 to 6 inches in diameter), stemmed, gills removed

GRILLED PLANTAINS

1 Combine oil, lemon juice, garlic, and salt in 1-gallon zipper-lock bag. Add mushrooms and toss to coat; press out as much air as possible and seal bag. Let sit at room temperature for 1 hour.

2 Cut four 12-inch square pieces of heavy-duty aluminum foil (or six 9-inch square pieces if using smaller mushrooms). Before grilling, remove mushrooms from marinade (do not pat dry) and place one on each foil square, gill side up. Fold foil around mushrooms and seal edges.

3A **FOR A CHARCOAL GRILL** Open bottom vent completely. Light large chimney starter three-quarters filled with charcoal briquettes (4½ quarts). When top coals are partially covered with ash, pour evenly over grill. Set cooking grate in place, cover, and open lid vent completely. Heat grill until hot, about 5 minutes.

3B **FOR A GAS GRILL** Turn all burners to high; cover; and heat grill until hot, about 15 minutes. Turn all burners to medium-high.

4 Clean and oil cooking grate. Place foil packets seam side up on grill and cook (covered if using gas) until juicy and tender, 9 to 12 minutes. Using tongs, unwrap mushrooms and transfer gill side up to grill; cook until grill-marked, 30 to 60 seconds. Transfer to platter and serve.

VARIATION

Grilled Marinated Portobellos with Tarragon
Substitute 2 teaspoons rice vinegar for lemon juice, reduce garlic to 1 clove, and add 1 tablespoon chopped fresh tarragon to marinade.

Grilled Plantains

SERVES 4 **TIME** 25 minutes

Why This Recipe Works Although plantains closely resemble bananas, these Latin American staples have a starchier texture and subtler flavor than bananas, making them a great option for a delicious grilled side dish. We prefer ripe, black-skinned plantains: They're softer, sweeter, and easier to peel than green ones, which is important because plantains must be peeled and oiled before grilling. By the time the plantains are streaked with grill marks, they will be cooked through, tender, and ready to serve.

- 2 large ripe plantains, peeled and halved lengthwise
- 2 tablespoons vegetable oil
- 1 teaspoon kosher salt

1 Gently toss plantains with oil and salt in bowl to coat.

2A FOR A CHARCOAL GRILL Open bottom vent completely. Light large chimney starter three-quarters filled with charcoal briquettes (4½ quarts). When top coals are partially covered with ash, pour evenly over grill. Set cooking grate in place, cover, and open lid vent completely. Heat grill until hot, about 5 minutes.

2B FOR A GAS GRILL Turn all burners to high; cover; and heat grill until hot, about 15 minutes. Turn all burners to medium-high.

3 Clean and oil cooking grate. Place plantains on grill and cook, turning as needed, until grill marks appear, 7 to 8 minutes. Serve.

Grilled Potatoes with Garlic and Rosemary

SERVES 4 **TIME** 45 minutes

Why This Recipe Works Grilled potatoes are a summer classic. For tender potatoes imbued with the smoky flavor of the grill and enlivened with the bold flavors of garlic and rosemary, we apply a potent infused oil to the potatoes not once but three times. Before cooking, we pierce the potatoes, skewer them, season them with salt, brush them with the garlic-rosemary oil, and precook them in the microwave. Then, before grilling, we brush them again with the infused oil. After grilling, we toss them with the oil yet again. This recipe works best with small potatoes that are about 1½ inches in diameter. If using medium potatoes, 2 to 3 inches in diameter, cut them into quarters. If the potatoes are larger than 3 inches in diameter, cut each potato into eighths. Since the potatoes are first cooked in the microwave, use wooden skewers.

- ¼ cup extra-virgin olive oil
- 9 garlic cloves, minced
- 1 teaspoon chopped fresh rosemary
- 1½ teaspoons kosher salt, divided
- 2 pounds small red potatoes, unpeeled, halved
- 6–8 (12-inch) wooden skewers
- 2 tablespoons chopped fresh chives

1 Heat oil, garlic, rosemary, and 1 teaspoon salt in 8-inch skillet over medium heat until sizzling, about 3 minutes. Reduce heat to medium-low and continue to cook until garlic is light blond, about 3 minutes. Pour mixture through fine-mesh strainer into small bowl; press on solids. Measure 1 tablespoon solids and 1 tablespoon oil into large bowl. Discard remaining solids and reserve remaining oil.

2 Poke each potato several times with skewer, then thread potatoes onto skewers. Brush potatoes with 1 tablespoon strained oil and sprinkle with remaining ½ teaspoon salt. Brush baking sheet with 1 tablespoon strained oil. Microwave potatoes, uncovered, until paring knife inserted into potato meets slight resistance, about 8 minutes, turning halfway through microwaving. Transfer potatoes to prepared baking sheet, brush with remaining 1 tablespoon strained oil, and season with salt and pepper to taste.

3A FOR A CHARCOAL GRILL Open bottom vent completely. Light large chimney starter filled with charcoal briquettes (6 quarts). When top coals are partially covered with ash, pour two-thirds evenly over half of grill, then pour remaining coals over other half of grill. Set cooking grate in place, cover, and open lid vent completely. Heat grill until hot, about 5 minutes.

3B FOR A GAS GRILL Turn all burners to high; cover; and heat grill until hot, about 15 minutes. Turn all burners to medium-high.

4 Clean and oil cooking grate. Place potatoes on grill (hotter side if using charcoal) and cook (covered if using gas) until grill marks appear, 3 to 5 minutes, flipping halfway through cooking. Move potatoes to cooler side of grill (if using charcoal) or turn all burners to medium-low (if using gas). Cover and cook until paring knife slips in and out of potatoes easily, 5 to 8 minutes.

5 Remove potatoes from grill. Slide potatoes off skewers into bowl with reserved garlic-oil mixture. Add chives, season with salt and pepper to taste, and toss until thoroughly coated. Serve.

VARIATION

Grilled Potatoes with Oregano and Lemon

Reduce garlic to 3 cloves, substitute 2 tablespoons chopped fresh oregano for rosemary, and add 2 teaspoons grated lemon zest to oil in skillet. Substitute 2 teaspoons chopped fresh oregano for chives and add additional 1 teaspoon grated lemon zest to potatoes when they come off grill.

Grilled Potato Foil Packs

SERVES 4 **TIME** 35 minutes

Why This Recipe Works The appeal of this campfire classic is partly convenience: All you need is fire, food, and tin foil, no pots or pans required. But the method has other virtues: Because the food is cooked in a contained environment over the fire, the technique combines freshness and clear flavors with the deep caramelized taste of grilling. We start with Yukon Golds, cut them into evenly sized wedges, and microwave them for a few minutes before grilling them. Tossing the potatoes with a little oil prevents them from sticking to the foil. A quick flip halfway through cooking on the grill ensures perfectly cooked, spotty brown potatoes. The contained cooking environment of the foil pack creates the perfect opportunity to add all kinds of flavors in our variations, from simple herbs to more creative ingredients like chorizo sausage or wine vinegar. To keep the packs from tearing, use heavy-duty aluminum foil.

- 2 pounds Yukon Gold potatoes, unpeeled
- 1 tablespoon olive oil
- 2 garlic cloves, peeled and chopped
- 2 teaspoons kosher salt
- 1 teaspoon minced fresh thyme
- ½ teaspoon pepper

1 Cut each potato in half crosswise, then cut each half into 8 wedges. Place potatoes in large bowl; cover; and microwave until edges of potatoes are translucent, 4 to 7 minutes, shaking bowl halfway through cooking. Drain potatoes well, then transfer to bowl. Gently toss potatoes with oil, garlic, salt, thyme, and pepper.

2 Cut four 14 by 10-inch sheets of heavy-duty aluminum foil. Working with one at a time, spread one-quarter of potato mixture over half of foil, fold foil over potatoes, and crimp edges tightly to seal.

3A FOR A CHARCOAL GRILL Open bottom vent completely. Light large chimney starter filled with charcoal briquettes (6 quarts). When top coals are partially covered with ash, pour evenly over grill. Set cooking grate in place, cover, and open lid vent completely. Heat grill until hot, about 5 minutes.

3B FOR A GAS GRILL Turn all burners to high; cover; and heat grill until hot, about 15 minutes. Leave all burners on high.

4 Clean cooking grate. Place packs on grill; cover; and cook until potatoes are completely tender, about 10 minutes, flipping halfway through cooking. Cut open foil and serve.

GRILLED SPANISH-STYLE POTATO FOIL PACKS

Making Potato Foil Packs

1 Microwave potatoes first to help them cook quickly on grill.

2 Arrange microwaved potatoes on foil, fold over, and crimp.

3 Flip packs halfway through grilling for evenly charred potatoes.

VARIATIONS

Grilled Spanish-Style Potato Foil Packs

Add 6 ounces thinly sliced cured chorizo sausage, 1 seeded and chopped red bell pepper, and 1 teaspoon paprika to microwaved potatoes as they are tossed in step 1.

Grilled Spicy Home Fry Potato Foil Packs

Omit chopped garlic. Add 1 teaspoon paprika, ½ teaspoon garlic powder, ½ teaspoon onion powder, and ¼ teaspoon cayenne pepper to microwaved potatoes as they are tossed in step 1.

Grilled Vinegar and Onion Potato Foil Packs

Microwave 1 halved and thinly sliced small onion with potatoes in step 1. Add 2 tablespoons white wine or red wine vinegar to microwaved potatoes as they are tossed in step 1.

Grilled Sweet Potatoes with Maple Chile Crisp

SERVES 4 to 6 **TIME** 2¾ hours plus 6 ½ hours cooling

Why This Recipe Works This recipe is inspired by the sweet potatoes with maple chile crisp served by chef, author, and educator Sean Sherman at Owamni in Minneapolis, Minnesota, a restaurant and community "committed to revitalizing Native American Cuisine and in the process . . . re-identifying North American Cuisine and reclaiming an important culinary culture long buried and often inaccessible." For our version, we roast sweet potatoes in the oven until fully tender before halving and grilling them; this hybrid cooking technique produces potatoes with exquisitely creamy centers and deeply caramelized edges with complex flavors and a pleasing range of textures. Using a firm metal spatula helps dislodge and maneuver the potatoes on the grill as they became handsomely charred. We love these potatoes drizzled with smoky-sweet, aromatic maple chile crisp. Light brown sugar can be substituted for the maple sugar and vegetable oil for the sunflower oil, if necessary. You can use an equal amount of table salt in place of the fine sea salt. This recipe makes a medium-spiced chile crisp. If you prefer your chile crisp slightly milder, reduce the arbol and chipotle chiles to two each. Using a metal bowl for the chili crisp in step 2 is important; a Pyrex or glass bowl could shatter when the hot oil is added in step 3. To serve a larger crowd, you can double the potato portion of the recipe.

GRILLED SWEET POTATOES WITH MAPLE CHILE CRISP

CHILE CRISP

- 3 dried chipotle chiles
- 3 arbol chiles
- 2 ancho chiles
- 2 guajillo chiles
- 2 dried New Mexico chiles
- 3 scallions, sliced thin
- 2 tablespoons maple sugar
- 3 garlic cloves, minced
- 1½ teaspoons fine sea salt
- 1½ cups sunflower oil

POTATOES

- 2 (12- to 16-ounce) white sweet potatoes, unpeeled, each lightly pricked with fork in 6 places
- 4 teaspoons sunflower oil, divided
- ½ teaspoon fine sea salt, divided
- ½ teaspoon flake sea salt
- 1 scallion, sliced thin on bias

1 **FOR THE CHILI CRISP** Adjust oven rack to middle position and heat oven to 400 degrees. Spread chipotle, arbol, ancho, guajillo, and New Mexico chiles on rimmed baking sheet. Roast until fragrant, 3 to 5 minutes. Let chiles cool completely on sheet, about 10 minutes.

2 Stem and seed chiles, then break chiles into 1- to 2-inch pieces. Working in batches, pulse chiles in spice grinder until pieces are no larger than ¼ inch, about 6 pulses. Transfer ground chiles to medium metal bowl and stir in scallions, sugar, garlic, and salt.

3 Heat oil in small saucepan over medium-high heat to 375 degrees. Carefully pour hot oil over chile mixture in bowl (mixture will bubble aggressively). Let sit, stirring occasionally, until cooled completely, about 30 minutes. Transfer chile crisp to jar and let sit for at least 4 hours before using. (Chile crisp will keep at room temperature for at least 1 month.)

4 **FOR THE POTATOES** Meanwhile, adjust oven rack to middle position and heat oven to 400 degrees. Line rimmed baking sheet with parchment paper and place potatoes on sheet. Bake potatoes until paring knife inserted in center meets no resistance, 1¼ to 1½ hours. Let potatoes cool completely, at least 2 hours. (Potatoes can be baked and refrigerated up to 2 days in advance.) Before grilling, cut potatoes in half lengthwise. Brush cut sides of potatoes with 2 teaspoons sunflower oil and sprinkle with ¼ teaspoon fine sea salt.

5A **FOR A CHARCOAL GRILL** Open bottom vent completely. Light large chimney starter filled with charcoal briquettes (6 quarts). When top coals are partially covered with ash, pour evenly over grill. Set cooking grate in place, cover, and open lid vent completely. Heat grill until hot, about 5 minutes.

5B **FOR A GAS GRILL** Turn all burners to high; cover; and heat grill until hot, about 15 minutes. Leave all burners on high.

6 Clean and oil cooking grate. Place potatoes cut side down on grill and cook until char-streaked and easily release from grill, 3 to 5 minutes. Brush skin sides of potatoes with remaining 2 teaspoons sunflower oil and sprinkle with remaining ¼ teaspoon fine sea salt. Flip potatoes and cook until lightly browned on skin side and heated through, 3 to 5 minutes.

7 Transfer potatoes to cutting board. Cut each potato in half lengthwise, then in half crosswise. Arrange potatoes on platter and spoon generous ½ cup chile crisp over top. Sprinkle with flake sea salt and scallion. Serve with extra chili crisp.

Blistered Shishito Peppers

SERVES 4 to 6 as an appetizer **TIME** 20 minutes

Why This Recipe Works Japanese shishito peppers boast thin skins; delicate flesh; and a fruity, grassy flavor reminiscent of jalapeño or serrano chiles, minus the heat. A cast-iron plancha on the grill blisters these beauties in a matter of minutes, for a supersimple one-bite snack or appetizer. Once they're done, just toss them with flake sea salt or other seasonings and then pick them up by the stem and devour them whole. You will need a cast-iron plancha measuring at least 20 by 10 inches.

- 8 ounces shishito peppers
- 1 tablespoon vegetable oil

1 Toss peppers with oil in bowl.

2A **FOR A CHARCOAL GRILL** Open bottom vent completely. Light large chimney starter filled with charcoal briquettes (6 quarts). When top coals are partially covered with ash, pour evenly over grill. Set cooking grate in place, center plancha on cooking grate, cover, and open lid vent completely. Heat grill with plancha until hot, about 5 minutes.

2B **FOR A GAS GRILL** Turn all burners to high; cover; and heat grill until hot, about 15 minutes. Center plancha on grill, cover, and heat for 5 more minutes. Leave all burners on high.

BLISTERED SHISHITO PEPPERS

3 Arrange peppers in even layer on plancha and cook, without moving, until skins are blistered on first side, 1 to 3 minutes. Flip peppers and continue to cook until blistered on second side, 1 to 2 minutes. Transfer to serving bowl and season with flake sea salt to taste. Serve immediately.

VARIATIONS

Blistered Shishito Peppers with Espelette, Smoked Paprika, and Lime

Combine 1 teaspoon ground dried Espelette pepper, 1 teaspoon smoked paprika, ½ teaspoon flake sea salt or kosher salt, and ¼ teaspoon grated lime zest in small bowl. Sprinkle over cooked peppers in serving bowl. Serve with lime wedges.

Blistered Shishito Peppers with Mint, Poppy Seeds, and Orange

Combine 1 teaspoon dried mint, 1 teaspoon poppy seeds, ½ teaspoon flake sea salt or kosher salt, and ¼ teaspoon grated orange zest in small bowl. Sprinkle over peppers in serving bowl. Serve with orange wedges.

GRILLED TOMATOES

Grilled Tomatoes

SERVES 4 to 6 **TIME** 45 minutes

Why This Recipe Works Grilling is a brilliant way to showcase summer tomatoes: Their flesh softens and gains concentrated sweetness while the smoky char of the grill adds another dimension of flavor. And tomatoes cook quickly, so you can grill them while your steak or other protein is resting and the coals are still hot. After halving the tomatoes, salt them to draw out their juice; less moisture means they brown better. Grill them cut side down first to caramelize them, then flip them over so the cradle-like skins hold the tomatoes together as they continue to soften. Fresh basil, salt and pepper, and their own reserved juices are all the seasoning they need. For the best results, use in-season, round tomatoes that are ripe yet a bit firm so that they will hold their shape on the grill. Plum tomatoes may be used, but they will be drier in texture. If using plum tomatoes, halve them lengthwise. Supermarket vine-ripened tomatoes will work but won't be as flavorful. This recipe can easily be doubled. These tomatoes are great on their own or for pasta, sandwiches, salads, soup, and sauces.

- 2 pounds ripe tomatoes, cored and halved along equator
- 1 tablespoon extra-virgin olive oil
- 1 teaspoon kosher salt
- ¼ teaspoon pepper
- 2 tablespoons torn fresh basil leaves
- 1 tablespoon extra-virgin olive oil

1 Toss tomatoes with oil, salt, and pepper in large bowl. Let stand for at least 15 minutes or up to 1 hour.

2A FOR A CHARCOAL GRILL Open bottom vent completely. Light large chimney starter filled with charcoal briquettes (6 quarts). When top coals are partially covered with ash, pour evenly over grill. Set cooking grate in place, cover, and open lid vent completely. Heat grill until hot, about 5 minutes.

2B FOR A GAS GRILL Turn all burners to high; cover; and heat grill until hot, about 15 minutes. Leave all burners on high.

3 Clean and oil cooking grate. Place tomatoes cut side down on grill (reserve any juice left behind in bowl). Cook (covered if using gas) until tomatoes are charred and beginning to soften, 4 to 6 minutes.

4 Using tongs or thin metal spatula, carefully flip tomatoes and cook (covered if using gas) until skin sides are charred and juice bubbles, 4 to 6 minutes. Transfer tomatoes to large plate and sprinkle with reserved juice, basil, oil, and flake sea salt to taste. Serve.

Easy Grilled Coleslaw

SERVES 4 **TIME** 30 minutes

Why This Recipe Works We love the fresh crunch of cold and creamy coleslaw, but grilling brings a welcome nuance to this side dish, taming the raw bite of cabbage. A modest amount of mayo seasoned with puckery cider vinegar binds the cabbage together. Carrot adds earthy sweetness, and fresh cilantro takes this slaw from workaday picnic classic to something a bit more spirited. Do not remove the core from the cabbage; it will keep the leaves intact on the grill.

- ½ head green cabbage, cut into 2 wedges through core
- 2 tablespoons extra-virgin olive oil
- 1½ teaspoons kosher salt
- 1 teaspoon pepper
- ¼ cup mayonnaise
- 1 shallot, minced
- 4 teaspoons cider vinegar
- 1 carrot, peeled and shredded
- 2 tablespoons minced fresh cilantro

1 Brush cabbage wedges with oil and sprinkle with salt and pepper.

2A FOR A CHARCOAL GRILL Open bottom vent completely. Light large chimney starter filled with charcoal briquettes (6 quarts). When top coals are partially covered with ash, pour evenly over grill. Set cooking grate in place, cover, and open lid vent completely. Heat grill until hot, about 5 minutes.

2B FOR A GAS GRILL Turn all burners to high; cover; and heat grill until hot, about 15 minutes. Leave all burners on high.

3 Clean and oil cooking grate. Place cabbage on grill and cook (covered if using gas), turning as needed, until cabbage is lightly charred on all sides, 8 to 12 minutes. Transfer cabbage to platter, tent with aluminum foil, and let rest while making dressing.

4 Whisk mayonnaise, shallot, and vinegar together in large bowl. Slice cabbage into thin strips, discarding core. Stir cabbage, carrot, and cilantro into mayonnaise mixture. Season with salt and pepper to taste. Serve.

EASY GRILLED COLESLAW

Smoky Potato Salad

SERVES 8 **TIME** 55 minutes

Why This Recipe Works For a summery potato salad that can be cooked on the grill from start to finish, we begin with halved red potatoes: The skin helps them stay intact, and their firm, waxy texture can stand up to the grill. We grill rounds of onion alongside the potatoes to add sweetness to the salad. Crispy bacon; fresh scallions; and a spicy, smoky vinaigrette with just a touch of mayo are the perfect match for this potato salad. Use small red potatoes, 1½ to 2 inches in diameter. If you don't have 2 tablespoons of fat in the skillet after frying the bacon, add olive oil to make up the difference.

- 6 slices bacon
- 3 tablespoons red wine vinegar
- 2 tablespoons mayonnaise
- 2 teaspoons minced canned chipotle chile in adobo sauce
- 2½ teaspoons kosher salt, divided
- ¾ teaspoon pepper, divided
- ¼ cup extra-virgin olive oil, divided
- 3 pounds small red potatoes, unpeeled, halved
- 1 large onion, sliced into ½-inch-thick rounds
- 4 scallions, sliced thin

1 Cook bacon in 12-inch skillet over medium heat until crispy, 7 to 9 minutes; transfer to paper towel–lined plate. Measure out 2 tablespoons bacon fat and set aside for brushing potatoes; reserve remaining bacon fat for another use. When cool enough to handle, crumble bacon. Whisk vinegar, mayonnaise, chipotle, 1 teaspoon salt, and ½ teaspoon pepper together in large bowl. Slowly whisk in 3 tablespoons oil until combined; set aside for serving.

2 Toss potatoes with 2 tablespoons reserved bacon fat and 1 teaspoon salt. Push toothpick horizontally through each onion round to keep rings intact while grilling. Brush onion with remaining 1 tablespoon oil and sprinkle with remaining ½ teaspoon salt and ¼ teaspoon pepper.

3A FOR A CHARCOAL GRILL Open bottom vent completely. Light large chimney starter three-quarters filled with charcoal briquettes (4½ quarts). When top coals are partially covered with ash, pour evenly over grill. Set cooking grate in place, cover, and open lid vent completely. Heat grill until hot, about 5 minutes.

3B FOR A GAS GRILL Turn all burners to high; cover; and heat grill until hot, about 15 minutes. Turn all burners to medium-high.

4 Clean and oil cooking grate. Place potatoes, cut side down, and onion on grill. Cover and cook until both are nicely charred and potatoes are easily pierced with tip of paring knife, 20 to 30 minutes, flipping halfway through cooking. Transfer potatoes and onion rounds to rimmed baking sheet as they finish cooking and let cool slightly.

5 When cool enough to handle, halve potatoes; remove toothpicks and chop onion rounds coarse. Add potatoes, onion, scallions, and bacon to dressing and toss to combine. Season with salt and pepper to taste. Serve warm or at room temperature.

Grilled Sweet Potato Salad

SERVES 4 to 6 **TIME** 55 minutes

Why This Recipe Works To bring together two summer traditions—potato salad and grilling—we use the grill both to steam and char sweet potatoes, so all the cooking is done outside. We first toss the potatoes with a spiced vinaigrette in a disposable aluminum pan; the vinaigrette generates steam and helps cook the potatoes through while also seasoning them. Once the potatoes are steamed, we transfer them from the pan to the hot cooking grate to give them some flavorful char. Threading toothpicks through the onion rounds keeps them intact and prevents them from falling through the grate during cooking. Buy medium-size sweet potatoes, 2 to 3 inches in diameter, so they'll fit neatly in the disposable aluminum pan.

- 3 tablespoons lime juice (2 limes), plus lime wedges for serving
- 2 tablespoons honey
- 2 teaspoons kosher salt, divided
- 1 teaspoon minced canned chipotle chile in adobo sauce
- ¾ teaspoon pepper, divided
- ½ teaspoon ground cumin
- ⅓ cup vegetable oil
- 1 small red onion, sliced into ½-inch-thick rounds
- 2½ pounds sweet potatoes, peeled and cut into ½-inch-thick rounds
- 1 (13 by 9-inch) disposable aluminum pan
- 2 ounces feta cheese, crumbled (½ cup)
- 3 scallions, sliced thin on bias
- ¼ cup coarsely chopped fresh cilantro

1 Whisk lime juice, honey, 1 teaspoon salt, chipotle, ¼ teaspoon pepper, and cumin together in bowl. Slowly whisk in oil.

2 Push toothpick horizontally through each onion round to keep rings intact while grilling. In large bowl, toss potatoes and onion rounds with ¼ cup vinaigrette, remaining 1 teaspoon salt, and remaining ½ teaspoon pepper to coat. Place onion rounds in bottom of disposable pan, layer potatoes over top, then pour in any remaining liquid from bowl. Cover pan tightly with aluminum foil.

3A **FOR A CHARCOAL GRILL** Open bottom vent completely. Light large chimney starter filled with charcoal briquettes (6 quarts). When top coals are partially covered with ash, pour evenly over grill. Set cooking grate in place, cover, and open lid vent completely. Heat grill until hot, about 5 minutes.

3B **FOR A GAS GRILL** Turn all burners to high; cover; and heat grill until hot, about 15 minutes. Leave all burners on high.

4 Clean and oil cooking grate. Place disposable pan on grill; cover; and cook until vegetables are tender, 20 to 25 minutes, shaking disposable pan halfway through cooking. Remove disposable pan from grill.

5 Transfer potatoes and onion to grill and cook (covered if using gas), turning as needed, until lightly charred and tender, 4 to 8 minutes. Transfer vegetables to platter. Remove toothpicks from onion rounds and separate rings. Pour remaining vinaigrette over vegetables and toss to coat. Sprinkle feta, scallions, and cilantro over top. Serve with lime wedges.

SMOKY POTATO SALAD

Grilled Peach and Tomato Salad with Burrata and Basil

SERVES 4 to 6 **TIME** 45 minutes plus 30 minutes cooling and draining

Why This Recipe Works Late summer's juiciest peaches and tomatoes mingle in a dish that's greater than the sum of its already wonderful parts. Grilling peaches enhances their aroma and sweetness; a little butter brushed on the cut halves keeps them from sticking to the grate and speeds browning. You'll grill them over high heat and then move them to a covered pan over indirect heat until they're fully softened. After cutting the grilled peaches into wedges, toss them with raw tomato chunks in a simple vinaigrette of white wine vinegar and extra-virgin olive oil. Creamy burrata cheese adds texture and richness to this stunning dish, which is also fabulous made with nectarines or plums. For the best results, use high-quality, ripe, in-season tomatoes and peaches. If burrata is unavailable, sliced fresh mozzarella makes a suitable substitute.

GRILLED SWEET POTATO SALAD

GRILLED PEACH AND TOMATO SALAD WITH BURRATA AND BASIL

PEACHES

- 1½ pounds ripe but slightly firm peaches (4 peaches), halved and pitted
- 2 tablespoons unsalted butter, melted
- 1 (13 by 9-inch) disposable aluminum pan

SALAD

- 12 ounces ripe tomatoes, cored and cut into ½-inch pieces
- 1½ teaspoons kosher salt, divided
- 5 tablespoons extra-virgin olive oil, divided
- 1 tablespoon white wine vinegar
- 8 ounces burrata cheese, room temperature
- ⅓ cup chopped fresh basil

1 **FOR THE PEACHES** Brush cut side of peaches with melted butter.

2A **FOR A CHARCOAL GRILL** Open bottom vent completely. Light large chimney starter three-quarters filled with charcoal briquettes (4½ quarts). When top coals are partially covered with ash, pour evenly over half of grill. Set cooking grate in place, cover, and open lid vent completely. Heat grill until hot, about 5 minutes.

2B **FOR A GAS GRILL** Turn all burners to high; cover; and heat grill until hot, about 15 minutes. Leave primary burner to high and turn off other burner(s).

3 Clean and oil cooking grate. Place peaches cut side down on hotter side of grill and cook (covered if using gas), moving peaches around as needed, until grill marks have formed, 5 to 7 minutes.

4 Transfer peaches cut side up to disposable pan and tent with aluminum foil. Place pan on grill (cooler side if using charcoal; turn all burners to medium if using gas). Cover and cook until peaches are very tender and paring knife slips in and out with little resistance, 10 to 15 minutes. Transfer peaches to cutting board, let cool slightly, then discard skins. Let peaches cool completely.

5 **FOR THE SALAD** While peaches cool, toss tomatoes with ½ teaspoon salt and let drain in colander for 30 minutes.

6 Cut each peach half into 4 wedges, then cut each wedge in half crosswise. Whisk ¼ cup oil, vinegar, and remaining 1 teaspoon salt together in large bowl. Add peaches and tomatoes and toss gently to combine; transfer to shallow serving bowl. Place burrata on top of salad and drizzle with remaining 1 tablespoon oil. Season with pepper to taste, then sprinkle with basil. Serve, breaking up burrata with spoon and allowing creamy liquid to meld with dressing.

Brined Grilled Zucchini with Mint Salsa Verde

SERVES 4 **TIME** 25 minutes plus 45 minutes brining

Why This Recipe Works A saltwater soak produces well-seasoned zucchini that can pick up color on the grill without drying out. We pair them with a punchy riff on salsa verde, packed with refreshing herbs, garlic and red pepper flakes for heat, and capers and vinegar for an acidic bite. Look for zucchini that are about 2 inches in diameter and do not brine them for more than 1 hour, or they will taste too salty. (You can remove them from the brine, pat them dry, and refrigerate them for up to 3 hours before cooking.) This is a perfect side dish for when you're firing up the grill for dinner. Grill the zucchini first; they're great served warm or even at room temperature.

- ½ cup plus 2 tablespoons kosher salt for brining
- 3 large zucchini (10 ounces each), halved lengthwise
- 1 cup finely chopped fresh mint
- 1 cup finely chopped fresh parsley
- ¼ cup extra-virgin olive oil
- 3 tablespoons white wine vinegar
- 2 tablespoons capers, rinsed and minced
- 2 garlic cloves, minced
- 1 teaspoon red pepper flakes

1 Dissolve salt in 1 quart water in large bowl. Add zucchini to brine and weigh down with plate to keep submerged. Let sit at room temperature for 45 minutes to 1 hour. Transfer zucchini to paper towel–lined plate and pat dry. Discard brine.

2A **FOR A CHARCOAL GRILL** Open bottom vent completely. Light large chimney starter filled with charcoal briquettes (6 quarts). When top coals are partially covered with ash, pour evenly over half of grill. Set cooking grate in place, cover, and open lid vent completely. Heat grill until hot, about 5 minutes.

2B **FOR A GAS GRILL** Turn all burners to high; cover; and heat grill until hot, about 15 minutes. Leave all burners on high.

3 Clean and oil cooking grate. Place zucchini, cut side down, on grill (hotter side if using charcoal) and cook until zucchini are well charred on bottom and flesh just begins to soften, 3 to 4 minutes. Flip zucchini and continue to cook until skin side is charred, about 2 minutes longer. (Zucchini should be slightly soft at edges but still firm at centers.) Transfer to serving platter.

4 Stir together mint, parsley, oil, vinegar, capers, garlic, and pepper flakes in small bowl. Season with salt to taste. Spoon salsa verde over zucchini and serve.

Grilled Zucchini and Corn Salad

SERVES 4 **TIME** 35 minutes

Why This Recipe Works To make the most of peak-season zucchini and corn, we brush them with a simple marinade of oil, garlic, and red pepper flakes before charring them on the grill. Leaving the zucchini in large planks allows it to pick up plenty of smoky flavor without turning to mush. After cutting the kernels from the cobs and slicing the zucchini into bite-size pieces, we toss them with the remaining spiced oil, along with fresh basil and lemon juice. A final sprinkling of feta cheese adds creamy, salty complexity. Serve warm or at room temperature.

- ⅓ cup extra-virgin olive oil
- 2 garlic cloves, minced
- 1 teaspoon kosher salt
- ½ teaspoon pepper,
- ¼ teaspoon red pepper flakes
- 2 ears corn, husks and silk removed
- 3 zucchini (8 ounces each), sliced lengthwise into ½-inch-thick planks
- 2 tablespoons chopped fresh basil
- 4 teaspoons lemon juice
- 2 ounces feta cheese, crumbled (½ cup)

1 Whisk oil, garlic, salt, pepper, and pepper flakes together in large bowl. Brush corn with 1 tablespoon oil mixture. Add zucchini to remaining oil mixture in bowl and toss to coat.

2A **FOR A CHARCOAL GRILL** Open bottom vent completely. Light large chimney starter filled with charcoal briquettes (6 quarts). When top coals are partially covered with ash, pour evenly over grill. Set cooking grate in place, cover, and open lid vent completely. Heat grill until hot, about 5 minutes.

2B **FOR A GAS GRILL** Turn all burners to high; cover; and heat grill until hot, about 15 minutes. Leave all burners on high.

3 Clean and oil cooking grate. Place corn and zucchini on grill; reserve any oil mixture remaining in zucchini bowl. Cook, turning as needed, until corn is lightly charred all over and zucchini is well browned and tender (not mushy), 10 to 16 minutes. Transfer corn and zucchini to cutting board as they finish cooking.

4 Cut kernels from cobs. Cut zucchini on bias into ½-inch-thick slices. Add vegetables to bowl with reserved oil mixture. Add basil and lemon juice and toss to combine. Season with salt and pepper to taste. Transfer salad to platter and sprinkle with feta. Serve.

Grilled Vegetable Ratatouille

SERVES 6 to 8 **TIME** 40 minutes

Why This Recipe Works A well-made ratatouille embodies the essence of flavors from the south of France, including firm eggplant, zucchini, caramelized onions, heady garlic, and garden-fresh herbs. Bringing the mixture together are the ripest of tomatoes. The prime season for all these vegetables happens to be prime grilling season, so why not cook them on the grill? A smoky char enhances the flavors of the ratatouille, and the heat of the grill fire helps evaporate all the excess moisture that would make the vegetables mushy. To ensure perfect doneness, we carefully monitor the grill time for each vegetable separately. Depending on the size of your grill, you may have to cook the vegetables in multiple batches. A rasp grater makes quick work of turning garlic into a paste.

- 1 red onion, cut into ½-inch-thick slices
- 3 zucchini or summer squash (8 ounces each), sliced lengthwise into ½-inch-thick planks
- 2 bell peppers, stemmed, seeded, and halved, each half cut into thirds
- 1 pound tomatoes, cored and halved
- 7 tablespoons extra-virgin olive oil, divided
- 2 pounds eggplant, sliced into ¾-inch-thick rounds
- 2 teaspoons kosher salt
- 1 teaspoon pepper
- 3 tablespoons sherry vinegar
- ¼ cup chopped fresh basil
- 1 tablespoon minced fresh thyme
- 1 garlic clove, minced to paste

1 Push toothpick horizontally through each onion round to keep rings intact while grilling. Brush onion, zucchini, bell peppers, tomatoes, and then eggplant with 3 tablespoons oil (eggplant will absorb more oil than other vegetables). Sprinkle vegetables with salt and pepper. Whisk remaining ¼ cup oil, vinegar, basil, thyme, and garlic together in large bowl.

2A FOR A CHARCOAL GRILL Open bottom vent completely. Light large chimney starter three-quarters filled with charcoal briquettes (4½ quarts). When top coals are partially covered with ash, pour evenly over grill. Set cooking grate in place, cover, and open lid vent completely. Heat grill until hot, about 5 minutes.

2B FOR A GAS GRILL Turn all burners to high; cover; and heat grill until hot, about 15 minutes. Turn all burners to medium-high.

GRILLED VEGETABLE RATATOUILLE

3 Clean and oil cooking grate. Place vegetables on grill and cook, turning once, until tender and streaked with grill marks, 10 to 12 minutes for onion, 8 to 10 minutes for eggplant and squash, 7 to 9 minutes for peppers, and 4 to 5 minutes for tomatoes. Transfer vegetables to cutting board as they finish cooking and let cool slightly.

4 When cool enough to handle, chop vegetables into ½-inch pieces and add to oil mixture; toss to coat. Season with salt and pepper to taste and serve warm or at room temperature.

Mechouia (Tunisian-Style Grilled Vegetables)

SERVES 4 to 6 **TIME** 1¼ hours

Why This Recipe Works For our take on this robustly flavored Tunisian dish of grilled vegetables, we start by halving the eggplant, zucchini, and plum tomatoes lengthwise and stemming and flattening the bell peppers; this exposes as much surface area to the heat as possible for good charring. We also score the eggplant and zucchini before putting them over the coals, so they release their excess moisture as they cook. A potent combination of coriander, caraway, cumin, paprika, and cayenne stands in for the traditional Tunisian spice blend tabil; the heat of the grill blooms the flavor of the spices so they don't taste raw or harsh. More of the spices, plus garlic, lemon, and a trio of herbs provide a bright, fresh-tasting dressing. Equal amounts of ground coriander and cumin can be substituted for the whole spices.

VINAIGRETTE

- 2 teaspoons coriander seeds
- 1½ teaspoons caraway seeds
- 1 teaspoon cumin seeds
- 5 tablespoons olive oil
- ½ teaspoon paprika
- ⅛ teaspoon cayenne pepper
- 3 garlic cloves, minced
- ¼ cup chopped fresh parsley
- ¼ cup chopped fresh cilantro
- 2 tablespoons chopped fresh mint
- 1 teaspoon grated lemon zest plus 2 tablespoons juice

VEGETABLES

- 2 bell peppers (1 red and 1 green)
- 1 small eggplant, halved lengthwise
- 1 large zucchini (10 ounces), halved lengthwise
- 2 shallots, unpeeled
- 4 plum tomatoes, cored and halved lengthwise
- 2 teaspoons kosher salt

1 FOR THE VINAIGRETTE Grind coriander seeds, caraway seeds, and cumin seeds in spice grinder until finely ground. Whisk ground spices, oil, paprika, and cayenne together in bowl. Measure out 3 tablespoons oil mixture and set aside for brushing vegetables.

2 Heat remaining oil mixture and garlic in 8-inch skillet over low heat, stirring occasionally, until fragrant and small bubbles appear, 8 to 10 minutes. Transfer to large bowl; let cool for 10 minutes; then whisk parsley, cilantro, mint, and lemon zest and juice into oil mixture. Season with salt to taste.

3 FOR THE VEGETABLES Slice ¼ inch off tops and bottoms of bell peppers and remove cores. Make slit down 1 side of each bell pepper and then press flat into 1 long strip, removing ribs and remaining seeds with knife as needed. Cut slits on cut sides of eggplant and zucchini, spaced ½ inch apart, in crosshatch pattern; be careful to cut down to but not through skin. Brush shallots and cut sides of bell peppers, eggplant, zucchini, and tomatoes with reserved oil mixture and sprinkle with salt.

4A FOR A CHARCOAL GRILL Open bottom vent completely. Light large chimney starter three-quarters filled with charcoal briquettes (4½ quarts). When top coals are partially covered with ash, pour evenly over grill. Set cooking grate in place, cover, and open lid vent completely. Heat grill until hot, about 5 minutes.

4B FOR A GAS GRILL Turn all burners to high; cover; and heat grill until hot, about 15 minutes. Turn all burners to medium-high.

5 Clean and oil cooking grate. Place vegetables cut side down on grill and cook, turning as needed, until tender and well browned and skins of bell peppers, eggplant, tomatoes, and shallots are charred, 8 to 16 minutes. Transfer vegetables to baking sheet as they finish cooking. Place bell peppers in bowl, cover with plastic wrap, and let steam to loosen skins.

6 When cool enough to handle, peel bell peppers, eggplant, tomatoes, and shallots. Chop all vegetables into ½-inch pieces and transfer to bowl with vinaigrette; toss to coat. Season with salt and pepper to taste, and serve warm or at room temperature.

Grilled Vegetable and Halloumi Salad

SERVES 4 to 6 **TIME** 35 minutes

Why This Recipe Works This warm, hearty salad pairs briny halloumi cheese with nicely charred eggplant, radicchio, and zucchini. Halloumi has a high melting point, making it perfect for grilling; the outside becomes beautifully charred and crisp in contrast to its chewy, warm interior. It takes just 5 to 10 minutes for the slabs of cheese and large pieces of vegetables to become perfectly browned, tender, and redolent with smoky flavor. Then, simply chop all the grilled goodies before tossing everything with a sweet and herbaceous honey and thyme vinaigrette, and dinner is served. If you like, grill some bread to serve alongside. The halloumi may stick to the grill at first, but as it continues to brown it will naturally release and flip easily.

GRILLED VEGETABLE AND HALLOUMI SALAD

- 3 tablespoons honey
- 1 tablespoon minced fresh thyme or rosemary
- 1½ teaspoons kosher salt, divided
- 1 garlic clove, minced
- ½ teaspoon grated lemon zest plus 3 tablespoons juice
- ⅛ teaspoon plus ½ teaspoon pepper, divided
- ¼ cup extra-virgin olive oil, divided
- 1 head radicchio (10 ounces), quartered
- 1 zucchini or summer squash (8 ounces), halved lengthwise
- 1 (8-ounce) block halloumi cheese, sliced into ½-inch-thick slabs
- 1 pound eggplant, sliced into ½-inch-thick rounds

1 Whisk honey, thyme, ½ teaspoon salt, garlic, lemon zest and juice, and ⅛ teaspoon pepper together in large bowl. Whisking constantly, slowly drizzle in 2 tablespoons oil; set aside for serving. Brush radicchio, zucchini, halloumi, and then eggplant with remaining 2 tablespoons oil (eggplant will absorb more oil than other vegetables). Sprinkle with remaining 1 teaspoon salt and remaining ½ teaspoon pepper.

2A **FOR A CHARCOAL GRILL** Open bottom vent completely. Light large chimney starter three-quarters filled with charcoal briquettes (4½ quarts). When top coals are partially covered with ash, pour evenly over grill. Set cooking grate in place, cover, and open lid vent completely. Heat grill until hot, about 5 minutes.

2B **FOR A GAS GRILL** Turn all burners to high; cover; and heat grill until hot, about 15 minutes. Turn all burners to medium-high.

3 Clean cooking grate, then repeatedly brush grate with well-oiled paper towels until grate is black and glossy, 5 to 10 times. Place vegetables and halloumi on grill. Cook (covered if using gas), turning as needed, until everything is softened and lightly charred, 3 to 5 minutes for radicchio, and about 10 minutes for eggplant, zucchini, and cheese. Transfer vegetables and halloumi to cutting board as they finish cooking. Let cool slightly, then cut into 1-inch pieces.

4 Rewhisk vinaigrette to combine, then add vegetables and halloumi and toss gently to coat. Season with salt and pepper to taste. Serve.

Grilled Panzanella

SERVES 4 to 6 **TIME** 55 minutes

Why This Recipe Works For our grilled take on this classic bread salad, we brush garlic oil onto red onion, red bell pepper, and zucchini (each cut into fairly large pieces for easy grilling), along with thickly sliced baguette. We use some of the oil as the base of a flavor-packed dressing and add vinegar, briny capers, and Dijon mustard. After the vegetables and bread come off the grill, tender and well charred, we cut everything into bite-size chunks and toss it with the dressing, cherry tomatoes, cucumber, and chopped fresh basil for a cooling, fresh contrast.

GARLIC OIL AND DRESSING

1 cup extra-virgin olive oil
3 garlic cloves, minced
⅓ cup white vinegar
2 tablespoons capers, minced, plus 1 tablespoon brine
1 teaspoon Dijon mustard
1 teaspoon kosher salt
½ teaspoon pepper

SALAD

1 red onion, halved and cut into ½-inch-thick wedges through root end
1 red bell pepper, stemmed, seeded, and cut into 2-inch planks
1 zucchini (8 ounces), quartered lengthwise
1 (12-inch) baguette, cut on bias into 4-inch-long, 1-inch-thick slices
½ seedless English cucumber, cut into ½-inch chunks
1 cup cherry tomatoes, halved
½ cup chopped fresh basil
1½ ounces Parmesan cheese, shredded (½ cup)

1 FOR THE GARLIC OIL AND DRESSING Whisk oil and garlic together in bowl. Measure out ⅓ cup garlic oil for brushing vegetables and bread. Whisk vinegar, capers and brine, mustard, salt, and pepper into remaining garlic oil; set dressing aside.

2 FOR THE SALAD Place onion, bell pepper, zucchini, and bread on rimmed baking sheet and brush all over with garlic oil.

3A FOR A CHARCOAL GRILL Open bottom vent completely. Light large chimney starter mounded with charcoal briquettes (7 quarts). When top coals are partially covered with ash, pour evenly over grill. Set cooking grate in place, cover, and open lid vent completely. Heat grill until hot, about 5 minutes.

GRILLED PANZANELLA

3B FOR A GAS GRILL Turn all burners to high; cover; and heat grill until hot, about 15 minutes. Leave all burners on high.

4 Clean and oil cooking grate. Place onion, bell pepper, and zucchini on grill and cook (covered if using gas), turning as needed, until well browned and tender, 6 to 12 minutes. Return vegetables to sheet as they finish cooking and season with salt and pepper.

5 Place bread slices on grill and cook, turning as needed, until golden brown and lightly charred, 2 to 4 minutes. Return to sheet and season with salt and pepper.

6 Cut grilled vegetables and bread slices into ¾-inch chunks and transfer to large bowl. Add cucumber, tomatoes, basil and ¾ cup dressing and toss to combine; let sit for 10 minutes for flavors to blend. Season with salt and pepper to taste. Transfer salad to serving platter and sprinkle with Parmesan. Serve, passing remaining reserved dressing separately.

Grilled Vegetable Platter

SERVES 4 to 6 **TIME** 55 minutes

Why This Recipe Works A bounteous assortment of grilled vegetables served with a citrus-kissed vinaigrette makes for a casual and fabulously charry spread. The vegetables are even better at room temperature than they are hot, so you can easily make this ahead, if you like. It makes an excellent starter to keep everybody happy at the outdoor table while you continue to grill up more goodies, or you can customize the platter with add-ons to make this the centerpiece of your meal. The burrata is a great start; its creamy insides will mingle with the vegetables on guests' plates. Also consider additions such as crusty bread slices toasted on the grill, marinated olives, marinated white beans, high-quality tuna packed in oil, and/or grilled lemon halves to squeeze over whatever you please. If burrata is unavailable, sliced fresh mozzarella makes a suitable substitute.

VINAIGRETTE

- 2 tablespoons lemon juice
- 4 teaspoons Dijon mustard
- 2 garlic cloves, minced
- 1 teaspoon kosher salt
- ¼ teaspoon pepper
- 6 tablespoons extra-virgin olive oil
- ¼ cup chopped fresh basil, plus basil leaves for garnish

PLATTER

- 2 red bell peppers
- 1 red onion, cut into ½-inch-thick rounds
- 4 plum tomatoes, cored and halved lengthwise
- 2 zucchini (8 ounces each), sliced lengthwise into ¾-inch-thick planks
- 3 tablespoons extra-virgin olive oil
- 1 pound eggplant, sliced into ½-inch-thick rounds
- 1 teaspoon kosher salt
- ½ teaspoon pepper
- 8 ounces burrata cheese, room temperature

1 **FOR THE VINAIGRETTE** Whisk lemon juice, mustard, garlic, salt, and pepper together in bowl. Whisking constantly, slowly drizzle in oil. Stir in basil and season with salt and pepper to taste. (Vinaigrette can be refrigerated for up to 2 days. Bring to room temperature and whisk to recombine before serving.)

2 **FOR THE PLATTER** Slice ¼ inch off tops and bottoms of bell peppers and remove cores. Make slit down 1 side of each bell pepper, then press flat into 1 long strip, removing ribs and remaining seeds with knife as needed. Cut strips in half crosswise (you should have 4 bell pepper pieces).

3 Push toothpick horizontally through each onion round to keep rings intact while grilling. Brush onion, bell peppers, tomatoes, and zucchini all over with oil, then brush eggplant with remaining oil (it will absorb more oil than other vegetables). Sprinkle vegetables with salt and pepper.

4A **FOR A CHARCOAL GRILL** Open bottom vent completely. Light large chimney starter filled with charcoal briquettes (6 quarts). When top coals are partially covered with ash, pour evenly over grill. Set cooking grate in place, cover, and open lid vent completely. Heat grill until hot, about 5 minutes.

4B **FOR A GAS GRILL** Turn all burners to high; cover; and heat grill until hot, about 15 minutes. Leave all burners on high.

5 Clean and oil cooking grate. Place vegetables on grill and cook, turning as needed, until skins of bell peppers and tomatoes are well browned and onions, eggplant, and zucchini are tender, 10 to 16 minutes. Transfer vegetables to baking sheet as they finish cooking. Place bell peppers in bowl; cover with plastic wrap; and let steam to loosen skins, about 5 minutes.

6 Remove toothpicks from onion and separate rings. When cool enough to handle, peel bell peppers, discarding skins; slice into 1-inch-thick strips. Arrange vegetables and burrata attractively on serving platter with lemon-basil vinaigrette. Garnish platter with basil leaves. Serve warm or at room temperature.

Ultimate Veggie Burgers

SERVES 12 **TIME** 2 hours and 50 minutes

Why This Recipe Works Veggie burgers shouldn't have to imitate hamburgers, but they do need to be hearty, flavorful, and able to travel from grill to bun without falling apart. A combination of lentils and bulgur gives these burgers just the right amount of chew. We add savory flavor with umami-rich cremini mushrooms and cashews, and use panko bread crumbs for the perfect binder. This recipe feeds a crowd; with a slight variation, you can freeze the patties to have on hand for whenever you need them. Canned lentils can be substituted for dried, though some flavor will be sacrificed. Use a 15-ounce can, drain the lentils in a fine-mesh strainer, and thoroughly rinse under cold running water before spreading them on paper towels and drying them as directed in step 1.

- ¾ cup dried brown lentils, picked over and rinsed
- 2 teaspoons kosher salt, plus extra for cooking lentils and bulgur
- ¾ cup medium-grind bulgur
- 2 tablespoons vegetable oil
- 2 onions, chopped fine
- 1 celery rib, chopped fine
- 1 small leek, white and light green parts only, halved lengthwise, chopped fine, and washed thoroughly
- 2 garlic cloves, minced
- 1 pound cremini or white mushrooms, trimmed and sliced ¼ inch thick
- 1 cup raw cashews
- ⅓ cup mayonnaise
- 2 cups panko bread crumbs
- ¼ teaspoon pepper
- 12 hamburger buns, toasted if desired

1 Bring 3 cups water, lentils, and 1 teaspoon salt to boil in medium saucepan over high heat. Reduce heat to medium-low and simmer, uncovered, stirring occasionally, until lentils are just beginning to fall apart, about 25 minutes. Drain in fine-mesh strainer. Line rimmed baking sheet with triple layer of paper towels and spread drained lentils over paper towels. Gently pat lentils dry with additional paper towels. Let lentils cool to room temperature.

2 While lentils simmer, bring 2 cups water and ½ teaspoon salt to boil in small saucepan. Stir bulgur into boiling water and cover immediately; let sit off heat until water is absorbed, 15 to 20 minutes. Drain in fine-mesh strainer, then use silicone spatula to press out excess moisture. Transfer bulgur to medium bowl and set aside.

3 Heat 1 tablespoon oil in 12-inch nonstick skillet over medium-high heat until shimmering. Add onions, celery, leek, and garlic and cook, stirring occasionally, until vegetables begin to brown, about 10 minutes. Spread vegetable mixture onto second rimmed baking sheet to cool; set aside. Heat remaining 1 tablespoon oil in now-empty skillet over high heat until shimmering. Add mushrooms and cook, stirring occasionally, until golden brown, about 12 minutes. Spread mushrooms on baking sheet with vegetable mixture; let cool to room temperature, about 20 minutes.

4 Pulse cashews in food processor until finely chopped, about 15 pulses (do not wash workbowl). Stir cashews into bowl with bulgur, then stir in mayonnaise, cooled lentils, and vegetable-mushroom mixture. Transfer half of mixture to now-empty food processor and pulse until coarsely chopped, 15 to 20 pulses (mixture should be cohesive but roughly textured). Transfer processed mixture to large bowl and repeat with remaining unprocessed mixture; combine with first batch.

5 Stir in panko, pepper, and salt. Line baking sheet with paper towels. Divide mixture into 12 portions, about ½ cup each, shaping each into tightly packed patty about 4 inches in diameter and ½ inch thick. Place patties on prepared sheet to absorb excess moisture. (Patties can be refrigerated for up to 3 days.)

6A **FOR A CHARCOAL GRILL** Open bottom vent completely. Light large chimney starter filled with charcoal briquettes (6 quarts). When top coals are partially covered with ash, pour evenly over grill. Set cooking grate in place, cover, and open lid vent completely. Heat grill until hot, about 5 minutes.

6B **FOR A GAS GRILL** Turn all burners to high; cover; and heat grill until hot, about 15 minutes. Leave all burners on high.

7 Clean and oil cooking grate. Place patties on grill and cook, without moving them, until well browned on first side, about 5 minutes. Flip patties and cook until second side is browned, about 5 minutes. Transfer burgers to platter and serve on buns.

VARIATION

Ultimate Veggie Burgers for the Freezer

Increase amount of panko bread crumbs to 2¼ cups. To freeze, stack patties, separated by parchment paper; wrap in plastic wrap; and place in zipper-lock freezer bag. Before cooking, thaw patties overnight in refrigerator on triple layer of paper towels, covered loosely. Once thawed, pat patties dry with paper towels and reshape to make sure they are tightly packed and cohesive.

ULTIMATE VEGGIE BURGERS

GRILLED PORTOBELLO BURGERS WITH GOAT CHEESE AND ARUGULA

Grilled Portobello Burgers with Goat Cheese and Arugula

SERVES 4 **TIME** 35 minutes

Why This Recipe Works When the king of mushrooms hits the grill, magic happens as its texture softens and its earthy, rich flavor deepens. Layer this portobello burger with melty goat cheese and peppery arugula, top it off with a tomato slice and smoky grilled onion, and you have a meatless burger featuring an irresistible combination of flavors and textures. Mushroom gills can have an off-flavor, so we scrape them out to avoid a muddy taste. Before cooking, we lightly score the smooth side of the mushroom with a crosshatch pattern to expedite the release of moisture and give the caps a more tender texture.

- 4 portobello mushroom caps (4 to 5 inches in diameter), gills removed
- 1 large red onion, sliced into ½-inch-thick rounds
- 3 tablespoons plus 1 teaspoon extra-virgin olive oil, divided
- 2 garlic cloves, minced
- 2 teaspoons minced fresh thyme
- ½ teaspoon kosher salt
- ¼ teaspoon pepper
- 2 ounces goat cheese, crumbled (½ cup)
- 1 cup baby arugula
- ¼ teaspoon balsamic vinegar
- 4 hamburger buns, toasted if desired
- 1 tomato, cored and sliced thin

1 Cut 1⁄16-inch-deep slits on top side of mushroom caps, spaced ½ inch apart, in crosshatch pattern. Push toothpick horizontally though each onion round to keep rings intact while grilling. Brush onion with 1 tablespoon oil and season with salt and pepper to taste. Combine 2 tablespoons oil, garlic, thyme, salt, and pepper in bowl.

2A FOR A CHARCOAL GRILL Open bottom vent completely. Light large chimney starter three-quarters filled with charcoal briquettes (4½ quarts). When top coals are partially covered with ash, pour evenly over grill. Set cooking grate in place, cover, and open lid vent completely. Heat grill until hot, about 5 minutes.

2B FOR A GAS GRILL Turn all burners to high; cover; and heat grill until hot, about 15 minutes. Turn all burners to medium-high.

3 Clean and oil cooking grate. Place mushrooms, gill side down, and onion on grill (and cover if using gas). Cook onion until lightly charred, 8 to 12 minutes, turning as needed. Meanwhile, cook mushrooms until lightly charred and gill side begins to soften, 4 to 6 minutes. Flip mushrooms, brush with oil-garlic mixture, and cook until second side is tender and browned, 4 to 6 minutes. Sprinkle with goat cheese and let cheese melt, about 2 minutes. As they finish cooking, transfer mushrooms and onion to platter and tent with aluminum foil.

4 Toss arugula with vinegar and remaining 1 teaspoon oil in bowl and season with salt and pepper to taste. Remove toothpicks from onion rounds and separate into rings. Place arugula and mushroom caps on bun bottoms. Top with tomato, onion, and bun tops. Serve.

Portobello Mushrooms

Although they don't appear to be full of moisture, portobello mushrooms can leach a lot of liquid after they're cooked, which makes for soggy hamburger buns and a messy sandwich. Leaving the caps on the grill until their excess moisture evaporates only makes them leathery and dry. Instead, simply use the tip of a sharp paring knife to lightly cut into the caps in a crosshatch pattern, which will help them release liquid as they cook. It may seem counterintuitive, but quickly shedding excess moisture helps the mushrooms stay moist and succulent on the grill.

ULTIMATE GRILLED VEGETABLE SANDWICH

GRILLED HALLOUMI WRAPS

Ultimate Grilled Vegetable Sandwich

SERVES 4 to 6 **TIME** 1¼ hours

Why This Recipe Works For a rich and hearty grilled vegetable sandwich, we use a medley of summer vegetables: eggplant, zucchini, red bell pepper, and red onion. We cut the vegetables into thin planks (or wedges for the onions) to maximize surface area for the most flavorful grill marks. We brush them with a garlicky olive oil and then grill them until tender but not mushy. Tossing the grilled eggplant and zucchini in a balsamic dressing imbues them with tangy flavor throughout and softens them to the perfect silky consistency. Thinly slicing the grilled bell pepper and onion prevents large, slippery pieces from falling out of the sandwich. We layer the vegetables in a big ciabatta loaf (hollowed out to keep everything contained) with fresh mozzarella and a punchy basil mayonnaise and then grill the whole thing again to toast it. Be sure to use fresh bread here; once ciabatta becomes stale, the crust becomes tough and the sandwich will be difficult to eat.

- 1 (1-pound) loaf ciabatta, halved horizontally
- ½ cup chopped fresh basil
- ⅓ cup mayonnaise
- ⅔ ounce Pecorino Romano cheese, grated (⅓ cup)
- 2 tablespoons capers, rinsed and chopped
- 1 teaspoon pepper, divided
- 6 tablespoons extra-virgin olive oil
- 5 garlic cloves, minced
- ¼ teaspoon red pepper flakes
- 1 zucchini, halved crosswise and sliced lengthwise ¼ inch thick
- 1 red bell pepper, stemmed, seeded, and quartered
- ½ small red onion, cut into 2 wedges through root end
- 1 pound eggplant, sliced into ¼-inch-thick rounds
- 2¼ teaspoons kosher salt, divided
- 1 tablespoon balsamic vinegar
- 8 ounces fresh mozzarella cheese, sliced into ¼-inch-thick rounds

1 Using your hands, hollow out ciabatta by removing inner crumb, leaving ¼-inch border on sides and bottom. Combine basil, mayonnaise, Pecorino, capers, and ½ teaspoon pepper in bowl.

2 Combine oil, garlic, and pepper flakes in 1-cup liquid measuring cup. Microwave, uncovered, until bubbling and fragrant, about 90 seconds. Brush zucchini, bell pepper, and onion all over with ¼ cup garlic oil, then brush eggplant with remaining oil (it will absorb more oil than other vegetables). Sprinkle vegetables with 2 teaspoons salt and remaining ½ teaspoon pepper.

3A **FOR A CHARCOAL GRILL** Open bottom vent completely. Light large chimney starter filled with charcoal briquettes (6 quarts). When top coals are partially covered with ash, pour evenly over grill. Set cooking grate in place, cover, and open lid vent completely. Heat grill until hot, about 5 minutes.

3B **FOR A GAS GRILL** Turn all burners to high; cover; and heat grill until hot, about 15 minutes. Leave all burners on high.

4 Clean and oil cooking grate. Place eggplant and zucchini on grill and cook (covered if using gas), turning as needed, until well-browned and tender, 6 to 9 minutes. Transfer eggplant and zucchini to large bowl as they finish cooking. Add 1 tablespoon garlic oil and vinegar and toss to combine.

5 Place bell pepper and onion on now-empty grill and cook (covered if using gas), turning as needed, until well browned and tender, 12 to 16 minutes. Transfer bell pepper and onion to cutting board; slice thin, then sprinkle with remaining ¼ teaspoon salt. (Grill will be used again in step 7.)

6 Brush ciabatta crust with remaining 1 tablespoon garlic oil. Spread mayonnaise mixture inside ciabatta. Build sandwich on ciabatta by layering mozzarella on bottom, followed by eggplant and zucchini, and finally bell pepper and onion. Wrap tightly in aluminum foil.

7 Transfer foil-wrapped sandwich to grill. Cook, pressing occasionally with spatula, until bread is dark golden brown and charred in spots, 2 to 6 minutes, flipping halfway through cooking (peel back small piece of foil to check bread color). Transfer to cutting board and let foil-wrapped sandwich rest for 5 minutes. Unwrap sandwich, slice, and serve.

Grilled Halloumi Wraps

SERVES 4 **TIME** 40 minutes

Why This Recipe Works Firm and easy to brown, halloumi cheese is a total natural on the grill. In these wraps, the cheese's salty richness is offset by crisp sumac-spiked onion, smoky-sweet grilled bell pepper, and peppery arugula. While the cheese and peppers cook, you'll steam some moistened pitas in a foil packet on the cooler side of the grill so that they'll be soft and flexible when it comes time to wrap. For a yogurt spread that's garlicky without being harsh, stir the garlic into the lemon juice to deactivate its alliinase before the yogurt is whisked in.

- 1 red onion, halved and sliced thin
- 3 tablespoons red wine vinegar
- 1 tablespoon ground sumac
- 1½ teaspoons kosher salt, divided
- ½ cup plain Greek yogurt
- 2 tablespoons lemon juice
- 1 garlic clove, minced
- 1 large red bell pepper
- 4 (8-inch) pitas
- 12 ounces halloumi cheese, sliced crosswise ½ inch thick
- 1 tablespoon extra-virgin olive oil
- ¼ teaspoon red pepper flakes
- 2 ounces (2 cups) baby arugula

1 Stir onion, vinegar, sumac, and ½ teaspoon salt in medium bowl until well combined. Whisk yogurt, lemon juice, garlic, and ½ teaspoon salt in small bowl until smooth.

2 Slice ¼ inch off top and bottom of bell pepper and remove core. Make slit down 1 side of bell pepper and then press flat, skin side down into 1 long strip. Remove ribs and remaining seeds with knife as needed.

3 Lightly moisten 2 pitas with water. Sandwich remaining pitas between moistened pitas and wrap tightly in lightly greased heavy-duty aluminum foil.

4A **FOR A CHARCOAL GRILL** Open bottom vent completely. Light large chimney starter filled with charcoal briquettes (6 quarts). When top coals are partially covered with ash, pour evenly over half of grill. Set cooking grate in place, cover, and open lid vent completely. Heat grill until hot, about 5 minutes.

4B **FOR A GAS GRILL** Turn all burners to high; cover; and heat grill until hot, about 15 minutes. Leave primary burner on high and turn off other burner(s).

5 Clean cooking grate, then repeatedly brush grate with well-oiled paper towels until grate is black and glossy, 5 to 10 times. Place halloumi and bell pepper, skin side up, on hotter side of grill. Cook, covered, until lightly browned on both sides, 6 to 10 minutes, flipping halfway through cooking. Meanwhile, place packet of pitas on cooler side of grill and cook, turning as needed, until warm throughout, about 5 minutes. Transfer halloumi and bell pepper to cutting board as they finish cooking.

6 Cut bell pepper into ½-inch pieces and transfer to second small bowl. Add oil, pepper flakes, and remaining ½ teaspoon salt and toss to combine. Lay each warm pita on 12-inch square of foil or parchment paper. Spread each pita with one-quarter of yogurt mixture. Place one-quarter of halloumi in middle of each pita. Top with pepper, onion, and arugula. Drizzle with any remaining onion liquid. Roll pita into cylinder. Wrap in foil and cut in half. Serve.

EGGPLANT AND MOZZARELLA PANINI

Eggplant and Mozzarella Panini

SERVES 4 **TIME** 50 minutes

Why This Recipe Works Filled with garden-fresh eggplant and tomatoes, melty mozzarella, and fragrant basil, these panini are sure to become a summertime favorite. Grilling lets the eggplant slices cook through without turning greasy and nicely chars the plum tomato halves. We turn the grilled tomatoes into a quick, chunky sauce to layer with the eggplant and slices of fresh mozzarella. The sandwiches become crisp and toasty when pressed between a hot plancha and a baking sheet weighted with a cast-iron skillet. You will need a 10- or 12-inch cast-iron skillet and a cast-iron plancha measuring at least 20 by 10 inches.

- 12 ounces plum tomatoes, halved and seeded
- 10 ounces eggplant, sliced into ¾-inch-thick rounds
- 5 tablespoons extra-virgin olive oil, divided
- 1 teaspoon kosher salt, divided
- ¼ teaspoon pepper, divided
- 8 (½-inch-thick) slices crusty bread
- ½ cup coarsely chopped fresh basil
- 1 tablespoon red wine vinegar
- 2 garlic cloves, minced
- 8 ounces fresh mozzarella cheese, sliced thin

1 Brush tomatoes and then eggplant with 3 tablespoons oil and sprinkle with ½ teaspoon salt and ⅛ teaspoon pepper. Brush remaining 2 tablespoons oil evenly over 1 side of each slice of bread. Lightly spray underside of rimmed baking sheet with vegetable oil spray.

2A **FOR A CHARCOAL GRILL** Open bottom vent completely. Light large chimney starter three-quarters filled with charcoal briquettes (4½ quarts). When top coals are partially covered with ash, pour evenly over grill. Set cooking grate in place, cover, and open lid vent completely. Heat grill until hot, about 5 minutes.

2B **FOR A GAS GRILL** Turn all burners to high; cover; and heat grill and until hot, about 15 minutes. Turn all burners to medium-high.

GRILLED VEGETABLE KEBABS

3 Clean and oil cooking grate. Place eggplant and tomatoes on grill and cook (covered if using gas) until eggplant is browned and tender and tomatoes are slightly charred, 8 to 10 minutes, flipping halfway through cooking. Transfer tomatoes to bowl and mash with fork. Stir in basil, vinegar, garlic, remaining ½ teaspoon salt, and remaining ⅛ teaspoon pepper.

4 Build 4 sandwiches on bread (with oiled sides on outside of sandwiches) by layering half of mozzarella on bottom, followed by tomato sauce and eggplant, and, finally, remaining mozzarella. Press gently on sandwiches to set.

5 Center plancha on now-empty grill. Cover and heat plancha for 5 minutes. Place sandwiches on plancha. Center prepared baking sheet, oiled side down, on top of sandwiches. Center 10- or 12-inch cast-iron skillet on sheet and cook until bread is golden and crisp on first side, about 3 minutes. Using 2 spatulas, flip sandwiches; replace sheet and skillet; and cook until second side is golden and crisp and cheese is melted, about 3 minutes. Serve immediately.

Grilled Vegetable Kebabs

SERVES 4 **TIME** 45 minutes

Why This Recipe Works Vegetables are often just the supporting characters on meat kebabs, but this recipe puts them in the starring role. The flavors and textures of sweet bell peppers, hearty zucchini, and meaty portobello mushrooms complement one another nicely. Before skewering and grilling the vegetables, we toss them with a simple mixture of olive oil, Dijon mustard, rosemary, and garlic. We also grill lemon quarters and then add some of their juice to the oil mixture. Then we drizzle this dressing over the kebabs and serve them with the remaining grilled lemon quarters. You will need eight 12-inch metal skewers for this recipe.

- ¼ cup extra-virgin olive oil
- 1 teaspoon Dijon mustard
- 1 teaspoon minced fresh rosemary
- 1 garlic clove, minced
- 1 teaspoon kosher salt
- ¼ teaspoon pepper
- 6 portobello mushroom caps (5 inches in diameter), quartered
- 2 zucchini (8 ounces each), halved lengthwise and sliced ¾ inch thick
- 2 red bell peppers, stemmed, seeded, and cut into 1½-inch pieces
- 2 lemons, quartered

1 Whisk oil, mustard, rosemary, garlic, salt, and pepper together in large bowl. Measure half of mixture into separate bowl and set aside for serving. Toss mushrooms, zucchini, and bell peppers with remaining oil mixture, then thread in alternating order onto eight 12-inch metal skewers.

2A FOR A CHARCOAL GRILL Open bottom vent completely. Light large chimney starter half-filled with charcoal briquettes (3 quarts). When top coals are partially covered with ash, pour evenly over grill. Set cooking grate in place, cover, and open lid vent completely. Heat grill until hot, about 5 minutes.

2B FOR A GAS GRILL Turn all burners to high; cover; and heat grill until hot, about 15 minutes. Turn all burners to medium.

3 Clean and oil cooking grate. Place kebabs and lemons on grill. Cook (covered if using gas), turning as needed, until vegetables are tender and well browned and lemons are juicy and slightly charred, 16 to 18 minutes. Transfer kebabs and lemons to platter, removing skewers.

4 Squeeze juice of 2 lemon quarters into reserved oil mixture and whisk to combine. Drizzle vegetables with dressing and serve with remaining grilled lemon quarters.

Grilled Tomato Gazpacho

SERVES 4 **TIME** 35 minutes plus 2 hours 25 minutes seasoning, cooling, and chilling

Why This Recipe Works For a riff on this refreshing chilled soup, we use grilled tomatoes, cooking them over high heat, so they brown and char quickly without softening too much. To let the smoky, charred flavor of the tomatoes stand out, we add just a few other vegetables—cucumber, garlic, shallot, and a serrano chile for some heat. A slice of white sandwich bread, blended in along with some extra-virgin olive oil, gives the soup body and richness, and sherry vinegar adds sweet acidity. Letting the gazpacho rest overnight helps meld the flavors. For the best results, use in-season, round tomatoes that are ripe yet a bit firm so that they will hold their shape on the grill. Plum tomatoes may be used, but they will be drier in texture. If using plum tomatoes, halve them lengthwise. Supermarket vine-ripened tomatoes will work but won't be as flavorful. If you have an abundance of tomatoes, this recipe can be doubled. For the ideal flavor, refrigerate the gazpacho overnight before serving. Red wine vinegar can be substituted for the sherry vinegar, if desired.

GRILLED TOMATO GAZPACHO

- 2 pounds ripe tomatoes, cored and halved along equator
- 1 tablespoon plus ½ cup extra-virgin olive oil, divided
- 1 tablespoon kosher salt, divided
- ¼ teaspoon pepper
- 1 small cucumber, peeled and cut into 1-inch pieces
- 1 slice hearty white sandwich bread, crust removed, torn into 1-inch pieces
- 1 small shallot, peeled and halved
- 1 small garlic clove, peeled and quartered
- 1 small serrano chile, stemmed and halved lengthwise
- 2 tablespoons minced fresh parsley
- 1 teaspoon sherry vinegar, plus extra for seasoning

1 Toss tomatoes with 1 tablespoon oil, 1 teaspoon salt, and pepper in large bowl. Let stand for at least 15 minutes or up to 1 hour.

2A FOR A CHARCOAL GRILL Open bottom vent completely. Light large chimney starter filled with charcoal briquettes (6 quarts). When top coals are partially covered with ash, pour evenly over grill. Set cooking grate in place, cover, and open lid vent completely. Heat grill until hot, about 5 minutes.

2B FOR A GAS GRILL Turn all burners to high; cover; and heat grill until hot, about 15 minutes. Leave all burners on high.

3 Clean and oil cooking grate. Place tomatoes cut side down on grill (reserve any juice left behind in bowl). Cook (covered if using gas) until tomatoes are charred and beginning to soften, 4 to 6 minutes. Using tongs or thin metal spatula, carefully flip tomatoes and cook (covered if using gas) until skin sides are charred and juice bubbles, 4 to 6 minutes. Transfer tomatoes to bowl and let cool completely.

4 When tomatoes are cool enough to handle, place in blender along with any reserved juice, cucumber, bread, shallot, garlic, serrano, and remaining 2 teaspoons salt; process for 30 seconds. With blender running, slowly drizzle in remaining ½ cup oil; continue to process until completely smooth, about 2 minutes longer. Strain soup through fine-mesh strainer into large measuring cup, using back of ladle or silicone spatula to press soup through strainer. Stir in parsley and vinegar. Add enough water to yield 4 cups of soup.

5 Cover and refrigerate for at least 2 hours to chill and develop flavors. Season with salt, pepper, and extra vinegar to taste. Serve.

Smoky Tomato and Eggplant Phyllo Pie

SERVES 4 to 6 **TIME** 1½ hours plus 30 minutes salting

Why This Recipe Works This visually stunning tart is an unexpected outdoor pleasure that would be equally welcome as part of a brunch spread as it would be at dinnertime. Paper-thin phyllo layers grill-bake to a beautiful golden color and shatteringly crisp texture. Tucked inside is a filling of eggplant and tomatoes layered between mozzarella and Parmesan. Grilling the eggplant and tomatoes before assembling the tart gives them deeper flavor and delightful char. Layering 12 sheets of phyllo creates a crust sturdy enough to stand up to the abundance of vegetables, and the mozzarella melts into the crust, insulating it from becoming soggy. Either fresh or block mozzarella works well here. To thaw phyllo dough, let it sit in the refrigerator overnight or on the counter for 4 to 5 hours; do not thaw in the microwave. If using a charcoal grill, you can substitute 2 wood chunks for the wood chip packet. You will need a 10-inch cast-iron skillet.

- 1 pound ripe tomatoes, cored and sliced ½ inch thick
- 2½ teaspoons kosher salt, divided
- ½ cup plus 1 tablespoon extra-virgin olive oil, divided
- 1 pound eggplant, sliced into ¼-inch-thick rounds
- ¼ teaspoon pepper, divided
- 3 garlic cloves, minced
- 2 teaspoons minced fresh oregano or ¾ teaspoon dried
- 2 cups wood chips
- 12 (14 by 9-inch) phyllo sheets, thawed
- 6 ounces mozzarella cheese, shredded (1½ cups)
- 2 tablespoons grated Parmesan cheese
- 1 tablespoon chopped fresh basil

1 Place tomato slices in single layer on double layer of paper towels and sprinkle with 1 teaspoon salt; let sit for 30 minutes. Place second double layer paper towels on top of tomatoes and press to dry tomatoes. Brush tomatoes with 1 tablespoon oil. Brush eggplant with 2 tablespoons oil and sprinkle with ½ teaspoon salt and ⅛ teaspoon pepper. Combine garlic, oregano, 1 tablespoon oil, remaining 1 teaspoon salt, and remaining ⅛ teaspoon pepper in bowl; set garlic oil aside.

2 Using large piece of heavy-duty aluminum foil, wrap wood chips in 8 by 4-inch foil packet. (Make sure chips do not poke holes in sides or bottom of packet.) Cut 2 evenly spaced 2-inch slits in top of packet.

3A FOR A CHARCOAL GRILL Open bottom vent halfway. Light large chimney starter mounded with charcoal briquettes (7 quarts). When top coals are partially covered with ash, pour two-thirds evenly over half of grill, then pour remaining coals over other half of grill. Place wood chip packet along 1 side of grill near border between hotter and cooler coals. Set cooking grate in place, cover, and open lid vent halfway. Heat grill until hot and wood chips are smoking, about 5 minutes.

3B FOR A GAS GRILL Remove cooking grate and place wood chip packet directly on primary burner. Set grate in place and turn all burners to high. Cover and heat grill until hot and wood chips are smoking, 15 to 25 minutes. Leave primary burner on high and turn other burner(s) to medium. (Adjust primary and secondary burners as needed to maintain grill temperature of 425 to 450 degrees.)

4 Clean and oil cooking grate. Place tomatoes on hotter side of grill and cook (covered if using gas) until charred and starting to soften, about 4 minutes; do not flip. Transfer tomatoes to platter. Place eggplant on hotter side of grill and cook (covered, if using gas), turning as needed, until browned and tender, 8 to 10 minutes. Transfer to platter with tomatoes.

5 Brush 10-inch cast-iron skillet with 1 tablespoon oil. Place 1 phyllo sheet in prepared skillet, then lightly brush phyllo with oil. Turn skillet 30 degrees and place second phyllo sheet on first phyllo sheet, leaving any overhanging phyllo in place. Brush second phyllo sheet with oil. Repeat turning skillet and layering remaining 10 phyllo sheets in pinwheel pattern, brushing each with oil (you should have 12 total layers of phyllo).

6 Sprinkle mozzarella evenly in center of phyllo in 9-inch circle. Shingle tomatoes and eggplant on top of mozzarella in concentric circles, alternating tomatoes and eggplant as you go. Brush garlic oil over vegetables and sprinkle with Parmesan.

7 Gently fold edges of phyllo over vegetable mixture, pleating every 2 to 3 inches as needed, and lightly brush edges with remaining oil. Place skillet on cooler side of grill; cover; and cook, covered, until phyllo is crisp and golden brown, 30 to 35 minutes. Let cool for 15 minutes. Sprinkle with basil. Cut into wedges and serve.

Grilled Soy Ginger–Glazed Tofu

SERVES 4 to 6 **TIME** 40 minutes plus 20 minutes draining

Why This Recipe Works Tofu has a soft, silky texture that contrasts nicely with the crisp, browned crust that results from a quick stint on the grill. For successful grilling, it's key to handle the tofu carefully and cut it into the right shape. Thick slabs maximize surface contact while being large enough to turn easily. We give the mild tofu a flavor boost with a nicely clingy soy sauce–based glaze spiked with chili-garlic sauce. You can use either firm or extra-firm tofu in this recipe. Dry sherry or white wine can be substituted for the mirin in this recipe. Be sure to handle the tofu gently on the grill, or it may break apart. Using two spatulas provides the best leverage for flipping the tofu.

GLAZE

- ⅓ cup soy sauce
- ⅓ cup water
- ⅓ cup sugar
- ¼ cup mirin
- 1 tablespoon grated fresh ginger
- 2 garlic cloves, minced
- 2 teaspoons cornstarch
- 1 teaspoon chili-garlic sauce

TOFU

- 28 ounces firm tofu, sliced lengthwise into three 1-inch-thick slabs
- 2 tablespoons vegetable oil
- 1 teaspoon kosher salt
- ½ teaspoon pepper
- ¼ cup minced fresh cilantro

1 FOR THE GLAZE Simmer soy sauce, water, sugar, mirin, ginger, garlic, cornstarch, and chili-garlic sauce in small saucepan over medium-high heat until thickened and reduced to ¾ cup, 5 to 7 minutes; transfer to bowl.

2 FOR THE TOFU Spread tofu over paper towel–lined baking sheet, let drain for 20 minutes, then gently press dry with paper towels. Brush tofu with oil and sprinkle with salt and pepper.

3A FOR A CHARCOAL GRILL Open bottom vent completely. Light large chimney starter filled with charcoal briquettes (6 quarts). When top coals are partially covered with ash, pour two-thirds evenly over half of grill, then pour remaining coals over other half of grill. Set cooking grate in place, cover, and open lid vent completely. Heat grill until hot, about 5 minutes.

3B **FOR A GAS GRILL** Turn all burners to high; cover; and heat grill until hot, about 15 minutes. Leave all burners on high.

4 Clean cooking grate, then repeatedly brush grate with well-oiled paper towels until grate is black and glossy, 5 to 10 times. Gently place tofu on grill, perpendicular to grate bars (on hotter part of grill if using charcoal). Cook (covered if using gas) until lightly browned on both sides, 6 to 10 minutes, gently flipping tofu halfway through cooking using 2 spatulas.

5 Slide tofu to cooler side of grill (if using charcoal) or turn all burners to medium (if using gas). Brush tofu with ¼ cup glaze and cook until well browned, 1 to 2 minutes. Flip tofu, brush with ¼ cup glaze, and cook until well browned, 1 to 2 minutes. Transfer tofu to platter, brush with remaining ¼ cup glaze, and sprinkle with cilantro. Serve.

VARIATIONS

Grilled Asian Barbecue–Glazed Tofu
Substitute following mixture for glaze: Simmer ⅓ cup hoisin sauce, ⅓ cup ketchup, 2 tablespoons rice vinegar, 1½ tablespoons soy sauce, 1½ tablespoons toasted sesame oil, 1 tablespoon grated fresh ginger, and 1 minced scallion in small saucepan over medium-high heat until thickened and reduced to ¾ cup, 5 to 7 minutes.

Grilled Honey-Mustard Tofu
Substitute ¾ cup Honey-Mustard Barbecue Sauce (page 389) for glaze.

Grilled Tofu with Charred Broccoli and Peanut Sauce

SERVES 4 **TIME** 35 minutes plus 20 minutes draining

Why This Recipe Works Microwave-fried crispy shallots bring savory onion flavor and irresistible texture to grilled tofu and broccoli in this weeknight standout. Instead of discarding the shallot-infused oil, we toss it with the broccoli wedges to add extra oomph before grilling them to the perfect level of char and crunch. Red curry paste spices up the slabs of tofu prior to grilling and also helps create a two-ingredient peanut sauce for serving that tastes far more complex than it is. All in all, a major flavor reward for a modest assembly of ingredients. Be sure to handle the tofu gently on the grill, or it may break apart. Using two spatulas provides the best leverage for flipping the tofu.

GRILLED SOY GINGER–GLAZED TOFU

- 28 ounces firm tofu, sliced lengthwise into four ¾-inch-thick slabs
- 5 tablespoons warm water
- ¼ cup creamy peanut butter
- 5 teaspoons Thai red curry paste, divided
- 3 shallots, sliced thin
- ½ cup plus 2 tablespoons vegetable oil, plus extra as needed
- 1½ pounds broccoli crowns, cut into 4 wedges if 3 to 4 inches in diameter or 6 wedges if 4 to 5 inches in diameter
- 1 teaspoon kosher salt, divided
- ¼ teaspoon pepper, divided

1 Spread tofu over paper towel–lined baking sheet, let drain for 20 minutes, then gently press dry with paper towels.

2 Whisk water, peanut butter, and 1 teaspoon curry paste in bowl until smooth; set aside for serving. Microwave shallots and oil in medium bowl for 5 minutes. Stir and continue to microwave in 2-minute increments until beginning to brown, 2 to 6 minutes. Stir and continue to microwave in 30-second increments until golden brown, 30 seconds to 2 minutes. Using slotted spoon, transfer shallots to paper towel–lined plate and season with salt to taste; reserve shallot oil. (You should have about 7 tablespoons reserved oil; if you have less, add vegetable oil to make 7 tablespoons.)

3 Toss broccoli with 5 tablespoons reserved shallot oil, ½ teaspoon salt, and ⅛ teaspoon pepper in bowl. Whisk remaining 4 teaspoons curry paste, remaining 2 tablespoons reserved shallot oil, remaining ½ teaspoon salt, and remaining ⅛ teaspoon pepper together in bowl. Brush tofu all over with curry paste mixture.

4A **FOR A CHARCOAL GRILL** Open bottom vent completely. Light large chimney starter filled with charcoal briquettes (6 quarts). When top coals are partially covered with ash, pour evenly over grill. Set cooking grate in place, cover, and open lid vent completely. Heat grill until hot, about 5 minutes.

4B **FOR A GAS GRILL** Turn all burners to high; cover; and heat grill until hot, about 15 minutes. Leave all burners on high.

5 Clean cooking grate, then repeatedly brush grate with well-oiled paper towels until grate is black and glossy, 5 to 10 times. Place broccoli and tofu on grill and cook (covered if using gas) until broccoli is charred in spots and tofu is well browned, 6 to 10 minutes, turning broccoli as needed and gently flipping tofu halfway through cooking. Serve tofu and broccoli with reserved peanut sauce and crispy shallots.

GRILLED TOFU WITH CHARRED BROCCOLI AND PEANUT SAUCE

GRILLED TOFU AND VEGETABLES WITH HARISSA

Grilled Tofu and Vegetables with Harissa

SERVES 4 to 6 **TIME** 35 minutes plus 20 minutes draining

Why This Recipe Works Spicy harissa complements the char of many grilled foods, and tofu slabs make an especially versatile canvas for this aromatic chile paste's complexity. Brushing the tofu with the harissa after grilling preserves the condiment's bright depth. The secret to a satisfying grilled vegetable platter is including a mixture of not just flavors but also textures and temperatures. Pleasantly bitter radicchio wedges, sweet bell peppers, and zesty red onions go on the grill alongside the tofu, and everything is topped off with juicy raw grape tomatoes and fresh mint. Be sure to handle the tofu gently on the grill, or it may break apart. Using two spatulas provides the best leverage for flipping the tofu.

- 28 ounces firm tofu, sliced lengthwise into four ¾-inch-thick slabs
- ¼ cup harissa
- 2 tablespoons water
- 1 tablespoon honey
- 2½ teaspoons kosher salt, divided
- 1 teaspoon pepper, divided
- ½ teaspoon grated lemon zest plus 2 tablespoons juice
- 1 large red onion, sliced into ½-inch-thick rounds
- 2 red, yellow, or orange bell peppers, halved lengthwise, stemmed, and seeded
- 3 tablespoons extra-virgin olive oil, divided
- 1 head radicchio (10 ounces), cut into 4 wedges through core
- 10 ounces grape tomatoes, halved
- ½ cup fresh mint or parsley leaves, torn

1 Spread tofu on paper towel–lined baking sheet, let drain for 20 minutes, then gently press dry with paper towels.

2 Whisk harissa, water, honey, ½ teaspoon salt, ¼ teaspoon pepper, and lemon zest and juice together in bowl. Push toothpick horizontally through each onion round to keep rings intact while grilling. Arrange bell peppers skin side up on cutting board and press to flatten with your hand.

3 Brush tofu with 1 tablespoon oil and sprinkle with 1 teaspoon salt and ¼ teaspoon pepper. Brush radicchio, onion, and bell peppers with remaining 2 tablespoons oil and sprinkle with remaining 1 teaspoon salt and remaining ½ teaspoon pepper.

4A **FOR A CHARCOAL GRILL** Open bottom vent completely. Light large chimney starter filled with charcoal briquettes (6 quarts). When top coals are partially covered with ash, pour evenly over grill. Set cooking grate in place, cover, and open lid vent completely. Heat grill until hot, about 5 minutes.

4B **FOR A GAS GRILL** Turn all burners to high; cover; and heat grill until hot, about 15 minutes. Leave all burners on high.

5 Clean cooking grate, then repeatedly brush grate with well-oiled paper towels until grate is black and glossy, 5 to 10 times. Place tofu and vegetables on grill. Cook (covered if using gas), flipping as needed, until vegetables are tender and lightly charred and tofu is lightly charred, 10 to 12 minutes. Transfer vegetables and tofu to serving platter as they finish grilling and tent with aluminum foil to keep warm

6 Remove toothpicks from onion rounds. Brush tofu with half of harissa mixture. Top with tomatoes, sprinkle with mint, and drizzle with remaining harissa mixture. Serve.

Grilled Barbecued Tempeh Burgers with Spicy Pickled Jicama

SERVES 4 **TIME** 35 minutes plus 1 hour pickling and marinating

Why This Recipe Works For a supereasy grilled veggie burger with rich, smoky flavor, turn to tempeh. Forming the burgers is as simple as halving two pieces of tempeh crosswise to make four planks. Marinating the tempeh in a mixture of barbecue sauce and water infuses it with flavor, and patting it dry before grilling ensures a crispy edge. For an extra boost of barbecue flavor, we brush both sides of each plank with additional sauce during the last few minutes of grilling. We top the burgers with peppery arugula and add sweet, spicy pickled jicama for a lively crunch.

- 1 cup cider vinegar
- ⅓ cup sugar
- ½ teaspoon kosher salt
- 6 ounces jicama, peeled and cut into 2-inch matchsticks (1½ cups)
- 1 jalapeño chile, stemmed, seeded, and sliced into thin rings
- 1½ cups barbecue sauce, divided, plus extra for serving
- ¼ cup water
- 2 (8-ounce) packages tempeh, cut in half crosswise
- 4 hamburger buns, toasted if desired
- 1 cup baby arugula

GRILLED BARBECUE TEMPEH AND VEGETABLE SKEWERS

1 Bring vinegar, sugar, and salt to simmer in small saucepan over medium-high heat, stirring occasionally, until sugar has dissolved. Off heat, stir in jicama and jalapeño; cover; and let cool to room temperature, about 1 hour. (Pickled jicama can be refrigerated in airtight container for up to 1 week.)

2 Whisk 1 cup barbecue sauce and water together in small bowl. Combine sauce mixture and tempeh in 1-gallon zipper-lock bag and toss to coat; press out as much air as possible and seal bag. Refrigerate for at least 1 hour, flipping bag occasionally. Before grilling, remove tempeh from marinade and pat dry with paper towels.

3A **FOR A CHARCOAL GRILL** Open bottom vent completely. Light large chimney starter filled with charcoal briquettes (6 quarts). When top coals are partially covered with ash, pour evenly over grill. Set cooking grate in place, cover, and open lid vent completely. Heat grill until hot, about 5 minutes.

3B **FOR A GAS GRILL** Turn all burners to high; cover; and heat grill until hot, about 15 minutes. Leave all burners on high.

4 Clean and oil cooking grate. Place tempeh on grill and cook (covered if using gas) until well browned, 8 to 12 minutes, turning as needed. Brush patties with ¼ cup barbecue sauce, flip, and continue to cook until sizzling and well browned, about 1 minute. Brush second side of patties with remaining ¼ cup sauce, flip, and continue to cook until well browned, about 1 minute. Serve burgers on buns, topped with pickled jicama and arugula, passing extra barbecue sauce separately.

Grilled Barbecue Tempeh and Vegetable Skewers

SERVES 4 **TIME** 35 minutes

Why This Recipe Works Tempeh, made from fermented soybeans, has a nicely chewy, hearty texture that makes for satisfyingly meaty skewers. Its neutral yet nutty flavor is a natural fit for barbecue sauce. In this recipe, the sauce plays double duty, serving as a sweet and smoky marinade for the tempeh as well as a glaze for the kebabs, so they become caramelized when grilled. You will need eight 12-inch metal skewers for this recipe.

- 1¼ cups barbecue sauce, divided
- 2 tablespoons extra-virgin olive oil
- 2 tablespoons water
- 1 pound tempeh, cut into 1½-inch pieces
- 1 pound cremini mushrooms, trimmed
- 2 red bell peppers, stemmed, seeded, and cut into 1-inch pieces
- 1 lemon, halved

1 Whisk ½ cup barbecue sauce, oil, and water together in large bowl. Add tempeh and mushrooms and toss to coat. Thread tempeh onto two 12-inch metal skewers, thread mushrooms onto three 12-inch metal skewers, and thread peppers onto three 12-inch metal skewers.

2A **FOR A CHARCOAL GRILL** Open bottom vent completely. Light large chimney starter filled with charcoal briquettes (6 quarts). When top coals are partially covered with ash, pour evenly over grill. Set cooking grate in place, cover, and open lid vent completely. Heat grill until hot, about 5 minutes.

2B **FOR A GAS GRILL** Turn all burners to high; cover; and heat grill until hot, about 15 minutes. Leave all burners on high.

3 Clean cooking grate, then repeatedly brush grate with well-oiled paper towels until grate is black and glossy, 5 to 10 times. Place lemon halves cut sides down on grill and cook (covered if using gas) until lightly charred, about 2 minutes; set aside for serving. Place skewered tempeh and vegetables on grill and cook (covered if using gas), turning as needed, until tempeh is well browned and vegetables are tender and lightly charred, 10 to 12 minutes.

4 Brush 1 side of skewers with ¼ cup barbecue sauce; flip sauced side down; and grill until sizzling and well browned, about 1 minute. Brush second side with ¼ cup sauce, flip skewers sauced side down, and cook until sizzling and well browned on second side, about 1 minute. Transfer to platter and serve with grilled lemons and remaining ¼ cup barbecue sauce.

8

Pizza, Breads + Desserts

PIZZA

BREADS

DESSERTS

IN DEPTH

Outdoor Baking

Many grilling recipes require you to have only a couple of tools handy—a pair of tongs, perhaps, and a platter. But for grill-baking, an outdoor setup like the one we suggest on page 24 is superuseful. Take pizza, for instance: Once the dough is ready, it takes mere minutes to assemble and grill a pizza, so organization is crucial. If you've given yourself the space and the tools to press out the dough and add the toppings, you—and your guests—will be amazed at how quickly and efficiently you can turn out top-quality pizzas. Another perk: Less time running back and forth to the kitchen means more time enjoying the food.

SET YOURSELF UP FOR SUCCESS

Here's what a grill station setup for pizza looks like:

- **Oil** for stretching dough
- **Tablespoon measure** for oil
- **Two rimmed baking sheets** for holding dough before and after shaping
- **Dough rounds**
- **Pizza peel** (In a pinch, tongs and an overturned rimmed baking sheet can be used to transfer the dough to and from the grill.)
- **Tongs and metal spatula** for flipping and moving the crust
- **Prepared toppings**
- **Cutting board**
- **Sharp chef's knife or pizza cutter**

This type of prep station is useful for other grill-baked items as well. If you're baking in a cast-iron skillet or Dutch oven, be sure to have **grill gloves** or **potholders** for removing the hot pan from the grill, and a **wire rack set in a rimmed baking sheet** as a place to park the pan while it cools. Keep a **fork** handy for popping any large bubbles that form in flatbreads. And have a **tub of soapy water** or at least a **damp towel** close by to wipe food-covered or oily hands before lifting the grill's lid handle.

Perfect Pizza Crust

THE RING OF FIRE

Though it sounds counterintuitive, a conventional single-level charcoal fire with the coals spread across the grill can cause pizza crust to burn at the center. This is because the pizza is not just subjected to heat from below; the curved kettle walls also reflect the heat inward, creating a hot spot at the center of the grill. For more even heat we arrange the coals in a **ring**, so the center of the pizza cooks through reflected heat only. This setup also works well for Grilled Flatbreads (page 365) and Mana'eesh Za'atar (page 368).

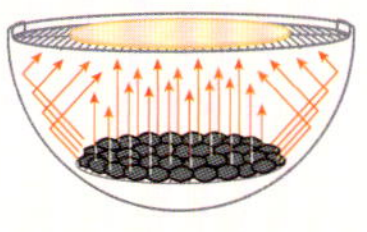

SINGLE LEVEL
Too hot in center

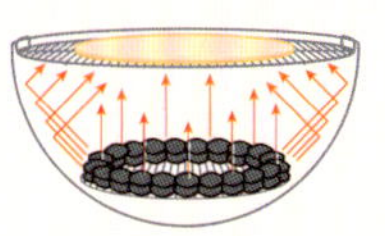

RING
Even heat

THE LEOPARDING EFFECT

A hallmark of pizzas baked in high-heat wood-fired pizza ovens is "leoparding," a pattern of deep brown spots on pizza crust that occurs as small blisters in the dough char. This dramatic browning is coveted for the extra dimension of flavor it adds to the pie. Here's how to get it in your outdoor gas pizza oven.

1 Preheat the oven on high to reach 800 to 850 degrees; this is crucial.

2 Once the pizza is in the oven, drop the temperature to low to ensure that the dough bakes through at the same rate as the cheese melts, and the blisters on the dough's surface become charred.

3 For the first 30 seconds of baking, don't move the pizza. This allows the bottom crust to firm up so that the peel can easily slide underneath for easy rotating.

4 After that, rotate the pizza every 20 to 30 seconds for even cooking. (If you have a single back-burner oven, rotate it a quarter-turn. If you have an L-shaped burner oven, rotate it a one-third turn.

5 The pizza should take 2 to 3 minutes to cook. If it takes longer, increase the oven temperature slightly while cooking.

6 Between pizzas, allow the oven to fully reheat to 800 to 850 degrees, 3 to 5 minutes.

BAKE IT OUTSIDE

These baked goods can be made from start to finish at the grill:

370 Big and Fluffy Biscuits
377 Charred Strawberry Dutch Baby
377 Cherry Spoon Cake
366 Easy Grilled Butternut Squash, Apple, and Goat Cheese Flatbreads
366 Easy Grilled Onion, Pear, and Prosciutto Flatbreads
371 Grilled Fresh Corn Cornbread with Charred Jalapeños and Cheddar
380 Orange Upside-Down Cake
382 Skillet Chocolate-Chip Cookie

Grilled Pizza

SERVES 4 to 6 **TIME** 1½ hours plus 24 hours rising

Why This Recipe Works Taking your pizza party outside is a winning move: The grill's heat produces a golden-brown pizza crust with flavorful grill marks in a matter of minutes. To prevent a hot spot at the center that would burn the crust, we place the coals in a ring around the perimeter of the grill (for more about this, see page 359). Our easy-to-stretch dough bakes up thin, with small air bubbles. Stretching the dough on a generously oiled baking sheet makes it less sticky and helps it crisp up over the flames. To make sure the toppings cook as quickly as the crust, we prewarm the sauce and use a combo of fast-melting fresh mozzarella and finely grated Parmesan. This recipe works best with high-protein bread flour such as King Arthur. It's important to use ice water to prevent the dough from overheating in the food processor. Because the ultrathin crust can't support much weight beyond sauce and cheese, go easy on toppings. Try one of our variations or scatter one of the following on the pies once they come off the grill: lightly dressed baby arugula, paper-thin prosciutto slices, strips of roasted red pepper, thinly sliced scallions or onion, or chopped or torn fresh herbs. Setting up a prep table (see page 358) will streamline the process by allowing you to shape the dough and top the pizzas grillside.

DOUGH

- 3 cups (16½ ounces) bread flour
- 1 tablespoon sugar
- ¼ teaspoon instant or rapid-rise yeast
- 1¼ cups plus 2 tablespoons (11 ounces) ice water
- 1 tablespoon extra-virgin olive oil, plus extra for counter, baking sheet, and dough balls
- 1½ teaspoons table salt

SAUCE

- 1 (14-ounce) can whole peeled tomatoes, drained with juice reserved
- 2 tablespoons extra-virgin olive oil
- 2 teaspoons minced fresh oregano
- ½ teaspoon sugar, plus extra for seasoning
- ½ teaspoon table salt
- ¼ teaspoon red pepper flakes

PIZZA

- ½ cup plus 1 tablespoon extra-virgin olive oil, divided, plus extra for drizzling
- 3 ounces Parmesan cheese, grated (1½ cups)
- 8 ounces fresh whole-milk mozzarella cheese, torn into bite-size pieces (2 cups)
- 3 tablespoons shredded fresh basil

1 FOR THE DOUGH Process flour, sugar, and yeast in food processor until combined, about 3 seconds. With processor running, slowly add ice water and process until dough is just combined and no dry flour remains, about 10 seconds. Let dough stand for 10 minutes.

2 Add oil and salt to dough and process until dough forms satiny, sticky ball that clears sides of bowl, 30 to 60 seconds. Transfer dough to lightly oiled counter and knead until smooth, about 1 minute. Divide dough into 3 equal pieces. Shape each piece into tight ball, transfer to well-oiled rimmed baking sheet (alternatively, place dough balls in individual well-oiled bowls), and coat top of each ball lightly with oil. Cover tightly with plastic wrap (taking care not to compress dough) and refrigerate for at least 24 hours or up to 3 days.

3 FOR THE SAUCE Pulse tomatoes in food processor until finely chopped, 12 to 15 pulses. Transfer to medium bowl and stir in reserved juice, oil, oregano, sugar, salt, and pepper flakes. Season with extra sugar and salt to taste, cover, and refrigerate until ready to use. (Sauce can be refrigerated for up to 3 days.)

4 One hour before cooking pizza, remove dough from refrigerator and let stand at room temperature.

5A FOR A CHARCOAL GRILL Open bottom vent halfway. Light large chimney starter three-quarters filled with charcoal briquettes (4½ quarts). When top coals are partially covered with ash, pour into ring around perimeter of grill, leaving 8-inch clearing in center. Set cooking grate in place, cover, and open lid vent halfway. Heat grill until hot, about 5 minutes.

5B FOR A GAS GRILL Turn all burners to high; cover; and heat grill until hot, about 15 minutes. Turn all burners to medium-high.

6 While grill is heating, transfer sauce to small saucepan and bring to simmer over medium heat. Cover and keep warm.

7 FOR THE PIZZA Clean and oil cooking grate. Pour ¼ cup oil onto center of rimmed baking sheet. Transfer 1 dough round to sheet and coat both sides of dough with oil. Using your fingertips and palms, gently press and stretch dough to form rough 12 by 8-inch oval of even thickness. Using both hands, gently grab corners of dough on long side of oval. Using fluid motion, lift dough, allowing it to stretch further into rough 16 by 12-inch oval, and carefully transfer to center of grill (oval will droop slightly). Cook (covered if using gas) until grill marks form on first side, 1 to 6 minutes. Using tongs and spatula, carefully peel dough from grate, then rotate dough 90 degrees and continue

GRILLED PIZZA

to cook (covered if using gas) until second set of grill marks appears, 1 to 6 minutes. Flip dough and cook (covered if using gas) until second side of dough is lightly charred in spots, 2 to 6 minutes. Using tongs or pizza peel, transfer crust to cutting board so that side that was grilled first is facing down. Repeat with remaining 2 dough rounds, adding 1 tablespoon oil to sheet for each round and keeping grill cover closed when not in use to retain heat.

8 Drizzle top of 1 crust with 1 tablespoon oil. Sprinkle one-third of Parmesan evenly over surface. Arrange one-third of mozzarella pieces, evenly spaced, on surface of pizza. Dollop one-third of sauce in evenly spaced 1-tablespoon mounds over surface of pizza.

9 Using pizza peel or overturned rimmed baking sheet, return pizza to center of grill (turn all burners to medium-low if using gas). Cover and cook until bottom is well browned and mozzarella is melted, 3 to 5 minutes, checking bottom and rotating frequently to prevent burning. Transfer pizza to cutting board, sprinkle with 1 tablespoon basil, drizzle lightly with extra oil, and season with salt to taste. Cut into wedges and serve. Repeat with remaining 2 crusts and remaining oil, cheese, sauce, and basil.

GRILLED PIZZA

VARIATIONS

Grilled Pizza with Fontina, Pecorino, and Scallions

Omit Parmesan and mozzarella. Combine 3 tablespoons of oil with 1 minced garlic clove in bowl. Chop basil rather than shredding it; combine basil, 3 tablespoons chopped fresh parsley, and 2 thinly sliced scallions in second bowl. Combine 1⅓ cups shredded fontina and 2 cups shredded Pecorino in third bowl. Set bowls aside. In step 8, brush each pizza with one-third of garlic oil, sprinkle with one-third of cheese mixture, and dollop with one-third of tomato sauce. In step 9, after grilling, sprinkle each pizza with one-third of scallion-herb mixture.

Grilled Pizza with Soppressata, Banana Peppers, and Hot Honey

In step 8, after topping each pizza with cheeses and sauce, scatter with 4 thin slices soppressata, cut into quarters, and 2 tablespoons sliced banana pepper rings. Drizzle with hot honey before serving.

Forming the Pizza Crust

1 Press and stretch dough out into 12 by 8-inch oval on oiled rimmed baking sheet.

2 Carefully transfer dough to center of grill.

Thin-Crust Pizza for the Outdoor Pizza Oven

MAKES two 13-inch pizzas or four 9½-inch pizzas
TIME 1¼ hours plus 1 hour resting

Why This Recipe Works Sure, this isn't a grilling recipe, but we couldn't resist including this Neapolitan-inspired pizza made in an outdoor pizza oven—it's a great example of the thrill of baking outdoors. You can customize this recipe to make two large or four small pizzas, depending on the size of your oven and your gathering. To prevent sticking, dust the pizza peel liberally with bread flour or semolina. Place the shaped dough on the peel, gently shake the peel, and dust with more flour as needed. Don't top your pizza until it's on the peel, right before baking. For tips on achieving a leoparding effect (deep-brown, flavorful charred spots) on your pizza, see page 359. Setting up a prep table (see page 358) will streamline the process by allowing you to shape the dough and top the pizzas grillside. This recipe makes extra sauce, which can be refrigerated for up to one week or frozen for up to one month.

- 1 (28-ounce) can whole peeled tomatoes, drained
- 1 tablespoon extra-virgin olive oil
- 1 teaspoon red wine vinegar
- 2 garlic cloves, minced
- 1 teaspoon table salt
- 1 teaspoon dried oregano
- ¼ teaspoon pepper
- 1 recipe Pizza Dough for the Outdoor Pizza Oven or Whole-Wheat Pizza Dough for the Outdoor Pizza Oven (page 364)
- 1 ounce Parmesan cheese, grated (½ cup)
- 8 ounces fresh whole milk-mozzarella cheese, torn into bite-size pieces (2 cups)

1 Process tomatoes, oil, vinegar, garlic, salt, oregano, and pepper in food processor until smooth, about 30 seconds. Transfer sauce to medium bowl and refrigerate.

2 Remove dough from refrigerator and divide in half (for two 13-inch pies) or quarters (for four 9½-inch pies). Shape each dough piece into smooth, tight ball. Place on lightly oiled rimmed baking sheet, spacing them at least 3 inches apart. Cover loosely with greased plastic wrap and let rest for 1 hour.

3 Preheat portable outdoor pizza oven on high to 800 to 850 degrees, 20 to 30 minutes. Coat 1 ball of dough generously with flour and place on well-floured counter. Using your fingertips, gently flatten into 8-inch disk, leaving 1 inch of outer edge slightly thicker than center.

THIN-CRUST PIZZA FOR THE OUTDOOR PIZZA OVEN

4A FOR TWO 13-INCH PIZZAS Using your hands, gently stretch disk into 12-inch round, working along edges and giving disk quarter turns as you stretch. Transfer dough to well-floured peel and stretch into 13-inch round. Using back of spoon or ladle, spread ⅓ cup tomato sauce in thin layer over surface of dough, leaving ½-inch border around edge. Sprinkle ¼ cup Parmesan evenly over sauce, followed by 1 cup mozzarella.

4B FOR FOUR 9½-INCH PIZZAS Using your hands, gently stretch disk into 9-inch round, working along edges and giving disk quarter turns as you stretch. Transfer dough to well-floured peel and stretch into 9½-inch round. Using back of spoon or ladle, spread 2 tablespoons tomato sauce in thin layer over surface of dough, leaving ¼-inch border around edge. Sprinkle 2 tablespoons Parmesan evenly over sauce, followed by ½ cup mozzarella.

5 Slide pizza carefully onto center of stone; reduce oven temperature to low; and bake until crust is spotty brown and cheese is bubbly and beginning to brown, 2 to 3 minutes, rotating pizza every 20 to 30 seconds. Remove pizza and place on wire rack for 5 minutes before slicing and serving. Repeat from step 3 to shape, top, and bake remaining pizza(s).

Pizza Dough for the Outdoor Pizza Oven

MAKES two 13-inch or four 9½-inch pizzas **TIME** 20 minutes, plus 24 hours resting

Why This Recipe Works We adapted our regular thin-crust pizza dough recipe for optimum performance in an outdoor pizza oven, adjusting the hydration level to 64 percent to make it easier to handle and shape, and omitting the sugar to reduce the risk of burning. A one- to three-day proof in the fridge minimizes air bubbles and develops flavor in the crust.

- 3 cups (16½ ounces) bread flour
- ½ teaspoon instant or rapid-rise yeast
- 1⅓ cups (10⅝ ounces) ice water
- 1 tablespoon extra-virgin olive oil
- 1½ teaspoons table salt

1 Pulse flour and yeast in food processor until combined, about 5 pulses. With processor running, slowly add ice water and process until dough is just combined and no dry flour remains, about 10 seconds. Let dough rest for 10 minutes.

2 Add oil and salt to dough and process until dough forms satiny, sticky ball that clears sides of bowl, 30 to 60 seconds. Transfer dough to lightly oiled surface and knead to form smooth, tight ball, about 30 seconds. Place seam side down in lightly greased large bowl, cover tightly with plastic wrap, and refrigerate for at least 24 hours or up to 3 days.

VARIATION

Whole-Wheat Pizza Dough for the Outdoor Pizza Oven

Reduce bread flour to 1 cup (5½ ounces), increase yeast to ¾ teaspoon, and add 1½ cups (8¼ ounces) whole-wheat flour in step 1. In step 2, reduce ice water to 1¼ cups (10 ounces), and increase oil to 2 tablespoons. Process and form dough and let rise as directed.

Topping Your Pizza

Careful prep and a light touch are the secrets to dressing up your pizza without making it soggy. Here are a few guidelines.

DELICATE VEGETABLES AND HERBS: Place leafy greens such as baby spinach and herbs such as basil beneath the cheese to shield them from the intense heat or add them raw atop the fully cooked hot pizza.

HARDY VEGETABLES: Aim for a maximum of 6 ounces per 13-inch pie or 3 ounces per 9½-inch pie, spread out in a single layer. Thinly slice and lightly sauté (or microwave for a minute or two along with a little olive oil) sturdy vegetables such as onions, peppers, and mushrooms.

MEATS: Use 4 ounces per 13-inch pie or 2 ounces per 9½-inch pie. We like to poach meats such as sausage (broken up into ½-inch chunks), pepperoni, or ground beef for 4 to 5 minutes in a wide skillet with ¼ cup of water, which helps render the fat while keeping the meat moist. Or simply drape paper-thin slices of prosciutto over the top of the finished pizza.

Grilled Flatbreads

MAKES 4 flatbreads **TIME** 50 minutes plus 1¾ hours rising and resting

Why This Recipe Works The beautifully blistered naans produced by tandoor ovens were our inspiration for these flatbreads. Yogurt, oil, and an egg yolk make these soft, rich, and pleasingly chewy. If garlic is your thing, check out the variation; it's used in four different ways for big allium flavor. This recipe works best with a high-protein all-purpose flour such as King Arthur. Do not use nonfat yogurt. It's important to use ice water to prevent the dough from overheating in the food processor.

- ½ cup (4 ounces) ice water
- ⅓ cup plain whole-milk yogurt
- 3 tablespoons vegetable oil
- 1 large egg yolk
- 2 cups (10 ounces) all-purpose flour
- 1¼ teaspoons sugar
- 1¼ teaspoons table salt
- ½ teaspoon instant or rapid-rise yeast
- 2 tablespoons unsalted butter, melted

1 In liquid measuring cup, combine ice water, yogurt, oil, and egg yolk. Process flour, sugar, salt, and yeast in food processor until combined, about 3 seconds. With processor running, slowly add water mixture and process until dough forms sticky ball that clears sides of bowl, 30 to 60 seconds. Transfer dough to lightly floured counter and knead until smooth, about 1 minute. Shape dough into tight ball and place in large, lightly oiled bowl. Cover with plastic wrap and let rise at room temperature for 30 minutes.

2 Using greased bowl scraper or your fingertips, fold partially risen dough over itself 8 times by gently lifting and folding edge of dough toward middle, turning bowl 90 degrees after each fold. Cover with plastic, let rise for 30 minutes, then repeat folding. Cover and let rise for 30 minutes longer.

3 Transfer dough to lightly floured counter and divide into 4 equal pieces. Shape each piece into tight ball, transfer to well-oiled rimmed baking sheet, and cover loosely with greased plastic. Let rest for 15 to 20 minutes.

4 Line rimmed baking sheet with floured parchment paper. Transfer 1 dough ball to lightly floured counter and sprinkle with flour. Using your hands and rolling pin, press and roll ball into 9-inch round of even thickness, sprinkling dough and counter with flour as needed to prevent sticking. Using fork, poke entire surface of round 20 to 25 times. Repeat with remaining dough, stacking rounds between pieces of floured parchment on prepared sheet.

GRILLED FLATBREADS

5A **FOR A CHARCOAL GRILL** Open bottom vent completely. Light large chimney starter filled with charcoal briquettes (6 quarts). When top coals are partially covered with ash, pour into ring around perimeter of grill, leaving 8-inch clearing in center. Set cooking grate in place, cover, and open lid vent completely. Heat grill until hot, about 5 minutes.

5B **FOR A GAS GRILL** Turn all burners to high; cover; and heat grill until hot, about 15 minutes. Leave all burners on high.

6 Clean and oil cooking grate. Place 2 flatbreads in center of grill and cook until bottoms are lightly charred, about 90 seconds. Flip flatbreads and grill until lightly charred on second side and cooked through, 1 to 2 minutes. (If flatbread puffs up, gently poke with fork to deflate.) Transfer flatbreads to platter, brush tops with half of melted butter, and cover loosely with aluminum foil. Repeat with remaining flatbreads and remaining butter. Serve immediately.

VARIATIONS

Hand-Mixed Grilled Flatbreads

Whisk flour, sugar, yeast, and salt together in large bowl. Using silicone spatula, fold water mixture into flour mixture, scraping up dry flour from bottom of bowl and pressing dough until cohesive and shaggy and all flour is incorporated. Proceed with step 2, increasing kneading time to 5 to 7 minutes. (Coat your hands with flour if dough begins to stick.)

Grilled Garlic Flatbreads

Microwave 3 thinly sliced garlic cloves with oil until garlic is golden and crisp, 2 to 3 minutes, stirring halfway through microwaving. Using fork, remove garlic and reserve. Add garlic oil to water mixture and crispy garlic to food processor with flour. Add 2 minced garlic cloves and ½ teaspoon garlic powder to butter before melting.

Easy Grilled Onion, Pear, and Prosciutto Flatbreads

SERVES 6 to 8 **TIME** 55 minutes

Why This Recipe Works For these savory-sweet-salty flatbreads, we grill the pears and onion directly on the grate first to soften, sweeten, and pick up char. Then we grill store-bought pizza dough on one side, flip it, and top it with the grilled goodies, along with some Brie. Once the cheese is melty, the flatbreads are ready to be draped with ribbons of pink prosciutto, drizzled with honey, and served. Make sure to flour the counter so that the dough doesn't stick as you work with it. For the best flavor and texture, serve the grilled flatbreads as soon as possible.

- 1 pound store-bought pizza dough, room temperature, divided into 2 equal pieces
- 1 red onion, sliced into ½-inch-thick rounds
- 2 ripe but firm Bartlett or Bosc pears, peeled, halved, and cored
- 5 tablespoons extra-virgin olive oil, divided
- ½ teaspoon table salt
- ¼ teaspoon pepper
- 6 ounces firm Brie cheese, sliced thin
- 4 ounces thinly sliced prosciutto
- 2 teaspoons minced fresh thyme
- Honey

1 Cover dough pieces loosely with plastic wrap and set aside. Push toothpick horizontally through each onion round to keep rings intact while grilling. Brush onion and pear halves with 1 tablespoon oil and sprinkle with salt and pepper.

2 Line rimmed baking sheet with floured parchment paper. Transfer 1 dough ball to lightly floured counter and sprinkle with flour. Using your hands and rolling pin, press and roll ball into 12 by 8-inch rectangle of even thickness, sprinkling dough and counter with flour as needed to prevent sticking. Transfer dough to prepared sheet, reshaping as needed; sprinkle with flour; and top with second sheet of parchment. Repeat with remaining dough and stack on top of first dough rectangle on prepared sheet.

3A **FOR A CHARCOAL GRILL** Open bottom vent completely. Light large chimney starter filled with charcoal briquettes (6 quarts). When top coals are partially covered with ash, pour evenly over grill. Set cooking grate in place, cover, and open lid vent completely. Heat grill until hot, about 5 minutes.

EASY GRILLED ONION, PEAR, AND PROSCIUTTO FLATBREADS

3B FOR A GAS GRILL Turn all burners to high; cover; and heat grill until hot, about 15 minutes. Leave all burners on high.

4 Clean and oil cooking grate. Place pear halves cut side down and onion on grill. Cook (covered if using gas), turning as needed, until both are tender and charred, about 8 minutes for pears and 20 minutes for onion. Transfer onion and pears to cutting board as they finish cooking. Remove toothpicks from onion rounds and discard any charred outer rings. Chop onion and slice pears thin.

5 Brush top of each dough rectangle with 1 tablespoon oil. Place dough oiled side down on grill and cook until undersides are spotty brown and top is covered with bubbles, 2 to 3 minutes (pop any large bubbles that form). Brush top of each flatbread with 1 tablespoon oil, then flip. Top dough with Brie, pear, and onion. Cover and cook until second side of flatbreads is spotty brown and cheese is melted, 3 to 5 minutes. Transfer to cutting board.

6 Top flatbreads with prosciutto and thyme and drizzle with honey. Cut into wedges and serve.

VARIATION

Easy Grilled Butternut Squash, Apple, and Goat Cheese Flatbreads

Omit prosciutto and thyme. Substitute 1 pound butternut squash, peeled, halved lengthwise, seeded, and sliced crosswise ½ inch thick, for onion; do not thread on toothpicks. Substitute 1 Granny Smith apple, peeled, halved, and cored, for pears. Substitute crumbled goat cheese for Brie and maple syrup for honey. Sprinkle flatbreads with ground sumac before serving.

MANA'EESH ZA'ATAR

GRILLED FLOUR TORTILLAS

Mana'eesh Za'atar

MAKES 3 flatbreads **TIME** 40 minutes plus 2¼ hours rising and resting

Why This Recipe Works Mana'eesh, a beloved street food in Lebanon, are typically baked in a very hot oven—a factor that makes these flatbreads a great candidate for grilling over fire. This version, topped with olive oil and the tangy, herbal spice blend za'atar, is a favorite. Poking the dough all over with a fork before baking helps prevent uneven puffing and promotes a chewy yet tender crust. Grilling the mana'eesh over medium-high heat encourages them to cook through inside while delicate bubbles form on top of the bread and the bottom turns an even golden brown. It's important to use ice water to prevent the dough from overheating in the food processor.

- ¾ cup plus 2 tablespoons (7 ounces) ice water
- 5 tablespoons extra-virgin olive oil, divided
- 2½ cups (12½ ounces) all-purpose flour
- 1½ teaspoons instant or rapid-rise yeast
- 1½ teaspoons table salt, divided
- 3 tablespoons za'atar

1 In liquid measuring cup, combine water and 2 tablespoons oil. Process flour, yeast, and 1 teaspoon salt in food processor until combined, about 3 seconds. With processor running, slowly add water mixture and process until dough forms sticky ball that clears sides of bowl, 30 to 60 seconds.

2 Transfer dough to lightly floured counter and knead until smooth, about 1 minute. Shape dough into tight ball and place in large, lightly oiled bowl. Cover with plastic wrap and let rise at room temperature until almost doubled in size, 2 to 2½ hours.

3 Transfer dough to clean counter and divide dough into 3 equal pieces. Shape each piece of dough into tight ball; cover loosely with greased plastic and let rest for 15 minutes. Combine za'atar with remaining 3 tablespoons oil and remaining ½ teaspoon salt in bowl.

4 Line rimmed baking sheet with floured parchment paper. Transfer 1 ball to lightly floured counter and sprinkle with flour. Using your hands and rolling pin, press and roll into 9-inch round of even thickness, sprinkling dough and counter with flour as needed to prevent sticking. Using fork, poke entire surface of round 20 to 25 times. Transfer dough to prepared sheet, reshaping as needed; sprinkle with flour; and top with second sheet of parchment. Repeat with remaining dough, stacking rounds between pieces of floured parchment on prepared sheet.

5A FOR A CHARCOAL GRILL Open bottom vent completely. Light large chimney starter three-quarters filled with charcoal briquettes (4½ quarts). When top coals are partially covered with ash, pour into ring around perimeter of grill, leaving 8-inch clearing in center. Set cooking grate in place, cover, and open lid vent completely. Heat grill until hot, about 5 minutes.

5B FOR A GAS GRILL Turn all burners to high; cover; and heat grill until hot, about 15 minutes. Turn all burners to medium-high.

6 Clean and oil cooking grate. Place 2 flatbreads in center of grill; cover; and cook until bottoms are lightly charred, about 90 seconds. Flip flatbreads and spread one-third of za'atar mixture (about 1½ tablespoons) over surface of each flatbread with back of dinner spoon, stopping ½ inch from edge. Firmly tap dough all over with your fingertips about 6 times. Cover and cook until lightly charred on second side and cooked through, 1 to 2 minutes. (If flatbread puffs up, gently poke with fork to deflate.) Transfer flatbreads to platter and tent with aluminum foil. Repeat with remaining flatbread and za'atar mixture. Slice or tear and serve.

Grilled Flour Tortillas

MAKES twelve 6-inch tortillas **TIME** 45 minutes plus 30 minutes chilling

Why This Recipe Works With an easy-to-roll dough and a superfast cooking time, flour tortillas are a natural for outdoor cooking, and they're very forgiving: These tortillas cook over a medium fire, but if yours is a little hotter or a little cooler because of what else you are grilling, you can adjust the time down or up by a minute or two. Just pay attention to the visual cues. Wrap these around any grilled protein and vegetables to make a meal.

- 2¾ cups (13¾ ounces) all-purpose flour
- 1½ teaspoons table salt
- 6 tablespoons (2½ ounces) vegetable shortening, cut into 6 pieces
- ¾ cup plus 2 tablespoons (7 ounces) warm tap water

1 Whisk flour and salt together in large bowl. Using your hands, rub shortening into flour mixture until mixture resembles coarse meal. Stir warm water into flour mixture with wooden spoon until incorporated and dough comes together. Transfer dough to clean counter and knead by hand to form smooth, cohesive ball, about 30 seconds. Divide dough into quarters and cut each quarter into 3 equal pieces (about 2 ounces each). Roll each piece into ball and transfer to plate. Cover with plastic wrap and refrigerate for at least 30 minutes or up to 3 days.

2 Line rimmed baking sheet with floured parchment paper. Using rolling pin, roll 1 piece of dough into 6-inch-round on lightly floured counter. Transfer tortilla to prepared sheet, reshaping as needed; sprinkle with flour; and top with second sheet of parchment. Repeat with remaining dough, stacking tortillas between pieces of floured parchment on prepared sheet.

3A FOR A CHARCOAL GRILL Open bottom vent completely. Light large chimney starter two-thirds filled with charcoal briquettes (4 quarts). When top coals are partially covered with ash, pour evenly over grill. Set cooking grate in place, cover, and open lid vent completely. Heat grill until hot, about 5 minutes.

3B FOR A GAS GRILL Turn all burners to high; cover; and heat grill and until hot, about 15 minutes. Turn all burners to medium.

4 Clean and oil cooking grate. Working quickly, transfer 6 tortillas to grill. Cook until surface begins to bubble and bottoms are lightly charred, about 1 minute. Flip tortillas and cook until puffed and bottom is lightly charred, about 1 minute. Transfer to plate and cover with dish towel. Clean and oil cooking grate. Repeat with remaining tortillas. Serve.

Shaping Flour Tortillas

1 Form dough into 12 equal balls and refrigerate.

2 Roll each ball into 6-inch circle.

BIG AND FLUFFY BISCUITS WITH ORANGE AND TARRAGON

Big and Fluffy Biscuits

MAKES 8 biscuits **TIME** 55 minutes

Why This Recipe Works There's nothing like tender, fluffy biscuits for breakfast (or any time)—hot off the grill. They're easy enough to throw together even before you've had your morning coffee. The one-bowl dough is portioned right into a cast-iron skillet, which means there's no fussy rolling or cutting required. The heavy skillet distributes the heat of the grill evenly to ensure crisp bottoms and nicely browned crusts. A little butter brushed on the tops of the biscuits before grill-baking enhances their rich flavor and promotes browning. Choose between the classic version or either of the citrus-herb variations, or try all three. You will need a 12-inch cast-iron skillet for this recipe.

- 3 cups (15 ounces) all-purpose flour
- 1 tablespoon baking powder
- ½ teaspoon baking soda
- 1 teaspoon table salt
- 8 tablespoons unsalted butter, cut into ½-inch pieces and softened, plus 1 tablespoon melted
- 4 tablespoons vegetable shortening, cut into ½-inch pieces
- 1¼ cups buttermilk

1A FOR A CHARCOAL GRILL Open bottom vent completely. Light large chimney starter mounded with charcoal briquettes (7 quarts). When top coals are partially covered with ash, pour into steeply banked pile against 1 side of grill. Set cooking grate in place, cover, and open lid vent completely. Heat grill until hot, about 5 minutes.

1B FOR A GAS GRILL Turn all burners to high; cover; and heat grill until hot, about 15 minutes. Leave primary burner on high and turn off other burners(s). (Adjust primary and secondary burners as needed to maintain grill temperature between 400 and 450 degrees.)

2 While grill heats, whisk flour, baking powder, baking soda, and salt together in large bowl. Using your hands, rub softened butter and shortening into flour until mixture resembles coarse meal. Stir buttermilk into flour mixture until just combined. Using greased ½-cup dry measuring cup, scoop out and drop 8 mounds of dough evenly into 12-inch cast-iron skillet. Brush biscuits with melted butter.

3 Place skillet on cooler side of grill. Cover and bake until biscuits are puffed and beginning to brown at edges, 20 to 30 minutes, rotating skillet halfway through baking. Transfer skillet to wire rack and let biscuits cool for at least 15 minutes. Serve.

VARIATIONS

Big and Fluffy Biscuits with Lemon and Dill

Whisk ⅓ cup minced fresh dill and 1 tablespoon grated lemon zest into flour mixture.

Big and Fluffy Biscuits with Orange and Tarragon

Whisk ⅓ cup minced fresh tarragon and 1 tablespoon grated orange zest into flour mixture.

Grilled Fresh Corn Cornbread with Charred Jalapeños and Cheddar

SERVES 6 to 8 **TIME** 1 hour and 10 minutes plus 30 minutes cooling

Why This Recipe Works We toast the cornmeal as well as grilling whole ears of corn to make a skillet cornbread that's hearty enough to take on the bold flavors of charred jalapeños and sharp cheddar. The batter is easy to mix outdoors, and the finished bread comes out lofty and golden, with a delectably crisp bottom and a cheese-laced top. It's the perfect side for ribs, steak, or really anything off the grill. Don't use stone-ground cornmeal. You will need a 10-inch cast-iron skillet for this recipe.

- 4 jalapeño chiles
- 2 ears corn, husks and silk removed
- 2¼ cups (11¼ ounces) cornmeal
- 1 tablespoon sugar
- 1 teaspoon baking powder
- 1 teaspoon baking soda
- ¾ teaspoon table salt
- 1½ cups sour cream
- ½ cup whole milk
- ¼ cup vegetable oil
- 5 tablespoons unsalted butter, melted, divided
- 2 large eggs
- 8 ounces sharp cheddar cheese, shredded (2 cups), divided

1A **FOR A CHARCOAL GRILL** Open bottom vent completely. Light large chimney starter mounded with charcoal briquettes (7 quarts). When top coals are partially covered with ash, pour into steeply banked pile against 1 side of grill. Set cooking grate in place, cover, and open lid vent completely. Heat grill until hot, about 5 minutes.

1B **FOR A GAS GRILL** Turn all burners to high; cover; and heat grill until hot, about 15 minutes. Leave primary burner on high and turn off other burners(s). (Adjust primary and secondary burners as needed to maintain grill temperature between 400 and 450 degrees.)

2 Clean and oil cooking grate. Place jalapeños and corn on hotter side of grill. Cook (covered if using gas), turning as needed, until jalapeños are blistered and charred in spots, 7 to 10 minutes, and corn is charred on all sides, 10 to 12 minutes. Transfer jalapeños to cutting board and let cool slightly; stem, seed, and chop fine. Transfer corn to cutting board and let cool slightly; cut kernels from corn. (You should have about 1½ cups.)

3 Place 10-inch cast-iron skillet on hotter side of grill. Add cornmeal; toast, stirring frequently, until fragrant, about 5 minutes. Transfer cornmeal to large bowl. Whisk sugar, baking powder, baking soda, and salt into cornmeal. Whisk in sour cream, milk, oil, 4 tablespoons melted butter, and eggs until combined. Stir in jalapeños, corn, and 1½ cups cheddar.

4 Brush skillet (it will still be warm) with remaining 1 tablespoon melted butter. Quickly scrape batter into skillet and smooth top. Sprinkle remaining ½ cup cheddar on top of batter. Place skillet on cooler side of grill; cover; and bake until top is golden brown and toothpick inserted into center comes out clean, 20 to 35 minutes, rotating skillet halfway through baking. Transfer skillet to wire rack and let cornbread cool for 30 minutes. Slice into wedges and serve.

GRILLED FRESH CORN CORNBREAD WITH CHARRED JALAPEÑOS AND CHEDDAR

No-Knead Dutch Oven Bread

MAKES 1 loaf **TIME** 1½ hours plus 13 hours rising, resting, and cooling

Why This Recipe Works The thrill of pulling a beautifully bronzed, rustic loaf from the oven is multiplied when you swap the oven for the grill. Grill-baking this slow-risen, no-knead dough in a preheated Dutch oven over the cooler side of the fire for about an hour produces a loaf with a chewy, open crumb, a golden top, and a deliciously dark and crusty bottom. We prefer to use a mild lager, such as Budweiser, here; strongly flavored beers will make this bread taste bitter. You can substitute ½ cup water for the beer if desired. This recipe works best with a high-protein bread flour such as King Arthur. You will need a 3- to 5-quart cast-iron Dutch oven; this size is important for helping the dough rise up, not out. Use a bowl that is at least 9 inches wide and 4 inches deep for the second proof in step 4.

- 2¾ cups (15⅛ ounces) bread flour
- 1½ teaspoons table salt
- ¼ teaspoon instant or rapid-rise yeast
- ¾ cup plus 2 tablespoons (7 ounces) water, room temperature
- ½ cup (4 ounces) mild lager, room temperature
- 1 tablespoon honey
- 1 tablespoon distilled white vinegar

1 Whisk flour, salt, and yeast together in large bowl. Using silicone spatula, fold water, beer, honey, and vinegar into flour mixture, scraping up dry flour from bottom of bowl and pressing dough until cohesive and shaggy and all flour is incorporated. Cover tightly with plastic wrap and let rise at room temperature for at least 8 hours or up to 18 hours.

2 Lay 18 by 12-inch sheet of parchment paper on counter and spray lightly with vegetable oil spray. Using greased bowl scraper or your fingertips, fold partially risen dough over itself 8 times by gently lifting and folding edge of dough toward middle, turning bowl 90 degrees after each fold. Flip dough seam side down in bowl, cover with plastic, and let rest for 15 minutes.

3 Turn out dough seam side up onto lightly floured counter and pat into rough 9-inch circle using your lightly floured hands. Using bowl scraper or your floured fingertips, lift and fold edge of dough toward center, pressing to seal. Repeat 6 more times (for a total of 7 folds), evenly spacing folds around circumference of dough. Press down on dough to deflate, then use bench scraper to gently flip dough seam side down.

4 Using both hands, cup side of dough farthest from you and pull dough toward you, keeping your pinky fingers and sides of palms in contact with counter and applying slight pressure to dough as it drags to create tension. (If dough slides across surface of counter without rolling, remove excess flour. If dough sticks to counter or your hands, lightly sprinkle counter or hands with flour.) Rotate dough ball 90 degrees, reposition dough ball at top of counter, and repeat pulling dough until taut, round ball forms, at least 4 more times. Transfer dough seam side down to center of prepared parchment and cover with inverted large bowl. Let rise until dough has doubled in volume and dough springs back minimally when poked gently with your finger, about 2 hours.

5A FOR A CHARCOAL GRILL Open bottom vent completely. Light large chimney starter mounded with charcoal briquettes (7 quarts). When top coals are partially covered with ash, pour into steeply banked pile against 1 side of grill. Set cooking grate in place and place 3- to 5-quart cast-iron Dutch oven and lid next to each other on grill grate at center of grill. Cover and open lid vent completely. Heat grill until hot, about 5 minutes.

5B FOR A GAS GRILL Place 3- to 5-quart cast-iron Dutch oven and lid next to each other on grill grate over primary burner. Turn all burners to high; cover; and heat grill until hot, about 15 minutes. Leave primary burner on high and turn off other burner(s). (Adjust primary and secondary burners as needed to maintain grill temperature between 450 and 500 degrees.)

6 Using sharp knife, make one 6-inch-long, ½-inch-deep slash with swift, fluid motion along top of loaf. Using parchment as sling, carefully transfer dough to hot Dutch oven. Working quickly, reinforce scoring in top of loaf if needed. Top Dutch oven with hot lid and slide to cooler side of grill. Cover and bake for 30 minutes.

7 Carefully remove Dutch oven lid and rotate pot 90 degrees. Continue to bake bread, covered, until loaf is golden brown and registers at least 205 degrees, 20 to 40 minutes. Using parchment sling, carefully remove loaf from hot pot and transfer to wire rack; discard parchment. Let cool completely, about 3 hours, before slicing.

NO-KNEAD DUTCH OVEN BREAD

Folding and Forming the Dough

1 Using greased bowl scraper or your fingertips, gently lift and fold edge of dough toward middle. Turn bowl 90 degrees; repeat 7 more times.

2 After dough has rested, turn onto lightly floured counter and pat into rough 9-inch circle.

3 Using bowl scraper or your floured fingertips, lift and fold edge of dough toward center, pressing to seal. Repeat 6 more times.

4 Cup dough with both hands and pull toward you, applying slight pressure. Rotate dough ball 90 degrees and repeat until taut round ball forms.

Rosemary Focaccia

MAKES 1 loaf **TIME** 45 minutes plus 3¼ hours rising, resting and cooling

Why This Recipe Works The aroma of this herb-spiked focaccia coming from your grill is as enticing as it is unexpected. To create the signature bubbly crumb, you'll use a no-knead mixing method with a highly hydrated dough and give it a good rise and a rest after shaping. Coating the skillet with plenty of olive oil protects the bread from scorching and gives the crust a rich flavor and delectable crunch while allowing for a light, airy crumb. You will need a 12-inch cast-iron skillet for this recipe.

- 2½ cups (12½ ounces) all-purpose flour
- 1¾ teaspoons kosher salt
- 1 teaspoon instant or rapid-rise yeast
- 1¼ cups (10 ounces) water, room temperature
- ¼ cup extra-virgin olive oil, divided
- 2 tablespoons fresh rosemary leaves
- 1 teaspoon flake sea salt

1 Whisk flour, kosher salt, and yeast together in large bowl. Using silicone spatula, fold water into flour mixture, scraping up dry flour from bottom of bowl and pressing dough until cohesive and shaggy and all flour is incorporated. Cover tightly with plastic wrap and let rise at room temperature until doubled in size, 2 to 4 hours. (Alternatively, refrigerate dough until doubled in size, 8 to 18 hours; let dough stand at room temperature for 1 hour before proceeding.)

2 Coat bottom and sides of 12-inch cast-iron skillet with 3 tablespoons oil. Using bowl scraper or your floured fingertips, lift and fold edge of dough toward center, pressing to seal. Repeat 6 more times (for a total of 7 folds), evenly spacing folds around circumference of dough. Use bench scraper to gently transfer dough seam side up into oiled skillet, then flip dough over. Cover loosely with greased plastic and let dough rest for 30 minutes.

3A FOR A CHARCOAL GRILL Open bottom vent completely. Light large chimney starter mounded with charcoal briquettes (7 quarts). When top coals are partially covered with ash, pour into steeply banked pile against 1 side of grill. Set cooking grate in place, cover, and open lid vent completely. Heat grill until hot, about 5 minutes.

3B FOR A GAS GRILL Turn all burners to high; cover; and heat grill until hot, about 15 minutes. Leave primary burner on high and turn off other burner(s). (Adjust primary and secondary burners as needed to maintain grill temperature between 450 and 500 degrees.)

4 Using your fingertips, gently press dough round into corners of skillet, taking care not to tear dough. (If dough resists stretching, let it relax for 5 to 10 minutes before trying to stretch it again.) Using fork, poke surface of dough 40 to 45 times. Brush surface of dough with remaining 1 tablespoon oil. Sprinkle rosemary and sea salt evenly over top; cover loosely with greased plastic; and let dough rest until slightly bubbly, about 10 minutes.

5 Place skillet on cooler side of grill; cover; and bake until top and sides are golden brown and edges are crispy, 25 to 30 minutes, rotating skillet halfway through baking. Transfer skillet to wire rack and let cool for 5 minutes. Remove focaccia from skillet and let cool on wire rack for 30 minutes. Serve warm or at room temperature.

Pull-Apart Dinner Rolls

MAKES 12 rolls **TIME** 1 hour plus 2 hours rising

Why This Recipe Works Buttery and rich yet light, these deceptively simple dinner rolls are sure to impress at your next cookout. The dough is easy to work with and can handle the variances of grill-baking. Thanks to the cast-iron skillet, the rolls turn out with a light, almost fried, crunchy crust that's reminiscent of pan pizza crust. That crust is optimized through baking the rolls in a ring formation so that the bottom and sides of each one make contact with the hot metal. Keep these rolls in the skillet after baking so they'll stay nice and warm while serving. You will need a 10-inch cast-iron skillet for this recipe.

DOUGH

- ¾ cup (6 ounces) warm tap water (110 degrees)
- 5 tablespoons unsalted butter, melted, divided
- 1 large egg yolk
- 2 cups (10 ounces) all-purpose flour, plus extra as needed
- 1⅛ teaspoons instant or rapid-rise yeast
- 1 teaspoon sugar
- 1 teaspoon table salt

EGG WASH

- 1 large egg white
- 1 teaspoon water
- ⅛ teaspoon table salt

1 FOR THE DOUGH Whisk water, 1 tablespoon melted butter, and egg yolk together in small bowl. In bowl of stand mixer, whisk flour, yeast, sugar, and salt together. Fit stand mixer with dough hook. With mixer on low speed, slowly add water mixture and mix until dough comes together, about 2 minutes. Increase speed to medium and mix until dough is smooth and elastic, about 8 minutes. (If after 4 minutes dough is still very sticky, add 1 to 2 tablespoons extra flour; dough should clear sides of bowl but stick to bottom.) Transfer dough to lightly floured counter and knead by hand to form smooth ball, about 1 minute.

2 Place dough in lightly greased large bowl; cover tightly with greased plastic wrap; and let rise until doubled in size, about 1 hour.

3 Brush 10-inch cast-iron skillet with 1 tablespoon melted butter. Transfer dough to lightly floured counter and shape into 12-inch log. Divide log into 12 equal pieces and cover with greased plastic. Working with 1 piece of dough at a time (keep other pieces covered), form into rough ball by stretching dough around your thumb and pinching edges together so that top is smooth. Place ball seam side down on clean counter and, using your cupped hand, drag in small circles until dough feels taut and round. Arrange dough balls around perimeter of skillet, leaving center empty. Brush dough balls with 1 tablespoon melted butter. Cover loosely with greased plastic and let rise until nearly doubled in size, about 1 hour.

4A **FOR A CHARCOAL GRILL** Open bottom vent completely. Light large chimney starter mounded with charcoal briquettes (7 quarts). When top coals are partially covered with ash, pour into steeply banked pile against 1 side of grill. Set cooking grate in place, cover, and open lid vent completely. Heat grill until hot, about 5 minutes.

4B **FOR A GAS GRILL** Turn all burners to high; cover; and heat grill until hot, about 15 minutes. Leave primary burner on high and turn off other burner(s). (Adjust primary and secondary burners as needed to maintain grill temperature between 450 and 500 degrees.)

5 **FOR THE EGG WASH** Beat egg white with water and salt in small bowl with fork. Brush rolls with egg wash. Place skillet on cooler side of grill; cover; and bake until rolls are golden brown, 10 to 15 minutes, rotating halfway through baking.

6 Transfer skillet to wire rack. Brush rolls with remaining 2 tablespoons melted butter. Let cool for 10 minutes. Serve.

PULL-APART DINNER ROLLS

CHARRED STRAWBERRY DUTCH BABY

Charred Strawberry Dutch Baby

SERVES 6 to 8 **TIME** 55 minutes

Why This Recipe Works This gorgeous pancake works equally well as a dessert, a weekend breakfast, or part of a brunch spread. Charring skewered, honey-brushed strawberries is a quick route to a sophisticated fruit topping: Chop them up and let them sit with lemon juice and more honey while the pancake puffs up crisp and golden in the skillet. For a real treat, serve this with whipped cream, mascarpone, or crème fraîche. Larger strawberries hold up better on the grill; smaller strawberries will also work, but you might need three skewers instead of two, and you should monitor the grill and pull them off before they collapse. You can use whole or low-fat milk instead of skim, but the Dutch baby won't be as crisp. You will need a 12-inch cast-iron skillet and two 12-inch metal skewers for this recipe.

- 1 pound strawberries (preferably 1 inch or larger), hulled
- 3 tablespoons honey, divided
- 1 cup (5 ounces) all-purpose flour
- ¼ cup (1 ounce) cornstarch
- 2 teaspoons grated lemon zest plus 1 teaspoon juice
- 1 teaspoon table salt
- 3 large eggs
- 1¼ cups skim milk
- 1 tablespoon unsalted butter, melted and cooled
- 1 teaspoon vanilla extract
- 2 tablespoons vegetable oil
- Confectioners' sugar

1 Thread strawberries onto two 12-inch metal skewers and brush with 1½ tablespoons honey. Whisk flour, cornstarch, lemon zest, and salt together in large bowl. In separate bowl, whisk eggs until frothy, then whisk in milk, melted butter, and vanilla until combined.

2A **FOR A CHARCOAL GRILL** Open bottom vent completely. Light large chimney starter filled with charcoal briquettes (6 quarts). When top coals are partially covered with ash, pour evenly over half of grill. Set cooking grate in place, cover, and open lid vent completely. Heat grill until hot, about 5 minutes.

2B **FOR A GAS GRILL** Turn all burners to high; cover; and heat grill until hot, about 15 minutes. Leave primary burner on high and turn other burner(s) to low. (Adjust primary and secondary burners as needed to maintain grill temperature around 400 degrees.)

3 Clean and oil cooking grate. Place strawberries on hotter side of grill and cook, turning as needed, until tender and charred, 3 to 5 minutes. Transfer strawberries to cutting board and let cool slightly, about 5 minutes. Remove strawberries from skewers and cut into quarters. Toss strawberries with remaining 1½ tablespoons honey and lemon juice in separate bowl.

4 Brush 12-inch cast-iron skillet with oil and place on hotter side of grill. Cover and heat skillet until oil is shimmering, about 5 minutes. Meanwhile, working quickly while skillet heats, whisk one-third of milk mixture into flour mixture until no lumps remain. Slowly whisk in remaining milk mixture until smooth.

5 Slide skillet to cooler side of grill. Pour batter into skillet. Cover and cook until Dutch baby puffs and turns golden brown along edges, 15 to 20 minutes, rotating skillet halfway through baking.

6 Transfer Dutch baby to cutting board using spatula. Dust with sugar and slice into wedges. Serve immediately, topped with charred strawberry mixture.

Cherry Spoon Cake

SERVES 8 to 10 **TIME** 1 hour plus 30 minutes cooling

Why This Recipe Works This unfussy dessert tops an easy stir-together batter with juicy fresh cherries. As it cooks in a skillet on the grill, the bottom and edges of this spoon cake brown nicely while the cherries sink into the batter and release their juices. You'll want to serve this in bowls, with spoons—and maybe with a scoop of vanilla ice cream on top. Frozen cherries may be substituted for fresh; thaw and drain the cherries before using. You will need a 12-inch cast-iron skillet for this recipe.

- 10 tablespoons unsalted butter, melted and cooled, divided
- 1½ cups (7½ ounces) plus 2 tablespoons all-purpose flour, divided
- 1½ cups (10½ ounces) sugar
- 2½ teaspoons baking powder
- ¾ teaspoon table salt
- 1½ cups milk
- 1 teaspoon grated orange zest
- 1 teaspoon vanilla extract
- 1 pound fresh sweet cherries, pitted and halved

1 Brush 12-inch cast-iron skillet with 2 tablespoons melted butter. Whisk 1½ cups flour, sugar, baking powder, and salt together in large bowl. Whisk milk, orange zest, vanilla, and remaining 8 tablespoons melted butter together in separate bowl. Whisk milk mixture into flour mixture until combined. Pour batter into prepared skillet. Toss cherries with remaining 2 tablespoons flour in separate bowl; set aside.

2A **FOR A CHARCOAL GRILL** Open bottom vent completely. Light large chimney starter three-quarters filled with charcoal briquettes (4½ quarts). When top coals are partially covered with ash, pour into steeply banked pile against 1 side of grill. Set cooking grate in place, cover, and open lid vent completely. Heat grill until hot, about 5 minutes.

2B **FOR A GAS GRILL** Turn all burners to high; cover; and heat grill until hot, about 15 minutes. Leave primary burner on medium-high and turn off other burner(s). (Adjust primary burner as needed to maintain grill temperature between 325 and 350 degrees.)

3 Place skillet on cooler side of grill and spoon cherry mixture evenly over batter. Cover and bake until top is golden brown and skewer inserted in center comes out clean, 45 to 55 minutes, rotating skillet halfway through baking. Transfer skillet to wire rack and let cool for at least 30 minutes. Serve.

CHERRY SPOON CAKE

Rustic Summer Fruit Tart

SERVES 4 to 6 **TIME** 1¼ hours plus 1 hour and 40 minutes chilling and cooling

Why This Recipe Works One of the best things about ripe summer fruits—their intense juiciness—can spell trouble when they're baked in a tart. Using a cast-iron skillet as a grill-top tart pan is a genius solution: The skillet captures the bubbling fruit juices and transforms them into an irresistible caramel-like glaze. It also acts like a pizza stone, absorbing heat to crisp the bottom crust before the fruit juices can sog it out. A simple mix of stone fruit and berries with a few tablespoons of sugar makes a quick, easy filling. Be sure to taste the fruit before adding sugar; use less sugar if the fruit is very sweet, more if it is tart. Do not add the sugar to the fruit until you're ready to fill and form the tart. It's important to use ice water to prevent the dough from overheating in the food processor. You will need a 10-inch cast-iron skillet for this recipe.

- 1½ cups (7½ ounces) all-purpose flour
- ½ teaspoon table salt
- 10 tablespoons unsalted butter, cut into ½-inch pieces and chilled
- 4–6 tablespoons (2 to 3 ounces) ice water
- 1 pound plums, apricots, peaches, and/or nectarines, halved, pitted, and cut into ½-inch wedges
- 5 ounces (1 cup) raspberries, blackberries, and/or blueberries
- ¼ cup (1¾ ounces) sugar, divided, plus extra sugar as needed

1 Process flour and salt in food processor until combined, about 5 seconds. Scatter butter over top and pulse until mixture resembles coarse sand and butter pieces are size of small peas, about 10 pulses. Continue to pulse, adding water 1 tablespoon at a time, until dough begins to form small curds that hold together when pinched with fingers, about 10 pulses.

2 Turn mixture onto lightly floured counter and gather into rectangular pile. Starting at farthest end, use heel of your hand to smear small amount of dough against counter. Continue to smear dough until all crumbs have been worked. Gather smeared crumbs together in another rectangular pile and repeat process.

3 Press dough into 6-inch disk, wrap tightly in plastic wrap, and refrigerate for 1 hour or up to 2 days. Before rolling out dough, let it sit on counter to soften slightly, about 10 minutes.

4 Spray 10-inch cast-iron skillet lightly with vegetable oil spray. Roll dough into 12-inch round between 2 large sheets of parchment paper. Remove top piece of parchment, loosely roll dough around rolling pin, and gently unroll it onto prepared skillet. Ease dough into skillet by gently lifting and supporting edge of dough with your hand while pressing into skillet bottom and corners with your other hand. Leave any overhanging dough in place.

5 Gently toss plums, raspberries, and 3 tablespoons sugar together in bowl; toss with additional sugar if needed. Transfer fruit to dough-lined skillet, mounding fruit slightly in middle. Fold in sides of dough over fruit, pleating every 2 to 3 inches as needed; gently pinch pleated dough to secure, but do not press dough into fruit. Brush dough with water and sprinkle evenly with remaining 1 tablespoon sugar.

6A **FOR A CHARCOAL GRILL** Open bottom vent completely. Light large chimney starter mounded with charcoal briquettes (7 quarts). When top coals are partially covered with ash, pour into steeply banked pile against 1 side of grill. Set cooking grate in place, cover, and open lid vent completely. Heat grill until hot, about 5 minutes.

6B **FOR A GAS GRILL** Turn all burners to high; cover; and heat grill until hot, about 15 minutes. Leave primary burner on high and turn off other burner(s). (Adjust primary and secondary burners as needed to maintain grill temperature between 450 and 475 degrees.)

7 Place skillet on hotter side of grill. Cover and bake for 10 minutes. Slide skillet to cooler side of grill; cover; and bake until crust is beginning to brown and juices are bubbling, 30 to 45 minutes, rotating skillet halfway through baking.

8 Transfer skillet to wire rack and let cool for 10 minutes. Gently slide tart onto rack using spatula and let cool until juices have thickened, at least 30 minutes. Serve.

RUSTIC SUMMER FRUIT TART

Smearing the Dough

1 Gather dough into rectangular pile. Starting at farthest end, use heel of your hand to smear small amount of dough against counter.

2 Continue to smear dough until all crumbs have been worked. Gather smeared crumbs together and repeat process.

ORANGE UPSIDE-DOWN CAKE

SKILLET BROWNIE

Orange Upside-Down Cake

SERVES 8 **TIME** 1¼ hours plus 1 hour 20 minutes cooling

Why This Recipe Works If you didn't make it yourself, you'd find it hard to believe this stunning cake came off a grill. The sturdy butter cake gets its richness and tang from sour cream. White sugar in the fruit layer contributes a clean sweetness that keeps the orange flavor front and center. A thin layer of orange marmalade brushed over the cooled cake makes for an extra-shiny and extra-citrusy finish. Peeling the oranges by hand (instead of cutting away the peel and pith with a knife) ensures perfectly round slices. You will need a 10-inch cast-iron skillet for this recipe.

- 1 pound small navel oranges, blood oranges, and/or Cara Cara oranges
- 10 tablespoons unsalted butter, melted, divided
- 1½ cups (10½ ounces) sugar, divided
- 1 teaspoon cornstarch
- ⅛ teaspoon plus ½ teaspoon table salt, divided
- 1 cup (5 ounces) all-purpose flour
- 1 teaspoon baking powder
- ½ cup sour cream
- 2 large eggs
- 1 teaspoon vanilla extract
- 2 tablespoons orange marmalade

1 Spray 10-inch cast-iron skillet lightly with vegetable oil spray, line with parchment paper, then grease parchment. Grate 2 teaspoons zest from 1 orange; set aside. Peel oranges by hand. Using sharp chef's knife or serrated knife, trim ends and slice oranges crosswise into ¼-inch-thick rounds, removing any seeds.

2 Pour 4 tablespoons melted butter into prepared skillet and swirl to evenly coat. Whisk ½ cup sugar, cornstarch, and ⅛ teaspoon salt together in bowl, then sprinkle mixture evenly over skillet bottom. Arrange orange slices in single layer over sugar mixture, nestling slices snugly together and pressing them flat (you may have fruit left over).

3 Whisk flour, baking powder, and remaining ½ teaspoon salt together in large bowl. Whisk sour cream, eggs, vanilla, reserved orange zest, and remaining 1 cup sugar in second large bowl until smooth, about 1 minute. Whisk remaining 6 tablespoons melted butter into sour cream mixture until combined. Whisk flour mixture into sour cream mixture until just combined. Pour batter over oranges in skillet and smooth top.

4A **FOR A CHARCOAL GRILL** Open bottom vent completely. Light large chimney starter three-quarters filled with charcoal briquettes (4½ quarts). When top coals are partially covered with ash, pour into steeply banked pile against 1 side of grill. Set cooking grate in place, cover, and open lid vent completely. Heat grill until hot, about 5 minutes.

4B FOR A GAS GRILL Turn all burners to high; cover; and heat grill until hot, about 15 minutes. Leave primary burner on medium-high and turn off other burner(s). (Adjust primary burner as needed to maintain grill temperature between 325 and 350 degrees.)

5 Place skillet on cooler side of grill. Cover and bake until golden brown and toothpick inserted in center comes out clean, 35 to 50 minutes, rotating skillet halfway through baking.

6 Transfer skillet to wire rack and let cool for 20 minutes. Run knife around edge of skillet to loosen cake, then invert cake onto serving platter. Discard parchment. Let cake cool for at least 1 hour. Microwave marmalade in bowl until fluid, about 20 seconds. Brush marmalade over top of cake. Serve.

Skillet Brownie

SERVES 8 to 12 **TIME** 1¼ hours plus 30 minutes cooling

Why This Recipe Works Grill-baking this brownie in a cast-iron skillet and slicing it into wedges creates the best of both worlds—a crispy edge and a fudgy middle—in every serving. Marshmallows dial up the fudgy texture, and bittersweet chocolate chunks stirred into the batter at the end stud the brownie with gooey pockets of lush melted chocolate. Using indirect heat prevents the chocolate from burning and gets this brownie to its sweet spot in about an hour. In step 2, you can substitute bittersweet or semisweet chocolate chips for the chopped bittersweet chocolate, if desired, but the results will be less gooey. You will need a 12-inch cast-iron skillet for this recipe.

- 2 ounces marshmallows (about 8 large marshmallows)
- ½ cup plus 2 tablespoons (10 ounces) warm tap water
- 4 tablespoons unsalted butter, cut into 4 pieces
- 2 ounces unsweetened chocolate, chopped fine
- ⅓ cup (1 ounce) Dutch-processed cocoa powder
- 2½ cups (17½ ounces) sugar
- ½ cup vegetable oil
- 2 large eggs plus 2 large yolks
- 2 teaspoons vanilla extract
- 1¾ cups (8¾ ounces) all-purpose flour
- 1 teaspoon table salt
- 6 ounces bittersweet chocolate, chopped

1 Combine marshmallows, warm water, butter, unsweetened chocolate, and cocoa in large bowl. Microwave at 50 percent power, stirring occasionally, until chocolate is fully melted and mixture is smooth, 2 to 4 minutes. Let cool for 5 minutes.

2 Spray 12-inch cast-iron skillet lightly with vegetable oil spray. Whisk sugar, oil, eggs and yolks, and vanilla into marshmallow mixture until fully combined. Gently whisk in flour and salt until just incorporated. Stir in bittersweet chocolate. Transfer batter to prepared skillet.

3A FOR A CHARCOAL GRILL Open bottom vent completely. Light large chimney starter mounded with charcoal briquettes (7 quarts). When top coals are partially covered with ash, pour into steeply banked pile against 1 side of grill. Set cooking grate in place, cover, and open lid vent completely. Heat grill until hot, about 5 minutes.

3B FOR A GAS GRILL Turn all burners to high; cover; and heat grill until hot, about 15 minutes. Leave primary burner on high and turn off other burner(s). (Adjust primary and secondary burners as needed to maintain grill temperature between 425 and 450 degrees.)

4 Place skillet on cooler side of grill. Cover and bake until toothpick inserted in center comes out with a few moist crumbs and batter attached (be careful not to overbake; brownie will continue to bake as it cools), 50 minutes to 1 hour 5 minutes, rotating skillet halfway through baking. Transfer skillet to wire rack and let cool for at least 30 minutes. Slice into wedges and serve.

VARIATIONS

Spiced Skillet Brownie

Add 1½ teaspoons ground cinnamon, ¼ teaspoon pepper, and ¼ teaspoon cayenne pepper to sugar mixture with flour.

Espresso-Walnut Skillet Brownie

Add 1½ teaspoons instant espresso powder to bowl with cocoa in step 1. Sprinkle batter with ⅓ cup chopped toasted walnuts before baking.

Skillet Chocolate Chip Cookie

SERVES 8 to 12 **TIME** 1 hour plus 20 minutes cooling

Why This Recipe Works Cast-iron skillet cookies are beloved for their crunchy crusts and soft interiors, and those qualities are enhanced when you grill-bake this giant shareable dessert. This recipe makes dual use of the grill, both to brown the butter and to bake the cookie. You can slide the skillet onto the grill while it's still hot right after cooking the main course, and then enjoy wedges of warm cookie for dessert. The chocolate chips might melt a bit, creating a marbled effect in the cookie. It'll be just as delicious, but if you want to avoid this, you can pop the chocolate chips in the freezer briefly before using them. You will need a 12-inch cast-iron skillet for this recipe.

- 12 tablespoons unsalted butter, divided
- ¾ cup packed (5¼ ounces) dark brown sugar
- ½ cup (3½ ounces) granulated sugar
- 2 teaspoons vanilla extract
- 1 teaspoon table salt
- 1 large egg plus 1 large yolk
- 1¾ cups (8¾ ounces) all-purpose flour
- ½ teaspoon baking soda
- 1 cup (6 ounces) semisweet chocolate chips

1A FOR A CHARCOAL GRILL Open bottom vent completely. Light large chimney starter mounded with charcoal briquettes (7 quarts). When top coals are partially covered with ash, pour evenly over half of grill. Set cooking grate in place, cover, and open lid vent completely. Heat grill until hot, about 5 minutes.

1B FOR A GAS GRILL Turn all burners to high; cover; and heat grill until hot, about 15 minutes. Leave primary burner on high and turn off other burner(s). (Adjust primary and secondary burners as needed to maintain grill temperature between 425 and 450 degrees.)

2 Place 12-inch cast-iron skillet on hotter side of grill and melt 9 tablespoons butter in skillet. Continue to cook, stirring constantly, until butter is dark golden brown and has nutty aroma and bubbling subsides, 4 to 6 minutes. Transfer browned butter to large bowl; set skillet aside. Whisk remaining 3 tablespoons butter into browned butter until completely melted.

3 Whisk brown sugar, granulated sugar, vanilla, and salt into butter until smooth. Whisk in egg and yolk until smooth, about 30 seconds. Let mixture sit for 3 minutes, then whisk for 30 seconds. Repeat process of resting and whisking 2 more times until mixture is thick, smooth, and shiny.

4 Whisk flour and baking soda together in separate bowl, then stir flour mixture into butter mixture until just combined, about 1 minute. Stir in chocolate chips, making sure no flour pockets remain. Transfer dough to now-empty skillet and press into even layer with spatula.

5 Place skillet on cooler side of grill. Cover and bake until light golden brown and edges are set, 15 to 25 minutes, rotating skillet halfway through baking. Transfer skillet to wire rack and let cool for at least 20 minutes. Slice into wedges and serve.

Glazed Rotisserie Pineapple with Salted Rum Butterscotch Sauce

SERVES 6 to 8 **TIME** 1¾ hours

Why This Recipe Works This stunning dessert really shows off what the grill rotisserie is all about. Turning a ripe pineapple over a hot fire caramelizes its surface to a golden brown and brings out an irresistible aroma reminiscent of a tropical cocktail. The heat penetrates to the inside of the fruit, unlocking its juices. The spiral-cut edges pick up glorious color while cradling the fantastic salted rum butterscotch sauce. This recipe can be doubled: Slide the first pineapple about three-quarters of the way down the skewer and then thread the second pineapple onto the skewer. Center the pineapples on the skewer, leaving a 1-inch gap between them. Use caution when threading the rotisserie skewer through the pineapple, as it will require some pressure to push the skewer through the core. We love the appearance and ridges of a spiral-cut pineapple; however, in step 2 you can simply trim the pineapple slightly further to remove the eyes. You will need a motorized rotisserie attachment. Our gas grill instructions are for a three-burner grill. If using a two-burner grill, cook with both burners turned to medium.

- 1 cup packed (7 ounces) light brown sugar
- ½ cup heavy cream
- 8 tablespoons unsalted butter, cut into 8 pieces and chilled, divided
- ½ teaspoon table salt
- 2 tablespoons dark rum
- ½ teaspoon vanilla extract
- 1 pineapple
- 1 (13 by 9-inch) disposable aluminum roasting pan (if using charcoal grill)

1 Cook sugar, cream, 4 tablespoons butter, and salt in medium saucepan over medium-high heat, stirring often with silicone spatula, until large bubbles burst on surface of sauce, about 4 minutes. Off heat, carefully stir in remaining 4 tablespoons butter until fully combined, about 1 minute. Stir in rum and vanilla. Transfer sauce to bowl and let cool for 30 minutes (sauce will thicken as it cools). (Sauce can be refrigerated for up to 1 week; reheat in microwave before serving.)

2 Using sharp knife, slice off crown and bottom of pineapple. Holding pineapple upright, pare off rind from top to bottom as thin as possible. Lay fruit on 1 side. Working around pineapple, cut shallow, diagonal V-shaped grooves just deep enough to remove eyes, following their natural spiral pattern.

3 Set pineapple upright on cutting board. Center beveled tip of rotisserie skewer on top of pineapple and carefully push skewer down through core of pineapple. Turn pineapple on its side and continue to thread it onto center of skewer. Attach rotisserie forks to skewer and insert tines into pineapple; secure forks by tightening screws.

4A **FOR A CHARCOAL GRILL** Open bottom vent completely and place disposable pan in center of grill. Light large chimney starter mounded with charcoal briquettes (7 quarts). When top coals are partially covered with ash, pour into 2 even piles on either side of disposable pan. Position rotisserie motor attachment on grill so that skewer runs parallel to coals. Cover; open lid vent completely; and heat grill until hot, about 5 minutes.

4B **FOR A GAS GRILL** Remove cooking grate. Position rotisserie motor attachment on grill and turn all burners to high. Cover and heat grill until hot, about 15 minutes. Turn outside burners to medium-high and turn off center burner. (Adjust outside burners as needed to maintain grill temperature between 450 and 500 degrees.)

5 Brush pineapple with ¼ cup sauce. Attach rotisserie skewer to motor and start motor. Cover and cook for 30 minutes.

6 Brush pineapple with ¼ cup sauce and continue to cook, covered, until tender and lightly charred, 15 to 30 minutes. Transfer pineapple, still on skewer, to cutting board. Using large wad of paper towels in each hand, carefully remove rotisserie forks and skewer from pineapple. Slice pineapple thin and serve with remaining sauce.

GLAZED ROTISSERIE PINEAPPLE WITH SALTED RUM BUTTERSCOTCH SAUCE

Spiral-Cutting a Pineapple

1 Holding pineapple upright, pare off rind from top to bottom as thin as possible. Lay fruit on side.

2 Working around pineapple, cut shallow, diagonal V-shaped grooves just deep enough to remove eyes, following their natural spiral pattern.

9

Sauces, Relishes + Rubs

SAUCES

GRILLING SAUCES

HERB SAUCES

CREAMY SAUCES

SALSAS AND GUACAMOLE

RELISHES

CHUTNEYS

SPICE RUBS

FLAVORED SALTS

Barbecue Sauces

In most of the country, "barbecue sauce" brings to mind a tangy-sweet, thick, tomato-based concoction. This style is modeled after Kansas City barbecue sauces, but in other regions of the barbecue belt, the sauces range from thin and vinegary to brash and mustardy, and the texture might be thick enough to cling to chicken parts or thin enough to soak into a plateful of shredded pork. Stick with tradition or mix and match your favorite type of sauce with your favorite kind of barbecue.

HONEY-MUSTARD BARBECUE SAUCE
EASTERN NORTH CAROLINA–STYLE BARBECUE SAUCE
NO-COOK BARBECUE SAUCE

No-Cook Barbecue Sauce

MAKES 1¼ cups **TIME** 6 minutes

This pantry sauce comes together in a flash and hits all the right tangy, tomatoey notes. A teaspoon of hot sauce balances the sweetness of the molasses with a bit of heat. Use a liquid smoke that contains nothing but smoke and water.

- 1 cup ketchup
- 3 tablespoons molasses
- 1 tablespoon cider vinegar
- 1 teaspoon hot sauce
- ⅛ teaspoon liquid smoke (optional)

Whisk all ingredients together in small bowl. (Sauce can be refrigerated for up to 5 days.)

VARIATIONS

No-Cook Honey-Scallion Barbecue Sauce

Omit molasses, hot sauce, and liquid smoke. Add 3 tablespoons honey, 2 teaspoons Dijon mustard, 2 finely chopped scallions, and ¾ teaspoon pepper.

No-Cook Five-Alarm Barbecue Sauce

Omit hot sauce and liquid smoke. Add 1 tablespoon minced canned chipotle chiles in adobo; 1 jalapeño chile, stemmed, seeded, and minced; and ¼ teaspoon cayenne pepper.

Easy All-Purpose Barbecue Sauce

MAKES 2½ cups **TIME** 30 minutes plus 30 minutes cooling

Grating and then sautéing an onion mellows and softens it, so it blends seamlessly into this easy barbecue sauce. Worcestershire sauce and ketchup add rich, savory flavor, and a combination of chili powder, cayenne pepper, and hot sauce provide just enough heat. Grate the onion on the large holes of a box or paddle grater.

- 2 tablespoons vegetable oil
- ½ cup grated onion
- 1 teaspoon garlic powder
- 1 teaspoon chili powder
- ¼ teaspoon cayenne pepper
- 1½ cups ketchup
- ¼ cup molasses
- 3 tablespoons Worcestershire sauce
- 3 tablespoons cider vinegar
- 2 tablespoons Dijon mustard
- 1 teaspoon hot sauce

1 Heat oil in medium saucepan over medium heat until shimmering. Add onion and cook, stirring occasionally, until softened, about 5 minutes. Stir in garlic powder, chili powder, and cayenne and cook until fragrant, about 30 seconds.

2 Stir in ketchup, molasses, Worcestershire, vinegar, mustard, and hot sauce and bring to simmer. Reduce heat to low and cook until flavors meld, about 5 minutes. Let cool completely before serving. (Sauce can be refrigerated for up to 5 days.)

VARIATIONS

Easy Bourbon Barbecue Sauce

Add ¼ cup bourbon to sauce with ketchup.

Easy Chipotle Barbecue Sauce

Substitute 1 tablespoon minced canned chipotle chile in adobo sauce for chili powder.

Easy Espresso Barbecue Sauce

Combine 2 tablespoons instant espresso powder and 1 tablespoon hot water in small bowl; let sit for 3 minutes. Add espresso mixture to sauce with ketchup.

Easy Hoisin and Ginger Barbecue Sauce

Omit chili powder, molasses, Worcestershire, and hot sauce. Add 1 tablespoon grated fresh ginger to saucepan with garlic powder. Stir 3 tablespoons hoisin sauce and 3 tablespoons soy sauce into sauce with ketchup.

Eastern North Carolina–Style Barbecue Sauce

MAKES about 2½ cups **TIME** 10 minutes

In eastern North Carolina, the barbecue sauce has a vinegary punch, a bit of spiciness, and plenty of salt. Its thin consistency allows it to soak into North Carolina Barbecue Pork (page 226) when the meat is very finely chopped. One 12-ounce bottle of Texas Pete Original Hot Sauce will yield more than enough for this recipe.

- 1½ cups cider vinegar
- 1 cup Texas Pete Original Hot Sauce
- ¼ cup packed light brown sugar
- 2 teaspoons kosher salt
- 1 teaspoon pepper
- 1 teaspoon red pepper flakes

Whisk all ingredients together in bowl. (Sauce can be refrigerated for up to 5 days.)

Lexington-Style Barbecue Sauce

MAKES about 2½ cups **TIME** 20 minutes plus 30 minutes cooling

The tangy barbecue sauce in Lexington, North Carolina, is the classic choice for soaking into rich, smoky North Carolina Barbecue Pork (page 226) when the meat is coarsely chopped. Simmering cider vinegar, ketchup, granulated garlic, pepper, red pepper flakes, and salt melds their flavors. The ketchup makes the sauce redder, a touch sweeter, and a bit thicker.

- 2 cups cider vinegar
- 1 cup ketchup
- 2 teaspoons granulated garlic
- 2 teaspoons pepper
- 1½ teaspoons kosher salt
- 1 teaspoon red pepper flakes

Combine all ingredients in small saucepan and bring to boil over medium-high heat. Reduce heat to medium-low and simmer for 5 minutes. Transfer sauce to bowl and let cool completely. (Sauce can be refrigerated for up to 5 days.)

Western South Carolina–Style Barbecue Sauce

MAKES 2 cups **TIME** 40 minutes

In Western South Carolina, they favor a ketchup and vinegar combo in sauce for pulled pork.

- 1 tablespoon vegetable oil
- ½ onion, minced
- 2 garlic cloves, minced
- ½ cup cider vinegar
- ½ cup Worcestershire sauce
- 1 tablespoon dry mustard
- 1 tablespoon dark brown sugar
- 1 tablespoon paprika
- 2 teaspoons kosher salt
- 1 teaspoon cayenne pepper
- 1 cup ketchup

Heat oil in 2-quart saucepan over medium heat. Add onion and garlic and cook until softened, about 5 minutes. Stir in cider vinegar, Worcestershire sauce, mustard, sugar, paprika, salt, and cayenne and bring to boil. Reduce heat to low; stir in ketchup; and cook, stirring occasionally, until thickened, about 15 minutes. (Sauce can be refrigerated for up to 5 days.)

MID–SOUTH CAROLINA MUSTARD SAUCE

Mid–South Carolina Mustard Sauce

MAKES 2½ cups **TIME** 10 minutes

In central South Carolina, the sauce for pulled pork puts the emphasis on mustard; it also tastes great on chicken.

- 1 cup cider vinegar
- 6 tablespoons Dijon mustard
- 2 tablespoons maple syrup or honey
- 4 teaspoons Worcestershire sauce
- 1 teaspoon hot pepper sauce
- 1 cup vegetable oil
- 4 teaspoons kosher salt

Whisk all ingredients together in bowl and season with pepper to taste. (Sauce can be refrigerated for up to 5 days.)

Kansas City Barbecue Sauce

MAKES 4 cups **TIME** 1½ hours

Kansas City barbecue is slathered with a thick, sweet, smoky, and sticky tomato-based sauce–the model for what much of America thinks of as barbecue sauce. We like our barbecue sauce extra-thick. If you like a thinner, smoother texture, the sauce can be strained after it has finished cooking. This sauce burns quickly and should not be used over direct heat when grilling.

- 2 teaspoons vegetable oil
- 1 onion, minced
- 4 cups chicken broth
- 1 cup root beer
- 1 cup cider vinegar
- 1 cup dark corn syrup
- ½ cup molasses
- ½ cup tomato paste
- ½ cup ketchup
- 2 tablespoons brown mustard
- 1 tablespoon hot sauce
- ½ teaspoon garlic powder
- ¼ teaspoon liquid smoke (optional)

Heat oil in saucepan over medium-high heat until shimmering. Add onion and cook until softened, about 5 minutes. Whisk in chicken broth, root beer, vinegar, corn syrup, molasses, tomato paste, ketchup, mustard, hot sauce, and garlic powder and bring to boil. Reduce heat to medium and simmer until mixture is thick and has reduced to 4 cups, about 1 hour. Stir in liquid smoke, if using. (Sauce can be refrigerated for up to 5 days.)

Oklahoma Barbecue Sauce

MAKES about 1½ cups **TIME** 45 minutes

The sharp, tangy sauce for Oklahoma barbecue is traditionally served on the side so as not to smother the meat or hide its flavor. This sauce goes particularly well with pulled pork.

- 1 tablespoon vegetable oil
- ½ small onion, chopped fine
- 1 tablespoon tomato paste
- 2 teaspoons paprika
- 1 cup ketchup
- ¾ cup cider vinegar
- 3 tablespoons brown sugar
- 1 tablespoon Worcestershire sauce
- ½ teaspoon celery salt

1 Heat oil in medium saucepan over medium heat until shimmering. Add onion and cook until softened, about 3 minutes. Stir in tomato paste and paprika and cook until paste begins to darken, about 1 minute.

2 Add ketchup, vinegar, brown sugar, Worcestershire, and celery salt and bring to boil. Reduce heat to medium-low and simmer until slightly thickened, 8 to 10 minutes. Transfer to bowl and let cool to room temperature. Season with salt and pepper to taste. (Sauce can be refrigerated for up to 5 days.)

Texas-Style Barbecue Sauce

MAKES 1¾ cups **TIME** 55 minutes plus 20 minutes cooling

Texas-style barbecue is largely about the dry rub; sauces are served in bottles on the side to be used as you wish. We combine the usual sauce ingredients—vinegar, brown sugar, molasses, etc.—with dry mustard, pepper, and chili powder for spiciness. Savory Worcestershire adds depth, while tomato juice provides tangy flavor and helps thin out the sauce. This peppery, tangy barbecue sauce works well with beef ribs (see page 242) as well as chicken and pork. Don't use blackstrap molasses in this sauce.

- 2 tablespoons unsalted butter
- ¼ cup minced onion
- 1½ teaspoons chili powder
- 1 clove garlic, minced
- 2 cups tomato juice
- ¾ cup distilled white vinegar, divided
- 2 tablespoons Worcestershire sauce
- 2 tablespoons molasses
- 1 tablespoon kosher salt
- 1 teaspoon minced canned chipotle chile in adobo sauce
- ½ teaspoon dry mustard mixed with 1 tablespoon water
- ¼ teaspoon pepper

1 Melt butter in small saucepan over medium heat. Add onion and cook, stirring occasionally, until softened, about 3 minutes. Stir in chili powder and garlic and cook until fragrant, about 20 seconds. Stir in tomato juice, ½ cup vinegar, Worcestershire, molasses, salt, chipotle, and mustard mixture. Increase heat to high and bring to simmer, then reduce heat to medium and continue to simmer, stirring occasionally, until sauce is slightly thickened and reduced to 1½ cups, 30 to 40 minutes.

2 Off heat, stir in pepper and remaining ¼ cup vinegar. Let cool to room temperature before serving. (Sauce can be refrigerated for up to 5 days.)

Blueberry Barbecue Sauce

MAKES about 2 cups **TIME** 30 minutes

This berry-based take on an American classic combines the bright, fruity flavor of blueberries with the tangy sweetness of barbecue sauce and the spicy kick of chipotle chiles in adobo sauce. We like to slather this sauce on chicken right off the grill.

- 1 tablespoon vegetable oil
- 1 shallot, chopped fine
- 2 tablespoons minced canned chipotle chile in adobo sauce
- 1 garlic clove, minced
- 10 ounces (2 cups) blueberries
- ⅔ cup packed brown sugar
- ½ cup balsamic vinegar
- 1 tablespoon Worcestershire sauce
- 2 teaspoons kosher salt
- ½ teaspoon pepper

1 Heat oil in large saucepan over medium heat until shimmering. Add shallot and cook, stirring often, until softened, 3 to 5 minutes. Stir in chipotle and garlic and cook until fragrant, about 30 seconds.

2 Stir in blueberries, sugar, vinegar, Worcestershire, salt, and pepper and bring to boil over medium-high heat. Carefully mash blueberries with potato masher and cook, stirring often, until berries have softened and liquid has thickened, 5 to 10 minutes. (Sauce can be refrigerated for up to 4 days.)

Honey-Mustard Barbecue Sauce

MAKES 2 cups **TIME** 30 minutes

This sweet-savory sauce goes with our Honey-Mustard Barbecued Baby Back Ribs (page 231); it's also particularly good on chicken or tossed with shredded cabbage for a simple slaw.

- 8 tablespoons unsalted butter
- 2 garlic cloves, minced
- ¾ cup honey
- ⅓ cup Dijon mustard
- ⅓ cup whole-grain mustard
- ¼ cup Worcestershire sauce

Melt butter in small saucepan over low heat. Stir in garlic and cook until fragrant, about 30 seconds. Whisk in honey, mustards, and Worcestershire. Remove sauce from heat and let cool to room temperature. Season with salt and pepper to taste. (Sauce can be refrigerated for up to 5 days.)

Grilling Sauces

A grilling sauce combines the clinging power and savory-sweet quality of barbecue sauce with wider-ranging flavor profiles. To make it happen, we start with quick-to-make thickener: caramel. Then we add spicy and sweet ingredients for a balanced flavor. All three sauces work equally well on pork and chicken; each yields enough to coat six to eight pieces (3 to 4 pounds) of meat, plus extra for the table. Because of their high sugar content, it's best to wait to apply these sauces until the last 5 minutes of grilling. Brush both sides of the meat with about ¼ cup of sauce, browning each side after brushing on the sauce. Pass the remaining ½ cup of sauce when serving.

ORANGE-CHIPOTLE GRILLING SAUCE

Orange-Chipotle Grilling Sauce

MAKES about 1 cup **TIME** 25 minutes

Orange marmalade, orange juice, chipotle chile in adobo, and vinegar give this sauce a balance of sweetness, tang, and smoky spice.

- ½ cup orange marmalade
- ¼ cup distilled white vinegar
- 1 tablespoon minced canned chipotle chile in adobo sauce
- 1 teaspoon kosher salt
- ½ teaspoon finely grated orange zest plus ⅓ cup juice
- ⅓ cup water
- ⅓ cup sugar

1 Whisk marmalade, vinegar, chipotle, salt, and orange zest and juice in medium bowl.

2 Place water in heavy-bottomed 2-quart saucepan; pour sugar in center of pan, taking care not to let sugar crystals adhere to sides of pan. Cover and bring mixture to boil over high heat; once boiling, uncover and continue to boil until syrup is thick and straw-colored, 3 to 4 minutes. Reduce heat to medium and continue to cook until syrup is golden amber, 1 to 2 minutes longer.

3 Quickly remove saucepan from heat and whisk in orange-chipotle mixture. Return to medium heat and cook, whisking constantly, until caramel has dissolved and sauce has thickened, about 2 minutes. (Sauce can be refrigerated for up to 4 days.)

Apple-Mustard Grilling Sauce

MAKES about 1 cup **TIME** 25 minutes

This sauce gets its rich, fruity flavor and mild heat from apple butter, whole-grain mustard, cider vinegar, and cayenne pepper.

- ⅔ cup apple cider or apple juice
- ⅓ cup apple butter
- 3 tablespoons whole-grain mustard
- 2 tablespoons cider vinegar
- 1 teaspoon dry mustard
- 1 teaspoon kosher salt
- ⅛ teaspoon cayenne pepper
- ⅓ cup water
- ⅓ cup sugar

1 Whisk cider, apple butter, whole-grain mustard, vinegar, dry mustard, salt, and cayenne in medium bowl.

2 Place water in heavy-bottomed 2-quart saucepan; pour sugar in center of pan, taking care not to let sugar crystals adhere to sides of pan. Cover and bring mixture to boil over high heat; once boiling, uncover and continue to boil until syrup is thick and straw-colored, 3 to 4 minutes. Reduce heat to medium and continue to cook until syrup is golden amber, 1 to 2 minutes longer.

3 Quickly remove saucepan from heat and whisk in apple-mustard mixture. Return to medium heat and cook, whisking constantly, until caramel has dissolved and sauce has thickened, about 2 minutes. (Sauce can be refrigerated for up to 4 days.)

Coconut–Red Curry Grilling Sauce

MAKES about 1 cup **TIME** 30 minutes

To give this sauce deep umami flavor and a spicy kick, we combine the caramel base with coconut milk, red curry paste, lime zest, and fish sauce.

- 1¼ cups canned coconut milk
- 1 tablespoon red curry paste
- 1 tablespoon fish sauce
- ½ teaspoon finely grated lime zest plus ¼ cup juice (2 limes)
- ⅓ cup water
- ⅓ cup sugar

1 Whisk coconut milk, curry paste, fish sauce, and lime zest and juice in medium bowl.

2 Place water in heavy-bottomed 2-quart saucepan; pour sugar in center of pan, taking care not to let sugar crystals adhere to sides of pan. Cover and bring mixture to boil over high heat; once boiling, uncover and continue to boil until syrup is thick and straw-colored, 3 to 4 minutes. Reduce heat to medium and continue to cook until syrup is golden amber, 1 to 2 minutes longer.

3 Quickly remove saucepan from heat and whisk in coconut–red curry mixture. Return to medium heat and cook, whisking constantly, until caramel has dissolved and sauce has thickened, 6 to 7 minutes. (Sauce can be refrigerated for up to 4 days.)

BASIL PESTO

Herb Sauces

Herb sauces–from chermoula to chimichurri to persillade to salsa verde–brighten meals in cuisines across the globe. Raw ingredients are the common element in all of these sauces; the grassy freshness of herbs and the bite of garlic add a summery punch to just about any grilled food you can think of.

Basil Pesto

MAKES 1¾ cups **TIME** 45 minutes

This iconic Italian sauce is packed with the sweet, subtle licorice notes of aromatic basil; the toasted aroma and buttery texture of pine nuts; the richness of olive oil; the savory bite of garlic; and the saltiness of Parmesan cheese. You can dollop it on anything off the grill, from pizza to chicken to vegetables. We prefer the flavor of Italian pine nuts here; the container should indicate where they're grown. The amount of processed Parmesan should be about 10 tablespoons.

- ½ cup pine nuts
- ¾ cup extra-virgin olive oil, divided
- 4 ounces fresh basil leaves and stems
- 1½ teaspoon kosher salt, plus salt for blanching basil
- 1¼ ounces Parmesan cheese
- 2 garlic cloves, peeled

1 Toast pine nuts and 1 tablespoon oil in 8-inch skillet over medium heat, stirring often, until light golden, 3 to 6 minutes. Spread pine nuts out on plate and let cool for 15 minutes.

2 Meanwhile, bring 2 quarts water to boil in medium saucepan. Remove and discard basil stems from leaves (you should have 4 cups leaves [3 ounces by weight]). Add basil leaves and 1 teaspoon salt to boiling water and cook until basil is wilted and bright green, 5 to 10 seconds. Using slotted spoon, transfer basil directly to salad spinner and spin to remove excess water. Spread basil on clean dish towel to dry. (If you don't have a salad spinner, drain basil on clean dish towel and thoroughly pat dry with paper towels.)

3 Process Parmesan in food processor until finely ground, about 30 seconds; transfer to medium bowl. Process garlic, pine nuts, basil, salt, and remaining oil in now-empty processor until smooth, about 1 minute, scraping down sides of bowl as needed. Transfer pesto to bowl with Parmesan and stir to combine. (Pesto can be refrigerated for up to 2 days.)

SAUCE VERTE

Sauce Verte

MAKES about ½ cup **TIME** 10 minutes

The French equivalent of salsa verde, this fresh herb sauce makes a great accompaniment to rich meats such as Grilled Lamb Shoulder Chops (page 94) and comes together in seconds in the food processor. We use equal amounts of parsley, mint, and tarragon; if you like, omit the tarragon and increase the amounts of parsley and mint to ¾ cup each.

- ½ cup fresh parsley leaves
- ½ cup fresh mint leaves
- ½ cup fresh tarragon leaves
- 1 small shallot, chopped
- 1 tablespoon capers, rinsed
- 1 garlic clove, peeled
- 1 anchovy fillet, rinsed and patted dry
- ½ teaspoon kosher salt
- ¼ cup extra-virgin olive oil
- 1 teaspoon finely grated lemon zest plus 1 tablespoon juice

Process parsley, mint, tarragon, shallot, capers, garlic, anchovy, and salt in food processor until coarsely chopped, about 5 seconds. Add oil and lemon zest and juice and process until sauce is uniform, about 5 seconds, scraping down sides of bowl as needed. (Sauce can be refrigerated for up to 2 days.)

Persillade

MAKES about 1¼ cups **TIME** 25 minutes

This classic French sauce has a bold flavor thanks to the combination of capers, cornichons, and raw garlic. It makes a great accompaniment to almost anything, but tastes especially terrific on beef. If you prefer, you can skip mincing the ingredients and use a food processor.

- ¾ cup minced fresh parsley
- ½ cup extra-virgin olive oil
- 6 tablespoons minced cornichons plus 1 teaspoon brine
- ¼ cup capers, rinsed and chopped coarse
- 3 garlic cloves, minced
- 1 scallion, minced
- 1 teaspoon sugar
- ½ teaspoon kosher salt
- ¼ teaspoon pepper

Combine all ingredients in small bowl. Let sit at room temperature until flavors have blended, about 10 minutes. (Sauce can be refrigerated for up to 2 days.)

Mint Persillade

MAKES about 1 cup **TIME** 10 minutes

We put a spin on classic persillade with mint, anchovies, and lemon zest and juice, making it the perfect zesty accompaniment for lean meats such as pork chops or chicken breasts.

- 1 cup fresh mint leaves
- 1 cup fresh parsley leaves
- 3 garlic cloves, peeled
- 3 anchovy fillets, rinsed and patted dry
- 1 teaspoon grated lemon zest plus 1 tablespoon juice
- 1 teaspoon kosher salt
- ⅛ teaspoon pepper
- ⅓ cup extra-virgin olive oil

Pulse mint, parsley, garlic, anchovies, lemon zest, salt, and pepper in food processor until finely chopped, 15 to 20 pulses. Add lemon juice and pulse briefly to combine. Transfer mixture to medium bowl and slowly whisk in oil until fully incorporated. (Sauce can be refrigerated for up to 2 days.)

Italian Salsa Verde

MAKES 1½ cups **TIME** 15 minutes

Lightly toasted bread is the secret to this sauce's thick, uniform texture; we process it with oil and lemon juice to create a smooth base for the sauce. Grassy parsley, briny capers, garlic, anchovy, and a pinch of salt round out the bright, assertive flavors.

- 2 slices white sandwich bread
- 1 cup extra-virgin olive oil
- ¼ cup lemon juice (2 lemons)
- 4 cups fresh parsley leaves
- 4 anchovy fillets, rinsed and patted dry
- ¼ cup capers, rinsed
- 2 small cloves garlic, minced
- ½ teaspoon kosher salt

1 Toast bread in toaster at lowest setting until surface is dry but not browned, about 15 seconds. Remove crust and cut bread into rough ½-inch pieces (you should have about 1½ cups).

2 Process bread pieces, oil, and lemon juice in food processor until smooth, about 10 seconds. Add parsley, anchovies, capers, garlic, and salt. Pulse until mixture is finely chopped (mixture should not be smooth), about 5 pulses. Transfer mixture to small bowl. (Sauce can be refrigerated for up to 2 days.)

VARIATIONS

Lemon-Basil Salsa Verde

Reduce amount of parsley to 2 cups and add 2 cups coarsely chopped fresh basil and 1 teaspoon grated lemon zest to food processor with parsley.

Salsa Verde with Arugula

Reduce amount of parsley to 2 cups and add 2 cups chopped arugula to food processor with parsley.

Argentinian Chimichurri Sauce

MAKES about 1½ cups **TIME** 20 minutes plus 1 hour resting

Chimichurri, featured prominently in Argentinian and Uruguayan cuisines, is known for its vibrant flavor and aroma. It's typically used as a marinade, dipping sauce, or condiment for grilled meats and seafood. We like to serve it with Grill-Roasted Beef Tenderloin (page 85). This chimichurri features three different herbs and a hearty amount of fresh garlic. Using fresh parsley and cilantro is key here, but dried oregano works just fine if it's first soaked in hot water to help release its flavor. Whisking in the olive oil by hand, rather than adding it to the food processor, helps preserve its fresh, fruity flavor.

- ¼ cup hot water
- 2 teaspoons dried oregano
- 2 teaspoons kosher salt
- 1⅓ cups fresh parsley leaves
- ⅔ cup fresh cilantro leaves
- 6 garlic cloves, minced
- ½ teaspoon red pepper flakes
- ¼ cup red wine vinegar
- ½ cup extra-virgin olive oil

Combine hot water, oregano, and salt in small bowl; let sit for 5 minutes to soften oregano. Pulse parsley, cilantro, garlic, and pepper flakes in food processor until coarsely chopped, about 10 pulses. Add water mixture and vinegar and pulse briefly to combine. Transfer mixture to medium bowl and slowly whisk in oil until incorporated and mixture is emulsified. Cover with plastic wrap and let sit at room temperature for at least 1 hour. (Sauce can be refrigerated for up to 2 days.)

Red Chimichurri Sauce

MAKES about ½ cup **TIME** 10 minutes plus 30 minutes resting

Paprika and red wine vinegar give this chimichurri a smoky, bright flavor that tastes great with beef, lamb, pork, chicken, and seafood.

- ¼ cup minced fresh parsley
- ¼ cup red wine vinegar
- ¼ cup extra-virgin olive oil
- 1 shallot, minced
- 1½ teaspoons paprika
- 1 garlic clove, minced
- ¼ teaspoon kosher salt
- ⅛ teaspoon red pepper flakes

Whisk all ingredients together in small bowl. Let sit at room temperature for at least 30 minutes to allow flavors to blend. Whisk to recombine before serving. (Sauce can be refrigerated for up to 2 days.)

Tarragon Chimichurri Sauce

MAKES about 1 cup **TIME** 10 minutes

Tarragon gives this chimichurri a unique, perfumed flair that complements poultry and fish.

- ½ cup minced fresh parsley
- ¼ cup extra-virgin olive oil
- 2 tablespoons minced fresh tarragon
- 2 tablespoons white wine vinegar
- 2 garlic cloves, minced
- ¼ teaspoon red pepper flakes

Combine all ingredients in bowl and season with salt and pepper to taste. Let sit at room temperature for at least 30 minutes to allow flavors to blend. (Sauce can be refrigerated for up to 2 days.)

Cranberry Chimichurri Sauce

MAKES about 1½ cups **TIME** 15 minutes plus 30 minutes resting

The surprising addition of minced sweet-tart dried cranberries gives this chimichurri a modern twist, perfect for fall grilling. This relish works well with pork, lamb, and poultry; it tastes especially good with grilled turkey.

- ¾ cup dried cranberries, minced
- ⅔ cup extra-virgin olive oil
- ½ cup chopped fresh cilantro leaves and stems
- ½ cup chopped fresh parsley
- 3 tablespoons red wine vinegar
- 1 shallot, minced
- 3 garlic cloves, minced
- 1½ teaspoons dried oregano
- 1 teaspoon kosher salt
- ½ teaspoon red pepper flakes
- ¼ teaspoon pepper

Combine all ingredients in small bowl. Let sit at room temperature for at least 30 minutes to allow flavors to blend. (Sauce can be refrigerated for up to 2 days.)

Chermoula Sauce

MAKES about 1 cup **TIME** 15 minutes plus 1 hour resting

Chermoula is a classic olive oil–based North African sauce featuring lots of fresh cilantro and a few aromatic spices. It's served alongside beef, lamb, chicken, seafood, and vegetables but is also enjoyed as a condiment or dipping sauce. This version has a bright, lemony flavor and a little kick from cayenne pepper. A food processor quickly combines the bulk of the ingredients, but we prefer whisk in the oil by hand to preserve its fresh, fruity flavor. A rasp-style grater makes quick work of turning the garlic into a paste.

- ¾ cup fresh cilantro leaves
- 4 garlic cloves, minced to paste
- 1 teaspoon ground cumin
- 1 teaspoon paprika
- ½ teaspoon kosher salt
- ¼ teaspoon cayenne pepper
- 3 tablespoons lemon juice
- ½ cup extra-virgin olive oil

Pulse cilantro, garlic, cumin, paprika, salt, and cayenne in food processor until coarsely chopped, about 10 pulses. Add lemon juice and pulse briefly to combine. Transfer mixture to medium bowl and slowly whisk in oil until incorporated and mixture is emulsified. Let sit at room temperature for at least 30 minutes to allow flavors to blend. (Sauce can be refrigerated for up to 2 days.)

MUSTARD-DILL SAUCE

Creamy Sauces

Creamy sauces make comfort foods even more comforting—think flaky, tender fish with tartar sauce or a blanket of "special sauce" on a juicy burger. They can also serve as a cooling counterpoint to spicy foods or add richness to lean foods, as with Mexican crema and tzatziki. But not all creamy sauces are cooling and white, or even dairy-based. Ají Amarillo and Ají Verde have outsize flavor profiles that belie their creamy texture, as do chile-and-tomato-based Romesco Sauce and simple, punchy Mustard-Dill Sauce.

Pub-Style Burger Sauce

MAKES about 1 cup **TIME** 8 minutes

This recipe is easily made from a few flavorful pantry ingredients, fresh chives, and garlic. Using mayonnaise for the base ensures that the sauce will be thick enough to spread onto toasted burger buns. Soy sauce, brown sugar, and Worcestershire round out the flavor profile.

- ¾ cup mayonnaise
- 2 tablespoons soy sauce
- 1 tablespoon packed dark brown sugar
- 1 tablespoon Worcestershire sauce
- 1 tablespoon minced fresh chives
- 1 garlic clove, minced
- ¾ teaspoon pepper

Whisk all ingredients together in small bowl. (Sauce can be refrigerated for up to 2 days.)

Tzatziki

MAKES 2 cups **TIME** 10 minutes plus 1 hour chilling

Serve this Mediterranean yogurt, garlic, and cucumber sauce with grilled chicken, fish, or vegetables. Don't substitute regular plain yogurt for the Greek yogurt or the sauce will be very watery.

- 1 cucumber, peeled, halved lengthwise, and seeded
- 1 cup plain whole-milk Greek yogurt
- 2 tablespoons extra-virgin olive oil
- 2 tablespoons finely chopped fresh mint and/or dill
- 1 small garlic clove, minced

Shred cucumber on large holes of box grater. Whisk yogurt, oil, mint, and garlic together in medium bowl. Stir in cucumbers and season with salt and pepper to taste. Cover and refrigerate until chilled, about 1 hour. (Sauce can be refrigerated for up to 2 days.)

Classic Tartar Sauce

MAKES about 1 cup **TIME** 25 minutes

This sauce tastes great on Grilled Southern Shrimp Burgers (page 209). Be sure to rinse the capers before mincing them or the sauce will have a strong, briny flavor. We prefer the flavor of regular mayonnaise; you can use low-fat mayonnaise (the sauce will taste a bit more harsh), but don't use nonfat mayonnaise.

- ¾ cup mayonnaise
- 1½ teaspoons minced shallot
- 2 tablespoons capers, rinsed and minced
- 2 tablespoons sweet pickle relish
- 1½ teaspoons distilled white vinegar
- ½ teaspoon Worcestershire sauce

Combine all ingredients in small bowl, let sit for 15 minutes, and season with salt and pepper to taste. (Sauce can be refrigerated for up to 5 days.)

LEMON-GARLIC SAUCE

Herb Yogurt Sauce

MAKES about ½ cup **TIME** 20 minutes

This yogurt sauce pairs well with fish, lamb, poultry, and vegetables and is easy to vary depending on the other flavors in the meal. We prefer to use whole-milk yogurt here for a well rounded flavor. You can use low-fat yogurt (the flavor of the sauce will taste a bit more harsh) but do not use nonfat yogurt. If using Greek yogurt, which is thicker, you will need to thin out the sauce with water or milk. A rasp-style grater makes quick work of turning the garlic into a paste.

- ½ cup plain whole-milk yogurt
- 2 tablespoons minced fresh dill, tarragon, basil, cilantro, or parsley
- ½ teaspoon grated lemon or lime zest plus 2 teaspoons juice
- 1 small garlic clove, minced to paste

Combine all ingredients in small bowl; refrigerate for 15 minutes. Season with salt and pepper to taste. (Sauce can be refrigerated for up to 2 days.)

Lemon-Garlic Sauce

MAKES about ½ cup **TIME** 20 minutes

This simple, creamy sauce can be dolloped on grilled fish, shrimp, asparagus, or potatoes. Fresh lemon zest and garlic mashed into a fine paste add a bright, aromatic flavor. A rasp-style grater makes quick work of turning the garlic into a paste.

- ½ cup mayonnaise
- 1 tablespoon minced fresh parsley
- ½ teaspoon grated lemon zest, plus lemon juice to taste
- 1 small garlic clove, minced to paste

Combine all ingredients in small bowl; refrigerate for 15 minutes. (Sauce can be refrigerated for up to 2 days.)

Creamy Lemon-Herb Sauce

MAKES about ½ cup **TIME** 25 minutes

We like to dollop this simple mayonnaise-based sauce on Grilled Salmon Burgers (page 210) or serve it with any grilled fish. Other fresh herbs such as cilantro, chives, tarragon, basil, marjoram, and chervil can be substituted for the parsley or thyme.

- ½ cup mayonnaise
- 2½ tablespoons lemon juice
- 1 tablespoon minced fresh parsley
- 1 tablespoon minced fresh thyme
- 1 large scallion, minced
- 1 teaspoon kosher salt

Combine all ingredients in small bowl; refrigerate for 15 minutes. (Sauce can be refrigerated for up to 2 days.)

Horseradish Cream Sauce with Chives

MAKES about 1 cup **TIME** 5 minutes

A classic accompaniment to beef tenderloin, this sauce also complements salmon. Using crème fraîche will give the sauce a milder, creamier flavor but sour cream works well too.

- 1 cup crème fraîche or sour cream
- 2 tablespoons prepared horseradish
- 2 tablespoons minced fresh chives
- Pinch kosher salt

Combine all ingredients in small bowl. (Sauce can be refrigerated for up to 1 day.)

Quick Mexican Crema

MAKES about 1¼ cups **TIME** 5 minutes

Thick, slightly tangy Mexican crema imparts a touch of richness to many dishes, from grilled vegetables to tacos and fajitas. If you can't find it, this quick version of crema works well as a substitute. If a looser crema is desired, add more milk as needed.

- ½ cup mayonnaise
- ½ cup sour cream
- 2 tablespoons lime juice
- 2 tablespoons milk

Whisk all ingredients together in small bowl. (Sauce can be refrigerated for up to 2 days.)

Ají Verde

MAKES about ¾ cup **TIME** 10 minutes

Our take on classic ají verde is mayonnaise-based and features huacatay, as well as grassy jalapeños, garlic, salty cotija cheese, and tangy lime juice. Huacatay is a Peruvian herb sometimes called black mint. You can find it jarred in supermarkets or online. If it's unavailable, increase the cilantro to 5 tablespoons. Serve this sauce with Peruvian Garlic-Lime Chicken (page 259).

- ½ cup mayonnaise
- 1 jalapeño chile, stemmed, seeded, and chopped coarse
- 3 tablespoons minced fresh cilantro
- 2 tablespoons grated cotija cheese
- 2 tablespoons lime juice
- 1 tablespoon jarred huacatay paste
- 1 garlic clove, minced

Combine all ingredients in blender and process until smooth, about 1 minute. (Sauce can be refrigerated for up to 1 week.)

Ají Amarillo

MAKES about ⅔ cup **TIME** 10 minutes

The yellow Peruvian chiles that give ají amarillo paste its name have fruity, habanero-like vibes with moderate heat. Lime juice, garlic, and huacatay accent the chile flavor in this sauce. Ají amarillo paste is available in supermarkets or online. If huacatay paste is unavailable, it can be omitted. Serve this sauce, along with ají verde, with Peruvian Garlic-Lime Chicken (page 259).

- ½ cup mayonnaise
- 2 tablespoons ají amarillo paste
- 1 tablespoon lime juice
- 1 garlic clove, minced
- 1 teaspoon jarred huacatay paste

Combine all ingredients in blender and process until smooth, about 1 minute. (Sauce can be refrigerated for up to 1 week.)

Mustard-Dill Sauce

MAKES about 1 cup **TIME** 5 minutes

This lush, potent sauce is perfect on salmon and salmon cakes. Use Dijon, honey, or grainy mustard, as desired. Depending on your choice of mustard, this sauce can be fairly hot.

- 1 cup mustard
- ¼ cup minced fresh dill

Combine mustard and dill in small bowl. (Sauce can be refrigerated for up to 2 days.)

Romesco Sauce

MAKES about 2 cups **TIME** 20 minutes

This sauce is traditionally served with fish but also goes well with chicken, meat, or vegetables and makes a great dip for rustic bread.

- 1–2 slices hearty white sandwich bread, crusts removed, bread lightly toasted and cut into ½-inch pieces (½ cup)
- 3 tablespoons slivered almonds, toasted
- 1¾ cups jarred roasted red peppers
- 1 small tomato, cored, seeded, and chopped
- 2 tablespoons extra-virgin olive oil
- 1½ tablespoons sherry vinegar
- 1 large garlic clove, minced
- 1 teaspoon kosher salt
- ¼ teaspoon cayenne pepper

Process bread and almonds in food processor until almonds are finely ground, 10 to 15 seconds. Add red peppers, tomato, oil, vinegar, garlic, salt, and cayenne. Process until mixture has texture similar to mayonnaise, 20 to 30 seconds. Season with salt to taste and transfer to serving bowl. (Sauce can be refrigerated for up to 2 days.)

PICO DE GALLO

Salsas and Guacamole

These popular condiments are equally at home as an accompaniment to grilled meats and as a main-event appetizer, with chips. You can customize the heat level of any of these salsas to your preferred spiciness. Some are raw, some have grilled components for a smoky element, and others achieve that effect on the stove, so you can have them ready ahead of time. Our guacamole recipes also offer you a choice of outdoor or indoor prep.

Pico de Gallo

MAKES about 1½ cups **TIME** 15 minutes plus 30 minutes draining

Salting the tomatoes and letting them sit in a colander for 30 minutes draws out and drains away excess moisture, which gives this pico de gallo its potent flavor. Garlic and onion provide bite, minced jalapeño adds heat, and lime juice and cilantro brighten up the mix. For a spicier salsa, add some or all of the jalapeño seeds and ribs. We serve this with our Grilled Steak Fajitas (page 80).

- 3 tomatoes, cored and chopped
- ½ teaspoon kosher salt
- ¼ cup finely chopped red onion
- ¼ cup chopped fresh cilantro
- 1 jalapeño chile, stemmed, seeded, and minced
- 1 tablespoon lime juice
- 1 garlic clove, minced

Toss tomatoes with salt in bowl; transfer to colander and let drain for 30 minutes. Combine drained tomatoes, onion, cilantro, jalapeño, lime juice, and garlic in bowl. Season with salt and pepper to taste.

Santa Maria Salsa

MAKES about 4 cups **TIME** 15 minutes plus 1½ hours draining and sitting

Unexpected ingredients like celery, dried oregano, and Worcestershire sauce transform this salsa. Salting and draining the tomatoes prevents the excess liquid from diluting the flavor, and jalapeños give it moderate heat. The distinct texture of each ingredient is part of this salsa's identity and appeal, so we don't recommend using a food processor. This salsa is the perfect partner for California Barbecued Tri-Tip (page 84).

- 2 pounds ripe tomatoes, cored and chopped
- 4 teaspoons kosher salt
- 2 jalapeño chiles, stemmed, seeded, and minced
- 1 small red onion, chopped fine
- 1 celery rib, chopped fine
- 1 garlic clove, minced
- ¼ cup lime juice (2 limes)
- ¼ cup chopped fresh cilantro
- ⅛ teaspoon dried oregano
- ⅛ teaspoon Worcestershire sauce

Toss tomatoes with salt in bowl; transfer to colander and let drain for 30 minutes. Combine drained tomatoes, jalapeños, onion, celery, garlic, lime juice, cilantro, oregano, and Worcestershire in large bowl and toss to combine. Let salsa sit for 1 hour for flavors to meld.

Salsa Roja

MAKES about 1½ cups **TIME** 45 minutes

This salsa is spicy enough to hold its own alongside any grilled meat. A dried ancho chile adds a welcome fruitiness. Instead of hydrating the ancho in water and then draining it, we process it in the blender and then combine it with a fresh tomato. Minced canned chipotle chile contributes a hint of smoke. Chiles vary in heat level, so adjust the amount of chipotle to your taste.

- 1 dried ancho chile, stemmed, seeded, and torn into ½-inch pieces
- 1 pound plum tomatoes, cored and halved, divided
- 1–3 teaspoons minced canned chipotle chile in adobo sauce, divided
- ¼ small onion, root end intact
- 1 jalapeño chile
- 1 large garlic clove, unpeeled
- ¼ cup coarsely chopped fresh cilantro leaves and stems
- 1½ teaspoons kosher salt

1 Process ancho pieces in blender until finely chopped, about 20 seconds. Add one-quarter of tomatoes and 1 teaspoon chipotle. Process on low speed, scraping down sides of blender jar if necessary, until tomatoes are finely chopped and ancho pieces are moistened, about 45 seconds. Let mixture sit for 15 minutes.

2 Meanwhile, line rimmed baking sheet with aluminum foil. Adjust oven rack 4 inches from broiler element and heat broiler. Place remaining tomatoes skin side down on prepared sheet. Add onion and jalapeño and broil until onion and jalapeño are blackened and tomatoes are beginning to turn spotty brown, 4 to 6 minutes. Flip onion and jalapeño, add garlic, and broil until all vegetables are blackened, 3 to 4 minutes.

3 Transfer jalapeño and garlic to cutting board; let cool. When cool enough to handle, peel garlic. Without peeling, stem and seed jalapeño. Add tomatoes, onion, jalapeño, garlic, cilantro, and salt to blender and process until smooth, about 2 minutes. Season with salt and up to 2 teaspoons additional chipotle to taste; process until smooth. Transfer to serving bowl and, if desired, stir in water, 1 teaspoon at a time, to loosen to drizzling consistency. (Salsa can be refrigerated for up to 5 days.)

Sweet and Smoky Grilled Tomato Salsa

MAKES about 3 cups **TIME** 55 minutes

Meaty plum tomatoes hold together well on the grill to give this salsa deep flavor. We start the halved tomatoes cut side down and then flip them cut side up—the skin acts as a cradle, keeping the juicy flesh intact as the tomatoes continue to cook and soften. Wood chips add a smoky note. For a spicier salsa, add some or all of the jalapeño seeds and ribs. Use this salsa to dress up any simple steak.

- 2 pounds plum tomatoes (10 to 12), cored and halved lengthwise
- 2 large jalapeño chiles
- 2 teaspoons vegetable oil
- 1 cup wood chips
- 3 tablespoons minced red onion
- 2 tablespoons chopped fresh cilantro
- 2 tablespoons extra-virgin olive oil
- 2 tablespoons lime juice, plus extra as needed
- 2 teaspoons kosher salt
- ½ teaspoon sugar, plus extra as needed
- ¼ teaspoon pepper

1 Toss tomatoes and jalapeños with vegetable oil to coat. Using large piece of heavy-duty aluminum foil, wrap wood chips in 8 by 4-inch foil packet. (Make sure chips do not poke holes in sides or bottom of packet.) Cut 2 evenly spaced 2-inch slits in top of packet.

2A **FOR A CHARCOAL GRILL** Open bottom vent completely. Light large chimney starter filled with charcoal briquettes (6 quarts). When top coals are partially covered with ash, pour evenly over grill. Place wood chip packet on coals. Set cooking grate in place, cover, and open lid vent completely. Heat grill until hot and wood chips are smoking, about 5 minutes.

2B **FOR A GAS GRILL** Remove cooking grate and place wood chip packet directly on primary burner. Set grate in place; turn all burners to high; cover; and heat grill until hot and wood chips are smoking, about 15 minutes. Leave all burners on high.

3 Clean and oil cooking grate. Place tomatoes, cut side down, and jalapeños on grill (away from wood chips). Cover and cook, turning as needed, until vegetables are nicely charred on both sides and tomato juices are bubbling, 8 to 12 minutes. Transfer vegetables to plate as they finish cooking and let cool for 10 minutes.

4 Stem, peel, and seed jalapeños, then chop fine. Pulse tomatoes in food processor until broken down but still chunky, about 6 pulses. Transfer tomatoes to bowl and stir in jalapeños, onion, cilantro, oil, lime juice, salt, sugar, and pepper. Season with additional lime juice and sugar to taste. Let salsa sit for 10 minutes for flavors to meld. (Salsa can be refrigerated for up to 3 days.)

Tomatillo Salsa

MAKES 2 cups **TIME** 45 minutes

Cooking softens tomatillos, which can be quite firm, and mellows their bracing acidity. We char half of the tomatillos under the broiler and leave the other half raw to give this salsa a clean, fresh flavor and subtle smoky nuances. The salsa comes together easily in the food processor and can be served with simple grilled chicken or fish. For a spicier salsa, add some or all of the jalapeño seeds and ribs.

- 1 pound tomatillos, husks and stems removed, rinsed well and dried, divided
- 1 teaspoon vegetable oil
- 1 small white onion, chopped
- 1 jalapeño chile, stemmed, halved, and seeded
- ½ cup fresh cilantro leaves
- 2 tablespoons lime juice
- 1 garlic clove, minced
- ½ teaspoon kosher salt
- 2 teaspoons extra-virgin olive oil

1 Adjust oven rack 6 inches from broiler element and heat broiler. Line rimmed baking sheet with aluminum foil. Toss half of tomatillos with vegetable oil and transfer to prepared sheet. Broil until tomatillos are spotty brown and skins begin to burst, 7 to 10 minutes. Transfer tomatillos to food processor and let cool completely.

GRILLED TOMATILLO SALSA

2 Halve remaining tomatillos and add to food processor with broiled tomatillos. Add onion, jalapeño, cilantro, lime juice, garlic, and salt. Pulse until slightly chunky, 16 to 18 pulses. Transfer to salsa bowl and let sit at room temperature for 15 minutes. Stir in olive oil and season with salt and sugar to taste. (Salsa can be refrigerated for up to 5 days.)

Grilled Tomatillo Salsa

MAKES about 2 cups **TIME** 30 minutes

Grilling tomatillos, scallions, and garlic softens and mellows them and adds deep flavor to this quick salsa. Try it with Grilled Chicken Nachos with Corn, Poblanos, and Black Beans (page 172).

- 1 pound tomatillos, husks and stems removed, rinsed well, and dried
- 9 scallions
- 6 garlic cloves, peeled and threaded onto wooden skewer
- 1 teaspoon plus 2 tablespoons extra-virgin olive oil, divided
- ¾ cup minced fresh cilantro
- 2 serrano chiles, stemmed, seeded, and minced
- 3 tablespoons lime juice, plus extra for seasoning (2 limes)
- ½ teaspoon sugar
- ⅛ teaspoon kosher salt
- ⅛ teaspoon ground cumin
- ⅛ teaspoon chipotle chile powder

1 Brush tomatillos, scallions, and garlic with 1 teaspoon oil.

2A FOR A CHARCOAL GRILL Open bottom vent completely. Light large chimney starter filled with charcoal briquettes (6 quarts). When top coals are partially covered with ash, pour evenly over half of grill. Set cooking grate in place, cover, and open lid vent completely. Heat grill until hot, about 5 minutes.

2B FOR A GAS GRILL Turn all burners to high; cover; and heat grill until hot, about 15 minutes. Leave all burners on high.

3 Clean and oil cooking grate. Place tomatillos, scallions, and garlic on hotter side of grill. Cover and cook, turning as needed, until vegetables are charred and softened, 8 to 10 minutes. Transfer vegetables to plate as they finish cooking and let cool.

4 Chop scallions coarse. Pulse scallions, tomatillos, garlic, cilantro, serranos, lime juice, sugar, salt, cumin, chipotle, and remaining 2 tablespoons oil in food processor until mixture is coarsely chopped, 4 to 6 pulses. Transfer to bowl and season with salt and extra lime juice to taste. (Salsa can be refrigerated for up to 5 days.)

Fresh Corn Salsa with Tomato

MAKES 3 cups **TIME** 45 minutes

Corn's natural sweetness makes it an exemplary foil for salsa's signature spicy chiles and tart citrus juice. Steeping raw corn kernels in boiling water with a touch of baking soda softens the corn and loosens the hulls so that the kernels become juicy and crisp, perfect for a bright, fresh salsa. Do not substitute frozen corn for fresh. For a spicier salsa, add some or all of the jalapeño seeds and ribs.

- 3 ears corn, kernels cut from cobs (2¼ cups)
- ¼ teaspoon baking soda
- ½ teaspoon kosher salt, plus extra for boiling corn
- 2 tablespoons lime juice
- 1 tablespoon vegetable oil
- ½ teaspoon honey
- 1 tomato, cored, seeded, and cut into ¼-inch pieces
- 1 shallot, minced
- 1 jalapeño chile, stemmed, seeded, and minced
- ¼ cup chopped fresh cilantro

1 Bring 2 cups water to boil in small saucepan over high heat. Stir in corn, baking soda, and ½ teaspoon salt; remove pan from heat and let sit for 10 minutes. Drain corn and let cool slightly, about 10 minutes.

2 Whisk lime juice, oil, honey, and salt together in bowl. Add corn, tomato, shallot, jalapeño, and cilantro to lime juice mixture and toss to combine. Let sit for 10 minutes. Season with salt and pepper to taste. (Salsa can be refrigerated for up to 1 day.)

VARIATIONS

Fresh Corn Salsa with Avocado and Toasted Cumin

Omit tomato and shallot. Add ½ teaspoon whole toasted cumin seeds and ⅛ teaspoon cayenne pepper to bowl with lime juice. Add 3 thinly sliced scallions and 1 avocado, halved, pitted, and cut into ¼-inch pieces, to salsa with corn.

Fresh Corn Salsa with Jicama and Pineapple

Omit tomato and jalapeño. Add ¾ cup pineapple, cut into ¼-inch pieces; ½ cup jícama, peeled and cut into ¼-inch pieces; and 1 minced serrano chile to salsa with corn.

Fresh Corn Salsa with Mango and Cucumber

Omit tomato, jalapeño, and cilantro. Add ¼ teaspoon chipotle chile powder to bowl with lime juice. Add ½ mango, peeled and cut into ¼-inch pieces; 1 small cucumber, peeled, halved lengthwise, seeded, and cut into ¼-inch pieces; and ¼ cup chopped fresh mint to salsa with corn.

Fresh Corn Salsa with Peach and Radishes

Omit tomato, jalapeño, and cilantro. Add 1 peach, peeled, halved, pitted and cut into ¼-inch pieces; 4 thinly sliced radishes; and ¼ cup chopped fresh basil to salsa with corn.

Toasted Corn and Black Bean Salsa

MAKES 5 cups **TIME** 25 minutes

This salsa gets its intense flavor from toasting corn, which is fast and easy to do. Do not substitute frozen corn for fresh. Be sure to use a nonstick skillet when toasting the corn. For a spicier salsa, add some or all of the jalapeño seeds and ribs

- 2 tablespoons extra-virgin olive oil, divided
- 2 ears corn, kernels cut from cobs
- 1 (15-ounce) can black beans, rinsed
- 1 red bell pepper, stemmed, seeded, and chopped fine
- 1 tomato, cored and chopped
- ½ jalapeño chile, seeded and minced
- 1 scallion, sliced thin
- 2 garlic cloves, minced
- 2 tablespoons lime juice
- 2 tablespoons minced fresh cilantro
- ½ teaspoon ground cumin

Heat 1 tablespoon oil in 12-inch nonstick skillet over medium-high heat until shimmering. Add corn and cook until golden brown, 6 to 8 minutes. Transfer corn to serving bowl and stir in remaining 1 tablespoon oil, beans, bell pepper, tomato, jalapeño, scallion, garlic, lime juice, cilantro, and cumin. Season with salt and pepper to taste. (Salsa can be refrigerated for up to 1 day.)

VARIATION

Spicy Toasted Corn and Black Bean Salsa

Add minced seeds from jalapeño and 4 teaspoons minced canned chipotle chile in adobo sauce to salsa.

PINEAPPLE-MANGO SALSA

PINEAPPLE-CUCUMBER SALSA

PINEAPPLE-WATERMELON SALSA

Avocado-Orange Salsa

MAKES about 1 cup **TIME** 10 minutes

Creamy avocado adds a cooling note to this lively salsa. It makes a fast, fresh accompaniment for grilled fish or chicken.

1 large orange, rind and pith removed and segments cut into ½-inch pieces
1 ripe avocado, pitted, peeled, and diced
2 tablespoons minced red onion
2 tablespoons minced fresh cilantro
4 teaspoons lime juice
1 small jalapeño chile, stemmed, seeded, and minced

Combine all ingredients in bowl. (Salsa can be refrigerated for up to 1 day.)

Mango-Mint Salsa

MAKES about 1 cup **TIME** 10 minutes

Combining sweet mango, tart lime juice, and spicy minced jalapeño, this easy-to-make salsa is a perfect foil to rich salmon. For a spicier salsa, add some or all of the jalapeño seeds and ribs.

1 mango, peeled, pitted, and cut into ¼-inch pieces
1 shallot, minced
3 tablespoons lime juice (2 limes)
2 tablespoons chopped fresh mint
1 jalapeño chile, stemmed, seeds reserved, and minced
1 tablespoon extra-virgin olive oil
1 garlic clove, minced
1 teaspoon kosher salt

Combine all ingredients in bowl. (Salsa can be refrigerated for up to 1 day.)

Pineapple Salsa

MAKES about 2 cups **TIME** 15 minutes

A food processor pulls this bright, juicy salsa together quickly. We use pineapple as the base of our salsa and finish it by stirring in some jalapeño chiles, fresh cilantro, red onion, garlic, lime juice, oil, salt, and pepper. Do not use canned pineapple in this recipe. For a spicier salsa, add some or all of the jalapeño seeds and ribs.

2 cups 1-inch pineapple pieces
3 jalapeño chiles, stemmed, seeded, and cut into ½-inch pieces

1 cup fresh cilantro leaves
¼ cup coarsely chopped red onion
2 garlic cloves, smashed and peeled
1 tablespoon lime juice
1 tablespoon extra-virgin olive oil
1 teaspoon kosher salt
½ teaspoon pepper

Pulse pineapple, jalapeños, cilantro, onion, and garlic in food processor until coarsely chopped, about 6 pulses, scraping down sides of bowl as needed. Transfer to serving bowl. Stir in lime juice, oil, salt, and pepper. (Salsa can be refrigerated for up to 1 day.)

VARIATIONS

Pineapple-Mango Salsa

Substitute ½ cup fresh chopped chives for cilantro. Reduce amount of pineapple to 1½ cups. Add 1½ cups 1-inch fresh mango pieces to food processor with remaining ingredients.

Pineapple-Cucumber Salsa

Substitute ½ cup fresh chopped mint for cilantro. Reduce amount of pineapple to 1½ cups. Stir 1 cup ¼-inch English cucumber pieces into salsa with lime juice.

Pineapple-Watermelon Salsa

Substitute ½ cup fresh basil leaves for cilantro and ½ habanero chile, seeded and cut into ½-inch pieces, for jalapeño. Reduce amount of pineapple to 1½ cups. Stir 1 cup ¼-inch watermelon pieces into salsa with lime juice.

Classic Guacamole

SERVES 8 **TIME** 15 minutes

Using a whisk to mix and mash the avocado creates a creamy yet chunky dip. We mince the onion and chile by hand with kosher salt; the coarse crystals break down the aromatics, releasing their juices and flavors and transforming them into a paste that's easy to combine with the avocado and other ingredients. A molcajete or mortar and pestle can be used to process the onion mixture. Be sure to use Hass avocados here; Florida, or "skinny," avocados are too watery. For a spicier salsa, add some or all of the serrano seeds and ribs.

2 tablespoons finely chopped onion
1 serrano chile, stemmed, seeded, and minced
1 teaspoon kosher salt
¼ teaspoon grated lime zest plus 1½–2 tablespoons juice
3 ripe avocados, halved, pitted, and cut into ½-inch pieces
1 plum tomato, cored, seeded, and cut into ⅛-inch dice
2 tablespoons chopped fresh cilantro

Place onion, serrano, salt, and lime zest on cutting board and chop until very finely minced. Transfer onion mixture to medium bowl and stir in 1½ tablespoons lime juice. Add avocados and, using sturdy whisk, mash and stir mixture until well combined with some ¼- to ½-inch chunks of avocado remaining. Stir in tomato and cilantro. Season with salt and up to additional 1½ teaspoons lime juice to taste. (Guacamole can be refrigerated, with plastic wrap pressed directly onto surface, for up to 1 day.)

Charred Guacamole

SERVES 6 to 8 **TIME** 40 minutes

Grilling the avocados, jalapeno, onion, and garlic gives this perennial favorite a more intense flavor. Since overheating avocados can bring out bitterness, we grill them just long enough for the hot grate to leave its marks. A combination of mashed and chopped avocados makes for a rustic texture. You can make this dip ahead and chill it for up to a day, but it also tastes great still slightly warm from the grill. Spoon it over Grilled Chicken and Vegetable Quesadillas (page 175), steak, or shrimp, or just scoop it up with chips. For a spicier guacamole, add some or all of the jalapeño seeds and ribs. You will need one 12-inch metal skewer. Be sure to use Hass avocados here; Florida, or "skinny," avocados are too watery.

1 jalapeño chile
¼ small red onion
2 garlic cloves, unpeeled
3 ripe but firm avocados, halved and pitted
2 tablespoons chopped fresh cilantro
¼ teaspoon grated lime zest plus 2 tablespoons juice, plus extra juice for seasoning
1 teaspoon kosher salt

1 Thread jalapeño, onion, and garlic onto 12-inch metal skewer.

2A FOR A CHARCOAL GRILL Open bottom vent completely. Light large chimney starter filled with charcoal briquettes (6 quarts). When top coals are partially covered with ash, pour evenly over grill. Set cooking grate in place, cover, and open lid vent completely. Heat grill until hot, about 5 minutes.

2B FOR A GAS GRILL Turn all burners to high; cover; and heat grill until hot, about 15 minutes. Leave all burners on high.

3 Clean and oil cooking grate. Place vegetable skewer on grill and cook (covered if using gas), turning occasionally, until vegetables are well charred, 4 to 6 minutes; transfer to cutting board. Place avocados cut side down on grill and cook (covered if using gas) until lightly charred, about 3 minutes; transfer to cutting board and let cool slightly, about 5 minutes.

4 Using paper towel, peel away skin from jalapeño, then remove stem and seeds and chop fine. Peel and mince garlic and chop onion fine. Combine vegetables with cilantro, lime zest and juice, and salt in large bowl.

5 Scoop flesh from 2 avocado halves directly into bowl with vegetable mixture. Using tines of fork, mash avocado until just combined. Scoop flesh from remaining 4 avocado halves onto cutting board and chop coarse. Gently fold chopped avocado into mashed avocado mixture until it has broken down just enough to coat other ingredients but is still chunky. Season with extra lime juice and salt to taste. (Guacamole can be refrigerated, with plastic wrap pressed directly onto surface, for up to 1 day.)

CHARRED GUACAMOLE

SUN-DRIED TOMATO AND BASIL RELISH

Relishes

With a flavorful relish on hand you can easily dress up a simple, quick-cooking grilled protein. Chunky like salsa, but generally less liquidy, relishes are especially good paired with cutlets, chops, steaks, and fish fillets. With the exception of the Cucumber-Ginger Relish, any of these recipes is a great make-ahead choice.

Sun-Dried Tomato and Basil Relish

MAKES about 1 cup **TIME** 10 minutes

A more intense, concentrated cousin to fresh tomato salsa, this quick relish starts with flavorful oil-packed jarred sun-dried tomatoes. Fresh basil and parsley add herbal depth, while balsamic vinegar and extra-virgin olive oil make it spoonable. The flavors go well with grilled pork tenderloin and boneless chicken breasts.

- ¼ cup oil-packed sun-dried tomatoes, rinsed and chopped fine
- ¼ cup chopped fresh basil
- ¼ cup chopped fresh parsley
- ¼ cup extra-virgin olive oil
- 2 tablespoons balsamic vinegar
- 1 small shallot, minced

Combine all ingredients in bowl and season with salt and pepper to taste. (Relish can be refrigerated for up to 3 days.)

Spicy Red Pepper Relish

MAKES about 1 cup **TIME** 40 minutes plus 20 minutes cooling

For acidity and added sweetness, we use equal parts white vinegar and sugar, which temper the chiles' heat. A quick simmer on the stovetop lets the sweet and spicy notes of the relish meld.

- 2 red bell peppers, stemmed, seeded, and cut into 1-inch pieces
- 2 jalapeño chiles, stemmed, seeded, and cut into 1-inch pieces
- 1 small onion, chopped
- 3 garlic cloves, peeled
- ½ cup distilled white vinegar
- ½ cup sugar
- 1 teaspoon yellow mustard seeds
- 1 teaspoon kosher salt

1 Pulse bell peppers and jalapeños in food processor until coarsely chopped into ¼-inch pieces, 8 to 10 pulses; transfer to large bowl. Pulse onion and garlic in now-empty food processor until coarsely chopped into ¼-inch pieces, about 10 pulses; transfer to bowl with bell pepper mixture.

2 Bring vinegar, sugar, mustard seeds, and salt to boil in Dutch oven over medium-high heat. Add vegetable mixture; reduce heat to medium; and simmer, stirring occasionally, until mixture has thickened, 15 to 18 minutes. Let relish cool for 20 minutes, then transfer to airtight container and let cool to room temperature. (Relish can be refrigerated for up to 1 week.)

Orange and Mint Relish

MAKES about 1 cup **TIME** 25 minutes

The trick to making a fresh orange relish is to drain the excess juice from the oranges before adding the other ingredients. Other herbs, such as parsley, cilantro, and basil, can be substituted for the mint. This relish tastes great on fish.

- 3 oranges, rind and pith removed and segments cut into ½-inch pieces
- ½ small shallot, minced
- 2 tablespoons chopped fresh mint
- 2 teaspoons lemon juice
- 2 teaspoons extra virgin olive oil

Place oranges in fine-mesh strainer set over medium bowl and drain for 15 minutes. Pour off all but 1 tablespoon orange juice from bowl; whisk in shallot, mint, lemon juice, and oil. Stir in oranges and season with salt and pepper to taste. (Relish can be refrigerated for up to 2 days.)

Cucumber-Ginger Relish

MAKES about 2 cups **TIME** 15 minutes

Our take on a cucumber relish starts with a punchy base of rice vinegar, lime juice, mustard, and a generous amount of grated fresh ginger. We add finely diced cucumber, as well as loads of mint and cilantro, and a minced serrano chile for fresh heat. For a spicier relish, add some or all of the serrano seeds and ribs. To keep the cucumbers crisp, serve this relish within 30 minutes of assembling it. Try it with Grill-Smoked Side of Salmon (page 292) or grilled whole fish such as trout or snapper.

- ½ cup rice vinegar
- 6 tablespoons extra-virgin olive oil
- ¼ cup lime juice (2 limes)
- 2 tablespoons whole-grain mustard
- 1 tablespoon grated fresh ginger
- ½ teaspoon kosher salt
- 1 English cucumber, seeded and cut into ¼-inch dice
- 1 cup minced fresh mint
- 1 cup minced fresh cilantro
- 1 serrano chile, stemmed, seeded, and minced

Whisk vinegar, oil, lime juice, mustard, ginger, and salt in bowl until smooth. Add cucumber, mint, cilantro, and serrano and stir to combine.

Pomegranate Relish

MAKES about 1½ cups **TIME** 8 minutes

The inspiration for the flavors here comes from the Middle East. This bright sauce offers a pleasant pop and welcome dimension to grilled lamb or pork dishes.

- ¾ cup pomegranate seeds
- ¾ cup chopped fresh parsley
- 1 shallot, minced
- ½ cup extra virgin olive oil
- 2 tablespoons lemon juice
- 2 garlic cloves, minced
- ¾ teaspoon kosher salt

Combine pomegranate seeds, parsley, shallot, extra-virgin olive oil, lemon juice, garlic, and salt in a small bowl. (Relish can be refrigerated for up to 2 days.).

Green Olive, Almond, and Orange Relish

MAKES about 1½ cups **TIME** 10 minutes

Olives and almonds make a chunky, rich-tasting relish, accented by fresh orange zest and mint. We use a food processor for quick chopping, but we stir in the orange juice and olive oil by hand to preserve the oil's fresh, fruity flavor. This relish tastes great on lamb, pork, chicken, and seafood.

- ½ cup pitted brine-cured green olives, chopped coarse
- ½ cup toasted slivered almonds
- 1 small garlic clove, minced
- 1 teaspoon grated orange zest plus ¼ cup juice
- ¼ cup extra-virgin olive oil
- ¼ cup minced fresh mint
- 2 teaspoons white wine vinegar
- Cayenne pepper

Pulse olives, nuts, garlic, and orange zest in food processor until finely chopped, 10 to 12 pulses. Transfer to bowl and stir in orange juice, oil, mint, and vinegar. Season with salt and cayenne to taste. (Relish can be refrigerated for up to 2 days.)

Sweet Mint-Almond Relish

MAKES about 1 cup **TIME** 10 minutes plus 1 hour resting

The combination of fresh mint and toasted almonds makes a delicious and sophisticated flavor that works well with lamb. Red wine vinegar and Dijon give the relish welcome acidity while red current jelly adds sweetness and body. Apple or apricot jelly can be substituted for the red currant jelly if necessary.

- ½ cup minced fresh mint
- ¼ cup sliced almonds, toasted and chopped fine
- ¼ cup extra-virgin olive oil
- 2 tablespoons red currant jelly
- 4 teaspoons red wine vinegar
- 2 teaspoons Dijon mustard

Combine all ingredients in bowl. Season with salt and pepper to taste. Let sit at room temperature for at least 1 hour for flavors to meld. (Relish can be refrigerated for up to 2 days.)

Preserved Lemon–Almond Sauce

MAKES 1 cup **TIME** 25 minutes

Almonds and extra-virgin olive oil balance the briny pungency of preserved lemons, a staple of Middle Eastern cuisine. Use this chunky relish-like sauce to punch up grilled beef, fish, and vegetables. Sliced almonds provide a delicate crunch; do not substitute slivered or whole almonds.

- 5 tablespoons extra-virgin olive oil, divided
- ¼ cup sliced almonds, chopped
- ½ cup minced fresh parsley
- 2 tablespoons finely chopped preserved lemon plus 2 tablespoons brine
- 2 tablespoons lemon juice
- ¼ teaspoon sugar

Combine 1 tablespoon oil and almonds in 8-inch skillet; toast over medium-high heat, stirring constantly, until almonds are golden brown, 1 to 2 minutes. Immediately transfer to bowl. Stir in parsley, preserved lemon and brine, lemon juice, sugar, and remaining ¼ cup oil. Let sit for 15 minutes for flavors to meld. Stir well before using. (Sauce can be refrigerated for up to 2 days.)

Caper-Currant Relish

MAKES about ½ cup **TIME** 15 minutes plus 20 minutes resting

We balance sweet currants, salty capers, fresh parsley, and savory garlic in this relish that's perfect for seafood such as scallops and swordfish, as well as poultry. Golden raisins can be substituted for the currants.

- 3 tablespoons minced fresh parsley
- 3 tablespoons extra-virgin olive oil
- 2 tablespoons capers, rinsed and chopped fine
- 2 tablespoons currants, chopped fine
- 1 garlic clove, minced
- 1 teaspoon grated lemon zest plus 2 tablespoons juice

Combine all ingredients in bowl; let sit for 20 minutes for flavors to meld. (Relish can be refrigerated for up to 2 days.)

KIMCHI-SCALLION SAUCE
PRESERVED LEMON–ALMOND SAUCE

Kimchi-Scallion Sauce

MAKES about 1 cup **TIME** 22 minutes

The craveable fermented tang of kimchi is the foundation for this quick, saucy relish. We chop the kimchi fine and then stir in savory soy sauce, sliced scallions, and bright rice vinegar and give the flavors 15 minutes to meld before serving. Cider vinegar or seasoned rice vinegar can be substituted for the unseasoned rice vinegar. Serve this with rich beef short ribs or salmon fillets.

- 6 scallions, sliced thin
- ⅓ cup finely chopped kimchi
- ¼ cup vegetable oil
- 4 teaspoons soy sauce
- 4 teaspoons unseasoned rice vinegar
- ¼ teaspoon sugar

Stir all ingredients together in bowl; let sit for 15 minutes for flavors to meld. Stir well before using. (Sauce can be refrigerated for up to 2 days.)

Scallion-Ginger Relish

MAKES about ⅔ cup **TIME** 10 minutes plus 30 minutes cooling and resting

Ginger, white pepper, and lime juice give this sauce a nice punch that highlights the grassy, mildly pungent flavor of fresh scallions. Neutral vegetable oil allows the flavors to shine through, and a dash of soy sauce rounds it out. This sauce tastes great on pork, chicken, and seafood.

- 6 scallions, white and green parts separated and sliced thin
- 2 teaspoons grated fresh ginger
- ½ teaspoon ground white pepper
- ½ teaspoon grated lime zest plus 2 teaspoons juice
- ¼ cup vegetable oil
- 2 teaspoons soy sauce

Combine scallion whites, ginger, pepper, and lime zest in heatproof bowl. Heat oil in small saucepan over medium heat until shimmering. Pour oil over scallion mixture. (Mixture will bubble.) Stir until well combined. Let cool completely, about 15 minutes. Stir in scallion greens, lime juice, and soy sauce. Let sit for 15 minutes for flavors to meld. (Relish can be refrigerated for up to 2 days.)

SPICED GREEN-TOMATO CHUTNEY

Chutneys

Made with fresh, frozen, or dried fruit, chutneys are cooked until they're thick, with a potent flavor that combines sweetness with acidity. Because pork has an affinity with fruit, a spoonful of any of these chutneys would taste great alongside grilled pork tenderloin or chops. They also pair well with the rich taste of grilled salmon.

Mango Chutney

MAKES about 1 cup **TIME** 35 minutes plus 30 minutes cooling

For a well-rounded chutney that highlights the luscious, rich flavor of mango, we start by blooming spices in oil. Some white wine vinegar in the infusing medium provides the pucker, and brown sugar and dried currants balance it out with sweetness. A little shallot brings some fresh allium flavor and savor; to moderate its raw bite, we soak the shallot in water while the chutney simmers and then drain and add it off the heat. A finishing sprinkle of mint brings all the flavors alive.

- 1 shallot, minced
- 3 tablespoons vegetable oil, divided
- 1 teaspoon grated fresh ginger
- ½ teaspoon ground coriander
- ¼ teaspoon dry mustard
- ¼ teaspoon ground turmeric
- ⅛ teaspoon cayenne pepper
- 1 ripe but firm mango, peeled, pitted, and cut into ½-inch pieces (1½ cups)
- 2 tablespoons white wine vinegar
- 1 tablespoon dried currants
- 1 tablespoon packed light brown sugar
- ½ teaspoon kosher salt
- 2 tablespoons coarsely chopped mint

Combine shallot and 2 cups water in bowl; set aside. Heat 1 tablespoon oil in small saucepan over medium heat until shimmering. Add ginger, coriander, mustard, turmeric, and cayenne and cook until fragrant, about 30 seconds. Stir in mango, ¼ cup water, vinegar, currants, sugar, and salt. Bring to simmer and cook, stirring occasionally, until mixture is thickened and reduced to about 1 cup, 10 to 15 minutes. Drain shallot and stir into chutney. Transfer to bowl and let cool for 30 minutes. Stir in mint and season with salt and pepper to taste. (Chutney can be refrigerated for up to 3 days.)

Spiced Green-Tomato Chutney

MAKES about 2 cups **TIME** 1 hour plus 2 hours cooling

Green tomatoes make the base of a flavor-packed chutney that gets sweet tartness from equal amounts of sugar and white vinegar. This chutney makes a wonderful counterpoint to rich meats such as pork shoulder.

- 2 pounds green tomatoes, cored and cut into 1-inch chunks
- ¾ cup sugar
- ¾ cup distilled white vinegar
- 2 teaspoons kosher salt
- 1 teaspoon coriander seeds
- ½ teaspoon red pepper flakes
- 2 teaspoons lemon juice

Bring tomatoes, sugar, vinegar, salt, coriander seeds, and pepper flakes to simmer in medium saucepan. Cook until thickened, about 40 minutes. Let cool to room temperature, about 2 hours. Stir in lemon juice just before serving. (Chutney can be refrigerated for up to 3 days.)

Peach and Double-Mustard Chutney

MAKES about 2½ cups **TIME** 40 minutes

Using frozen fruit makes for an easy-prep chutney. We combine frozen peaches with two types of mustard—Dijon and whole-grain mustard—along with sugar, vinegar, shallot, and a bit of salt, for flavors that pop. We cook the mixture until a spatula dragged across the pot bottom leaves a trail that gradually fills in; this ensures that once the chutney cools, it is just the right thickness. There's no need to thaw the peaches before using. We like the combination of Dijon, which provides heat, and whole-grain mustard, which adds texture, but you can use just one type of mustard, if desired.

- 10 ounces frozen peaches, cut into ½-inch pieces (about 2½ cups)
- ¼ cup sugar
- ¼ cup cider vinegar
- 1 shallot, minced
- 1 tablespoon Dijon mustard
- 1 tablespoon whole-grain mustard
- 1 teaspoon kosher salt

Combine all ingredients in medium saucepan. Cover and bring to boil over high heat. Adjust heat to rapid simmer and cook, uncovered, until thickened and spatula drawn across bottom of saucepan leaves trail that slowly fills in, 8 to 10 minutes (mixture will thicken as it cools; do not overreduce). Let cool for 15 minutes. (Chutney can be refrigerated for up to 3 days.)

Blueberry-Ginger Chutney

MAKES about 2 cups **TIME** 40 minutes

Blueberries, sugar, vinegar, grated fresh ginger, and a bit of salt and pepper make a chutney with a complex backbone, a punch of brightness, and subtle warmth. We cook the mixture, gently pressing on the blueberries to make sure they burst, until thickened enough that a spatula drawn across the bottom of the pot leaves a trail that slowly fills in; once cooled, the chutney is perfectly spoonable. If using frozen blueberries, there's no need to thaw them before cooking.

- 10 ounces (2 cups) fresh or frozen blueberries
- ¼ cup sugar
- ¼ cup white wine vinegar
- 1 tablespoon grated fresh ginger
- 1 teaspoon kosher salt
- ½ teaspoon pepper

Combine all ingredients in medium saucepan. Cover and bring to boil over high heat. Adjust heat to rapid simmer and cook, uncovered, gently pressing blueberries occasionally with spatula to make sure they've burst, until thickened and spatula drawn across bottom of saucepan leaves trail that slowly fills in, 8 to 10 minutes (mixture will thicken as it cools; do not overreduce). Let cool for 15 minutes. (Chutney can be refrigerated for up to 3 days.)

Burst Cherry Tomato and Jalapeño Chutney

MAKES about 2½ cups **TIME** 40 minutes

A shot of fish sauce gives an umami backbone to this bright tomato chutney. We simmer all the ingredients together, pressing on the tomatoes as the mixture cooks to ensure that they burst and help thicken the chutney. Since the chutney thickens as it cools, we take it off the heat when it is just shy of a spoonable texture. Be sure to use cherry tomatoes; grape tomatoes won't break down as much and will produce a drier sauce. For a spicier salsa, add some or all of the jalapeño seeds and ribs.

- 12 ounces cherry tomatoes
- ¼ cup sugar
- ¼ cup red wine vinegar
- 1 tablespoon fish sauce
- 3 garlic cloves, minced
- 1 jalapeño chile, stemmed, seeded, and minced

Combine all ingredients in medium saucepan. Cover and bring to boil over high heat. Adjust heat to rapid simmer and cook, uncovered, gently pressing tomatoes occasionally with spatula to make sure they've burst, until thickened and spatula drawn across bottom of saucepan leaves trail that slowly fills in, 8 to 10 minutes (mixture will thicken as it cools; do not overreduce). Let cool for 15 minutes. (Chutney can be refrigerated for up to 3 days.)

Spice Rubs

Spice rubs season steaks and roasts before grilling and help the meat develop a delicious browned crust while on the grill. In some regional barbecue traditions, such as Texas barbecue, spice-rubbed ribs and brisket are served on their own—no sauce needed. But even if you plan to use sauce, applying a spice rub first lays down the foundation for deep barbecue flavor. All of these rubs can be stored in an airtight container for up to three months.

Barbecue Spice Rub

MAKES about 1 cup **TIME** 10 minutes

You can adjust the proportions of spices in this all-purpose rub or add or subtract a spice, as you wish. This recipe was developed using Diamond Crystal kosher salt. If you have Morton kosher salt, which is denser, use 3 tablespoons.

- ¼ cup paprika
- ¼ cup kosher salt
- 2 tablespoons chili powder
- 2 tablespoons ground cumin
- 2 tablespoons packed dark brown sugar
- 1 tablespoon dried oregano
- 1 tablespoon granulated sugar
- 1 tablespoon pepper
- 1 tablespoon white pepper
- 1–2 teaspoons cayenne pepper

Combine all ingredients in small bowl.

Tex-Mex Spice Rub

MAKES about 1 cup **TIME** 10 minutes

This cumin-based rub has an aromatic flavor with just a hint of cocoa, making it perfect for beef, pork, or poultry. This recipe was developed using Diamond Crystal kosher salt. If you have Morton kosher salt, which is denser, use 1 tablespoon.

- ¼ cup ground cumin
- 2 tablespoons chili powder
- 2 tablespoons ground coriander
- 2 tablespoons dried oregano
- 2 tablespoons garlic powder
- 4 teaspoons kosher salt
- 2 teaspoons unsweetened cocoa powder
- 1 teaspoon cayenne pepper

Combine all ingredients in small bowl.

CLASSIC STEAK RUB

Classic Steak Rub

MAKES about ⅓ cup **TIME** 5 minutes

This earthy, herbal rub is a popular steakhouse seasoning that works well on beef, lamb, and pork.

- 2 tablespoons peppercorns
- 3 tablespoons coriander seeds
- 4 teaspoons dried dill
- 2 teaspoons red pepper flakes

Process peppercorns and coriander seeds in spice grinder until finely ground, about 30 seconds; transfer to small bowl. Stir in dill and pepper flakes.

Cajun Spice Rub

MAKES about 1 cup **TIME** 10 minutes

This brightly colored paprika-based spice rub tastes great on pork and poultry. This recipe was developed using Diamond Crystal kosher salt. If you have Morton kosher salt, which is denser, use 1½ tablespoons.

- ½ cup paprika
- 2 tablespoons kosher salt
- 2 tablespoons garlic powder
- 1 tablespoon dried thyme
- 2 teaspoons ground celery seeds
- 2 teaspoons pepper
- 2 teaspoons cayenne pepper

Combine all ingredients in small bowl.

Curry-Cumin Spice Rub

MAKES about ½ cup **TIME** 10 minutes

This fragrant, yellow-tinged rub works well with lamb, pork, chicken, and seafood.

- 2 tablespoons ground cumin
- 2 tablespoons curry powder
- 2 tablespoons chili powder
- 1 tablespoon ground allspice
- 1 tablespoon pepper
- 1 teaspoon ground cinnamon

Combine all ingredients in small bowl.

Jamaican Jerk Spice Rub

MAKES about 1 cup **TIME** 10 minutes

This classic spice rub works well on pork, chicken, and seafood. This recipe was developed using Diamond Crystal kosher salt. If you have Morton kosher salt, which is denser, use 2 tablespoons.

- ¼ cup packed brown sugar
- 3 tablespoons kosher salt
- 3 tablespoons ground coriander
- 2 tablespoons ground ginger
- 2 tablespoons garlic powder
- 1 tablespoon ground allspice
- 1 tablespoon pepper
- 2 teaspoons cayenne pepper
- 2 teaspoons ground nutmeg
- 1½ teaspoons ground cinnamon

Combine all ingredients in bowl.

Herb Spice Rub

MAKES about 1 cup **TIME** 10 minutes

This mild aromatic rub is given depth with a dash of ground cloves (or allspice) and works well with lamb, pork, or chicken.

- ¼ cup dried thyme
- ¼ cup dried rosemary
- ¼ cup pepper
- 12 bay leaves, ground in a spice grinder or finely crumbled
- 1 teaspoon ground cloves or ground allspice

Combine all ingredients in small bowl.

Herbes de Provence

MAKES about 6 tablespoons **TIME** 5 minutes

This classic aromatic blend of dried herbs from southern France lends a balanced, herby flavor to grilled poultry, pork, tomatoes, or potatoes.

- 2 tablespoons dried thyme
- 2 tablespoons dried marjoram
- 2 tablespoons dried rosemary
- 2 teaspoons fennel seeds

Combine all ingredients in small bowl.

Flavored Salts

Store-bought flavored finishing salts (which are used as a final flourish for a dish, providing pops of crunchy, mineral salinity) are great but expensive. The good news is that these salts are supereasy to make. Some flavored salts can be made by simply stirring ingredients together, while others require being heated up to infuse the salt with flavor. Flavoring salt with fresh herbs takes a bit more time in order for the salt to draw moisture out of the herbs via osmosis. All of these flavored salts can be stored in an airtight container for up to two months.

Fresh Herb Salt

MAKES about ½ cup **TIME** 10 minutes plus 36 hours drying

This technique works well with most herbs. If you try it with an herb that isn't in the list below, just remember to use less if the herb is potent and more if the herb is mild. This aromatic and colorful salt tastes good on nearly everything, from vegetables such as grilled zucchini or corn to beef. Try it on our Ultimate Charcoal-Grill Steaks (page 50).

- ½ cup coarse or flake sea salt
- 1 cup thinly sliced fresh chives, dill, or tarragon; or 1½ cups finely chopped fresh basil; or ¼ cup finely chopped fresh makrut lime leaves.

1 Line rimmed baking sheet with parchment paper. Combine salt and herbs in large bowl. Pick up handful of salt mixture and rub between your hands to disperse herbs throughout salt. Repeat until thoroughly combined, about 30 seconds. Transfer mixture to prepared sheet and spread into even layer.

2 Place sheet in 50- to 70-degree location away from direct sunlight. Let mixture sit until completely dry, 36 to 48 hours, raking mixture with fork every 12 hours to ensure herb dries evenly.

3 Rub mixture between your hands to break up any clumps of dried herbs and evenly distribute herbs throughout salt. Transfer to airtight container.

Cumin-Sesame Salt

MAKES about 6 tablespoons **TIME** 20 minutes

This mild and fragrant salt tastes great on grilled chicken, seafood, pork, and lamb as well as on grilled vegetables such as carrots, cauliflower, and mushrooms. This recipe was developed using Diamond Crystal kosher salt. If you have Morton kosher salt, which is denser, use 1½ tablespoons.

- 2 tablespoons cumin seeds
- 2 tablespoons sesame seeds
- 2 tablespoons kosher salt

Toast cumin seeds and sesame seeds in 8-inch skillet over medium heat, stirring occasionally, until fragrant and sesame seeds are golden brown, 3 to 4 minutes. Transfer to spice grinder and let cool for 10 minutes. Pulse seeds until coarsely ground, about 6 pulses. Transfer to bowl and stir in salt.

Chili-Lime Salt

MAKES about ½ cup **TIME** 25 minutes

This zesty flavored salt tastes great on vegetables, chicken, seafood, and tofu. This recipe was developed using Diamond Crystal kosher salt. If you have Morton kosher salt, which is denser, use 3 tablespoons.

- ¼ cup kosher salt
- 2 tablespoons plus 2 teaspoons chili powder
- 1½ teaspoons grated lime zest

Combine salt, chili powder, and lime zest in bowl, then spread onto large plate. Microwave, stirring occasionally, until zest no longer clumps, about 2 minutes. Let cool to room temperature, about 15 minutes.

Smoked Salt

MAKES about ½ cup **TIME** 15 minutes

This intensely flavored salt tastes great on lamb and beef, and you can sprinkle it on burgers or on grilled vegetables and fruit such as eggplant, asparagus, potatoes, and pineapple. This recipe was developed using Diamond Crystal kosher salt. If you have Morton kosher salt, which is denser, use 6 tablespoons.

- ½ cup kosher salt
- 1 teaspoon liquid smoke

Combine salt and liquid smoke in bowl, then spread onto large plate. Microwave, stirring occasionally, until only slightly damp, about 2 minutes. Let sit until completely dry and cool, about 10 minutes.

Sriracha Salt

MAKES about ½ cup **TIME** 20 minutes

This spicy salt tastes great on all kinds of meat; you can also use it to season guacamole or coat the rim of a margarita glass. This recipe was developed using Diamond Crystal kosher salt. If you have Morton kosher salt, which is denser, use 6 tablespoons.

- ½ cup kosher salt
- ⅓ cup sriracha

Combine salt and sriracha in bowl, then spread on large plate. Microwave, stirring occasionally, until only slightly damp, 6 to 8 minutes. Let sit until completely dry and cool, about 10 minutes.

Conversions + Equivalents

Some say cooking is a science and an art. We would say that geography has a hand in it too. Flours and sugars manufactured in the United Kingdom and elsewhere will feel and taste different from those manufactured in the United States. So we cannot promise that the loaf of bread you bake in Canada or England will taste the same as a loaf baked in the States, but we can offer guidelines for converting weights and measures. We also recommend that you rely on your instincts when making our recipes. Refer to the visual cues provided.

The recipes in this book were developed using standard U.S. measures following U.S. government guidelines. The charts below offer equivalents for U.S. and metric measures. All conversions are approximate and have been rounded up or down to the nearest whole number.

EXAMPLE

1 teaspoon = 4.9292 milliliters, rounded up to 5 milliliters
1 ounce = 28.3495 grams, rounded down to 28 grams

Volume Conversions

U.S.	METRIC
1 teaspoon	5 milliliters
2 teaspoons	10 milliliters
1 tablespoon	15 milliliters
2 tablespoons	30 milliliters
¼ cup	59 milliliters
⅓ cup	79 milliliters
½ cup	118 milliliters
¾ cup	177 milliliters
1 cup	237 milliliters
1¼ cups	296 milliliters
1½ cups	355 milliliters
2 cups (1 pint)	473 milliliters
2½ cups	591 milliliters
3 cups	710 milliliters
4 cups (1 quart)	0.946 liter
1.06 quarts	1 liter
4 quarts (1 gallon)	3.8 liters

Weight Conversions

OUNCES	GRAMS
½	14
¾	21
1	28
1½	43
2	57
2½	71
3	85
3½	99
4	113
4½	128
5	142
6	170
7	198
8	227
9	255
10	283
12	340
16 (1 pound)	454

Conversions for Common Baking Ingredients

Because measuring by weight is far more accurate than measuring by volume, and thus more likely to achieve reliable results, in our recipes we provide ounce measures in addition to cup measures for many ingredients. Refer to the chart below to convert these measures into grams.

INGREDIENT	OUNCES	GRAMS
Flour		
1 cup all-purpose flour*	5	142
1 cup cake flour	4	113
1 cup whole-wheat flour	5½	156
Sugar		
1 cup granulated (white) sugar	7	198
1 cup packed brown sugar (light or dark)	7	198
1 cup confectioners' sugar	4	113
Cocoa Powder		
1 cup cocoa powder	3	85
Butter †		
4 tablespoons (½ stick, or ¼ cup)	2	57
8 tablespoons (1 stick, or ½ cup)	4	113
16 tablespoons (2 sticks, or 1 cup)	8	227

* U.S. all-purpose flour, the most frequently used flour in this book, does not contain leaveners, as some European flours do. These leavened flours are called self-rising or self-raising. If you are using self-rising flour, take this into consideration before adding leavening to a recipe.

† In the United States, butter is sold both salted and unsalted. We generally recommend unsalted butter. If you are using salted butter, take this into consideration before adding salt to a recipe.

Oven Temperature

FAHRENHEIT	CELSIUS	GAS MARK
225	105	¼
250	120	½
275	135	1
300	150	2
325	165	3
350	180	4
375	190	5
400	200	6
425	220	7
450	230	8
475	245	9

Converting Temperatures from an Instant-Read Thermometer

We include doneness temperatures in many of the recipes in this book. We recommend an instant-read thermometer for the job. Refer to the table above to convert Fahrenheit degrees to Celsius. Or, for temperatures not represented in the chart, use this simple formula:

Subtract 32 degrees from the Fahrenheit reading, then divide the result by 1.8 to find the Celsius reading.

EXAMPLE

"Roast chicken until thighs register 175 degrees."

TO CONVERT

175°F – 32 = 143°

143° ÷ 1.8 = 79.44°C, rounded down to 79°C

Nutritional Information for Our Recipes

We calculate the nutritional values of our recipes per serving; if there is a range in the serving size, we used the highest number of servings to calculate the nutritional values. We entered all the ingredients, using weights for important ingredients such as meat, cheese, and most vegetables. We also used our preferred brands in these analyses. We did not include additional salt or pepper for food that's "seasoned to taste."

1. Beef	CAL	TOTAL FAT (G)	SAT FAT (G)	CHOL (MG)	SODIUM (MG)	CARBS (G)	FIBER (G)	TOTAL SUGAR (G)	PROTEIN (G)
Char-Grilled Steaks	439	32	13	150	414	1	0	0	35
Grilled Sugar Steak	422	19	8	141	460	9	0	8	50
Grilled Porterhouse or T-Bone Steaks	470	27	9	190	700	1	0	0	53
with Garlic	470	27	9	190	700	1	0	0	53
Grilled Cowboy-Cut Rib Eyes	557	45	19	146	489	1	0	0	37
Grilled Flank Steak	211	10	4	84	291	2	0	2	26
Bacon-Wrapped Filet Mignon	718	54	20	190	594	13	0	13	43
Ultimate Charcoal-Grilled Steaks	467	23	9	169	529	0	0	0	60
Grilled Boneless Beef Short Ribs	364	29	12	110	353	0	0	0	26
Grilled Steakhouse Steak Tips	519	37	10	122	924	10	1	7	39
Grilled Beef Teriyaki	595	18	5	143	2515	36	1	28	53
Grilled Bourbon Steaks	687	47	19	148	702	9	0	4	40
Grilled Flank Steak with Garlic-Shallot-Rosemary Marinade	377	26	7	103	403	2	0	0	32
with Garlic-Ginger-Sesame Marinade	377	26	7	103	401	1	0	0	32
with Garlic-Chile Marinade	377	26	7	103	401	2	0	0	32
Grilled Marinated Skirt Steak	351	24	6	73	1418	10	1	7	25
Grilled Thai Curry Marinated Skirt	358	27	9	73	857	7	0	6	24
Grilled Hoisin-Scallion Marinated Skirt Steak	366	25	6	73	1413	12	1	9	25
Grilled Black Pepper-Honey Marinated Skirt Steak	354	24	6	73	1297	12	1	10	25

1. Beef (cont.)	CAL	TOTAL FAT (G)	SAT FAT (G)	CHOL (MG)	SODIUM (MG)	CARBS (G)	FIBER (G)	TOTAL SUGAR (G)	PROTEIN (G)
Grilled Shell Sirloin Steak with New Mexican Chile Rub	282	19	7	88	312	5	1	3	23
with Ancho Chile-Coffee Rub	281	19	7	88	290	5	1	2	23
with Spicy Chipotle Chile Rub	275	18	7	88	285	4	1	2	23
Grilled Spice-Rubbed Chuck Steaks	600	41	15	190	751	3	1	1	55
Kalbi (Korean Grilled Flanken-Style Short Ribs)	1382	124	54	259	595	11	0	8	50
Steak and Potato Salad with Grilled Lemon Dressing	981	73	24	153	1223	38	6	4	48
Grilled Strip Steaks and Zucchini with Olive Vinaigrette	682	53	17	167	1128	8	3	6	43
Grilled Strip Steak and Potatoes with Blue Cheese Butter	1233	83	35	332	1541	42	5	2	76
Beef Tenderloin with Pear, Grilled Onion, and Blue Cheese Salad	480	27	9	125	780	14	3	7	44
Grilled Steak and Kale Salad	717	54	15	143	836	10	5	4	48
Grilled Cumin-Rubbed Flank Steak with Mexican Street Corn	559	32	10	149	775	22	3	7	49
Flank Steak with Grilled Guacamole Salad	663	50	11	116	1007	19	9	5	40
Nam Tok (Grilled Thai Beef Salad)	237	10	4	77	556	11	3	4	26
Japanese Steakhouse Steak and Vegetables	734	56	25	171	1109	14	3	6	44
Beef Satay with Spicy Peanut Dipping Sauce	193	12	3	39	571	7	1	5	14
Beef Kebabs with Lemon-Rosemary Marinade	487	34	10	118	749	12	2	7	32
with Red Curry Marinade	330	16	3	55	1230	16	3	8	28
with North African Marinade	320	16	3	55	940	14	3	8	28
Shashlik-Style Beef Kebabs	470	34	10	121	572	8	1	5	32
Grilled Beef and Chorizo Skewers	410	31	10	100	1210	4	1	2	27
Grilled Flank Steak Pinwheels with Prosciutto and Provolone	430	25	10	142	741	2	0	0	46
with Spinach and Pine Nuts	370	22	7	105	600	3	1	1	39
with Sun-Dried Tomatoes and Capers	380	22	9	115	640	4	1	1	40
Tacos al Carbón	389	19	5	84	546	26	5	2	30
Grilled Skirt Steak Tacos with Roasted Poblanos	559	24	8	98	921	52	8	10	38
Mesquite-Grilled Tacos Rasurados	1259	89	34	201	1222	56	6	6	56
Grilled Steak Fajitas	821	48	10	98	1413	59	4	8	40
Grilled Steak Sandwiches	909	71	18	109	972	33	2	2	34
Grilled Free-Form Beef Wellington with Balsamic Reduction	669	46	16	213	652	21	2	7	40
Baltimore Pit Beef with Tiger Sauce	700	41	13	164	685	34	3	2	47
Grill-Roasted Top Sirloin with Garlic and Rosemary	442	30	11	150	476	1	0	0	39
with Shallot and Tarragon	442	30	11	150	476	1	0	0	39
California Barbecued Tri-Tip	305	19	6	101	367	2	0	0	31
Grill-Roasted Beef Tenderloin	420	21	7	160	680	1	0	0	20
Smoked Beef Tenderloin	380	22	6	125	500	2	1	0	41

2. Pork and Lamb

2. Pork and Lamb	CAL	TOTAL FAT (G)	SAT FAT (G)	CHOL (MG)	SODIUM (MG)	CARBS (G)	FIBER (G)	TOTAL SUGAR (G)	PROTEIN (G)
Easy Grilled Boneless Pork Chops	357	19	6	128	473	2	0	1	42
Grilled Thin-Cut Pork Chops	179	13	7	64	223	1	0	1	13
with Thyme and Ginger	409	26	11	158	402	1	0	0	41
Spicy Grilled Thin-Cut Pork Chops with Cilantro and Lime	409	26	11	158	402	1	0	1	41
Mediterranean Grilled Thin-Cut Pork Chops	410	26	11	158	411	1	0	1	41
Grilled Thick-Cut Bone-In Pork Chops	488	29	11	191	813	1	0	0	53
Grilled Lamb Shoulder Chops	610	50	22	145	160	0	0	0	39
Grilled Lamb Rib or Loin Chops	250	14	4	80	90	0	0	0	30
Rosticciana (Tuscan Grilled Pork Ribs)	1256	109	33	333	965	1	0	0	65
with Grilled Radicchio	570	50	13	105	720	7	1	1	23
Grilled Pork Cutlets	373	25	6	97	366	3	0	3	32
with Rosemary and Red Wine Vinegar	364	25	6	97	364	1	0	1	32
with Cilantro and Lime	364	25	6	97	363	2	0	1	32
Grilled Citrus-Marinated Pork Cutlets	240	14	3.5	85	230	4	3	1	24
Garlic-Lime Grilled Pork Tenderloin Steaks	280	15	2	95	450	6	0	4	31
Lemon-Thyme Grilled Pork Tenderloin Steaks	280	15	2	95	450	6	0	4	31
Spicy Orange-Ginger Grilled Pork Tenderloin Steaks	280	15	2	95	450	6	0	4	31
Grilled Hoisin-Glazed Pork Chops with Pineapple Salsa	449	22	6	104	868	30	3	20	33
Grill-Smoked Thick-Cut Pork Chops	696	31	10	235	985	30	1	25	71
Spice-Rubbed Pork Tenderloin with Grilled Tomato–Ginger Salsa	220	10	2	70	350	8	2	4	24
Orange-Glazed Pork Tenderloin Roast	350	4.5	1.5	140	700	32	0	28	46
Miso-Glazed Pork Tenderloin Roast	370	6	1.5	140	1360	25	0	20	47
Sweet and Spicy Hoisin-Glazed Pork Tenderloin Roast	330	7	2	140	1650	15	0	9	47
Smoked Bourbon Pork Tenderloin	260	5	2	93	1244	9	0	7	31
Barbecued Country-Style Ribs	360	10	3	110	720	35	2	30	33
St. Louis Barbecued Pork Steaks	547	29	10	147	629	23	1	17	42
Grilled Pork Cutlets and Zucchini with Feta and Mint	276	16	7	208	535	4	1	3	28
Molasses-Glazed Pork Chops and Sweet Potatoes with Red Cabbage Slaw	775	36	8	127	1192	63	8	32	51
Mojo Grilled Pork Chops with Black Bean and Orange Salad	600	33	6	75	810	36	10	9	38
Grilled Lamb Shoulder Chops with Zucchini and Corn Salad	1115	93	33	221	991	17	3	8	54
Grilled Pork Tenderloin with Broccolini and Hazelnut Browned Butter	640	45	17	205	740	7	5	1	54
Grilled Honey-Ginger Pork Tenderloin and Plums	447	25	13	186	697	17	1	15	45
Grilled Spice-Rubbed Pork Tenderloins with Charred Fingerling Potato Salad	620	29	3.5	140	960	40	6	8	50
Pork Tenderloin and Peach Kebabs with Brown Rice Salad	557	21	4	105	889	56	4	17	39
Pinchos Morunos (Spanish Grilled Pork Kebabs)	570	41	6	168	596	4	1	0	45
Grilled Pork Kebabs with Hoisin and Five-Spice	265	9	2	106	464	10	1	5	34
with Sweet Sriracha Glaze	259	8	2	105	442	11	0	10	33
with Barbecue Glaze	253	8	2	105	447	9	0	8	34

2. Pork and Lamb (cont.)	CAL	TOTAL FAT (G)	SAT FAT (G)	CHOL (MG)	SODIUM (MG)	CARBS (G)	FIBER (G)	TOTAL SUGAR (G)	PROTEIN (G)
Shish Kebab with Mint, Rosemary, and Garlic Marinade	550	41	13	112	522	11	3	6	33
with Sweet Curry-Buttermilk Marinade	414	24	11	113	581	15	4	9	35
with Cilantro, Raisin, and Garam Masala Marinade	568	41	13	112	524	16	3	10	33
with Parsley, Ginger, and Warm Spices Marinade	556	41	13	112	526	13	4	6	34
Grilled Pork Tacos with Tomatillo-Avocado Salsa	762	31	6	140	1106	66	8	8	55
Tacos al Pastor	545	29	8	105	990	39	6	9	34
Grilled Pork Banh Mi	570	34	6	90	1280	34	2	14	29
Grilled Rosemary Pork Loin	200	10	2	70	410	1	0	0	26
Grill-Roasted Bone-In Pork Rib Roast	350	21	4.5	110	660	0	0	0	38
Cuban-Style Grill-Roasted Pork	844	36	11	167	1232	77	1	69	52
Grilled Rack of Lamb with Garlic and Herbs	967	90	38	189	140	1	0	0	36
Grilled Butterflied Leg of Lamb	240	12	3	105	360	0	0	0	33
Grilled Bone-In Leg of Lamb with Charred-Scallion Sauce	648	50	17	160	791	3	1	0	44
Rotisserie Leg of Lamb with Cauliflower and Grape Salad	580	33	9	185	1660	14	3	8	57
for a Gas Grill	580	33	9	185	1660	12	3	8	57

3. Poultry	CAL	TOTAL FAT (G)	SAT FAT (G)	CHOL (MG)	SODIUM (MG)	CARBS (G)	FIBER (G)	TOTAL SUGAR (G)	PROTEIN (G)
Grilled Boneless, Skinless Chicken Breasts	306	9	1	145	1150	9	0	9	45
Grilled Bone-In Chicken Breasts	270	6	1	160	660	0	0	0	50
Grilled Chicken Wings	192	7	2	56	174	25	0	25	9
BBQ Wings	250	16	4.5	135	970	3	1	1	22
Creole Grilled Chicken Wings	240	16	4.5	135	940	2	0	0	22
Tandoori Grilled Chicken Wings	240	16	4.5	135	940	1	0	0	22
Smoked Chicken Parts	898	62	16	333	864	27	0	25	56
Grilled Honey Mustard–Glazed Boneless, Skinless Chicken Breasts	419	10	2	146	613	36	1	35	46
Grilled Coconut Curry–Glazed Boneless, Skinless Chicken Breasts	320	9	4.5	125	1250	20	0	17	40
Grilled Spicy Hoisin-Glazed Boneless, Skinless Chicken Breasts	310	5	1	125	1350	23	0	19	39
Grilled Miso Sesame–Glazed Boneless, Skinless Chicken Breasts	310	8	1.5	125	1280	17	0	14	40
Grilled Molasses Coffee–Glazed Boneless, Skinless Chicken Breasts	330	4.5	1	125	940	30	0	29	39
Grilled Citrus Chicken	507	31	3	145	731	12	2	7	46
Grilled Chicken Caprese	445	25	9	162	678	5	1	2	48
Monterey Chicken	605	30	13	202	906	22	2	19	61
Grilled Pesto Chicken	928	59	13	274	1053	4	1	0	91
Sweet and Tangy Barbecued Chicken	860	55	15	255	961	25	1	20	64
Barbecued Dry-Rubbed Chicken	515	35	10	170	545	6	1	5	43
Grilled Jerk Chicken	921	66	16	255	1122	15	2	8	66
Peri Peri Grilled Chicken	874	61	16	255	994	12	3	6	67
Thai-Style Grilled Chicken with Spicy Sweet-and-Sour Dipping Sauce	739	33	8	174	1082	52	2	43	59

3. Poultry (cont.)	CAL	TOTAL FAT (G)	SAT FAT (G)	CHOL (MG)	SODIUM (MG)	CARBS (G)	FIBER (G)	TOTAL SUGAR (G)	PROTEIN (G)
Grilled Chicken with Adobo and Sazón	584	44	11	164	738	3	0	0	41
Best Grilled Chicken Thighs with Mustard and Tarragon	363	27	7	156	561	3	1	0	27
with Gochujang	376	27	7	156	596	4	1	2	28
with Garam Masala	420	34	8	156	556	2	0	0	26
Grilled Mojo Chicken	573	45	11	192	757	6	1	2	35
Grilled Chicken Cobb Salad	811	56	13	322	1364	16	10	4	62
Grilled Spiced Chicken and Carrots with Bulgur	854	49	10	170	1022	49	10	6	58
Grilled Chicken Panzanella	559	29	7	95	1076	38	3	10	35
Grilled Chicken and Pita Salad	591	30	5	145	1368	31	7	11	51
Grilled Chicken and Cabbage with Lemony Browned Butter Dressing	614	41	16	206	963	14	6	5	49
Grilled Chicken, Shishitos, and Tomatoes with Miso-Garlic Butter	544	22	9	175	835	43	15	5	52
Grilled Garam Masala Chicken with Radicchio and Naan	894	57	16	261	1163	24	2	3	69
Grilled Chicken Thighs with Mango Slaw	520	29	5	132	1063	36	4	30	29
Go-To Grilled Chicken Kebabs	263	13	2	142	702	4	1	3	31
with Harissa, Aleppo Pepper, and Mint	250	13	2	140	340	1	0	1	30
with Red Curry Paste and Lime	250	13	2	140	390	1	0	1	30
Barbecued Chicken Kebabs	317	10	3	149	536	24	1	20	32
Grilled Chicken Souvlaki with Green Peppers and Onion	567	26	5	131	910	37	5	7	48
Grilled Chicken Satay	385	22	3	142	589	14	2	7	33
Grilled Chicken Tacos with Salsa Verde	384	10	2	124	797	31	5	5	42
Grilled Chicken Fajitas with Cilantro-Lime Sour Cream	753	33	7	134	1042	69	5	8	46
Grilled Chicken Nachos with Corn, Poblanos, and Black Beans	508	20	5	86	876	48	6	7	33
Grilled Chicken and Vegetable Quesadillas	320	22	7	35	570	21	1	2	12
Grilled Chicken Sandwiches with Red Curry Slaw	827	45	7	160	1696	51	3	18	52
Chicken Spiedies	516	29	4	86	496	31	1	1	31
Easy Grill-Roasted Whole Chicken	695	50	14	231	1064	0	0	0	57
Grill-Roasted Butterflied Chicken	680	47	13	231	1066	4	0	3	48
with Barbecue Spice Rub	720	46	13	225	1469	17	2	13	57
with Ras el Hanout Spice Rub	700	46	13	225	1050	11	4	6	57
Grilled Wine-and-Herb-Marinated Chicken	886	57	15	231	1410	12	1	8	58
Thai Grilled Cornish Hens with Chili Dipping Sauce	946	54	15	384	1697	45	1	39	67
Barbecue-Glazed Cornish Hens	810	49	14	350	1710	27	2	22	61
Hoisin and Ginger–Glazed Cornish Hens	820	53	14	350	1760	23	2	15	61
Smoked Turkey Breast	309	5	1	122	2632	16	2	13	48
Simple Grill-Roasted Turkey	517	21	5	251	1150	2	0	0	76

4. Burgers, Sausage, and Ground Meat	CAL	TOTAL FAT (G)	SAT FAT (G)	CHOL (MG)	SODIUM (MG)	CARBS (G)	FIBER (G)	TOTAL SUGAR (G)	PROTEIN (G)
Classic Beef Burgers	613	38	16	144	567	23	1	3	42
Grilled Well-Done Burgers	677	43	18	140	688	29	1	4	40
Smashed Burgers	619	43	15	104	710	27	1	5	30
Grind-Your-Own Sirloin Burgers	835	56	26	235	732	23	1	3	56
for the Freezer	835	56	26	235	732	23	1	3	56
Grind-Your-Own Ultimate Beef Burgers	726	46	19	187	699	23	1	3	55
for the Freezer	726	46	19	187	699	23	1	3	55
Grilled New Mexican Green Chile Cheeseburgers	467	31	13	129	624	9	2	4	37
Grilled Jucy Lucy Burgers	436	28	11	121	480	9	1	2	35
Grilled Bayou Burgers with Spicy Mayonnaise	870	67	22	148	1333	28	2	5	38
Grilled Teriyaki Pork Burgers	904	54	16	129	1700	64	3	25	38
Bún Chả	403	17	6	54	1641	45	3	10	18
Grilled Harissa Lamb Burgers	724	53	19	128	631	26	2	5	33
Grilled Lamb Kofte	470	39	13	88	469	8	2	3	24
Grilled Adana-Style Kebabs	534	37	13	83	656	28	4	4	23
Grilled Arayes with Parsley-Cucumber Salad	940	72	25	135	1390	36	5	6	39
Classic Turkey Burgers	564	32	13	161	599	24	1	4	44
Grilled Turkey Burgers with Spinach and Feta	438	22	9	130	527	24	1	3	35
with Miso and Ginger	340	9	6	70	530	26	0	5	40
with Herbs and Goat Cheese	390	14	9	80	400	24	0	4	44
Grind-Your-Own Turkey Burgers	586	32	10	149	789	25	1	4	47
for the Freezer	586	32	10	149	789	25	1	4	47
Grilled Southern Shrimp Burgers	268	12	2	279	468	4	1	1	35
Grilled Salmon Burgers	370	27	5	81	382	1	0	0	29
Chili Cheese Dogs	997	61	26	160	2053	58	4	11	53
Grilled Beer Brats and Onions	339	14	3	18	682	39	3	4	11
Grilled Sausages with Bell Peppers and Onions	630	20	6	45	1486	75	5	10	37
Grilled Sausages and Polenta with Arugula Salad	400	25	6	35	1030	23	1	2	23

5. Barbecue	CAL	TOTAL FAT (G)	SAT FAT (G)	CHOL (MG)	SODIUM (MG)	CARBS (G)	FIBER (G)	TOTAL SUGAR (G)	PROTEIN (G)
Lexington-Style Pulled Pork	325	19	7	96	627	8	1	6	27
South Carolina Pulled Pork	450	26	9	120	706	19	1	16	35
Kalua Pork	369	24	8	120	612	2	0	2	34
Tennessee Pulled Pork Sandwiches	190	7	2.5	70	610	9	0	7	22
Hoecakes	310	5	2	50	710	55	1	6	8
North Carolina Barbecue Pork	389	26	9	128	637	1	0	0	36
South Carolina Smoked Fresh Ham	420	17	6	160	990	10	0	9	52
Barbecued Baby Back Ribs	320	17	6	110	920	5	2	2	36
Chicago-Style Barbecued Baby Back Ribs	390	16	5	100	980	31	1	26	32
Honey-Mustard Barbecued Baby Back Ribs	540	28	13	115	1370	41	1	35	25
South Dakota Corncob-Smoked Baby Back Ribs	360	15	5	100	790	24	1	18	32
Barbecued Pork Spareribs	1140	90	29	300	510	21	2	17	60
Memphis-Style Barbecued Spareribs	780	62	20	210	1410	10	1	7	42
Kansas City–Style Barbecued Spareribs	400	19	7	125	870	19	0	17	40
Blood Bros.–Inspired Gochujang-Glazed Spareribs	460	25	7	125	1410	19	1	14	42
Chinese-Style Barbecued Spareribs	1060	68	21	215	2580	62	0	51	47
Texas Smoked Sausages	1150	67	23	174	2197	83	3	6	49
Shredded Barbecued Beef	509	27	12	152	791	22	1	18	44
Texas-Style Smoked Beef Ribs	670	25	10	321	1193	2	1	0	110
Barbecued Flat-Cut Brisket	740	55	22	235	612	13	0	12	45
Texas-Style Barbecued Whole Brisket	670	45	17	215	1220	1	1	0	62
Kansas City Barbecued Brisket	748	56	22	235	721	15	1	12	45
Barbecued Burnt Ends	796	55	22	235	690	28	0	25	45
Barbecued Pulled Chicken	878	57	15	320	873	32	2	24	58
with Peach Sauce	902	57	15	320	876	38	1	26	58
for a Crowd	520	16	3.5	290	1170	26	1	21	61
Smoked Barbecued Chicken Wings	390	28	11	190	1780	7	1	5	26
Barbecued Chicken Thighs	781	51	14	297	893	27	1	19	51
Alabama Barbecued Chicken	380	28	6	90	490	3	0	3	26
Pollo a la Brasa (Peruvian Rotisserie Chicken)	820	63	16	235	1140	4	1	1	57
Beer Can Chicken	600	37	10	173	794	16	6	2	46
Peruvian Garlic-Lime Chicken	590	40	11	195	1780	4	1	0	50
Smoked Prime Rib with Horseradish Sauce	967	88	34	183	743	2	1	1	40
Barbecued Glazed Pork Roast	540	23	4.5	115	1370	41	0	35	41
Holiday Smoked Turkey	542	20	5	251	1275	9	1	6	76

6. Seafood	CAL	TOTAL FAT (G)	SAT FAT (G)	CHOL (MG)	SODIUM (MG)	CARBS (G)	FIBER (G)	TOTAL SUGAR (G)	PROTEIN (G)
Gambas a la Plancha	150	6	1	190	320	2	0	0	21
Grilled Chipotle Shrimp	309	13	2	371	606	4	1	1	46
Spicy Grilled Jalapeño-Lime Shrimp Skewers	222	12	2	214	965	4	0	1	24
Grilled Caribbean Shrimp Skewers	210	9	1.5	215	1240	6	0	3	23
Grilled Red Chile–Ginger Shrimp Skewers	180	5	1	215	1430	7	1	3	25
Grilled Shrimp Skewers with Chili Crisp and Napa Cabbage Slaw	420	29	3.5	215	400	11	4	3	28
Grilled Shrimp Tacos with Jicama Slaw	466	18	5	266	833	44	10	4	36
Grilled Shrimp, Corn, and Avocado Salad	540	33	4.5	285	930	29	8	7	37
Grilled Shrimp Boil Foil Packs	739	47	24	383	903	37	4	6	46
Grilled Clams, Mussels, or Oysters with Soy-Citrus Sauce	70	0.5	0	15	1580	3	0	0	11
Grilled Scallops with Chile-Lime Vinaigrette	470	36	4.5	40	1150	19	0	10	21
with Basil Vinaigrette	850	83	11	40	1370	12	0	3	21
with Barbecue Sauce Vinaigrette	470	36	4.5	40	1260	17	0	8	21
Grilled Bacon-Wrapped Scallops	597	42	17	138	1596	12	1	1	42
Grilled Lobsters	520	37	22	345	1450	9	0	0	35
with Tarragon-Chive Butter	520	37	22	345	1430	9	0	0	35
Grilled Lobster Tails	299	19	11	235	645	6	0	0	26
Paella on the Grill	813	31	8	205	1350	76	4	5	53
Perfect Grilled Salmon	517	38	8	115	505	1	0	1	41
Grilled Honey Mustard–Glazed Salmon	640	30	7	125	2090	35	0	32	50
Grilled Maple Soy–Glazed Salmon	646	35	7	125	1745	33	1	28	49
Grilled Salmon Caesar Salad	1096	76	15	133	1121	45	4	6	57
Grilled Salmon with Charred Red Cabbage Slaw	540	37	7	95	720	16	4	8	37
Smoked Salmon Tacos	927	43	8	91	1070	95	4	44	40
Wood-Grilled Salmon Fillets	860	56	13	218	525	2	0	2	81
Barbecued Wood-Grilled Salmon Fillets	847	53	12	218	583	6	0	5	81
Lemon-Thyme Wood-Grilled Salmon Fillets	425	27	6	109	486	2	0	2	41
Grill-Smoked Side of Salmon	468	30	6	104	471	9	0	8	39
Grilled Swordfish Steaks	417	25	5	150	556	1	0	0	45
Grilled Swordfish Salmoriglio	499	33	6	150	648	4	1	1	45
Grilled Swordfish Tacos with Grilled Pineapple Slaw	610	25	3.5	100	630	63	6	19	35
Grilled Swordfish Skewers with Caponata	310	18	3	75	684	15	4	9	24
Grilled Swordfish and Pineapple Skewers with Couscous	896	45	7	112	1392	82	8	28	45
Grilled Tuna Steaks with Red Wine Vinegar–Mustard Vinaigrette	533	32	4	88	639	3	1	2	56
with Chermoula Vinaigrette	520	29	4.5	90	220	3	0	2	56
with Provençal Vinaigrette	546	33	5	90	661	4	1	2	56
with Soy-Ginger Vinaigrette	561	35	5	88	600	4	1	2	56
Grilled Tuna Steaks with Cucumber-Mint Farro Salad	610	28	5	45	820	53	6	6	38

6. Seafood (cont.)	CAL	TOTAL FAT (G)	SAT FAT (G)	CHOL (MG)	SODIUM (MG)	CARBS (G)	FIBER (G)	TOTAL SUGAR (G)	PROTEIN (G)
Grilled Blackened Red Snapper Fillets	322	15	6	96	509	4	2	0	42
Grilled Red Curry Mahi-Mahi with Pineapple Salsa	277	9	1	145	196	12	1	8	37
Grilled Cod and Summer Squash Packets	438	29	4	73	1036	14	4	7	34
Grilled Halibut with Spicy Orange and Fennel Salad	430	30	4.5	85	750	9	2	6	33
Grilled Whole Trout with Marjoram and Lemon	496	25	5	187	752	2	0	1	62
with Lime and Coriander	497	25	5	187	753	2	1	1	62
with Orange and Fennel	496	25	5	187	753	2	0	1	62
Grilled Stuffed Trout	420	24	7	120	850	7	3	4	41
Grilled Whole Red Snapper	473	19	3	126	218	0	0	0	70

7. Vegetables and Vegetarian Mains	CAL	TOTAL FAT (G)	SAT FAT (G)	CHOL (MG)	SODIUM (MG)	CARBS (G)	FIBER (G)	TOTAL SUGAR (G)	PROTEIN (G)
Grilled Artichokes with Lemon Butter	184	16	8	31	507	10	5	1	3
Grilled Asparagus	70	6	3.5	15	95	4	2	2	3
with Chili-Lime Butter	70	6	3.5	15	100	5	2	2	3
with Cumin Butter	70	6	3.5	15	95	5	2	2	3
with Garlic Butter	70	6	3.5	15	95	5	2	2	3
with Orange-Thyme Butter	70	6	3.5	15	95	4	2	2	3
Grill-Roasted Bell Peppers with Sherry Vinaigrette	190	15	2	0	300	12	4	7	2
with Rosemary	190	15	2	0	300	12	4	7	2
Grilled Broccoli with Lemon and Parmesan	241	17	4	6	640	18	7	4	10
with Sweet Chili Sauce	250	19	3	0	598	18	6	7	7
Grilled Butternut Squash	120	7	1	0	190	15	3	3	1
Spicy Grilled Butternut Squash with Garlic and Rosemary	140	7	1	0	190	20	3	7	1
Grilled Cabbage	252	21	3	0	600	18	6	10	3
Grilled Carrots with Feta-Herb Sauce	382	26	8	35	761	30	8	14	10
Grill-Roasted Whole Cauliflower with Tahini-Yogurt Sauce	315	22	4	2	529	27	5	16	8
Grilled Corn with Basil and Lemon Butter	250	17	8	30	390	23	3	4	4
with Honey Butter	270	17	8	30	390	29	3	10	4
with Chipotle-Cilantro Butter	250	17	8	30	400	23	3	4	4
with New Orleans "Barbecue" Butter	250	17	8	30	240	24	3	4	4
with Spicy Old Bay Butter	250	17	8	30	340	23	3	4	4
Elote	249	14	3	11	277	29	3	10	7
Grilled Eggplant with Yogurt Sauce	133	11	2	2	336	9	4	5	2
Baba Ghanoush	246	22	3	0	476	12	6	5	4
Grilled White Mushrooms	112	9	3	10	394	6	2	3	5
Grilled Marinated Portobello Mushrooms	140	14	2	0	75	3	1	1	1
with Tarragon	140	14	2	0	75	2	1	1	1
Grilled Plantains	170	7	1	0	280	29	2	13	1

7. Vegetables and Vegetarian Mains (cont.)	CAL	TOTAL FAT (G)	SAT FAT (G)	CHOL (MG)	SODIUM (MG)	CARBS (G)	FIBER (G)	TOTAL SUGAR (G)	PROTEIN (G)
Grilled Potatoes with Garlic and Rosemary	336	17	2	0	587	42	5	2	5
with Oregano and Lemon	290	14	2	0	460	38	4	3	5
Grilled Potato Foil Packs	208	4	1	0	540	40	5	2	5
Grilled Spanish-Style Potato Foil Packs	343	14	4	27	709	44	6	3	11
Grilled Spicy Home Fry Potato Foil Packs	209	4	1	0	539	41	5	2	5
Grilled Vinegar and Onion Potato Foil Packs	221	4	1	0	597	42	5	3	5
Grilled Sweet Potatoes with Maple Chile Crisp	637	58	8	0	567	29	5	9	3
Blistered Shishito Peppers	30	2.5	0	0	0	2	1	1	0
with Espelette, Smoked Paprika, and Lime	30	2.5	0	0	95	3	1	1	0
with Mint, Poppy Seeds, and Orange	40	2.5	0	0	200	5	2	2	1
Grilled Tomatoes	142	8	1	0	605	18	6	12	4
Easy Grilled Coleslaw	210	17	2.5	5	550	11	4	6	2
Smoky Potato Salad	286	16	4	16	534	30	3	3	7
Grilled Sweet Potato Salad	339	15	3	11	583	47	6	14	5
Grilled Peach and Tomato Salad with Burrata and Basil	341	28	11	48	530	14	2	11	10
Brined Grilled Zucchini with Mint Salsa Verde	180	15	2	0	570	10	3	5	4
Grilled Zucchini and Corn Salad	286	23	5	17	620	17	3	7	7
Grilled Vegetable Ratatouille	107	5	1	0	725	16	6	9	3
Mechouia (Tunisian-Style Grilled Vegetables)	168	12	2	0	546	15	6	8	3
Grilled Vegetable and Halloumi Salad	251	18	6	34	506	19	4	13	7
Grilled Panzanella	540	41	7	8	579	34	3	6	11
Grilled Vegetable Platter	397	34	10	37	684	16	5	9	12
Ultimate Veggie Burgers	383	15	2	3	411	52	5	6	13
for the Freezer	383	15	2	3	411	52	5	6	13
Grilled Portobello Burgers with Goat Cheese and Arugula	306	18	5	10	345	27	2	6	10
Ultimate Grilled Vegetable Sandwich	592	37	11	46	989	46	5	9	19
Grilled Halloumi Wraps	437	25	13	80	1188	36	5	6	20
Eggplant and Mozzarella Panini	663	44	18	87	973	40	7	10	29
Grilled Vegetable Kebabs	169	14	2	0	525	11	4	6	3
Grilled Tomato Gazpacho	348	31	4	0	755	17	4	8	4
Smoky Tomato and Eggplant Phyllo Pie (Cast Iron Skillet)	420	30	7	20	920	29	3	4	12
Grilled Soy Ginger–Glazed Tofu	307	17	2	0	798	17	3	11	24
Grilled Asian Barbecue–Glazed Tofu	240	14	2	0	1380	14	0	8	14
Grilled Honey-Mustard Tofu	270	16	5	15	450	17	0	13	12
Grilled Tofu with Charred Broccoli and Peanut Sauce	640	52	5	0	650	20	5	6	25
Grilled Tofu and Vegetables with Harissa	240	13	1.5	0	590	19	3	8	14
Grilled Barbecued Tempeh Burgers with Spicy Pickled Jicama	615	15	3	0	1311	95	4	56	29
Grilled Barbecue Tempeh and Vegetable Skewers	430	12	1.5	0	920	62	1	34	18

8. Pizza, Breads, and Desserts	CAL	TOTAL FAT (G)	SAT FAT (G)	CHOL (MG)	SODIUM (MG)	CARBS (G)	FIBER (G)	TOTAL SUGAR (G)	PROTEIN (G)
Grilled Pizza	799	46	14	55	702	63	3	4	32
with Fontina, Pecorino, and Scallions	708	33	12	64	1330	73	5	11	28
with Soppressata, Banana Peppers, and Hot Honey	750	44	12	50	1580	65	3	5	25
Thin-Crust Pizza for the Outdoor Pizza Oven	730	25	11	55	2350	94	4	4	30
Pizza Dough for the Outdoor Pizza Oven	450	9	1	0	910	85	3	0	14
Whole-Wheat Pizza Dough for the Outdoor Pizza Oven	400	9	1.5	0	910	71	7	0	13
Grilled Flatbreads	440	20	7	65	750	56	2	2	10
Hand-Mixed Grilled Flatbreads	440	20	7	65	750	56	2	2	10
Grilled Garlic Flatbreads	440	20	7	65	750	58	2	2	10
Easy Grilled Onion, Pear, and Prosciutto Flatbreads	350	18	6	35	840	35	2	9	13
Easy Grilled Butternut Squash, Apple, and Goat Cheese Flatbreads	310	15	5	10	580	35	2	7	9
Mana'eesh Za'atar	323	12	2	0	264	46	2	0	7
Grilled Flour Tortillas	170	6	1.5	0	300	25	1	0	3
Big and Fluffy Biscuits	390	21	10	35	590	43	1	2	7
with Lemon and Dill	390	21	10	35	590	43	2	2	7
with Orange and Tarragon	390	21	10	35	590	43	2	2	7
Grilled Fresh Corn Cornbread with Charred Jalapeños and Cheddar	530	35	15	121	442	42	2	7	13
No-Knead Dutch Oven Bread	210	1	0	0	460	42	1	2	7
Rosemary Focaccia	220	7	1	0	520	34	1	0	5
Pull-Apart Dinner Rolls	140	5	3	30	230	19	1	0	3
Charred Strawberry Dutch Baby	420	14	4	150	690	63	3	26	1
Cherry Spoon Cake	340	13	8	35	300	54	3	16	5
Rustic Summer Fruit Tart	380	20	12	50	210	46	3	16	5
Orange Upside-Down Cake	420	19	11	95	410	60	3	16	5
Skillet Brownie	480	22	8	60	220	73	2	50	6
Spiced Skillet Brownie	480	22	8	60	220	73	2	50	6
Espresso-Walnut Skillet Brownie	500	24	9	70	220	73	2	50	6
Skillet Chocolate Chip Cookie	340	12	10	60	260	46	1	29	4
Glazed Rotisserie Pineapple with Salted Rum Butterscotch Sauce	300	17	11	45	160	36	1	33	1

9. Sauces, Relishes, and Rubs	CAL	TOTAL FAT (G)	SAT FAT (G)	CHOL (MG)	SODIUM (MG)	CARBS (G)	FIBER (G)	TOTAL SUGAR (G)	PROTEIN (G)
No-Cook Barbecue Sauce (per 1 tablespoon)	25	0	0	0	110	7	0	6	0
No-Cook Honey-Scallion BBQ Sauce (per 1 tablespoon)	20	0	0	0	115	0	0	4	0
No-Cook Five-Alarm BBQ Sauce (per 1 tablespoon)	25	0	0	0	100	6	0	5	0
Easy All-Purpose Barbecue Sauce (per 1 tablespoon)	25	0.5	0	0	115	5	0	4	0
Easy Bourbon Barbecue Sauce (per 1 tablespoon)	25	0.5	0	0	105	4	0	4	0
Easy Chipotle Barbecue Sauce (per 1 tablespoon)	25	0.5	0	0	115	5	0	4	0
Easy Espresso Barbecue Sauce (per 1 tablespoon)	25	0.5	0	0	110	5	0	4	0
Easy Hoisin and Ginger Barbecue Sauce (per 1 tablespoon)	25	0.5	0	0	170	5	0	2	0
Eastern North Carolina–Style Barbecue Sauce (per 1 tablespoon)	15	0	0	0	220	3	0	1	0
Lexington-Style Barbecue Sauce (per 1 tablespoon)	10	0	0	0	105	2	0	1	0
Western South Carolina–Style Barbecue Sauce (per 1 tablespoon)	25	0.5	0	0	190	4	0	3	0
Mid–South Carolina Mustard Sauce (per 1 tablespoon)	60	6	0	0	180	1	0	1	0
Kansas City Barbecue Sauce (per 1 tablespoon)	35	0	0	0	90	7	0	7	0
Oklahoma Barbecue Sauce (per 1 tablespoon)	30	0.5	0	0	140	6	0	5	0
Texas-Style Barbecue Sauce (per 1 tablespoon)	20	1	0	0	190	2	0	2	0
Blueberry Barbecue Sauce (per 1 tablespoon)	15	0	0	0	75	2	0	2	0
Honey-Mustard Barbecue Sauce (per 1 tablespoon)	60	3	2	10	130	7	0	0	0
Orange-Chipotle Grilling Sauce (per 1 tablespoon)	35	0	0	0	75	10	0	9	0
Apple-Mustard Grilling Sauce (per 1 tablespoon)	35	0	0	0	130	7	1	6	0
Coconut–Red Curry Grilling Sauce (per 1 tablespoon)	20	0	0	0	130	4	0	4	0
Basil Pesto (per 1 tablespoon)	80	8	5	0	85	0	0	0	0
Sauce Verte (per 1 tablespoon)	70	7	1	0	115	2	0	0	1
Persillade (per 1 tablespoon)	50	6	0	0	110	1	0	0	0
Mint Persillade (per 1 tablespoon)	45	5	0.5	0	180	1	0	0	0
Italian Salsa Verde (per 1 tablespoon)	100	10	1.5	0	105	2	0	0	1
Lemon-Basil Salsa Verde (per 1 tablespoon)	100	10	1.5	0	105	2	0	0	1
Salsa Verde with Arugula (per 1 tablespoon)	100	10	1.5	0	105	2	0	1	3
Argentinian Chimichurri Sauce (per 1 tablespoon)	45	4.5	0.5	0	200	1	0	0	0
Red Chimichurri Sauce (per 1 tablespoon)	70	7	1	0	35	1	0	0	0
Tarragon Chimichurri Sauce (per 1 tablespoon)	35	3.5	0	0	20	0	0	0	0
Cranberry Chimichurri Sauce (per 1 tablespoon)	70	6	1	0	50	4	0	3	0
Chermoula Sauce (per 1 tablespoon)	70	7	1	0	35	1	0	0	0

9. Sauces, Relishes, and Rubs (cont.)	CAL	TOTAL FAT (G)	SAT FAT (G)	CHOL (MG)	SODIUM (MG)	CARBS (G)	FIBER (G)	TOTAL SUGAR (G)	PROTEIN (G)
Pub-Style Burger Sauce (per 1 tablespoon)	80	8	1	5	220	1	0	1	0
Tzatziki (per 1 tablespoon)	20	1.5	1	0	10	0	0	0	1
Classic Tartar Sauce (per 1 tablespoon)	70	8	1	5	110	1	0	1	0
Herb Yogurt Sauce (per 1 tablespoon)	10	0.5	0	0	25	1	0	1	1
Lemon-Garlic Sauce (per 1 tablespoon)	90	10	1.5	5	90	0	0	0	0
Creamy Lemon-Herb Sauce (per 1 tablespoon)	90	10	1.5	5	210	1	0	0	0
Horseradish Cream Sauce with Chives (per 1 tablespoon)	60	6	3.5	20	20	1	0	1	1
Quick Mexican Crema (per 1 tablespoon)	50	5	1.5	5	45	1	0	0	0
Ají Verde (per 1 tablespoon)	70	7	1.5	5	85	0	0	0	0
Ají Amarillo (per 1 tablespoon)	70	8	1	5	220	0	0	0	0
Mustard-Dill Sauce (per 1 tablespoon)	15	0	0	0	360	0	0	0	0
Romesco Sauce (per 1 tablespoon)	20	1	0	0	75	1	0	1	0
Pico De Gallo (per 1/4 cup)	15	0	0	0	120	3	1	2	1
Santa Maria Salsa (per 1/4 cup)	15	0	0	0	290	3	1	2	1
Salsa Roja (per 1/4 cup)	25	0	0	0	310	5	2	2	1
Sweet and Smoky Grilled Tomato Salsa (per 1/4 cup)	45	3	0	0	210	4	1	2	1
Tomatillo Salsa (per 1/4 cup)	40	2.5	0	0	70	4	1	3	1
Grilled Tomatillo Salsa (per 1/4 cup)	70	4.5	0.5	0	25	6	2	3	1
Fresh Corn Salsa with Tomato (per 1/4 cup)	30	1.5	0	0	110	4	1	2	1
with Avocado and Toasted Cumin (per 1/4 cup)	50	4	0.5	0	85	5	2	1	1
with Jicama and Pineapple (per 1/4 cup)	35	1.5	0	0	75	6	1	2	1
with Mango and Cucumber (per 1/4 cup)	35	1.5	0	0	75	6	1	2	1
with Peach and Radishes (per 1/4 cup)	35	1.5	0	0	75	5	1	3	1
Toasted Corn and Black Bean Salsa	40	2	0	0	80	5	1	1	1
Spicy Toasted Corn and Black Bean Salsa (per 1/4 cup)	40	2	0	0	80	5	1	1	1
Avocado-Orange Salsa (per 1/4 cup)	100	7	1	0	4	10	4	4	1
Mango-Mint Salsa (per 1/4 cup)	80	4	1	0	180	11	0	2	0
Pineapple Salsa (per 1/4 cup)	45	2	0	0	190	7	1	5	0
Pineapple-Mango Salsa (per 1/4 cup)	40	1.5	0	0	125	7	1	5	0
Pineapple-Cucumber Salsa (per 1/4 cup) (per 1/4 cup)	40	2	0	0	190	7	1	3	0
Pineapple-Watermelon Salsa	30	1	0	0	95	5	1	5	1
Classic Guacamole (per 1/4 cup)	130	11	1.5	0	150	8	5	1	2
Charred Guacamole (per 1/4 cup)	120	11	1.5	0	150	7	5	1	2
Sun-Dried Tomato and Basil Relish (per 1 tablespoon)	40	4	0.5	0	5	1	0	0	0
Spicy Red Pepper Relish (per 1 tablespoon)	25	0	0	0	85	6	0	5	0
Orange and Mint Relish (per 1 tablespoon)	15	0.5	0	0	5	2	0	2	0
Cucumber-Ginger Relish (per 1 tablespoon)	30	2.5	3	0	40	1	0	0	0
Pomegranate Relish (per 1 tablespoon)	50	5	0.5	0	35	1	0	1	0

9. Sauces, Relishes, and Rubs (cont.)	CAL	TOTAL FAT (G)	SAT FAT (G)	CHOL (MG)	SODIUM (MG)	CARBS (G)	FIBER (G)	TOTAL SUGAR (G)	PROTEIN (G)
Green Olive, Almond, and Orange Relish (per 1 tablespoon)	40	4	0	0	40	0	0	0	1
Sweet Mint-Almond Relish (per 1 tablespoon)	45	4	0	0	15	2	0	2	0
Preserved Lemon–Almond Sauce (per 1 tablespoon)	50	5	0.5	0	170	1	0	0	0
Caper-Currant Relish (per 1 tablespoon)	60	5	0.5	0	50	2	0	6	0
Kimchi-Scallion Sauce (per 1 tablespoon)	35	3.5	0.5	0	95	1	0	0	0
Scallion-Ginger Relish (per 1 tablespoon)	100	11	0	0	65	1	0	0	0
Mango Chutney (per 1 tablespoon)	40	2.5	0	0	35	4	0	2	0
Spiced Green-Tomato Chutney (per 1 tablespoon)	25	0	0	0	75	6	0	6	0
Peach and Double-Mustard Chutney (per 1 tablespoon)	5	0	0	0	45	2	0	2	0
Blueberry-Ginger Chutney (per 1 tablespoon)	10	0	0	0	35	2	0	0	0
Burst Cherry Tomato and Jalapeño Chutney (per 1 tablespoon)	5	0	0	0	40	1	0	1	0
Barbecue Spice Rub (per 1 teaspoon)	10	0	0	0	290	2	1	1	0
Tex-Mex Spice Rub (per 1 teaspoon)	5	0	0	0	105	1	0	0	0
Classic Steak Rub (per 1 teaspoon)	5	0	0	0	0	1	1	0	0
Cajun Spice Rub (per 1 teaspoon)	5	0	0	0	140	1	1	0	0
Jamaican Jerk Spice Rub (per 1 teaspoon)	10	0	0	0	210	2	0	1	0
Curry-Cumin Spice Rub (per 1 teaspoon)	5	0	0	0	20	1	1	0	0
Herb Spice Rub (per 1 teaspoon)	5	0	0	0	0	1	0	0	0
Herbes de Provence (per 1 teaspoon)	5	0	0	0	0	1	0	0	0
Fresh Herb Salt (per 1 teaspoon)	0	0	0	0	1700	0	0	0	0
Cumin-Sesame Salt (per 1 teaspoon)	10	0.5	0	0	380	0	0	0	0
Chili-Lime Salt (per 1 teaspoon)	0	0	0	0	580	0	0	0	0
Smoked Salt (per 1 teaspoon)	0	0	0	0	1120	0	0	0	0
Sriracha Salt (per 1 teaspoon)	5	0	0	0	1220	1	0	1	0

Index

NOTE: Page references in *italics* indicate photographs.

C

G

L

M

N

T